Corporate Financial Reporting and Analysis

Second Edition

ASISH K. BHATTACHARYYA
Formerly, Professor, Finance and Control
Indian Institute of Management Calcutta

PHI Learning Private Limited
Delhi-110092
2025

*In fond memory of **Shri Asoke K. Ghosh** (October 1942 – February 2024), Founder Chairman and Managing Director of PHI Learning, whose vision endlessly inspires.*

The Legacy Continues....

Published by Pushpita Ghosh, PHI Learning Private Limited, Rimjhim House, 111, Patparganj Industrial Estate, Delhi-110092 and Printed by Mudrak, C-55, Sector 65, Noida, U.P.-201301

₹1195.00

CORPORATE FINANCIAL REPORTING AND ANALYSIS, Second Edition
Asish K. Bhattacharyya

ISBN-978-93-88028-87-5 (Print Book)
ISBN-978-93-88028-88-2 (e-Book)

The export rights of the book are vested solely with the publisher.

Contents

Preface

The First Edition of the book, published last year, was well received by the instructors and students of various business schools and their overwhelming response encouraged me to revise and bring out the second edition. Based on the feedback and suggestions of instructors, four new chapters have been added on financial instruments, non-financial liabilities, business combination and consolidated financial statements and the last chapter to discuss some important topics in brief, including lease accounting. Lease accounting is discussed based on the principles and methods stipulated in Ind AS 116, which is applicable from April 1, 2019. Instructors feel that all those topics, which are relatively complex, require simple presentation for the students specialising in Finance for their clear understanding of the basic principles, thus explained lucidly.

Some of them have found this book suitable for Financial Statement Analysis course as well, which many business schools offer as a compulsory course to the students specialising in Finance.

I hope the readers of the book will acquire more knowledge and skill through this enlarged new edition.

I am thankful to a large number of students and professors of various business schools who have enriched me by providing ideas on how to improve the contents. I will fail in my duty if I do not mention the names of Professors Arpita Ghosh, Manju Jaiswall, Sudhir Jaiswall (all from IIM Calcutta), Ashish Varma, Puja Aggarwal, Sachin Choudhry, Vandana Gupta (all from IMT Ghaziabad), and Priti Sharma (from IMT-CDL, Ghaziabad).

I look forward to receive feedback from students and instructors. They can reach me at phi@phindia.com or asish.bhattacharyya@gmail.com.

Asish K. Bhattacharyya

Preface to the First Edition

In today's business environment, corporate financial reporting is an essential activity, which helps the management in understanding the position, progress and prospects of business with respect to industry. In the present book, all the aspects pertaining to the subject are covered. It is designed as per the AICTE Model Curriculum for Management published in January 2018.

During the course of my teaching, I realised that the management students without accounting background face many difficulties in understanding and mastering the subject. Also, the instructors find it hard to teach Financial Accounting to those students effectively. Thus, I derived my motivation from an urge to present complex accounting principles stipulated in Ind AS in a language and form so that even the students with non-accounting background are able to comprehend the subject with great ease. For instance, formats of balance sheet and statements of profit and loss prescribed in the Companies Act, 2013 are explained before explaining the accounting cycle. Besides, additional assignments are provided for classroom discussion, and also, to test students for their knowledge and understanding of accounting concepts. I hope the readers will find the organisation of the book and chapter assignments useful.

I am thankful to a large number of students and professors of various business schools who have enriched me by providing ideas on how to improve the material. I will fail in my duty if I do not mention the names of Professors Arpita Ghosh, Manju Jaiswall, Sudhir Jaiswall (all from IIM Calcutta), Ashish Varma, Puja Aggarwal, Sachin Choudhry (all from IMT Ghaziabad), and Priti Sharma (from IMT-CDL, Ghaziabad).

I look forward to receive feedback from students and instructors. They can reach me at phi@phindia.com or asish.bhattacharyya@gmail.com.

Asish K. Bhattacharyya

CHAPTER 1

The Conceptual Framework

Learning Objectives

The objective of this chapter is to provide an understanding of the corporate financial reporting environment and the basic principles of financial reporting. After reading this chapter, you will develop understanding of the following:

- How transactions and other events change assets, liabilities and net worth of an entity
- Difference between bookkeeping and accounting
- The role of Generally Accepted Accounting Principles (GAAP) and accounting standards in bringing comparability of financial statements and consistency in applying accounting principles and methods from year to year
- The purpose and content of balance sheet and statement of profit and loss
- Difference between equity capital and debt capital
- Firm structures, including limited liability company and limited liability partnership
- Importance of financial reporting

NOTES

INTRODUCTION

Motivation for Learning Financial Accounting

Every business entity issues financial statements periodically, at least annually. If you visit the website of any listed company, in the section 'investors', financial statements for the current period and earlier periods are available. This is so because anyone who has an interest in the company wants to know the sustainability and the growth potential of the company, and financial statements provide the information that is used as the starting point to assess the same. If you aspire to be an entrepreneur after completing Management Programme, you should have a clear understanding of how financiers (e.g., venture capitalist) and others use information given in financial statements to evaluate the risks of funding of your venture or doing business with you. If you want to make a career in the finance sector (e.g., career as a financial analyst with a financial institution), you must be proficient in using the information provided in financial statements. If you decide to make a career in non-finance sector (e.g., manufacturing and service sectors), you will be required to analyse financial statements of the partners (e.g., vendors and customers) and competitors of the company that you will serve in order to evaluate their sustainability and growth, and strategy. Therefore, there is no surprise that every Management Programme includes a compulsory course on Financial Accounting.

Like any other technical subject, financial accounting has its own jargons, accounting principles and methods. Therefore, it is not difficult to learn financial accounting. Being a business language, learning financial accounting is similar to learning any other language, which requires learning vocabulary and grammar.

The accounting principles and methods discussed in this book are applicable to not-for-profit organisations, with modifications.

NATURE OF FINANCIAL ACCOUNTING

Nature of Transactions and Other Events

Transaction refers to exchange of goods, services and funds. A transaction changes the assets or/and liabilities. Assets are economic resources that are controlled by an entity (an individual or an organisation). A liability is the amount that the entity owes to outsiders. Outsiders, in case of an organisation, refer to entities other than owners. For example, you have ₹1,00,000 and that is the only asset that you own. You buy a refrigerator on credit for ₹40,000. The value of your assets has gone up to ₹1,40,000 and you have assumed a liability of ₹40,000. The composition of your assets has also changed. Events, other than transactions, also change assets and liabilities. For example, suppose you are enjoying dinner with your family in a fine dining restaurant in an upmarket close to your residence. A baby in your family spoils the costly attire of a lady sitting in the next table. You promise her to compensate for the loss, which is estimated to be ₹50,000. You have the reputation of always honouring your commitments. Therefore, by promising the lady to compensate for the loss, you have assumed a liability. Similarly, you may lose wealth due to fire in the premises in which you keep your furniture or burglary in a bank in which the burglar empties the vault in which you keep your gold ornaments.

In effect, transactions and other events that affect your assets and liabilities might change the value of your wealth. You measure your wealth by deducting the amount of your liabilities from the value of your assets. Your wealth was reduced by ₹50,000 when you promised the lady to compensate her for the loss estimated to be ₹50,000.

Some transactions reduce assets or increase liabilities. For example, you pay ₹20,000 for a dinner hosted by you to your close friends to celebrate completion of your MBA Programme successfully. This will reduce your assets (cash), if you pay the bill in cash or

NOTES

increase your liabilities, if you pay the bill using your credit card. In any case, your wealth is reduced by ₹20,000.

A transaction or event does not change your wealth if it equally affects your assets and liabilities, wealth is neither reduced nor increased. For example, if you purchase a refrigerator on credit, your wealth remains unchanged.

In financial accounting (hereafter accounting) jargon, the term 'net worth' is used to refer to that part of the wealth of the owners which is invested in the business entity. The terms 'net worth' and 'equity' are used interchangeably. The term 'net worth' has also come in common use. For example, we say 'high net worth individuals' to refer to affluent individuals.

Self-Test Questions

Self-test question 1.1

Fill in the blanks:

(i) The asset that S. Limited (SL) owns is valued at ₹10,00,000 and the amount that it owes to others (liabilities) is ₹2,00,000. The net worth of the company is ₹......................

(ii) Preetam purchases an apartment for ₹2 crore. He partly finances the transaction by taking a bank loan of ₹1.5 crore. Preetam's net worth increases by ₹...........................

(iii) Neetu paid her college fees of ₹15 lakhs. This....................... her net worth by ₹15 lakhs. [Choose the right word from 'reduced' and 'increased'].

Self-test question 1.2

Indicate whether the following statements are true (T) or false (F):

(i) Transactions necessarily change net worth.

(ii) Events other than transactions might affect assets and/or liabilities.

(iii) Increase in liabilities without change in the value of assets reduces net worth.

(iv) Credit purchase of an asset reduces net worth.

(v) Cash purchase of an asset increases net worth.

Bookkeeping and Accounting

Bookkeeping

Bookkeeping is the record keeping aspect of accounting. It is recording the economic effect of transactions and other events on the assets, liabilities, and net worth of an entity. It is the financial information infrastructure of an entity. Accurate bookkeeping facilitates day-to-day operations and preparation of financial statements.

Accounting

Accounting refers to the process of preparation and presentation of financial statements based on data accumulated, organised and stored through the bookkeeping process. It is said that accounting begins where bookkeeping ends. However, with the increase in the use of computer and accounting software (e.g., Tally), the distinction between bookkeeping and accounting has blurred. The accounting software, which records the transactions and events and produces financial statements in the given format, is extensively used by small and mid-size entities. In large entities, accounting is concerned with issues related to formulation of accounting policy, measurement of assets and liabilities, and disclosures. Measurement often involves estimation, which requires developing perceptions about the economic consequences of complex transactions and events.

Accounting policy

Accountants formulate accounting policy. Accounting policies are the specific principles, bases, conventions, rules and practices applied by an entity in preparing and presenting financial statements. For example, an entity formulates accounting policies on how stock of finished goods at the end of the accounting period will be measured, and at what point in the process of selling goods, revenue will be recognised and measured. Accounting policies must conform to Generally Accepted Accounting Principles (GAAP).

GAAP

Generally Accepted Accounting Principles (GAAP) are codified in accounting standards, which are issued by a designated body. In India, the Institute of Chartered Accountants of India issues accounting standards. Accounting standards control accounting policies. This ensures *comparability* of financial statements of different entities operating in the same industry, as all the entities are required to apply the same accounting principles and methods. Entities are not permitted to change accounting policies voluntarily. Therefore, they apply the same accounting principles and methods *consistently* from year to year. This ensures that financial statements for different years are comparable. Mandatory application of GAAP facilitates analysing the performance and financial position of the same entity over number of years and comparing the performance and financial position of peers.

Accounting period and fiscal year

Usually, complete set of financial statements are prepared annually. The annual period is called *fiscal year*. In India, companies are required to adopt the fiscal year that begins on April 1 and ends on March 31 of the next year. The fiscal year 2017–2018 refers to the period from April 1, 2017 to March 31, 2018. Listed companies are required to prepare abridged financial statements on quarterly and half-yearly basis. The generic term 'accounting period' is used to refer to the period for which the financial statements are prepared.

Self-Test Questions

Self-test question 1.3

Indicate whether the following statements are true (T) or false (F):

(i) The boundary between bookkeeping and accounting has been blurred with the extensive use of computer and accounting software.

(ii) In accounting, measurement of assets and liabilities does not involve estimation.

(iii) Net worth of an entity is affected by the management's perception about the economic consequences of transactions and other events.

(iv) Generally Accepted Accounting Principles (GAAP) codified in accounting standards control accounting policy.

(v) The terms 'comparability' and 'consistency' are used interchangeably.

Complete Set of Financial Statements

The basic financial statements are balance sheet and the statement of profit and loss. A complete set of financial statements also includes statement of changes in equity, statement of cash flows, and notes to accounts.

Balance sheet

Balance sheet provides information on assets, liabilities and equity of the entity at the balance sheet date. Equity is viewed as the claim of owners on the assets of the entity. Liabilities are viewed as claims of outsiders on the assets of the entity. As per the contemporary Generally Accepted Accounting Principles (GAAP), all assets and liabilities do not qualify for recognition in the balance sheet. For example, core competence (accumulated institutional knowledge and unique processes), which provides competitive advantage to a business firm is not recognised in the balance sheet. Intangible assets, except computer software, developed internally are not recognised in the balance sheet.

Increase in equity, adjusted (reduced/increased) for fresh investment and/or withdrawals by owners, measures the profit or loss for the accounting period.

Recognition refers to the process of including an item in basic financial statements (balance sheet and statement of profit and loss). It is the depiction of the item in words and monetary terms.

NOTES

ILLUSTRATION 1.1 Profit or Loss

The equity of James Limited (JL) as at March 31, 2017 was ₹5,00,000. During 2017–18, owners introduced fresh equity capital of ₹2,00,000. Equity as at March 31, 2018 was ₹9,00,000.

Required

How much profit JL earned during the accounting period 2017–1018?

Solution

During the accounting period 2017–18, JL earned a profit of (₹9,00,000 – 2,00,000 – 5,00,000) or ₹2,00,000.

Statement of profit and loss

Statement of profit and loss presents the operating result of the entity for the accounting period covered by the statement. It details how the entity earned profit or incurred loss. It provides information on income, expenses incurred to earn the income, finance cost (e.g., interest on borrowings) and tax expense. Income of entities primarily comes from revenue. *Revenue* is income arising in the course of an entity's ordinary activities. For example, revenue of an entity that operates in non-finance sector is the income from sale of goods and services. Examples of expenses are cost of goods that have been sold during the accounting period, salaries and wages, travelling expenses, communication expenses and electricity charges. Excess of total income over total expenses, including finance cost and tax expense, is profit. Excess of total expenses, including finance cost and tax expense, over total income is loss.

The term 'net income' is often used to refer to profit. Negative net income represents loss.

Statement of profit and loss is discussed in detail in Chapter 4.

Statement of changes in equity for the period

Statement of changes in equity reconciles the equity as at the beginning of the accounting period and the same as at the end of the accounting period.

Statement of changes in equity is discussed in detail in Chapter 3.

Cash flow statement

Cash flow statement presents cash inflows and outflows during the accounting period and reconciles opening (at the beginning of the accounting period) and closing (at the end of the accounting period) cash balances. It establishes a link between balance sheet and the statement of profit and loss.

Notes to accounts

Notes provide summary of accounting policy; narrative descriptions or disaggregations of items presented in balance sheet, changes in equity, statement of profit and loss and cash flow statement; and information about items that do not qualify for recognition in those statements.

NOTES

Key Terms
Accounting, accounting period, accounting policy, accounting standard, asset, balance sheet, bookkeeping, equity, fiscal year, GAAP, liability, loss, net income, net worth, profit, recognition, revenue, and transaction

Self-Test Questions

Self-test question 1.4

Fill in the blanks:

(i) The equity of Kasturi Limited (KL) as at March 31, 2017 was ₹6,00,000. During 2017–18, owners introduced fresh equity capital of ₹2,00,000 and withdrawn ₹50,000. Equity as at March 31, 2018 was ₹9,00,000. Profit earned by KL during the year 2017–18 was ₹...............

(ii) The terms 'equity' and ....are used interchangeably.

(iii) ....assets generated internally are not recognised in the balance sheet.

(iv) Income from sale of goods and services by an entity operating in a non-finance sector is called...........................

(v) The process of including an item in basic financial statements is called.................

Self-test question 1.5

Indicate whether the following statements are true (T) or false (F):

(i) The terms 'income' and 'net income' are used interchangeably.

(ii) Computer software created internally is not recognised in the balance sheet.

(iii) Profit is the excess of total income over total expenses, excluding tax expense.

(iv) Cash flow statement reconciles opening cash balance and closing cash balance.

(v) Note to accounts is not a component of the complete set of financial statements.

SUMMARY

Transaction refers to exchange of goods, services and funds. A transaction changes the assets and/or liabilities and might change net worth. Similarly, some events, other than transactions, change the assets and/or liabilities and might change net worth. A transaction or event does not change the net worth if it equally affects assets and liabilities; wealth is neither reduced nor increased.

Bookkeeping is the record keeping aspect of accounting. Accounting refers to the process of preparation and presentation of financial statements based on data accumulated, organised and stored through the bookkeeping process. In large entities, accounting is concerned with issues related to formulation of accounting policy, measurement of assets and liabilities, and disclosures. Measurement often involves estimation, which requires developing perceptions about the economic consequence of complex transactions and events.

Accountants formulate accounting policy. Accounting policies must conform to Generally Accepted Accounting Principles (GAAP), which are codified in accounting standards. This ensures comparability and consistency.

Basic financial statements are balance sheet and the statement of profit and loss. A complete set of financial statements also includes statement of changes in equity, statement of cash flows, and notes to accounts.

CASE STUDY 1.1 Use of Information in Balance Sheet and Statement of Profit and Loss

Santosh started a fashion business (named it Santosh & Juthika, in short, SJ) on April 1, 2015 with investment in cash of ₹10,00,000. SJ maintained accounting books to record transactions and other events that would affect its assets and liabilities, and consequently, equity. It did well in 2015–16. Its equity during the period increased to ₹15,00,000. SJ's balance sheet as at March 31, 2016, showed that its assets and liabilities were ₹20,00,000 and ₹5,00,000, respectively. It had no borrowing on that date. SJ's statement of profit and loss for the year 2015–16 showed that

NOTES

the revenue for that year was ₹45,00,000 and expenses totalled ₹40,00,000. The net profit was (₹45,00,000 – ₹40,00,000) or ₹5,00,000. Assume tax expense was zero.

SJ applied for loan from Small Industries Development Bank of India (SIDBI) for setting up a small manufacturing unit. SIDBI sanctioned loan of ₹15,00,000 and disbursed the same on April 1, 2016. As per the terms of the loan, interest at the rate of 10 percent is payable annually on March 31 every year and the loan is repayable in five equal instalments starting from March 31, 2018.

SJ's balance sheet as at March 31, 2017, showed that its assets and liabilities were ₹45,00,000 and ₹20,00,000, respectively. Liabilities included outstanding balance (₹15,00,000) of the amount borrowed from SIDBI. SJ's statement of profit and loss for the year 2016–17 showed that the revenue for that year was ₹90,00,000 and expenses, including tax expense and finance cost, totalled ₹80,00,000. The finance cost for the year was (₹15,00,000 × 0.10) or ₹1,50,000. The net profit was (₹90,00,000 – ₹80,00,000) or ₹10,00,000. Assume tax expense was zero.

Santosh is scouting around for an angel investor who will invest in the equity capital of SJ. Angel investors are High Net Worth (HNI) individuals who have-high risk appetites and look for opportunities to invest in startups.

Question

What information in balance sheets and statements of profit and loss of SJ is useful to angel investors in deciding whether to invest in the equity of SJ? What additional information angel investors will require to decide whether to investment or not in the equity of SJ? [Assume that the income tax rate is 40 percent of taxable income for both the years.]

Solution

(i) Angel investors are primarily interested to assess the growth potential of the business and Return on Invested Capital (ROIC). The capital invested in the business is the total of equity capital and borrowings.

From the balance sheets of SJ, we find that the amount of invested capital as at March 31, 2016 was ₹15,00,000 and the same as at March 31, 2017 was (₹25,00,000 + 15,00,000) or ₹40,00,000. The invested capital at the commencement of the business (April 1, 2015) was ₹10,00,000. Thus, average invested capital for 2015–16 was [(₹10,00,000 + 15,00,000)/2] or ₹12,50,000; and average invested capital for 2016–17 was [(₹15,00,000 + 40,00,000)/2] or ₹27,50,000.

For computing the ROIC, we have to calculate the operating profit, which is the profit before tax and finance cost. Therefore, the profit should be adjusted by finance cost (net of tax). Thus, the operating profit was

Year 2015–16: ₹5,00,000; and

Year 2016–17: [₹10,00,000 + (1,50,000 – 1,50,000 × 0.40)] or ₹10,90,000.

ROIC was:

Year 2015–16: [(₹5,00,000/12,50,000) × 100] or 40%; and

Year 2016–17: [(₹10,90,000/27,50,000) × 100] or 39.64%.

Revenue growth for the year 2016–17 was [(90,00,000/45,00,000) × 100] or 200%.

(ii) Information given in (i) is historical. It helps in assessing the management's ability to use the resource (capital) productively. However, angel investors are interested in the future of SJ. For this, they need to collect information to assess the future of the fashion industry. Moreover, they will also compare the performance of SJ and other startup firms in the fashion industry to decide whether they would invest in SJ, and if, they decide to invest in SJ, they have to plan the amount also that they should invest and the terms and conditions of investment.

Investment in equity will give the angel investor ownership right and he/she will be the co-owner of SJ with Santosh. He/she may or may not directly participate in the management.

NOTES

ACTIVITY

Download the latest financial statements of a non-finance company of your choice from its website and study the items in the balance sheet and the statement of profit and loss. You may not be able to understand the sources of all the items. But this will give you a general understanding of the nature of balance sheet and the statement of profit and loss.

CAPITAL AND FIRM STRUCTURES

Capital

Translating a business idea, which is developed by an entrepreneur, into a business venture requires resources (capital). If the entrepreneur's own resource is insufficient to finance the business, he/she will convince others to invest in the venture by explaining the high probability of the venture's success and growth in investment. At the early stage of the venture, investment is exposed to high risk because the chance of failure is high. At that stage, the entrepreneur gets the support from family members, friends, angel investors (affluent individuals) and venture capitalist (a type of private equity). As the venture succeeds, initial investors, particularly angel investors and venture capitalists, exit the venture and new investors, who are willing to take moderate risks, join as owners by contributing to the equity capital of the entity. Capital is also provided by lenders and other creditors, who do not want to take business risks. Capital provided by lenders is often referred to as *debt capital*.

BOX 1.1 Equity Capital and Debt Capital

Capital provided by owners is called *equity capital* and capital provided by lenders is called *debt capital*.

Investment in equity capital is defined as the residual interest in the assets of the entity after deduction of liabilities. In a situation of liquidation, assets are first used to settle liabilities and residual assets are distributed to owners. It is exposed to business risks in the sense that return on investment in equity capital depends on the business performance.

Return on investment in debt capital (interest) is predetermined. Investment in debt capital is exposed to credit risks, that is, the risk that the entity may fail to honour its commitment to pay interest and repay the loan as per the terms and conditions of the contract.

Self-Test Questions

Self-test question 1.6

Fill in the blanks:

(i) Economic resources being used in a business entity are called.....................

(ii) Affluent individuals who have high-risk appetites and invest in startup are called..................

(iii) Investors in startups are the entrepreneur, affluent individuals and ....

(iv) Investment in the equity capital of a firm is exposed to ....risks.

(v) Investment in the debt capital of a firm is exposed to ....risks.

Firm Structures

Choice of the firm structure depends on the amount of capital required at different stages of the venture's growth and the entrepreneur's strategy to share the risks and rewards incidental to the business with other investors. In this section, we shall briefly discuss different firm structures.

NOTES

Sole proprietorship

If a venture requires small amount of capital, the entrepreneur floats a sole-proprietorship firm. In the case of a sole-proprietorship firm, an individual (the entrepreneur) provides the equity capital (owners capital) and other investors (e.g., financial institutions) provide debt capital. The proprietor has personal liability for all obligations assumed by the firm. The liability of the proprietor is unlimited in the sense that it is not limited to his/her equity contribution to the firm. Creditors, including lenders, can recover their claims from the personal estate of the owner. This firm structure is suitable for small businesses such as a kirana store (a small shop selling groceries and sundries).

Self-Test Questions

Self-test question 1.7

Fill in the blanks:

(i) In sole-proprietorship business, equity capital is provided by ....

(ii) The liability of the owner is ....[Choose between the words 'limited' and 'unlimited'.]

Partnership firm

Partnership structure is suitable for professional firms and other small business firms, which require small amount of capital. More than one individual (called partners) provide equity capital. Partnerships are governed by the Indian Partnership Act, 1938. Every partner is jointly and severally liable for all obligations assumed by the firm. The liability of the each partner is unlimited. Internal governance (e.g., capital contribution, profit sharing and retirement) is regulated by an agreement between the partners.

Self-Test Questions

Self-test question 1.8

Fill in the blanks:

(i) In a partnership firm, capital is provided by ....

(ii) The liability of the a partner is ....[Choose between the words 'limited' and 'unlimited'.]

Limited Liability Partnership (LLP)

The Limited Liability Partnership (LLP) is governed by the Limited Liability Partnership Act, 2008. The LLP is a legal entity separate from partners. It enjoys perpetual succession. Each partner is an agent of the LLP. The liability of partners is limited in the sense that the liability of the LLP is met out of the property of the LLP and partners are not required to inject additional capital to settle the liabilities of the firm. A partner is personally liable for his/her wrongful acts or admissions. But, he/she is not liable for wrongful acts or omissions of other partners. An LLP is run like a general partnership and has similar degree of management flexibility. It facilitates partnership among individuals who operate in different geographic locations and may not be closely known to each other. Most large professional firms of accountants, lawyers, etc. adopt the LLP structure.

NOTES

BOX 1.2 Perpetual Succession

Perpetual succession is the continuation of an incorporated entity such as the LLP and limited liability company (discussed below), despite the death, bankruptcy, insanity of an owner (member in case of a company, and partner in case of LLP) or change in owners or an exit from the business of any owner, or any transfer of shares.

Self-Test Questions

Self-test question 1.9

Indicate whether the following statements are true (T) or false (F):

(i) The liability of partners in a Limited Liability Partnership (LLP) is unlimited.
(ii) A LLP enjoys perpetual succession.
(iii) A partner is not personally liable for his/her wrongful acts or omissions or the acts or omissions of other partners.

Limited Liability Company

Limited liability companies (also called *joint stock companies*) in India are governed by the Companies Act, 2013. The liability of a limited liability company (hereafter, company) is limited to the value of assets that it holds. Consequently, the liability of equity shareholders, who are deemed owners, is limited to the unpaid amount of the contribution to the equity capital of the company committed by them. In other words, the liability is limited to the unpaid amount on the number of equity shares issued to them. Investors in equity capital are called *members*.

ILLUSTRATION 1.2 Limited Liability

Sewa Limited (SL) allotted 100 shares to Rumela. The issue price of each share is ₹150. As per the terms of issue, Rumela paid ₹100 and ₹50 are payable, as and when the company will call for payment.

Required

What is the liability of Rumela?

Solution

Rumela's liability is limited to ₹50 per share or ₹5,000 in total, which is the uncalled amount on shares allotted to her.

A company incorporated under the Companies Act, 2013 is a juridical person. It has an identity separate from investors in the company. It enjoys perpetual succession. Therefore, shareholders can freely transfer their shares without the permission of the company. A company can enter into contracts and can sue and be sued in its own name. A company acts through its Board of Directors, which delegates some powers, particularly those related to day-to-day operation, to the Chief Executive Officer (CEO). Directors are elected by equity shareholders using their voting rights. Under the Indian Companies Act, one share has one vote. Memorandum of Association, which is the most important public document, specifies among other things, the objects that the company will pursue and the address of its registered office. Internal governance of a company is guided by its Articles of Association.

Capital provided to a company belongs to the company. Use of the capital is decided by the company. Investors provide capital to a company in exchange of claims on economic resources (assets) of the company.

NOTES

Companies can be classified into three categories—private companies, public limited companies and listed public companies. One person company is considered as a private limited company.

Private limited company

Private limited companies are also called *closely-held companies*. The Companies Act, 2013 does not allow a private limited company to have more than 200 members and does not allow it to invite public to invest in its equity capital. Therefore, its growth might be constrained by shortage of capital. The cost to comply with regulations of a private limited company is much lower than that of a public company.

One-person company

One-Person Company (OPC) means a company which has only one member. OPC gives the young businessmen all benefits of a private limited company. It means they will have access to credits, bank loans, limited liability, legal protection for business, access to market, etc., all in the name of a separate legal entity. The compliance cost is quite low as OPC enjoys large number of exemptions from complying with the provisions of the Companies Act, 2013.

Public limited company

A public limited company is allowed to invite public to contribute to its equity capital and there is no restriction on the number of members. However, the Companies Act 2013 stipulates large number of prescriptions, proscriptions and disclosure requirements to protect the interest of shareholders, who cannot participate in the management of the company directly. Therefore, the compliance cost is higher than that in the case of a private limited company.

Listed company

A share in a company is *liquid,* and hence, attractive if a seller can always find a buyer and a buyer can always find a seller. Therefore, public limited companies usually list shares issued by them in recognised stock exchanges (e.g., the Bombay Stock Exchange and the National Stock Exchange). A company whose securities are listed in a recognised stock exchange is called a *listed company* or a *publicly traded company*. The securities and Exchange Board of India (SEBI) is responsible for protecting the interest of shareholders of a listed company and efficient operation of capital markets (stock exchanges). A listed company is required to comply with all the regulations issued by SEBI, including the Code of Corporate Governance, in addition to the requirements under the Companies Act 2013. Therefore, the compliance cost of a listed company is much higher than that of an unlisted company.

BOX 1.3 Preference Share Capital

Companies can issue preference shares. Investors in preference shares have a preferential claim (relative to the claim of equity shareholders) on assets of the company and on profit. They are entitled for a pre-determined dividend if the company earns profit. Their claim is senior to the claim of equity shareholders but subordinate to the claim of creditors (including investors in debt capital).

A senior claim gets preference in settlement over a subordinate claim. Under Indian Accounting Standards (Ind AS), preference shares are classified as debt or equity, depending on the terms of the issue. Redeemable preference shares are classified as *debt.* In India, companies cannot issue preference shares other than redeemable preference shares.

NOTES

Key Terms
Angel investors, articles of association, board of directors, business risks, capital, closely held company, credit risks, debt capital, joint stock company, juridical person, limited liability company, limited liability partnership, listed company, memorandum of association, one person company, partner, perpetual succession, preference share capital, private equity, private limited company, public limited company, publicly traded company, sole proprietor

Self-Test Questions

Self-test question 1.10

Indicate whether of the following statements are true (T) or false (F):

(i) A limited liability company can sue and can be sued in its own name.
(ii) A private limited company can invite public to contribute to its equity capital.
(iii) Compliance cost of a public limited company is higher than that of a private limited company.
(iv) Investment in equity shares of a listed company is attractive because it is liquid.
(v) Redeemable preference share capital is a component of equity capital of a company.

SUMMARY

Translating a business idea into a business venture requires resources (capital). At the early stage of the venture, investment is exposed to high risk. At that stage, the entrepreneur gets the support from family members, friends, angel investors and venture capitalist (a type of private equity). As the venture succeeds, initial investors, particularly angel investors and venture capitalists, exit the venture and new investors, who are willing to take moderate risks, join as owners by contributing to the equity capital of the entity. Debt capital is also provided by lenders. Investment in equity capital of a business entity is exposed to business risks. Investment in debt capital of a business entity is exposed to credit risk.

Choice of the firm structure depends on the amount of capital required at different stages of the venture's growth and the entrepreneur's strategy to share the risks and rewards incidental to the business with other investors. In sole proprietorship, equity capital is provided by one individual. In partnership, equity capital is provided by more than one individual called partners. The liability of the sole proprietor and partners is unlimited. A Limited Liability Partnership (LLP) enjoys perpetual succession and the liability of the partners is limited. A limited liability company (hereafter, company) is a juridical person and enjoys perpetual succession. It acts through Board of Directors. The liability of equity shareholders (called members) is limited. A private limited company cannot invite public to contribute to its shareholders and cannot have more than 200 members. There is no such restriction for a public limited company. A public limited company whose shares are listed in a stock exchange is called a listed company (also called publicly traded company). A one-person company is a private limited company.

FINANCIAL STATEMENTS

Objective of Financial Reporting

The objective of financial reporting is to provide financial information, which is useful in making decisions about providing resources to the entity, to the existing and potential investors, lenders and other creditors. Those decisions involve (i) decisions to buy, sell or hold equity and debt instruments (e.g., corporate bond); (ii) decisions to provide or settle loans and other forms of credit; and (iii) decisions needed to exercise rights while holding investments such as in the case of a company, rights of equity shareholders to vote on or otherwise influence management's actions.

Investors and potential investors, lenders and creditors use information in financial statements along with other information such as general economic conditions and expectations, political events and political climate, and industry and company outlooks, for deciding resource allocation.

NOTES

Self-Test Questions

Self-test question 1.11

Indicate whether the following statements are true (T) or false (F):

(i) The primary objective of financial reporting is to provide financial information to the management and the Board of Directors of the company.

(ii) Financial statements provide information that is sufficient to decide buy, hold or sell equity shares and corporate bonds.

(iii) Equity shareholders of a company use information provided in financial statements to decide voting on various decisions placed before them.

(iv) Equity shareholders of a company use information provided in financial statements to evaluate management in its stewardship function.

Users of Financial Statements

Table 1.1 provides the list of users of financial statements:

TABLE 1.1

List of Users of Financial Statements

S. No.	Users	Objectives
		A. Primary Users
1.	Investors and potential investors, and their advisors	The objectives are to (i) value the equity of the company in order to assess whether the equity share of the company is overvalued or undervalued; (ii) forecast the possible movement in equity share prices of the company and its peers; and (iii) evaluate the management of the company in its stewardship function.
2.	Lenders and other creditors	The objective is to assess credit risks in lending or providing credit over different time frames (e.g., short-term and long-term).
		B. Others
3.	Managers and Board of Directors	The objectives are to (i) evaluate the effectiveness of their decisions in organising and allocating resources and the effectiveness of risk management; and (ii) identify candidates for mergers and acquisitions, usually with the help of investment bankers.
4.	Employees	The objective is to assess the stability and growth of the company, as employees' career prospect, future bonus and variable pay depend on the same.
5.	Citizens and government	The objectives are to assess: (i) the stability and growth of the companies, as their discontinuance might have a significant social impact; (ii) the impact of the policy decisions (e.g., providing subsidy) on the performance of companies operating in a particular industry; and (iii) whether a company has avoided paying duties and taxes payable by it.

NOTES

Self-Test Questions

Self-test question 1.12

Indicate whether the following statements are true (T) or false (F):

(i) The primary users of financial statements are investors, potential investors, lenders and other creditors.

(ii) Investors and potential investors use the information provided in financial statements to value equity.

(iii) Lenders and other creditors use the information provided in financial statements to assess business risks.

(iv) Board of Directors uses the information provided in financial statements to evaluate effectiveness of its decision to allocate resources.

(v) Lower-level employees do not find the information provided in financial statements relevant.

SUMMARY

The objective of financial reporting is to provide information to investors, potential investors, lenders and other creditors. Investors and potential investors use the information provided in financial statements to value equity, and lenders and other creditors use the information to evaluate credit risks. However, information available in financial statements is not sufficient for their decision-making. They collect additional information about the business environment (economic, legal, political, technological and social) and use the same along with information available in financial statements for taking economic decisions. Other users of financial statements are managers and Board of Directors, employees, citizens and government.

ANSWERS TO SELF-TEST QUESTIONS

1.1 (i) ₹8,00,000; (ii) Zero; (iii) Reduced
1.2 (i) F; (ii) T; (iii) T; (iv) F; (v) F
1.3 (i) T; (ii) F; (iii) T; (iv) T; (v) F
1.4 (i) ₹1,50,000; (ii) Net worth; (iii) Intangible; (iv) Revenue; (v) Recognition
1.5 (i) F; (ii) F; (iii) F; (iv) T; (v) F
1.6 (i) Capital; (ii) Angel investors; (iii) Venture capital funds; (iv) business; (v) Credit
1.7 (i) Individual; (ii) Unlimited
1.8 (i) Partners; (ii) Unlimited
1.9 (i) F; (ii) T; (iii) F
1.10 (i) T; (ii) F; (iii) T; (iv) T; (v) F
1.11 (i) F; (ii) F; (iii) T; (iv) T
1.12 (i) T; (ii) T; (iii) F; (iv) T; (v) F

ASSIGNMENTS

Multiple Choice Questions

1. Indicate which of the following statements are true (T) and which are false (F):

   (i) Company financial report is primarily targeted towards existing and potential investors and creditors.

   (ii) The liability of an equity shareholder of private limited company is unlimited.

   (iii) A limited liability partnership does not enjoy perpetual succession.

   (iv) Interest-free credits do not form part of invested capital of a firm.

   (v) Net worth of a business entity may be viewed as owners' claim on the assets of the entity.

(vi) Events other than transactions entered by a business entity might affect the assets and liabilities of the entity.
(vii) Publicly traded companies should necessarily be public limited companies.
(viii) Venture capital funds invest in the equity capital of startups with a plan to exit at a later date.

NOTES

2. Fill in the blanks:
(i) A private limited company is also known as .... company.
(ii) A private limited company cannot have more than .... members.
(iii) The claim of owners on the assets of a business entity is called ....
(iv) The terms equity and .... are used interchangeably.
(v) Financial statements are primarily aimed at ....
(vi) The equity capital, long-term debt and short-term debt of a company as at March 31, 2018 were ₹5,00,000, ₹3,00,000, and ₹2,00,000, respectively. The interest-free credit on that date was ₹1,00,000. The invested capital in the company as at March 31 2018 was ....

Accounting Conventions

CHAPTER

2

Learning Objectives

The objective of this chapter is to provide an understanding of the basic principles of financial reporting. After reading this chapter, you will develop understanding of the following:

- Accounting conventions and their applications
- Qualitative characteristics of financial statements

NOTES

ACCOUNTING CONVENTIONS

Accounting rules are subject to well-accepted accounting conventions. Table 2.1 presents the same.

TABLE 2.1

Accounting Conventions

S. No.	Convention	Description
1.	Accounting entity	An accounting entity is an area of economic interest of a particular individual or group. It may be the business unit itself (e.g., a limited liability company), or the defined part of a business unit (e.g., a division), or an amalgamation of related business units (e.g., a holding company) depending on the user's needs. It can also be a non-business group (e.g., person, club and government). According to the entity convention, all transactions and other events are recorded from the point of view of the entity itself, and not from the perspective of stakeholders (e.g., owners). Therefore, an entity records the amount due to owners as claims (equity capital) on assets it controls.
2.	Money measurement	According to this convention, all transactions and other events should be measured in terms of money. Measurement of transactions and events in a common unit of measurement is essential for aggregation and summarisation. There is a lot of debate on whether measurement should be based on the purchasing power of money. However, current accounting rules require companies to measure transactions and other events at nominal amount, without any adjustment for inflation.
3.	Going concern	Unless otherwise stated, users of financial statements assume that the entity is a going concern. An entity is a going concern, if it has neither the intention nor the need to liquidate itself in the foreseeable future, usually one year from the balance sheet date. The going concern convention is important because entities hold assets (e.g., plant and machinery) that are valuable to them only and have relatively significantly low value to others. The entities unlock the value of such an asset through use. Therefore, if the company ceases to exist, the value is lost. The rules for measurement of assets, particularly fixed assets (e.g., property, plant and equipment), of a going concern are likely to be different from the rules for measurement of assets of an entity which is not a going concern.
4.	Cost	Traditionally, financial statements are prepared and presented based on historical cost. Assets are recorded at acquisition cost. Liabilities are recorded at the amount of proceeds received in exchange for an obligation. In some circumstances, for example, income tax liabilities are recorded at the amount of cash expected to be paid to satisfy the liability in the normal course of business. However, accounting practice is shifting its focus from the cost convention. For example, investment in equity shares issued by another entity and derivative instruments are measured at their fair value at the balance sheet date. ***Fair value*** is the price at which the entity can sell the asset or transfer the liability at an arm's length transaction.
5.	Realisation	The realisation convention is closely related to the cost convention. According to this convention, an asset should be recorded at historical cost, and any change in value should be recognised at the time the firm realises or disposes of the asset. An unrealised

(*Contd.*)

NOTES

TABLE 2.1

Accounting Conventions (*Contd.*)

S. No.	Convention	Description
		gain should not be recognised. For some assets and liabilities, the current accounting principles contravene this convention. For example, Ind AS permits companies to measure property, plant and equipment at fair value. Similarly, it mandates measurement of some specified assets (investment in equity held for trading) at fair value and recognise the increase or decrease in the fair value in profit or loss.
6.	Accrual	According to the accrual convention, income is recognised as it is earned and expenditure is recognised, either as an asset or as an expense, when it is incurred. In contrast, under cash basis of accounting, income is recognised when cash is received and expenditure is recognised when cash is paid.
7.	Matching	According to the matching convention, in order to present true and fair view of the operating result, accounting principles and methods should ensure matching income and expenses to the extent possible. In the past, the focus was on reporting profit or loss, and therefore, the matching principle was the overriding principle for the preparation and presentation of financial statements. However, with shift of focus to the balance sheet, the matching principle is no more the overriding principle. As per the current accounting principle, an expenditure, from which no asset can be recognised, should be recognised as an expense for the period in which the expenditure is incurred. For example, no asset is recognised from expenditure during the research phase, and accordingly, research expenditure is recognised as an expense for the period in which it is incurred, although it has no cause and effect relationship with the revenue earned during that period.
8.	Periodicity	Entities are expected to operate for a fairly long period. It may be assumed that an entity has an indefinite life. The indefinite life is subdivided into smaller time units to measure and understand the performance and financial position of the entity and timely dissemination of financial information. The convention is to issue a complete set of financial statements at an interval of 12 months. The 12-month period is called the *fiscal year or the accounting year.* Listed companies are required (by governing regulations) to publish abridged financial statements on a quarterly basis.
9.	Conservatism (also called prudence)	Estimation is at the centre of accounting measurement. It requires judgement. Prudence is the exercise of caution when making judgements under conditions of uncertainty. Traditionally, according to the conservatism convention, in a situation of uncertainty, it is preferable to understate profit and assets rather than overstating the same. The operating rules are: (i) An entity should not anticipate income and should provide for all estimated losses. (ii) Faced with the choice between two methods of valuing an asset, the accountant should choose a method that leads to the lesser value. The underlying principle is that bad news should travel fast and good news may be delayed. The principle of prudence is good from creditors' perspective, who assess credit risks, but not so from investors' perspective, who forecast performance to value equity. The contemporary thought is that the application of prudence does not allow overstatement or understatement of assets, income, liabilities and expenses.

Self-Test Questions

Self-test question 2.1

Indicate whether the following statements are true (T) or false (F):

(i) GAAP cannot be applied in preparing and presenting financial statements of a sub-unit of a company because as per the 'accounting entity' convention, it cannot be treated as an accounting entity.

(ii) 'Money measurement' convention requires entities to measure transactions and other events at nominal amount, without any adjustment for inflation.

(iii) In accounting, 'going concern' implies that in the long-term (say, in next ten years). the entity will not get liquidated.

(iv) As per GAAP, all assets and liabilities are measured at historical cost.

(v) Some contemporary accounting practices violate the 'realisation' convention.

(vi) Accrual convention allows recognition of revenue when the invoice is preferred on the customer for supply of goods without waiting for realisation of the amount due from it.

(vii) 'Matching' is the overriding accounting principle under GAAP.

(viii) Listed companies are required (by governing regulations) to publish abridged financial statements on a quarterly basis.

(ix) The 'prudence' convention, the underlying principle of which is that bad news should travel fast and good news may be delayed, protects investors from manager's temptation to disclose good news early and delay disclosure of bad news.

NOTES

Key Terms

Accounting entity, accrual, conservatism, fair value, going concern, historical cost, holding company, prudence, true and fair view

SUMMARY

Accounting rules are subject to well-accepted accounting conventions. According to the entity convention, all transactions and other events are recorded from the point of view of the entity itself, and not from the perspective of stakeholders (e.g., owners). According to 'money measurement' convention, all transactions and other events should be measured in terms of money. As per 'going concern' convention, unless otherwise stated, financial statements are prepared on the assumption that the entity is a going concern, which means it has neither the intention nor the need to liquidate itself in the foreseeable future. Under the 'cost' convention, financial statements are prepared and presented based on historical cost. However, contemporary accounting practices are shifting from the cost conventions. According to 'realisation' convention, unrealised gains should not be recognised. Some contemporary accounting practices violate this convention. According to the accrual convention, income is recognised as it is earned and expenditure is recognised either as an asset or as an expense, when it is incurred. According to the matching convention, in order to present true and fair view of the operating result, accounting principles and methods should ensure matching income and expenses, to the extent possible. According to the 'periodicity' convention, a complete set of financial statements is issued at an interval of 12 months. According to 'conservatism' convention, in a situation of uncertainty, it is preferable to understate profit and assets rather than overstating the same.

QUALITATIVE CHARACTERISTICS OF FINANCIAL STATEMENTS

The qualitative characteristics identify the types of information that are likely to be most useful to the primary users (existing and potential investors, lenders and other creditors) of financial statements. The Conceptual Framework For Financial Reporting issued by the International Accounting Standards Board (IASB), which guides formulation of accounting standards, describes qualitative characteristics.

NOTES

Table 2.2 presents the qualitative characteristics.

TABLE 2.2

Qualitative Characteristics of Financial Statements

S. No.	Qualitative characteristic	Description
		A. Fundamental Qualitative Characteristics
1.	Relevance	Financial information is relevant if it has predictive value or confirmatory value, and thus, is capable of making a difference in the decisions made by users. Financial information has predictive value if it can be used as an input in predicting the future financial position, performance, earning capacity, cash flows, etc. of the entity. It has confirmatory value if it provides feedback on past evaluation. Usually, information having predictive value has confirmatory value also.
2.	Faithful representation	Financial statements report economic phenomena in words and numbers. Financial information must faithfully represent the phenomena that it purports to represent. Therefore, financial statements must report substance of an economic phenomenon instead of merely providing information about its legal form. For example, in some situations, in substance, a sale and buy-back transaction is a financing transaction and not a sale transaction, and therefore, such a transaction should be reported as financing transaction. Faithful representation requires that the information should be complete, neutral and free from error. Completeness implies that the information should include all necessary descriptions and explanations to enable the user to understand the phenomenon. Neutrality implies that the information should be free from bias in the sense that it is not slanted, weighted, emphasised, deemphasised or otherwise manipulated to increase the probability that users will receive the financial information favourably or unfavourably. Neutrality is supported by the exercise of prudence. Measurement uncertainties affect faithful representation. Therefore, it is important that notes to financial statements explain uncertainties surrounding estimates.
		B. Enhancing Qualitative Characteristics
3.	Comparability	Comparability implies that information about a reporting entity can be compared with similar information about other entities and with similar information about the same entity for another period or another date. Consistency refers to using the same methods for the same items either from period to period within a reporting entity or in a single period across entities. Consistency helps in achieving comparability.
4.	Verifiability	Verifiability means that different knowledgeable and independent observers could reach consensus, although not necessarily complete agreement, that a particular depiction is a faithful representation. If a particular measure cannot be verified, disclosures may be needed in the notes to the financial statements to enable users of financial statements to understand the assumptions used.
5.	Timeliness	Timeliness means having information available to decision-makers in time to be capable of influencing their decisions.
6.	Understandability	Financial information should be understandable to those users, who have a reasonable knowledge of business and economic activities and who review and analyse the information diligently. Classifying, characterising and presenting information clearly and concisely make it understandable.

NOTES

BOX 2.1 Materiality

Information is material if omitting it or misstating it could influence decisions of the primary users (investors and potential investors, lenders and creditors) of financial statements. Materiality is an *entity-specific aspect of relevance* based on the nature or magnitude, or both, of the items to which the information relates in the context of an individual entity's financial report. Assessing materiality is a matter of judgement.

Materiality is an entity-specific aspect; the threshold of magnitude is decided by the entity. But sometimes, the regulator establishes threshold. For example, the Indian Companies Act, 2013 requires that any item under which income or expenses exceed 1 percent of the revenue from operations of the company or ₹10,00,000, whichever is higher, shall be shown as a separate and distinct item in the statement of profit and loss.

An example of materiality by nature is the reporting of a new segment irrespective of the amount of income or profit earned by the segment during the reporting period. Omission of this information is expected to influence the decisions of the primary users, as the information helps in assessing the risks and opportunities facing the entity.

Self-Test Questions

Self-test question 2.2

Indicate whether the following statements are true (T) or false (F):

(i) Usually, information having predictive value has confirmatory value also.

(ii) Faithful representation requires that a transaction should be accounted for based on its economic substance rather than on its legal form.

(iii) Information in financial statements loses relevance in the absence of complete disclosure (in notes to accounts) of details of each item on the face of balance sheet and the statement of profit and loss.

(iv) Accuracy in bookkeeping is essential for achieving the quality of faithful representation.

(v) Fundamental qualitative characteristics may be sacrificed to some extent for the sake of improving understandability, as most retail investors do not have the skills and knowledge, which are required for analysing complex financial statements.

(vi) Materiality of an item in the balance sheet and statement of profit and loss is determined with reference to its magnitude only.

Cost Constraints on Useful Financial Reporting

Financial reporting imposes costs; its benefits should justify these costs. Assessing whether the benefits of providing information justify the related costs will usually be more qualitative than quantitative. In applying the cost constraint, standard setters assess whether the benefits of reporting information are likely to justify the costs incurred to provide and use that information. When making this assessment, they consider whether one or more qualitative characteristics might be sacrificed to some degree to reduce cost. An entity is not allowed to take the plea that it has not complied with an accounting standard because the cost of compliance is higher than the benefits that users of financial statements would derive from compliance of the standard.

Self-Test Questions

Self-test question 2.3

Indicate whether the following statements are true (T) or false (F):

(i) An entity may decide not to apply an accounting principle stipulated in the applicable accounting standard if it estimates that the cost of collecting the relevant information and/or the negative impact of disclosing the same on its competitive advantage exceeds the benefits to primary users of financial statements.

(ii) Standard setters consider sacrificing one or more qualitative characteristics to reduce the cost of financial reporting.

NOTES

Key Terms
Faithful representation, materiality, neutrality, relevance, verifiability

SUMMARY

The qualitative characteristics identify the types of information that are likely to be most useful to the primary users (existing and potential investors, lenders and other creditors) of financial statements. Fundamental qualitative characteristics are 'relevance' and 'faithful representation'. Financial information is relevant if it has predictive value or confirmatory value, and thus, is capable of making a difference in the decisions made by users. Financial information must faithfully represent the phenomena that it purports to represent. Therefore, financial statements must report substance of an economic phenomenon instead of merely providing information about its legal form. Faithful representation requires that the information should be complete, neutral and free from error. Enhancing qualitative characteristics are comparability, verifiability, timeliness and understandability.

Materiality is an *entity-specific aspect* of *relevance* based on the nature or magnitude, or both, of the items to which the information relates in the context of an individual entity's financial report. Information is material if omitting it or misstating it could influence decisions of the primary users of financial statements. Assessing materiality is a matter of judgement.

Financial reporting imposes costs; its benefits should justify these costs. Standard setters, while formulating accounting standards, assess whether the benefits of reporting information are likely to justify the costs incurred to provide and use that information.

EXAMPLES OF APPLICATION OF ACCOUNTING CONVENTIONS AND QUALITATIVE CHARACTERISTICS

Accrual Accounting

Accrual accounting helps in providing true and fair view of (i) activities undertaken during the period and (ii) assets (e.g., trade receivables) and liabilities (trade creditors) at the end of the period. Table 2.3 presents examples of accrual accounting.

TABLE 2.3

Examples of Accrual Accounting

S. No.	Element in financial statements	Accounting principle
1.	Sales of goods and services	An entity recognises income from sale of goods and services when it fulfills the performance obligation and collection is reasonably certain. It does not wait for realisation of cash.
2.	Expenditure	An entity recognises an asset or expense when the expenditure is incurred (e.g., goods and services received) without waiting for outflow of economic resources (e.g., cash).
4.	Pre-paid expenses	An entity recognises expense (e.g., rent and insurance premium) paid in advance as an asset, as service against that payment will be received in future.
5.	Deferred revenue (also called, unearned revenue)	An entity recognises a liability (deferred revenue) for the amount received from a customer before the entity fulfills one or more performance obligations.
6.	Interest	An entity recognises interest income and interest expense on time proportion basis. It recognises accrued interest income as an asset and accrued interest expense as a liability.

NOTES

S. No.	Element in financial statements	Accounting principle
7.	Depreciation of an item of Property, Plant and Equipment (PP&E) and amortisation of an item of intangible assets	Depreciation is the allocation of cost less estimated residual value of an item of PP&E over the intended period of use. Residual value is the value that the entity expects to realise on disposing the asset after its useful life. Depreciation is the allocation of capitalised expenditure to different periods that benefit from the expenditure. This method of allocation of capitalised expenditure is often referred to as ***long-term accrual***. In case of intangible assets, the term 'amortisation' is used instead of depreciation.

CASE STUDY 2.1 Sale of Goods

Nirvana Limited (NL) is a manufacturer of ayurvedic medicines. It sells its medicines through dealers located across India. It gives three months credit to its dealers. Most dealers pay well in time, but sometimes, dealers delay the payment. However, they invariably pay within six months from the date of invoice. Dealers use their own transport to collect the medicines from the factory gate.

Question

When should NL record the sale?

Solution

Sale is complete immediately on delivery of medicines to the transporter of the dealer, as the transporter acts as the agent of the dealer. Past payment pattern from dealer shows that the payments due from dealers are realised. Therefore, NL reasonably expects that payments would be realised against each invoice. Therefore, sale should be recorded on the date of invoice and simultaneously amount due from dealers should be recorded.

CASE STUDY 2.2 Expenses

Nirvana Limited (NL) is a manufacturer of ayurvedic medicines. It obtains most of ingredients from plants, whose leaves and fruits have medicinal properties. Plant growers are local inhabitants of hilly areas in Himachal Pradesh and Uttarakhand in India. Employees of NL collect ingredients and transport to the factory through a logistic company, which specialises in transportation of medicines at appropriate temperature.

NL is a new generation company and takes pride in publishing its financial statements by April 30, that is, within one month from the close of the accounting year. The logistic company submits some of invoices for the transportation services rendered in March after the Board of Directors of NL approves issue of the financial statements.

Question

How should NL account for the transportations expenses incurred in the year 2017–18, for which invoices are not received from the logistic company by April 30, 2018, the date on which the Board of Directors will approve financial statements?

Solution

NL has a contract with the logistic company, which specifies rates at which the logistic company charges NL for its services. NL should estimate the expenses for which invoices are not received. It should recognise a liability for the estimated amount of expenses in its balance sheet as at March 31, 2018 and include the amount in the transportation expenses to be recognised in the statement of profit and loss for the year 2017–18.

NOTES

CASE STUDY 2.3 Pre-paid Expenses

Nirvana Limited (NL) is a manufacturer of ayurvedic medicines. Its factories are located in the industrial areas in Ghaziabad and Manesar. It has taken on lease the factory building constructed by a real estate developer. At the insistence of the real estate developer, the lease contract is for eleven months. However, for past ten years, the contract is renewed without any dispute. As per the terms of the contract, lease rent is payable on quarterly basis immediately before the commencement of the contract. On March 31, 2018, NL paid ₹10,00,000 towards lease rent for the quarter ending June 30, 2018.

Question

How should NL account for the lease rent paid on March 31, 2018 in its financial statements for the year 2017–18?

Solution

NL should recognise ₹10,00,000 paid towards lease rent for the quarter ending June 30, 2018 as an asset (pre-paid rent) in its balance sheet as at March 31, 2018 and adjust the rent expense to be recognised in the statement of profit or loss for the year 2017–18.

CASE STUDY 2.4 Deferred Revenue

Vanu Automobiles Limited (VAL) is an automobile dealer. It sold 20 cars on March 31, 2018 for ₹2 crore with free maintenance for one year. It provides maintenance services at a price after one year from the date of sale.

Question

How should VAL account for the sale in its financial statements for the year 2017–18?

Solution

VAL should allocate a part of the selling price of ₹2 crore to maintenance services to be offered to its customers free of charge. It should estimate the maintenance charge based on its experience of charging customers for maintenance of new cars, which are not covered under the contract for free maintenance for one year. That part of the selling price, which is allocated to maintenance service, should be recognised as deferred revenue, which is a liability, in the balance sheet as at March 31, 2018 and the balance amount should be recognised as revenue in statement of profit and loss for the year 2017–18.

CASE STUDY 2.5 Interest

On June 30, 2017, Singham Limited (SL) borrowed ₹1,00,000 at the interest rate of 10 percent per annum payable at six monthly intervals. There is a moratorium on repayment of the loan. The loan is to be repaid in five yearly instalments starting from June 30, 2020. It paid interest of ₹5,000 on December 31, 2017. Interest of ₹5,000 is payable on June 30, 2018.

Question

How should SL account for the interest on loan?

Solution

The entity should recognise interest for three months (January 1, 2018 to March 31, 2018), which is ₹2,500, as accrued interest, which is a liability, in the balance sheet dated March 31, 2018. The amount of interest to be recognised in the statement of profit and loss is (₹5,000 + 2,500) or ₹7,500.

NOTES

CASE STUDY 2.6 Depreciation

On April 1, 2017, Moon Beam Limited (MBL) purchased a vehicle for ₹10,00,000. It estimates that it will use it for 10 years. It estimates the residual value at zero.

Question

How MBL should account for depreciation on the vehicle?

Solution

MBL will allocate (₹10,00,000 – 0) or ₹10,00,000 over the useful life of the vehicle (ten years). One of the acceptable depreciation methods is to allocate ₹1,00,000 uniformly to all the ten years. This is called the *straight-line method of depreciation*. Using this method, the MBL should recognise the vehicle at ₹9,00,000 in the balance sheet dated March 31, 2018 and it should recognise depreciation of ₹1,00,000 as an expense in the statement of profit and loss for the year 2017–18. MBL may choose any other acceptable method of depreciation.

Self-Test Questions

Self-test question 2.4

Fill in the blanks:

(i) In 2017–18, an entity invoiced customers for goods sold for ₹1,000 crore, but it could realise only ₹950 crore from those customers during 2017–18. The revenue should be recognised in the statement of profit and loss for the year 2017–18 at ₹...............

(ii) SM Limited started business on April 1, 2017. It pays monthly rent for the office building in advance, that is at the end of the previous month. The rent is ₹10,000 per month. Its cash book shows that it paid ₹1,30,000 in the ₹2017–18 towards rent. The office rent to be recognised in the statement of profit and loss for the year 2017–18 should be ₹.................

(iii) KS Limited sells designer ladies attire. It provides free dry cleaning services for two years to its existing customers and charges those who are not in its existing customers' list. During 2017–18, it sold goods for ₹100 crore and estimated that the fair value of free maintenance service that it would provide for attires sold during the year was ₹2 crore. The revenue for the year 2017–18 should be recognised at ₹...............

(iv) On October 1, 2017, MN Limited gave ₹10,00,000 to one of its vendors as loan repayable after two year. The agreed interest rate is 10 percent per annum payable annually. The interest income to be recognised in statement of profit and loss for the year 2017–18 at ₹....................

(v) VT Limited purchased five cars on April 1, 2017 for ₹60,00,000. It intends to use the car for five years. The market price of used five-year old car of the same model is ₹2,00,000. Assuming that the entity uses straight line method of depreciation for vehicles, the carrying amount of the five vehicles in the balance sheet as at March 31, 2018 should be ₹....................

NOTES

Prudence

Prudence is the exercise of caution in making judgements under conditions of significant uncertainty to ensure that assets, liabilities, incomes and expenses are neither overstated nor understated. In a situation of uncertainty when it is difficult to formulate judgements, it is better to understate the asset rather than overstating it. The working rule is that loss should be recognised immediately when estimated, but profit or gain should not be recognised until realised or realisable.

Table 2.4 presents examples of the applications of the principle of prudence.

TABLE 2.4

Applications of the Principle of Prudence

S. No.	Element in financial statements	Accounting principle
1.	Measurement of stock-in-trade, finished goods and work-in-progress	An entity measures stock of 'goods-in-trade', finished goods and Work-In-Progress (WIP) at the lower of cost or Net Realisable Value (NRV). The NRV is the amount that the entity expects to realise by selling the goods in the next or a subsequent period, adjusted for direct expenses in selling the goods. This results in recognition of the estimated loss, in the current period, that it will incur in the next or subsequent periods while selling the goods. For example, if the cost of production of finished goods in stock is ₹20,000 and the estimated NRV is ₹18,000, the stock of finished goods is measured at ₹18,000. On the other hand, if the estimated NRV is ₹22,000, the stock of finished goods is measured at ₹20,000.
2.	Onerous contract	*Executory contract* is a contract under execution, or where one or more parties have not yet performed their duties as stipulated in the contract document. Onerous contract is an executory contract in which the unavoidable costs of meeting the obligations under the contract exceed the economic benefits expected to be received under it. An entity recognises the estimated loss on an onerous contract in the current period by simultaneously recognising a liability and an expense.
3.	Impairment loss	An entity recognises impairment loss when it estimates that an item of asset will not be able to recover its carrying amount either through use or through sale. For example, the carrying amount, which is cost less accumulated depreciation and accumulated impairment loss, of an asset is ₹10,00,000. The entity estimates that it will be able to recover ₹8,00,000. It reduces the carrying amount of the asset to ₹8,00,000 in the balance sheet and recognises impairment loss of ₹2,00,000 in the statement of profit and loss.
4.	Intangible assets	An entity does not recognise internally generated intangible assets, except computer software, in the balance sheet, as estimate of their value is not verifiable, and therefore, the information can be misleading. It does not recognise any asset from expenditures on advertising, training and research. An asset from expenditure incurred during the development (of a product or process) is recognised in the balance sheet if certain stringent criteria specified in the relevant accounting standard (Ind AS 38, Intangible Assets) are met.

NOTES

CASE STUDY 2.7 Onerous Contract

New Electricals Limited (NEL) accepted an order for constructing a seaport in Gujarat coast. Before execution of a turnkey contract, execution of which is scheduled to commence in July 2018, NEL estimates that it will incur a loss of ₹50 crore due to sudden change in input prices. In other words, the contract has become onerous due to increase in input prices. If NEL does not execute the contract, it will have to pay a penalty of ₹20 crore.

Question

What liability should NEL recognise on account of the onerous contract?

Solution

NEL will prefer not to execute the contract and pay penalty, as the amount of penalty is lower than the amount of the estimated loss. Therefore, it should recognise a liability of ₹20 crore, which is the amount of the penalty in the balance sheet dated March 31, 2018 and should recognise a loss of ₹20 crore on account of the onerous contract in the statement of profit and loss for the year 2017–18.

Self-Test Questions

Self-test question 2.5

Fill in the blanks:

(i) BK Limited is in the retail business and sells garments. The cost of goods in stock as at March 31, 2018 is ₹50 crore. The management estimates that it will realise only ₹45 crore in 2018–19. The stock should be carried in the balance sheet as at March 31, 2018 at ₹.................

(ii) At the end of the year 2017–18, the management of CD Construction Limited estimates that a turnkey contract for the construction of an elevated road, construction of which is yet to commence, has become onerous and it will incur a loss of 50 crore. The penalty payable if, the entity does not execute the contract is ₹20 crore. The management has decided to execute the contract to avoid reputation loss. The entity should provide liability on this account in the balance sheet dated March 31, 2018 at ₹..............

(iii) The carrying amount of an asset as at March 31, 2018 is ₹10 crore. The management estimates that it will be able to recover ₹2 crore by selling the asset and it will recover ₹8 crore if, it uses the asset. The entity should recognise impairment loss in its statement of profit and loss for the year 2017–18 at ₹.................

Substance over Form

Transactions and other events are recorded and presented in financial statements based on their economic substance, which might be different from the legal form of the transaction. This is important to present a true and fair view of the performance and financial position of the reporting entity.

Table 2.5 presents examples of the application of the principle of substance over form.

NOTES

TABLE 2.5

Application of the Principle of Substance over Form

S. No.	Element in financial statements	Accounting principle
1.	Lease	Lease is a contract that conveys the right to use an asset for a period of time in exchange for consideration. Although a leasing arrangement is legally viewed as a contract similar to hiring an asset (e.g., vehicles) by the user for all or a part of economic life of the asset, the lessee accounts for a non-cancellable lease that is classified as a finance lease as a financing transaction. A financial lease is essentially a leasing arrangement in which the rewards and risks incidental to ownership of the asset are substantially transferred to the lessee. The relevant accounting standard provides a list of indicators, which that indicates that the lease is a finance lease. The lessee recognise the asset and a corresponding liability.
2.	Redeemable preference shares	The claim of an investor in the preference share capital of a company is subordinate to the claims of creditors, but senior to the claim of equity shareholders. A claim is subordinate to another claim when settlement of that other claim gets priority over the settlement of the claim. That other claim is said to be senior to the claim. In the case of redeemable preference shares, the company is under obligation to repay the capital as per the agreement. Therefore, redeemable preference share capital is recognised as liability.
3.	Sale and buy-back arrangement	In some transactions involving sale and buy-back of the goods, significant risks and rewards of ownership are not transferred to the buyer. Although the legal form of those transactions is sale of goods, they are not presented as such in financial statements.
4.	Barter transaction	In barter transaction, which involves exchange of similar goods, neither of the parties recognises sale and expenses in its statement of profit and loss. This is because exchange of similar goods has no commercial substance in the sense that the transaction does not have any material impact on the cash flows of the parties concerned. A barter transaction involving exchange of dissimilar goods is accounted for as a sale/purchase transaction.

CASE STUDY 2.8 Sale and Buy-back

On December 5, 2017, Moon Light Limited (MLL) sold 10,000 shares of Infosys technologies Limited, which are actively traded in Bombay Stock Exchange (BSE) and National Stock Exchange (NSE), to Sun Shine Limited (SSL) for ₹984.40 per share, which is the market price on that date. As per the contract, MLL will buy-back the shares on December 4, 2018 at ₹1,102.53 per share.

Question

How should the transaction be presented by MLL and SSL in their respective balance sheets as at March 31, 2017?

Solution

The legal form of the transaction is a sale transaction. However, in substance, it is a financing transaction. SSL has financed MLL (₹984.40 × 10,000) or ₹98,44,000 at an interest of (₹1,102.53 – 984.40) × 10,000 or ₹11,81,300, which is 12 percent of ₹98,44,000. As the buy-back is at a pre-specified price, MLL retains the risk (loss due to downward movement of the share price) and reward (gain due to upward movement of the share price) incidental to the ownership of the shares. SSL will earn interest at the rate of 12 percent per annum on the loan extended to MLL.

MLL should recognise the sale proceeds of ₹98,44,000 as borrowings in its balance sheet dated March 31, 2018. SSL should recognise the purchase price of ₹98,44,000 as loan in its balance sheet dated March 31, 2018.

NOTES

CASE STUDY 2.9 Barter Transaction, Similar Goods

Ghaziabad Dairy Limited (GDL) is located in Raj Nagar, Ghaziabad, which is a constituent of the National Capital Region (NCR). Delhi Dairy Limited (DDL) is located in Masoodpur, Delhi, which is also a constituent of NCR. The distance between the two is 50 km. GDL has customers in Delhi and DDL has customers in Ghaziabad. Under an agreement between GDL and DDL, GDL supplies 1,000 litre of milk to the customers of DDL located in Ghaziabad and DDL supplies 1,000 litre of milk to the customers of GDL located in Delhi.

Question

How should the transaction between GDL and DDL be recorded in the books of GDL and DDL?

Solution

The barter transaction between GDL and DDL involves exchange of similar goods. Therefore, no sale and purchase should be recognised either by GDL or DDL from the transaction between them. However, both GDL and DDL should recognise revenue based on invoices preferred by their customers, including customers located in Delhi/Ghaziabad, for supply of milk. The total cost of production of milk is matched with total revenues in the statement of profit and loss.

CASE STUDY 2.10 Barter Transaction, Dissimilar Good

Bengaluru InfoTech Limited (BIL) sells Internet advertising space to Kolkata InfoTech Limited (KIL) in exchange for Internet advertising space provided by KIL. KIL sells Internet advertising space at the rate of ₹2,000 per unit for cash (or an asset easily convertible into cash) in non-barter transactions. BIL does not sell Internet advertising space for cash (or an asset easily convertible into cash).

Question

How do BIL and KIL account for the transaction between them?

Solution

Although Internet advertising space that BIL sells to KIL appears to be similar to the Internet advertising space provided by KIL, in all likelihood they are different. Therefore, this is a case of barter of dissimilar goods. The sale and purchase should be recognised at the fair value. It should be presumed that the fair value of the non-monetary asset or service exchanged is more clearly evident than the fair value of the barter assets or service received.

As KIL sells Internet advertising space in non-barter transactions at the rate of ₹2,000 per unit for cash, it should measure the sale and purchase applying the rate of ₹2,000 per unit and recognise the same in the statement of profit and loss. BIL does not sell the Internet advertising space in non-barter transactions for cash. Therefore, it is unable to measure the fair value of the transaction reliably. Consequently, it is not permitted to recognise the sale and purchase arising from the barter transaction.

NOTES

Key Terms

Amortisation, deferred revenue, depreciation, executory contract, impairment loss, lease, long-term accrual, net realisable value, onerous contract, pre-paid expenses, redeemable preference share, residual value, useful life

Self-Test Questions

Self-test question 2.6

Fill in the blanks:

(i) On March 31, 2018, KP Consultants Limited (KPCL) has taken on lease an equipment for a lease rent of ₹1 crore per month for a lease term of five years. The lease rent will increase at 10 percent in each subsequent year. The lessee classifies the lease as a finance lease. The present value of the lease rent estimated by applying the rate at which KPCL can borrow additional fund is ₹48 crore. The asset (equipment) and the liability (borrowings) should be recognised in the balance sheet as at March 31, 2018 at ₹.......................

(ii) On March 31, 2018, HJ Limited (HJL) sold to PQ Limited (PQL) 100 shares issued by a well-known company at ₹1,000 per share, the market price on that date, with an arrangement to buy-back the shares at a price of ₹1,100 per share after one year. The shares are actively traded in NSE. HJL should recognise the sale proceeds as ....in its financial statements for the year 2017–18.

(iii) FG Limited (FGL) and DE Limited (DEL) are in the business of home delivery of milk. In an arrangement between the two companies, FGL serves the customers of DEL located near FGL's manufacturing unit and DEL serves the customers of FGL located near DEL's manufacturing unit. As per the agreement, 12,000 litre of milk in a year is exchanged. The fair value of milk is ₹100 per litre. FGL and DEL should recognise the purchase and sale from this exchange transaction at ₹...............

SUMMARY

Accrual accounting helps in providing true and fair view of (i) activities undertaken during the period and (ii) assets (e.g., trade receivables) and liabilities (e.g., trade creditors) at the end of the period. Under accrual accounting system, an entity recognises income when earned and expenses when incurred without waiting for cash inflows and outflows. Examples are recognition of income from sale of goods and services when it fulfills the performance obligation and collection is reasonably certain, recognition of pre-paid expenses as an asset, recognition of accrued interest on investment as an asset, recognition of accrued interest on borrowings as a liability, recognition of deferred revenue as a liability, and recognition of depreciation.

Prudence is the exercise of caution in making judgements under conditions of significant uncertainty to ensure that assets, liabilities, incomes and expenses are neither overstated nor understated. In a situation of uncertainty when it is difficult to formulate judgements, it is better to understate the asset rather than overstating it. Examples of application of the principle of prudence are valuing finished goods at the lower of cost and net realisable value, providing liability for onerous contracts, and recognising impairment loss. Under this principle, internally generated intangible assets, other than computer software, are not recognised as assets in the balance sheet.

Under the principle of 'substance over form', transactions and other events are recorded and presented in financial statements based on their economic substance, which might be different from the legal form of the transaction. Examples of the application of this principle are recognising a lease transaction as a financing transaction, recognising redeemable preference shares as liabilities, and recognising some sale and lease back transactions as financing transactions. Under this principle, barter transactions involving similar goods and services are not recognised as sale and purchase.

ACTIVITY

Download the financial statements of a non-finance company of your choice and go through its accounting policy.

ANSWERS TO SELF-TEST QUESTIONS

2.1 (i) F; (ii) T; (iii) F; (iv) F; (v) T; (vi) T; (vii) F; (viii) T; (ix) T

2.2 (i) T; (ii) T; (iii) T; (iv) T; (v) F; (vi) F

2.3 (i) F; (ii) T

2.4 (i) ₹1,000 crore; (ii) ₹1,20,000; (iii) ₹98 crore; (iv) ₹50,000; (v) ₹50,00,000

2.5 (i) ₹45 crore; (ii) ₹50 crores; (iii) ₹2 crore

2.6 (i) ₹48 crore; (ii) Borrowings; (iii) ₹Zero

NOTES

ASSIGNMENTS

Multiple Choice Questions

1. Indicate whether the following statements are true (T) or false (F):
   - (i) Amount invested in a company through redeemable preference shares is included in measuring the equity in the balance sheet of a company.
   - (ii) Stock of finished goods at the end of the accounting period is valued at cost to determine the carrying amount of the same in the balance sheet.
   - (iii) Core competence of a business firm is not recognised as an asset in its balance sheet.
   - (iv) Barter transactions involving exchange of similar goods and services are ignored in preparing financial statements.
   - (v) An investor who does not have knowledge of economics, business and accounting finds it difficult to understand the information provided in financial statements, particularly of large companies, which enter into complex transactions.
   - (vi) 'Decision usefulness' is the overriding principle in the preparation and presentation of financial statements.
   - (vii) Information is reliable only if it is free from material error or bias.
   - (viii) Materiality is determined with reference to the size of the item and nothing else.
   - (ix) Contemporary financial accounting practice ignores inflation while measuring assets and liabilities at historical cost.
   - (x) Only those expenses that are incurred to earn the revenue for the period are recognised in the profit and loss account for the period.
   - (xi) Application of the principle of prudence results in understatement of profit.
   - (xii) A business enterprise has the complete discretion to formulate its accounting policy.
2. Fill in the blanks:
   - (i) Information is reliable only when it is ....
   - (ii) In a transaction involving sale and buy-back of an actively traded share, if the buy-back is at the market price of the share at the buy-back date, the transaction is recognised as a .... transaction.
   - (iii) Application of the principle of .... results in recognition of deferred revenue as a liability in the balance sheet of a business firm.
   - (iv) When the management estimates that execution of a contract, execution of which is yet to commence, will incur a loss, the contract is classified as .... contract.

Analytical Questions

1. Explain why equity capital is called *risk capital*. If debt capital is 80 percent of the total capital employed in a firm, will it be correct to say that the debt capital is exposed to credit risk only? Is the notion of 'safe debt level' appropriate in determining the capital structure?
2. "The photographic analogy for the balance sheet is snap shot and for the statement of profit and loss and cash flow statement is a motion picture." Explain.
3. Elucidate the statement that "in the preparation and presentation of financial statements accountants always balance between 'relevance and reliability'."
4. Do you believe that harmonisation of accounting practices across the globe is a prerequisite for the movement of capital across the globe? Present your views in the form of a note.
5. "Politics is inherent to the accounting standard setting process." Explain.

ANNEXURES

ANNEXURE 1: ACCOUNTING POLICY AND ACCOUNTING ESTIMATES

Accounting policies are the specific principles, bases, conventions, rules and practices applied by an entity in preparing and presenting financial statements.

For example, an entity formulates an accounting policies on how stock of finished goods at the end of the accounting period will be measured, and at what point in the process of selling goods, income from sales of goods will be recognised and measured.

An entity rarely selects an accounting policy that deviates from accounting principles and methods stipulated in accounting standards. Entities are not allowed to change accounting policy voluntarily. Accounting policy is changed when it is required by a new or revised accounting standard

NOTES

or by a statute. Change in the accounting policy is applied retrospectively unless the new or revised standard includes the transition provision. Retrospectively implies that the new policy is applied to transactions and events of earlier years and equity, assets and liabilities at the beginning of the current year is restated to reflect the cumulative effect of the application of the new accounting policy to transactions and events of earlier years.

The use of reasonable estimates is an essential part of the preparation of financial statements, because uncertainties inherent in business activities do not allow precise measurement of many items in financial statements. Estimation involves judgements based on the latest available, reliable information. Examples of items that involve estimation are: bad debt, fair value of financial assets, useful life of a building and warranty obligations. Estimates change with the flow of new information. The effect of change in estimate is applied prospectively, that is, in the current year and in subsequent years.

ANNEXURE II: TRUE AND FAIR VIEW

Financial statements provide a true and fair view of the financial position and performance of the reporting entity only if it meets the required qualitative characteristics of financial statements. Often, an enterprise, in preparing and presenting financial statements, balances between different qualitative characteristics. Let us take an example. Entities are required to provide information about different operating segments. The objective is to provide information to enable readers of financial statements to understand business risks from the perspective of the board of directors of the company. Therefore, entities use the internal management information system to identify segments for external reporting. This accounting policy enhances the relevance, but compromises with comparability. *A reporting enterprise must ensure that financial statements meet the minimum threshold of all the qualities mentioned in the text.*

Generally, financial statements provide a true and fair view if:

(a) it is free from any material error and bias;
(b) it is prepared using the appropriate accounting policy and applicable accounting standards; and
(c) it is presented in the format prescribed by the regulator or, in the absence of a prescribed format, it is prepared in a manner that facilitates analysis of the financial position and the performance of the reporting entity.

True and fair view override

"True and fair view override" allows an entity to deviate from the principles and methods stipulated in various accounting standards, if the management forms the judgement that the application of principles and methods stipulated in accounting standards would impair the true and fair view of the financial position and performance of the entity. However, it is very rare that the accounting policy of an entity deviates from accounting standards. If, an accounting policy of an entity deviates from the applicable accounting standard, the entity provides detailed reasons for the deviation.

ANNEXURE III: ACCOUNTING STANDARDS

Accounting standards control accounting policy of entitles by stipulating accounting principles and methods. In India, the Institute of Chartered Accountants of India (ICAI) issues accounting standards. Non-corporate entities follow the accounting standards issued by ICAI. An accounting standard becomes a part of the law that governs registered companies when the government of India notifies it for application by companies. In USA, accounting standards, known as US GAAP, are issued by the Financial Accounting Standards Board (FASB). Every country/territory (e.g., the European Union) has a body that issues accounting standards.

Setting accounting standard is a political process in which all stakeholders get involved. Therefore, accounting standards stipulate accounting principles and methods, which are acceptable to all stakeholders. Accounting standards are to be applied in practice. Therefore, practicality is an important consideration in formulating accounting standards. They may not prescribe the conceptually most appropriate accounting principles and methods. Accounting standards are revised from time to time based on feedback from stakeholders, development in economic models and reduction in cost of collecting and processing information.

Accounting standards stipulate accounting principles and do not prescribe specific rules. An entity applies accounting principles and methods stipulated in accounting standards based on its interpretation of those principles and the environment in which it operates. Generally, a shared understanding of the principles evolves over time through discussion and debate between various stakeholders (e.g., auditors, financial analysts, regulators, and prepares of financial statements). However, sometimes different interpretations by different stakeholders lead to controversy.

Accounting Fundamentals

CHAPTER

3

LEARNING OBJECTIVES

The objective of this chapter is to provide an understanding of the relationship between assets, equity and liabilities. After reading this chapter, you will be able to understand the following:

- Accounting equation
- Difference between equity and liabilities
- Elements in the balance sheet
- Monetary and non-monetary assets
- Financial and non-financial assets
- Equity and components of equity
- Constructive obligation
- Income and expenses
- Discretionary expenses
- Difference between expenditure and expense
- Double entry bookkeeping principles and rules
- Face value, book value and market value of shares

NOTES

ACCOUNTING EQUATION

The following identity, known as the *accounting equation,* presents the relationship between assets, equity and liabilities:

$$\text{Assets} = \text{Equity} + \text{Liabilities} \tag{3.1}$$

This relationship between assets, equity and liabilities forms the basis of bookkeping and accounting. It can be interpreted from the following two different perspectives:

Perspective 1: Assets of an entity are financed by owners' capital and credit extended by outsiders (loan and credit extended by vendors etc.); and

Perspective 2: There are two types of claimants on the assets of an entity—owners and outsiders.

BOX 3.1 Difference between Equity and Liabilities

Equity: Equity is owners' investment in the entity. The owners collectively decide whether to withdraw the amount invested by them or withdraw the surplus generated by the business. Therefore, it is said that an entity has unconditional discretion to return the amount invested in the equity or to pay a return on the same. For example, in case of a company, distribution of surplus, which belongs to equity shareholders, is decided by equity shareholders collectively, that is, by the company, at the Annual General Meeting. An individual equity shareholder cannot ask the company to pay its share in the net profit.

Liability: Liability represents the entity's obligation to outsiders, that is, to those who are not owners. The entity has no practical ability to avoid settling the obligation. For example, when an entity borrows money, it commits to pay interest and repay the loan as per agreed terms. It has no option but to honour the contract. If it fails, the lender can take legal recourse to realise the amount due to it.

Owners' claim is residual. In a situation of liquidation of the entity, obligations to outsiders are settled first and then, if any asset is left, it is distributed to owners. Accounting equation written in the following form better explains that equity is the residual claim:

$$\text{Equity} = \text{Assets} - \text{Liabilities} \tag{3.2}$$

It is evident from the accounting equation that:

(i) If the total amount of liabilities increases without any change in the total amount of assets, equity reduces and, if the total amount of liabilities decreases without any change in the total amount of assets, equity increases:

(ii) If the total amount of assets increases without any change in the total amount of liabilities, equity increases and, if the total amount of assets decreases without any change in the total amount of liabilities, equity decreases.

Double-entry bookkeeping is based on the above relationship between assets, equity and liabilities.

CASE STUDY 3.1 Increase in Liabilities

The balance sheet of AV Limited (AVL) as at March 31, 2018 has been placed before the board of directors for approval. It shows, assets at ₹100 crores, liabilities at ₹80 crores and equity at ₹20 crores. During discussion in the board, it is decided that a liability for the claim from an important customer should be recognised, because AVL has to settle the claim to the satisfaction of the customer, even if the claim might not be enforceable in the court of law. The board decides to recognise the claim at ₹20 lakhs.

Question

What will be the amount of equity in the balance sheet on recognition of the liability?

Solution

As there is no change in the amount of assets recognised in the balance sheet, equity will be reduced by ₹20 lakhs. Therefore, after recognition of liability towards the claim by the customer, the balance sheet will show assets at ₹100 crores, liabilities at ₹80.20 crores and equity at ₹19.80 crores.

NOTES

Key Terms
Asset, equity, liability

Self-Test Questions

Self-test question 3.1

Fill in the blanks:

(i) As at the beginning of the day, the equity of SN Limited (SNL) was ₹1,00,000. During the day SNL purchased equipment for ₹50,000 on credit. There was no other transaction during the day and no event occurred, which might affect the assets and liabilities of the company. The equity at the end of the day was ₹..................

(ii) The balance sheet of PK Limited (PKL) as at March 31, 2018 shows a cash balance of ₹5,00,000. However, on physical counting before finalisation of accounts, the internal auditor has found a shortage of ₹20,000. It is unlikely that the insurance company will accept the claim. The equity should be ....by ₹20,000. [Choose the right word from the words: increased/decreased.]

(iii) The balance sheet of PK Limited (PKL) as at March 31, 2018 shows a cash balance of ₹5,00,000. However, on physical counting before finalisation of accounts, the internal auditor found a shortage of ₹30,000. It is unlikely that the insurance company will accept the claim. However, the amount is recoverable from the cashier. The equity should be .... [Choose the right word from the words: increased/decreased.] by ₹...........

SUMMARY

Accounting equation, which depicts the relationship between assets, liabilities and equity, is the basis on which accounting principles and methods are developed. An economic resource that the entity controls is an asset of the entity. Equity is the claim of owners on the assets of the company. Liabilities are the claims of outsiders on the assets of the company. The entity has no option but to settle a liability. The entity has unconditional discretion to repay investment in equity and to pay a return on equity.

ELEMENTS IN BALANCE SHEET

The balance sheet is presented in two segments. The upper segment of the vertical statement presents assets and the lower segment presents equity and liabilities as at the balance sheet date, which is the last date of the accounting period. Table 3.1 presents the balance sheet structure.

TABLE 3.1

Balance Sheet as at March 31, 2017

(Amount in ₹ crores)

Particulars	HUL	Infosys	Suzlon
ASSETS			
Total Assets	14,751	79,885	14,226
EQUITY AND LIABILITIES			
Equity (Owners' claim)	6,490	68,017	1,022
Liabilities (Outsiders' claim)	8,261	11,868	13,204
Total	14,751	79,885	14,226

Accounting standards prescribe the criteria for the recognition and measurement of assets and liabilities in the balance sheet.

Asset

Entities use various resources to create value. For example, they use natural resources, infrastructure created by the government or local authority, infrastructure created by other entities and resources acquired or developed by it. However, in accounting, all the assets that an entity uses do not fit into the accounting definition of assets.

Asset is defined as

"An asset is a present economic resource controlled by the entity as a result of past events."

An economic resource is a right that has the potential to produce economic benefits. An entity controls an economic resource if, it has the present ability to direct the use of the economic resource and obtain the economic benefits that flow from it. Usually, control comes with ownership, but not necessarily so. For example, an entity controls an asset obtained through finance lease, although it does not own it. Finance lease is a long-term, non-cancellable lease under which the rewards and risks incidental to the ownership of the asset is substantially transferred to the lessee. Assets arise from past events in the sense that the entity acquires an asset through a transaction (e.g., purchase) or event (e.g., government grant) occurred in past.

Natural resources, items of infrastructure created by the government or local authority are not assets for the entity, because the entity has no right to direct the use of those resources.

Examples of assets

Examples of assets are:

(i) Property, plant and equipment (e.g., land, building, roads and culverts, plant and machinery, furniture and fixtures, computers and vehicles);

(ii) Intangible assets (e.g., goodwill, product brand, license, right to use other's asset, and software);

(iii) Investments (e.g., investment in equity shares issued by another entity, investment in units of mutual funds, long-term fixed deposits with banks, and investment in investment properties);

(iv) Inventories (e.g., stock of raw materials, components, stores and spare parts, work-in-progress, finished goods and stock-in-trade);

(v) Receivables (e.g., trade receivables, i.e., the amount due from customers);

(vi) Loans (e.g., loans to vendors and loan to employees);

(vii) Advances (e.g., advances to suppliers);

(viii) Deposits (e.g., security deposits with public utilities); and

(ix) Cash and cash equivalents (e.g., cash in hand, cheques in hand, fixed deposits with bank for a period of three months or less, and investment in treasury bills of three months or less duration).

NOTES

Monetary and non-monetary assets

Monetary assets are money held and assets to be received in fixed or determinable amounts of money. Examples are cash on hand, bank deposits, deposits with other entities, loan given to other entities and receivables. In contrast, non-monetary assets are the assets for which it is not possible to precisely determine the money value. Examples are property, plant and equipment, intangible assets and inventories.

Financial assets

A financial asset is a contractual claim to receive cash or another financial asset. Examples are receivables from customers, deposits with banks and other entities, outstanding loan disbursed to another entity, investments in equity shares issued by another entity, and investments in corporate bonds.

Non-financial assets

A non-financial asset is an asset that cannot be classified as a financial asset. Examples are items of property, plant and equipment, stock of finished goods, stock of raw material, and intangible assets (e.g., brand, copyright, patent, and license). Advance paid to a vendor is a non-financial asset, as the vendor will settle the advance by supplying the agreed goods or by rendering agreed services.

Self-Test Questions

Self-test question 3.2

Indicate whether the following statements are true (T) or false (F):

(i) A road, which is constructed by the local development authority for use by HJ Limited (HJL) for transporting people and goods to and from its factory from and to the nearby railway siding and adjoining villages, is an asset of HJL, because it is used exclusively by HJL, as the connecting road does not cater for the needs of any other organisation.
(ii) A building taken on a lease, classified as finance lease, is an asset of the lessee.
(iii) An entity controls a resource if it has the ability to direct its use.
(iv) Pre-paid rent is a non-monetary asset.
(v) 'Trade receivables' is a non-monetary asset.
(vi) All financial assets are monetary assets.
(vii) Advance paid to a vendor is a non-monetary asset.

Liabilities

A liability is a present obligation of the entity to transfer an economic resource (e.g., cash, asset, and services) as a result of past events.

An entity has a present obligation to transfer an economic resource if both: (a) the entity has no practical ability to avoid the transfer; and (b) the obligation has arisen from past events, in other words, the entity has received the economic benefits (e.g., amount borrowed from a bank), or conducted the activities (e.g., purchased goods on credit) that establish the extent of its obligation.

Liability arises from contractual obligation, application of law and constructive obligation.

No practical ability to avoid transfer of economic resources

An entity has no practical ability to avoid a transfer if, for example, the transfer is legally enforceable, or any action necessary to avoid the transfer would cause significant business disruption or would have economic consequences significantly more adverse than the transfer itself.

Constructive obligation

Many obligations are legally enforceable as a consequence of a contract (e.g., borrowings

NOTES

from banks and amount due to vendors), legislation (e.g., income tax liability) or similar means. Obligations can also arise from an entity's customary practices, published policies or specific statements that require the transfer of an economic resource. If the entity has no practical ability to act in a manner inconsistent with those practices, policies or statements, the entity has an obligation. The obligation that arises in such situations is often described as a *constructive obligation*.

Examples of liabilities

Examples of liabilities are outstanding amount against borrowings from financial institutions, outstanding amount of borrowings from public through issuance of debentures or other types of bonds, outstanding amount against public deposits received, interest accrued on borrowings, trade creditors (amount due to suppliers of goods and services), amount due to employees, amount due to owners (e.g., unpaid dividend), amount due to vendors and employees, progress payments received from customers and amount due against tax liability.

Financial and non-financial liabilities

Financial liabilities are those which arise from contractual arrangements and are to be settled by payment of cash or transfer of a financial instrument (e.g., cheque drawn on a bank). Non-financial liabilities are those which are to be settled by transferring an asset, other than cash or financial instrument, or by delivering services. For example, amount outstanding against borrowings from a bank is a financial liability, as the loan is to be repaid in cash or by issuing a cheque. Advance received from a customer with purchase order is a non-financial liability, as the liability will be settled by delivering goods or rendering services.

CASE STUDY 3.2 Constructive Obligation

Fashion Point Limited (FPL) manufactures and sells women's attire. It has its own retail stores across India. As per the contractual terms, it refunds the price paid for an item if it is returned within seven days. However, as a practice that the company followed from the inception of the business, it takes back sold items and refund the price if the goods are returned within three weeks. In March 2018, FPL's sale was ₹100 crores. The management estimates that items sold for ₹5 lakhs will be returned within a week from the date when the sales occurred and items for ₹20 lakhs will be returned within three weeks from the date when the sales occurred. FPL publishes financial statements of an accounting year (which ends on March 31) by next April 5.

Question

What should be the amount for which liability on this account should be recognised in the balance sheet of FPL dated March 31, 2018, which will be issued in April 5, 2018?

Solution

Legal obligation is to take back items sold for ₹5 lakhs and refund the price. However, the entity cannot avoid the obligation of taking back items sold for ₹20 lakhs and refund the price, which is arising from the customary practice. If, the entity stops the practice abruptly, the business would be affected adversely. Therefore, FPL should recognise the liability on this account for (₹5 +20 lakhs) or ₹25 lakhs in the balance sheet dated March 31, 2018.

Note: If, FPL decides to publish the financial statements in the later part of May 2018 or afterwards, it would provide the liability in the balance sheet dated March 31, 2018 for the items actually returned in April 2018.

NOTES

CASE STUDY 3.3 Constructive Obligation

DB Limited (DBL) has a manufacturing plant in Balasore in Odisha (India). Many of the employees working in the plant come from a nearby village. The local body (Panchayat) of the village requested the company to construct a community centre in the village with sports facilities, a TV and a small computer centre. This will be used by the village residents to hold meetings, elders to spend time at leisure, youth to learn and practice indoor games, and farmers to gather agricultural information disseminated by experts using digital platforms. The Panchayat could persuade the local MLA and Balasore District Magistrate to request the chairman of the company to consider the Panchayat's request favourably. The board of directors of DBL in its meeting held on February 10, 2018 had decided to accept the request of the Panchayat. It was decided to provide funds to the Panchayat for constructing the community centre, which would be the asset of the Panchayat. It would provide management and supervisory support. The cost was estimated at ₹50 lakhs. The company had informed the board's decision to the Panchayat.

Construction of the community centre is not within the corporate social responsibility (CSR) programmes/projects approved by the board.

Question

Should DBL recognise liability on this account in its balance sheet dated March 31, 2018?

Solution

The communication to the Panchayat of the board's decision has resulted in a constructive obligation, because non-fulfillment of the commitment would hurt the reputation of the company, which in turn would adversely affect the relationships with stakeholders (e.g., government and local community) and consequently would aversely affect the business. Therefore, by announcing the board's decision, DBL has assumed a liability and it has no practical ability to avoid the transfer of funds to the Panchayat. Therefore, DBL should recognise a liability, measured at ₹50 lakhs, in its balance sheet dated March 31, 2018.

Self-Test Questions

Self-test question 3.3

Indicate whether the following statements are true (T) or false (F):

(i) An obligation is not a liability if the entity has practical ability to avoid settling the same.

(ii) An obligation is not a liability if the management estimates that it is less than probable, that is, less likely that economic resources will outflow the entity to settle the obligation.

(iii) All liabilities are contractual obligations.

(iv) Advance received from a customer along with the purchase order is a financial liability.

(v) Security deposit received from a contractor, which is refundable on satisfactory completion of the contract, is a financial liability.

Equity (Net Worth)

The terms equity, net assets and net worth are used interchangeably. Equity is the owners' investment in the entity. The following is the formal definition of equity:

"Equity is the residual interest in the assets of the entity after deducting all its liabilities'. It represents owners' claim on the assets of the entity."

The definition focuses on the fact that the claim of owners is subordinate to other claims against the assets of the entity.

Largely, equity is the total of: (i) The contribution by the owner; and (ii) Profit retained in the entity over its life. However, there are other items that are included in equity. Examples are (i) equity component of compound financial instruments (e.g., optionally convertible bonds) and (ii) fair value (at the grant date) of options, granted to employees, to purchase entity's share at a pre-specified price (called exercise price) on or before a specified date (called exercise date) under the Employees Stock Ownership Plan (ESOP).

When an entity accumulates losses more than the contribution from the owners, the net worth might be negative. In a company with negative net worth, the total amount of liabilities exceeds the total value of assets.

NOTES

Key Terms
Constructive obligation, equity, finance lease, financial asset, financial liability, net assets, net worth, liability, monetary asset, non-financial asset, non-financial liability, non-monetary asset

Self-Test Questions

Self-test question 3.4

Indicate whether the following statements are true (T) or false (F):

(i) Equity is owners' investment in the entity.
(ii) The terms equity, net assets and net worth are used interchangeably.
(iii) Negative net worth of an entity implies that the carrying amount of assets is lower than the total amount of liabilities.
(iv) An entity cannot have negative net worth at the commencement of its operation.

SUMMARY

The balance sheet is presented in two segments. The upper segment of the vertical statement presents assets and the lower segment presents equity and liabilities as at the balance sheet date. An asset is a present economic resource controlled by the entity as a result of past events. An economic resource is a right that has the potential to produce economic benefits. An entity controls an economic resource if, it has the present ability to direct the use of the economic resource and obtain the economic benefits that flow from it. Assets are classified into monetary assets and non-monetary assets, and also into financial assets and non-financial assets.

A liability is a present obligation of the entity to transfer an economic resource (e.g., cash, asset, and services) as a result of past events. An entity has a present obligation to transfer an economic resource if (a) the entity has no practical ability to avoid the transfer; and (b) the obligation has arisen from past events. Liability arises from contractual obligation, application of law and constructive obligation.

Equity is the owners' investment in the entity.

ELEMENTS IN THE STATEMENT OF PROFIT AND LOSS

Income

The following is the formal definition of income:

Income is defined as "increases in assets or decreases in liabilities that result in increases in equity, other than those relating to contributions from holders of equity claims."

Incomes include amounts generated by transactions and other events, including changes in the carrying amount of assets and liabilities. Income includes gains.

Examples of income from transactions are:

(i) Revenue from sale of goods and services,
(ii) Interest and dividend income from investments in financial assets,
(iii) Rent earned from investment property,
(iv) Export incentive receivable from the government,
(v) Gain from the sale of an item of property, plant and equipment,
(vi) Gain from the sale of investment, and
(vii) Extinguishment of interest liability in loan restructuring.

Examples of income from events are: (i) Revaluation gains from the revaluation of a class of property, plant and equipment; (ii) Gains from the change in fair value of a financial asset measured at fair value; and (iii) Government grant.

NOTES

Self-Test Questions

Self-test question 3.5

Indicate whether the following statements are true (T) or false (F):

(i) Equity increases due to income only.
(ii) Government grant received by an entity is not its income.
(iii) Income arises when the fair value of an asset, which is measured at fair value, changes upwards.
(iv) Income arises from the waiver of overdue interest by the lender.
(v) Fine imposed and recovered from an employees due to violation of code of conduct is income.
(vi) Goods and service tax (GST), which is collected on behalf of the government, is income.

Expenses

The following is the formal definition of expenses:

Expenses are decreases in assets or increases in liabilities that result in decreases in equity, other than those relating to distributions to holders of equity claims.

Expenses include amounts generated by transactions and other events, including changes in the carrying amount of assets and liabilities. Expenses include losses.

Examples of expenses from transactions are:

(i) Cost of goods sold,
(ii) Operating expenses, such as employee cost, goods and service tax (GST), logistic costs, rent, rates and taxes, maintenance expenses, electricity expenses, insurance expenses, advertising expenses, selling expenses, travelling expenses, training expenses and research and development expenses,
(iii) loss on sale of an item of property, plant and equipment,
(iv) Loss on sale of investment,
(v) Interest expense and other financing costs, and
(vi) Tax expense, which is not truly an expense arising from transactions, as it is a levy by government.

Examples of expenses from events are:

(i) Loss on revaluation of a class of property, plant and equipment,
(ii) Depreciation and impairment of an item of property, plant and equipment,
(iii) Impairment of financial assets,
(iv) Loss from the change in fair value of a financial asset measured at fair value, and
(v) Loss due to fraud, embezzlement, accidents etc.

Dividend is not an expense as it is distribution of profit to shareholders, the deemed owners of the company.

Discretionary expenses

Expenses, which do not have cause and effect relation with revenue that is recognised in the statement of profit and loss of the current period, are called discretionary expenses. Examples are advertisement expenses, training expenses and research expenses. An entity may cut those expenses in the current period without adversely affecting the revenue for the current period. Consequently, the entity may improve current period's performance by cutting down those expenses. However, reduction in discretionary expenses is likely to affect the future earning capacity of the entity adversely.

Self-Test Questions

Self-test question 3.6

Indicate whether the following statements are true (T) or false (F):

(i) Dividend is an expense.
(ii) Discretionary expenses do not benefit the entity.
(iii) Income tax payable by a company is an expense.
(iv) Loss due to fire is an expense.

Expenditure and Expense

Expenditure refers to the act of spending economic resources. It results in either reduction in asset or increase in liability. For example, spending in cash results in reduction of cash. Similarly, acquiring an asset or service on credit results is increase in liability.

If the entity recognises an asset from the expenditure, the amount of equity (i.e., assets minus liabilities) does not change and, therefore, no expense is recognised. For example, if the expenditure is incurred for purchasing an item of property, there is no change in the amount of equity, and consequently, no expense is recognised.

If the entity does not recognise an asset from the expenditure, the amount of equity (i.e., assets minus liabilities) reduces and, therefore, expense is recognised. For example, accounting standards do no permit recognition of an asset from expenditure on advertising, training and research, and consequently, expenditures on those items are recognised as expenses for the period in which the expenditures are incurred.

Expense for a year might arise from a transaction of a past year, when an asset was recognised from that transaction and its cost is allocated to the current year. An example is depreciation of equipment.

Self-Test Questions

Self-test question 3.7

Indicate whether the following statements are true (T) or false (F):

(i) Expenditure results in recognition of either assets or expenses.
(ii) Expenditure decreases equity.
(iii) Terms expenditure and expense are used interchangeably.
(iv) Expenses for an accounting period may arise from transactions of past years.

CASE STUDY 3.4 Asset/Expense

Bahar Limited (BL) is in merchandising business. It purchases goods in trade (i.e., goods which the company buys and sells) for ₹5,00,000 on credit.

Required

How does the transaction affect economic resources and claims on those resources?

Solution

The transaction results in increase in asset (goods in trade) and liability (amount due to the supplier) by ₹5,00,000, and thus, does not change equity. However, as per the current accounting practice, the transaction is recorded differently.

Current accounting practice

As per the current accounting practice, when an entity purchases goods in trade, it does not recognise an asset from the expenditure. It recognises an expense (purcase of goods in trade), which is later matched with income from sales. Both sales and purchase are recognised in the statement of profit and loss. The entity estimates the closing stock of goods at the end of the period and recognises an asset (stock-in-trade) in the balance sheet.

Therefore, as per the current accounting practice, liability (trade creditor) has increased by ₹5,00,000, without any change in asset. And, the equity is reduced by ₹5,00,000 and expense (purchase) is recognised at ₹5,00,000. In this case, liability (trade creditor) has increased by ₹5,00,000 and purchase is recognised at ₹5,00,000.

NOTES

CASE STUDY 3.5 Income

Bahar Limited (BL) of case study 3.4 has sold part of the 'goods in trade' purchased earlier (*see* case study 3.4) for ₹4,00,000 on credit.

Required

How does the transaction affect economic resources and claims on those resources?

Solution

The transaction results in decrease in an item of asset (goods in trade); increase in another item of asset (receivables from customers) by ₹4,00,000. Thus, it does not change equity. However, as per the current accounting practice, the transaction is recorded differently.

Current accounting practice

As per the current accounting practice, when a company sells goods in trade, it recognises the receipt or receivables as income because goods in trade purchased had not been recognised as an asset. Accordingly, in this case, BL recognises an asset (trade receivable) at ₹4,00,000, resulting in increase in the total amount of assets in the balance sheet by that amount. There is no change in the total amount of liabilities. Consequently, equity has increased by ₹4,00,000, and income (sales) of ₹4,00,000 is recognised.

CASE STUDY 3.6 Recognition of Closing Stock

Bahar Limited (BL) (see case studies 3.4 and 3.5) estimates the value of stock of 'goods-in-trade' at the end of the year which is ₹2,00,000.

Required

How does recognition of closing stock in the balance sheet affect economic resources and claims on those resources?

Solution

Recognition of the asset (stock of goods-in-trade) in the balance sheet increases the amount of total assets by ₹2,00,000, and consequently increases equity by that amount.

Net effect of purchase, sale and recognition of closing stock

The net effect of the transactions in case studies 3.4 and 3.5, and recognition of stock in case study 3.6 is that the equity has increased by ₹1,00,000, which is profit for the period. It may be verified as follows:

Sales of ₹4,00,000; Cost of sales ₹3,00,000; profit ₹1,00,000. Cost of sales is calculated by deducting the value of stock-in-trade at the end of the period from purchase (₹5,00,000 – 2,00,000). Profit is calculated by deducting cost of sales from sales.

NOTES

Key Terms
Discretionary expense, expenditure, expense, gain, government grant, income

CASE STUDY 3.7 Loss Due to Embezzlement

On December 25, 2017, Ashok, the cashier of Parama Limited, left with cash amounting to ₹4,00,000. In fact, he absconded. He was covered under the fidelity insurance taken by the company. Therefore, the company lodged a claim with the concerned insurance company. The insurance company accepted the claim on the same day for ₹3,00,000 as the insurance cover was for ₹3,00,000 only.

Required

How should the embezzlement by Ashok and acceptance of claim by the insurance company be presented in the financial statement of Parama Limited?

Solution

The embezzlement by Ashok and the corresponding acceptance of the insurance claim by the insurance company have resulted in derecognition of cash (₹4,00,000) and recognition of an asset (insurance claim of ₹3,00,000) in the balance sheet. As a result, the total amount of assets is reduced by ₹1,00,000, without any change in liabilities. Consequently, the amount of equity is reduced by ₹1,00,000. The reduction in equity results in recognising an expense (loss due to embezzlement by Ashok) in the statement of profit and loss for the period.

SUMMARY

Income is defined as increases in assets or decreases in liabilities that result in increases in equity, other than those relating to contributions from holders of equity claims. Income includes gain. Expenses are decreases in assets or increases in liabilities that result in decreases in equity, other than those relating to distributions to holders of equity claims. Expenses include losses. Expenses, which do not have cause and effect relation with revenue that is recognised in the statement of profit and loss of the current period, are called discretionary expenses. Expenditure refers to the act of spending economic resources. It results in either reduction in asset or increase in liability. Entity recognises either an asset or an expense from expenditure. Expense for a year might arise from a transaction of a past year, when an asset was recognised from that transaction and its cost is allocated to the current year. An example is depreciation of equipment.

DOUBLE ENTRY BOOKKEEPING

Double Entry Principle

The principle of double entry bookkeeping is that for every debit (written as Dr.), there is a credit (Cr.). Therefore, if the economic effects of transactions and events for a particular period (say, accounting year) are recorded correctly, the total of amounts in debit and total of the amounts in credit at the end of the period shall agree. This is the beauty of double-entry bookkeeping.

Recognition of income and recognition of corresponding increase in asset or de-recognition of liability are simultaneous. Similarly, recognition of expenses and recognition of liability or de-recognition of asset are simultaneous.

NOTES

Double-Entry Rules

The double entry bookkeeping rules flows from the accounting equation, which is as follows:

$$\text{Assets} = \text{Equity} + \text{Liabilities} \quad (3.3)$$

The accounting equation tells us that increase in the total amount of assets results either increase in the total amount of equity or in increase in the total amount of liabilities. Similarly, decrease in the total amount of assets results in either decrease in the total amount of equity or decrease in the total amount of liabilities.

According to the accounting convention, asset account is debited for increase in the amount of asset. Every debit has a credit. Therefore, there should be corresponding credit to either the equity account or the liability account. It implies that increase in liability should be credit. Similarly, increase in equity should be credit.

If increase in asset is debit, logically, decrease in asset should be credit. With the same logic, decrease in liability should be debit and decrease in equity should be debit.

Incomes increase equity, therefore, income is credit. Similarly, expenses decrease equity, therefore, expense is debit (Table 3.2).

TABLE 3.2

Double Entry Bookkeeping: Debit-credit Rules

S. No.	Element in financial statements	Increase	Decrease
1.	Asset	Debit	Credit
2.	Equity	Credit	Debit
3.	Liability	Credit	Debit
4.	Income	Credit	Debit
5.	Expense	Debit	Credit

Alternative Debit-Credit Rules

Accountants classify account heads into three different categories: Personal account, Real account, and Nominal account. An account with a natural person or juridical person (incorporated entity, such as LLP and limited liability company) is classified as Personal Account; An asset (other than amount due from a natural or juridical person) is classified as Real account; and Income account and Expense account are classified as Nomial Account.

Table 3.3 presents the debit-credit rules based on this classification.

TABLE 3.3

Alternative Debit/Credit Rules

S. No.	Account classification	Debit/Credit Rules
1.	Personal	Debit the receiver and credit the giver.
2.	Real	Debit what comes in and credit what goes out.
3.	Nominal	Debit expenses and credit incomes.

ILLUSTRATION 3.1

Apply debit-credit rules to following transactions entered into by Joy Tea (JT) during December 2017:

(i) Started business with cash of ₹10,00,000.
(ii) Deposited ₹8,00,000 in bank.
(iii) Paid office rent for December 2017 and January 2018 at the rate of ₹20,000 per month in cash.

NOTES

(iv) Purchased office furniture for ₹2,00,000 on credit. The amount is payable within three months from the date of purchase.
(v) Purchased merchandise for ₹5,00,000 on credit.
(vi) Paid ₹50,000 towards advertising in cash.
(vii) Paid ₹5,00,000 to the supplier of merchandise by issuing cheque.
(viii) Paid ₹20,000 towards conveyance expenditure in cash.
(ix) Sold part of the goods for ₹7,00,000 on credit.
(x) Withdrew ₹1,00,000 from bank for office use.
(xi) Paid ₹5,000 towards telephone charges in cash.
(xii) Paid ₹2,000 towards electricity charges in cash.
(xiii) Paid ₹30,000 towards salaries in cash.

Solution

TABLE 3.4

Application of Debit and Credit Rules

Transaction No.	Debit	Credit	Explanation	Amount (₹)
(i)	Cash	Equity	Asset (cash) and Equity (owner's investment) increased	10,00,000
(ii)	Bank	Cash	Composition of assets changed, amount due from bank increased and cash reduced;	8,00,000
(iii)	(a) Rent (b) Pre-paid rent	Cash	Rent is an expense; Pre-paid rent (rent for January 2018) is an asset, as benefits from this expenditure will be received in future; Cash (asset) is decreased	(a) 20,000 (b) 20,000
(iv)	Office furniture	Creditors (supplier)	Office furniture (asset) increased and Creditors (liability) also increased.	2,00,000
(v)	Purchase of goods in trade	Trade creditors	Purchase of goods-in-trade is an expense; Trade creditors is a liability, which has increased.	5,00,000
(vi)	Advertising expense	Cash	Advertising expense is an expense; Cash is an asset, which is reduced.	50,000
(vii)	Trade creditors	Bank	Liability (Trade creditors) is reduced; and asset (bank balance) is also reduced.	5,00,000
(viii)	Conveyance expenses	Cash	Conveyance expense is an expense; Cash is an asset, which is reduced.	20,000
(ix)	Trade debtors	Sales	Trade debtors (the amount due from the buyer) is an asset, which is increased; Sales, which is income, is credited.	7,00,000
(x)	Cash	Bank	Cash (asset) is increased and bank balance (asset) is reduced.	1,00,000
(xi)	Telephone charges	Cash	Telephone charges is an expense; Cash is an asset, which is reduced.	5,000
(xii)	Electricity charges	Cash	Electricity charges is an expense; Cash is an asset, which is reduced.	2,000
(xiii)	Salaries	Cash	Salaries is an expense; Cash is an asset, which is reduced.	30,000

Note: For item (v): As per the contemporary accounting practice purchase of merchandise is accounted for as an expense (Purchase of goods-in-trade Account) and not as an asset (in this case, goods-in-trade). At the end of the period, stock of each item is counted and valued applying measurement bases prescribed in the relevant accounting standard (Ind AS2). It is recognised as an asset in the balance sheet. Similarly, in case of purchase of raw material, 'Purchase of raw material' Account is debited. [See case studies 3.4 to 3.6 above.]

BOX 3.2 Cash Book, General Ledger and Trial Balance

The general ledger is the principal book of accounts. Account heads [e.g., Purchase of raw materials Account, Sale of goods Account, Employee benefits Account and Vehicles Account] to record transactions and economic consequences of events related to assets, equity, liabilities, incomes and expenses are maintained in the general ledger. Cash and bank transactions are recorded directly in the 'Cash Book'. Cash account and bank account are not maintained in the general ledger. Periodically, net balance (amount) in different accounts in the general ledger and cash book are calculated. If the total of amounts in debit is higher than the total amounts in credit, it is said the account has a debit balance. For example, if in an Account, the total of debits is ₹1000 and total of credits is ₹800, the Account has a debit balance of ₹200. Similarly, if the total of amounts in credit is higher than the total amounts in debit, it is said the account has a credit balance. After balancing the accounts in the general ledger and cash book, a statement listing the debit and credit balances in various account heads is prepared. This statement is known as the Trial Balance. The total of the debit balances agree with the total of the credit balances. Preparation of the Trial Balance is the starting point for preparing financial statements.

NOTES

Key Terms
Cash book, credit, debit, general ledger, trial balance

Self-Test Questions

Self-test question 3.8

Apply debit-credit rules to following transactions entered into by PC Limited (PCL) during May 2018:

(i) Started business with cash of ₹15,00,000.
(ii) Deposited ₹13,00,000 in bank.
(iii) Paid office rent for May 2018 and June 2018 at the rate of ₹30,000 per month in cash.
(iv) Purchased office furniture for ₹3,00,000 on credit. The amount is payable within three months from the date of purchase.
(v) Purchased merchandise for ₹10,00,000 on credit.
(vi) Paid ₹1,00,000 towards advertising in cash.
(vii) Paid ₹6,00,000 to the supplier of merchandise by issuing cheque.
(viii) Paid ₹20,000 towards conveyance expenditure in cash.
(ix) Sold part of the goods for ₹8,00,000 on credit.
(x) Withdrew ₹1,00,000 from bank for office use.
(xi) Paid ₹10,000 towards telephone charges in cash.
(xii) Paid ₹8,000 towards electricity charges in cash.
(xiii) Paid ₹30,000 towards salaries in cash.

SUMMARY

The double entry bookkeeping rules flows from the accounting equation. According to the accounting convention, asset account is debited for increase in the amount of asset. Every debit has a credit. Increase in asset is debit and decrease in asset is credit. Increase in liability is credit and decrease in liability is debit. Increase in equity is credit and decrease in equity is debit. Income is credit and expense is debit.

Trial balance lists out the balances in various accounts in the general ledger and cash book. The total of debit balances agree with the total of credit balances, because of the rule that every debit has a credit.

NOTES

FACE VALUE, BOOK VALUE, AND MARKET VALUE

Authorised Capital and Face Value

The authorised capital of a company is the maximum amount of share capital, measured at face value, that the company is authorised to issue to its shareholders. The *Memorandum of Association*, which is the constitutional document that a company submits to the government while filing the application for registration, mentions the amount of authorised capital. Part of the authorised capital can (and frequently does) remain unissued.

The authorised capital may be increased by the vote of the company's shareholders at a general meeting, provided this is permitted by the *Articles of Association*, which describes the internal regulation of a company. Authorised capital has no economic significance. Higher the authorised capital, higher is the registration fees and stamp duty. Usually, a company that has ambition to grow as a large company signals the ambition by mentioning high authorised capital in the Memorandum of Association.

Face value (also called *par value*) of share is calculated by dividing the authorised capital by the number of parts in which the authorised capital is divided by the company. It is at the discretion of the company to decide the face value.

Authorised capital does not limit the capacity of the company to mobilise equity capital from public. A company can issue shares at a premium, that is at a price, which is higher than the face value.

CASE STUDY 3.8 Face value of shares

Both Ishita Limited (IL) and Jassi Limited (JL) have an authorised capital of ₹10,00,000. IL has decided to divide its authorised capital into 1,00,000 shares. JL has decided to divide its authorised capital into 10,000 shares.

Required

Determine the face value of shares to be issued by IL. Also, determine the face value of shares to be issued by JL.

Solution

Face value of share of IL: ₹10,00,000/1,00,000 = ₹10

Face value of share of JL: ₹10,00,000/10,000 = ₹100

CASE STUDY 3.9 Share premium

Both Ishita Limited (IL) and Jassi Limited (JL) in case study 3.8 have decided to issue all the shares to mobilise ₹1 crore from the market.

Required

Determine the premium per share. Also, discuss how the amount mobilised by IL and JL will be presented in their respective balance sheets.

Solution

The issue prices of shares are as follows:

IL: (₹1,00,00,000/1,00,000) = ₹100 per share

JL: (₹1,00,00,000/10,000) = ₹1,000 per share

Share premium per share is as follows:

IL: ₹100 (Issue price) – 10 (Face value) = ₹90

JL: ₹1,000 (Issue price) – 100 (Face value) = ₹900

In the balance sheet of both the companies, the amount mobilised will be presented as follows:

Equity

Share capital (Issued, subscribed and paid up)	₹10,00,000
Reserves and surplus (Securities premium)	₹90,00,000
Total Equity	₹1,00,00,000

Self-Test Questions

Self-test question 3.9

Indicate whether the following statements are true (T) or false (F):

(i) Authorised capital mentioned in the Memorandum of Association filed at the time of registration of the company cannot be changed later.

(ii) Authorised capital limits the capacity of the company to mobilise equity capital from public.

(iii) Face value of shares has no economic significance.

(iv) A company at its discretion can decide the face value of shares.

Book Value and Market Value

Book value of equity is the balance sheet amount of equity. Book value per share is calculated by dividing the balance sheet amount of equity by the number of outstanding shares. Number of outstanding shares is number of shares allotted, reduced by the number of shares bought back by the company from shareholders. Book value is affected by the past transactions and other events and also by the recognition and measurement principles.

Market value per share (also called share price) is the price at which the shares are being traded in stock exchanges. Market value of equity (also called market capitalisation) is calculated by multiplying number of outstanding shares by the share price. Market value reflects the market's perception (perception of investors and potential investors collectively) about the cash flows that the company will generate in future and risks and timing of those cash flows. Risk is the chance that actual cash flows will differ from expected cash flows. Market value of equity usually differs from the book value of equity.

Self-Test Questions

Self-test question 3.10

Indicate whether the following statements are true (T) or false (F):

(i) Book value of equity can be used as a proxy for the market value of equity.

(ii) The gap between the book value per share and the share price in the capital market is likely to be larger for a company that create value by managing intangible assets than that of a company that uses tangible assets to create value.

(iii) Market capitalisation represents the market value of equity.

(iv) Book value of equity is the estimated amount that will be available for distribution to equity shareholders in a situation of liquidation of the company.

NOTES

Key Terms

Authorised capital, book value, face value, market capitalisation, market value, par value

SUMMARY

The authorised capital of a company is the maximum amount of share capital, measured at face value, that the company is authorised to issue to its shareholders. Face value (also called par value) of share is calculated by dividing the authorised capital by the number of parts in which the authorised capital is divided by the company. It is at the discretion of the company to decide the face value. Authorised capital does not limit the capacity of the company to mobilise equity capital from public. A company can issue shares at a premium, that is at a price, which is higher than the face value. Book value of equity the balance sheet amount of equity. Book value per share is calculated by dividing the balance sheet amount of equity by the number of outstanding shares. Market value per share (also called share price) is the price at which the shares are being traded in stock exchanges. Market value of equity (also called market capitalisation) is calculated by multiplying number of outstanding shares by the share price.

ANSWERS TO SELF-TEST QUESTIONS

3.1 (i) Zero; (ii) Decreased; (iii) Increased/Decreased, and zero

3.2 (i) F; (ii) T; (iii) T; (iv) T; (v) F; (vi) F; (vii) T

3.3 (i) T; (ii) T; (iii) F; (iv) F; (v) T

3.4 (i) T; (ii) T; (iii) T; (iv) T

3.5 (i) F; (ii) F; (iii) T; (iv) T; (v) T; (vi) F

3.6 (i) F; (ii) F; (iii) T; (iv) T

3.7 (i) T; (ii) F; (iii) F; (iv) T

3.8 Table is given below:

Transaction No.	Debit	Credit	Explanation	Amount (₹)
(i)	Cash	Equity	Asset (cash) and Equity (owner's investment) increased.	15,00,000
(ii)	Bank	Cash	Composition of assets changed, amount due from bank increased and cash reduced.	13,00,000
(iii)	(a) Rent (b) Pre-paid rent	Cash	Rent is an expense; Pre-paid rent (rent for June 2018) is an asset, as benefits from this expenditure will be received in future; Cash (asset) is decreased.	(a) 30,000 (b) 30,000
(iv)	Office furniture	Creditors (supplier)	Office furniture (asset) increased and Creditors (liability) also increased.	3,00,000
(v)	Purchase of goods in trade	Trade creditors	Purchase of goods-in-trade is an expense; Trade creditors is a liability, which has increased.	10,00,000
(vi)	Advertising expense	Cash	Advertising expense is an expense; Cash is an asset, which is reduced.	1,00,000
(vii)	Trade creditors	Bank	Liability (Trade creditors) is reduced; and asset (bank balance) is also reduced.	6,00,000
(viii)	Conveyance expenses	Cash	Conveyance expense is an expense; Cash is an asset, which is reduced.	20,000
(ix)	Trade debtors	Sales	Trade debtors (the amount due from the buyer) is an asset, which is increased; Sales, which is an income, is credited.	8,00,000
(x)	Cash	Bank	Cash (asset) is increased and bank balance (asset) is reduced.	1,00,000
(xi)	Telephone charges	Cash	Telephone charges is an expense; Cash is an asset, which is reduced.	10,000
(xii)	Electricity charges	Cash	Electricity charges is an expense; Cash is an asset, which is reduced.	8,000
(xiii)	Salaries	Cash	Salaries is an expense; Cash is an asset, which is reduced.	30,000

3.9 (i) F; (ii) F; (iii) T; (iv) T

3.10 (i) F; (ii) T; (iii) T; (iv) F

NOTES

ASSIGNMENTS

Multiple Choice Questions

1. Tick the correct answer.

(i) Which of the following is an essential characteristic of an asset?
  (a) The claim to an asset's benefit is legally enforceable.
  (b) An asset is tangible.
  (c) An asset is obtained at a cost.
  (d) An asset provides future benefits.

(ii) In the accounting equation:
  (a) Equity and assets are dependent variables.
  (b) Assets and liabilities are dependent variables.
  (c) Equity and liabilities are dependent variables.
  (d) None of the above.

(iii) The intangible assets are:
  (a) Fictitious assets that will not result in flow of economic benefits to the enterprise.
  (b) Non-monetary assets without physical substance
  (c) Non-monetary current assets without physical substance
  (d) None of the above.

(iv) Trade receivables, that is, the amount due from a customer is a:
  (a) Monetary asset.
  (b) Non-monetary asset.
  (c) Monetary financial asset.
  (d) None of the above.

(v) Purchase of goods (for sale) for ₹10,000 results in:
  (a) Increase in equity by ₹10,000, if the purchase is on credit.
  (b) Increase in equity by ₹10,000, if the purchase is on cash basis.
  (c) Decrease in equity by ₹10,000.
  (d) None of the above.

(vi) Sale of goods (stock-in-trade) for ₹10,000 leads to:
  (a) Decrease in equity by ₹10,000.
  (b) Increase in equity by the difference between ₹10,000 and the cost at which the goods were purchased if the cost was lower than ₹10,000.
  (c) Increase in equity by ₹10,000.
  (d) None of the above.

(vii) Payment of ₹5,000 towards salaries and wages results in:
  (a) Increase in equity by ₹5,000.
  (b) Decrease in equity by ₹5,000.
  (c) Decrease in equity by ₹5,000. if it does not include any advance payment of salaries and wages.
  (d) None of the above.

(viii) Payment of dividend by a company results in:
  (a) Decrease in equity that represents a loss.
  (b) Decrease in equity that represents distribution to owners.
  (c) Decrease in equity that represents an expense.
  (d) None of the above.

2. Group the following items into assets, liabilities, equity, income and expenses:

(i) Capital: ₹10,00,000
(ii) Withdrawal by the owner: ₹1,00,000
(iii) Land: ₹5,00,000
(iv) Building: ₹5,00,000
(v) Sales: ₹20,00,000
(vi) Purchases: ₹12,00,000
(vii) Railway siding: ₹2,00,000
(viii) Interest received: ₹50,000
(ix) Wages: ₹40,000
(x) Salaries: ₹1,20,000
(xi) Insurance claim receivable: ₹30,000
(xii) Furniture and fixtures: ₹1,50,000
(xiii) Depreciation for the year: ₹50,000
(xiv) Repairs and maintenance: ₹60,000

(xv) Interest on investment accrued but not due: ₹25,000
(xvi) Interest on loan accrued but not due: ₹30,000
(xvii) Trade receivables: ₹5,00,000
(xviii) Patent: ₹1,00,000
(xix) Copyright: ₹3,00,000
(xx) Prepaid expenses: ₹50,000
(xxi) Insurance premium: ₹1,00,000
(xxii) Loan: ₹5,00,000
(xxiii) Public deposit: ₹3,00,000
(xxiv) Conveyance charges: ₹34,000
(xxv) Travelling expenses: ₹1,50,000
(xxvi) Telephone charges: ₹2,00,000
(xxvii) Advance from customers: ₹5,00,000
(xxviii) Insurance claim: ₹3,00,000
(xxix) Bad debt: ₹20,000
(xxx) Discount received: ₹40,000
(xxxi) Closing stock of finished goods: ₹90,000
(xxxii) Goodwill: ₹5,00,000
(xxxiii) Brand: ₹45,00,000
(xxxiv) Discount allowed: ₹2,00,000
(xxxv) Research expenses: ₹10,00,000
(xxxvi) In-process research: ₹80,00,000
(xxxvii) Customers' list: ₹50,000
(xxxviii) Subsidy received from the government to meet expenses: ₹1,00,000
(xxxix) Subsidy received from the government to meet the cost of equipment: ₹1,00,000
(xL) Export incentives received: ₹2,00,000

CHAPTER 4

Balance Sheet Structure and Assets

LEARNING OBJECTIVES

The objective of this chapter is to provide an understanding of the structure of balance sheet and classification of assets. After reading this chapter, you will develop the understanding of the following:

- The balance sheet format (Schedule III, Division II) provided in the Companies Act, 2013 for non-finance companies (other than electricity companies), which have adopted Ind AS
- Purpose of balance sheet
- Balance sheet structure
- Grouping of assets and liabilities under different categories
- Deferred tax assets and deferred tax liabilities
- Current and non-current classification of assets and liabilities
- Events occurring after the balance sheet date

Schedule III to the Companies Act provides the format for presenting balance sheet and statement of profit and loss by non-finance companies (other than electricity companies), which apply Indian Accounting Standard (Ind AS) in the preparation and presentation of financial statements. Ind AS is fully convergent with the International Financial Reporting Standards (IFRS).

Schedule III (Division II) is available at the website of the Ministry of Corporate Affairs (http://ebook.mca.gov.in/Actpagedisplay.aspx?PAGENAME=17919).

PURPOSE OF THE BALANCE SHEET

Balance sheet is a snapshot statement of the financial position of a company at the end of the accounting period, i.e., at the balance sheet date. It lists assets, equity (owners' claim) and liabilities (outsiders' claim). In a way, it is a stock statement. Non-finance companies categorise assets and liabilities into 'current' (short-term) and 'non-current' (long-term) categories. Finance companies present assets and liabilities in order of liquidity. This chapter focuses on the balance sheet structure of non-finance companies.

In order to avoid cluttering of information, assets and liabilities are grouped under different categories and presented on the face of the balance sheet. Breakup of each item on the balance sheet and explanations related to those items are provided in notes to accounts.

Users of financial statements analyse information in balance sheet to assess the financial health of the company. This information, when analysed in conjunction with the information provided in the statement of profit and loss, helps in developing a perspective on the ability of the company to utilise the infrastructure productively and to manage working capital efficiently, which is necessary for forecasting future cash flows. Working capital is the capital that is being used for the day-to-day operation of the entity.

Notes to accounts

Accounting Standards (Ind ASs), Schedule III (Division II) and some other laws that are applicable to the company require disclosure of specified information for each item of asset, equity and liabilities. Companies disclose that information in notes to accounts. Notes are numbered for cross-referencing. Notes to accounts also include disclosure of accounting policy, clarificatory notes and disclosure of items of assets and liabilities that cannot be recognised in the balance sheet as per the applicable Accounting Standards (Ind ASs).

Due to space constraints, in this text, disclosure requirements have not been discussed in detail. Readers may refer to Schedule III (Division II) reproduced in Chapter 8 to get an understanding of disclosures required under the Companies Act, 2013.

Self-Test Questions

Self-test question 4.1

Indicate whether the following statements are true (T) or false (F):

(i) Balance sheet is a stock statement.

(ii) Balance sheet is a snapshot statement because it does not provide information on assets, liabilities and equity in great detail.

(iii) Balance sheet is similar to a geographical map, which provides adequate details of the geography of a particular location without cluttering information.

(iv) The degree of relevance of information provided in notes to accounts is lower than the information provided on the face of the balance sheet.

(v) Information in balance sheet is useful in assessing the productivity of capital invested in the entity.

(vi) In a way, equity shareholders and lenders own a firm jointly, and therefore, their claim on assets of the firm is proportional.

SUMMARY

Balance sheet is a snapshot statement of the assets, liabilities and equity at the balance sheet date. In order to avoid cluttering of information, details of different categories of assets, liabilities and equity are not provided on the face of the balance sheet. Detailed break up of every item on the face of the balance sheet is provided in notes to accounts. Notes to accounts also disclose additional information for better understanding the information provided on the face of the balance sheet. Entities classify assets and liabilities into current and non-current categories in order to enhance the usefulness of the information.

BALANCE SHEET STRUCTURE

Balance sheet has two segments. Assets are presented in the upper segment and equity and liabilities are presented in the lower segment. Table 4.1 presents the balance sheet structure.

TABLE 4.1

Balance Sheet Structure

(Amount in ₹ crore)

Particulars	HUL	Infosys	Suzlon
ASSETS			
Total assets	14,751	79,885	14,226
EQUITY AND LIABILITIES			
Equity (Owners' claim)	6,490	68,017	1,022
Liabilities (Outsiders' claim)	8,261	11,868	13,204
Total	14,751	79,885	14,226

Notes:

(i) Figures for HUL (Hindustan Unilever Limited) are taken from the stand-alone balance sheet as at March 31, 2017.

(ii) Figures for Infosys (Infosys Limited) are taken from the stand-alone balance sheet as at March 31, 2017.

(iii) Figures for Suzlon (Suzlon Energy Limited) are taken from the stand-alone balance sheet as at March 31, 2017.

Observations

Although the information provided in Table 4.1 is very inadequate for financial analysis, it is enough to conclude that the financial health of Suzlon is quite weak, as almost 93 percent of its assets (in value) is financed by liabilities, which are to be settled by the company, sooner or later, and that will result in outflow of economic resources. The financial health of HUL and Infosys is quite strong. In case of HUL, only 56 percent of assets is financed by liabilities, and the same is 15 percent in case of Infosys.

Self-Test Questions

Self-test question 4.2

Indicate whether the following statements are true (T) or false (F):

(i) Balance sheet reflects the relationship between assets, liabilities and equity as depicted by the accounting equation.

(ii) Even limited information on total assets, total liabilities and equity is helpful in broadly assessing the financial health of the entity.

(iii) In a way, the balance sheet provides information on resources held by the entity at the balance sheet date and the sources of financing those resources.

(iv) In a way, balance sheet provides information on assets held by the entity at the balance sheet date and claims on those assets.

Components of Assets, Equity and Liabilities

Table 4.2 presents the broad categories of assets, equity and liabilities.

NOTES

TABLE 4.2

Balance Sheet Structure

(Amount in ₹ crores)

	HUL	Infosys	Suzlon
ASSETS			
Non-current assets	5,340	32,203	6,901
Current assets	9,411	47,682	7,325
Total	14,751	79,885	14,226
EQUITY			
Equity share capital	216	1,148	1,005
Other equity	6,274	66,869	17
Total	6,490	68,017	1,022
LIABILITIES			
Non-current liabilities	1,059	82	4,339
Current liabilities	7,202	11,786	8,865
Total	8,261	11,868	13,204
Grand total	14,751	79,885	14,226

Note: The figures are based on stand-alone balance sheets as at March 31, 2017 of respective companies.

Table 4.2 provides more information than what Table 4.1 provides. Table 4.2 provides information on what proportion of assets is 'current assets' and what proportion of liabilities is 'current liabilities'. Balance sheet also presents information on financial and non-financial assets separately.

Classification of assets and liabilities into current and non-current categories

Current assets are those assets that management expects to consume or realise within a short period. Assets, which the entity holds for sale, are always classified as current assets. *Current liabilities* are those liabilities that the management expects to settle within a short period. Operating liabilities are normally part of the working capital and are used in the company's normal operating cycle. Therefore, they are classified as current liabilities even if the management does not expect to settle them within twelve months after the balance sheet date.

Short period for the purpose of classifying assets and liabilities into current and non-current categories is the period of twelve months after the balance sheet date or the normal operating cycle, whichever is longer. If, normal operating cycle cannot be estimated reliably, it is considered to be twelve months after the balance sheet date. For a manufacturing company, *operating cycle* is the period from the point of time of receiving raw materials to the point of time when cash is realised from customers. For example, if the raw material holding period is 3 months, work-in-process remains on the shop floor for 9 months, finished goods remain in the warehouse for 2 months and the average collection period from customers is 3 months, the operating cycle is (3 + 9 + 2 + 3) or 17 months or approximately 510 days.

For analysing financial statements, as a thumb rule, analysts consider short-term as the period of twelve months after the balance sheet date.

Non-current assets are those assets that cannot be classified as current assets, and *non-current liabilities* are those liabilities that cannot be classified as current liabilities.

Non-current assets do not include assets that entity holds for sale.

Examples of non-current assets

Table 4.3 presents the list of non-current assets of HUL, Infosys and Suzlon.

NOTES

TABLE 4.3

Non-current Assets as at March 31, 2017

(Amount in ₹ crore)

Particulars	HUL	Infosys	Suzlon
Property, plant and equipment	3,654	8,605	926
Capital-work-in-progress	203	1,247	73
Investment property	0	0	34
Goodwill	0	0	643
Other intangible assets	370	0	186
Intangible assets under development	0	0	56
Investment in subsidiaries, associates and joint ventures	254		
Financial assets			
Investments	6	15,334	3,167
Trade receivables			35
Loans	198	5	1,129
Other financial assets	114	216	620
Non-current tax assets (Net)	311	5,454	0
Deferred tax assets (Net)	160	346	0
Other non-current assets	70	996	32
Total	5,340	32,203	6,901

Notes:

(i) The information is based on the stand-alone balance sheets of the companies as at March 31, 2017.

(ii) Components of each item presented on the face of balance sheet are disclosed in notes to accounts. In addition, notes provide information to be disclosed under the Companies Act, 2013 and as required by accounting standards. Notes also include explanatory statements.

The notes to accounts provide further breakup of each class of assets and disclose information about each item of non-current assets.

Examples of current assets

Table 4.4 provides list of current assets held by HUL, Infosys and Suzlon as at March 31, 2017.

TABLE 4.4

Current Assets as at March 31, 2017

(Amount in ₹ crore)

Particulars	HUL	Infosys	Suzlon
Inventories	2,362	0	2,276
Financial assets			
Investment	3,519	9,643	481
Trade receivables	928	10,960	2,307
Cash and cash equivalents	572	19,153	153
Bank balances other than cash and cash equivalents mentioned above	1,099		0
Loans	0	310	1,787
Other financial assets	306	5,403	103
Current tax assets (net)	0	0	15
Other current assets	553	2,213	203
Assets held for sale	72	0	0
Total	9,411	47,682	7,325

Notes:

(i) The information is based on the stand-alone balance sheets of the companies as at March 31, 2017.

(ii) Components of each item presented on the face of balance sheet are disclosed in notes to accounts. In addition, notes provide information to be disclosed under the Companies Act, 2013 and as required by accounting standards. Notes also include explanatory statements.

(iii) Infosys included all bank balances in cash equivalents.

NOTES

Self-Test Questions

Self-test question 4.3

Indicate whether the following statements are true (T) or false (F):

(i) Any asset that the management does not expect to consume or realise within twelve months after the balance sheet date or within the normal operating cycle is classified as a non-current asset.

(ii) An item of property, plant and equipment that the entity holds to sell is classified as current asset.

(iii) Deferred tax asset (net) is a non-current asset.

(iv) Trade receivables are current assets.

(v) Usually, the operating cycle of a company operating in service industry is shorter than that of a company operating in the manufacturing sector.

SUMMARY

Current assets are those assets that the management expects to consume or realise within a short period. However, an asset held for sale (e.g., stock-in-trade) is always classified as current asset, irrespective of the period for which the entity expects to hold. Current liabilities are those liabilities that the management expects to settle within a short period. Operating liabilities are normally part of the working capital and are used in the company's normal operating cycle, and therefore, they are classified as current liabilities. Assets and liabilities, which cannot be classified as current, are classified as non-current.

Balance Sheet of Financial Institutions

This chapter discusses the structure of balance sheet of non-finance companies. Non-finance companies classify assets and liabilities into current and non-current categories, which is not appropriate for financial institutions, because they do not supply goods or services within a clearly identifiable operating cycle.

They present assets and liabilities in increasing or decreasing order of liquidity, which provides information that is reliable and more relevant than a current/non-current presentation. Table 4.5 below provides the structure of balance sheet of the State Bank of India Ltd. as at March 31, 2017

The government is contemplating a separate format for the presentation of financial statements by non-banking finance companies. Formats for presenting financial statements by banking companies and insurance companies are provided by respective laws applicable to them.

TABLE 4.5

Balance Sheet of SBI (stand-alone) as at March 31, 2017

Particulars	Amount (₹ crore)
CAPITAL AND LIABILITIES	
CAPITAL	797
Reserves and surplus	1,87,489
Deposits	20,44,751
Borrowings	3,17,694
Other liabilities and provisions	1,55,235
Total	27,05,966
ASSETS	
Cash and balances with Reserve Bank of India	1,27,998
Balances with banks and money at call and short notice	43,974
Investments	7,65,990
Advances	15,71,077
Fixed assets (PP&E and Intangible Assets)	42,919
Other assets	1,54,008
Total	27,05,966

NOTES

ASSETS AND THEIR CLASSIFICATION

Table 4.6 presents types of assets and their classification.

TABLE 4.6

Assets and Their Classification

S. No.	Assets	Current	Non-current
NON-FINANCIAL ASSETS			
1.	Property, plant and equipment		✓
2.	Capital work-in-progress		✓
3.	Investment property		✓
4.	Goodwill and other intangible assets		✓
5.	Intangible assets under development		✓
6.	Biological assets other than bearer plants		✓
7.	Raw material (inventory)	✓	✓
8.	Work-in-progress (inventory)	✓	✓
9.	Finished goods (inventory)	✓	
10.	Stock-in-trade (inventory)	✓	
11.	Stores and spares (inventory)	✓	✓
12.	Loose tools (inventory)	✓	✓
13.	Current tax assets (Net)	✓	✓
14.	Non-current assets held for sale	✓	
15	Other non-financial assets	✓	✓
FINANCIAL ASSETS			
16.	Investments in financial assets (Financial asset)	✓	✓
17.	Trade receivables (Financial asset)	✓	✓
18.	Loans (Financial asset)	✓	✓
19.	Margin money deposit with banks against guarantee (Financial asset)	✓	✓
20.	Cash and cash equivalents (Financial asset)	✓	
21.	Bank balances other than (19 above) (Financial asset)	✓	✓
22.	Other financial assets	✓	✓
23.	Deferred tax asset (net)		✓

Note: Assets at serial numbers 7, 8, 11 to 13, 15 to 19, 21 and 22 are classified into current and non-current based on the management's judgement whether those will be consumed within twelve months after the balance sheet date or normal operating cycle, whichever is longer.

Non-Financial Assets

Property, Plant and Equipment

Property, plant and equipment (PP&E) are tangible items, which an entity:

(i) holds for use in the production or supply of goods or services, for rental to others, or for administrative purposes, and

(ii) expects to use during more than one period.

PP&E provides infrastructure. Entities do not hold items of PP&E for sale.

Table 4.7 provides components of property, plant and equipment of HUL, Infosys and Suzlon.

NOTES

TABLE 4.7

Components of Property, Plant and Equipment as at March 31, 2017

Net block (₹ in *crore*)

Particulars	HUL	Infosys	Suzlon
Freehold land	58	1,093	107
Leasehold land	27	633	30
Site development			25
Buildings	1,075	4,106	404
Plant and equipment	2,423	729	289
Wind research and measuring equipment			12
Furniture and fixtures	33	454	22
Vehicles	0	10	12
Office equipment	38	297	25
Computer equipment		1,283	
Total	3,654	8,605	926

Notes:

(i) The information is based on the stand-alone balance sheets of the companies as at March 31, 2017.

(ii) The table provides information on 'net block', which is the gross block of assets that the company holds at the balance sheet date, less accumulated depreciation and accumulated impairment loss up to that date.

(iii) Gross block is the acquisition cost of the assets that the company holds as at the balance sheet date, if the company has adopted the cost model. All the three companies listed in the table have adopted the cost model. Entities have an option to use the fair value model.

(iv) Companies provide information on additions and adjustments to gross block, and additions and adjustments to accumulated depreciation and impairment loss. Adjustments are usually required when the company disposes of an item of asset or write back the impairment loss recognised in earlier periods.

Observations

As it is evident from Table 4.7, different companies operating in different industries require different infrastructure. Infrastructure requirements differ among entities in the same industry, as the requirement also depends on the entity's strategy. For example, investment in plant and machinery will be much lower of an FMCG company that has outsourced manufacturing than investment in plant and machinery by another FMCG company that manufactures products in-house.

Self-Test Questions

Self-test question 4.4

Indicate whether the following statements are true (T) or false (F):

(i) Items of property, plant and equipment are classified as non-current assets.

(ii) In a way, property, plant and equipment (PP&E) provide infrastructure for operation, and therefore, it is not a part of working capital.

(iii) The carrying amount of property, plant and equipment as a percentage of the total carrying amount of all the assets varies in a narrow range among the firms operating in the same industry.

(iv) For companies using the cost model for measuring property, plant and equipment, gross block presented in the balance sheet is the total acquisition cost of all the items of PP&E acquired over the life of the company.

(v) An item of furniture that the entity does not intend to use for more than one financial year is not classified as property, plant and equipment.

Capital Work-In-Progress

When an item of PP&E is being constructed in-house and it is not ready for use at the balance sheet date, all the expenses incurred till the balance sheet date are accumulated under capital work-in-progress. Similarly, when an item of PP&E is not yet installed or not ready for use, the cost of the same is carried in the balance sheet as capital work-in-progress. The amount accumulated under capital work-in-progress is transferred to PP&E when the item is ready for use.

Capital advance

Amount paid in advance to the entity that has been awarded contract to produce or supply an item of PP&E (called capital advance) is not included in capital work-in-progress. It is included in other non-current asset.

Self-Test Questions

Self-test question 4.5

Indicate whether the following statements are true (T) or false (F):

(i) Capital advance is included in capital work-in-progress.

(ii) A printing press that is installed but not ready for use at the balance sheet date, as test run is not complete, is included in property, plant and equipment and not in capital work-in-progress.

(iii) A building under construction is included in capital work-in-progress.

(iv) Furniture received, but yet to be allocated to different employees is included in capital work-in-progress.

(v) Capital work-in-progress is classified as 'non-current asset'.

Investment Property

Investment property is the property (land or a building—or part of a building—or both), which the entity holds to earn rentals or for capital appreciation or both. The entity does not use it in the production or supply of goods or services or for administrative purposes; or holds it for sale in the ordinary course of business.

Self-Test Questions

Self-test question 4.6

Indicate whether the following statements are true (T) or false (F):

(i) An entity, which is in the business of leasing out buildings on short-term basis, classifies all the buildings that it intends to lease out as investment property.

(ii) An entity providing residential accommodation to its employees and recovering a nominal amount towards rent should classify residential quarters that are allotted to employees or earmarked for future allotment as 'investment property'.

(iii) A piece of land in a fast developing locality, which is acquired by the entity on March 31, 2018, but it is undecided about its future use, should be presented as 'investment property' in the balance sheet date dated March 31, 2018.

(iv) Investment property is classified as 'non-current asset'.

(v) A newly constructed office building, which is temporarily let out for six-months, should be presented as 'investment property' in the balance sheet and not as 'property, plant and equipment'.

Intangible Assets

An intangible asset is an identifiable non-monetary asset without physical substance.

Monetary assets are money held and assets to be received in fixed or determinable amounts of money. For example, 'trade receivable', which is the total amount receivable from sale of goods and services, is a monetary asset. Therefore, trade receivable is not an intangible asset.

An intangible asset is identifiable if it can be sold, transferred, licensed, rented or exchanged separately from the entity or it arises from contractual or other legal rights.

Examples

Common examples of intangible assets are computer software, goodwill, patents, copyrights, product brand, motion picture films, customer lists, fishing licences, customer or supplier relationships, customer loyalty, market share and marketing rights.

The GAAP does not permit recognition of internally generated intangible assets, other than computer software, in the balance sheet. However, it allows recognition of intangible assets that are acquired directly or in a transaction involving business combination. For example, although FMCG companies create and manage product brands by investing significant amount on product promotion, it is not permitted to recognise product brand generated by such investment.

Goodwill

Goodwill is the established reputation of a business. It is an amorphous intangible asset, which includes all intangible assets that cannot be identified separately such as relationship with customers, employees, government, local community, and vendors. The GAAP does not permit recognition of internally generated goodwill. It allows recognition of goodwill from a transaction involving business combination. It is measured at excess of purchase consideration over the fair value of net assets (fair value of assets minus fair value of liabilities).

CASE STUDY 4.1 Goodwill

S InfoTech Limited (SIL) acquired K InfoTech Limited (KIL), which is a five-year old company, to build its capabilities in artificial intelligence. It paid ₹100 crore towards purchase consideration. The fair value of net assets is ₹60 crore.

Question

Should SIL recognise goodwill? If it recognises goodwill, at what value the goodwill should be measured?

Solution

The GAAP does not permit recognition of internally generated goodwill. However, it allows recognition of goodwill from a transaction involving business combination. Therefore, SIL should recognise goodwill from the transaction involving acquisition of KIL. The goodwill should be measured at the excess of purchase consideration over the fair value of net assets acquired in the transaction. SIL should recognise the goodwill at (₹100 – 60) or ₹40 crore.

CASE STUDY 4.2 Capital Reserve

N Infrastructure Limited (NIL) acquired P Builders Limited (PBL), which is in the real estate business and known for its capabilities of constructing high-quality green office spaces. After the death of Dr. Rakesh, the promoter of PBL, his only son, Rajesh, who is settled in the USA, decided to sell the business immediately. Without scouting for a buyer, Rajesh approached NIL to buy the business. NIL agreed to acquire PBL due to its technological capabilities. NIL paid ₹100 crores towards purchase consideration. The fair value of net assets (fair value of assets minus fair value of liabilities) is ₹120 crore.

Question

Should NIL recognise goodwill?

Solution

The question of recognising goodwill does not arise, as the fair value of net assets is higher than the purchase consideration. The GAAP requires that the excess of the fair value of net assets over the purchase consideration should be recognised in the balance sheet as capital reserve. In fact, the transaction resulted in a gain of (₹120 – 100) or ₹20 crore leading to increase in equity. The GAAP prohibits distribution of this gain to owners (equity shareholders of a company). Therefore, it requires the gain of ₹20 crore to be recognised as capital reserve, as a component of other equity.

NOTES

Self-Test Questions

Self-test question 4.7

Indicate whether the following statements are true (T) or false (F):

(i) P Limited (PL), which purchased a product brand called 'baboon' from T Limited (TL) on December 15, 2017, should recognise the brand in its balance sheet dated March 31, 2018.

(ii) S Limited, which earns royalty from its subsidiaries for use of the highly valued corporate brand 'Soman' that is built over 100 years, should recognise the corporate brand in its balance sheet.

(iii) Goodwill arising from a business combination transaction is recognised in the balance sheet.

(iv) 'Trade receivables' is an intangible asset because it is not a tangible asset.

(v) Computer software is an intangible asset.

Intangible Assets under Development

The GAAP does not permit recognition of an asset from expenditure during the research phase. Development phase begins after the research phase is over. Usually, entities do not recognise an asset from expenditure during the development phase.

The GAAP permits recognition of an asset (intangible asset under development) if and only if, an entity can demonstrate all of the following:

(i) the technical feasibility of completing the intangible asset so that it will be available for use or sale; (ii) its intention to complete the intangible asset and use or sell it; (iii) its ability to use or sell the intangible asset; (iv) how the intangible asset will generate probable future economic benefits (e.g., by selling the intangible asset or its output); (v) the availability of technical and financial capabilities to complete the development and to use or sell the intangible asset; and (vi) its ability to measure reliably the development.

Self-Test Questions

Self-test question 4.8

Indicate whether the following statements are true (T) or false (F):

(i) A pharmaceutical company, which is engaged in basic research and spends, on an average, 10 percent of revenue towards research expenses, should capitalise research expenses and recognise it under the heading 'intangible assets under development' on the ground of materiality.

(ii) New Age Limited (NAL), which is spending significant amount to develop the prototype of a sophisticated equipment invented by it, which if installed in a housing society or an office complex with an area of up to five acres will purify the air in the complex, should capitalise the expenditure even though it is not sure of the economic viability of the product.

(iii) Most companies do not recognise assets from expenses incurred during development phase, as it is difficult to meet the conditions set out in the GAAP for capitalising those expenses.

Biological Assets Other than Bearer Plants

A *biological asset* is a living animal or plant. Examples are sheep, dairy cattle, cotton plants, tea bushes, sugarcane and trees in a timber plantation.

A *bearer plant* is a living plant, which (i) is used in the production or supply of agricultural produce; (ii) is expected to bear produce for more than one period; and (iii) has a remote likelihood of being sold as agricultural produce, except for incidental scrap sales. Examples of bearer plants are tea bushes, cotton plants, oil palms, fruit trees, and grape vines.

Bearer plants are included in property, plant and equipment. Livestock (living animals held for breeding purpose) is an example of biological asset that is not a bearer plant and is not included in property, plant and equipment.

Self-Test Questions

Self-test question 4.9

Indicate whether the following statements are true (T) or false (F):

(i) Biological assets are included in property, plant and equipment.

(ii) Livestock is not included in property, plant and equipment because it is not a bearer plant.

(iii) Grape vine is not included in property, plant and equipment because it is not a bearer plant.

Inventories

Inventories are assets (i) held for sale in the ordinary course of business; (ii) in the process of production for such sale; or (iii) in the form of materials or supplies to be consumed in the production process or in the rendering of services.

Inventories include: (i) Goods purchased and held for resale, including, for example, merchandise purchased by a retailer and held for resale, or land and other property held for resale by a real estate developer; (ii) Finished goods produced, or work in process (WIP) being produced, by the entity; (iii) Materials (e.g., raw material and components, stores and spares) and supplies awaiting use in the production process; and (iv) Lose tools.

Some use the terms 'work-in-process' and 'work-in-progress' interchangeably. Others reserve the term 'work-in-progress' for 'capital work-in-progress'.

Self-Test Questions

Self-test question 4.10

Indicate whether the following statements are true (T) or false (F):

(i) Capital work-in-progress is a component of inventories.

(ii) Inventory items are always classified as current assets.

(iii) Some items of stores and spares, which meet the definition of property, plant and equipment (PP&E), are not included in inventories.

(iv) An item of property, plant and equipment, which the entity holds for sale, is included in inventories.

(v) Residential apartments that a real estate developer holds for sale are classified as inventories.

Current Tax Assets (Net)

If the amount of tax already paid in respect of current and prior periods exceeds the amount of tax due for those periods, then such excess is recognised as an asset. The excess tax paid (presented as current tax assets) may not be recovered/realised within one year from the balance sheet date and if so, the same should be presented under non-current assets. An entity should evaluate whether current tax assets meets the definition of current assets or not and should accordingly present the same.

NOTES

Self-Test Questions

Self-test question 4.11

Indicate whether the following statements are true (T) or false (F):

(i) Advance tax paid for the assessment year related to the current financial year is a component of current tax asset.

(ii) Refund of tax intimated by the tax authority after assessment, but not received until the balance sheet date is included in current tax asset.

(iii) Current tax asset is always classified as current asset.

Assets Held for Sale

Inventories

Assets that an entity holds for sale in the normal course of business are included in inventories. For example, an entity holds for sale stock-in-trade and finished goods, which are components of inventories. Work-In-Process (WIP) is usually classified as current asset, although the entity does not hold the same as it is. However, WIP that the management does not expect to complete within twelve months after the balance sheet date or within the normal operating cycle should be classified as non-current asset.

Non-current assets held for sale

Entities also hold non-current assets (e.g., items of PP&E) for sale, e.g., when it decides to retire those assets permanently from use. Non-current assets held for sale are classified as current assets.

The GAAP requires that an entity should classify a non-current asset as held for sale if its carrying amount will be recovered principally through a sale transaction rather than through continuing use. The asset must be available for immediate sale in its present condition subject only to terms that are usual and customary for sales of such assets and its sale must be highly probable. Thus, an entity should not classify an asset as a non-current asset held for sale, if the entity intends to sell it in a distant future. Sale of 'non-current assets held for sale' should be completed within one year from the date of classification.

Key Terms

Asset held for sale, bearer plant, biological assets, capital advance, capital work-in-progress, current tax asset, goodwill, gross block, intangible assets under development, inventory, investment property, livestock, monetary asset, net block, work-in-process

Self-Test Questions

Self-test question 4.12

Indicate whether the following statements are true (T) or false (F):

(i) An item of property, plant and equipment (PP&E) that the entity holds for sale is classified as current asset.

(ii) A particular group of plant and machinery that is used to produce a particular product that has to be discontinued from April 1, 2020 as per new environmental norms, should be presented as 'non-current assets held for sale', in the balance sheet dated March 31, 2018, as the Board of Directors, in its meeting held on December 20, 2017, decided to sell the assets included in that group immediately after April 1, 2020.

(iii) Stock-in-trade is always classified as current asset.

(iv) WIP is always classified as current asset.

Other Non-Financial Assets

Examples of other non-financial assets are capital advances and other advances (including advances for materials), and prepaid expenses.

NOTES

SUMMARY

Property, plant and equipment (PP&E) are tangible items, which an entity: (i) holds for use in the production or supply of goods or services, for rental to others, or for administrative purposes; and (ii) expects to use during more than one period. Investment property is the property, which the entity holds to earn rentals or for capital appreciation or both. The entity does not use it in the production or supply of goods or services or for administrative purposes; or holds it for sale in the ordinary course of business. Capital work-in-progress represents the cost of items PP&E under construction and those, which are yet to be ready for use. An intangible asset is an identifiable non-monetary asset without physical substance. Internally developed intangible assets, other than computer software, are not recognised in the balance sheet. Goodwill arises from a transaction involving business combination. Intangible assets under development represents expenditure incurred during development phase and not recognised as expense. Bearer plants are included in PP&E. Biological assets, other than bearer plants, such as livestock, are presented as a separate line item in the balance sheet. Inventories are assets: (i) held for sale in the ordinary course of business; (ii) in the process of production for such sale; or (iii) in the form of materials or supplies to be consumed in the production process or in the rendering of services. The amount excess of the tax already paid in respect of current and prior periods over the amount of tax due for those periods is recognised as current tax asset. Items of PP&E held for sale are not included in PP&E and presented separately as 'assets held for sale'.

Financial Assets

Investments in Financial Assets

Investment represents assets that the entity holds to earn return through capital appreciation, and by receiving interest, dividend, rent, etc.

Examples of investment in financial assets are investments in

(i) equity shares issued by another company,
(ii) mutual funds,
(iii) corporate bonds,
(iv) sovereign bonds,
(v) treasury bills, and
(vi) commercial papers.

Trade Receivable

'Trade receivable' is the total amount receivable from sale of goods and services.

Loan

There is a difference between loan and advance. Loan is repayable, in cash or by issuing another financial asset like cheque drawn on a bank, usually with interest. Examples of loan are security deposit, loan to employees, loan to vendors, and loan to subsidiaries.

On the other hand, amount paid in advance before it is due (e.g., advance to suppliers of goods and services) is not repayable in cash or by issuing another financial asset. The counter party settles the advance by delivering goods or rendering services.

Loan is a financial asset. Advance paid against future delivery of goods and services is a non-financial asset.

Self-Test Questions

Self-test question 4.13

Indicate whether the following statements are true (T) or false (F):

(i) Advance to employees for purchase of a house is classified as loan and is a financial asset.
(ii) Security deposit with a customer, e.g., in capital infrastructure projects, is classified as loan.
(iii) Loan is a financial asset while advances paid to vendors and other are non-financial assets.

NOTES

Margin Money

While issuing guarantee, the bank asks the client to deposit some money as counter security. The money so deposited is called the *margin money*. For example, a bank may stipulate that a client has to deposit 25 percent of the guarantee amount in fixed deposit for a tenure that matches with the validity period of the guarantee.

Cash and Cash Equivalents

Cash

Cash includes cash on hand and demand deposits with banks.

Cash equivalent

Cash equivalents are short-term, highly liquid investments that are readily convertible to known amounts of cash and they are subject to an insignificant risk of changes in value.

Cash equivalent includes cheques in hand; bank balances (in savings accounts and current accounts); an investment in a debt security that has a short maturity of, say three months or less from the date of acquisition (e.g., investment in treasury bills issued by the government); and term deposits with banks that have an original maturity of three months or less.

Bank balances (including term deposits) held as margin money or security against borrowings are neither in the nature of demand deposits nor readily available for use by the entity, and accordingly, do not meet the definition of cash equivalents.

Key Terms
Margin money, cash, cash equivalent

Bank Balances other than those Included in Cash Equivalents

Bank deposits with original maturity of more than three months but less than 12 months are classified as current assets.

Investments in term deposits (with banks) with original maturity of more than twelve months, but with remaining maturity of less than 12 months after the balance sheet date are classified as current assets.

Investments in term deposits (with banks) with the remaining maturity of more than 12 months after the balance sheet date are classified as non-current assets.

Self-Test Questions

Self-test question 4.14

Indicate whether the following statements are true (T) or false (F):

(i) Investments in equity instruments, which the entity intends to sell within three months from the date of purchase, are classified as cash equivalents.
(ii) Bank deposits of original maturity of three years, but less than three months after the balance sheet date are classified as cash equivalent.
(iii) Bank balances held as margin money are always classified as non-current asset.
(iv) Cheques in hand are included in cash equivalent.
(v) Cash and cash equivalent are current assets.

Other Financial Assets

Examples of other financial assets are security deposits with customs, port trust, excise and other government authorities, export incentives receivables and input credits due under Goods and Service Tax (GST).

NOTES

SUMMARY

Common financial assets are investments in financial assets, trade receivables, loans, cash and cash equivalents, and bank deposits. Cash equivalents are short-term, highly liquid investments that are readily convertible to known amounts of cash and they are subject to an insignificant risk of changes in value. Bank deposits with original maturity of three months or less are included in cash equivalents.

DEFERRED TAX ASSETS

Accounting principles and policy for computing taxable income as per income tax law (hereafter, tax accounting) differ from accounting principles for the preparation of financial statements (hereafter, financial accounting). Income tax liability for a particular year (called *current tax liability*) is determined based on the taxable income. Taxable income for a particular year might not match with the net profit reported in the statement of profit and loss due to differences in financial accounting and tax accounting.

Some differences are permanent, while others are temporary. For example, permanent difference arises because penalty paid for violation of statutory laws is not deductible in computing the taxable income. Temporary differences reverse in future. For example, differences in depreciation methods and rates cause temporary difference, which reverses in future because the total depreciation allowed in computing taxable income over the useful life of the asset is same as the total depreciation charged in financial accounting over the useful life of the asset.

Temporary differences create deferred tax assets and liabilities. Permanent differences do not result in recognition of deferred tax asset or deferred tax liability as they do not reverse in future.

ILLUSTRATION 4.1 Deferred Tax Asset and Deferred Tax Liability

The following is the fact pattern:

(i) Taxable income of KP Limited (KPL) for the financial year 2017–18 is ₹1,00,00,000.

(ii) The net profit of the company reported in the statement of profit and loss for that year is ₹1,20,00,000.

(iii) The difference of ₹20,00,000 between reported profit and taxable income is a temporary difference, which will reverse in the year 2018–19.

(iv) The estimated net profit for the financial year 2018–19 is ₹1,00,00,000. No temporary or permanent difference between taxable income and reported net profit will arise except the reversal of the temporary difference recorded in the year 2017–18.

(v) Assume that the income tax rate for the financial year 2017–18 (assessment year 2018–19) and 2018–19 is 0.35 percent.

Required

Explain the concept of deferred tax liability with reference to the above facts.

Solution

The current tax liability for the financial year 2017–18 is (₹1,00,00,000 × 0.35) or ₹35,00,000. If we apply the tax rate to the reported net profit, the tax liability comes to (₹1,20,00,000 × 0.35) or ₹42,00,000. Thus, KPL's current tax liability is lower than what is payable on its net profit by (₹42,00,000 – 35,00,000) or ₹7,00,000. The temporary difference, which will reverse in the next year, has caused deferment of income tax liability of ₹7,00,000 to 2018–19. Lower income tax paid for the year 2017–18 will result in increase in tax liability in 2018–19. In accordance with the principle of accrual accounting, KPL should recognise deferred tax liability, measured at ₹7,00,000, in its balance sheet dated March 31, 2018. Tax expense recognised in the statement of profit and loss is the total of current tax and deferred tax. Tax expense for the financial year 2017–18 is (₹35,000 + 7,000) or ₹42,000.

NOTES

In the year 2018–19, the temporary difference for the year 2017–18 will reverse. In the absence of any new permanent or temporary difference, the taxable income will be (₹1,00,00,000 + 20,00,000) or ₹1,20,00,000. The amount of ₹20,00,000 is added to the reported net profit due to the reversal of the temporary difference of the previous year (2017–18). The current tax liability for the financial year 2018–19 will be (₹1,20,00,000 × 0.35) or ₹42,00,000. If we apply the tax rate to the reported net profit, the tax liability comes to (₹1,00,00,000 × 0.35) or ₹35,00,000. Thus, KPL's current tax liability for the year 2018–19 will be higher than what is payable on its net profit by ₹7,00,000 because it paid less income tax in the year 2017–18, and thus, accumulated an addition.

Deferred tax liability of ₹7,00,000 recognised in the balance sheet as at March 31, 2018 will be derecognised in the year 2018–19. Tax expense to be recognised in the statement of profit and loss for the year 2018–19 is (₹42,00,000 – 7,00,000) or ₹35,00,000.

Deferred tax asset and deferred tax liability

Deferred tax assets arise when the entity accumulates future deductions from taxable income. Deferred tax liabilities arise when the entity accumulates future additions to taxable income. Income tax law allows deduction of current year's losses (called carry forward losses) for a specified number of future years. Therefore, when entity carries forward losses that are deductible in future, deferred tax asset arises.

Deferred tax liabilities and deferred tax assets are netted for presenting in the balance sheet.

Sometimes, deferred tax asset may be quite large. For example, the deferred tax asset (net) of Infosys as at March 31, 2017 was ₹327 crore.

Self-Test Questions

Self-test question 4.15

Indicate whether the following statements are true (T) or false (F):

(i) Deferred tax asset is classified as 'non-current asset'.

(ii) A temporary difference reverses in future years, while a permanent difference does not reverse in future years.

(iii) Provision for bad debt is not allowed as a deduction in computing taxable income, but bad debt is allowed as a deduction when the amount receivable is written off; and this results in recognition of deferred tax asset.

(iv) Both temporary and permanent differences result in recognition of deferred tax asset/deferred tax liability.

SUMMARY

Deferred tax asset and deferred tax liability arise due to temporary differences between tax accounting and financial accounting. Temporary differences reverse in future, while permanent differences do not reverse. Deferred tax asset also arises from accumulated carry forward losses and tax credits. Deferred tax asset is classified as non-current asset.

ANSWERS TO SELF-TEST QUESTIONS

4.1 (i) T; (ii) T; (iii) T; (iv) F; (v) F; (vi) F

4.2 (i) T; (ii) T; (iii) T; (iv) T

4.3 (i) F; (ii) T; (iii) T; (iv) F; (v) T

4.4 (i) T; (ii) T; (iii) F; (iv) F; (v) T

4.5 (i) F; (ii) F; (iii) T; (iv) F; (v) T

4.6 (i) F; (ii) F; (iii) T; (iv) T; (v) F

4.7 (i) T; (ii) F; (iii) T; (iv) F; (v) T

4.8 (i) F; (ii) F; (iii) T

4.9 (i) F; (ii) T; (iii) F

4.10 (i) F; (ii) F; (iii) T; (iv) F; (v) T

4.11 (i) T; (ii) F; (iii) F

4.12 (i) T; (ii) F; (iii) T; (iv) F

4.13 (i) T; (ii) T; (iii) T

4.14 (i) F; (ii) F; (iii) F; (iv) T; (v) T

4.15 (i) T; (ii) T; (iii) T; (iv) F

ASSIGNMENTS

Multiple Choice Questions

1. Tick the correct answer.
   (i) The intangible assets are:
   (a) Fictitious assets that will not result in flow of economic benefits to the enterprise.
   (b) Non-monetary assets without physical substance.
   (c) Non-monetary current assets without physical substance.
   d) None of the above.
   (ii) Receivable, that is, the amount due from a customer is a:
   (a) Monetary current asset.
   (b) Non-monetary current asset.
   (c) Fixed asset.
   (d) None of the above.
   (iii) An asset is classified as a non-current asset or current asset based on:
   (a) The utility of the asset.
   (b) Whether the asset is movable or not.
   (c) Its intended use.
   (d) None of the above.
   (iv) Current assets are:
   (a) Assets that are expected to be realised within twelve months of the balance sheet date.
   (b) Assets that are expected to be realised or consumed in the normal course of the enterprise's operating cycle.
   (c) Assets that are expected to be realised within twelve months of the balance sheet date, and also assets that are expected to be realised or consumed in the normal course of the operating cycle of the enterprise.
   (d) None of the above.
2. State whether the following statements are true (T) or false (F):
   (i) Usually, monetary assets are classified as *current assets* or *investments*.
   (ii) Investments are necessarily assets that are held by an enterprise for the accretion of wealth through distribution or for capital appreciation.
   (iii) Current assets are necessarily short-term assets.
   (iv) Both the terms *intangible asset* and *fictitious asset* represent an asset that has no physical substance, and these two terms are used interchangeably.
   (v) Non-current assets are those assets that are intended to be used either for production or for administrative purposes.

Analytical Questions

1. 'A' has entered into an irrevocable agreement to purchase machinery from 'B & Co.' for ₹1,00,000. Should 'A' recognise the asset and the corresponding liability?
2. 'A & Co.' while launching its new product, 'Zoom' toothpaste, incurred expenditure of ₹1 million on advertisement. The Managing Director of the company proposes that the expenditure be shown as an asset on the balance sheet; however, the accountant disagrees. Who is right?
3. "Users of financial statements assume that the enterprise is a going concern." Comment as this statement.
4. The CESC has installed a transformer within the premises of the factory owned by Mr. A. who paid an amount of ₹50,000 to the CESC towards the cost of the transformer and installation charges. As per the agreement, the ownership of the transformer lies with CESC. Should this expenditure of ₹50,000 be treated as an asset?
5. Human resource is not shown as an asset in the balance sheet though managers claim that it is the most important asset of an enterprise. What could be the reasons for not recognising human resource as an asset on the balance sheet?
6. An analyst asserts: "If the normal operating cycle of a firm is significantly long, classification of assets into current and non-current does not provide any meaningful insight". Do you agree with this statement? Justify your answer.
7. Swaroop Limited (SL) manufactures and sells compressors of various capacities, including large compressors that are used in oil exploration. The auditor of the company argues that it has no well-defined normal operating cycle for the following reasons:
   (a) Its collection period (i.e., the period between the dispatch of goods and collection of receivables) is erratic. It varies between two months and nine months.

NOTES

(b) Its production cycle varies between two months to eighteen months although the production cycle for each type of compressor is well defined.

(c) The auditor proposes that the classification of assets into current or non-current should be based on the 12-month criterion. Do you agree? Explain your position on this issue.

ANNEXURE

EVENTS OCCURRING AFTER THE BALANCE SHEET DATE

1. ADJUSTING EVENTS

To a significant extent, financial reporting information is based on estimates, judgements and models of the financial effects on an entity of transactions and other events and circumstances that have happened or that exist, rather than on exact depictions of those effects. Management develops its perception about the economic consequences of transactions and other events based on information collected by it using reasonable efforts. Information gathered by it is likely to be incomplete, because collection of complete information may involve more than reasonable costs and efforts, and the time required to collect the complete information may delay publishing the financial statements. Therefore, management takes into consideration additional evidence (about the conditions at the balance sheet date) provided by events unfolded after the balance sheet date but before approval by the board of directors for issuance of financial statements. Events that provide additional evidence are called adjusting events. For example, bankruptcy of a customer after the balance sheet date is an adjusting event and the net amount that the entity expects to recover from the customer is adjusted taking into account the information related to bankruptcy and the receivable from the customer, which is recognised in the balance sheet, is measured at that adjusted amount.

2. NON-ADJUSTING EVENTS

Events that are indicative of conditions that arose after the balance sheet date are *non-adjusting events.* Assets and liabilities are not adjusted for non-adjusting events. For example, a fire in a factory on the first day of the next accounting year is a non-adjusting event. The carrying amount of assets in the factory should not be adjusted for the damage caused by the fire. There is an exception to the rule. If the non-adjusting event destroys the fulcrum of the business and invalidates the "going concern" assumption, the assets and liabilities are measured based on the assumption that the entity was not a going concern at the balance sheet date. For example, if a company had only a manufacturing facility, which is destroyed by fire after the balance sheet date and the company did not have any insurance cover for the risk of fire, the survival of the company is difficult and the management has to reassess the validity of the assumption that the company was a going concern at the balance sheet date.

Companies disclose non-adjusting events, if material, in the financial report, usually in the board of director's report. The disclosure provides information about the nature of the event and estimate of its financial effect. If a company is unable to make an estimate of the financial effect, it should state that such an estimate could not be made.

The following are the examples of non-adjusting events, which should be disclosed in the Board of Director's report:

(i) Major business combination after the balance sheet date;

(ii) Announcing a plan to discontinue an operation;

(iii) Major purchase or disposal of assets, or acquisition of major assets by the government;

(iv) Commencement of a major restructuring;

(v) Major change in exchange rates;

(vi) Major change in tax rates;

(vii) Issuance of significant guarantees on behalf of third parties; and

(viii) Commencement of major litigation arising of events that occurred after the balance sheet date.

CHAPTER

5

Equity, Liabilities, Recognition and Measurement

LEARNING OBJECTIVES

The objective of this chapter is to provide an understanding of the format of statement of changes in equity, classification of equity and liabilities and general principles of recognition and measurement of assets and liabilities. After reading this chapter, you will develop understanding of the following:

- The format of statement of changes in equity (Schedule III, Division II) provided in the Companies Act, 2013 for non-finance companies (other than electricity companies), which have adopted Ind AS
- Current and non-current classification of liabilities
- Presentation of earlier comparative periods
- General principles of recognition, derecognition and measurement of assets and liabilities
- Components of 'other equity'

Schedule III to the Companies Act provides the format for presenting balance sheet and statement of profit and loss by non-finance companies (other than electricity companies), which apply Indian Accounting Standards (Ind AS) in the preparation and presentation of financial statements. Ind AS is fully convergent with the International Financial Reporting Standards (IFRS).

Schedule III (Division II) is available at the website of the Ministry of Corporate Affairs (http://ebook.mca.gov.in/Actpagedisplay.aspx?PAGENAME=17919).

NOTES

EQUITY

Equity has two components—equity share capital and other equity (see Table 5.1).

TABLE 5.1

Equity as at March 31, 2017

(Amount in ₹ crore)

Particulars	HUL	Infosys	Suzlon
Equity share capital	216	1,148	1,005
Other equity	6,274	66,869	17
Total	6,490	68,017	1,022

Notes:

(i) The information is based on the stand-alone balance sheets of the companies as at March 31, 2017.

(ii) Components of each item presented on the face of balance sheet are disclosed in notes to accounts. In addition, notes provide information to be disclosed under the Companies Act, 2013 and as required by accounting standards. Notes also include explanatory statements.

Share Capital

Share capital shows the aggregate amount of the face value of outstanding equity shares to the extent paid up (called *paid-up share capital*).

Outstanding equity shares refer to the number of equity shares issued and subscribed reduced by the number of equity shares bought back by the company. *Issued share capital* refers to the number of shares offered to investors. *Subscribed share capital* refers to the number of shares allotted against share applications received, expressing desire to participate. *Paid-up share capital* refers to the aggregate amount of money received against the face value of shares subscribed by and allotted to investors.

The Companies Act, 2013 does not permit return of face value of shares to the shareholders.

Self-Test Questions

Self-test question 5.1

Fill in the blanks:

(i) CP Limited (CPL) issued 1,00,000 equity shares with face value of ₹10 each at ₹150 per share. The amount of paid-up share capital in the balance sheet will increase by ₹..........

(ii) The balance sheet of N M Limited (NML) as at April 1, 2018 shows number of subscribed and paid-up shares at 1,50,000. During the year 2018–19, NML bought back 50,000 shares. The number of outstanding shares as at Mach 31, 2019 is ....

Other Equity

Other equity includes all components of equity, other than share capital (see Table 5.2).

NOTES

TABLE 5.2

Components of Other Equity as at March 31, 2017

(Amount in ₹ crore)

Particulars	HUL	Infosys	Suzlon
Capital reserve	4	54	23
Capital redemption reserve	6	0	15
Securities premium reserve	116	2,208	8,842
Employees stock options outstanding amount	30	120	55
General reserve	2,187	11,087	854
Retained earnings	3,953	49,957	(9,734)
Business transfer adjustment reserve	0	3,448	
Foreign currency monetary items translation difference	0	0	(66)
Equity component of compound financial instruments	0	0	29
Other reserves	9	0	0
Items of other comprehensive income			
Remeasurement of defined benefit plans	(32)	0	0
Fair value change of equity instruments through OCI	0	(5)	0
Fair value change of debt instruments through OCI	1	0	0
Cash flow hedge	0	39	0
Other items of other comprehensive income	0	(39)	0
Total	6,274	66,869	17.59

Notes:

(i) The information is based on the stand-alone balance sheets of the companies as at March 31, 2017.

(ii) Figures in bracket show negative amount.

(iii) Components of each item presented on the face of balance sheet are disclosed in notes to accounts. In addition, notes provide information to be disclosed under the Companies Act, 2013 and as required by accounting standards. Notes also include explanatory statements.

The following are the components of other equity:

(i) share application money pending allotment to the extent not refundable;
(ii) equity component of compound financial instruments;
(iii) reserves and surplus: Capital reserve, Securities premium reserve, Retained earnings; and other reserves;
(iv) debt instruments through other comprehensive income;
(vi) equity instruments through other comprehensive income;
(vii) effective portion of Cash Flow Hedge;
(viii) revaluation surplus;
(ix) exchange difference on translating the financial statements of a foreign operation
(x) other items of other comprehensive income; and
(xi) money received against share warrants.

Share Application Money Pending Allotment, to the Extent Not Refundable

Application money, which is received with applications for contributing to the equity capital of the company, is adjusted to the money payable on allotment of shares. Companies issue prospectus to invite public to contribute to its equity capital. It provides information that are required to be provided as per the law and regulations to enable prospective investors to understand past performance, nature of business and business risks. It also indicates the number of shares on offer and the share price. If the applications received are for more number of shares than that is on offer, the application money is refunded to those to whom shares could not be allotted. The application money that is not refundable is recognised in other equity.

NOTES

The application money to the extent refundable is separately shown under 'other financial liabilities'.

Self-Test Questions

Self-test question 5.2

Indicate whether the following statements are true (T) or false (F):

(i) Application money received with share application is considered to be a part payment of the share price payable on allotment.

(ii) If the shares are not allotted by the balance sheet date, the total amount of the share application money received is presented as a liability in the balance sheet.

Equity Component of Compound Financial Instruments

A compound financial instrument (e.g., debentures with an option to convert into equity shares) has both equity and liability component. The GAAP requires splitting the two components. The equity component is recognised as 'equity component of compound financial instrument' and presented under 'other equity'. The liability component' is presented as a part of 'Borrowings'.

Reserves and Surplus

'Reserves and surplus' represent the income retained in the business over the life of the entity. Reserves and surplus are classified into capital reserve and revenue reserve. Generally revenue reserve is created out of profit from day-to-day operation of business, and capital reserve is created out of capital profit.

Capital reserve is not available for distribution to shareholders. A revenue reserve that is created for a specific purpose is also not available for distribution to shareholders.

Securities Premium Reserve

When a company issues shares at a premium, that is, at a price above the face value of shares, the excess over the face value of the shares allotted is credited to the 'securities premium reserve'. The Companies Act, 2013 (Section 78) restricts the use of securities premium reserve. For example, it cannot be used for payment of dividend, but can be used for issuing bonus shares and buying-back own shares.

Free Reserve (also called General Reserve)

'Free reserve' means such as reserve which is available for distribution as dividend. Free reserves do not include (i) any amount representing unrealised gains, notional gains or revaluation of assets, whether shown as a reserve or otherwise, or (ii) any change in carrying amount of an asset or of a liability recognised in equity, including surplus in the statement of profit and loss on measurement of the asset or the liability at fair value.

All revenue reserves are not free reserves.

Capital Redemption Reserve

Under the Companies Act, 2013, capital redemption reserve is required to be created in the following two situations:

(i) Under the provisions of Section 55 of the Act, where the redemption of preference shares is out of profits, an amount equal to nominal value (also called *face value*) of shares redeemed is to be transferred to a reserve called *capital redemption reserve.*

(ii) Under Section 69 of the Act, if the buy-back of shares is out of free reserves, the nominal value of the shares so purchased is required to be transferred to capital redemption reserve from distributable profit.

The Companies Act, 2013 restricts the use of capital redemption reserve. For example, it cannot be used for payment of dividend, but can be used for issuing bonus shares.

Debenture Redemption Reserve

According to Section 71 of the Companies Act, 2013 where a company issues debentures, it is required to create a debenture redemption reserve for the redemption of such debentures. The company is required to credit adequate amounts, out of its profits every year to debenture redemption reserve, until such debentures are redeemed. On redemption of the debentures for which the reserve is created, the amounts no longer necessary to be retained in this account need to be transferred to the General Reserve.

Share Options Outstanding Account

Ind AS Schedule III requires that 'Share Options Outstanding Account' to be shown as a part of 'Reserve and Surplus' under 'Other Reserves'.

The companies grant stock options (ESOP) as part of compensation to their employees. The ESOP gives an employee the right to buy company's shares at a specified price (called *exercise price*) on or before a specified date (called *exercise date*). Fair value of the ESOP at the grant date is allocated to accounting periods covered by the vesting period, which is the period of time for which the employee must work for the employer to be entitled to exercise the options granted to him/her. Fair value allocated to an accounting period is recognised as an expense (employee benefits) for the period with corresponding credit to 'share option outstanding account'. When the option is exercised, the amount lying in the credit of 'share option outstanding account' is transferred to share capital (to the extent of face value of shares issued) and securities premium account.

ILLUSTRATION 5.1 ESOP

The fair value of each ESOP covering one share, at the grant date, is ₹30, exercise price is ₹100, face value of each share is ₹10 and number of ESOPs granted is 100. The grant date is March 31, 2018. The exercise date is March 31, 2019. There is no vesting period. The option will be exercised on March 31, 2019.

Required

Explain how the ESOP should be presented in financial statements for the years 2017–18 and 2018–19?

Solution

The fair value of 100 ESOPs is (₹30 × 100) or ₹3,000. The fair value of the ESOP (₹3,000) should be recognised as an expense (included in employee benefits) in the statement of profit and loss for the year 2017–18, and the same should be recognised in the balance sheet as at March 31, 2018 as a part of other equity under the heading 'share option outstanding account.

The option is exercised in the year 2018–19. The amount (₹3,000) lying in 'share option outstanding account' is transferred to the securities premium account. The company has received (₹100 × 100) or ₹10,000 from the employees towards the share price. Of this, (₹10 × 100) or ₹1,000 is recognised as share capital and balance ₹9,000 is recognised as securities premium account.

If the parent issues its shares against the ESOP and the company has no obligation, the fair value of the option is considered as contribution of the parent to meet a part of employees' expenses of the company. Exercise of the option does not result in increase in the number of equity shares issued, subscribed and paid up by the company. Consequently, on exercise of the option, the credit balance of 'share option outstanding account' is transferred to another line item in 'other equity'.

Foreign Currency Monetary Items Translation Difference

Foreign currency monetary items

Foreign currency monetary item refers to (i) an asset to be realised in specified or determinable amount of foreign currency; and (ii) a liability to be settled by paying a specified or determinable amount of foreign currency.

Foreign currency and functional currency

Foreign currency is a currency other than the functional currency of the entity. Functional currency is the currency of the primary economic environment in which the entity operates. The primary economic environment in which an entity operates is normally the one in which it primarily generates and expends cash. For example, in most situations, the functional currency of Indian companies is INR.

Translation difference

A foreign currency monetary item is translated into functional currency at the time of initial recording, at the end of each accounting period and at the time of settlement. Foreign currency translation difference arises when the amount receivable or payable in foreign currency is translated into functional currency after initial recognition.

ILLUSTRATION 5.2 Foreign Currency Translation Difference

On April 1, 2017, TP Limited (TPL) purchases equipment from a supplier located in the USA for US$ 1,00,000. The amount is to be paid on April 1, 2018.
Assume that the exchange rate between INR and US$ was (i) on April 1, 2017, 1 US$ = ₹68; (ii) on March 31, 2018, 1 US$ = ₹69; and (iii) on April 1, 2018, 1 US$ = ₹68.90.

Required

Explain foreign currency translation difference with reference to the facts presented above.

Solution

(i) On April 1, 2017, the transaction should be recorded at (1,00,000 × 68) or ₹68,00,000. Both asset (equipment) and liability (amount payable to the supplier) are to be recorded at ₹68,00,000.

(ii) On March 31, 2018, the amount outstanding to the supplier is US$ 1,00,000. This should be measured for recognition in the balance sheet as at March 31, 2018 at (1,00,000 × 69) or ₹69,00,000. This results in foreign currency translation difference of (₹69,00,000 – 68,00,000) or ₹1,00,000. The liability in INR has gone up resulting in decrease in equity. Therefore, the foreign currency translation difference is an expense.

(iii) On April 1, 2018, TPL will buy US$ 1,00,000 at (1,00,000 × 68.90) or ₹68,90,000 to pay US$ 1,00,000 to the vendor. In effect, it paid ₹68,90,000 to settle the liability recognised in the balance sheet at ₹69,00,000. Thus, the settlement has resulted in the foreign currency translation difference of (₹69,00,000 – ₹68,90,000) or ₹10,000. It has resulted in reduction in liability by ₹69,00,000 and reduction in asset (cash) by ₹68,90,000, and consequently, increase in equity by ₹10,000. Therefore, the foreign currency translation difference is an income.

Accounting for foreign currency translation difference

With certain exceptions, under the GAAP (Ind AS), the foreign currency translation difference is recognised in the statement of profit and loss as an expense or income depending on whether the translation of the foreign currency monetary item has resulted in decrease in equity or increase in equity.

Exception to the accounting rule

An entity that has adopted Ind AS for the first-time is permitted to continue the policy adopted for accounting for exchange differences arising from translation of long-term foreign currency monetary items recognised in the financial statements for the period ending immediately before the beginning of the first Ind AS financial reporting period as per the previous GAAP (AS). The previous GAAP allows entities to accumulate exchange differences arising from translation of long-term foreign currency monetary items in 'Foreign currency monetary items translation difference' and amortise the same over the balance period of such asset or liability, by recognition as income or expense in each such period.

Suzlon, which adopted Ind AS from April 1, 2016, decided to apply the earlier accounting policy.

Business Transfer Adjustment Reserve

Infosys has created 'business transfer adjustment reserve' on account of transition to Ind AS, wherein profit from transfer in business between entities under common control is taken to reserve.

Retained Earnings

'Retained earnings' represents the profit that the company has earned till date from the date of its formation, and not distributed to shareholders as dividend or buy-back of shares, and not appropriated to any specified reserve.

A negative amount of retained earnings is reported as accumulated deficit and presented as a deduction from reserves and surplus.

Self-Test Questions

Self-test question 5.3

Indicate whether the following statements are true (T) or false (F):

(i) 'Reserve and surplus' represents accumulated (retained) profit and other gains from transactions and other events over the life of the company.

(ii) The terms 'revenue reserve' and 'free reserve' are used interchangeably.

(iii) Securities premium reserve arises only when the company issues shares at a price higher than their face value.

(iv) The Companies Act, 2013 restricts the use of capital redemption reserve.

(v) Debenture redemption reserve can never be used for distribution of dividend, even after redemption of debentures.

(vi) 'Share options outstanding account' represents the fair value of ESOPs at the grant date.

(vii) Foreign currency monetary item translation difference is not presented in the balance sheet under the broad heading 'other equity' under Ind AS (the extant GAAP).

(viii) The 'term retained earnings' does not represent the profit that the company has earned till date from the date of its formation, and not distributed to shareholders as dividend.

(ix) Entities cannot have negative retained earnings.

(x) Exchange difference arises when a foreign currency asset or liability is translated into functional currency at the balance sheet date, and also, when the entity settles a foreign currency liability or realises a foreign currency receivable.

Items of Other Comprehensive Income

Items of other comprehensive income that are presented as separate line items in 'other Equity' are:

(a) debt instruments through other comprehensive income;

(b) equity instruments through other comprehensive income;

(c) effective portion of cash flow hedge;

(d) revaluation surplus; and

(e) exchange difference on translating the financial statements of a foreign operation.

Money Received against Share Warrants

Ind AS 33, Earnings per Share, defines 'warrants' as "financial instruments, which give the holder the right to acquire equity shares." Share warrant is in the nature of call option, which gives the right to the holder, but no obligation, to buy the underlying shares at the exercise price at or within the exercise date.

Generally, listed companies issue share warrants to promoters and others in terms of the Guidelines for preferential issues, viz. SEBI (Issue of Capital and Disclosure Requirements),

Guidelines, 2009. Effectively, money received against share warrants (upfront payment by the warrant holder) is the total of part payment for shares to be issued in future and the premium (called *option premium*) paid for the right to buy shares at a later date. If the warrant holder does not exercise the right, the amount is forfeited. The money received against share warrant is presented as a separate line item under the broad heading 'other equity'.

ILLUSTRATION 5.3 Money Received against Share Warrant

SV Limited (SVL) issued share warrant to its promoter for 10,000 equity shares for a consideration of ₹100 per equity share of face value of ₹10. The terms of issue require 25 percent of the total consideration to be paid upfront. The warrant holder exercised the right within the specified period.

Required

Explain the accounting for money received against share warrant.

Solution

₹25 per share, which is paid upfront by the promoter, is the total of premium (called *option premium*) for acquiring the right to buy 10,000 shares at a specified price (₹100, including the option premium) and part payment of the share price. SVL will present (₹25 × 10,000) or ₹2,50,000, received on issuance of share warrant as 'money received against share warrant' under other equity. On receipt of the remaining ₹75 per share on exercise of the share warrant, ₹10 per share will be recognised as share capital and balance ₹65 per share will be recognised as 'securities premium account' under other equity. Thus, (₹10 × 10,000) or ₹1,00,000 should be recognised as share capital and (₹65 × 10,000) or ₹6,50,000 should be recognised as 'securities premium account'. 'Money received against share warrant' should be transferred to 'securities premium account'.

Self-Test Questions

Self-test question 5.4

Indicate whether the following statements are true (T) or false (F):

(i) Share warrant is a type of derivative instrument (call option, i.e., the option to buy shares).

(ii) Money received against share warrant is the total of option premium and part payment of money to be received on issue of shares when the option will be exercised.

(iii) On issue of shares the money received against share warrant is transferred to the securities premium reserve.

SUMMARY

Equity has two components—share capital and other equity. Share capital shows the aggregate amount of the face value of outstanding equity shares, to the extent paid up (called *paid-up share capital*). Other equity primarily consists of share premium reserve and profit (including gains) accumulated retained over the life of the entity. Other elements of other equity are share application money pending allotment to the extent not refundable, equity component of compound financial instruments, foreign currency monetary items translation reserve, share options outstanding account, money received against share warrants and items of other comprehensive income. Reserves and surplus are classified into capital reserve and revenue reserve. Generally speaking, revenue reserve is created out of profit from day-to-day operation of business and capital reserve is created out of capital profit.

Key Terms

Bonus share, call option, capital redemption reserve, compound financial instrument, exchange difference, ESOP, face value, foreign currency monetary item translation difference, free reserve, general reserve, nominal value, option premium, other comprehensive income, other equity, paid up share capital, prospectus, reserves and surplus, retained earnings, revenue reserve, securities premium reserve, share application money, share options outstanding account, share warrant

NOTES

LIABILITIES AND THEIR CLASSIFICATIONS

Non-current and current liabilities of HUL, Infosys and Suzlon are presented in Table 5.3 and Table 5.4.

TABLE 5.3

Non-current Liabilities as at March 31, 2017

(Amount in ₹ crore)

Particulars	HUL	Infosys	Suzlon
Financial liabilities			
Borrowing	0	0	4,039
Other financial liabilities (not included in provision)	71	40	202
Provisions	485	0	58
Non-current tax liabilities (net)	296	0	0
Other non-current liabilities	207	42	40
Total	1,059	82	4,339

Notes:

(i) The information is based on the stand-alone balance sheets of the companies as at March 31, 2017.

(ii) Components of each item presented on the face of balance sheet are disclosed in notes to accounts. In addition, notes provide information to be disclosed under the Companies Act, 2013 and as required by accounting standards. Notes also include explanatory statements.

TABLE 5.4

Current Liabilities as at March 31, 2017

(Amount in ₹ crore)

Particulars	HUL	Infosys	Suzlon
Financial liabilities			
Borrowings	0	0	1,976
Trade payables	6,006	269	4,654
Other financial liabilities (not included in provision)	181	5,056	679
Other current liabilities	628	2,349	869
Provisions	387	350	687
Income tax liabilities (net)	0	3,762	0
Total	7,202	11,786	8,865

Notes: Same as given in Table 5.3.

Table 5.5 presents the types of liabilities and their classification.

Table 5.5

Liabilities and Their Classification

S. No.	Liabilities	Current	Non-current
1.	Borrowings	✓	✓
2.	Trade payables	✓	✓
3.	Other financial liabilities, not included in provisions	✓	✓
4.	Provisions	✓	✓
5.	Current tax liability (net)	✓	✓
6	Deferred revenue and advance from customers	✓	✓
7.	Other non-financial liabilities	✓	✓
8.	Deferred tax liability (net)		✓

Note: Liabilities at serial numbers 1 to 5 and 7 are classified into current and non-current based on management's judgement on whether those will be settled within 12 months after the balance sheet date or normal operating cycle, whichever is longer.

BOX 5.1 Current Liabilities

An entity shall classify a liability as current when

(i) it expects to settle the liability in its normal operating cycle;
(ii) it holds the liability primarily for the purpose of trading;
(iii) the liability is due to be settled within 12 months after the reporting period; or
(iv) it does not have an unconditional right to defer settlement of the liability for at least 12 months after the reporting period. Terms of a liability that could, at the option of the counterparty, result in its settlement by the issue of equity instruments do not affect its classification.

An entity should classify all other liabilities as non-current.

An issued debt instrument (e.g., debentures) that the entity intends to repurchase soon to make a gain from short-term movements in interest rates is an example of a liability held for trading.

Financial Liabilities not Included in Provision

Borrowings

Borrowings represent the outstanding amount against the amount borrowed by the company from financial institutions, non-financial institutions and public.

Borrowing includes term loan from banks and other parties; deferred payment liabilities (e.g., purchase of equipment with the terms that payment would be made over next five years); deposits (e.g., deposits from public and deposits from customers); loans from related parties (e.g., loan from the group company and loan from directors); redeemable preference shares; and liability component of compound financial instruments (e.g., liability component of optionally convertible bonds).

Current maturities of long-term debt (borrowing) are presented as a separate line item under the broad heading 'other financial liabilities'.

Long-term and short-term borrowings

Long-term debt is specified in Ind AS Schedule III as a borrowing having a period of more than 12 months at the time of origination. Borrowing that cannot be classified as long-term debt is classified as short-term debt. Therefore, all short-term borrowings are classified as current liability. Long-term liabilities are usually repayable in tranches.

BOX 5.2 Secured and Unsecured Borrowings

When the company provides a collateral to the lender, for example, by pledging some asset (e.g., an item of PP&E) in order to reduce the lender's credit risk, the company classifies the borrowing as 'secured borrowing'. On default by the company in repayment of the amount borrowed or interest thereon, the lender has the right to sell the asset and recover the amount due to it. In case of unsecured borrowings, the company does not provide any collateral.

Self-Test Questions

Self-test question 5.5

Indicate whether the following statements are true (T) or false (F):

(i) Redeemable preference shares are classified as borrowings.
(ii) Borrowings against the personal guarantee of the promoter are classified as 'secured borrowings'.
(iii) Public deposits are presented in the balance sheet under the broad heading 'borrowings'.
(iv) Borrowings having a period of more than 12 months at the time of origination are classified as long-term borrowings.
(v) Current maturities of long-term debt (borrowing) are presented as a separate line item under the broad heading 'borrowings'.

Trade Payables

Trade payables represent the amount due to suppliers of goods and services, which the company consumes in the normal course of business, against claims received from them and accepted by the company.

Trade payables do not include amounts due under contractual obligations or statutory payables. For example, trade payables do not include amount due in respect of contribution to provident fund, contractually reimbursable expenses, and towards purchase of capital goods (e.g., items of PP&E).

Self-Test Questions

Self-test question 5.6

Indicate whether the following statements are true (T) or false (F):

(i) Trade creditors include liability towards goods and services received, but for which claims from suppliers are not received.

(ii) Trade payables do not include amounts due under contractual obligations towards purchase of capital goods.

(iii) Trade payables include statutory payables.

Other Financial Liabilities (Not Included in Provision)

The items, which meet the definition of financial liabilities as per Ind AS 32, Financial Instruments, such as contingent consideration (usually arises in transactions involving business combination), derivative contracts, financial guarantee contracts issued, contractually reimbursable expenses, etc. are presented under other financial liabilities. Other common examples include outstanding salaries and wages, current maturities of long-term debt, interest accrued, unpaid dividends, application money received for allotment of securities to the extent refundable and interest accrued thereon, unpaid matured deposits and interest accrued thereon, and unpaid matured debentures and interest accrued thereon.

Interest accrued on financial liabilities forms part of its carrying amount whether it is at amortised cost (i.e., as per effective interest method), or at fair value. Accordingly, an entity may not present 'Interest Accrued' separately from the related financial liability.

BOX 5.3 Accruals

Accruals are the liabilities to pay for goods or services that have been received or supplied (but not received) but have not been paid, invoiced or formally agreed with the supplier. Supplier includes employees. Although it is sometimes necessary to estimate the amount or timing of accruals, the uncertainty is generally much less than for provisions. Examples of accruals are liability for profit sharing bonus for 2017–18, payable in 2018–19; and services received from a supplier before the close of the accounting year, but invoice is not received before the Board of Directors approves the financial statements.

Accruals are reported as a part of other payables and are not included in provisions.

Self-Test Questions

Self-test question 5.7

Indicate whether the following statements are true (T) or false (F):

(i) Unpaid dividend is a liability, but dividend proposed by the Board of Directors is not a liability.

(ii) An entity may not present 'Interest Accrued' separately from the related financial liability.

(iii) Application money received for allotment of securities to the extent refundable and interest accrued thereon is presented as a part of equity and not as a liability.

(iv) Financial guarantee contracts issued are recognised as a liability, although they are in the nature of contingent liabilities.

(v) Unpaid matured debentures are classified as borrowing.

NOTES

SUMMARY

Borrowings represent the outstanding amount against the amount borrowed by the company from financial institutions, non-financial institutions and public. Borrowings include redeemable preference shares and liability component of compound financial instruments. Current maturities of long-term debt (borrowing) are presented as a separate line item under the broad heading 'other financial liabilities'. Interest accrued on financial liabilities forms part of its carrying amount whether it is at amortised cost (i.e., as per effective interest method), or at fair value. Accordingly, an entity may not present 'Interest Accrued' separately from the related financial liability. Accruals are liabilities to pay for goods or services that have been received or supplied (but not received) but have not been paid, invoiced or formally agreed with the supplier.

Key Terms
Accruals, financial guarantee contracts, interest accrued, long-term borrowing, provision, short-term borrowing, trade payables

Non-Financial Liabilities not Included in Provision

Current Tax Liabilities (Net)

If amount of tax due in respect of current and prior periods exceeds the amount of tax already paid for those periods then such excess is recognised as a liability.

Deferred Revenue and Advance from Customers

Deferred revenue (Unearned income)

Deferred revenue (also called, *unearned income*) is the money received from customers before fulfilment of performance obligations.

For example, 'deferred revenue' is recognised by an entity that sells subscriptions of magazines/journals. It does not recognise the full subscription for one or more years as revenue for the accounting period in which it has received the subscription, if it has not supplied all the issues of the journal during that period. It recognises a part of the subscription as 'deferred revenue' (liability) for the number of issues it owes to the customer. Liability will be extinguished gradually with the supply of remaining issues of the journal. Similarly, entities that sell insurance (e.g., health insurance) and provide services (e.g., telecom services) recognise 'deferred revenue' as a liability.

Advance from customers

Accountants make a distinction between 'deferred revenue' and 'advance from customers'. Advance from customers is also money received from the customers before fulfilment of performance obligations. But, the money received is not in the nature of revenue (like insurance premium or subscription for journals or pre-paid mobile charges). Money received is in the nature of advance with order (for supplying goods and services) to enable the seller to mobilise resources (e.g., in capital goods industry or consultancy services) or to ensure commitment for the acceptance of the goods and services to be supplied by the seller.

Self-Test Questions

Self-test question 5.8

Indicate whether the following statements are true (T) or false (F):

(i) There is no difference between deferred revenue and advance from customers.

(ii) Advance received from customers with purchase order for supply of equipment is classified as advance from customers.

(iii) An automobile dealer, who provides free maintenance services for one year to the customers and allocates a portion of the revenue earned by selling cars to revenue from maintenance services to be provided in future, should present that part of revenue in the balance sheet as 'advance from customers'.

NOTES

Key Terms
Advance from customers, current tax liability, deferred revenue, unearned revenue

Other Non-Finance Liabilities (Not Included in Provision)

Deferred revenue, and advance from customers are presented as other non-financial liabilities in the balance sheet. Another example is statutory claims (e.g., tax deducted at source) outstanding.

SUMMARY

If amount of tax due in respect of current and prior periods exceeds the amount of tax already paid for those periods, then such excess is recognised as a liability. *Deferred revenue* (also called *unearned income*) is the money received from customers before fulfilment of performance obligations. Advance from customers is also money received from the customers before fulfilment of performance obligations, but the money received is not in the nature of revenue.

Provisions

A provision is a liability of uncertain timing or amount. Provisions are distinguished from other liabilities, such as trade payables and accruals, because there is uncertainty about the timing or amount of the future expenditure required in settlement.

Examples of provision are provision for employee benefits (pension, medical, compensated absences and others); provision for statutory levy contested by the company; provision for product warranty; provision for post-sales support to client (usually, in information technology industry); provision for performance guarantee, maintenance and warranty and liquidated damages (usually, in capital goods industry) and provision for decommissioning cost that the company will incur after an equipment (e.g., oil rig) is retired from use permanently.

Self-Test Questions

Self-test question 5.9

Indicate whether the following statements are true (T) or false (F):

(i) There is no difference in the nature of provisions and accruals.

(ii) Provisions are liabilities, estimates of which are surrounded by uncertainties.

(iii) Provisions are liabilities, settlement of which might not require outflow of economic resources.

Deferred Tax Liabilities (Net)

Please see Chapter 4 for discussion on deferred tax liabilities.

CONTINGENT LIABILITIES AND COMMITMENTS

Contingent Liabilities

Contingent liabilities are not recognised in the balance sheet. These are disclosed in notes below the balance sheet.

A liability recognised in the balance sheet is a present obligation. An obligation is a present obligation if

(i) the entity has no practical ability to avoid settling the obligation, and

(ii) it is probable, in the sense that it is more likely than not that the economic resources will outflow to settle the obligation.

A contingent liability is a possible obligation, existence of which will be confirmed only by the occurrence or non-occurrence of one or more uncertain future events not wholly within the control of the entity. For example, possible obligation arises from a performance guarantee issued by a holding company on behalf of its subsidiary, as the obligation will be confirmed only if the subsidiary fails to perform as per the terms of the contract.

Contingent liabilities also include an obligation, which is not recognised in the balance sheet because it is not probable that an outflow of economic resources will be required to settle the obligation. For example, the management does not recognise a liability for damage claimed by a customer for a defective product, which is under arbitration, if it estimates that it is not probable that an outflow of economic resources will be required to settle the obligation.

Management does not recognise a present obligation in the balance sheet and discloses it as a contingent liability if it is unable to measure the amount of the obligation with sufficient reliability. For example, an automobile manufacturer may not recognise the liability arising from defective air bags supplied with cars manufactured during the last quarter of the financial year, as it is unable to estimate the liability reliably until the publication of the financial statements.

Examples of contingent liabilities

(i) Guarantees given on behalf of third parties (e.g., subsidiaries and associates), other than financial guarantees, and

(ii) Claims (against the company) by employees, tax authorities, customers and others, which have not been accepted and acknowledged as debt by the company, and are under dispute resolution proceedings (e.g., legal and arbitration).

Financial guarantee

Financial guarantee is recognised in the balance sheet as a liability.

A *financial guarantee contract* is a contract for compensating the holder of a debt instrument only for a loss that it incurs because a specified debtor fails to make specified payment. The contract does not compensate the holder for more than the actual loss it incurs.

CASE STUDY 5.1 Financial Guarantee

Investor Z buys debentures issued by KM Limited (KML). At the same time, it obtains a guarantee from a bank (SMI) that, if KML fails to make payment of the full amount due on the maturity of the debentures, then the bank will pay the shortfall to Z.

Questions

What is the nature of the guarantee and how SMI should present it in the balance sheet?

Solution

The guarantee issued by SMI is a 'financial guarantee contract' because SMI will compensate Z for a loss that it might incur if KML fails to redeem the debentures in full on maturity. SMI should recognise the financial guarantee as a liability in its balance sheet.

NOTES

Key Terms
Contingent liability, Financial guarantee, Commitments

Self-Test Questions

Self-test question 5.10

Indicate whether the following statements are true (T) or false (F):

(i) There is a thin difference between contingent liability and provision.

(ii) Liability arising from issuance of financial guarantee is a contingent liability, but extant GAAP requires entities to recognise liability for financial guarantee contracts issued by them.

(iii) Whether a liability against a demand from the Income Tax Department, which is under appeal, should be recognised in the balance sheet as a provision or should be disclosed as a contingent liability depends on the perspective developed by the management, hence judgemental.

Commitment

The term 'commitment' simply implies future liability for contractual expenditure. The following commitments are disclosed separately in notes below the balance sheet:

(i) Estimated amount of contracts remaining to be executed on capital account

(ii) Uncalled liability on shares and other investments partly paid, and

(iii) Other commitments (specify nature).

'Other commitments' would include all expenditure-related contractual commitments apart from capital commitments such as commitments arising from long-term contracts for purchase of raw material, employee contracts, lease commitments, etc.

Self-Test Questions

Self-test question 5.11

Indicate whether the following statements are true (T) or false (F):

(i) In most situations, commitments at the balance sheet date get translated into a contractual liability at a later date.

(ii) Commitments are not contingent liabilities.

SUMMARY

Contingent liability is a possible obligation, existence of which will be confirmed only by the occurrence or non-occurrence of one or more uncertain future events not wholly within the control of the entity; or a liability, settlement of which is unlikely (not probable) to result in outflow of economic benefits; or an obligation, the amount of which cannot be measured with sufficient reliability. Contingent liabilities are not recognised in the balance sheet. These are disclosed in notes below the balance sheet. A commitment is not a contingent liability.

PRESENTATION OF EARLIER COMPARATIVE PERIODS

Two balance sheets

Companies are required to present at least two balance sheets, two statements of profit and loss and two cash flow statements to provide comparative information for the previous period. For example, the balance sheet as at March 31, 2018 provides information on assets, equity and liabilities as at March 31, 2018, and also, the same information as at March 31, 2017.

Prior period errors

Errors occur primarily due to misinterpretation of an accounting policy or law, error in calculations, error in applying an applicable accounting standard or a fraud committed in an earlier period, which could not be detected.

Restatement of financial statements

Ind AS 8, Accounting Policies, Changes in Accounting Estimates and Errors require retrospective adjustments to effect changes in accounting policies, to the extent practicable, except when the transition provisions in another Ind AS require otherwise. Ind AS 8 also requires restatements to correct prior period errors retrospectively, to the extent practicable.

Restatement of financial statements and the third balance sheet

Companies restate financial statements when an accounting policy is applied retrospectively or an error occurred in a prior period; and that had materially affected the balances of assets, equity and liabilities in the balance sheet.

When a company applies an accounting policy retrospectively or makes a restatement of items in the financial statements or when it reclassifies items in its financial statements, it presents three balance sheets. The third balance sheet is the balance sheet as at the beginning of the earliest comparative period presented. For example, if the entity changes its accounting policy in 2018–19, it should present three balance sheets—balance sheet dated March 31, 2019; balance sheet dated March 31, 2018; and balance sheet dated March 31, 2017. The balance sheets as at March 31, 2018 and as at March 31, 2017 show the cumulative effect of the application of the new accounting policy retrospectively on assets, equity and liabilities.

CASE STUDY 5.2 Rectification of Errors and Three Balance Sheets

While preparing the financial statements of NM Limited (NML) for the year ended March 31, 2018, the Chief Accounts Officer (CAO) has detected an error occurred in the year 2013–14. In 2013–14, NML did not recognise a liability for dismantling and restoration of site for equipment installed in that year. Ind AS 16, Property, Plant and Equipment stipulates that the liability should be provided and the amount so provided should be added to the acquisition cost of the asset. The liability should be measured at the present value of estimated cash outflows to dismantle the equipment and restore the site at the end of the useful life of the equipment. In every subsequent year, the liability increases due to unwinding of the discount rate. The amount by which the liability increases is recognised as finance cost in the statement of profit and loss. The CAO estimates the liability at ₹10 crore as at March 31, 2014. The CAO and the auditor concur that the error had materially affected the balances of asset, equity and liabilities presented in the balance sheet as at March 31, 2017.

Question

How should NML correct the error?

Solution

NML has to restate the financial statements.

The error of not providing liability for dismantling the equipment and restoring the site had resulted in understatement of liabilities, understatement of the asset (gross block and net block of the equipment) and overstatement of equity (reserves and surplus) in the balance sheet as at March 31, 2014. Consequently, the balances in the balance sheets dated March 31,

NOTES

2015, March 31, 2016 and March 31, 2017 were incorrect. NML has to estimate the cumulative effect of the error on the balances of assets, equity and liabilities in the balance sheet dated March 31, 2016. The corrected balances should be taken as opening balances for restating the statement of profit and loss for the year 2016–17 and balance sheet as at March 31, 2017. The financial statements for the year 2017–18 should be prepared based on the restated balance sheet of 2016–17.

Ind AS1, Presentation of Financial Statements, and Schedule III (Division II) of the Companies Act, 2013 requires that NML in its financial statements for the year 2017–18 should present the balance sheet as at March 31, 2016, in addition to balance sheets at March 31, 2017 and March 31, 2018.

Key Terms
Prior-period error, restatement

Self-Test Questions

Self-test question 5.12

Indicate whether the following statements are true (T) or false (F):

(i) Prior-period errors might arise from incorrect interpretation of laws and regulations.
(ii) Cumulative effect of correcting a prior period error on assets, liabilities and equity must be considered in the preparation and presentation of current year's financial statements.
(iii) Restatement of earlier period's financial statements requires presentation of three balance sheets and three statements of profit and loss.
(iv) Change in accounting policy arising from issuance of a new or revised accounting standard always requires the entity to apply the revised accounting policy retrospectively.

SUMMARY

Entities are required to present comparative figures of the previous accounting year in financial statements. In a way, they present two balance sheets, two statements of profit and loss and two cash flow statements. However, if the entity, in the current year, revises accounting policy or identifies an error occurred in a prior year, it is required to present three balance sheets. The third balance sheet reflects the opening balances of the previous year incorporating cumulative effect of the revised accounting policy retrospectively or correcting the error in the year in which the error occurred.

STATEMENT OF CHANGES IN EQUITY

Statement of changes in equity provides reconciliation between equity at the commencement of the accounting period and the same at the end of the period. It is presented in two parts—(i) equity share capital; and (ii) other equity. The formats are provided in Schedule III (Division II) of the Companies Act, 2013.

Equity share capital

Balance at the beginning of the reporting period	Changes in equity share capital during the year	Balance at the end of the reporting period

NOTES

Other equity

	Components of other equity (Reconciliation for each component is required)							
	1	2	3	4	5	6	7	8
Balance at the beginning of the reporting period								
Changes in accounting policy or prior period errors								
Restated balance at the beginning of the reporting period								
Total comprehensive income for the year								
Dividends								
Transfer to retained earnings								
Any other change (to be specified)								
Balance at the end of the reporting period								

Changes in accounting policy and prior period errors

Retrospective adjustments and retrospective restatements are not changes in equity, but they are adjustments to the opening balance of retained earnings, except when an Ind AS requires retrospective adjustment of another component of equity. Paragraph Ind AS 1, Presentation of Financial Statements requires disclosure in the statement of changes in equity of the total adjustment to each component of equity resulting from changes in accounting policies, and separately from corrections of errors. These adjustments are disclosed for each prior period and the beginning of the period.

RECOGNITION AND DERECOGNITION OF ASSETS AND LIABILITIES

Recognition

Recognition is inclusion of an item of asset or liability in the balance sheet.

Relevant accounting standard, which stipulates accounting principles and methods for a particular class of assets or liabilities, provides the recognition criteria for that class of assets or liabilities in detail.

As a general principle, an item of asset or liability is *not recognised* if

(i) There is an uncertainty whether the asset or liability exists, and in case of an intangible asset, whether the asset is separable from goodwill.

Some assets, for example, rights to benefit from items such as know-how and customer or supplier relationships, are not contractual or other legal rights. Therefore, there is uncertainty about the existence of the asset.

Similarly, for some liabilities, it may be unclear whether a past event causing an obligation has occurred. For example, if another party claims compensation from the entity for an act of wrongdoing, it may be uncertain whether the entity committed the act.

(ii) There is only a low probability that an inflow (in case of an asset) or outflow (in case of a liability) of economic benefits will result.

(iii) The level of uncertainty in estimating the amount at which the asset or a liability is to be measured is so high that the resulting information has little relevance.

(iv) The cost of recognition (e.g., cost of collecting the information) outweighs the benefits to users.

Dercognition

Derecognition is the removal of all or part of a previously recognised asset or liability from an entity's balance sheet.

Relevant accounting standard, which stipulates accounting principles and methods for a particular class of assets or liabilities, provides the derecognition criteria for that class of asset or liability in detail.

General principle

As a general principle, an asset is normally derecognised when the entity loses control of all or part of the previously recognised asset; and a liability is normally derecognised when the entity has no longer a present obligation for all or part of the previously recognised liability.

Self-Test Questions

Self-test question 5.13

Indicate whether the following statements are true (T) or false (F):

(i) GAAP does not permit recognition of internally generated intangible assets because of uncertainties surrounding their existence and measurement.

(ii) Amount due from a customer is recognised as an asset immediately after completing the performance obligation, even if there is significant uncertainty about collectability of the amount.

(iii) There is no thumb rule that a customer's claim that is under arbitration should be disclosed as a contingent liability and no provision should be recognised in the balance sheet.

(iv) Costs and benefits of collecting information are assessed by the standard setter, and therefore, auditor adversely comments on the balance sheet if the management does not recognise a liability on the ground that the cost of collecting information for estimating the liability exceeds the benefits to the primary users of financial statements.

(v) An entity derecognises a land that has been acquired by the government for public purpose.

MEASUREMENT OF ASSETS AND LIABILITIES

Measurement is the process of quantifying, in monetary terms, information about an entity's assets, liabilities, equity, income and expenses.

A measurement basis is an identified feature of an item being measured (e.g., historical cost, fair value or fulfilment value). Relevant accounting standard, which stipulates accounting principles and methods for a particular class of assets or liabilities, stipulates the measurement basis that is to be used to measure that particular class of assets or liabilities at the initial measurement, and in subsequent measurement.

Initial measurement and subsequent measurement

Initial measurement refers to measurement when the asset or liability is initially recognised. *Subsequent measurement* refers to the measurement when the item continues to be recognised in subsequent balance sheets. For example, a building is purchased on January 15, 2018. It is initially recognised on January 15, 2018. It is subsequently recognised in the balance sheet dated March 31, 2018 and in the subsequent balance sheets. Initial measurement of the building refers to the measurement of the building on January 15, 2018, and subsequent measurement refers to the measurement of the building to estimate the carrying amount of the asset in the balance sheet dated March 31, 2018 and in the subsequent balance sheets.

Historical Cost

Measures based on historical cost provide monetary information about assets or liabilities, using information derived from the transaction or event that created them. The historical cost measures of assets or liabilities do not reflect changes in prices. However, the measures do reflect changes such as the consumption or impairment of assets and the fulfilment of liabilities.

Historical Cost of Non-financial Assets

Examples of non-financial assets

Examples of non-financial assets are property, plant and equipment, intangible assets, and advance paid to vendors.

Measurement principle

The historical cost of a non-financial asset at the time of the asset's acquisition or construction is the cost incurred to acquire or construct the asset, including both the consideration given and the transaction costs incurred.

In subsequent measurement, the amount is adjusted for, if and when applicable, depreciation and amortisation (consumption of the economic resource that constitutes the asset); and impairment (that part of the historical cost of the asset, which is no longer recoverable).

Self-Test Questions

Self-test question 5.14

Indicate whether the following statements are true (T) or false (F):

(i) The historical cost of an item of property, plant and equipment is the cost of acquisition.

(ii) The historical cost of an item of property, plant and equipment, in subsequent measurement, is the acquisition cost less accumulated depreciation and accumulated impairment loss.

(iii) The historical cost of advance paid to a vendor is the amount paid to the vendor.

Historical Cost of Non-financial Liabilities

Example of a non-financial liability

An example of non-financial liability is the advance received from customers against orders for supply of goods or services, deferred revenue and current tax liability.

Measurement principles

The historical cost of a non-financial liability at the time it is incurred is the value of the consideration received, comprising the consideration less the transaction costs incurred in taking it on.

That amount is adjusted over time to depict, if and when applicable

(i) accrual of interest

(ii) fulfilment of the liability (e.g., by delivering the goods or services), and

(iii) any excess in the estimated cash outflows over the net consideration received (onerous liabilities). As a result, the carrying amount of a liability is increased when it becomes so onerous that the historical consideration is no longer sufficient to depict the requirement to fulfil the liability.

An *onerous contract* is an executory contract in which the aggregate cost required to fulfil the agreement is higher than the economic benefit to be obtained from it. An *executory contract* is a contract in which neither of the parties have fulfilled their promises.

NOTES

CASE STUDY 5.3 Onerous Contract

FG Shipbuilders Limited (FGSL) has received a contract for building a ship on November 30, 2016. It has received an advance of ₹30,00,000 from the customer. Before executing the contract, FGSL estimates that the aggregate cost required for executing the project is higher than the economic benefit to be obtained from it. Therefore, it decides not to honour the contract and pay the penalty specified in the contract. The amount of penalty payable is ₹50,00,000.

Question

What is the liability to be recognised in the balance sheet as at March 31, 2017?

Solution

The contract is onerous because the aggregate cost required for executing the project is higher than the economic benefit to be obtained from it. The penalty payable (₹50,00,000) is more than the advance received against the contract (₹30,00,000). Had the contract not been identified as onerous, the liability against the advance should have been recognised at ₹30,00,000. As FGSL has identified the contract as an onerous contract, it increases the liability to ₹50,00,000.

Self-Test Questions

Self-test question 5.15

Indicate whether the following statements are true (T) or false (F):

(i) The historical cost, at initial measurement, of advance received from a customer is the amount received from the customer.

(ii) Historical cost of advance received from a customer, at subsequent measurement, is the amount received as advance less the amount adjusted against amount due from the customer on account of goods and services delivered to him/her.

(iii) If the penalty payable on non-fulfilment of promises in a contract is higher than the advance received from the client, and the entity decides not to execute the contract, as the contract is assessed as an onerous contract, the entity should recognise the liability towards the client at the amount of the penalty.

Historical Cost of Financial Assets and Financial Liabilities

Nature of financial assets and financial liabilities

A financial asset is a *contractual claim* to receive cash or another financial asset. A financial liability is a *contractual obligation* to deliver cash or another financial asset.

Derivative instruments are recognised as a financial asset or financial liability depending on whether the price movement is favourable or unfavourable to the entity.

The above definitions are not technical definitions of financial assets and financial liabilities provided in Ind AS 32, Financial Instruments: Presentation, but adequate to understand the basic characteristics of those assets and liabilities.

Examples of financial assets and liabilities

Examples of financial assets are investment in equity shares issued by another company, investment in bond issued by another company, investment in units of mutual funds, deposits with banks, loan given to another entity and receivables from customers.

Examples of financial liabilities are bonds issued by the entity, borrowings from bank and amount payable to suppliers of goods and services.

Measurement principle

The historical cost of a financial asset (sometimes referred to as *amortised cost*) is initially the value of the consideration given to acquire the asset plus the transaction costs (incurred by the investor) relating to the acquisition. The historical cost of a financial liability (again, sometimes referred to as amortised cost) is initially the value of the consideration received to take on the liability less the transaction costs (incurred by the issuer/borrower) incurred in taking it on.

The subsequent carrying amount of financial assets and financial liabilities measured using amortised cost reflects subsequent changes such as the accrual of interest, changes in the estimates of cash flows (including the impairment of financial assets) and payments or receipts, but does not reflect subsequent changes in prices caused by other factors.

BOX 5.4 Effective Interest Rate and Amortised Cost

Effective interest rate

Ind AS 109, Financial Instruments, defines Effective Interest Rate (EIR) as, "the rate that exactly discounts estimated future cash payments or receipts through the expected life of the financial asset or financial liability to the gross carrying amount of a financial asset or to the amortised cost of a financial liability."

For example, when a company sells a bond at a premium, the EIR is lower than the coupon rate (which is the promised rate of interest on the face value of the bond). This is so because the amount of the bond premium is amortised to interest expense over the life of the bond. Similarly, if a bond is issued at a discount, the EIR will be higher than the coupon rate. The method is to find out the interest rate that will discount the cash outflows (periodical interest payments and repayment of the principal at maturity) to the amount received on issue of the bond at premium. This interest is called *Internal Rate of Return (IRR)*.

Amortised cost

Amortised cost is defined in Ind AS 109, Financial Instruments, as the amount at which the financial asset or financial liability is measured at initial recognition minus principal repayments, plus or minus the cumulative amortisation using the effective interest method of any difference between that initial amount and the maturity amount and, for financial assets, adjusted for any loss allowance.

CASE STUDY 5.4 Effective Interest Rate

An entity has issued a bond with face value of ₹100, maturity of 5 years and coupon rate of 5 percent payable annually, at the face value of ₹100. The transaction cost is ₹2. The bond will be redeemed at the end of the 5th year.

Question

What is the effective interest rate? Calculate the interest to be recognised in the statement of profit and loss for the years 1 to 5 and the amortised cost at which the liability will be measured at the end of each year.

Solution

Effective interest rate: The net amount received is ₹98. The effective interest rate is 5.47 percent, which equates future cash outflows (year 1 to 4: ₹5 each year-end and ₹105 at the end of 5th year.) to ₹98.

Effective interest for year 1 and amortised cost at the end of year 1: Effective interest for year 1 is ₹98 × 0.0547 or ₹5.36. Interest expense is recognised at ₹5.36 and the difference between the interest expense recognised and the actual interest payment (₹5), that is, ₹0.36 is added to the carrying amount of the liability. Therefore, the amortised cost (carrying amount) at the end of year 1 is ₹98.36.

NOTES

Effective interest for year 2 and amortised cost at the end of year 2: Interest expense for year 2 is ₹98.36 × 0.0547 or ₹5.38. Amortised cost of the liability at the end of year 2 is [₹98.36 + (5.38 – 5)] or ₹98.74.

Effective interest for year 3 and amortised cost at the end of year 3: Interest expense for year 3 is ₹98.74 × 0.0547 or ₹5.40. Amortised cost of the liability at the end of year 3 is ₹99.14.

Effective interest for year 4 and amortised cost at the end of year 4: Interest expense for year 4 is: ₹99.14 × 0.0547 or ₹5.42. Amortised cost of the liability at the end of year 4 is ₹99.56.

Effective interest for year 5 and amortised cost at the end of year 5: Interest expense for year 5 is: ₹99.56 × 0.0547 or ₹5.44. Amortised cost of the liability at the end of year 5 is ₹100.00.

On maturity of the bond at the end of year 5, the entity will repay ₹100 (the face value of the bond) and the liability will be derecognised.

Amortised cost of investment

The calculations will be exactly same for an investor who buys the identical bond at ₹98, including the transaction cost. The carrying amount of the investment will gradually increase and it will be ₹100 at maturity. The entity will receive cash of ₹100 and the investment will be derecognised.

Self-Test Questions

Self-test question 5.16

Fill in the blanks:

(i) E Limited (EL) borrowed ₹1,00,000 from a bank and paid processing fee of 5 percent. At initial recognition, the amortised cost of the loan is ₹............

(ii) B Bank Limited (BBL) disbursed loan of ₹1,00,000 and received processing fee of 5 percent. At initial recognition, the amortised cost of the loan is ₹............

(iii) K Limited (KL) purchased a corporate bond from the market for ₹1,00,000 and incurred transaction cost of 5 percent. At initial recognition, the amortised cost of the loan is ₹............

(iv) N Limited (NL) purchased debentures issued by KD Limited (KDL) at ₹900 (adjusted for transaction cost) per debenture. The face value of each debenture is ₹1,000 and the coupon rate is 12 percent per annum. The effective interest rate will be .... than the coupon rate. [Choose from the words 'higher' and 'lower'.]

Fair Value

Fair value is the price that would be received to sell an asset, or paid to transfer a liability, in an orderly transaction between market participants at the measurement date. Fair value reflects the perspective of market participants, that is, the asset or the liability is measured using the same assumptions that market participants would use while pricing the asset or the liability if those market participants act in their economic best interest.

If the fair value of an asset or a liability can be observed in an active market, the process of fair value measurement is simple and easy to understand, and the fair value is verifiable. If the fair value cannot be observed, valuation techniques (sometimes including the use of cash flow-based measurements) may be needed to estimate that fair value.

For example, it is simple to estimate the fair value of 1,000 equity shares of Infosys as at March 31, 2018. It is estimated by multiplying the share price as at March 31, 2018 in NSE/BSE by the number of shares (1,000). On the other hand, the fair value of specialised equipment is not observable in an active market because no active market usually exists for that equipment. Estimating the fair value will require applying some valuation technique.

NOTES

When a valuation technique is used to estimate the fair value, the inputs into the process may be subjective and it may be difficult to verify both the inputs and the validity of the process itself. Ind AS 113, Fair value Measurement, provides detailed guidance on how to estimate fair value.

BOX 5.5 Active Markets

Active market is a market in which transactions for the asset or liability take place with sufficient frequency and volume to provide pricing information on an ongoing basis. Example of active market is stock exchanges such as National Stock Exchange (NSE) and Bombay Stock Exchange (BSE). Active markets are usually not available for non-financial assets and liabilities.

Self-Test Questions

Self-test question 5.17

Indicate whether the following statements are true (T) or false (F):

(i) Fair value is the exit price.
(ii) The terms 'fair value' and 'market value' are used interchangeably.
(iii) Fair value of equity shares issued by a closely held company is less reliable than that of the shares issued by a listed company.
(iv) The price in a recent transaction involving sale and purchase of a villa in a particular locality necessarily reflects the fair value of similar villas in the same locality.

Value in Use and Fulfilment Value

Value in use and fulfilment value are entity-specific values.

Value in use is the present value of the cash flows that an entity expects to derive from the continuing use of an asset and from its ultimate disposal.

Fulfilment value is the present value of the cash flows that an entity expects to incur as it fulfils a liability.

Value in use and fulfilment value cannot be directly observed and are determined using cash flow-based measurement techniques.

ANSWERS TO SELF-TEST QUESTIONS

5.1 (i) ₹10,00,000; (ii) 1,00,000
5.2 (i) T; (ii) F
5.3 (i) T; (ii) F; (iii) T; (iv) T; (v) F; (vi) T; (vii) T; (viii) T; (ix) F; (x) T
5.4 (i) T; (ii) T; (iii) T
5.5 (i) T; (ii) F; (iii) T; (iv) T; (v) F
5.6 (i) F; (ii) T; (iii) F
5.7 (i) T; (ii) T; (iii) F; (iv) T; (v) F
5.8 (i) F; (ii) T; (iii) F
5.9 (i) F; (ii) T; (iii) T
5.10 (i) F; (ii) T; (iii) T
5.11 (i) T; (ii) T
5.12 (i) T; (ii) T; (iii) F; (iv) F
5.13 (i) T; (ii) F; (iii) F; (iv) T; (v) T
5.14 (i) T; (ii) T; (iii) T
5.15 (i) T; (ii) T; (iii) T
5.16 (i) ₹95,000; (ii) ₹95,000; (iii) ₹1,05,000; (iv) Higher
5.17 (i) T; (ii) F; (iii) T; (iv) F

ASSIGNMENTS

Multiple Choice Questions

1. Tick the correct answer.
   (i) Current liabilities are:
   (a) Liabilities that are due to be settled within twelve months of the balance sheet date.
   (b) Liabilities that are expected to be settled in the normal course of the operating cycle of the enterprise.
   (c) Liabilities that are due to be settled within twelve months of the balance sheet date, and also liabilities that are expected to be settled in the normal course of the operating cycle of the enterprise.
   (d) None of the above.
   (ii) A provision is a:
   (a) Liability of uncertain timing.
   (b) Liability of uncertain timing and amount.
   (c) Liability of uncertain amount.
   (d) None of the above.
2. State whether the following statements are true (T) or false (F):
   (i) The current part of a long-term liability should be classified as a current liability.
   (ii) The degree of uncertainty surrounding 'provision' is higher as compared to the degree of uncertainty surrounding 'accruals'.
   (iii) Short-term bank borrowings should be classified as *secured loans*, and not current liabilities.
   (iv) Any change in policy should be given effect retrospectively while the effect of any change in accounting estimate should be accounted in the period of change or in subsequent periods.
   (v) The fact that a liability is used to fund trading activities does make that liability one that is held for trading.

Analytical Questions

1. 'A' has entered into an irrevocable agreement to purchase machinery from B & Co. for ₹1,00,000. Should 'A' recognise the asset and the corresponding liability?
2. On January 1, 2013, Damodaran Limited (DL) borrowed ₹1,00,00,000 from Universal Bank Limited (UBL). The loan is repayable on September 30, 2017. The company has approached the bank to roll over the loan for another period of two years. If the bank agrees to the proposal, the repayment date will be shifted to September 30, 2019. On the date of the board meeting, which is convened to consider and approve financial statements for 2017, the Board of Directors is informed that the core committee of the bank that considers the restructuring proposal has recommended acceptance of the proposal, and it is pending for approval by the Board of Directors. In the balance sheet dated December 31, 2017, DL classifies the borrowing as a non-current liability. Is DL right in classifying the liability as a non-current liability? Explain your position on this issue.

Statement of Profit and Loss

CHAPTER

6

Learning Objectives

The objective of this chapter is to provide an understanding of the structure and components of the statement of profit and loss. After reading this chapter, you will develop understanding of the following:

- Format of the statement of profit and loss
- Presentation principles
- Total comprehensive income, other comprehensive income, and profit or loss
- Revenue, other operating income and other income
- Finance cost
- Interest expense
- Exceptional items
- Discontinued operation
- Basic EPS and Diluted EPS
- Gross profit, EBIT, EBITDA and NOPAT

NOTES

FORMAT OF THE STATEMENT OF PROFIT AND LOSS

Purpose of the Statement of Profit and Loss

The statement of profit and loss presents the operating results of the entity for the accounting period covered by the statement. It also presents incomes, gains and losses from transactions (not arising from operating decisions) and other events. It provides information on incomes and expenses, which analysts use in conjunction with information available in the balance sheet, to assess the earning capacity of the entity.

Table 6.1 presents the structure of statement of profit and loss provided in Schedule III (Division II) of the Companies Act, 2013.

TABLE 6.1

Statement of Profit and Loss (Schedule III, Division II Format)

S. No	Particulars	Amount
I	Revenue from operations	
II	Other income	
III	Total income (I + II)	
IV	Expenses	
V	Profit/(loss) before exceptional items and tax (I – IV)	
VI	Exceptional items	
VII	Profit/(loss) before tax (V – VI)	
VIII	Tax expense	
IX	Profit (loss) for the period from continuing operations (VII – VIII)	
X	Profit/(loss) from discontinued operations	
XI	Tax expense of discontinued operations	
XII	Profit/(loss) from discontinued operations after tax (X – XI)	
XIII	Profit/(loss) for the period (IX + XII)	
XIV	Other comprehensive income	
	A (i) Items that will not be reclassified to profit or loss	
	(ii) Income tax relating to items that will not be reclassified to profit or loss	
	B (i) Items that will be reclassified to profit or loss	
	(ii) Income tax relating to items that will be reclassified to profit or loss	
XV	Total comprehensive income for the period (XIII + XIV) (comprising profit (loss) and other comprehensive income for the period)	
XVI	Earnings per equity share (for continuing operation):	
	(1) Basic	
	(2) Diluted	
XVII	Earnings per equity share (for discontinued operation):	
	(1) Basic	
	(2) Diluted	
XVIII	Earnings per equity share (for discontinued and continuing operations):	
	(1) Basic	
	(2) Diluted	

ACTIVITY

Download the statement of profit and loss of a company and carefully go through the items in the statement with their explanatory notes.

NOTES

Presentation Principles

Classification of Expenses

The GAAP (Ind AS) requires entities to present an analysis of expenses recognised in profit or loss using a classification based on the nature of expense method.

In the analysis based on the 'nature of expense' method, an entity aggregates expenses within profit or loss according to their nature (for example, depreciation, purchases of materials, transport costs, employee benefits and advertising costs), and does not reallocate them among functions within the entity. This method is simple to apply because no allocations of expenses to functional classifications are necessary.

The second form of analysis is the 'function of expense' or 'cost of sales' method and classifies expenses according to their function as part of cost of sales or, for example, the costs of distribution or administrative activities. The GAAP does not permit this method of presentation.

Materiality and Aggregation

The GAAP requires an entity to present separately each material class of similar items. An entity should present separately items of a dissimilar nature or function unless they are immaterial except when required by law.

When items of income or expense are material, an entity should disclose their nature and amount separately. Schedule III (Division II) requires companies to disclose by way of notes any item of income or expenditure which exceeds one percent of the revenue from operations or ₹10,00,000, whichever is higher, in addition to the consideration of 'materiality'.

Comparative Information

Entities present comparative information in respect of the preceding period for all amounts reported in the current period's financial statements. For example, statement of profit and loss for the year 2018–2019 should present information for 2018–2019, and also, for 2017–2018.

Self-Test Questions

Self-test question 6.1

Indicate whether the following statements are true (T) or false (F):

(i) Indian companies use 'natural classification method' in presenting expenses in the statement of profit and loss.

(ii) 'Functional classification method' requires allocation of expenses to different functions, which is judgemental.

(iii) The materiality threshold provided in Schedule III is arbitrary.

(iv) Entities should assess materiality of information based on magnitude and nature.

(v) Aggregation of items in the statement of profit and loss account might result in sacrificing some important details.

SUMMARY

Indian companies are required to use 'natural classification method' for presenting expenses in the statement of profit and loss. They are not permitted to use the 'functional classification method'. Income and expenses that are material should be presented separately. Entities present comparative information in respect of the preceding period for all amounts reported in the current period's financial statements.

NOTES

TOTAL COMPREHENSIVE INCOME, OTHER COMPREHENSIVE INCOME AND PROFIT OR LOSS

Total Comprehensive Income

Ind AS 1, Presentation of Financial Statements, defines total comprehensive income as: "*Total comprehensive income is the change in equity during a period resulting from transactions and other events, other than those changes resulting from transactions with owners in their capacity as owners.*" Total comprehensive income is the total of profit or loss for the period and 'other comprehensive income'.

Profit or Loss

Ind AS 1, Presentation of Financial Statements, defines profit and loss as: "*Profit or loss is the total of income less expenses, excluding the components of other comprehensive income.*" Analysts consider profit or loss to measure the performance of the entity.

In some other territories (e.g., the U.S.A.), the term 'net income' is used to denote profit.

Although the matching principle is applied to determine the profit or loss, some expenses may not have cause and effect relationship with revenue recognised in the statement of profit and loss. For example, discretionary expenses, such as advertising, research and training expenses have no cause and effect relationship with revenue.

Other Comprehensive Income (OCI)

Ind AS 1, Presentation of Financial Statements, defines other comprehensive income as: *Other comprehensive income comprises items of income and expense (including reclassification adjustments) that are not recognised in profit or loss as required or permitted by other Ind ASs.*"

Standard setters have not used any well-defined criterion to decide which of the items of gains or losses should be included in other comprehensive income. Generally, gains or losses that do not arise from operating decisions or unrealised gains that the entity does not intend to realise in foreseeable future are accumulated in equity through other comprehensive income.

Reclassification adjustments are the amounts reclassified to profit or loss in the current period that were recognised in other comprehensive income in the current or previous periods and accumulated in equity.

Examples of Other Comprehensive Income

There are nine types of gains and losses that are accumulated in equity through other comprehensive income. We are providing three examples to provide an understanding of the nature of other comprehensive income.

(a) **Revaluation gain:** The gain from revaluation of items of property, plant and equipment is accumulated in equity through other comprehensive income. On disposal of the asset, cumulative gain or loss is transferred directly (without routing through the statement of profit and loss) to the retained earnings in the balance sheet.

(b) **Remeasurement of defined benefit plan:** Under a defined benefit plan for post-retirement benefits to employees, the obligation of the employer is to pay to employees the benefits specified in the plan. Example of defined benefit is pension equal to 50 percent of last pay drawn to those who complete 20 years of service. Employers create a fund or take insurance policy (called *plan asset*), which is used to settle the obligation periodically. The liability is measured at the present value (PV) of the obligation less the fair value (FV) of the plan asset. The PV of the obligation is estimated based on the actuarial valuation involving significant demographic and financial assumptions. The PV changes every year due to actuarial gain or loss and other reasons. Actuarial gain or loss results from (i) experience adjustments (the effects of differences between the previous actuarial assumptions and what has actually occurred); and (ii) the effects of changes in actuarial assumptions. The change in the liability due to actuarial gain or loss and changes in other assumptions are recognised in equity through other comprehensive income. This reduces volatility in the profit reported from year to year.

(c) **Fair value changes in debt instruments through other comprehensive income:** Measurement, subsequent to initial recognition, of investments in debt instruments, depends on the characteristic of the debt instrument and the business model of the entity. If the contractual terms of the debt instrument give rise on specified dates to cash flows that are solely payments of principal and interest on the principal amount outstanding (SPPI criterion), it is said that the debt instrument meets the SPPI criterion. A basic lending arrangement meets the SPPI criterion. If the entity holds an investment in debt instrument with an intention to sell, if required, the investment is measured at fair value. Gains or losses arising from change in the fair value of investments are recognised in equity through other comprehensive income. Cumulative gains and losses recognised in other comprehensive income and accumulated in the separate component of equity, are reclassified from equity to profit or loss when the investment is derecognised on sale or otherwise.

NOTES

Key Terms
Other comprehensive income, profit, loss, revaluation gain, total comprehensive income

Self-Test Questions

Self-test question 6.2

Indicate whether the following statements are true (T) or false (F):

(i) The terms 'total comprehensive income' and 'other comprehensive income' are used interchangeably.
(ii) Most analysts use total comprehensive income to measure the performance of the entity.
(iii) The terms 'profit' and 'net income' are used interchangeably.
(iv) Matching principle ensures that only those expenses, which have cause and effect relationship with revenue, are recognised in the statement of profit and loss.

SUMMARY

The GAAP does not allow inclusion of some specified items of income, gain and loss in profit or loss. It requires items to be accumulated in equity through other comprehensive income. The total of profit or loss and other comprehensive income is called *total comprehensive income.* Analysts consider profit or loss to evaluate the performance of the entity.

ELEMENTS OF PROFIT AND LOSS

Revenue from Operations and Other Income

Schedule III (Division II) requires an entity to disclose separately in the notes (i) sale of products (including excise duty); (ii) sale of services; and (iii) other operating revenues.

Revenue from Operations

Ind AS 115, Revenue From Contracts With Customers, defines revenue as: *"Income arising in the course of an entity's ordinary activities."* Ordinary activities imply core activities.

Non-finance entities earn revenue by selling goods or rendering services. Banks and non-banking finance companies (NBFC) primarily earn revenue from return on investments (e.g., interest on loan and dividend) and fees from non-fund based services (e.g., issue of bid bond and performance guarantee, issue of 'letter of credit', collection of export bills and merchant banking). Insurance companies earn revenue in the form of insurance premium by selling insurance policies and from return on investments (e.g., interest and dividend).

An entity recognises revenue when it fulfills the performance obligation and it is reasonably certain that it will collect the amount due from the customer.

Revenue does not include amount collected on other's behalf, as the amount collected on others' behalf does not increase equity. Therefore, in an agency relationship, only the commission earned by the entity is revenue.

Revenue should be presented as net of Goods and Service Tax (GST), as the GST is collected by the entity on behalf of the government. Earlier, excise duty used to be included in revenue and recognised as expense because it was a levy on the entity, while sales tax recovered from customers did not form part of revenue, as entities used to collect sales tax on behalf of the government.

Other Operating Income

Other operating income arises from a company's operating activities, which cannot be classified as revenue, and it does not arise from sale of goods or rendering of services. It arises from either entity's principal or ancillary revenue-generating activities. For example, income from sale of scrap and export incentives are classified as 'other operating income'. Similarly, interest earned on credit sales is classified as 'other operating revenue'.

Other Income

Other income is the income other than operating income, that is, income not earned from entity's ordinary activities. Examples of other income of non-finance companies are interest income, dividend income, gains or losses from sale of fixed assets retired permanently from use and gains and losses arising from change in fair value of financial assets that are measured at 'Fair Value Through Profit or Loss' (FVTPL).

Difference between other operating revenue and other income

Whether a particular income constitutes 'other operating revenue' or 'other income' is to be decided based on the facts of each case and detailed understanding of the company's activities.

CASE STUDY 6.1 Other Operating Income and Other Income

S Limited (SL) is primarily engaged in manufacturing and sale of industrial and consumer products. It has also one real estate division. The real estate division is continuously engaged in leasing of real estate properties. K Limited (KL) is a consumer products company, which owns a 10-storey building. The company currently does not need one floor for its own use and has given the same temporarily on rent.

Question

How SL and KL should classify the rent earned by them?

Solution

Rent earned by SL is arising from its operation because its real estate division is in the business of leasing out real estate properties. However, it is not arising from the core activity of selling products. Therefore, SL should classify the rent arising from leasing of real estate as 'other operating revenue'. On the other hand, KL has temporarily leased out one storey of its 10-storey building. Therefore, rent earned is not an income from operating activities of the company. KL should classify the rent earned as 'other income'.

NOTES

Key Terms
Revenue, other operating income, other income

Self-Test Questions

Self-test question 6.3

Indicate whether the following statements are true (T) or false (F):

(i) The lease rent earned by R Limited (RL), which is a retailer of branded fashion garments, by leasing 20 percent of space in its showrooms located across India to retailers of fashion accessories, should be recognised as 'other income'.

(ii) N Limited (NL) primarily sells new and old cars. The income earned by the company from maintenance and repair services, which it provides to its customers, should be recognised as 'other operating income'.

(iii) Gains and losses from change in fair value of investments in equity instruments, which the entity holds for trading, should be recognised as 'other income'.

(iv) Proceeds from sale of items of property, plant and equipment, which Q Limited (QL) permanently retires from use, should be recognised as 'revenue from operations' because QL sells some items in every fiscal year.

(v) Export incentives should be recognised as 'other operating income'.

SUMMARY

Income from core activities of the entity is recognised as revenue. Income, which is not from core activities, but from the principal or ancillary revenue-generating activities is classified as other operating income. Other income is the income other than operating income, that is, income not earned from entity's ordinary activities.

Finance Cost

As per Note 4 of the General Instructions for the Preparation of the Statement of Profit and Loss, disclosure of finance costs is to be bifurcated under the following:

(i) Interest

(ii) Dividend on redeemable preference shares

(iii) Exchange differences regarded as an adjustment to borrowing costs; and

(iv) Other borrowing costs (specify nature)

Exchange Difference Regarded as Adjustment to Borrowing Cost

Ind AS 23, Borrowing Costs, stipulates that borrowing cost includes 'exchange differences regarded as an adjustment to borrowing costs'. It provides guidance on how to estimate the amount for adjustment to borrowing costs.

Exchange loss

The entity should estimate the notional amount of savings arising from the decision to borrow in foreign currency. If the amount of savings is more than the loss arising on translating the foreign currency liability (borrowing) due to change in the exchange rate, the entire amount of exchange difference should be considered as borrowing cost. If the amount of savings is lower than the loss arising on translating the foreign currency liability due change in the exchange rate, the amount of exchange difference to the extent of notional savings in interest should be considered as borrowing cost.

NOTES

ILLUSTRATION 6.1 Exchange Difference Regarded as Adjustment to Borrowing Cost

The notional saving due to differential interest rate between foreign currency borrowing and notional INR borrowing is ₹2000. Exchange difference, which is a loss/expense is ₹1,500.

Required

How much should be added to the borrowing cost?

Solution

The exchange difference, which is a loss, being lower than the notional savings in interest, the entire amount of the exchange difference should be added to the borrowing cost.

ILLUSTRATION 6.2 Exchange Difference Regarded as Adjustment to Borrowing Cost

The notional saving due to differential interest rate between foreign currency borrowing and notional INR borrowing is ₹2000. Exchange difference, which is a loss/expense is ₹2,500.

Required

How much should be added to the borrowing cost?

Solution

The exchange difference, which is a loss, being higher than the notional savings in interest, out of the total exchange difference, only an amount equal to the notional savings (₹2,000) should be added to the borrowing cost and balance (₹500) should be recognised as exchange difference (expense) in the statement of profit and loss.

Exchange gain: Exchange gain cannot be adjusted to actual interest because such an adjustment will result in the recognising interest at an amount that is lower than the actual interest on the borrowing. Where there is an unrealised exchange loss, which is treated as an adjustment to interest, and subsequently there is a realised or unrealised gain in respect of the settlement or translation of the same borrowing, the gain to the extent of the loss previously recognised as an adjustment should also be recognised as an adjustment to interest.

Importance of adjustment of exchange loss to borrowing cost: Adjustment of the borrowing cost for the exchange difference is important because a part of the borrowing cost that is directly attributable to the production or construction of an asset (production or construction of which takes more than a year) should be capitalised. On the other hand, no part of the exchange difference can be capitalised.

BOX 6.1 Meaning of the Term 'Capitalise'

When expenditure is capitalised, it is recognised in the balance sheet as a new asset (e.g., property, plant and equipment) or as increase in the carrying amount of an existing asset. Consequently, the recognition of the expenditure in the statement of profit and loss is delayed. Expenditure that is capitalised is allocated to the statement of profit and loss over the useful life of the asset.

ILLUSTRATION 6.3 Exchange Difference Regarded as Adjustment to Borrowing Cost

INR is the functional currency of S Limited (SL). SL borrowed AC (foreign currency) 1,000 on April 1, 2017 for two years at an interest rate of 5 percent per annum. Interest is payable at the end of the second year along with repayment of the principal.

Required

Calculate the total borrowing cost on the foreign currency borrowing of AC 1,000 for the year 2017–18.

Solution

Exchange rates: The exchange rate for 2017–18 is as follows:

April 1, 2017: AC 1.00: ₹2.00; March 31, 2018: AC 1.00: ₹2.20; Average for the year: AC 1.00: ₹2.15

Notional borrowing: SL could borrow in India ₹2,000 with identical terms at the interest rate of 7 percent per annum, that is, interest of ₹140 per annum.

1. *Actual interest payment*
   SL calculates the interest payable as follows:
   Interest: AC (1,000 × 0.05) or AC 50; Applying average rate, the interest is ₹(50 × 2.15) or ₹107.50
2. *Exchange loss*
   SL calculates the foreign exchange loss for the year ended March 31, 2018 on the translation of the principal amount outstanding and accrued interest as follows:
   Principal is 1,000 × (2.20 – 2.00) or ₹200; Accrued interest is 50 × (2.20 – 2.15) or ₹2.50; Total foreign exchange loss is ₹202.50.
3. *Notional savings in interest*
   (₹140 – 107.50) or ₹32.50
4. *Exchange loss adjustment*
   Foreign exchange loss, to the extent of savings in interest, is to be adjusted to the borrowing cost. Therefore, only ₹32.50 will be added to the borrowing cost for the year 2017–18 and balance (₹202.50 – 32.50) or ₹170 should be recognised as an expense in the line item 'exchange difference' in the statement of profit and loss for the year 2017–18. Thus, the total borrowing cost on the foreign currency borrowing of AC 1,000 for the year 2017–18 is ₹140.

NOTES

Key Terms
Capitalisation, exchange gain, exchange loss, interest

Other Borrowing Costs

Other borrowing costs would include commitment charges, loan processing charges, guarantee charges, loan facilitation charges, discounts/premium on borrowings, other ancillary costs incurred in connection with borrowings, or amortisation of such costs, etc. Such finance costs do not meet the definition of transaction costs directly attributable to issue of a financial liability and are, therefore, not included as a part of 'effective interest rate'. These should be presented under 'Other borrowing costs'.

Self-Test Questions

Self-test question 6.4

Indicate whether the following statements are true (T) or false (F):

(i) Dividend on redeemable preference shares, paid or not, is recognised as borrowing cost.

(ii) Transaction costs incurred for borrowing are included in interest, as companies are required to use effective interest method for recognising interest.

(iii) The GAAP requires that a part of exchange loss arising from translating liabilities (including accrued interest) that arise from foreign currency borrowing should be added to actual interest payable to the lender.

(iv) Interest on borrowings in foreign currency can be lower or higher than the actual interest payable to the lender.

(v) Interest on borrowings in foreign currency cannot be lower than the actual interest payable to the lender, but can be higher than that.

(vi) The GAAP allows capitalisation of borrowing cost in certain situations, but it does not permit capitalisation of exchange difference.

SUMMARY

Dividend in redeemable preference shares is included in borrowing costs. Exchange loss, not exceeding the notional savings, should be added to the actual interest payable on foreign currency borrowings. Exchange gain is not adjusted to interest on foreign currency borrowing.

NOTES

Depreciation, Amortisation and Depletion

Depreciation on PP&E

Depreciation is charged on all the items of property, plant and equipment (PP&E), except land. Usually, no depreciation is charged on land, except in certain cases (e.g., land used for landfill) because the land has indefinite useful life. Land is called a non-depreciable asset. Depreciation is charged on all depreciable assets from the date when it is ready for use. It does not matter whether the asset is put to use. Similarly, depreciation should be charged on an asset, which is retired from use. However, no depreciation should be charged on an item of PP&E, which is classified as 'non-current asset held for sale'.

Nature of depreciation

Depreciation is allocation of the depreciable amount of the useful life of an item of property, plant and equipment. Depreciable amount is the acquisition cost less estimated residual value. For example, if the acquisition cost is ₹10,00,000 and estimated residual value is ₹1,00,000, the depreciable amount is ₹9,00,000. Useful life is the period over which the entity intends to use the asset. If the useful life is 10 years, then the depreciable amount is allocated to 10 accounting years using an appropriate depreciation method.

Depreciation methods

Various depreciation methods are available for charging depreciation. In theory, a company should choose the method that will match depreciation with the pattern in which benefits will be derived from the use of a particular class of assets. However, in practice, it is difficult to march depreciation with benefits from the use of the asset. Most common depreciation method is *Straight-Line Method (SLM)*. Under SLM, the depreciable amount is uniformly allocated over the useful life of the asset. For example, if the depreciable amount is ₹10,00,000 and useful life is 10 years, ₹1,00,000 is allocated to each year in which the asset will be used. The amount so allocated is called *depreciation charge* and is included in expenses for the year.

Another common depreciation method is the *reducing balance method*. Under this method, the depreciation rate is applied to the Written Down Value (WDV) to determine the depreciation to be charged each year. The WDV is the acquisition cost less accumulated depreciation. The WDV reduces every year. For example, if the depreciable amount is ₹10,00,000 and depreciation rate is 25 percent, depreciation for first three years will be (a) 1st year: (₹10,00,000 × 0.25) or ₹2,50,000; (b) 2nd year: (₹7,50,000 × 0.25) or ₹1,87,500; and (c) 3rd year: (₹5,62,500 × 0.25) or ₹1,40,625. This example shows that under this method, depreciation is reduced for every subsequent year, exponentially. It is quite obvious that the depreciation rate under the 'reducing balance method' ought to be higher than the depreciation rate under SLM because the depreciable amount is to be allocated over the useful life under both the methods.

For some equipment like heavy earth moving equipment, useful life is expressed in terms of expected number of hours of use or expected units of production. In these cases, depreciation rate is expressed as per hour or per unit. For example, if the depreciable amount of the asset is ₹50,00,000 and useful life is 50,000 hours, the depreciation rate is (₹50,00,000/50,000) or ₹100 per hour. If, in a particular year, the asset is used for 10,000 hours, depreciation to be charged is (₹100 × 10,000) or ₹10,00,000. Although, as a general rule, depreciation should be charged on an asset even if it has remained idle in a particular financial year, when depreciation is charged based on the number of hours used or number of units produced, no depreciation is charged in the financial year when the asset was idle.

Depreciation on revalued assets

Depreciable amount changes when an asset is revalued. It is measured at the revalued amount less estimated residual value.

Depreciation under the Companies Act, 2013

The Companies Act, 2013 (Schedule II) provides indicative useful lives of various types of PP&E. It also stipulates that the residual value should not be more than the original cost. However, a company can estimate useful life, which might be different from the indicative useful life. Companies provide explanatory note when they estimate useful life of an asset, which is different from the indicative useful life.

Amortisation of Intangible Assets

Amortisation refers to the depreciation of intangible assets. An intangible asset, for which the useful life can be estimated, is amortised over its estimated useful life. An intangible asset that has indefinite useful life, in the sense that its useful life cannot be estimated reliably, is not amortised. It is tested for impairment every year. Examples of such assets are product brand and licence that is renewed automatically on payment of a nominal fee.

Key Terms
Depletion, depreciation, impairment

Depletion

Depletion refers to the allocation of the cost of natural resources to financial periods. As with depreciation, depletion gives the owner of the resources a way to account for the reduction in the natural resource reserves. Examples of natural or wasting resources are timber, coal, oil and precious metals (e.g., gold).

The cost of natural resources is the total of acquisition cost of the lease, development costs and restoration costs. Exploration costs are expensed as incurred.

Depletion rate is calculated by dividing the cost of the natural resource, reduced by estimated salvage value, by the total estimated units available for the natural resource.

Self-Test Questions

Self-test question 6.5

Indicate whether the following statements are true (T) or false (F):

(i) Usually no depreciation is charged on land.
(ii) Depreciation for a particular accounting year has no direct cause and effect relationship with revenue earned during that year.
(iii) Charging depreciation should commence from the date when the asset is put to use.
(iv) The terms 'depreciation', 'amortisation' and 'depletion' are used interchangeably.
(v) No depreciation should be charged on an item of PP&E that is classified as 'held for sale'.
(vi) The cost of a product brand is not amortised because it has indefinite useful life.

SUMMARY

Depreciation is allocation of depreciable amount over the useful life of an item of PP&E. Depreciation should be charged on an item of PP&E, except land, from the date it is available for use. Depreciation should be charged even if the asset remains idle in a particular accounting year. No depreciation is charged on an item of PP&E classified as 'held for sale'. Companies choose from various depreciation methods available. Most common methods are straight-line method, written down value method, and number of production hours/units method.

Cost of an intangible asset is amortised over its useful life. However, intangible assets with indefinite useful life are not amortised. They are tested for impairment every year.

Depletion is allocation of the cost of natural resource to different financial years.

Exceptional Items

The term 'exceptional items' is not defined either in Schedule III (Division II) or in

Ind AS. In practice, entities apply the following working definition to classify items of income and expenses as exceptional items:

Exceptional items are expenses and/or incomes, which arise from normal operations of the entity, but either do not occur regularly or are not within the normal range (in terms of the amount of the item).

Analysts exclude exceptional items from profit or loss to measure the performance of the entity.

Examples

The following are the examples of exceptional items: (i) Write-down of inventories to net realisable value or of property, plant and equipment to recoverable amount, as well as reversals of such write-down; (ii) Restructuring of the activities of an entity and reversals of any provisions for the costs of restructuring; (iii) Disposals of items of property, plant and equipment, which do not occur in the normal course of operation; (iv) Disposals of investments; (v) Discontinued operations; (vi) Litigation settlements; and (vii) Other reversals of provisions.

Extraordinary item

Ind AS 1, Presentation of Financial Statements, prohibits entities from presenting any items of income or expense as extraordinary items, in the statement of profit and loss or in the notes.

Earlier, entities used to present those items as extraordinary items that arise from transactions and events that are clearly distinct from ordinary activities of the entity such as earthquake disaster.

Self-Test Questions

Self-test question 6.6

Indicate whether the following statements are true (T) or false (F):

(i) No income or expense can be classified as extraordinary item.
(ii) Exceptional items are non-recurring incomes and expenses.
(iii) Sale of an investment property is an exceptional item.
(iv) Sale of an item of PP&E retired from use in the normal course of business is an exceptional item.
(v) Restructuring expense is an exceptional expense.

Discontinued Operations

Analysts exclude profit or loss from discontinued operation from the profit or loss for the period in assessing the performance of the entity.

Definition

Ind AS 105, Non-current Assets Held for Sale and Discontinued Operations, defines the term 'discontinued operations' as a component of an entity that either has been disposed of or is classified as held for sale and:

(i) represents a separate major line of business or geographical area of operations.
(ii) is part of a single coordinated plan to dispose of a separate major line of business or geographical area of operations, or
(iii) is a subsidiary acquired exclusively with a view to resale.

Component of an entity

A component of an entity comprises operations and cash flows that can be distinguished clearly, both operationally and financial reporting purposes, from the rest of the entity.

NOTES

Discontinuing products or product lines

Abandoning or discontinuing products or product lines or replacing them with newer products do not constitute a discontinued operation. They are a part of the normal evolution of business.

Closure of facilities

Closure of facilities within a business segment might not meet the definition of discontinued operation.

CASE STUDY 6.2 Discontinued Operation

P Limited (PL) has five different operating segments, one of which solely produces ayurvedic healthcare products. All the facilities for growing herbs and producing healthcare products are located in Himachal Pradesh in India. Manufacturing facilities of other operating segments are also located in Himachal Pradesh. In December 2017, PL decided to dispose of the ayurvedic healthcare segment.

Question

Does the healthcare segment meet the definition of discontinued operation?

Solution

The ayurvedic healthcare segment meets the definition of a component of business and represents a separate major line of business. Therefore, it qualifies for reporting as a discontinued operation.

CASE STUDY 6.3 Discontinued Operation

Z Limited (ZL) has three business segments—ice cream, chocolate and beverages. In December 2017, it decides to stop production of some varieties of dark chocolates and replace them by varieties of fruit and nuts chocolate bars.

Question

Does discontinuance of the production of dark chocolates meet the definition of discontinued operation?

Solution

Discontinuance of some varieties of dark chocolates does not meet the definition of discontinued operation because the production of the black chocolates does not meet the definition of a 'major line of business', and also, does not meet the definition of 'component' of the entity, as its cash flows cannot be distinguished clearly. It is quite likely that there was no dedicated facility for producing black chocolates, and the facility was used or can be used for producing other varieties of chocolates.

CASE STUDY 6.4 Discontinued Operation

K Limited (KL) has four operating segments—cigarettes, hotel, paper and paperboards, and food products. In December 2017, KL decides to close down one of its four facilities for manufacturing paper and paperboards on productivity and cost considerations and continue other facilities, which produce paper and paperboards.

NOTES

Key Terms
Component of an entity, discontinued operation

Question

Does closure of the facility meet the definition of discontinued operation?

Solution

The closure of the facility does not meet the definition of discontinued operation, as the component (business of paper and paperboards) of the entity will continue to operate with other facilities.

Measurement

Ind AS 105, Non-current Assets Held for Sale and Discontinued Operations, stipulates that an entity should measure a non-current asset (or disposal group) classified as held for sale at the lower of its carrying amount and fair value less costs to sell.

Presentation and Disclosure

An entity needs to separately disclose profit or loss from discontinued operations on the face of statement of profit and loss.

Ind AS 105, Non-current Assets Held for Sale and Discontinued Operations, requires a single amount in the statement of profit and loss comprising the total of: (i) post-tax profit or loss of discontinued operations; and (ii) post-tax gain or loss recognised on the measurement to fair value less costs to sell or on the disposal of the assets or disposal group(s) constituting the discontinued operation.

The standard also requires an entity to present an analysis of a single amount either in notes or on the face of the statement of profit and loss:

(i) the revenue, expenses and pre-tax profit or loss of discontinued operations.

(ii) the gain or loss recognised on the measurement to fair value less costs to sell or on the disposal of the assets or disposal group(s) constituting the discontinued operation.

(iii) the related income tax expense as required by Ind AS 12, Income Taxes.

If the above analysis is presented in the Statement of Profit and Loss, then it shall be presented in a section identified as relating to discontinued operations, i.e., separately from continuing operations.

Self-Test Questions

Self-test question 6.7

Indicate whether the following statements are true (T) or false (F):

(i) Closure of one of the facilities, which are used for manufacturing a particular product, should be classified as discontinued operation.

(ii) Discontinuance of SX brand of palm oil, while continuing to produce other brands of the same oil, should be classified as a discontinued operation because discontinuance will result in closure of some facilities to reduce the capacity of producing palm oil.

(iii) Items of PP&E of a discontinued operation should be measured at the lower of their carrying amount and fair value less costs to sell.

SUMMARY

Discontinued operations is a component of an entity that either has been disposed of or is classified as held for sale and (i) represents a separate major line of business or geographical area of operations, (ii) is part of a single coordinated plan to dispose of a separate major line of business or geographical area of operations, or (iii) is a subsidiary acquired exclusively for resale. Gains and losses of discontinued operations are presented separately in the statement of profit and loss. Items of PP&E of a discontinued operation are measured at the lower of their carrying amount and fair value less costs to sell.

NOTES

Tax Expense

Tax expense has two components—current tax and deferred tax.

Current tax

Current tax is the amount of income taxes payable (recoverable) in respect of the taxable income (tax loss) computed as per tax laws applicable to the entity for the current period. Any interest on shortfall in the payment of advance income tax is in the nature of finance cost, and hence, should not be clubbed with the current tax. Any penalties levied under income tax laws should not be classified as current tax. Penalties, which are compensatory in nature, should be treated as interest and other tax penalties should be classified under 'Other Expenses'. Excess/Short provision of tax relating to earlier years should be separately disclosed.

Deferred tax

Deferred tax is the difference between deferred tax liability (net of deferred tax asset) at the end of the period and the same at the beginning of the period. For example, if the deferred tax liability (net of deferred tax asset) at the end of the current period is ₹1,500 and it was ₹1,000 at the beginning of the current period, the deferred tax expense is ₹500 for the current period.

EARNINGS PER SHARE

Schedule III (Division II) of the Companies Act, 2013 requires companies to disclose Earnings Per Share (EPS) below the statement of profit and loss. Ind AS 33, Earnings Per Share, stipulates that an entity that discloses earnings per share shall calculate and disclose earnings per share in accordance with that standard.

There are two types of EPS—basic EPS and diluted EPS.

Even if there is loss in a particular year, EPS has to be presented. It would show a negative figure.

Basic EPS

'Basic earnings per share' is calculated by dividing profit or loss attributable to equity shareholders (the numerator) by the weighted average number of equity shares outstanding (the denominator) during the period.

Profit or loss attributable to equity shareholders

Profit or loss (after tax) from continuing operations is used for computing EPS. Profit or loss from discontinuing operations and other comprehensive income are not included in the profit or loss for computing EPS.

Weighted average number of shares

The weighted average number of equity shares outstanding during the period is the number of equity shares outstanding in the beginning of the period, adjusted by the number of equity shares bought back or issued during the period multiplied by a time-weighting factor. The time-weighting factor is the number of days that the shares are outstanding as a proportion of the total number of days in the period. For additional shares where no consideration received (e.g., bonus issue), time weighted average number of shares from beginning of year/date of issue of shares with consideration should be considered.

NOTES

ILLUSTRATION 6.4 Weighted Average Number of Shares

PQ Limited (PQL) provides the following information for calculating the weighted average number of shares for calculating Basic EPS for the year 2017–18:

(i) Number of outstanding shares as at April 1, 2017 (beginning of the year): 1,250
(ii) Number of shares bought back on June 30, 2017: 250
(iii) Number of new shares issued on September 30 to settle a liability: 1,000
(iv) Balance as at March 31, 2018: 2,000

Required

Calculate the weighted average number of shares for computing Basic EPS.

Solution

The weighted average number of shares is (3/12 × 1,250 + 3/12 × 1,000 + 6/12 × 2,000) or 1,562.50.

Diluted EPS

Dilution is a reduction in EPS or an increase in loss per share resulting from the assumption that convertible instruments (e.g., convertible debentures) are converted, that options or warrants are exercised, or that ordinary shares are issued upon the satisfaction of specified conditions.

Dilutive potential equity shares

The first step in calculating Diluted EPS is to assess whether the issue of potential equity shares will dilute the EPS. If it dilutes the EPS, the potential equity share is called *dilutive potential equity share.*

Earnings for the purpose of calculating dilutive EPS

Earnings for the purpose of calculating dilutive EPS is the profit or loss considered for calculating Basic EPS, adjusted for increase in earnings, if any, due to avoidance of the expenses associated with the instrument (e.g., convertible bond).

Number of equity shares

For the purpose of calculating diluted earnings per share, the number of equity shares should be the weighted average number of equity shares calculated for computing Basic EPS, plus the weighted average number of equity shares that would be issued on the conversion of all the dilutive potential equity shares into equity shares. It is assumed that dilutive potential equity shares have been converted into ordinary shares at the beginning of the period. However, if the date of issue is later, the same is considered.

ILLUSTRATION 6.5 Basic and Diluted EPS

At the end of 2017–18, NM Limited (NML) had 10,00,000 equity shares of face value of ₹1 each. In 2016–17, NML had issued 1,000, 10 percent convertible bonds with face value of ₹100 at par. Each bond is convertible into 20 equity shares on demand. Both equity shares and convertible bonds were outstanding for the whole year (2017–18). NML's equity share price is ₹4.50 per share. Net profit (after tax expense) for the year was ₹5,25,000, of which ₹25,000 (after tax expense) was from discontinuing operations. The tax rate applicable to the company is 40 percent.

Required

Calculate basic EPS and diluted EPS for the year 2017–18.

Solution

Basic EPS

Net profit (after tax expense) from continuing operations is to be considered for computing EPS. Basic EPS = (₹5,00,000/10,00,000) or ₹0.50 per share.

Diluted EPS

Conversion of the bond is not rational because face value of each bond is ₹100. While after conversion, the market value of 20 equity shares would be (20 × ₹4.5) or ₹90. Yet, for computing diluted EPS, we have to assume that convertible bonds were converted in the beginning of the year.

The first step is to assess whether the potential equity shares (convertible debentures) are dilutive. On conversion, interest on the bond will be saved, and to that extent, profit will increase. Interest after tax is 1000 × ₹100 × 0.10 × (1 – 0.40) = ₹6,000.

Increase in number of equity shares will be 1,000 × 20 = 20,000

Net profit per incremental equity share = (₹6,000/20,000) = ₹0.30

The bond is dilutive because net profit per incremental equity share of ₹0.30 is lower than the basic EPS of ₹0.50.

The second step is to calculate diluted EPS.

Diluted EPS = (₹5,00,000 + 6,000)/(10,00,000 + 20,000) = ₹0.496 per share

Self-Test Questions

Self-test question 6.8

Fill in the blanks:

(i) Number of outstanding equity shares as at April 1, 2017 was 10,000. Number of bonus shares (i.e., shares issued without consideration) issued on October 1, 2017 was 2,000. The weighted average number of shares for calculating the basic EPS for the year 2017–18 is...............equity shares.

(ii) Number of outstanding equity shares as at April 1, 2017 was 10,000. Number of shares bought back on October 1, 2017 was 2,000. The weighted average number of shares for calculating the basic EPS for the year 2017–18 is...............equity shares.

(iii) Basic EPS for the year 2017–18 is ₹0.60 per share. There are 100 outstanding optionally convertible debentures with face of ₹1,000 and coupon rate of 12 percent per annum. Each debenture can be converted into 100 equity shares. The tax rate is 40 percent. The convertible debentures are ....[Choose between the words 'dilutive' and 'non-dilutive'.]

(iv) Weighted average number of equity shares of BV Limited (BVL) for computing the basic EPS for the year 2017–18 is 20,000. The basic EPS for the year 2017–18 is ₹0.70 per share. There are 100 outstanding optionally convertible debentures with face of ₹1,000 and coupon rate of 10 per cent per annum. Each debenture can be converted into 100 equity shares. The tax rate is 40 percent. The diluted EPS for the year 2017–18 is ₹...........

PROFIT MEASURES

We shall discuss profit measures with reference to the statements of profit and loss of HUL, Infosys and Suzlon for the year ended March 31, 2017, presented in Table 6.2.

TABLE 6.2

Statement of Profit and Loss for the Year Ended on March 31, 2017

(Amount in ₹ crores, except for EPS)

Particulars	HUL	Infosys	Suzlon
INCOME			
Revenue from operations	34,487	59,289	9,229
Other operating income	0	0	17
Other income	526	3,062	401
Total income	35,013	62,351	9,647

(Contd.)

TABLE 6.2

Statement of Profit and Loss for the Year Ended on March 31, 2017 (*Contd.*)

(Amount in ₹ crores, except for EPS)

Particulars	HUL	Infosys	Suzlon
EXPENSES			
Cost of material consumed	11,363	0	5,874
Purchase of stock-in-trade	4,166	0	492
Changes in inventories of finished goods (including stock-in-trade) and work-in-progress	156	0	(824)
Excise duty	2,597	0	0
Employee benefits expenses	1,620	30,944	415
Cost of technical sub-contractors	0	4,809	0
Cost of software packages and others	0	1,235	0
Communication expenses	0	372	7
Consultancy and professional charges	0	538	73
Finance costs	22	0	931
Depreciation and amortisation expenses	396	1,331	414
Other expenses	8,538	2,546	1,373
Total expenses	28,858	43,413	8,755
Profit before exceptional items and tax	6,155	18,938	892
Exceptional items	241	0	(536)
Profit before tax	6,396	18,938	356
Tax expenses:			
Current tax	(1,865)	(5,068)	0
Deferred tax credit/(charge)	(41)	(52)	0
Profit for the year (A)	4,490	13,818	356
OTHER COMPREHENSIVE INCOME			
Items that will not be reclassified subsequently to profit or loss:			
Remeasurement of the net defined benefit plans	(32)	(42)	(10)
Equity instruments through other comprehensive income*	0	(5)	
Income tax related to items that will not be reclassified subsequently to profit or loss:			
Remeasurement of the net defined benefit plans	11		0
Items that will be reclassified subsequently to profit or loss:			
Fair value changes on cash flow hedges (net)		39	0
Fair value of debt instruments through other comprehensive income*	1	(10)	0
Income tax related to items that will be reclassified subsequently to profit or loss:			
Fair value of debt instruments through other comprehensive income	0		0
Other comprehensive income, net of tax for the year (B)	(20)	(18)	(10)
Total comprehensive income for the year (A + B)	4,470	13,800	346
EARNINGS PER SHARE:			
Basic (₹)	20.75	60.16	0.71
Diluted (₹)	20.74	60.15	0.71

Notes:

(i) Figures for HUL (Hindustan Unilever Limited) are taken from the stand-alone statement of profit and loss for the year ended March 31, 2017.

(ii) Figures for Infosys (Infosys Limited) are taken from the stand-alone statement of profit and loss for the year ended March 31, 2017.

(iii) Figures for Suzlon (Suzlon Energy Limited) are taken from the stand-alone statement of profit and loss for the year ended March 31, 2017.

* Infosys has provided the details of income tax in notes to accounts.

Gross Profit

Gross profit = Revenue from operations – Cost of goods sold

Cost of goods sold is also referred to as 'cost of sales'.

Gross profit ratio (%) = (Gross profit/Revenue from operations) × 100

Gross profit ratio is useful in assessing the efficiency in manufacturing or procurement of goods sold.

As evident from Table 6.2, it is difficult to calculate gross profit, as the figure for cost of goods sold is not available. Even we cannot estimate the cost of goods sold because in the absence of the required information, we shall not be able to allocate cost of employee benefits, depreciation and other expenses to manufacturing activities.

Earnings before Interest and Tax (EBIT)

Often, analysts calculate Earnings Before Interest and Tax' (EBIT) to revenue from operations to calculate the margin earned by the entity. This is not appropriate, as EBIT includes other income and excludes tax expense, which should be viewed as any other expense for operating business. EBIT from continued operation should be calculated.

Table 6.3 presents the EBIT of HUL, Infosys and Suzlon for the year 2016–17. Income tax rate is estimated at 34 percent.

TABLE 6.3

EBIT for the Year 2016–17

(Amount in ₹ crores)

Particulars	HUL	Infosys	Suzlon
Profit before exceptional items and tax (A)	6,155	18,938	892
Finance costs (B)	22	0	931
EBIT (A + B)	6,177	18,938	1,823

Although EBIT is widely used to measure operating profit, we should remember that EBIT does not measure operating profit, as it includes non-operating income (called other income) and excludes income tax.

Earnings before Interest, Tax, Depreciation and Amortisation (EBITDA)

Analysts use Earnings Before Interest, Tax, Depreciation and Amortisation (EBITDA) as a proxy cash profit. It is a useful measure of performance, particularly in capital-intensive industry, where depreciation constitutes an important component of total expense. In difficult time, an entity should earn at least the cash profit for survival.

Table 6.4 presents the EBITDA of HUL, Infosys and Suzlon for the year 2016–17.

TABLE 6.4

EBITDA for the Year 2016–17

(Amount in ₹ crores)

Particulars	HUL	Infosys	Suzlon
Profit before exceptional items and tax (A)	6,155	18,938	892
Add: finance costs (B)	22	0	931
Add: depreciation and amortisation (C)	396	1,331	414
EBITDA (A + B + C)	6,573	20,269	2,237

NOTES

Key Terms
EBIT, EBITDA, Gross profit, NOPAT, NOPLAT

EBITDA to total income ratios of different companies operating in the same industry with the similar business model are comparable, as EBITDA ignores financing decisions, age of facilities and tax rates. A weakness of EBITDA is that it understates the effects that capital structure and capital expenditure or CAPEX spending have on a business.

Net Operating Profit after Tax (NOPAT)

Net Operating Profit After Tax (NOPAT) measures operating profit. It is also called Net Operating Profit Less Adjusted Tax (NOPLAT).

A major part of non-operating income (called other income) comes from return on investments primarily, in financial assets. Therefore, other income should be excluded while measuring operating profit. However, if income, other than return on investments, is material, then that may be included in operating income. Operating profit should be calculated before interest, but after tax expense. NOPAT is the profit available to all investors.

Table 6.5 presents the NOPAT of HUL, Infosys and Suzlon for the year 2016–17.

TABLE 6.5

NOPAT for the Year 2016–17

(Amount in ₹ crores)

Particulars	HUL	Infosys	Suzlon
Profit (after tax) from continuing operation (A)	4,490	13,818	356
Less: exceptional items × (1 – 0.34) (B)	159	0	(354)
Less: other income × (1 – 0.34) (C)	347	2.021	265
Add: finance costs × (1 – 0.34) (D)	15	0	614
NOPAT (A – B – C + D)	3,999	11,797	1,059

Corporate tax rate for domestic companies was little more than 34 percent. We have used tax rate of 34 percent. When tax rates are different for different slabs of taxable income, marginal tax rate should be used.

Self-Test Questions

Self-test question 6.9

Indicate whether the following statements are true (T) or false (F):

(i) Gross profit ratio is useful in assessing the efficiency in manufacturing or procurement of goods sold.
(ii) EBIT measures operating profit.
(iii) EBITDA is used as a proxy for cash profit, but it is not a measure of cash flow from operating activities.
(iv) NOPAT measures operating profit.

ANSWERS TO SELF-TEST QUESTIONS

6.1 (i) T; (ii) T; (iii) T; (iv) T; (v) T
6.2 (i) F; (ii) F; (iii) T; (iv) F
6.3 (i) F; (ii) F; (iii) T; (iv) F; (v) T
6.4 (i) T; (ii) T; (iii) T; (iv) F; (v) T; (vi) T
6.5 (i) T; (ii) T; (iii) F; (iv) F; (v) T; (vi) T
6.6 (i) T; (ii) T; (iii) T; (iv) F; (v) T
6.7 (i) F; (ii) F; (iii) T
6.8 (i) 12,000; (ii) 9,000; (iii) Non-dilutive; (iv) ₹0.67
6.9 (i) T; (ii) F; (iii) T; (iv) T

NOTES

ASSIGNMENTS

Multiple Choice Questions

Quiz

1. (i) Which of the following formulas is most appropriate for computing expenses?
   - (a) Payments + Beginning prepaid + Ending outstanding
   - (b) Payments + Beginning prepaid + Ending outstanding – Ending prepaid – Beginning outstanding
   - (c) Payments + Ending outstanding – Beginning outstanding
   - (d) Payments + Beginning prepaid – Bnding prepaid

   (ii) Which of the following statements is correct?
   - (a) An expense represents the expenditure incurred during the period and from which no asset could be recognised.
   - (b) An expense represents the portion of an asset allocated to the current period.
   - (c) An expense represents an element of cost of goods or services sold during the period.
   - (d) An expense represents either the expenditure incurred during the period and from which no asset could be recognised or the portion of an asset allocated to the current period or an element of cost of goods or services sold during the period.

   (iii) Which of the following statements is correct?
   - (a) Exceptional items are distinguished by their unusual nature and by the infrequency of their occurrence.
   - (b) Exceptional items are distinguished by their unusual nature.
   - (c) Exceptional items are distinguished by the infrequency of their occurrence.
   - (d) Exceptional items are distinguished by their magnitude and infrequency of their occurrence.

   (iv) Which of the following statements is correct?
   - (a) Prior period item arises due to difference in actual amount and the estimated amount of an expense or income recognised in one of the earlier years based on that estimate.
   - (b) Prior period item arises due to revision of estimate of an expense or income recognised in one of the earlier years based on that estimate due to unfolding of new information.
   - (c) Prior period item arises due to a fundamental error in calculation or in interpretation of a law or a contract, etc., which occurred in one of the earlier years.
   - (d) Prior period item arises due to a fundamental error in calculation, which occurred in one of the earlier years.

2. State whether the following statements are true (T) or false (F):
   - (i) Increase in equity due to fresh contribution from owners represents income for the period.
   - (ii) Discretionary expenses recognised in the statement of profit and loss usually do not have any direct cause and effect relationship with revenue recognised in the statement of profit and loss.
   - (iii) Revenue represents income from core activities of the enterprise.
   - (iv) Profit from sale of an item of fixed assets is included in revenue.
   - (v) Usually, recognition of revenue results in simultaneous recognition of one or more current assets.
   - (vi) For a commission agent, only the commission earned is revenue.
   - (vii) Interest earned on loans and advances by a financial institution is recognised as other income.
   - (viii) Advertisement expenditure is usually considered as deferred revenue expenditure.
   - (ix) Revaluation gain is an item of other comprehensive income.
   - (x) Asset-liability measurement approach recognises the concepts of deferred revenue expenditure and fictitious asset.
   - (xi) NOPLAT is not affected by the capital structure of the entity.
   - (xii) EPS is not affected by the capital structure of the entity.

CHAPTER 7

The Accounting Cycle Journal, Cash Book, General Ledger and Trial Balance

LEARNING OBJECTIVES

The objective of this chapter is to provide an understanding of the mechanics of recording transaction in account books. After reading this chapter, you will be able to understand the following:

- Accounting cycle
- Journalisation of transactions
- Purpose of Journal Proper and recording of transactions in the same
- Purpose of Purchase Day Book and recording of transactions in the same
- Purpose of Sales Day Book and recording of transactions in the same
- Purpose of Cash Book and recording of transactions in the same
- Purpose of General Ledger and posting of transactions in the same
- Balancing Accounts in the General Ledger
- Preparation of Trial Balance
- Potential errors in Trial Balance

THE ACCOUNTING CYCLE

Accounting involves recording of transactions and other events in a manner that facilitates preparation and presentation of financial statements. Accounting cycle refers to the cycle starting with recording of opening entries (balances carried forward from the previous reporting period) in the general ledger, and ends with the preparation of financial statements. Following steps are involved in the preparation of financial statements:

1. Recording of opening entries in the general ledger
2. Recording of transactions and events in the journal (Journalisation)
3. Posting journal entries in appropriate accounts in the general ledger
4. Balancing the accounts in the general ledger
5. Preparing the trial balance
6. Recording adjustment entries
7. Preparing adjusted trial balance
8. Recording closing entries to prepare financial statements

Transactions and other events are recorded in the journal in a chronological order. Account heads, in accordance with accounts classification, are opened in the general ledger and journal entries are posted in the general ledger. Accounts in the general ledger are balanced periodically. Usually, entities prepare a trial balance, a statement that periodically lists balances in different ledger accounts. At the end of the reporting period, adjustment entries are passed to adjust revenue and expenses for matching expenses with revenue. A revised trial balance is prepared and closing entries are passed to close nominal accounts and prepare profit and loss accounts. Balances that appear in the general ledger after preparation of the statement of profit and loss are aggregated and classified for presentation in the balance sheet.

With rapid progress in information technology, computer-aided accounting, often with the use of standard software packages, has become common even among small firms. Therefore, bookkeeping does not require any special skill. The only important requirement is to record the proper accounting code in original documents which form the basis of bookkeeping.

NOTES

Key Terms
Accounting cycle, general ledger, journal, trial balance

Self-Test Questions

Self-test question 7.1

Indicate whether the following statements are true (T) or false (F):

(i) Transactions and other events are recorded in the journal in a chronological order.
(ii) Preparation of Trial Balance is the starting point in the preparation of financial statements.
(iii) Appropriate codification of account heads is important for recording transactions correctly.

JOURNALISATION

General Principles

The four phases in the accounting process are presented in Figure 7.1.

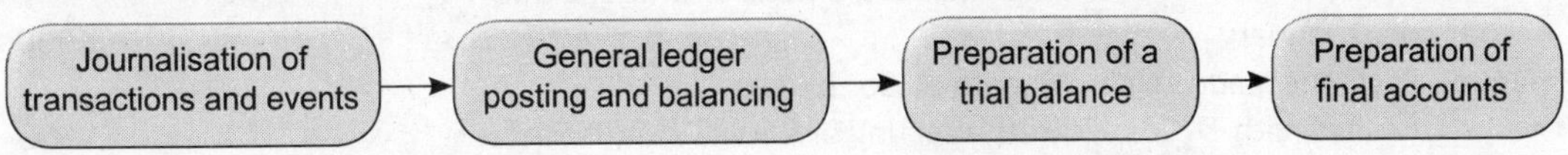

FIGURE 7.1 Four phases of accounting process.

NOTES

In the first phase, the transactions and events are analysed and recorded in the journal. Accountants use the following types of journals for recording different types of transactions and events:

1. **Purchase Day Book:** To record transactions relating to credit purchases of goods in trade.
2. **Sales Day Book:** To record transactions relating to credit sales.
3. **Purchase Return Book:** To record transactions relating to purchase return.
4. **Sales Return Book:** To record transactions relating to sales return.
5. **Cash Book:** To record cash, bank and discount transactions.
6. **Journal Proper:** To record other transactions for which no specific journal is maintained, and for recording entries to rectify mistakes in books of accounts.

Transactions and other events are recorded in the journal in a *chronological order.* The ledger folio in which the transaction is posted in the general ledger is entered in the journal for cross-referencing. In addition, the Journal Proper provides a brief narration of the transaction or the event. Papers or documents that evidence the transaction or the other event recorded in a journal should support each entry in the journal. Those papers and documents are known as **vouchers.**

Journal Proper

Case Study 7.1 shows recording of transactions in the journal proper. However, in practice, many of those transactions should be recorded in special journals mentioned above.

CASE STUDY 7.1

Record the Following Transactions of A & Co. in Journal Proper Form

2018			₹
Jan. 1	*Assets:*	Cash-in-hand	500
		Cash in bank	8,000
		Stock of goods	4,000
		Machinery	20,000
		Furniture	5,000
		Roy & Co. (amount due to A & Co.)	2,000
		Sen & Co. (amount due to A & Co.)	3,000
	Liabilities:	Loan from State Bank of India (SBI)	10,000
		Amount due to Vishwanath & Co.	5,000
Jan. 2	Bought goods on credit from Patel & Co.		2,000
Jan. 3	Sold goods for cash to Bose & Co.		500
Jan. 4	Sold goods to Roy & Co. on credit		1,000
Jan. 5	Received from Roy & Co. in full settlement of amount due on 1 January		1,900
Jan. 6	Payment made to Vishwanath & Co. by cheque (Vishwanath & Co. allowed discount of ₹50)		4,950
Jan. 8	Old furniture sold for cash (book value, ₹300)		350
Jan. 10	Bought goods for cash		1,000
Jan. 11	Received cheque from Sen & Co., deposited in bank		3,000
Jan. 12	Paid for repairs to machinery		200

Jan. 13	Bought goods from Vishwanath & Co. on credit	2,000
	Paid cartage on these goods	100
Jan. 14	Received cheque from Roy & Co., deposited in bank (discount allowed to them, ₹50)	950
Jan. 17	Paid cheque to Viswanath & Co.	2,000
Jan. 18	Bank intimates that cheque received from Roy & Co. has been returned unpaid	950
Jan. 19	Sold goods for cash to Dey & Co.	2,000
Jan. 21	Cash deposited in bank	1,000
Jan. 22	Paid municipal taxes in cash	100
Jan. 25	Borrowed from New Age Investment Co., for erecting own premises (amount deposited with bank)	20,000
Jan. 26	Paid for advertisements	500
Jan. 29	Sold old newspapers	50
Jan. 31	Paid rent by cheque	500
	Paid salaries for the month	500
	Drawn by Mr. A out of bank for personal use	500

Solution

JOURNAL

Date	Particulars	Ledger folio	Dr. Amount (₹)	Cr. Amount (₹)
2018				
Jan. 1	Cash a/c	Dr.	500	
	Bank a/c	Dr.	8,000	
	Stock a/c	Dr.	4,000	
	Machinery a/c	Dr.	20,000	
	Furniture a/c	Dr.	5,000	
	Roy & Co.	Dr.	2,000	
	Sen & Co.	Dr.	3,000	
	To loan from SBI account	Cr.		10,000
	To Vishwanath & Co.	Cr.		5,000
	To capital (balancing figure, residual amount)	Cr.		27,500
	(being the assets and liabilities brought forward from the previous reporting period)			
Jan. 2	Purchases a/c	Dr.	2,000	
	To Patel & Co. a/c	Cr.		2,000
	(being goods purchased from Patel & Co. as per bill no. ... dated ...)			
Jan. 3	Cash a/c	Dr.	500	
	To sales a/c	Cr.		500
	(being goods sold for cash to Bose & Co. as per cash memo no...)			
Jan. 4	Roy & Co. a/c	Dr.	1,000	
	To sales a/c	Cr.		1,000
	(being goods sold to Roy & Co. as per invoice no ... dated...)			
Jan. 5	Cash a/c	Dr.	1,900	
	Discount a/c	Dr.	100	
	To Roy & Co.	Cr.		2,000
	(being the amount of ₹1,900 received in full and final settlement of ₹2,000)			

NOTES

Date	Particulars	Ledger folio	Dr. Amount (₹)	Cr. Amount (₹)
Jan. 6	Vishwanath & Co. a/c	Dr.	5,000	
	To bank a/c	Cr.		4,950
	To discount a/c	Cr.		50
	(being the amount paid by cheque to Vishwanath & Co. towards settlement of ₹5,000)			
Jan. 8	Cash a/c	Dr.	350	
	To furniture a/c	Cr.		300
	To profit on sale of furniture	Cr.		50
	(being profit on sale of old furniture, book value ₹300, payment received in cash)			
Jan. 10	Purchases a/c	Dr.	1,000	
	To cash a/c	Cr.		1,000
	(being purchase of goods for cash as per cash memo no...)			
Jan. 11	Bank a/c	Dr.	3,000	
	To Sen & Co. a/c	Cr.		3,000
	(being cheque no. ... received from Sen & Co. and deposited in bank)			
Jan. 12	Repairs to Machinery a/c	Dr.	200	
	To cash a/c	Cr.		200
	(being the amount paid for repairs to machinery as per bill no.........)			
Jan. 13	Purchases a/c	Dr.	2,000	
	To Vishwanath & Co	Cr.		2,000
	(being goods purchased from M/s. Vishwanath & Co. as per invoice no...)			
Jan. 13	Freight Inward a/c	Dr.	100	
	To cash a/c	Cr.		100
	(being freight paid on goods purchased from Vishwanath & Co.)			
Jan. 14	Bank a/c	Dr.	950	
	Discount a/c	Dr.	50	
	To Roy & Co. a/c	Cr.		1,000
	(being amount received from Roy & Co. vide cheque no... dated ... drawn on ...., discount allowed ₹50)			
Jan. 17	Vishwanath & Co. a/c	Dr.	2,000	
	To bank a/c	Cr.		2,000
	(being amount paid to Vishwanath & Co. vide cheque no. ... dated... drawn on ...)			
Jan. 18	Roy & Co. a/c	Dr.	1,000	
	To bank a/c	Cr.		950
	To discount a/c	Cr.		50
	(being cheque no. ... dated.... drawn on... received from Roy & Co. returned by bank unpaid)			
Jan. 19	Cash a/c	Dr.	2,000	
	To sales a/c	Cr.		2,000
	(being goods sold for cash to Dey & Co. vide cash receipt no ...)			

NOTES

Date	Particulars	Ledger folio	Dr. Amount (₹)	Cr. Amount (₹)
Jan. 21	Bank account	Dr.	1,000	
	To cash a/c	Cr.		1,000
	(being cash deposited with bank)			
Jan. 22	Municipal taxes a/c	Dr.	100	
	To cash	Cr.		100
	(being municipal taxes paid vide cash memo no.....)			
Jan. 25	Bank a/c	Dr.	20,000	
	To loan from New Age Investment Co.	Cr.		20,000
	(being amount borrowed for erecting own premises, received vide cheque no. ... dated ... drawn on ...)			
Jan. 26	Advertisements a/c	Dr.	500	
	To cash a/c	Cr.		500
	(being amount towards advertisement in... vide cash memo no....)			
Jan. 29	Cash a/c	Dr.	50	
	To sale of newspapers	Cr.		50
	(being old newspapers sold)			
Jan. 31	Rent a/c	Dr.	500	
	To bank a/c	Cr.		500
	(being rent for the month of Jan. paid vide cheque no. ... dated... drawn...)			
Jan. 31	Salaries a/c	Dr.	500	
	To cash a/c	Cr.		500
	(being salaries for the month of Jan. paid)			
Jan. 31	Capital a/c	Dr.	500	
	To bank a/c	Cr.		500
	(being amount drawn by Mr. A for private use vide cheque no... dated... drawn ...)			

In Case Study 7.1, we recorded all types of transactions in a Journal Proper. However, in practice, cash and bank transactions are recorded in a Cash Book, credit purchases are recorded in a Purchase Day Book, credit sales are recorded in a Sales Day Book, and *only* the following types of transactions are recorded in the journal proper:

1. *Opening entries:* At the commencement of the reporting period, opening balances of assets, liabilities and equity are journalised to record *carry forward balances* in the books of accounts for the period. Opening entries will be discussed in detail in Chapter 8.
2. *Closing entries:* At the close of the reporting period, while preparing the profit and loss account, revenue, gain, expense and loss accounts are closed by transferring their balances in the general ledger to the profit and loss account through the journal proper, called *closing entries*. (Closing entries will be discussed in detail in Chapter 8).
3. *Rectification entries:* An error that occurred while recording a transaction or event is rectified through the journal proper.
4. *Transfer entries:* Transfer from one account head to another account head is made through the journal proper.
5. *Adjustment entries:* At the close of a reporting period, expenses and revenue are adjusted to match expenses with revenue for the period. Usually, such entries pertain to outstanding expenses, prepaid expenses, interest on capital, and depreciation. Adjustment entries are recorded in the journal proper.

NOTES

6. *Dishonouring of cheques and other negotiable instruments:* Non-payment or dishonouring of negotiable instruments (promissory notes, bill of exchange and cheques) is taken on record through the journal proper.
7. *Miscellaneous entries:* Transactions other than credit purchases, credit sales and cash and bank transactions are recorded through the journal proper.

Self-Test Questions

Self-test question 7.2

Fill in the blanks: [Choose between the words debiting and crediting.]

(i) Introduction of capital in the firm by owners in the form of cash is recorded by..................Cash account and ....Capital account.

(ii) Purchase of stock-in-trade on credit is recorded by..........................Trade Creditors account (name of the seller) and ....Purchases account.

(iii) Depositing cash in the bank is recorded by..........................Cash account and ....Bank account.

(iv) Sale of goods on credit is recorded by..........................Trade Receivables (name of the customer) and..............................Sales account.

(v) Amount received from a customer by cheque against amount due from it is recorded by..................Trade Receivable account (name of the customer) and ....Bank account.

(vi) Payment of salary by cash is recorded by..................Cash account and .... Salary account.

(vii) Payment to a supplier of goods by cheque against amount due to it is recorded by..................Trade Creditors account (name of the supplier) and........................ Bank account.

(viii) Amount borrowed from a bank (received in cheque) is recorded by .... Loan account and ....Bank account.

(ix) Withdrawal of cash from bank is recorded by ....Cash account and ....Bank account.

(x) Received from a customer ₹10,000 by cheque against ₹12,000 due from it in full and final settlement is recorded by .... Bank account by ₹10,000,..................... Discount allowed account by ₹2,000, and ....Trade Receivables account (name of the customer) by ₹12,000.

Purchase Day Book

In view of the large number of transactions, a separate journal entitled, 'Purchase Day Book' is maintained by enterprises to record credit purchases. However, credit purchases, other than purchases of stock-in-trade or materials being used in the manufacturing process, are not recorded in the purchase day book. Similarly, cash transactions are not recorded in this journal.

Entities also maintain a 'Purchase Return Book' to record return of goods to suppliers. The following case study presents the format of a 'purchase day book'.

CASE STUDY 7.2

A & Co. deals in ladies garments. The rough book of the firm shows the following transactions for the month of January 2018:

Jan. 1 *Purchased from B & Co. on credit:*
10 cotton salwar suits @ ₹500 per suit
10 silk salwar suits @ ₹1,500 per suit
Less: Trade discount @ 10%

Jan. 10 *Purchased in cash from C & Co:*
2 cotton salwar suits @ ₹150 per suit

Jan. 15 *Purchased a calculator for office use from D & Co. on credit for ₹500*

Jan. 20 *Purchased from Y & Co. on credit:*
10 cotton sarees @ ₹600 per saree
10 silk sarees @ ₹2,000 per saree
Less: Trade discount @ 10%

Jan. 31 Purchased 10 cotton suit lengths @ ₹300 per suit length from Z & Co. on credit.

Prepare the purchase day book of A & Co. for the month of January 2018.

Solution

A & CO.: PURCHASE DAY BOOK

Date	Particulars	Ledger folio	Amount (₹)	Net Amount (₹)
2018				
Jan. 1	*M/s B & Co.*			
	10 cotton salwar suits @ ₹500		5,000	
	10 silk salwar suits @ ₹1,500		15,000	
			20,000	
	Trade discount @ 10%		(2,000)	18,000
Jan. 20	*M/s Y & Co.*			
	10 cotton sarees @ ₹600		6,000	
	10 silk sarees @ ₹2,000		20,000	
			26,000	
	Trade discount @ 10%		(2,600)	23,400
Jan. 31	*M/s Z & Co.*			
	10 cotton suit lengths @ ₹300			3,000
	Total			44,400

Note: Transactions pertaining to cash purchase (10 January) and credit purchase of calculator (15 January) have not been recorded in the purchase day book.

The total of the purchase day book is posted periodically to the general ledger through the journal proper. The journal entry for January 2018 should be as follows:

Purchase Account	Dr.	₹44,400
To B & Co. a/c	Cr.	₹18,000
To Y & Co. a/c	Cr.	₹23,400
To Z & Co. a/c	Cr.	₹3,000

When an entity maintains subsidiary ledger for creditors, the journal entry from the purchase day book should be as follows:

Purchases a/c	Dr.	₹44,400
To trade creditors a/c	Cr.	₹44,400

BOX 7.1 Subsidiary Ledger

Usually, the number of transactions being large, personal accounts of individual creditors, debtors, employees and other counter parties is not maintained in the general ledger. Personal accounts of individuals are maintained in a subsidiary ledger that does not form a part of the main books of accounts. Only the *control account* is maintained in the general ledger. The balance in the control account at a particular date reflects the amount of liability or asset that has arisen from a particular type of transaction. For example, *Trade Creditors Account* shows the amount due to suppliers of goods. Individual accounts in the subsidiary ledger are posted from day books, journal proper, and cash book. The aggregate of balances in individual accounts in the subsidiary ledger should agree with the balance appearing in the control account in the general ledger. Subsidiary ledgers are known as *Memorandum Book* because accounting entries in those ledgers do not form a part of the double-entry accounting system. Subsidiary ledgers are usually maintained for transaction such as trade debtors, advance to employees, advances from customers, and other transactions where a large number of personal accounts are required to be maintained by the firm.

NOTES

Sales Day Book

Enterprises record credit sales of stock-in-trade in a **sales day book**. The mechanics of posting entries from the sales day book to the general ledger and the subsidiary ledger for debtors are similar to those of postings from the purchase day book. The following case study presents the format of a sales day book:

CASE STUDY 7.3

A & Co. deals in ladies garments. The rough book of the firm shows the following transactions for January 2018:

Jan. 2 *Sold to Alpha & Co. on credit:*
5 cotton salwar suits @ ₹600 per suit
5 silk salwar suits @ ₹1,800 per suit
Less: Trade discount @ 10%

Jan. 3 *Sold old furniture to M & Co. for ₹100 on credit*

Jan. 8 *Sold to Beta & Co. on credit:*
5 cotton salwar suits @ ₹600 per suit
5 silk salwar suits @ ₹1,800 per suit
Less: Trade discount @ 10%

Jan. 15 *Sold two silk sarees to M/s. Beauty for ₹2,500 in cash*

Jan. 31 *Sold to Gamma & Co. on credit:*
10 cotton sarees @ ₹800 per saree
10 silk sarees @ ₹2,500 per saree
Less: Trade discount @ 10%

Prepare the sales day book of A & Co. for January 2018.

Solution

A & CO.: SALES DAY BOOK

Date	Particulars	Ledger folio	Amount (₹)	Net Amount (₹)
2018				
Jan. 2	*M/s Alpha & Co.*			
	5 cotton salwar suits @ ₹600		3,000	
	5 silk salwar suits @ ₹1,800		9,000	
			12,000	
	Trade discount @ 10%		(1,200)	10,800
Jan. 8	*M/s Beta & Co.*			
	5 cotton salwar suits @ ₹600		3,000	
	5 silk salwar suits @ ₹1,800		9,000	
			12,000	
	Trade discount @ 10%		(1,200)	10,800
Jan. 31	*M/s Gamma & Co.*			
	10 cotton sarees @ ₹800		8,000	
	10 silk sarees @ ₹2,500		25,000	
			33,000	
	Trade discount @ 10%		(3,300)	29,700
	Total			51,300

Periodical posting of the total of the sales day book to the general ledger should be made through the following journal entry:

Trade receivables a/c	Dr. ₹51,300	
To sales a/c		Cr. ₹51,300

NOTES

Postings to personal accounts of trade debtors should be made in the subsidiary ledger for trade debtors. As in the case of the purchase day book, the aggregate of balances in personal accounts in the subsidiary ledger should agree with the balance in the trade receivables account in the general ledger.

Enterprises also maintain a 'Sales Return Book' to record inward return of goods from customers.

Cash Book

Cash and bank transactions are recorded directly in the 'Cash Book'. A cash book is primarily a journal. It also serves the purpose of a ledger account and, therefore, the cash account and bank account are not maintained in the general ledger. Balances in the cash book are taken directly to the trial balance that lists balances in various account heads in the general ledger. Thus, a cash book serves the dual purpose of maintaining a journal to record cash and bank transactions, and also maintaining cash and bank accounts in the general ledger. The following are the different types of cash books that are being maintained by enterprises:

1. **Single-column cash book.** It records only cash receipts and cash payments.
2. **Double-column cash book.** It provides additional information on discount received and discount allowed.
3. **Three-column cash book.** It has an additional column to record bank transactions.

The following case study presents a single-column cash book.

CASE STUDY 7.4

Record the following cash transactions entered into by A & Co. in January 2018 in a single-column cash book.

Jan. 1	Cash-in-hand	1,000
Jan. 6	Received from B & Co.	600
Jan. 10	Paid rent	500
Jan. 15	Sold goods for cash	2,000
Jan. 27	Purchased furniture for cash	1,200
Jan. 31	Paid salaries	800

A double-column cash book provides additional information on discount received and discount allowed. There are additional columns for discount on both debit and credit sides of the cash book. The total of discount columns are posted in the **discount account** in the general ledger. A double-column cash book is presented below:

Solution

A & CO.: CASH BOOK

Date	Receipts Particulars	LF	Dr. Amount (₹)	Date	Payments Particulars	LF	Cr. Amount (₹)
2018							
Jan. 1	To balance b/d		1,000	Jan. 10	By rent a/c		500
Jan. 6	To B & Co. a/c		600	Jan. 27	By furniture a/c		1,200
Jan. 15	To sales a/c		2,000	Jan. 31	By salaries a/c		800
				Jan. 31	By balance c/d		1,100
			3,600				3,600
Feb. 1	To balance b/d		1,100				

NOTES

CASE STUDY 7.5

A & Co. commenced business on January 1, 2010 with a cash balance of ₹2,000 as capital. He had the following cash transactions for January 2010. Prepare the cash book.

		₹
Jan. 1	Purchased furniture	200
Jan. 2	Purchased goods	300
Jan. 4	Sold goods	400
Jan. 6	Paid to B & Co.	500
	Allowed discount	20
Jan. 15	Received from C & Co.	600
	Allowed discount	30
Jan. 20	Purchased calculator	200
Jan. 31	Paid salaries	500

Solution

A&CO.: CASH BOOK

Dr.	**Receipts**					**Payments**			**Cr.**
Date	**Particulars**	**LF**	**Discount (₹)**	**Cash (₹)**	**Date**	**Particulars**	**LF**	**Discount (₹)**	**Cash (₹)**
2018									
Jan. 1	To capital a/c			2,000	Jan. 1	By furniture a/c			200
Jan. 4	To sales a/c			400	Jan. 2	By purchases a/c			300
Jan. 15	To C & Co. a/c		30	600	Jan. 6	By B & Co. a/c		20	500
					Jan. 20	By calculator a/c			200
					Jan. 31	By salaries a/c			500
					Jan. 31	By balance c/d			1,500
Total			30	3,000	Total			20	3,000
2010									
Feb. 1	To balance b/d			1,500					

In a three-column cash book, additional columns are provided to enter bank transactions. This helps dispense with the bank account in the general ledger. However, in case an entity operates more than one bank account, it is better to have a separate bank book or bank accounts in the general ledger. The following case study presents a three-column cash book.

CASE STUDY 7.6

A commenced business as A & Co. on January 1, 2018 with a cash balance of ₹2,000. Record the transactions for January 2018 in a cash book with discount and bank columns.

		₹
Jan. 1	Deposited cash with bank	1,500
Jan. 4	Received cheque from B & Co.	1,000
Jan. 5	C & Co. is paid by cheque. He allowed a discount of ₹20	330
Jan. 6	Received cheque from M & Co. after allowing a discount of ₹50	450
Jan. 10	Goods sold in cash to R & Co.	500
Jan. 12	Cash drawn for office use	500
Jan. 15	Paid for office expenses in cash	500
Jan. 25	Paid salaries for January in cash	500
Jan. 25	Cheque received from Y & Co.	400
Jan. 31	Cheque received from Y & Co. returned unpaid by bank	400

Solution

A&CO.: CASH BOOK

Dr.	**Receipts**						**Payments**				**Cr.**
Date	**Particulars**	**LF**	**Discount (₹)**	**Cash (₹)**	**Bank (₹)**	**Date**	**Particulars**	**LF**	**Discount (₹)**	**Cash (₹)**	**Bank (₹)**
2018						2018					
Jan. 1	To capital			2,000		Jan. 1	By cash	C		1,500	
Jan. 1	To bank	C			1,500	Jan. 5	By C & Co.		20		330
Jan. 4	To B & Co.				1,000	Jan. 12	By cash	C			500
Jan. 6	To M & Co.		50		450	Jan. 15	By office expenses			500	
Jan. 10	To sales			500		Jan. 25	By salaries			500	
Jan. 12	To bank	C		500		Jan. 31	By Y & Co.				400
Jan. 25	To Y & Co.				400	Jan. 31	By balance c/d			500	2,120
			50	3,000	3,350				20	3,000	3,350
Feb. 1	To balance b/d			500	2,120						

'C' denotes "Contra", that is, there is a corresponding entry on the other side in the bank/cash column.

Petty Cash Book

As a matter of convenience, an imprest (a predetermined amount of cash) is sanctioned to some individuals authorised to make payments of small amounts of high frequency. Examples of such payments are: postage, conveyance, carriage, and stationery. The individual so authorised maintains a cash book known as a *petty cash book*. The individual periodically recoups his 'imprest' by submitting an account of payments released to him during the period. A petty cash book usually has multiple columns to accommodate different types of payments.

SUMMARY

Accounting involves recording of transactions and other events in a manner that facilitates preparation and presentation of financial statements. Accounting cycle refers to the cycle starting with recording of opening entries (balances carried forward from the previous reporting period) in the general ledger, and ends with the preparation of financial statements. Transactions and other events are recorded in the journal in chronological order. Account heads, in accordance with accounts classification, are opened in the general ledger and journal entries are posted in the general ledger. Accounts in the general ledger are balanced periodically. Usually, entities prepare a trial balance—a statement that periodically lists balances in different ledger accounts. At the end of the reporting period, adjustment entries are passed to adjust revenue and expenses for matching expenses with revenue. A revised trial balance is prepared and closing entries are passed to close nominal accounts and prepare the statement of profit and loss. Balances that appear in the general ledger, after preparation of the statement of profit and loss, are aggregated and classified for presentation in the balance sheet. Accountants use different types of journals, such as Purchase Day Book, Sales Day Book, Purchase Return Book, Sales Return Book, and Cash Book.

Journal Proper is used to record opening entries, closing entries, rectification entries, transfer entries, adjustment entries, dishonouring of cheques, and other negotiable instruments and miscellaneous entries which are not recorded in day books or cash book.

NOTES

Key Terms
Cash book, contra entry, journalisation, negotiable instruments, petty cash book, promissory note, purchase day book, sales day book, subsidiary ledger

GENERAL LEDGER AND TRIAL BALANCE

General Ledger

The general ledger is the principal book of accounts. Journal entries are the bases for

NOTES

preparing the general ledger. After recording transactions in journals, the next phase in the accounting process is to post entries in appropriate account heads in the general ledger. Periodically, accounts in the general ledger are balanced. For example, if in a particular account the total of the debit side comes to ₹10,000 and the total of the credit side comes to ₹8,000, the account shows a debit balance of ₹2,000. Thus, a debit balance of ₹2,000 reflects that the total of the debit side exceeds the total of the credit side by ₹2,000. Financial statements are prepared on the basis of balances in ledger accounts at the end of the accounting period. Case Study 7.7 explains the process of posting transactions from journals to accounts in the general ledger. Accounts in the general ledger are often termed as **ledger accounts.**

CASE STUDY 7.7

From the information provided in Case Study 7.1, prepare ledger accounts in the general ledger of A & Co.

Solution

A & CO.: GENERAL LEDGER

Capital Account

Dr. | | | | | | | **Cr.**

Date	Particulars	LF	Amount (₹)	Date	Particulars	LF	Amount (₹)
2018				2018			
Jan. 31	To bank a/c		500	Jan. 1	By balance b/d		27,500
Jan. 31	To balance c/d		27,000				
			27,500				27,500
				Feb. 1	By balance b/d		27,000

Cash Account

Dr. | | | | | | | **Cr.**

Date	Particulars	LF	Amount (₹)	Date	Particulars	LF	Amount (₹)
2018				2018			
Jan. 1	To balance b/d		500	Jan. 10	By purchase a/c		1,000
Jan. 3	To sales a/c		500	Jan. 11	By repairs to machinery a/c		200
Jan. 5	To Roy & Co.		1,900	Jan. 13	By freight inward a/c		100
Jan. 8	To sundries a/c		350	Jan. 21	By bank a/c		1,000
Jan. 19	To sales a/c		2,000	Jan. 22	By municipal taxes a/c		100
Jan. 29	To sale of newspapers a/c		50	Jan. 26	By advertisement a/c		500
				Jan. 31	By salaries a/c		500
				Jan. 31	By balance c/d		1,900
			5,300				5,300
Feb. 1	To balance b/d		1,900				

Bank Account

Dr. | | | | | | | **Cr.**

Date	Particulars	LF	Amount (₹)	Date	Particulars	LF	Amount (₹)
2018				2018			
Jan. 1	To balance b/d		8,000	Jan. 6	By Vishwanath & Co. a/c		4,950
Jan. 11	To Sen & Co. a/c		3,000	Jan. 17	By Vishwanath & Co. a/c		2,000
Jan. 14	To Roy & Co.		950	Jan. 18	By Roy & Co. a/c		950
Jan. 21	To cash a/c		1,000	Jan. 31	By rent a/c		500
Jan. 25	To loan from New Age Inv. Co. a/c		20,000	Jan. 31	By capital a/c		500
				Jan. 31	By balance c/d		24,050
			32,950				32,950
Feb. 1	To balance b/d		24,050				

NOTES

Stock of Goods Account

Dr. | | | | | | | Cr.

Date	Particulars	LF	Amount (₹)	Date	Particulars	LF	Amount (₹)
2018				2018			
Jan. 1	To balance b/d		4,000	Jan. 31	By balance c/d		4,000
			4,000				4,000
Feb. 1	To balance b/d		4,000				

Machinery Account

Dr. | | | | | | | Cr.

Date	Particulars	LF	Amount (₹)	Date	Particulars	LF	Amount (₹)
2018				2018			
Jan. 1	To balance b/d		20,000	Jan. 31	By balance c/d		20,000
			20,000				20,000
Feb. 1	To balance b/d		20,000				

Furniture Account

Dr. | | | | | | | Cr.

Date	Particulars	LF	Amount (₹)	Date	Particulars	LF	Amount (₹)
2018				2018			
Jan. 1	To balance b/d		5,000	Jan. 8	By cash a/c		300
				Jan. 31	By balance c/d		4,700
			5,000				5,000
Feb. 1	To balance b/d		4,700				

Roy & Co. Account

Dr. | | | | | | | Cr.

Date	Particulars	LF	Amount (₹)	Date	Particulars	LF	Amount (₹)
2018				2018			
Jan. 1	To balance b/d		2,000	Jan. 5	By cash a/c		1,900
Jan. 4	To sales a/c		1,000	Jan. 5	By discount a/c		100
Jan. 18	To bank a/c		950	Jan. 14	By bank a/c		950
				Jan. 14	By discount a/c		50
				Jan. 31	By balance c/d		950
			3,950				3,950
Feb. 1	To balance b/d		950				

Sen & Co. Account

Dr. | | | | | | | Cr.

Date	Particulars	LF	Amount (₹)	Date	Particulars	LF	Amount (₹)
2018				2018			
Jan. 1	To balance b/d		3,000	Jan. 11	By bank a/c		3,000
			3,000				3,000

Loan from SBI Account

Dr. | | | | | | | Cr.

Date	Particulars	LF	Amount (₹)	Date	Particulars	LF	Amount (₹)
2018				2018			
Jan. 31	To balance c/d		10,000	Jan. 1	By balance b/d		10,000
			10,000				10,000
				Feb. 1	By balance b/d		10,000

Vishwanath & Co. Account

Dr. | Cr.

Date	Particulars	LF	Amount (₹)	Date	Particulars	LF	Amount (₹)
2018				2018			
Jan. 6	To bank a/c		4,950	Jan. 1	By balance b/d		5,000
Jan. 6	To discount a/c		50	Jan. 13	By purchases a/c		2,000
Jan. 17	To bank a/c		2,000				
			7,000				7,000

Purchases Account

Dr. | Cr.

Date	Particulars	LF	Amount (₹)	Date	Particulars	LF	Amount (₹)
2018				2018			
Jan. 2	To Patel & Co. a/c		2,000	Jan. 31	By balance c/d		5,000
Jan. 10	To cash a/c		1,000				
Jan. 11	To Vishwanath & Coa/c		2,000				
Feb. 1	To balance b/d		5,000				5,000

Patel & Co. Account

Dr. | Cr.

Date	Particulars	LF	Amount (₹)	Date	Particulars	LF	Amount (₹)
2018				2018			
Jan. 31	To balance c/d		2,000	Jan. 2	By purchases a/c		2,000
			2,000				2,000
				Feb. 1	By balance b/d		2,000

Sales Account

Dr. | Cr.

Date	Particulars	LF	Amount (₹)	Date	Particulars	LF	Amount (₹)
2018				2018			
Jan. 31	To balance c/d		3,500	Jan. 3	By cash a/c		500
				Jan. 4	By Roy & Co. a/c		1,000
				Jan. 19	By cash a/c		2,000
			3,500				3,500
				Feb. 1	By balance b/d		3,500

Discount Account

Dr. | Cr.

Date	Particulars	LF	Amount (₹)	Date	Particulars	LF	Amount (₹)
2018				2018			
Jan. 5	To Roy & Co.		100	Jan. 6	By Vishwanath & Co. a/c		50
Jan. 14	To Roy & Co.		50	Jan. 31	By balance c/d		100
			150				150
Feb. 1	To balance b/d		100				

Profit on Sale of Furniture Account

Dr. | Cr.

Date	Particulars	LF	Amount (₹)	Date	Particulars	LF	Amount (₹)
2018				2018			
Jan. 31	To balance c/d		50	Jan. 8	By cash a/c		50
			50				50
				Feb. 1	By balance b/d		50

NOTES

Repairs to Machinery Account

Dr. Cr.

Date	Particulars	LF	Amount (₹)	Date	Particulars	LF	Amount (₹)
2018				2018			
Jan. 12	To cash a/c		200	Jan. 31	By balance c/d		200
			200				200
Feb. 1	To balance b/d		200				

Freight Inward Account

Dr. Cr.

Date	Particulars	LF	Amount (₹)	Date	Particulars	LF	Amount (₹)
2018				2018			
Jan. 13	To cash a/c		100	Jan. 31	By balance c/d		100
			100				100
Feb. 1	To balance b/d		100				

Municipal Taxes Account

Dr. Cr.

Date	Particulars	LF	Amount (₹)	Date	Particulars	LF	Amount (₹)
2018				2018			
Jan. 22	To cash a/c		100	Jan. 31	By balance c/d		100
			100				100
Feb. 1	To balance b/d		100				

Loan from New Age Inv. Co. Account

Dr. Cr.

Date	Particulars	LF	Amount (₹)	Date	Particulars	LF	Amount (₹)
2018				2018			
Jan. 31	To balance c/d		20,000	Jan. 25	By bank a/c		20,000
			20,000				20,000
				Feb. 1	By balance b/d		20,000

Advertisement Account

Dr. Cr.

Date	Particulars	LF	Amount (₹)	Date	Particulars	LF	Amount (₹)
2018				2018			
Jan. 26	To cash a/c		500	Jan. 31	By balance c/d		500
			500				500
Feb. 1	To balance b/d		500				

Sale of Newspapers Account

Dr. Cr.

Date	Particulars	LF	Amount (₹)	Date	Particulars	LF	Amount (₹)
2018				2018			
Jan. 31	To balance c/d		50	Jan. 29	By cash a/c		50
			50				50
				Feb. 1	By balance b/d		50

NOTES

Rent Account

Dr.							Cr.
Date	**Particulars**	**LF**	**Amount (₹)**	**Date**	**Particulars**	**LF**	**Amount (₹)**
2018				2018			
Jan. 31	To bank a/c		500	Jan. 31	By balance c/d		500
			500				500
Feb. 1	To balance b/d		500				

Salaries Account

Dr.							Cr.
Date	**Particulars**	**LF**	**Amount (₹)**	**Date**	**Particulars**	**LF**	**Amount (₹)**
2018				2018			
Jan. 31	To cash a/c		500	Jan. 31	By balance c/d		500
			500				500
Feb. 1	To balance b/d		500				

Trial Balance

After balancing the accounts in the general ledger, a statement listing the debit and credit balances in various account heads in the general ledger is prepared. This statement is known as *the trial balance*. The total in the debit column of the trial balance should agree with the total in the credit column. This is because in the double-entry system, for each transaction or event, the total of the amounts debited to various accounts equals the total of amounts credited to various accounts. The trial balance forms the basis of preparing the statement of profit and loss and the balance sheet. The following is the trial balance prepared from the account balances appearing in the solution to Case Study 7.7.

A & Co.: Trial Balance as on 31 Jan 2018

Sl. No.	Particulars	Ledger folio	Dr. Amount (₹)	Cr. Amount (₹)
1	Capital a/c			27,000
2	Cash a/c		1,900	
3	Bank a/c		24,050	
4	Stock of goods a/c		4,000	
5	Machinery a/c		20,000	
6	Furniture a/c		4,700	
7	Roy & Co. a/c		950	
8	Loan from SBI a/c			10,000
9	Patel & Co. a/c			2,000
10	Loan from New Age Inv. Co. a/c			20,000
11	Purchases a/c		5,000	
12	Sales a/c			3,500
13	Discount a/c		100	
14	Profit on sale of furniture a/c			50
15	Repairs to machinery a/c		200	
16	Freight inward a/c		100	
17	Municipal taxes a/c		100	
18	Advertisement a/c		500	
19	Sales of newspapers a/c			50
20	Rent a/c		500	
21	Salaries a/c		500	
			62,600	62,600

Usually, debit balances in the trial balance represent either assets or expenses and credit balances represent equity or liability or income.

Errors not detected by trial balance

Matching of the debit side total with the credit side total of the trial balance is not a conclusive proof of the correctness of books of accounts. The trial balance fails to disclose errors that do not affect the agreement of the trial balance. Following are examples of errors not disclosed by the trial balance:

1. *Errors of omission:* These comprise omission in recording a transaction or other event in books of original entry. If only one aspect of the transaction is recorded, the partial omission throws the trial balance out of agreement.
2. *Errors of commission:* These pertain to incorrect recording of a transaction or other event in books of original entry. For example, a purchase of ₹10,000 is recorded as a purchase of ₹1,00,000. If recording of a transaction is partially incorrect, it throws the trial balance out of agreement.
3. *Clerical errors:* These errors relate to posting of an entry in a wrong account with the correct amount, and the correct side does not throw the trial balance out of agreement. For example, a credit purchase of ₹1,000 from Shyam is credited wrongly to the account of Shyam Lal.
4. *Compensating errors:* A compensating error is one that is counterbalanced by another error or errors of the same amount either in the same account or other accounts. For example, omission of posting an entry of ₹1,500 on the debit side is compensated by underposting of ₹1,500 on the credit side.
5. *Errors of principle:* An error of principle arises by reason of a transaction being recorded in a fundamentally incorrect manner. For example, conversion of a temporary shed into a permanent building is recorded as repair and maintenance of building.

Self-Test Questions

Self-test question 7.3

Prepare a trial balance from the balances in various account extracted from General Ledger as at March 31, 2018:

Particulars	Amount (₹)
Capital	1,24,000
Furniture	20,000
Equipment	40,000
Bank balance	1,00,000
Cash balance	10,000
Trade receivables	50,000
Trade creditors	30,000
Loan outstanding	50,000
Purchase of goods in trade	3,00,000
Sale	4,00,000
Carriage inward	6,000
Carriage outward	8,000
Employee benefits expenses	40,000
Advertisement	5,000
Travelling expenses	6,000
Communication expenses	10,000
Discount received	1,000
Discount allowed	2,000
Repairs and maintenance	3,000
Electricity and power	5,000

NOTES

Key Terms
Balancing ledger accounts

SUMMARY

The general ledger is the principal book of accounts. After recording transactions in journals, the next phase in the accounting process is to post entries in appropriate account heads in the general ledger. Periodically, accounts in the general ledger are balanced. After balancing the accounts in the general ledger, a statement listing the debit and credit balances in various accounts in the general ledger is prepared. This statement is known as the *trial balance*. The total in the debit column of the trial balance should agree with the total in the credit column. This is because, in the double-entry system, for each transaction or event, the total of the amounts debited to various accounts equals the total of amounts credited to various accounts. The trial balance forms the basis of preparing the profit and loss account and the balance sheet.

ANSWERS TO SELF-TEST QUESTIONS

7.1 (i) T; (ii) T; (iii) T

7.2 (i) Debiting, Crediting (ii) Crediting, Debiting; (iii) Crediting, Debiting; (iv) Debiting, Crediting (v) Crediting, Debiting; (vi) Crediting, Debiting; (vii) Debiting, Crditing; (viii) Crediting, Debiting; (ix) Debiting, Crediting; (x) Debiting, Debiting, Crediting

7.3 Trial Balance as at March 31, 2018

Particulars	Dr. Amount (₹)	Cr. Amount (₹)
Capital		1,24,000
Furniture	20,000	
Equipment	40,000	
Bank balance	1,00,000	
Cash balance	10,000	
Trade receivables	50,000	
Trade creditors		30,000
Loan outstanding		50,000
Purchase of goods in trade	3,00,000	
Sale		4,00,000
Carriage inward	6,000	
Carriage outward	8,000	
Employee benefits expenses	40,000	
Advertisement	5,000	
Travelling expenses	6,000	
Communication expenses	10,000	
Discount received		1,000
Discount allowed	2,000	
Repairs and maintenance	3,000	
Electricity and power	5,000	
Total	6,05,000	6,05,000

ASSIGNMENTS

Multiple Choice Questions

1. Tick the correct answer:

(i) A cash book:
 (a) Is a journal.
 (b) Is a ledger account.
 (c) Serves the dual purpose of journal and ledger account.
 (d) None of the above.

(ii) A purchase day book is used:
 (a) To record only credit purchases.
 (b) To record only credit purchases of stock-in-trade and materials being used; in manufacturing activities.
 (c) To record credit as well as cash purchases.
 (d) For none of the above.

(iii) Dishonouring of cheques and other negotiable instruments received are taken in books through:
 (a) Sales day book.
 (b) Journal proper.
 (c) Journal proper or cash book.
 (d) None of the above.

(iv) A government grant received by a company results in:
 (a) Increase in liability.
 (b) Increase in asset.
 (c) Increase in asset and equity.
 (d) None of the above.

(v) Sale of goods, purchased for ₹8,000, on credit for ₹10,000 results in:
 (a) A gain of ₹2,000 and increase in current assets and equity by ₹2,000.
 (b) A gain of ₹2,000 and increase in current assets and liability by ₹2,000.
 (c) An increase in asset and liability by ₹2,000.
 (d) None of the above.

(vi) A trial balance fails to disclose:
 (a) Errors in casting the books of subsidiary records.
 (b) Errors in balancing the account.
 (c) Errors in posting from the book of subsidiary record to the ledger.
 (d) None of the above.

2. State whether the following statements are true (T) or false (F):

(i) A bank account is a real account.
(ii) A prepaid insurance account is a nominal account.
(iii) A cash account is a real account.
(iv) A capital account is a personal account.
(v) An asset account should be credited for increase in its carrying amount.
(vi) Journals record transactions in chronological order while entries in general ledger are analytical.
(vii) Debtors' account can never be credited.
(viii) A trial balance discloses all types of errors.
(ix) A credit purchase of plant should be recorded in the purchase day book.
(x) Purchase of goods (stock-in-trade) is usually recorded as an asset.
(xi) Cash book is both a journal and a ledger.

3. Against each item in the following list, indicate whether it should usually show a debit balance or a credit balance. If it shows a debit balance, indicate by marking 'D' against it and if it shows a credit balance, indicate by marking 'C' against it. Also, classify each item into current asset (CA), non-current asset (NCA), current liability (CL), non-current liability (NCL), valuation allowance (V), income (I), and expense (E).

S. No.	The Accounts Head	S. No.	The Accounts Head
(i)	Share capital	(xxi)	Penalty paid
(ii)	Share premium	(xxii)	Power expenses
(iii)	Land	(xxiii)	Advertisement expenses
(iv)	Salaries and wages	(xxiv)	Depreciation
(v)	Sales	(xxv)	Training expenses
(vi)	Telephone charges	(xxvi)	Research expenses
vvii)	Conveyance	(xxvii)	Goodwill
(viii)	Travelling expenses	(xxviii)	Bad debt
(ix)	Purchases	(xxix)	Accumulated depreciation
(x)	Provident fund contribution	(xxx)	Provision for doubtful debts
(xi)	Prepaid insurance	(xxxi)	Provision for income tax
(xii)	Advances from customers	(xxxii)	Loan from bank
(xiii)	Sales return	(xxxiii)	Interest due but not paid
(xiv)	Purchase return	(xxxiv)	Trade debtors
(xv)	Discount allowed	(xxxv)	Trade creditors
(xvi)	Building	(xxxvi)	Loss by fire
(xvii)	Interest income	(xxxvii)	Investment in a subsidiary company
(xviii)	Royalty received	(xxxviii)	Investment in 180-day treasury bills
(xix)	Land development	(xxxix)	Cash in hand
(xx)	Interest paid	(xL)	Bank overdraft

Analytical Question

1. Do you agree that the concept of subsidiary ledgers has helped in allocation of duties and analysis and scrutiny of accounts in the general ledger? Explain your views on the issue.

Problem

1. The following are the transactions entered into by Mr. A during April 2018:

April 1 Opening balances:
Stock-in-trade: ₹1,000.
Amount due from Alpha & Co.: ₹2,000.
Cash-in-hand: ₹500.
Cash-in at bank: ₹1,000.
Amount due to B & Co.: ₹2,000.
A brought in cash, ₹10,000.
A deposited ₹8,000 in the bank.

2 A purchased goods for ₹2,000 on credit from Y & Co.
A purchased goods for ₹1,000 on credit from B & Co.

3 A purchased furniture for ₹3,000 on credit from R & Co.
A purchased goods for ₹3,000 on credit from C & Co.

4 A sold goods to Alpha & Co. for ₹2,000 on credit.

5 A received a cheque for ₹20,000 from New India Investment Co., towards loan.
A purchased goods for ₹500 in cash.
A paid ₹100 towards conveyance charges.
A purchased electrical fittings for ₹500.

6 A withdrew ₹1,000 from the bank for office use.
A purchased goods for ₹3,000 from M & Co. on credit.

7 A paid ₹500 towards office expenses.

8 A sold goods for ₹3,000 to Gamma & Co. on credit.

9 A paid ₹1,950 by cheque to Y & Co. Y & Co. allowed a discount of ₹50.

10 A paid ₹100 towards cartage inward.
A purchased goods for ₹8,000 from Y & Co. on credit.
A purchased furniture for ₹15,000 from R & Co. on credit.
A paid ₹3,000 to R & Co. by cheque.

April 11 A received a cheque for ₹1,950 from Alpha & Co. He allowed a discount of ₹50.
A sold goods for ₹8,000 to Delta & Co. on credit.
A paid ₹100 towards freight outward.
A paid ₹200 towards conveyance charges.

NOTES

12 A withdrew ₹1,000 from the bank towards personal expenses.
13 A paid ₹200 towards travelling expenses.
A paid ₹1,000 to B & Co. by cheque.
A received a cheque of ₹3,000 from Gamma & Co.
15 The bank informed that the cheque received from Gamma & Co. was returned unpaid by his banker. The banker levied a service charge of ₹20.
16 A received a bank demand draft of ₹2,900 from Gamma & Co. towards full and final settlement of the amount due from them.
A purchased goods for ₹2,000 on credit from B & Co.
17 A received a cheque of ₹7,900 from Delta & Co. A discount of ₹100 was allowed.
18 A sold goods for ₹500 to Mr. Z on cash basis.
A sold goods for ₹2,000 to Delta & Co. on credit.
19 A paid Y & Co. ₹7,900 by cheque. A discount of ₹100 was allowed.
20 A withdrew ₹2,000 for office use.
21 A purchased goods for ₹3,000 from Y & Co. on credit.
22 A paid ₹15,000 to R & Co. by cheque.
23 A paid insurance premium of ₹1,200 by cheque.
24 A paid rent of ₹2,000 by cheque.
25 A sold goods for ₹3,000 to Alpha & Co. on credit.
A sold goods for ₹2,000 to Beta & Co. on credit.
26 A paid ₹200 towards conveyance charges.
27 A sold goods for ₹500 to Mr. Z on cash basis.
28 A purchased goods for ₹1,000 from X & Co. on cash basis.
29 A received ₹2,950 from Alpha & Co. by cheque. A discount of ₹50 was allowed.
31 A paid ₹1,000 in cash towards wages.
A paid ₹1,500 in cash towards salaries.

Required: Record the above transactions appropriately in the cash book (with discount and bank columns), purchase day book, sales day book and journal proper. Also, prepare the trial balance after posting the transactions in the general ledger.

Completion of the Accounting Cycle Preparation of Profit and Loss Account and Balance Sheet

CHAPTER

8

LEARNING OBJECTIVES

The objective of this chapter is to provide an understanding of the mechanics of preparing balance sheet and the statement of profit and loss. After reading this chapter, you will develop understanding of the following:

- Journal entries for rectification of errors
- Use of suspense account
- Adjustment entry for closing stock
- Adjustment entries for accruals
- Adjustments for pre-paid expenses and deferred revenue
- Estimating the provision for doubtful debts and its accounting
- Estimating the provision for discount to be allowed to debtors and its accounting
- Accounting for depreciation
- Method for computing gain or loss on the sale of an item of PP&E after retirement
- Preparation of bank reconciliation statement and its use, and
- Preparation of manufacturing account, trading account and profit and loss account
- Preparation of balance sheet.

INTRODUCTION

The final phase in an accounting cycle is the preparation of the statement of profit and loss and the balance sheet. The statement of profit and loss is prepared by matching *income* and *expenses*, and the balance sheet is prepared by listing out *assets* and *liabilities*. The trial balance provides the raw data that are analysed and adjusted for preparing financial statements. In this chapter, we shall see various types of adjustments that are commonly carried out by business enterprises in preparing financial statements. We shall also study the process of preparing the statement of profit and loss and the balance sheet.

RECTIFICATION OF ERRORS

Errors might creep in while recording transactions and events. Errors may be classified into *errors of principles* and *errors in bookkeeping*. Errors of principles are those errors that arise due to wrong application of accounting principles in recording transactions and events. For example, expenditure that should be capitalised has been recorded as 'repair and maintenance of property, plant and equipment. Examples of bookkeeping errors are omission in recording a transaction, entering a wrong amount in subsidiary books, wrong casting of a ledger and errors of posting.

In bookkeeping, rectification of an error requires making an appropriate entry to neutralise the effect of the error and to restore the correct position.

Suspense Account

Error in only one account head results in disagreement of the trial balance. Let us take the following example:

When adding up the sales daybook, a mistake occurred, resulting in the total being ₹1,000 less than the correct total.

This error resulted in short credit to the sales account, and as a consequence, the credit side total of the trial balance is lower than the debit side total of the trial balance. It is assumed that individual accounts of customers are opened in the general ledger and each transaction is posted to the debit of the personal account of the concerned customer. Therefore, an error in the sales daybook did not result in a mistake in the debit side of the trial balance. Whenever there are such disagreements due to errors in only one account head, the difference in the trial balance is put in the suspense account. In this case, the suspense account will show a credit balance, because the debit side total of the trial balance is higher by ₹1,000 as compared to the credit side total.

The rectification entry should close the suspense account. The entry should be as follows:

Suspense a/c	Dr. ₹1,000	
To sales a/c		Cr. ₹1,000

In practice, the trial balance should agree in spite of the error described earlier, because only the total account (trade debtors' a/c) of customers is opened in the general ledger and debited with reference to the total of the sales daybook. As a result, the trial balance will agree and will not give an error in casting the sales daybook. However, such errors get detected, because the total of the individual account balance amounts in the subsidiary ledger of trade debtors does not agree with the balance in the trade debtor account in the general ledger. The following correction entry should be passed to rectify the error:

Trade debtors a/c	Dr. ₹1,000	
To sales a/c		Cr. ₹1,000

NOTES

ILLUSTRATION 8.1 A sale of goods for ₹6,000 to Ms. Rajani was entered in the purchase daybook.

The error must have resulted in wrong debit to the 'purchase a/c' and wrong credit to the 'trade creditors a/c' by ₹6,000. This is to be neutralised by the following entry:

Trade creditors a/c	Dr. ₹6,000	
To purchase a/c		Cr. ₹6,000

The following correct entry should be incorporated:

Trade debtors a/c	Dr. ₹6,000	
To sales a/c		Cr. ₹6,000

Both the entries should be clubbed and the following entry should be passed:

Trade creditors a/c	Dr. ₹6,000	
Trade debtors a/c	Dr. ₹6,000	
To purchasers a/c		Cr. ₹6,000
To sales a/c		Cr. ₹6,000

Personal accounts in subsidiary ledgers should be corrected.

ILLUSTRATION 8.2 Legal charges of ₹10,000 paid on purchase of building debited to legal expenses a/c.

This is an error of principle—legal charges should have been debited to the building a/c. The credit entry was correct. Therefore, a rectification entry should neutralise the debit to the legal expenses a/c and should incorporate the correct debit to the building a/c. The following rectification entry should be passed:

Building a/c	Dr. ₹10,000	
To legal expenses a/c		Cr. ₹10,000

ILLUSTRATION 8.3 ₹1,000 written off as depreciation on plant and machinery has not been debited to depreciation a/c.

We may assume that the plant and machinery a/c was correctly credited. Therefore, this error must have resulted in disagreement of the debit side total with the credit side total of the trial balance. The total of the debit side is short by ₹1,000. The suspense a/c should show a debit balance of ₹1,000. The following rectification entry should be passed:

Depreciation a/c	Dr. ₹1,000	
To suspense a/c		Cr. ₹1,000

This entry incorporates the correct debit to the depreciation account and closes the suspense a/c.

ILLUSTRATION 8.4 Discount allowed of ₹240 had been posted to the credit of discount received account as ₹420.

This error resulted in short debit of ₹240 and excess credit of ₹420. Thus, the total of the credit side of the trial balance must be in excess of the debit side total by ₹660. The suspense a/c should show a debit balance of ₹660. The following rectification entry should be passed:

Discount received a/c	Dr. ₹420	
Discount allowed a/c	Dr. ₹240	
To suspense a/c		Cr. ₹660

ILLUSTRATION 8.5 The cost of a new van of ₹5,000 had been debited to the purchases a/c.

This error does not result in disagreement between the debit side total and credit side total of the trial balance. The following rectification entry should be passed:

Motor van a/c	Dr. ₹5,000	
To purchases a/c		Cr. ₹5,000

NOTES

Errors Detected in a Subsequent Period

When errors are detected in a subsequent reporting period, cumulative effect of correcting the error should be reflected in the opening balances of the previous year and the statement of the profit and loss and balance sheet of the previous year is restated. A third balance sheet of the previous to the previous year is presented, which shows the corrected figures of assets, equity and liabilities. For example, if error occurred in 2014–15 and is detected in 2017–18, new balance sheet as at March 31, 2016 shall be prepared. The balance sheet will show the corrected figures of assets, equity and liabilities. Statement of profit and loss for the year 2016–17 and balance sheet as at March 31, 2017 should be restated taking the opening balances from the corrected balance sheet as at March 31, 2016.

Key Terms

Suspense account

Self-Test Questions

Self-test question 8.1

Fill in the blanks: [Choose between the word debited and credited and calculate amounts, if required.]

(i) ₹2,000 received from a past customer, whose account was written off as bad debt, was credited to trade creditors account. In order to rectify the error, bad debt recovered a/c should be ....and trade creditors a/c should be ....by ₹...............

(ii) A machine was purchased in exchange of an old machine and paying ₹20,000. The price of the new machine is ₹50,000. The cost of the new machine was recorded at ₹20,000. In order to rectify the error, the Machine a/c should be........................₹ .... and Sale of Machine a/c should be...........................by ₹.....................

(iii) ₹80,000 spent on repair of a machine was added to its cost. In order to rectify the error, the Machine a/c should be........................₹................... and Repair and Maintenance a/c should be ....by ₹..............

(iv) A customer paid ₹18,000 in the full and final settlement of ₹20,000. The customer's a/c was closed by transferring the amount to Discount Received a/c. In order to rectify the error, Discount Allowed a/c should be ....by ₹............... and Discount Received a/c should be ....by ₹...........

SUMMARY

Errors of principles are those, which arise due to wrong application of accounting principles in recording transactions and other events. Examples of bookkeeping errors are: omission in recording a transaction, entering a wrong amount in subsidiary books, wrong casting of a ledger, and errors of posting. In bookkeeping, rectification of an error requires making an appropriate entry to neutralise the effect of the error and to restore the correct position. Error in only one account head results in disagreement of the trial balance. Whenever there are such disagreements, the difference in the trial balance is put in the suspense account. When errors are detected in a subsequent reporting period, opening balances of the previous year is corrected.

ADJUSTMENTS

Introduction

The accrual system of accounting requires adjustments for accrued income and outstanding expenses (accruals). Moreover, preparation of a profit and loss account requires matching of income and expenses. These require adjustments for income received in advance and prepaid expenses. Some more adjustments are required to present a true and fair view of the operating result for the reporting period and the financial position at the end of the reporting period. Adjustment entries are passed through the journal proper and an 'adjusted trial balance' is drawn incorporating the adjustments. The adjusted trial balance forms the basis of preparing financial statements.

Closing Stock Inventories

Purchase of stock-in-trade, raw material and components are recorded as expense under the head purchases (e.g., purchase of stock-in-trade, and purchase of raw materials). Therefore, assessment of the value of stock-in-hand at the end of the reporting period and recognition of the same as an asset in the balance sheet is necessary to match the cost of goods sold and the revenue for the reporting period.

Usually, closing stock of inventory is recorded in the books of accounts through the following entry:

Stock a/c	Dr. ₹50,000	
To profit and loss a/c		Cr. ₹50,000

This entry is a part of the closing entries required to close the income and expenses accounts in the general ledger, and for constructing the statement of profit and loss. We shall study closing entries in a subsequent section.

The 'closing stock account' appears in the general ledger through the closing entry, and therefore, does not find a place in the trial balance which lists out account balance in the general ledger before posting of closing entries. The closing stock is an asset, and appears as such in the balance sheet. The closing stock balance is carried forward to the next reporting period as 'opening stock'. Transactions and events during the reporting period leave the balance in this account untouched, so it appears in the trial balance prepared at the end of the reporting period. Opening stock is added to purchases for determining the cost of goods that were available for sale, or the cost of materials that were available for consumption. Therefore, opening stock is treated as a 'nominal account' while preparing the profit and loss account.

In the traditional two-sided form ('T' form) of a profit and loss account, the opening and closing stock appears as follows:

Statement of Profit and Loss of...
For the Period Ending ...(incomplete)

Expenses	Amount (₹)	Income	Amount (₹)
To purchases	70,000	By sales	1,00,000
To opening stock	20,000	By closing stock	30,000

In the vertical form of the statement of profit and loss, the opening and closing stocks appear as follows:

Sales		₹1,00,000
Cost of goods sold:		
Purchases	₹70,000	
Opening stock	₹20,000	
	₹90,000	
Closing stock	(₹30,000)	₹60,000

Although it is not the normal practice, it is possible to pass the following entry before preparing the trial balance:

Closing stock a/c	Dr. ₹50,000	
To purchase a/c		Cr. ₹50,000

The result of this entry is to reduce the purchase account and to take on record the amount of closing stock. In case this entry is passed, the trial balance will show both opening stock and closing stock. The purchase account in the trial balance will show purchases adjusted for closing stock. Therefore, no adjustment will be required for closing stock in the statement of profit and loss. Moreover, closing entries will not include an entry for closing stock. The closing stock in the trial balance will find a place in the balance sheet and it will not appear in the profit and loss account.

Accruals

Accrual represents liabilities for which the amount is not certain, for example, services received but not invoiced by the supplier. In this situation, the reporting entity estimates the liability and passes the following adjustment entry:

Appropriate expense a/c	Dr. ₹1,00,000	
To outstanding liabilities a/c		Cr. ₹1,00,000

The term *accrued* also signifies that an expense has been incurred or income has been earned, but the due date for payment or receipt of the same falls in the next reporting period. Adjustments are to be made for accrued expenses and accrued income. The following adjustment entries are required to bring these expenses and income in the books of accounts:

Appropriate expense a/c	Dr. ₹50,000	
To expenses accrued a/c		Cr. ₹50,000
Income accrued a/c	Dr. ₹70,000	
To appropriate income a/c		Cr. ₹70,000

Examples of accrued expenses are rent, interest, rates and taxes and wages outstanding at the end of the reporting period. Examples of accrued income are interest on securities, professional fees and rents earned but not received until the end of the reporting period. Expenses accrued is presented as a liability and income accrued is presented as an asset in the balance sheet.

These adjustment entries are reversed at the commencement of the next reporting period. The following are the reversal entries

Expenses accrued a/c	Dr. ₹50,000	
To appropriate expense a/c		Cr. ₹50,000
Appropriate income a/c	Dr. ₹70,000	
To income accrued a/c		Cr. ₹70,000

Reversal entries close the expenses accrued account (appearing as a liability in the balance sheet of the previous period) and income accrued account (appearing as an asset in the balance sheet of the previous period). These reversal entries also result in recognition of expenditure and income carried forward from the previous period.

The expense (say wages account) will have the following entries:

Wages Account

Expenses	Amount (₹)	Income	Amount (₹)
To cash (actual amount paid)	90,00,000	By wages accrued a/c (reversal entry)	80,000
To wages accrued a/c	1,00,000	By balance c/d (expense for the year)	90,20,000
	91,00,000		91,00,000

The same result is obtained as follows:

Cash paid towards wages during the current period	₹90,00,000
Wages accrued during the current period	1,00,000
	₹91,00,000
Included in the previous period's expense as accrual	80,000
Expense to be recognised in the statement of profit and loss for the current period	₹90,20,000

NOTES

Prepaid Expenses and Deferred Revenue

Sometimes expenditure is incurred to receive services over a period that falls in more than one reporting period. The amount, which is allocated to services to be received in the next or subsequent reporting periods is termed as *prepaid expenses*. An example of prepaid expenses is insurance premium. The following adjustment entry is passed to record the prepaid amount:

Prepaid expenses a/c	Dr. ₹80,000	
To appropriate expense a/c		Cr. ₹80,000

The result of this entry is to recognise an asset in the form of a prepaid expense and to reduce the expenditure account by the amount allocated to a subsequent reporting period. The balance in the expenditure account represents expense for the current reporting period.

Sometimes income is received in advance. For example, subscription is received to cover a period that spills over to the next reporting period. The following accounting entry is passed for the amount of income received in advance:

Appropriate income a/c	Dr. ₹60,000	
To Deferred revenue a/c		Cr. ₹60,000

The result of this entry is to recognise a liability in the form of 'deferred revenue' and to reduce the income by the amount allocated to the next reporting period. The reduced balance in the income account represents the amount that pertains to the current reporting period.

These adjustment entries are reversed at the commencement of the next reporting period. Reversal entries close the prepaid expenses a/c and deferred revenue a/c. These entries also result in recognition of expenditure and income carried forward from the previous period.

Expenses on Materials other than Stock-in-Trade

Materials purchased for expenses such as stationery, advertisement materials and manufacturing stores are debited directly to respective expense accounts. Therefore, at the end of the reporting period, the following adjustment entry is required to bring the stock of materials in hand in the books:

Stock of materials a/c	Dr. ₹10,000	
To appropriate expense a/c		Cr. ₹10,000

The stock of materials is an asset recognised in the balance sheet. The entry is reversed at the commencement of the next reporting period. A reversal entry closes the stock of material a/c and results in recognition of expenditure carried forward from the previous period.

Self-Test Questions

Self-test question 8.2

Fill-in the blanks:

(i) In practice, the value of goods-in-trade lying in the stock at the end of the accounting period (called closing stock)......................................in the Trial Balance. [Choose between, 'appear' and 'does not appear'.]

(ii) In practice, the value of goods-in-trade lying in the stock at the beginning of the accounting period (called opening stock)......................................in the Trial Balance. [Choose between, 'appear' and 'does not appear'.]

(iii) The pre-paid insurance amount in the Trial Balance as at March 31, 2018 is ₹30,000. The Trial Balance also shows insurance expense at ₹2,40,000. The entity pays Insurance premium for the insurance policy that covers one year on July 1 every year. The balance sheet as at March 31 will show pre-paid insurance at ₹.................... and the statement of profit and loss will show insurance premium at ₹........................ .

(iv) In practice, the term outstanding liability is used to refer to............................... .

(v) The balance sheet as at April 1, 2017 shows deferred revenue at ₹10 lakhs. The entity estimated that in the balance sheet, as at March 31, 2018 deferred revenue should be recognised at ₹15 lakhs. The Trial balance as at March 31, 2018 shows revenue at ₹50 crores. 'Deferred revenue' is not appearing as an item in the Trial Balance. Revenue should be recognised in the statement of profit and loss for 2017–18 at ₹........................ .

SUMMARY

The management based on physical counting estimates the value of the closing stock at the balance sheet date, and an adjustment entry is passed to record the closing stock in the balance sheet as an asset. The closing stock in the balance sheet of the previous period appears as opening stock in the trial balance of the current period. In preparing financial statements for the current period, the opening stock in the trial balance is treated as a nominal account. *Accrual* represents liabilities for which the amount is not certain. The management estimates the amount of liability records the same in the books by passing an adjustment entry. The term 'accrued' also signifies that an expense has been incurred or income has been earned, but the due date for payment or receipt of the same falls in the next reporting period. Adjustments are made for accrued expenses and accrued income. *These adjustment entries are reversed at the commencement of the next reporting period.* A prepaid expense is recorded in the books as an asset through an adjustment entry. Similarly, deferred revenue is recorded in the books as a liability through an adjustment entry. *These adjustment entries are reversed at the commencement of the next reporting period.* Materials purchased for expenses, such as stationery, advertisement materials and manufacturing stores are debited directly to respective expense accounts. Therefore, at the end of the reporting period, the adjustment entries are passed to bring the stock of materials in hand in the books.

PROVISIONS FOR DOUBTFUL DEBTS AND DISCOUNT

Provision (Valuation Allowance) for Doubtful Debts

Enterprises often fail to recover a part of the amount due from their customers. Certain events, such as bankruptcy of a customer, confirm the non-recoverability of the amount due from a particular customer. The enterprise passes the following entry to recognise the loss:

Bad debt a/c	Dr. ₹50,000	
To trade debtors a/c		Cr. ₹50,000

This journal entry records the bad debt in the general ledger and simultaneously reduces the balance in the 'trade debtors' account' in the general ledger. An appropriate entry is incorporated in the subsidiary ledger of debtors against the particular customer's account to reduce the balance due from him. Bad debt is an expense, and it appears in the trial balance. It is taken to the statement of profit and loss directly from the trial balance.

Entities usually recognise a provision (also called valuation allowance) for doubtful debts. 'Provision for doubtful debts' is not a liability. It is a reduction of trade receivables. It is presented as a deduction from 'trade debtors' in the balance sheet. An entity tests trade receivables for impairment based on relevant, reasonable and supportable information about future expectations. For example, the trial balance of A & Co. as on March 31, 2018 shows ₹1,00,000 as trade debtors. A & Co. decides to provide 10 percent towards doubtful debts. The provision required is 10 percent of ₹1,00,000, that is, ₹10,000. The trial balance shows no provision against doubtful debts. The provision will be recognised through the following closing entry:

Profit and loss a/c	Dr. ₹10,000	
To provision for doubtful debts a/c		Cr. ₹10,000

NOTES

The provision is presented in the balance sheet as follows:

Balance Sheet of A & Co. as on March 31, 2018 (incomplete)

Liabilities	(₹)	Assets		(₹)
		Trade debtors	1,00,000	
		Provision for doubtful debts	(10,000)	90,000

The provision for doubtful debts cannot be used for any purpose other than reducing trade debtors for doubtful debts. Let us assume that there is an opening balance of ₹10,000 in the 'provision for doubtful debts a/c'. During the current reporting period, A & Co. has identified a bad debt of ₹4,000. The following entry should be passed to recognise the bad debt:

Provision for doubtful debt a/c	Dr. ₹4,000	
To trade debtors a/c		Cr. ₹4,000

This entry reduces trade debtors by ₹4,000, and simultaneously reduces the provision for doubtful debts by the same amount. Assume that at the end of the period, the trial balance shows ₹2,00,000 against trade debtors. A & Co. decides to provide for doubtful debts at the rate of 10 percent of trade debtors. Thus, the provision required is 10 percent of ₹2,00,000, that is, ₹20,000. The new provision required is calculated as follows:

Provision required	₹20,000
Existing provision	(₹6,000)
New provision required	₹14,000

The following closing entry should be passed to increase the balance in the provision for the doubtful debts a/c to ₹20,000:

Profit and loss a/c	Dr. ₹14,000	
To provision for doubtful debts a/c		Cr. ₹14,000

This entry also results in reduction of profit for the reporting period by ₹14,000. The provision of ₹20,000 is shown as a deduction from trade debtors in the balance sheet. If the opening balance in the 'provision for doubtful debt a/c' after adjustment for bad debts is in excess of the required provision, the excess should be credited to the profit and loss account.

Provision (Valuation Allowance) for Discounts

Sometimes entities create a provision for estimated amount of cash discounts to be offered to trade debtors. The objective is to charge the current reporting period with the estimated cash discounts to be allowed to trade debtors on sales during the current period and to reduce the carrying amount of trade debtors in the balance sheet. Provision for discounts is calculated with reference to good debtors, that is, the amount of trade debtors adjusted for provision for doubtful debts. For example, the trial balance of A & Co. as at March 31, 2018 shows an amount of ₹1,00,000 against trade debtors. The enterprise decides to provide for doubtful debts at the rate of 10 percent of trade debtors, and for discount at the rate of 2 percent of trade debtors. The provision required should be calculated as follows:

Provision for doubtful debts	10 percent of ₹1,00,000 = ₹10,000
Provision for discount	2 percent of (₹1,00,000 – ₹10,000) = ₹1,800

Trade debtors should be presented in the balance sheet as follows:

Balance Sheet of A & Co. as at March 31, 2018 (incomplete)

Liabilities	(₹)	Assets		(₹)
		Trade debtors	1,00,000	
		Provision for doubtful debts	(10,000)	
			90,000	
		Provision for discounts	(1,800)	88,200

Self-Test Questions

Self-test question 8.3

Indicate whether the following statements are true (T) or false (F):

(i) Provision for doubtful debts is a valuation allowance and not a liability.

(ii) Provision for doubtful debts measure impairment based on future expectations.

(iii) The Trial Balance shows Debtors at ₹10,00,000. The entity decides to create bad debt provision at 5 percent and a provision for discount at 2 percent. Assuming that there were no opening balances in these two accounts, the balance sheet will show Provision for doubtful debts at ₹50,000 and Provision for discount at ₹20,000.

(iv) Excess provision written back in the current year is recognised as income for the current period.

(v) Recognition of bad debt reduces the amount of trade receivables in the ledger, but recognition of provision for doubtful debts does not result in the same.

Key Terms

Provision for discount, provision for doubtful debts, valuation allowance

SUMMARY

The loss arising from non-recovery of amount due from customers is recorded as *bad debt*. Recording of "bad debt" reduces the balance in the 'trade debtors' account. Bad debt is an expense, and it appears in the trial balance. It is taken to the statement of profit and loss directly from the trial balance. Entities usually recognise a provision for doubtful debts. "Provision for doubtful debts" is not a liability. It is a reduction of trade receivables. If a provision for doubtful debts exists, the amount of bad debt is adjusted against the provision. If the opening balance in the 'provision for doubtful debt a/c' after adjustment for bad debts is in excess of the required provision, the excess should be credited to the profit and loss account. Sometimes, entities create a provision for estimated amount of cash discount to be offered to trade debtors. Provision for discount is calculated with reference to good debtors, that is, the amount of trade debtors adjusted for provision for doubtful debts.

PROVISION FOR DEPRECIATION (AMORTISATION)

The provision for depreciation (amortisation, in case of intangible assets) represents the reduction in the carrying amount of a depreciable asset.

The balance sheet should show the gross block (acquisition cost) of the asset and accumulated depreciation (at the balance sheet date) separately. Therefore, provision for depreciation is made by the following adjustment entry:

Depreciation a/c	Dr. ₹1,00,000	
To provision for depreciation a/c		Cr. ₹1,00,000

The 'provision for depreciation' is presented in the balance sheet as a deduction from the gross amount of the asset, and the balance in the depreciation account is transferred to the statement of profit and loss. The balance in the provision for depreciation account represents accumulated depreciation on assets being held by the enterprise.

ILLUSTRATION 8.6

The trial balance of A & Co. as at March 31, 2018 shows the following balance amounts:

Plant and machinery	₹1,00,000	(Debit balance)
Building	₹50,000	(Debit balance)
Provision for depreciation:		
Plant and machinery	₹10,000	(Credit balance)
Building	₹2,500	(Credit balance)

NOTES

A & Co. provides for depreciation at the rates of 10 percent of original cost on plant and machinery and 5 percent on building. A & Co. should pass the following closing entry:

	Dr.	Cr.
Profit and loss a/c (depreciation)	Dr. ₹12,500	
To provision for depreciation on plant and machinery a/c		Cr. ₹10,000
To provision for depreciation on building a/c		Cr. ₹2,500

The provision for depreciation should appear on the balance sheet as follows:

Balance Sheet of A & Co. as at March 31, 2018 (incomplete)

Liabilities	Amount	(₹)	Assets	Amount	(₹)
			Plant and machinery	1,00,000	
			Accumulated depreciation	(20,000)	80,000
			Building	50,000	
			Accumulated depreciation	(5,000)	45,000

It is possible to pass the following entry before extracting the adjusted trial balance:

	Dr.	Cr.
Depreciation on plant and machinery a/c	Dr. ₹10,000	
Depreciation on building	Dr. ₹2,500	
To provision for depreciation on plant and machinery a/c		Cr. ₹10,000
To provision for depreciation on building a/c		Cr. ₹2,500

The trial balance will show depreciation for the current reporting period, and also provision for depreciation including depreciation for the current reporting period. The balance in the depreciation a/c, which represents the depreciable amount allocated to the current period, is transferred to the statement of profit and loss through a closing entry. The balance in the provision for depreciation a/c, which represents depreciation accumulated at the end of the current period is presented in the balance sheet as a deduction from the gross block of the asset.

Retirement or Disposal of a Depreciable Asset

On sale or disposal of an item of a depreciable asset, the carrying amount of the asset is withdrawn from the asset account. Similarly, accumulated depreciation on the item sold or disposed of is withdrawn from the provision for depreciation account. The PP&E account and the provision for depreciation account, after these adjustments, will show the cost of assets the entity is holding, and the provision for depreciation account will show the amount of accumulated depreciation on those assets.

On disposal of a depreciable asset, the difference between the net disposal proceeds and the carrying amount (net book value) of the asset represents profit (loss) on disposal. The profit (loss) on disposal should be credited (debited) to the statement of profit and loss as other income (loss). On disposal of a previously revalued item of an item of PP&E, the loss, if related to an increase which was previously recognised in equity as revaluation reserve, may be charged directly to the revaluation reserve, to the extent that the same has not been subsequently reversed or utilised.

ILLUSTRATION 8.7

The following are the details of a machine disposed of on June 30, 2017:

Gross book value	₹1,00,000
Accumulated depreciation	₹60,000
Disposal proceeds	₹45,000

The profit on disposal is the difference between the disposal proceeds and the carrying amount (gross book value – accumulated depreciation). Therefore, in this case, profit on disposal is (₹45,000 – ₹40,000), that is, ₹5,000. The profit is to be credited to the statement of profit and loss as 'other income'.

Accounting Entries to Record the Transaction

Date	Particulars	Dr.	Cr.
June 30, 2017	Cash a/c To sale of machinery a/c (being the amount realised on disposal of machine no. ...)	Dr. ₹45,000	Cr. ₹45,000
June 30, 2017	Sale of machinery a/c To machinery a/c (being cost of the machine no. ... transferred to sale of machinery a/c)	Dr. ₹1,00,000	Cr. ₹1,00,000
June 30, 2017	Provision for depreciation a/c To sale of machinery a/c (being the accumulated depreciation on machine no. ... transferred to the sale of machinery a/c)	Dr. ₹60,000	Cr. ₹60,000
June 30, 2017	Sale of machinery a/c To profit on sale of machinery a/c (being profit on sale of machine no. ...)	Dr. ₹5,000	Cr. ₹5,000
March 31, 2018	Profit on sale of machinery a/c To profit and loss a/c (being profit on sale of machinery transferred to profit and loss account)	Dr. ₹5,000	Cr. ₹5,000

Notes:

1. It is assumed that the reporting period closes on March 31, 2018.
2. To keep computation simple, depreciation is not charged for the year 2017–18.

ILLUSTRATION 8.8

The following are the details of a machine disposed of on December 31, 2017:

Date of purchase	January 1, 2012
Useful life expected at the time of acquisition	10 years
Cost of acquisition	₹1,00,000
Method of depreciation	Straight-line method
Date of revaluation	December 31, 2016
New carrying amount on revaluation	₹90,000
Disposal proceeds	₹55,000

Carrying amount as on December 31, 2016 after charging depreciation for the year 2016:

$$₹1,00,000 - ₹10,000 \times 5 = ₹50,000$$

$$\text{Revaluation gain} = ₹90,000 - ₹50,000 = ₹40,000$$

The balance in revaluation reserve at the date of disposal is ₹40,000.
The carrying amount of the asset as at the date of disposal:

$$₹90,000 - \text{Depreciation for 2017} = ₹90,000 - (₹90,000/5) = ₹72,000$$

Loss on disposal:

$$₹72,000 - ₹55,000 = ₹17,000$$

The loss of ₹17,000 should be recognised against the balance in the revaluation reserve accumulated in the balance sheet. The remaining balance in the revaluation reserve (₹23,000) should be transferred from revaluation reserve to general reserve.

NOTES

Self-Test Questions

Self-test question 8.4

Indicate whether the following statements are true (T) or false (F):

(i) Provision for depreciation is a valuation allowance.

(ii) Balance sheet presents gross block of PP&E held by the entity at the balance sheet date and accumulated depreciation on those assets separately.

(iii) The loss on sale of a discarded machine acquisition cost of which is ₹1,00,000, at ₹30,000 is ₹70,000.

(iv) If, revaluation reserve pertaining to an item of PP&E machine exceeds the loss on the sale of the machine, the loss is not recognised in the statement of profit and loss.

(v) Gain or loss on the sale of an item of PP&E, which is revalued, is measured at the difference between the sale proceeds and the carrying amount, which is the difference between the fair value at the revaluation date and depreciation accumulated subsequent to revaluation.

SUMMARY

The provision for depreciation represents the amount of depreciation accumulated up to the balance sheet date. It is presented in the balance sheet as a deduction from the acquisition cost (gross block) of the asset. Depreciation for the current period is an expense and is so recognised in the statement of profit and loss for the current period. On sale or disposal of an item of a depreciable asset, the cost of the asset is withdrawn from the asset account. Similarly, accumulated depreciation on the item sold or disposed of is withdrawn from the provision for depreciation account. The PP&E account and the provision for depreciation account, after these adjustments, show the cost of assets the entity is holding, and the amount of accumulated depreciation on those assets, respectively. On disposal of a depreciable asset, the difference between the net disposal proceeds and the carrying amount (net book value) of the asset represents profit (loss) on disposal. The profit (loss) on disposal is presented in the statement of profit and loss as other income (loss). On disposal of a previously revalued item of PP&E, the loss, if related to an increase which was previously recognised in equity as revaluation reserve, may be charged directly to the revaluation reserve, to the extent that the same has not been subsequently reversed or utilised.

BANK RECONCILIATION STATEMENT

Introduction

A bank statement provides a mirror image of the bank account being maintained in the general ledger or cash book. A debit entry in the bank account (e.g., for cheque deposited) is reflected by the bank by a credit entry in the constituent's account being maintained in its account books. A bank statement is a copy of the constituent's account in the bank book and provides a mirror image of the bank account being maintained in the general ledger or cash book. Therefore, ideally a debit balance in the bank account should agree with the credit balance in the bank statement and vice versa.

However, in practice, rarely do these two balance amounts agree. Therefore, periodical reconciliation between them is important. The statement, which explains the differences between these two balances, is known as the *bank reconciliation statement*.

Reasons for Differences

Differences may arise on account of the following:

1. Cheques issued by the entity but not yet presented to the bank for payment.
2. Cheques deposited with the bank but not yet collected.

3. Interest allowed by the bank but not yet recorded in the books of the entity.
4. Interest and expenses charged by the bank but not yet recorded in the books of the entity.
5. Interests and dividend collected by the bank as per standing instruction of the entity but not yet recorded in the books of the entity.
6. Direct payments by the bank as per the standing instructions of the entity but not yet recorded in the books of the entity.
7. Direct payments received by the bank, for example, from a customer of the enterprise, not recorded in the books of the entity.
8. Dishonouring of a bill discounted with the bank, not yet recorded in the books of the entity.
9. Bills collected by the bank, not yet recorded in the books of the entity.
10. An error committed by the bank.
11. An error in writing the cash book.

Items (1), (2) and (10) do not require any adjustment in the bank account being maintained by the enterprise. The bank credits the constituent's account only when the cheque deposited is collected, and it debits the constituent's account only when payment is made against the cheque issued by the constituent on presentation by the holder of the cheque or in case of an account payee cheque, by the party in whose favour the cheque is issued. Therefore, the difference that arises due to reasons at items (1) and (2) above is only temporary. An error committed by the bank has to be corrected by the bank in its books of account, so no correction is required in the books of the enterprise. However, differences due to reasons at items (3) to (9) above require incorporation of various transactions in the books of the entity. Similarly, error in the cash book should also be corrected.

The final bank reconciliation statement, prepared after incorporating all transactions and correcting errors in the cash book, should exhibit only items (1), (2) and (10).

Advantages

The chief advantages of preparing a bank reconciliation statement at short intervals, say fortnightly, are as follows:

1. It brings out any error in the bank's records or in the cash book.
2. It brings out any undue delay in collection of cheques and other instruments deposited with the bank.
3. It is a control against embezzlement.
4. It summarises information that is available from the bank statement only.

Presentation

Illustrations 8.9 and 8.10 explain the presentation of information in a bank reconciliation statement:

ILLUSTRATION 8.9

On December 31, 2017, the bank column of the cash book of A & Co. shows a debit balance of ₹5,000, while the bank statement shows a credit balance of ₹4,850. On examination of the cash book and bank statement, it was found that

(a) a cheque of ₹2,000 deposited with the bank on December 1, 2017 was yet to be collected on that date.
(b) cheques amounting to ₹3,000 issued and recorded in the cash book are yet to be presented to the bank for payment.
(c) a cheque for ₹500 had been dishonoured prior to December 31, 2017, but not recorded in the cash book.

NOTES

(d) a dividend of ₹200 collected by the bank directly has not been recorded in the cash book.
(e) bank charges of ₹50 have not been recorded in the cash book.
(f) a cheque of ₹800 drawn by A & Co. Limited had been wrongly debited by bank in A & Co.'s account.

Required

(i) To prepare a bank reconciliation statement.
(ii) To make appropriate adjustments in the cash book.
(iii) To prepare a bank reconciliation statement after adjustments at (ii) above

Solution

(i)

A & Co.: Bank Reconciliation Statement as on December 31, 2017

Balance as per cash book			₹5,000
Add:	Cheques issued not yet presented	₹3,000	
	Dividend collected not yet recorded in the cash book	200	3,200
			8,200
Less:	Cheques deposited not yet collected	₹2,000	
	Cheque dishonoured not yet recorded in the cash book	500	
	Bank charges not yet recorded in the cash book	50	
	Cheque wrongly debited by bank	800	₹3,350
Balance as per bank statement			₹4,850

(ii)

A & Co.: Cash Book, Bank Column (incomplete)

Dr. Date	Receipts Particulars	LF	Amount (₹)	Date	Payments Particulars	LF	Cr. Amount (₹)
2017				2017			
Dec. 31	To balance b/d		5,000	Dec. 31	By trade debtors (cheque dishonoured)		500
	To dividend received a/c		200		By bank charges		50
					By balance c/d		4,650
			5,200				5,200
2018							
Jan. 1	To balance b/d		4,650				

(iii)

A & Co.: Bank Reconciliation Statement as on December 31, 2017

Balance as per cash book			₹4,650
Add:	Cheques issued not yet presented		3,000
			7,650
Less:	Cheques deposited not yet collected	₹2,000	
	Cheque wrongly debited by bank	800	2,800
Balance as per bank statement			₹4,850

ILLUSTRATION 8.10

According to the bank column of the cash book of B & Co., there was a bank balance of ₹3,000 overdrawn as on December 31, 2017. On investigation, it is found that:

(a) a cheque for ₹3,000 was deposited with the bank but not yet collected.
(b) a cheque for ₹5,000 was issued but not yet presented.
(c) a dividend of ₹700 directly collected by the bank has not been recorded in the cash book.
(d) bank charges of ₹500 have not been recorded in the cash book.
(e) a cheque of ₹1,000 had been dishonoured by the bank, but no entry has been made in the cash book.

NOTES

Key Terms
Bank reconciliation statement

Required

(i) To prepare a bank reconciliation statement.
(ii) To make appropriate adjustments in the cash book.
(iii) To prepare a bank reconciliation statement after adjustments at (ii) above.

Solution

(i)

B & Co.: Bank Reconciliation Statement as on December 31, 2017

Balance as per cash book (overdrawn)			₹3,000
Add:	Cheques deposited but not collected	₹3,000	
	Bank charges not yet recorded in the cash book	500	
Cheque dishonoured not yet recorded in the cash book		1,000	4,500
			7,500
Less:	Cheques issued but not yet presented	₹5,000	
	Dividend directly collected by bank	700	5,700
Balance as per bank statement (overdrawn)			1,800

(ii)

A & Co.: Cash Book, Bank Column (incomplete)

Dr. Date	Receipts Particulars	LF	Amount (₹)	Date	Payments Particulars	LF	Cr. Amount (₹)
2017				2017			
31 Dec.	To dividend received a/c		700	31 Dec.	By balance b/d		3,000
	To balance c/d		3,800		By trade debtors (cheque dishonoured)		1,000
					By bank charges		500
			4,500				4,500
					By balance c/d		3,800

(iii)

B & Co.: Bank Reconciliation Statement as on December 31, 2017

Balance as per cash book (overdrawn)		₹3,800
Add:	Cheques deposited but not yet collected	3,000
		6,800
Less:	Cheques issued but not yet presented	5,000
	Balance as per bank statement (overdrawn)	₹1,800

Self-Test Questions

Self-test question 8.5

Indicate whether the following statements are true (T) or false (F):

(i) Internal control system requires preparation of bank reconciliation statement, at least monthly, as a safeguard against embezzlement.
(ii) Bank reconciliation statement reflects wrong debits and credits by the bank.
(iii) Bank reconciliation statement provides information that is important to correctly measure assets, equity, liabilities, incomes and expenses.
(iv) Bank reconciliation statement, which includes items other than cheques issued and not presented and cheques deposited and not collected, reflects poor bookkeeping.

NOTES

SUMMARY

Entities periodically reconcile the balance as per the bank statement and the balance as per the cash book. The statement which explains the differences between these two balances is known as the bank reconciliation statement. Final bank reconciliation statement prepared after correcting errors and omissions in recording transactions shows the following three items: (i) cheques issued by the enterprise but not yet presented to the bank for payment, (ii) cheques deposited with the bank but not yet collected, and (iii) errors committed by the bank. The chief advantage of preparing a bank reconciliation statement at short intervals, say fortnightly, is that it is a control against embezzlement.

PREPARATION OF BALANCE SHEET AND STATEMENT OF PROFIT AND LOSS

Published statement of profit and loss does not present manufacturing account, trading account and profit and loss account separately. However, for our understanding, we shall discuss those separately. The manufacturing account shows the cost of goods manufactured and the trading account shows the gross profit earned during the reporting period. The profit and loss account shows the net profit/loss for the period.

Expenses recognised in the manufacturing account are the cost of raw materials and components consumed, manufacturing wages and other manufacturing expenses, including depreciation on factory assets. Expenses recognised in the trading account are opening stock of finished goods, cost of goods manufactured, purchases of finished goods and all other expenses attributable to bringing the finished goods to the condition and location of sale. Incomes recognised in the trading account is sales of goods. Closing stock is presented on the income side of the trading account, as purchase is recognised as an expense, without adjustment for the closing stock. The profit and loss account is credited with the gross profit, other operating income and extraordinary income. It is debited with operating expenses, financing charges, tax expenses and losses incurred during the reporting period.

The following case studies explain the technique of preparing the profit and loss account from the trial balance and other relevant information.

For easier understanding, we have used T format (also called horizontal format) for presenting manufacturing, trading and profit and loss account, and balance sheet. We must remember that the formats provided in Schedule III of the Companies Act, 2013 are vertical formats.

CASE STUDY 8.1

From the following trial balance prepare: (a) Manufacturing Account; (b) Trading and Profit and Loss Account; and (c) Balance Sheet.

Trial Balance as at March 31, 2016

Particulars	(₹)	(₹)
Wages	20,000	
Opening stock—Raw materials	5,710	
Purchases	88,274	
Carriage inward	3,686	
Repairs	6,000	
Salaries—factory	2,100	
Salaries—general	1,000	
Rates and taxes	2,240	
Travelling expenses	3,550	
Insurance—factory	700	

Particulars	(₹)	(₹)
Insurance—general	80	
Bad debts	410	
General expenses	2,942	
Carriage outward	9,424	
Other assets	1,13,884	
Drawings	1,000	
Opening stock—Finished goods	56,000	
Opening stock—work-in-progress	1,000	
Sales		1,74,000
Opening Profit and Loss Account Balance		12,000
Capital		1,31,000
Sale of scrap		1,000
	3,18,000	3,18,000

Closing stocks: Raw materials: ₹5,272; Finished goods: ₹34,324; Work-in-progress: ₹10,000

Solution

Manufacturing Account for the year ended March 31, 2016

Debit		(₹)	Credit	(₹)
To Raw materials consumed:			By sale of scrap	1,000
Op. stock	5,710		By Closing WIP	10,000
Add: Purchases	88,274		By Trading A/C	
			(Cost of goods manufactured t/f)	1,11,198
Less: Cl. Stock	5,272	88,712		
To Op. WIP		1,000		
To Wages		20,000		
To Carriage inward		3,686		
To Repairs		6,000		
To Salaries—factory		2,100		
To Insurance—factory		700		
		1,22,198		1,22,198

Trading and Profit and Loss Account for the year ended March 31, 2016

Debit	(₹)	Credit	(₹)
To Op. Stock of finished goods	56,000	By Sales	1,74,000
To Manufacturing a/c			
(Cost of goods manufactured)	1,11,198	By Cl. Stock of finished goods	34,324
To Gross profit c/d	41,126		
	2,08,324		2,08,324
To Salaries—general	1,000	By Gross profit b/d	41,126
To Rent and taxes	2,240		
To Travelling expenses	3,550		
To Insurance—general	80		
To Bad debts	410		
To General expenses	2,942		
To Carriage outward	9,424		
To Net profit transferred to			
Capital a/c	21,480		
	41,126		41,126

Balance sheet as at March 31, 2016

Particulars	(₹)	(₹)
EQUITY AND LIABILITIES		
Equity		
Capital Account:		
Opening balance	1,31,000	
Less: Drawings	1,000	1,30,000
Profit and Loss Account		
Opening balance	12,000	
Add: Current year's profit	21,480	33,480
Non-current liabilities		Nil
Current liabilities		Nil
Total		1,63,480
ASSETS		
Non-Current Assets		
Other assets		1,13,884
Current assets		
Closing stock		
Raw materials	5,272	
Work-in-progress	10,000	
Finished goods	34,324	49,596
Total		1,63,480

CASE STUDY 8.2

The following is the trial balance of Anindita as on March 31, 2016:

Particulars	Debit Amount (₹)	Credit Amount (₹)
Fixed assets	54,000	
Depreciation on fixed assets	6,000	
Cost of goods sold	1,11,600	
Closing stock	8,400	
Trade debtors	40,000	
Trade creditors		19,400
Bills payable		1,120
Bills receivables	2,000	
12 percent Investments (Purchased on 1.7.2015)	10,000	
Interest on investments		900
Accrued interest on investments	300	
Interest	500	
Loan from bank		800
Cash in hand	1,000	
Cash at bank	2,000	
Drawings	2,000	
Interest on drawings		200
Interest on capital	8,000	

Particulars	Debit Amount (₹)	Credit Amount (₹)
Capital		87,800
Sales		1,46,000
Return inward	2,000	
Carriage outward	400	
Discount allowed	400	
Discount received		200
Bad debts	1,300	
Rent	720	
Outstanding rent		120
Insurance	540	
Prepaid insurance	180	
Other office and administrative expenses	2,640	
Selling and distribution expenses	8,980	
Provision for doubtful debts		5,300
Provision for discount on debtors		1,120
Total	2,62,960	2,62,960

Solution

Notes:

(i) The trial balance is an adjusted trial balance. Therefore, no further adjustment is required for preparing profit and loss account and balance sheet.

(ii) Discount allowed is adjusted against the 'Provision for discount on debtors'.

(iii) Bad debt is adjusted against the 'Provision for doubtful debts'.

(iv) In absence of adequate information, investments are classified as 'Non-current assets'. It is not necessary that all investments are non-current assets. Investments that are a part of the trading portfolio and investments that the entity intends to sell within one year after the balance sheet date should be classified as current assets.

(v) In absence of adeq muate information, 'loan from bank' is classified as 'Non-current liability'. It is not necessary that all loans are non-current assets. Short-term loans and part of long-term loan that is payable within twelve months after the balance sheet date are classified as current liabilities.

Trading and Profit and Loss Account for the year ended March 31, 2016

Expenses	(₹)	Income		(₹)
To Cost of goods sold	1,11,600	By sales	1,46,000	
To Gross Profit c/d	32,400	Less return	2,000	1,44,000
	1,44,000			1,44,000
To Carriage outward	400	By Gross Profit b/d		32,400
To Insurance	540	By Discount		200
To Rent	720	By Interest on drawings		200
To Office and Administrative Expenses	2,640	By interest		900
To Selling and Distribution Expenses	8,980			
To Interest	500			
To Depreciation	6,000			
To Interest on capital	8,000			
To Net profit transferred to Capital a/c	5,920			
	33,700			33,700

NOTES

Balance Sheet as at March 31, 2016

Particulars	(₹)	(₹)
ASSETS		
Non-current Assets		
Fixed Assets		54,000
Investments		10,000
Current assets		
Closing stock		8,400
Debtors	40,000	
Less: Provision for doubtful debts	4,000	
	36,000	
Less: Provision for discount	720	35,280
Bills receivables		2,000
Pre-paid insurance		180
Interest accrued		300
Cash in hand		1,000
Cash at bank		2,000
Total		1,13,160
CAPITAL AND LIABILITIES		
Capital		
Opening balance	87,800	
Add: Net profit	5,920	
Less: drawings	2,000	91,720
Non-current liabilities		
Loan from bank		800
Current Liabilities		
Creditors		19,400
Bills payable		1,120
Outstanding rent		120
Total		1,13,160

CASE STUDY 8.3

A bookkeeper has submitted to you the following trial balance as at March 31, 2016, wherein the totals of debit and credit balances are not equal:

Particulars	Debit Amount (₹)	Credit Amount (₹)
Creditors	10,000	
Bills payable		560
Loan from bank	5,000	
Capital Account	45,400	
Sales		63,000
Purchase returns	500	
Discount earned	100	
Bad debt recovered	350	
Interest on investments	300	
Fixed assets	30,000	
Opening stock	7,500	
Debtors		20,500
Bills receivables	1,000	
Investments	5,000	
Cash in hand	500	
Cash in bank	1,000	
Drawings		900

Particulars	Debit Amount (₹)	Credit Amount (₹)
Purchases	52,500	
Sales returns		1,000
Carriage inward	140	
Freight outward		200
Duty paid on purchases		160
Primary packing expenses	200	
Rent paid		300
Insurance paid	360	
Office and administrative expenses	1,320	
Discount allowed		200
Bad debts	500	
Interest on loan from bank		250
Delivery expenses	660	
Selling and distribution expenses	1,000	
Income tax paid	100	
Value added tax (VAT) collected	200	
Loose tools	200	
Apprentice premium received		50
Commission received		30
Total	1,63,830	87,150

Required

(i) Redraft the trial balance correctly as at March 31, 2016

(ii) Prepare a Trading and Profit and Loss Account for the year ended March 31, 2016 and Balance Sheet as at March 31, 2016 after taking into account the following adjustments:

- (a) Closing stock was valued at ₹4,000
- (b) Rent outstanding for March 2016 ₹60
- (c) Insurance unexpired on March 31, 2016 ₹90
- (d) Accrued interest on investment amounted to ₹150
- (e) One-third of the commission received in respect of work to be done next year
- (f) ₹125 is due for interest on bank loan
- (g) Loose tools are valued at ₹80
- (h) Provide for depreciation on fixed assets @10 percent per annum

Solution

Trial Balance as at March 31, 2016

Particulars	Debit Amount (₹)	Credit Amount (₹)
Creditors		10,000
Bills payable		560
Loan from bank		5,000
Capital Account		45,400
Sales		63,000
Purchase returns		500
Discount earned		100
Bad debt recovered		350
Interest on investments		300
Fixed assets	30,000	
Opening stock	7,500	
Debtors	20,500	
Bills receivables	1,000	
Investments	5,000	
Cash in hand	500	
Cash in bank	1,000	
Drawings	900	
Purchases	52,500	
Sales returns	1,000	
Carriage inward	140	

Particulars	Debit Amount (₹)	Credit Amount (₹)
Freight outward	200	
Duty paid on purchases	160	
Primary packing expenses	200	
Rent paid	300	
Insurance paid	360	
Office and administrative expenses	1,320	
Discount allowed	200	
Bad debts	500	
Interest on loan from bank	250	
Delivery expenses	660	
Selling and distribution expenses	1,000	
Income tax paid	100	
Value added tax (VAT) collected		200
Loose tools	200	
Apprentice premium received		50
Commission received		30
Total	1,25,490	1,25,490

Trading and Profit and Loss Statement for the year ended March 31, 2016

Expenses	(₹)	(₹)	Income	(₹)	(₹)
To Opening Stock		7,500	By Sales	63,000	
To Purchase	52,500		*Less:* Returns	1,000	62,000
Less: Returns	500	52,000	By closing stock		4,000
To Duty on purchases		160			
To carriage inward		140			
To packaging expenses		200			
To Gross Profit c/d		6,000			
		66,000			66,000
To Freight outward		200	By Gross Profit b/d		6,000
To Rent	300		By commission	30	
Add: Rent outstanding	60	360	*Less:* Deferred commission	10	20
To Interest on loan	250		By Interest on investment	300	
Add: Interest unpaid	125	375	*Add:* Accrued interest	150	450
To Discount		200	By discount		100
To Insurance	360		By Apprentice Premium		
Received		50			
Less: Pre-paid insurance	90	270	By bad debt recovered		350
To Delivery expenses		660	By net loss transferred to Capital a/c		1,035
To Selling and Distribution expenses		1,000			
To Office and Administrative expenses		1,320			
To Bad debt		500			
To Depreciation on fixed assets		3,000			
To Loss on revaluation of loose tools		120			
		8,005			8,005

Balance Sheet as at March 31, 2016

Particulars	(₹)	(₹)
CAPITAL AND LIABILITIES		
Capital		
Opening balance	45,400	
Less: Net loss	1,035	
	44,365	
Less: Drawings	900	
Less: Income tax	100	43,365
Liabilities		
Loans		
Bank loan	5,000	
Add: Interest on loan	125	5,125
Current Liabilities		
Creditors		10,000
Bills payable		560
VAT collected		200
Deferred Commission		10
Outstanding rent		60
Total		59,320
ASSETS		
Fixed assets		
Fixed assets	30,000	
Less: Depreciation	3,000	27,000
Investments		
Investments		5,000
Current Assets		
Closing stock		4,000
Debtors		20,500
Bills receivables		1,000
Pre-paid insurance		90
Loose tools (₹200 – 120)		80
Interest accrued on investments		150
Cash at bank		1,000
Cash in hand		500
Total		59,320

Note: In sole proprietorship business, income tax paid by the business is considered personal drawing of the owner, because income tax is levied on the owner based on his/her total taxable income. Business income is only a part of his/her total income. In case of companies, income tax is levied on the company based on its taxable income. Therefore, in case of companies, income tax is treated as an expense and net profit is calculated after deducting income tax expense.

NOTES

CASE STUDY 8.4

On April 1, 2015 Suraj acquired a business as a going concern from Chandni for a sum of ₹28,000. He took stock valued at ₹2,400, furniture and fittings valued at ₹2,540, building valued at 12,000 and trade debtors ₹2,560. He undertook to pay trade creditors amounting to ₹2,560.

In addition to the sum paid for the business, Suraj paid ₹2,000 into a business bank account. At the end of the year (March 31, 2016), in addition to the balances arising from the above, the following balances were extracted from Suraj's books:

	Amount (₹)
Sales	86,980
Purchases	55,230
Carriage inward	1,250
Wages and salaries	8,700
Advertising	4,680
Rates and insurance	1,950
Electricity	870
Sundry office expenses	420
Debtors	6,580
Creditors	2,160
Cash in hand and balance at bank	560
Drawings	10,400
Discounts allowed to customers	560

Prepare Suraj's Trading and Profit and Loss Account for the year ended March 31, 2016 and a Balance Sheet as at that date, after taking into account the following additional information:

(i) Stock as at March 31, 2016 was valued at ₹4,560.

(ii) Building is to be depreciated by 5 percent and furniture and fittings by 20 percent of book value.

(iii) Wages and salaries ₹450 were outstanding.

(iv) Rates ₹300 were prepaid

(v) Provision for doubtful debts is to be made at 5 percent on sundry debtors.

Solution

Working Notes

1. Goodwill

	Amount (₹)
Assets taken over from Chandni	
Stock	2,400
Furniture and fittings	2,540
Buildings	12,000
Trade debtors	2,560
Total	19,500
Less: Trade creditors taken over	2,500
Net assets taken over	17,000
Purchase consideration	28,000
Goodwill (Purchase consideration less net assets taken over)	11,000

2. Adjusted Trial Balance

Particulars	**Debit (₹)**	**Credit (₹)**
Capital (₹28,000 + 2,000)		30,000
Goodwill	11,000	
Opening stock	2,400	
Furniture and fittings	2,540	
Building	12,000	

NOTES

Particulars	Debit (₹)	Credit (₹)
Debtors	6,580	
Prepaid rates	300	
Creditors		2,160
Outstanding wages and salaries		450
Cash in hand and balance at bank	560	
Drawings	10,400	
Sales		86,980
Purchases	55,230	
Carriage inward	1,250	
Wages and salaries (₹8,700 + 450)	9,150	
Advertising	4,680	
Rates and insurance (₹1,950 – 300)	1,650	
Electricity	870	
Sundry office expenses	420	
Discounts allowed to customers	560	
Total	1,19,590	1,19,590

Profit and Loss Account of Suraj for the year ended March 3, 2016

Expenses	Amount (₹)	Income	Amount (₹)
To opening stock	2,400	By sales	86,980
To purchases	55,230	By closing stock	4,560
To Carriage inward	1,250		
To Gross profit c/d	32,660		
	91,540		91,540
To wages and salaries	9,150	By Gross profit b/d	32,660
To Advertising	4,680		
To Rates and insurance	1,650		
To Electricity	870		
To Sundry office expenses	420		
To Discount allowed	560		
To Depreciation Building	600		
To Depreciation F&F	508		
To Provision for doubtful debts	329		
Net profit transferred to Capital a/c	13,893		
	32,660		

Notes:

(i) When a single account is maintained for 'wages and salaries', it is appropriate to assume that both wages and salaries are indirect expenses. Therefore, the expense should be recognised in the statement of profit and loss and not in the trading account.

(ii) IFRS and Ind AS (Indian equivalent of IFRS) requires all discounts, including cash discount, should be deducted from sales. Therefore, it is more appropriate to deduct discount allowed from sales than presenting the same as an expense.

Balance Sheet of Suraj as at March 31, 2016

	Amount (₹)	Amount (₹)
EQUITY AND LIABILITIES		
Capital		
As at April 1, 2016	30,000	
Add: Net profit for the year 2015–16	13,893	
	43,893	
Less: Drawings	10,000	33,983
Non-Current Liabilities		Nil

NOTES

Current liabilities		
Sundry creditors		2,160
Outstanding wages and salaries		450
Total		36,103
ASSETS		
Non-current assets		
Property, plant and equipment		
Building	12,000	
Less: Depreciation	600	11,400
Furniture and Fittings	2,540	
Less: Depreciation	508	2,032
Intangible assets		
Goodwill		11,000
Current assets		
Stock-in-trade		4,560
Sundry debtors	6,580	
Less: Provision for doubtful debts	329	6,251
Pre-paid rates and insurance		300
Cash and bank balance		560
Total		36,103

CASE STUDY 8.5

From the following trial balance of Manorama, prepare the Manufacturing, Trading and Profit and Loss Account for the year ended March 31, 2016, and a Balance Sheet as on that date after giving effect to the adjustments given below:

Trial Balance of Manorama as at March 31, 2016

Particulars	Debit Amount (₹)	Credit Amount (₹)
Capital account as at April 1, 2015		36,600
Drawings account	5,000	
Purchases	1,05,250	
Rates and taxes	1,250	
Salaries	5,000	
Carriage	1,000	
Fuel and cool	700	
Factory insurance	300	
Advertisement	1,000	
Factory power	800	
Bad debt written off	500	
Cash discount allowed	100	
Sundry expenses	175	
Opening stock—Raw materials	3,000	
Opening stock—Finished goods	2,500	
Patents	600	
Postage and telegrams	650	
Wages	1,750	
Cash discount received		750
Factory buildings	10,000	
Furniture and fixtures	2,575	
Plant and Machinery	4,750	
Sundry debtors	9,350	

Particulars	Debit Amount (₹)	Credit Amount (₹)
4% Government promissory notes (Subscribed on April 1, 2015)	1,000	
Sundry creditors		5,250
Sales		1,26,650
Cash in hand	2,275	
Cash at bank	9,725	
Total	1,69,250	1,69,250

Note: Closing stock as at March 31, 2016:
Raw materials: ₹2,500
Finished goods: ₹2,000

Adjustments:

(i) Depreciation/amortisation to be provided at the following rates:
Plant and Machinery: 10% Patents: 10%
Building: $2^1/_2$% Furniture: 5%

(ii) Provide 2.5% on debtors for doubtful debts

(iii) Purchase invoice aggregating ₹1,250 were omitted to be entered in the purchase daybook.

(iv) Debtors include ₹250 due from the proprietor.

(v) The amount of ₹250 received in respect of a private loan advanced by the proprietor was wrongly credited to sundry debtors account.

(vi) Purchase invoices of the value of ₹3,750 were entered in the purchase daybook on March 29, 2016, but the goods in respect thereof were received on April 3, 2016.

(vii) An amount of ₹175 received from a debtor was wrongly credited to sales account.

(viii) The annual interest on Government promissory notes accrued due on March 31, 2016, but was collected only in April 2016.

(ix) Carriage includes ₹400 towards outward charges.

Solution

Manufacturing, Trading and Profit and Loss Account
for the year ended March 31, 2016

Debit	(₹)	Credit	(₹)
To Raw materials consumed:		By factory cost of goods produced	
Opening stock	3,000	c/d	1,08,185
Purchases (1,05,250 + 1,250)	1,06,500		
Carriage inward (1,000 – 400)	600		
	1,10,100		
Less: Closing stock (2,500 + 3,750)	6,250		
	1,03,850		
To Wages	1,750		
To Fuel and coal	700		
To Factory insurance	300		
To Factory power	800		
To Depreciation—Plant and Machinery	475		
To Depreciation—Patent	60		
To Depreciation—Factory Building	250		
	1,08,185		1,08,185
To Opening stock—FG	2,500		
To Cost of goods produced b/d	1,08,185	By sales (1,26,650 – 175)	1,26,475
To Gross profit c/d	17,790	By Closing stock—FG	2,000
	1,28,475		1,28,475

Debit	(₹)	Credit	(₹)
To rent, rates and taxes	1,250	By Gross profit b/d	17,790
To salaries	5,000	By Discount received	750
To Depreciation		By Interest on Government promissory notes	40
F&F	129		
To Sundry expenses	175		
To Postage and Telegram	650		
To Advertisement	1,000		
To Carriage outwards	400		
To Bad debts	500		
To Provision for doubtful debts[1]	229		
To Discount allowed	100		
To Net profit transferred to Capital Account	9,147		
	18,580		18,580

Note: 1. Provision for Doubtful debts: 2.5 percent on (₹9,350 – 250 due from the proprietor + 250 received against private loan – 175 received from debtors, but wrongly credited to sales = ₹9,175)

Balance Sheet as at March 31, 2016

	Amount (₹)	Amount (₹)
CAPITAL AND LIABILITIES		
CAPITAL		
As on April 1, 2015	36,600	
Introduction of fresh capital[1]	250	
Net profit	9,147	
	45,997	
Less: Drawings[2] (5,000 + 250)	5,250	40.747
Liabilities		
Non-Current Liabilities		Nil
Current Liabilities		
Sundry creditors (5,250 + 1,250)		6,500
		47,247
ASSETS		
Non-Current Assets		
Property, Plant and Equipment		
Factory Building	10,000	
Less: Depreciation @2.5%	250	9,750
Plant and Machinery	4,750	
Less: Depreciation @ 10%	475	4,275
Furniture and fixtures	2,575	
Less: Depreciation @ 5%	129	2,446
Intangible Assets		
Patents	600	
Less: Amortisation @ 10%	60	540
Current Assets		
Inventories:		
Raw materials (2,500 + 3,750)		6,250
Finished goods		2,000
Sundry Debtors[3]	9,175	
Less: Provision for doubtful debts	229	8,946
4 percent Government Promissory Notes		1,000
Accrued interest on Government Promissory Notes		40
Cash at Bank		9.725
Cash in hand		2,275
		47,247

Notes:

1. The amount of ₹250 received in respect of a private loan advanced by the proprietor (wrongly credited to sundry debtors account) and retained in the business is considered fresh introduction of capital.
2. ₹250 due from the proprietor (wrongly included in debtors) is considered drawings.
3. See note under manufacturing, trading and profit and loss account.

CASE STUDY 8.6

After making necessary adjustments given below, prepare trading and profit and loss account for the year ending December 31, 2017 and the balance sheet as on that date from the following trial balance extracted from the books of Prem Jaipuria:

Trial Balance as at December 31, 2017

	(₹)		(₹)
Drawings	6,300	Capital	1,50,000
Cash in hand	3,870	Discount received	2,985
Bills receivables	1,860	9 percent loan account	15,000
Land and building	30,000	Purchase returns	1,455
Depreciation on land and building	2,580	Sales	2,81,505
Furniture	5,130	Provision for bad debts	4,650
Wages	46,875	Sundry creditors	18,675
Discount	3,960		
Office expenses	6,525		
Stock on December 31, 2009	60,255		
Purchase (adjusted)	1,35,375		
Stock on December 31, 2010	63,705		
Carriage	5,175		
General Expenses	7,680		
Sales returns	1,920		
Plant	18,600		
Depreciation on plant	3,000		
Taxes	3,630		
Debtors	65,745		
Bad debts	1,380		
Insurance	705		
	4,74,270		4,74,270

Adjustments:

(i) Stock at the end includes stock received on consignment ₹3,500.

(ii) Depreciation on plant was calculated at 10 percent p.a. on the straight-line method instead of the written down value method.

(iii) Debtors included:

  (a) Amount due from Sound Ltd. ₹3,745 considered as definitely good

  (b) Amount due from Hopeless Ltd. ₹2,000 considered as definitely bad

  (c) Amount due from Rambharose Ltd. ₹100 considered definitely doubtful

(iv) It was decided to make provision for doubtful debts at 5 percent on debtors.

(v) Stock of ₹10,000 was burnt by fire on 20 December; claim of ₹4,000 is acceptable by the insurance company.

(vi) Loan of ₹4,000 was paid on June 30, 2010 and ₹5,000 was paid on September 30, 2010.

(vii) Depreciate furniture at 5 percent p.a.

NOTES

Solution

Trading and Profit and Loss Account for the year ending December 31, 2017

Dr.	(₹)	(₹)	Cr.	(₹)	(₹)
To Stock		60,255	By Sales	2,81,505	
To purchase (1)	1,35,375		*Less:* Returns	1,920	2,79,585
Add: Stock on consignment wrongly deducted	3,500		By loss by fire (abnormal loss)		10,000
	1,38,875				
Less: Returns	1,455	1,37,420			
To Wages		46,875			
To Carriage		5,175			
To Depreciation on plant (4) (3,000 – 840)		2,160			
To Gross profit		37,700			
		2,89,585			2,89,585
To Office expenses		6,525	By Gross profit		37,700
To General expenses		7,680	By discount received		2,985
To Taxes		3,630			
To Insurance		705			
To To discount allowed		3,960			
To Interest on Loan (2)		1,868			
To Provision for doubtful debts (3)		2,680			
To Loss by fire		6,000			
To Depreciation on land and building		2,580			
To Depreciation on furniture		256			
To Net profit		4,801			
		40,685			40,685

Balance Sheet as on December 31, 2017

Equity and Liabilities	(₹)	(₹)	Assets	(₹)	(₹)
Capital	1,50,000		Building	32,580	
Less: Drawings	6,300		*Less:* Depreciation	2,580	30,000
Add: profit	1,43,700		Plant	21,600	
	4,801	1,48,501	*Less:* Depreciation	2,160	19,440
Loan	15,000		Furniture	5,130	
Add: Interest		16,868	*Less:* Depreciation	256	4,874
outstanding	1,868				
Sundry Creditors		18,675	Stock	63,705	
			Less: Stock on consignment	3,500	60,205
			Insurance claim		4,000
			Bills receivable		1,860
			Debtors (₹65,745 – 2,000)	63,745	
			Less: Provision	3,950	59,795
			Cash in hand		3,870
		1,84,044			1,84,044

Working notes:

1. If stock at the end appears in the trial balance, then it is taken to only one place. Since it is an asset, it is taken to balance sheet. In this case, adjustment entry must have been made as follows:

Stock account	Dr. ₹63,705	
To Purchase account		Cr. ₹63,705

Since by mistake stock at the end includes the stock received on consignment, purchases by the above entry have unnecessarily been reduced by ₹3,500. In order to restore the correct position, ₹3,500 will be deducted from stock and added to purchases.

2. Interest on loan:

Loan on January 1, 2017 must be ₹24,000 because, after making two payments of ₹5,000 and ₹4,000, ₹15,000 are still outstanding. Therefore, interest is as follows:

Interest at 9 percent on ₹24,000 for 6 months, i.e,. from January to June	₹1,080.00
Interest at 9 percent on ₹20,000 (i.e., 24,000 – 4,000) for 3 months, i.e,. from June to September	450.00
Interest on 9 percent on ₹15,000 (i.e., 20,000 – 5,000) for 3 months, i.e,. from September to December	337.50
Total interest	₹1,867.50

3. (a) Provision for doubtful debts:

Total debtors as per trial balance	₹65,745
Less: "Definitely good debts" (do not require any provision)	3,745
	62,000
Less: "Definitely bad debts" (do not require any provision)	2,000
	60,000
Less: "Definitely doubtful debts" (require full provision and will be added later on)	1,000
	₹59,000
Provision at 5 percent on ₹59,000	2,950
Add: "Definitely doubtful debts"	1,000
Total provision required	₹3,950

New provision for doubtful debts required:

Provision as per trial balance	₹4,650
Less adjustment for bad debts (in trial balance)	1,380
Less adjustment fro bade debt (Adjustments iii(b))	2,000
Balance after adjustments	1,270

New provision required (Required provision – balance after adjustments for bade debts)
= (₹3,950 – 1,270) = ₹2,680

Adequate provision is created by debiting profit and loss account by ₹2,680. As bad debts have been adjusted against the provision, those are not recognised as expenses in the profit and loss account.

(b) Figure of debtors (₹65,745) in the trial balance is not adjusted for bad debt (₹2,000) indicated in adjustments at iii(b). Therefore, the carrying amount of debtors in the balance sheet is at (₹65,745 – 2,000) or ₹63,745.

4. Depreciation on plant:

Value plant on December 31, 2017 (after depreciation)	18,600
Add: Depreciation provided during the year	3,000
Value of plant on January 1, 2017	21,600
Depreciation at 10 percent p.a. on ₹21,600 on w.d.v. method	2,160

Excess depreciation provided during the year is (₹3,000 – ₹2,160) ₹840. Adjustment entry is:

Plant account	Dr. ₹840	
To Depreciation account		Cr. ₹840

NOTES

CASE STUDY 8.7

The following balance amounts on March 31, 2018, are extracted from the books of Mr. Amritlal, a manufacturer-cum-trader:

	₹
Stock of raw materials, April 1, 2017	25,500
Stock of work-in-progress, April 1, 2017	30,700
Stock of finished goods, April 1, 2017	40,500
Stock of stores (factory), April 1, 2017	2,100
Cash in hand	1,600
Cash in bank	32,800
Purchase of raw materials	3,12,000
Purchase of finished goods	1,27,400
Purchase of factory stores	12,300
Factory wages	2,94,600
Salary of works manager	15,000
Office salaries and wages	86,400
Carriage inwards (raw materials)	32,300
Carriage inwards (finished goods)	10,600
Carriage outwards	3,700
Rent and rates (factory)	2,800
Rent and rates (general)	2,400
Electric charges (factory)	3,800
Electric charges (general)	1,700
Insurance (factory)	2,100
Insurance (general)	700
Travelling expenses	4,300
Brokerage on purchases (raw materials)	3,100
Commission on sales	2,600
Advertisement	12,400
Sales	10,36,500
Return outward (finished goods)	12,200
Return inwards (finished goods)	23,700
Repairs and renewals (factory)	8,500
Trade expenses	10,200
Provision for bad debts	2,600
Bad debts	1,800
Plant and machinery	3,26,400
Furniture and fixtures	57,300
Sundry trade debtors	65,800
Sundry trade creditors	1,53,400
Loose tools	8,400
Bills receivable	4,600
Bills payable	5,400
Loan on mortgage (October, 2005 @6% p.a.)	1,20,000
Income tax (for 2004–05 financial year)	10,000
Income tax (in advance for 2005–06)	8,000
Amritlal's capital	2,80,000
Amritlal's drawings	22,000

In addition, you are given the following information and particulars:

1. Closing stock on March 31, 2018:

	(₹)
Raw materials	28,700
Work-in-progress	33,300
Finished goods	43,800
Factory stores	2,900

2. Purchase of finished goods for ₹500 utilised for private use of Amritlal has not been duly adjusted.
3. Two bills receivable for ₹200 and ₹300, respectively, has been dishonoured and await adjustment.
4. A quarter of advertisement represents payment in advance to advertising agents.
5. Depreciation on plant and machinery and furniture and fixture @10 percent and loose tools @20 percent to be provided.
6. Provision for bad debts should be maintained at 5 percent of the debtors.
7. Interest on mortgage for 6 months to be provided.

Required

Prepare a manufacturing account, trading and profit and loss account for the year ending March 31, 2006 and the balance sheet as at that date.

Solution

Sri Amritlal Manufacturing, Trading and Profit and Loss Account for the Year ended March 31, 2017

Expenses		(₹)	**Income**		(₹)
To cost of materials consumed:			By factory cost of finished goods c/d		7,14,220
Opening stock	25,500				
Purchases	3,12,000				
Carriage inwards	32,300				
Brokerage	3,100				
	3,72,900				
Less closing stock	28,700	3,44,200			
To wages		2,94,600			
To factory overheads:					
Salary of works manager	15,000				
Rent and rates	2,800				
Electric charges	3,800				
Insurance	2,100				
Repairs and renewals	8,500				
Depreciation:					
Plant	32,640				
Loose tools	1,680				
Stores consumed					
(2,100 + 12,300 – 2,900)	11,500	78,020			
		7,16,820			
Less adjustment for WIP:					
Closing	33,300				
Opening	30,700	2,600			
		7,14,220			7,14,220
To opening stock (finished goods)		40,500	By sales	10,36,500	
To cost of finished goods b/d		7,14,220	*Less:* Returns	23,700	10,12,800
To purchase of finished goods	1,27,400		By closing stock		43,800
Less: Returns	12,200				
	1,15,200				
Less: Private consumption	500	1,14,700			
To carriage inward		10,600			
To gross profit c/d		1,76,580			
		10,56,600			10,56,600
			By gross profit b/d		1,76,580

NOTES

Expenses		(₹)	Income	(₹)
To office administration expenses:				
Office salaries and wages	86,400			
Rent and rates	2,400			
Electric charges	1,700			
Insurance	700			
Trade expenses	10,200			
Depreciation on furniture	5,730	1,07,130		
To selling and distribution expenses:				
Travelling expenses	4,300			
Commission	2,600			
Advertisement (12,400 – 3,100)	9,300			
Carriage outwards	3,700			
Provision for bad debts (3,315 + 1,800 – 2,600)	2,515	22,415		
To interest on loan		3,600		
To net profit transferred to capital a/c		43,435		
		1,76,580		1,76,580

Balance Sheet as on 31 March, 2017

Capital and Liabilities		(₹)	Assets		(₹)
Capital account:			*Fixed assets (Non-current assets):*		
Opening	2,80,000		Plant and machinery	3,26,400	
Add: Net profit	43,435		*Less:* Depreciation	32,640	2,93,760
	3,23,435		Furniture and fixtures	57,300	
Less: Drawings (22,000 + 500)	22,500		*Less:* Depreciation	5,730	51,570
	3,00,935		Loose tools	8,400	
Less: Income tax	18,000	2,82,935	*Less:* Depreciation	1,680	6,720
Mortgage loan		1,20,000	*Current assets:*		
Current liabilities:			*Inventories:*		
Outstanding interest on loan		3,600	Raw materials	28,700	
Sundry creditors		1,53,400	Work-in-progress	33,300	
Bills payable		5,400	Finished goods	43,800	
			Factory stores	2,900	1,08,700
			Trade receivables (65,800 + 200 + 300)	66,300	
			Less: Provision for doubtful debts	3,315	62,985
			Bills receivable (4,600 – 200 – 300)		4,100
			Cash in bank		32,800
			Cash in hand		1,600
			Prepaid advertisement		3,100
		5,65,335			5,65,335

Note: Advance income tax is considered as drawings by the proprietor, because in case of a sole proprietorship concern the tax law does not make a difference between the firm and the proprietor and levies tax on the total income of the proprietor.

SUMMARY

Usually, regulators do not require segmentation of profit and loss account into manufacturing account, trading account, and profit and loss account. However, entities often prefer this segmentation. The manufacturing account shows the cost of goods manufactured and the trading account shows the gross profit earned during the reporting period. The profit and loss account shows the net profit/loss for the period. The manufacturing account is debited with the cost of raw materials and components consumed, manufacturing wages and other manufacturing expenses, including depreciation on factory assets. The trading account is debited with the opening stock of finished goods, cost of goods manufactured, purchases of finished goods, and all other expenses attributable to bringing the finished goods to the condition and location of sale. The trading account is credited with the amount of sales and the closing stock. The profit and loss account is credited with the gross profit, other operating income and extraordinary income. It is debited with operating expenses, financing charges, tax expenses, and losses incurred during the reporting period.

CLOSING ENTRIES

Closing entries refer to those entries that are passed to transfer balance amounts in nominal accounts appearing in the adjusted trial balance to the manufacturing account, trading account and profit and loss account. The closing entries close nominal accounts in the general ledger. The remaining account balance amounts represent either assets or liabilities that appear in the balance sheet. The following case study shows closing entries:

CASE STUDY 8.8

Pass closing entries required for preparing the profit and loss account from assumed figures.

Solution

Journal

Date	Particulars	Ledger folio	Dr. Amount (₹)	Cr. Amount (₹)
2017				
March 31	Manufacturing a/c		9,10,000	
	To stock of raw material a/c			50,000
	To stock of working progress a/c			80,000
	To purchases of raw material a/c			6,00,000
	To wages a/c			1,20,000
	To electric power a/c			60,000
	(being the accounts in the trial balance to be transferred to the manufacturing a/c, debit side)			
March 31	Manufacturing a/c		65,250	
	To provision for depreciation on plant and machinery a/c			62,250
	To provision for depreciation on factory building			3,000
	(being provision for depreciation on plant and machinery at the rate of 15 percent and on building at the rate of 5 percent)			
March 31	Stock (closing) of raw material a/c		60,000	
	Stock (closing) of working progress a/c		85,000	
	To manufacturing a/c			1,45,000
	(being the value of a stock in hand as on March 31, 2000)			

NOTES

Date	Particulars	Ledger folio	Dr. Amount (₹)	Cr. Amount (₹)
March 31	Trading a/c		8,30,250	
	To manufacturing a/c			8,30,250
	(being the transfer of cost of goods manufactured during the accounting period)			
March 31	Trading a/c		16,20,000	
	To stock of finished goods a/c			2,00,000
	To purchases of finished goods a/c			14,00,000
	To freight inward a/c			20,000
	(being the accounts in the trial balance transferred to the trading a/c, debit side)			
March 31	Sales a/c		30,00,000	
	Goods lost by fire a/c		20,000	
	To trading a/c			30,20,000
	(being the accounts in the trial balance transferred to the trading a/c, credit side)			
March 31	Stock (closing) of finished goods a/c		2,20,000	
	To trading a/c			2,20,000
	(being the value of stock in hand as on March 31, 2000)			
March 31	Trading a/c		7,89,750	
	To profit and loss a/c			7,89,750
	(being the transfer of gross profit)			
March 31	Profit and loss a/c		5,94,000	
	To salaries a/c			1,50,000
	To rates and taxes a/c			30,000
	To electricity charges a/c			25,000
	To office rent a/c			30,000
	To travelling expenses a/c			1,00,000
	To insurance premium a/c			1,35,000
	To advertisement expenses a/c			42,000
	To bad debts a/c			10,000
	To discount a/c			5,000
	To general expenses a/c			36,000
	To post and telegram a/c			15,000
	To loss by fire a/c			2,000
	To loss on sale of plant and machinery			4,000
	To audit fees			10,000
	(being the various expense accounts transferred to the profit and loss a/c)			
March 31	Bad debt recovered a/c		2,000	
	To profit and loss a/c			2,000
	(being the bad debts recovered a/c transferred to the profit and loss a/c)			
March 31	Profit and loss a/c		51,900	
	To provision for depreciation on furniture and fixtures a/c			10,500
	To provision for doubtful debts a/c			30,000
	To provision for discount a/c			11,400
	(being various provisions created for the accounting year ending March 31, 2000 as per details below: Depreciation on F&F @10% Provision for doubtful debts @5% Provision for discount @2%			
March 31	Profit and loss a/c		1,45,850	
	To capital a/c			1,45,850
	(being the transfer of net profit to the capital a/c)			

PROFIT AND LOSS APPROPRIATION ACCOUNT

The profit and loss appropriation account shows the appropriation of profit brought forward from the previous period and profit (loss) earned incurred during the period. Appropriation takes the form of transfer to reserves, interest on capital and distribution to owners, such as payment of dividend in case of a limited liability company.

ANSWERS TO SELF-TEST QUESTIONS

8.1 (i) credited, debited, ₹2000; (ii) debited, ₹30,000, credited, ₹30,000; (iii) credited, ₹80,000, debited, ₹80,000; (iv) debited, ₹2,000, credited, ₹2,000

8.2 (i) does not appear; (ii) appear; (iii) ₹60,000, ₹2,10,000; (iii) accruals; (iv) ₹49.85 crores

8.3 (i) T; (ii) T; (iii) F; (iv) T; (v) T

8.4 (i) T; (ii) T; (iii) F; (iv) T; (v) T

8.5 (i) T; (ii) T; (iii) T; (iv) T

ASSIGNMENTS

Multiple Choice Questions

1. Tick the right answer.
   (i) A suspense account is opened
      (a) when the debit side total does not agree with the credit side total of the trial balance.
      (b) when the debit side total does not agree with the credit side total, and the error could not be located till the preparation of the trial balance.
      (c) when the debit side total and credit side total of the trial balance agree due to compensating error.
      (d) when an error has occurred in adding up balances appearing in the trial balance.
   (ii) Closing stock is recorded in the books of accounts through
      (a) an adjustment entry.
      (b) a closing entry.
      (c) a closing entry or by adjusting purchases through an adjustment entry.
      (d) an opening entry.
   (iii) Accruals are recorded in the books of accounts through
      (a) an adjustment entry.
      (b) a closing entry.
      (c) an opening entry.
      (d) either a closing entry or an opening entry.
   (iv) While making the trading and profit and loss accounts
      (a) only nominal accounts are transferred to the trading and profit and loss accounts.
      (b) only nominal accounts and opening stock are transferred to the trading and profit and loss accounts.
      (c) all nominal and real accounts are transferred to the trading and profit and loss accounts.
      (d) only real accounts are transferred to the trading and profit and loss accounts.
   (v) The balance sheet should show the
      (a) bank balance as per the bank statement.
      (b) bank balance as per the cash book.
      (c) bank balance either as per the bank statement, or as per the cash book, at the discretion of the management.
      (d) bank balance as per the cash book, adjusted for cheques deposited but not collected till the balance sheet's date.
2. Indicate whether true (T) or false (F):
   (i) Wages should be debited to the trading account.
   (ii) Freight outward should be debited to the trading account.
   (iii) Loss of stock by fire, before adjustment for insurance claims, should be credited to the trading account.
   (iv) Prepaid expenses are a part of current assets.

NOTES

(v) Closing stock, when appearing in the trial balance, should be taken directly to the balance sheet.

(vi) Prior-period adjustment should be taken directly to the balance sheet.

(vii) Provision for doubtful debts is a liability.

(viii) No depreciation should be charged if an item of depreciable has not been used during the reporting period.

(ix) Gross profit measures the performance of the enterprise in the market place.

(x) A change in depreciation method is a change in accounting estimate.

3. Fill in the blanks

(i) The balance sheet dated December 31, 2005 shows expenses accrued (outstanding liability) on account of travelling expenses at ₹20,000. The balance in the travelling expenses account in the general ledger for the year 2006 shows a debit balance of 5,00,000. The management estimates expenses accrued (outstanding liability) on account of travelling as at December 31, 2006 is at ₹30,000. The amount of travelling expenses to be recognised as an expense in the income statement for the year 2006 is ₹.............. .

(ii) Sunny Limited (SL) pays insurance premium for the manufacturing facility on 1 April every year. The insurance policy covers a period of one year. During the years 2005 and 2006, SL paid ₹24,00,000 and ₹30,00,000 towards insurance premium. SL should recognize ₹.............. as insurance expense in the income statement for the year 2006 and should recognize ₹.............. as .... in the balance sheet as at December 31, 2006.

(iii) The balance sheet dated December 31, 2005 of Ruksha Limited (RL) shows Receivables (gross) and Provision for doubtful debts at ₹5,00,000 and ₹25,000 respectively. During the year 2006, RL has written off ₹5,000 as bad debt against the provision for doubtful debts. The balance as at December 31, 2006 in the 'Receivables a/c' in the general ledger is ₹8,00,000. RL, as a policy, maintains a provision for doubtful debts at 5 percent of the balance in the receivables a/c. RL has decided that from the year 2006, it will provide for discount (that it allows to customers for payment before the due date) at 1 percent of the balance in receivables a/c without violating the accounting convention. The income statement of RL for the year 2006 should be debited by ₹.............. for 'Provision for doubtful debts' and by ₹.............. for 'Provision for discount'.

(iv) Mona Limited (ML) is in merchandising business. There was no stock of goods at the beginning of the year 2006. During the year 2006, it purchased 1,00,000 units of goods in which it trades for ₹20,00,000. It incurred ₹40,000 towards freight inward and ₹2,00,000 towards wages to make the goods ready for sale. At the end of the year, 5,000 units were in stock. The closing stock of 5,000 units should be valued at ₹.............. .

(v) Yashmin Limited (YL) is in merchandizing business. The stock of goods at the beginning of the year 2006, was valued at ₹1,20,000. During the year 2006, it purchased 1,00,000 units of goods in which it trades for ₹30,00,000. It incurred ₹50,000 towards freight inward, ₹2,00,000 towards wages to make the goods ready for sale and ₹30,000 towards freight outward. During the year 2006. At the end of the year 5,000 units were in stock. During the year 5,000 units were lost by fire for which the insurance company has accepted a claim of ₹1,50,000. The revenue for the year is recognized at ₹40,00,000. The gross profit for the year 2006 is ₹.............. .

(vi) Diya Limited (DL) manufactures small motors for farm use. On July 1, 2006, it sold a machine that was purchased on January 1, 2000. The cost of the machine was ₹10,00,000. DL follows straight line method of depreciation. The depreciation rate for plant and equipment is 10 percent. The income statement for the year shows that DL incurred a loss of ₹20,000 on the sale of the machine. DL sold the machine for ₹.............. .

(vii) The bank reconciliation statement for the year 2006 shows: cheques issued but not presented ₹1,50,000, cheques received but not credited, cheques deposited but dishonoured ₹20,000, dividends directly collected by bank ₹10,000, and bank charges not recorded in the cash book ₹5,000. The bank balance (credit balance) as at December 31, 2006, as per cash book, is ₹5,00,000. The bank balance of ₹.............. should be shown as a .... in the balance sheet as at December 31, 2006.

(viii) Mallika Limited (ML) assesses its tax liability for the year 2006 at ₹10,00,000. It estimates that the deferred tax liability as at December 31, 2006 at ₹2,50,000 as against the deferred tax liability of ₹2,15,000 recognized in the balance sheet as at December 31, 2005. ML should recognize the tax expense in the income statement for the year 2006 at ₹........... .

Analytical Questions

1. The finance director of a large company was not quite agreeable to the audit committee's suggestion that bank reconciliation statements should be prepared fortnightly instead of the present practice of preparing bank reconciliation statement quarterly. What should be the appropriate frequency for the preparation of the bank reconciliation statement? Prepare a note explaining your position.
2. Withdrawal of the concept of 'extraordinary items' is a sharp shift from an age old accounting practice. Prepare a note explaining the possible reason for this change in approach.
3. According to an analyst "Deferred tax liability is nothing but an accrual. Therefore, it should be treated as a debt in analysing financial statements". Do you agree? Explain your view on this issue.

Problems

1. Pass journal entries to rectify the following errors:
   (a) A cheque of ₹1,000 received for loss of stock by fire had been deposited in the proprietor's bank account.
   (b) An item of purchase of ₹236 was entered in the purchase daybook as ₹326.
   (c) The cost of a motor car purchased for ₹1,50,000 had been debited to the purchase account.
   (d) ₹1,200 received from a debtor was debited to the sundry debtors account.
   (e) The sales daybook was undercast by ₹500.
   (f) Discount of ₹200 allowed to a customer was debited to the sundry debtors account.
   (g) Wages of ₹10,000 paid towards construction of a building for internal use was debited to the wages account.
   (h) ₹500 spent on repairs to machinery was debited to the plant and machinery account.
   (i) ₹325 paid for freight on machinery was debited to the freight account for ₹532.
2. The cash book of Alpha Ltd. shows a bank balance of ₹25,800, which is not in agreement with the balance appearing in the bank statement issued by the bank. An examination of the cash book and bank statement disclosed the following:
   (a) Cheques deposited amounting to ₹5,000 not yet collected.
   (b) Cheques issued amounting to ₹7,500, not yet presented for payment.
   (c) A cheque for ₹1,200 received from a customer, returned by the bank but not recorded in the cash book.
   (d) Dividend amounting to ₹750 collected directly by the bank.
   (e) Bank charges of ₹500 debited by the bank.
   (f) A cheque for ₹2,500 issued by Alpha & Co. wrongly debited by the bank.
   (g) A bill amounting to ₹2,000 discounted, subsequently dishonoured by the bank but not recorded in the cash book.

   Required:
   (i) Prepare the bank reconciliation statement.
   (ii) Pass necessary adjustment entries.
   (iii) Prepare the bank reconciliation statement after adjustment.
3. The bank statement issued by the bank shows an overdraft of ₹10,000 in the account of Gamma Ltd. This balance is not in agreement with the balance as per the cash book. An examination of the cash book and bank statement disclosed the following:
   (a) Cheques deposited amounting to ₹6,000 not yet collected.
   (b) Cheques issued amounting to ₹8,000 not yet presented.
   (c) Dividend amounting to ₹1,200 collected directly by the bank.
   (d) Bank charges of ₹400 debited by the bank.
   (e) A cheque of ₹1,500 received from a customer, returned by the bank but not recorded in the cash book.

   Required:
   (i) Prepare the bank reconciliation statement.
   (ii) Pass necessary adjustment entries.
   (iii) Show the bank balance that appears in the balance sheet.

NOTES

4. The following balances are extracted from the ledger of Daulatram Faquirchand for the year ended December 31, 2005.

		(₹)
Daulatram Faquirchand capital account		2,00,000
Daulatram Faquirchand drawing account (Dr.)		15,000
Purchases less returns		16,50,260
Rates and taxes		2,500
Salaries		35,240
Lighting		6,210
Office rent		6,300
Electric power		25,600
Reserve account		12,500
Travelling expenses		2,220
Insurance (fire)		1,500
Advertisement expenses		37,750
Sales less returns		18,35,200
Bad debts written off		9,050
Discounts (debit balance)		4,225
General expenses		1,12,665
Postage and telegrams		3,200
Carriage inwards		5,120
Stock-in-trade:		
Raw materials	16,800	
Finished good	23,400	40,200
Wages		32,212
Factory land and buildings		25,650
Plant and machinery		40,000
Sundry creditors		35,420
Furniture and fixtures		31,200
Sundry debtors		65,210
Cash in hand		1,218
Cash in bank		22,040

You are required to make out the manufacturing, trading, and profit and loss accounts and balance sheet after taking into account the following additional information:

1. The stock-in-trade on December 31, 2005 was raw materials: ₹15,767, finished goods: ₹8,333.
2. Provide depreciation at 10 percent on plant and machinery, 5 percent on furniture and fixtures and 2.5 percent on land and buildings.
3. Provide 2.5 percent for discounts on debtors and create provision at 10 percent for bad debts.
4. Sundry creditors include an amount of ₹2,000 realised from Mr. Sadhuram, whose account had been written off two years back.
5. Insurance was paid in advance up to June 30, 2006.
6. One machine whose value in the books as on January 1, 2005 stood at ₹12,000 was disposed of on September 30, 2005 for ₹8,750 in part exchange for a new machine costing ₹19,000 and an invoice for the net amount of ₹10,250 was entered in the books. No depreciation need be provided on machinery disposed of during the year.
7. The following expenditure was outstanding but no provision had been made in the books; audit fees ₹1,200, salaries ₹3,000; electric power 2,500; and advertisement ₹1,800.
8. A deposit of ₹5,000 received from one of the debtors was credited to his personal account. (Ignore fractions of a rupee in the calculations.)

5. Mr. A, a shopkeeper, had prepared the following trial balance from his ledger as on March 31, 2006:

	Dr. (₹)	Cr. (₹)
Purchases	3,10,000	
Sales		4,15,000
Stock of goods as on April 1, 2005	50,000	
Cash in hand	2,100	
Cash in bank	12,000	
Mr. A's capital		2,88,600
Drawings	4,000	
Rates and taxes	5,000	
Salaries	32,000	
Postage	11,500	
Salesmen's commission	35,000	
Insurance	9,000	
Advertising	17,000	
Furniture and fittings	22,000	
Printing and stationery	3,000	
Motor car	48,000	
Bad debts	2,000	
Cash discounts	4,000	
General expenses	14,000	
Carriage inwards	10,000	
Carriage outwards	22,000	
Wages	20,000	
Outstanding liability for expenses	11,000	
Sundry creditors		40,000
Sundry debtors	1,00,000	
	7,43,600	7,43,600

Additional information:

(a) Cost of goods in stock as on March 31, 2006: ₹1,45,000.
(b) Mr. A had withdrawn goods worth ₹5,000 during the year.
(c) Printing and stationery expenses of ₹11,000 relating to the 2004–2005 accounting year had not been provided in that year, but were paid in this year by debiting outstanding liabilities.
(d) Purchases include purchase of furniture worth ₹10,000.
(e) Debtors include ₹5,000 bad debts.
(f) Creditors include a balance of ₹4,000 to the credit of LM Corporation in respect of which it has been decided and settled with the party to pay only ₹1,000.
(g) Sales include goods worth ₹15,000 sold out to SM & Co. on approval and remaining unsold as on March 31, 2006. The cost of the goods was ₹10,000.
(h) Provision for bad debts is to be created at 5 percent of sundry debtors.
(i) Depreciate furniture and fittings by 10 percent and the motor car by 20 percent.
(j) Salesmen are entitled to a commission of 10 percent on total sales.

Required: Prepare the trading and profit and loss accounts for the year ended on March 31, 2006 and the balance sheet as on that date.

6. The books of Mr. X, a trader in tea, showed the following balances as on March 31, 2006:

	(₹)		(₹)
Opening stock of tea	1,00,000	Commission to sales manager	32,400
Purchases: Tea	4,00,000	Furniture and fittings	35,000
Salaries paid	80,000	Air conditioners	30,000
Buildings	95,000	Sundry debtors	1,00,000
Cash in hand	2,000	Sundry creditors	80,000

NOTES

	(₹)		(₹)
Cash in bank	1,35,000	Loan on mortgage	70,000
Rent, rates and taxes	15,000	Interest paid on above	3,000
Insurance premium paid	3,000	Prepaid expenses	4,000
Miscellaneous receipts	10,000	Drawings	18,000
Sales	7,20,000	Bills payable	30,000
Cash discount allowed	4,750	Bank charges	2,000
Bad debts	3,250	Legal charges	6,000
Repairs: Buildings.	2,900	Motor vehicles	80,000
Miscellaneous expenses	8,700	Travelling and conveyance	10,000
Advertisement	20,000		

Additional information:

(a) Closing stock: ₹55,000

(b) Legal charges include ₹5,000 for cost of stamps and registration of a new building acquired during the year.

(c) Purchases include 4,000 kg tea valued at ₹22,000 which was found totally spoiled. The insurance claim lodged in this respect is expected to realise ₹15,000.

(d) Travelling and conveyance include proprietor's personal travelling for which he is to be charged ₹4,800.

(e) Loan on mortgage bears interest @12 percent p.a. with monthly interests. The loan was taken on June 1, 2005. One instalment of ₹10,000 was repaid on December 1, 2005.

(f) The sales manager is entitled to a commission of 7½ percent on total sales. However, the actual bad debts incurred during the year are deductible from such commission entitlements.

(g) Debtors include:
   (i) ₹10,000 due from M & Co. (creditor include ₹18,000 due to the same party).
   (ii) ₹5,000 due on account of sale of furniture.
   (iii) Bad debts of ₹2,000.

(h) Provision for bad debts is to be created @2 percent of net outstanding debtors.
   (i) Depreciation is chargeable as follows:
   (i) Buildings @2½%
   (ii) Furniture and fittings @10%
   (iii) Air conditioners @15%
   (iv) Motor vehicles @20%

(j) Miscellaneous receipts represent sale proceeds of furniture, the written-down value of which was ₹12,000.

(k) Prepaid expenses include insurance premium of ₹1,000 for the period from April 1, 2005 to September 30, 2005 paid in 2004–2005.

(l) Bills payable include a bill of ₹10,000 which fell due on March 31, 2006 and was paid by the bank as per standing instructions. The bank charges in this connection amounted to ₹100.

(m) The balance as per the bank as on March 31, 2006 was ₹1,24,900.

Required: Prepare the trading and profit and loss accounts for the year ended on March 31, 2006 and the balance sheet as on that date.

Accounts of Limited Liability Companies
Accounting for Shares and Debentures

CHAPTER

9

LEARNING OBJECTIVES

The objective of this chapter is to provide an understanding of the accounting for shares and debentures. After reading this chapter, you will develop understanding of the following:

- Types of share capital
- Nature of debenture and types of debentures
- Accounting for issue of shares at par
- Accounting for issue of shares at a premium
- Nature of sweat equity shares
- Forfeiture and reissue of forfeited shares
- Share split and bonus share
- Right issue and pricing rights
- Buy back of shares
- Redemption of preference shares
- Accounting for debentures
- Accounting for premium and discount on issue of debentures
- Accounting for premium on redemption of debentures
- Purchase of debentures in open market

NOTES

INTRODUCTION

A company incorporated under the Companies Act, 2013, is referred to as a *limited-liability company,* because the liability of its members is limited to the amount that they have agreed to contribute to the company by way of share capital. In case of a company limited by guarantee, the liability of its members is limited to the amount specified in the Memorandum of Association. The following are other chief advantages of incorporation:

1. An incorporated company is a distinct legal entity independent of its members and, therefore, its liabilities are not members' liabilities and its assets are not members' assets.
2. An incorporated company never dies—it continues to own its assets even if the membership changes and all directors change at the same time.
3. The share of an incorporated company is a movable property, so its shares are easily transferable.
4. Only the shares in a company (in contrast to shares in partnership firms) can be listed in capital markets anywhere in the world.

The two most common forms of companies are *public limited companies* and *private limited companies*. A private limited company cannot have more than 200 members. Promoters and equity shareholders are members of a limited liability company. It is required to restrict the transfer of shares and to prohibit any invitation to the public to subscribe for any shares in, or debentures of the company. Any company that is not a private limited company is a public limited company.

Other types of body corporate are *statutory corporations* and *guarantee companies*.

Any seven or more persons can form a public limited company, while any two or more persons can form a private limited company. The two most important documents that a company seeking incorporation has to file with the Registrar of Companies are:

- Memorandum of association
- Articles of association

A memorandum of association states, among other things:

1. The name of the company.
2. The state in which the registered office of the company is to be situated.
3. The objects for which the company is proposed to be incorporated and any matter considered necessary for furtherance thereof.
4. Authorised capital, which is, the amount of share capital with which the company is to be registered and the division thereof into shares of fixed amount.

Articles of association provide the constitution of the internal management of the company and describe the relationship between the members and the Board of Directors, and also the relationship among members. Articles have always been held subordinate to the memorandum. Table 'L' of Schedule I to the Companies Act, 2013 provides a set of clauses that will apply when a company does not have its own articles of association, or its articles are silent on the point.

In this chapter, we shall study accounting for shares and debentures. Discussion on legal aspects is beyond the scope of this text.

TYPES OF SHARE CAPITAL

A company can issue two types of share capital—*equity share capital* and *preference share capital*.

Holders of preference share capital have preferential rights on profit. They have a right to be paid a fixed amount or an amount calculated at a fixed rate before any profit is distributed to holders of equity share capital. Similarly, holders of this class of capital have a preferential right in respect of share capital. On a winding up or repayment of capital, they have the right to be paid the amount of the capital paid and any fixed premium or premium on any fixed scale, as specified in the memorandum or articles of the company.

Preference shares may be either *cumulative* or *non-cumulative*. If there are no or inadequate profits in one or more years and the arrears of dividends are to be carried forward and paid out of the profits of subsequent years before any profit is distributed to equity shareholders, the preference shares are said to be *cumulative*. In case of *non-cumulative* preference shares, unpaid dividend is not accumulated and the right of preference shareholders to receive dividend for the year lapses. In the absence of any clear provision in the articles of the company, preference shares are always deemed to be cumulative preferential shares. If holders of this class of shares have a right to participate in the surplus profit after distribution to equity shareholders and also in the surplus on winding up, the preference shares are known as *participating preference shares*. As a general principle, preference shares are assumed to be non-participating.

No company can issue any preference share which is irredeemable, or is redeemable after the expiry of a period of 20 years from the date of the issue. Preference shareholders are not creditors. However, redeemable preference share capital is classified as *liability* and not as *equity*.

Share capital other than preference share capital is known as *equity share capital*. Holders of equity shares provide the risk capital, and their rights are *subordinate* to the rights of the holders of preference share capital. A company may issue equity share capital (a) with voting rights or (b) with differential rights as to dividend, voting or otherwise in accordance with such rules and subject to such conditions as may be prescribed by the central government.

Self-Test Questions

Self-test question 9.1

Indicate whether the following statements are true (T) or false (F):

(i) Equity shareholders are deemed owners of the company.
(ii) Preference shareholders enjoy voting rights.
(iii) Redeemable preference shares are presented in the balance sheet as a part of equity.
(iv) Unless indicated otherwise, preference shares are deemed to be cumulative.

DEBENTURES

Companies Act, 2013 and SEBI (Issue and Listing of Debt Securities) Regulations 2008 regulate the issue of debentures by companies. Companies are permitted to issue only secured redeemable debentures. The date of redemption should not exceed 10 years from the date of issue. However, a company engaged in the setting up of infrastructure projects may issue secured debentures for a period exceeding 10 years but not exceeding 30 years.

Companies borrow from the financial market by issuing debentures. A *debenture* is a document that either creates a debt or acknowledges the same under the seal of the company. Thus, a debenture represents a liability and debenture-holders are creditors. Interest on debentures is a charge against profit. The usual features of debentures are as follows:

- A debenture is usually in the form of a certificate issued under the seal of the company.
- The certificate is generally an acknowledgement of indebtedness.
- A debenture provides for a specified sum on a specified date.
- A debenture provides for payment of interest at a fixed rate until the principal sum is paid back.
- A debenture, as a rule, is one of a series, yet a single debenture is not uncommon.

Usually, a fixed charge on assets, or a floating charge on assets that are circulating or liquid in nature secures debentures. A *floating charge* allows the company to use the charged assets in the course of business. A charge on assets is not valid unless registered with the Registrar of Companies. Therefore, a debenture shows the certificate registering

NOTES

Key Terms
Bearer debentures, convertible debentures, fixed charge, floating charge, naked debentures, non-convertible debentures, perpetual debentures, secured debentures

the charge. It is also customary to create a trusteeship in favour of one or more persons in case of mortgaged debentures. The trustees of debenture-holders have all powers of a mortgagee of a property and can act in whatever way they think necessary to safeguard the interest of debenture-holders. The following are the different classes of debentures:

1. *Redeemable debentures:* In the case of a redeemable debenture, on expiry of the term of the loan, the company has a right to pay back the debenture-holders and have its properties released from the mortgage charges. Redeemed debentures can be reissued. Upon such reissue, the person entitled to the debentures has the same rights as if the debentures had never been redeemed.
2. *Perpetual debentures:* A debenture that contains no clause as to payment or that contains a clause that it shall not be paid back, is known as a *perpetual* or *irredeemable debenture.*
3. *Simple or naked debentures:* Unsecured debentures are known as *simple* or *naked debentures.*
4. *Registered debentures and bearer debentures:* Registered debentures are registered in the names of its holders. Therefore, any transfer should be registered with the company, and only by executing a regular transfer deed can transfer be effected. Companies may issue bearer debentures that are transferable like negotiable instruments, by simple delivery. A person to whom a bearer debenture is transferred becomes its holder and is entitled to recover the principal and interest when due.

The following are the differences between shareholders and debenture-holders:

1. A shareholder is a member of the company and has ownership rights, whereas a debenture-holder is simply a creditor of the company. Therefore, a shareholder has the *voting right* whereas a debenture-holder has *no right to vote* at any meeting of the company.
2. A debenture-holder is entitled to a *fixed rate of interest* which the company must pay irrespective of whether it has earned a profit or not. Shareholders are entitled to get dividend that represents *distribution of profit.*
3. Unless the debentures are perpetual, the company can pay back the debenture-holder, but shareholders cannot be paid back as long as the company is a going concern, except in the manner provided in the Companies Act, 2013.
4. The claim of debenture-holders is senior to the claim of shareholders.

Convertible and non-convertible debentures

Debentures are of two types Convertible and Non-Convertible. The convertible debentures are the ones that can be converted into equity shares at a later time. This convertibility provides attraction to the investor but yield lower interest rates. Non-convertible debentures (NCD) does not convert into equity shares thus can yield a higher interest rate.

Self-Test Questions

Self-test question 9.2

Indicate whether the following statements are true (T) or false (F):

(i) In India companies are not permitted to issue irredeemable debentures.
(ii) Debenture is a type of corporate bond.
(iii) Debenture holders are creditors.
(iv) A fixed charge allows the company to use the charged assets in the course of business.
(v) Non-convertible debentures usually carry interest rate higher than that of convertible debentures.

NOTES

SUMMARY

Companies borrow money from public by issuing debentures. Indian companies are permitted to issue only secured redeemable debentures. The redemption period cannot exceed ten years. However, a company engaged in the setting up of infrastructure projects may issue secured debentures for a period exceeding 10 years but not exceeding 30 years. Debentures can be secured by fixed charge or floating charge.

PROSPECTUS

A *prospectus* is a document inviting deposits from the public or inviting offers from the public for the subscription to shares or purchase of debentures. Application forms for shares and debentures cannot be issued unless a prospectus accompanies them. The Companies Act, 2013, specifies the contents of a prospectus. It discloses the details of the particular issue of shares or debentures and also the history, future prospects and the details of promoters and directors of the company. The Companies Act, 2013, provides stringent penalties for misstatements in the prospectus.

ACCOUNTING FOR ISSUE OF SHARES

Accounting for Issue of Shares at Par

Issue of shares at par connotes that subscribers to the share capital shall contribute only the face value of the share. For example, if the authorised capital of a company is divided into shares of ₹10 each, the subscribers shall contribute only ₹10 to the company. Usually, subscribers are required to pay a part of the total amount payable with the application, a part on allotment, and the balance when called by the company. Allotment implies the acceptance of the application by the company. Commonly, the Board of Directors is authorised to allot shares in a board meeting. Case Study 9.1 presents the accounting at each stage of issuing shares at par.

CASE STUDY 9.1

Anu Ltd. (AL) is authorised to issue 10,000 shares of ₹100 each. On April 1, 2017, AL issued 5,000 shares of ₹100 each payable as follows:

₹20 on application
₹40 on allotment
₹20 on September 1, 2017
₹20 on February 1, 2018

On 25 June, it received applications for 5,000 shares. All applications were accepted and allotment was made on July 1, 2017. All sums due on allotment were received on July 15, 2017. Payments on first call were received on 15 September and second call was received on 15 February, except for 400 shares, payment for which was not received till March 31, 2017. Journalise the transactions, and also show how the share capital should be shown on the balance sheet as on March 31, 2018.

Solution

Journal Entries of AL

Date	Particulars	(₹)	(₹)
June 25, 2017	Bank a/c	Dr. 1,00,000	
	To share application and allotment a/c		Cr. 1,00,000
	(being share application money received on 5,000 shares)		
July 1, 2017	Share application and allotment a/c	Dr. 3,00,000	
	To share capital a/c		Cr. 3,00,000

Date	Particulars	(₹)	(₹)
	(being shares allotted to all the 5,000 applicants vide Board of Directors' resolution No. ... dated..., the amount transferred to share capital account, ₹20 on application and ₹40 on allotment)		
July 15, 2017	Bank a/c	Dr. 2,00,000	
	To share application and allotment a/c		Cr. 2,00,000
	(being amount due on share allotment, received on 5,000 shares allotted vide board resolution No. ... dated...)		
Sept. 1, 2017	Share first call a/c	Dr. 1,00,000	
	To share capital a/c		Cr. 1,00,000
	(being amount due from members in respect of first call on 5,000 shares allotted vide Board of Directors' resolution No. ...dated...)		
Sept. 15, 2017	Bank a/c	Dr. 1,00,000	
	To share first call a/c		Cr. 1,00,000
	(being receipt of amount due on first call from members)		
Feb. 1, 2018	Share second call a/c	Dr. 1,00,000	
	To share capital a/c		Cr. 1,00,000
	(being amount due from members in respect of second call on 5,000 shares allotted vide Board of Directors' resolution No. ... dated...)		
Feb. 15, 2018	Bank a/c	Dr. 92,000	
	To share second call a/c		Cr. 92,000
	(being amount received from 4,600 members in respect of second call on 5,000 shares allotted vide Board of Directors' resolution No. ... dated...)		

Balance Sheet of AL as on March 31, 2018 (incomplete)

Liabilities	Amount (₹)	Assets	Amount (₹)
Share capital			
Authorised			
10,000 shares of ₹100 each	10,00,000		
Issued and subscribed	5,00,000		
5,000 shares of ₹100 each fully called up			
Less: Calls unpaid	(8,000)		
	4,92,000		

It is important to note that the credit balance in the share capital account represents the amount of issued and subscribed capital and not the paid-up capital. Paid-up capital is arrived at by deducting the calls' unpaid amount from the amount of issued and subscribed capital. The debit balance in the call account represents the amount of calls unpaid.

Self-Test Questions

Self-test question 9.3

Indicate whether the following statements are true (T) or false (F):

(i) Excess of share application money on shares allotted is adjusted against amount due on allotment.

(ii) Share capital in the balance sheet shows paid up capital.

(iii) Companies cannot ask prospective shareholders to submit full share price with share application.

(iv) Only the board of directors can decide allotment of shares.

(v) An individual, who has applied for shares, can ask for refund of money after allotment.

Issue of Shares at a Premium and at a Discount

Issue of shares at a premium

Companies may issue securities at a premium. For example, a company may issue shares with a face value of ₹100 at ₹1,000, that is, at a premium of ₹900. According to Section 52 of the Companies Act, 2013, where a company issues security at a premium, whether for cash or otherwise, a sum equal to the aggregate amount of the premium should be transferred to an account to be called *the securities premium account.* The securities premium account is treated as share capital. Provisions of the Companies Act relating to the reduction of share capital are applicable to the reduction of the securities premium account. However, a company can apply the securities premium account for the following purposes specified in the Companies Act, 2013:

1. In paying up securities of the company to be issued to members of the company as fully paid bonus securities.
2. In writing off the preliminary expenses of the company. Preliminary expenses include expenditure incurred on the formation of the company and those relating to issue of shares and debentures. Examples are legal expenses, expenses on printing of memorandum of association and other documents, and underwriting commission.
3. In writing off the expenses of, or the commission paid or discount allowed on, any issue of shares or debentures of the company.
4. In providing for the premium payable on redemption of any redeemable preference shares or any debentures of the company.
5. For the purchase of its own shares or other securities under Section 68.

Issue of shares at a discount

Section 53 of the Companies Act 2013 provides that companies cannot issue shares at a discount other than as sweat equity shares.

Self-Test Questions

Self-test question 9.4

Indicate whether the following statements are true (T) or false (F):

(i) Companies are permitted to issue shares at a premium, but not at a discount.
(ii) Premium received on issue of shares can be used for payment of dividend.
(iii) Premium received on issue of shares can be used for issue of bonus shares.
(iv) Premium received on issue of shares can be used for buying back of own shares.
(v) Companies determine the price for issuing shares based on market demand.

Issue of Sweat Equity Shares

Sweat equity shares refer to the equity shares issued by the company to employees or directors at a discount or for consideration other than cash for providing know-how or making available rights in the nature of intellectual property rights or value additions, by whatever name called.

Section 54 of the Companies Act 2013 provides that a company may issue sweat equity shares *of a class of shares already issued* if the following conditions are fulfilled:

1. The issue of sweat equity shares is authorised by a special resolution passed by the company in its general meeting.
2. The resolution specifies the number of shares, current market price, consideration, if any, and the class or classes of directors or employees to whom such equity shares are to be issued.

NOTES

3. Not less than one year has, on the date of issue, elapsed since the date on which the company was entitled to commence business.
4. The sweat equity shares of a company whose equity shares are listed on a recognised stock exchange are issued in accordance with the regulations issued by the Securities and Exchange Board of India (SEBI) in this behalf.

Accounting

The Accounting value of sweat equity shares is their fair value as determined by the registered value.

When sweat equity shares have been issued for a no-cash consideration or at a discount, the difference between the fair value and the consideration received is recognised as an expense (employee benefits). However, if sweat equity shares are issued against consideration in the form of a depreciable or amortisable asset, the asset is recognised in the balance sheet and the difference between the fair value of sweat equity shares and the fair value of the assets received is recognised as expense.

This provision allows a company to issue equity shares at a discount or even without consideration to its employees and directors. This provision is very helpful for new-technology companies in which directors and employees bring with them knowledge which benefits other shareholders. Therefore, it is quite normal for these companies to issue shares to directors and employees at a huge discount as compensation for the intangible assets that they bring in with them.

Self-Test Questions

Self-test question 9.5

Indicate whether the following statements are true (T) or false (F):

(i) Companies can issue sweat equity to any of its employees.
(ii) Sweat equity cannot be issued at a discount.
(iii) A company may issue sweat equity shares only of a class of shares already issued.
(iv) Usually, start-ups and new-technology companies issue sweat equity.
(v) Sweat equity shares are recorded at fair value.

Forfeiture and Reissue of Shares

Articles of association of companies usually authorise directors to forfeit shares of a member on account of non-payment of call or interest thereon after serving him or her a prior notice as prescribed by the articles. Directors may either cancel forfeited shares or reissue those shares at a discount. However, the discount allowed should not exceed the amount forfeited on those shares. For example, a company may reissue forfeited shares of ₹100 each, on which the member failed to pay the call amount of ₹40 after paying ₹60 on application and allotment, at a discount not exceeding ₹60.

On forfeiture of shares issued at a premium, the balance in the share premium account should not be disturbed. For example, a member had paid ₹40 towards share capital and ₹10 towards premium and subsequently failed to pay the balance of ₹60. On forfeiture, only ₹40 would be considered as the amount forfeited, and ₹10 per share would continue to remain in the share premium account. However, if the share premium is not received, the 'share premium account' should be reversed. Subsequently, the Board of Directors may reissue the forfeited shares at the face value. For example, a share (face value ₹100) was issued at ₹120. Application money of ₹40 was received, but the allottee failed to pay ₹80 (including premium of ₹20). The company forfeits the share. On reissue, the company may allow a discount of ₹40 on the face value. Thus, it can issue the share at ₹60 and credit the 'share capital' by ₹100. It is not necessary to issue the share at a premium, though the original issue was at a premium of ₹20.

If shares originally issued at a discount are forfeited, the proportionate amount of discount should be written off. On reissue, the discount proportionate to the shares reissued should be reinstated.

On reissue of forfeited shares, the amount forfeited reduced by the amount of discount allowed (in excess of discount allowed on the original issue) on reissue is transferred to the capital reserve account. In effect, the difference between the total amount (total of the amount forfeited and the amount received on reissue) received on forfeited shares and the amount that ought to be received as per terms of original issue should be transferred to the capital reserve account. For example, ₹80 (including ₹20 towards premium) had been forfeited on shares originally issued at ₹120 (₹100 + premium of ₹20) due to failure, on the part of the original allottee, to pay ₹40 towards call money. The forfeited shares are now issued at ₹90. The total amount received on forfeited shares is ₹80 + ₹90, i.e., ₹170 (as against ₹120), which ought to be received as per the original terms of issue. Therefore, ₹50 should be transferred to the capital reserve account. Let us take another example. ₹60 had been forfeited on shares that were originally issued at ₹90 (₹100 – discount of ₹10). The shares are now issued at ₹60. On reissue, ₹60 + ₹60 – ₹90, that is, ₹30 should be transferred to the capital reserve account.

CASE STUDY 9.2

A Ltd. invited applications for 10,000 shares of ₹100 each at a discount of ₹6 per share, payable as follows:

On application	₹25
On allotment	₹35
On first and final call	₹34

The company accepted all the 9,000 applications received. The entire money was received except the first and final call on 100 shares. The company has forfeited those 100 shares and subsequently reissued 50 shares at ₹90 per share, as fully paid. Pass entries in the journal proper and show how balances in the ledger account should be exhibited in the balance sheet. [Please note that companies are not allowed to issue shares at a discount, except sweat equity.]

Solution

Journal Entries of A Ltd.

Particulars	₹	₹
Bank a/c	Dr. 2,25,000	
To share application and allotment a/c		Cr. 2,25,000
(being application money received for 9,000 shares at the rate of ₹25 per share)		
Share application and allotment a/c	Dr. 5,40,000	
Discount on shares a/c	Dr. 54,000	
To share capital a/c		Cr. 5,94,000
(being allotment of 9,000 shares of ₹100 each at a discount of ₹6 per share vide Board of Directors' resolution No. ... dated..., ₹25 received with application, ₹35 due on allotment)		
Bank a/c	Dr. 3,15,000	
To share application and allotment a/c		Cr. 3,15,000
(being receipt of amount due on allotment on 9,000 shares allotted vide Board of Directors' resolution No. ... dated...)		
Share first and final call a/c	Dr. 3,06,000	
To share capital a/c		Cr. 3,06,000
(being amount due on 9,000 shares at the rate of ₹34 per share vide Board of Directors' resolution No. ... dated...)		
Bank a/c	Dr. 3,02,600	
To share first and final call a/c		Cr. 3,02,600
(being amount received at the rate of ₹35 per share on 8,900 shares)		
Share capital a/c*	Dr. 10,000	
To share first and final call a/c		Cr. 3,400

NOTES

Particulars		₹	₹
To discount on share a/c	Cr.		600
To share forfeited a/c	Cr.		6,000
(being forfeiture of 100 shares on which ₹94 have been called up and on which first and final call to the extent of ₹3,400 is in arrears vide Board of Directors' resolution No. ... dated...)			
Bank a/c	Dr.	4,500	
Discount on shares a/c	Dr.	300	
Share forfeited a/c	Dr.	200	
To share capital a/c	Cr.		5,000
(being the reissue of 50 shares of ₹100 each at ₹90 per share vide Board of Directors' resolution No. ... dated...)			
Share forfeited a/c**	Dr.	2,800	
To capital reserve a/c	Cr.		2,800
(being profit remaining after reissue of 50 shares, transferred to capital reserve a/c)			

* Note that share capital was credited by ₹100 × 100, that is ₹10,000 for 100 shares. The total credit is being reversed on forfeiture.

** The total amount received on each reissued forfeited share is ₹60 + ₹90, that is, ₹150, as against ₹94, which ought to be received as per the original terms. Therefore, (₹150 – ₹94) × 50, that is ₹2,800 is transferred to the capital reserve account.

Balance Sheet of A Ltd. as on ... (incomplete)

Liabilities	Amount (₹)	Assets	Amount (₹)
Share capital		Bank	8,47,100
Authorised capital		Discount on shares	53,700
Issued and subscribed		(8,950 × ₹6)	
8,950 shares of ₹ 100 each	8,95,000		
Add shares forfeited	3,000		
	8,98,000		
Capital reserve	2,800		
	9,00,800		9,00,800

CASE STUDY 9.3

A Ltd. was registered on March 1, 2017 with an authorised capital of 1,00,000 shares of ₹100 each. The company offered 50,000 shares to the public at an issue price of ₹110. From the following particulars, record the transactions in the journal proper and show how balance amounts in ledger accounts should be shown in the balance sheet as on March 31, 2018. Assume that the reporting year ends on March 31, 2018.

Details of transactions

2017

Apr. 4 Received applications for 70,000 shares with a payment of ₹20 per share.

Apr. 20 Allotment was made as per details given below:

35,000 shares were allotted in full.

10,000 shares were allotted to those who had applied for 20,000 shares.

5,000 shares were allotted to those who had applied for 15,000 shares.

Amount due on allotment ₹40 (including premium of ₹10).

The Articles provide that the surplus money on application after adjustment of the money due on allotment was to be retained against further calls to be made.

May 15 Balance of amount due on allotment received in full.

Sept. 15 Made first call of ₹30 per share, payable on September 30, 2017.

Sept. 30 Amount due on first call received in full except from Mr. Raman, who applied for 1,000 shares and to whom allotment was made in full.

Dec. 1 Made final call of ₹20 per share, payable on December 15, 2017.

Dec. 15 Amount due on final call received in full except from Mr. Raman.

2018

Jan. 30 Board decided to forfeit the shares allotted to Mr. Raman.

Mar. 1 Board decided to reissue the forfeited shares at ₹90.

Solution

Journal of A Ltd.

Date	Particulars	₹	₹
Apr. 4, 2017	Bank a/c	Dr. 14,00,000	
	To share application and allotment a/c		Cr. 14,00,000
	(being application money received for 70,000 shares at the rate of ₹20 per share)		
Apr. 20, 2017	Share application and allotment a/c	Dr. 30,00,000	
	To share capital a/c		Cr. 25,00,000
	To share premium a/c		Cr. 5,00,000
	(being allotment of 50,000 shares vide Board of Directors resolution No. ... dated..., ₹20 per share received with application, ₹40 due on allotment—₹30 on account of capital and ₹10 on account of premium)		
May 15, 2017	Bank a/c	Dr. 16,00,000	
	To share application and allotment a/c		Cr. 16,00,000
	(being receipt of amount due on allotment of 50,000 shares allotted vide Board of Director's resolution No. ... dated...)		
Sept. 15, 2017	Share first call a/c	Dr. 15,00,000	
	To share capital a/c		Cr. 15,00,000
	(being amount due on 50,000 shares at the rate of ₹30 per share vide Board of Directors' resolution No. ... dated...)		
Sept. 30, 2017	Bank a/c	Dr. 14,70,000	
	To share first call a/c		Cr. 14,70,000
	(being amount received at the rate of ₹30 on 49,000 shares)		
Dec. 1, 2017	Share final call a/c	Dr. 10,00,000	
	To share capital a/c		Cr. 10,00,000
	(being final call due on 50,000 shares at the rate of ₹20 per share vide Board of Directors' resolution No. ... dated...)		
Dec. 15, 2017	Bank a/c	Dr. 9,80,000	
	To share final call a/c		Cr. 9,80,000
	(being amount received against the final call on 50,000 shares vide Board of Directors' resolution No. ... dated...)		
Jan. 20, 2018	Share capital a/c	Dr. 1,00,000	
	To share first call a/c		Cr. 30,000
	To share final call a/c		Cr. 20,000
	To share forfeited a/c		Cr. 50,000
	(being forfeiture of 1,000 shares on which ₹100 have been called up and on which the first call is in arrears to the extent of ₹30,000 and second call is in arrears to the extent of ₹20,000, vide Board of Directors' resolution No. ... dated...)		

NOTES

Key Terms
Allotment, forfeiture of shares, preliminary expenses, sweat equity share

Date	Particulars		Dr.	Cr.
Mar. 1, 2018	Bank a/c	Dr.	90,000	
	Shares forfeited a/c	Dr.	10,000	
	To share capital			1,00,000
	(being the reissue of 1,000 shares of ₹100 each at ₹90 per share vide Board of Directors' resolution No. ... dated...)			
Mar. 1, 2018	Share forfeited a/c	Dr.	40,000	
	To capital reserve a/c*			40,000
	(being balance in share forfeited account, after adjustment for discount on the reissue of forfeited shares transferred to capital reserve account)			

* Total amount received on each forfeited share is ₹(60 + 90), that is, ₹150, as against ₹110, which ought to be received as per the terms of the original offer. Therefore, the amount transferred to the capital reserve account is ₹(150 – 110) × 1,000, that is, ₹40,000.

Balance Sheet of 'A' Ltd. as on March 31, 2018 (incomplete)

Liabilities	Amount (₹)	Assets	Amount (₹)
Share capital		Bank	55,40,000
Authorised			
1,00,000 shares of ₹100 each	1,00,00,000		
Issued and subscribed			
50,000 shares of ₹ 100 each fully called up	50,00,000		
Share premium	500,000		
Capital reserve	40,000		
	55,40,000		55,40,000

Self-Test Questions

Self-test question 9.6

Indicate whether the following statements are true (T) or false (F):

(i) Shares on which the allotment money or call money remains unpaid can be forfeited.
(ii) Companies are not permitted to issue forfeited shares at a discount.
(iii) Companies are not permitted to issue forfeited shares at a price below the original issue price.
(iv) Gains on reissue of forfeited shares is capital profit.

SUMMARY

Companies can issue shares at par or at a premium, but not at a discount. Companies are permitted to issue sweat equity shares at a discount or without consideration to their employees and directors. Premium received on issue of shares at a premium is recognised in the balance sheet as 'securities premium reserve'. Companies cannot use securities premium reserve for payment of dividend, but can use it for issue of bonus shares or for buying back own shares. Sweat equity shares are accounted for at fair value.

SHARE SPLIT AND BONUS SHARES

Share Split

A company, if authorised by its Articles of association, may in a General Meeting decide to subdivide (split) or consolidate the shares into those of a smaller or higher denomination

NOTES

than that fixed by the memorandum of association. However, the company must continue to maintain the same proportion between the paid-up and unpaid amount, as it was in the case of the original shares. For example, a company with an authorised capital of ₹1,00,000 divided into 10,000 equity shares of ₹10 each, may decide to subdivide its shares into two shares of ₹5 each.

Usually, companies subdivide shares to increase the number of shares floating in the capital market. Subdivision also enhances liquidity when shares are traded at such a high price that investors find it difficult to participate in trade. For example, 1,00,000 shares of ₹10 each of 'A' Ltd. are outstanding on December 31, 2000. The market capitalisation as on that date is ₹100 million, that is, the shares are traded at ₹1,000 per share. The company decides to subdivide the shares into two shares of ₹5 each. This should not increase market capitalisation. However, this will increase the number of outstanding shares to 2,00,000 shares, resulting in reduction of the market price per share to ₹500. However, in practice, subdivision will make the shares more attractive, and this might enhance the price marginally. For instance, on August 17, 2010 the stock of Housing Development Finance Corporation (HDFC) was trading at ₹3,011.45. The company split the share in a ratio of 1 : 5 and the share price closed at ₹621.20 on August 18, 2010 (post-split).

Companies may convert fully paid shares into stock and stock into shares. *Stock is the consolidation of the share capital into one unit divisible into aliquant parts.*

Self-Test Questions

Self-test question 9.7

Indicate whether the following statements are true (T) or false (F):

(i) Stock split enhances the attractiveness of the shares by enhancing liquidity.

(ii) Stock split creates value for shareholders as market capitalisation increases significantly after stock split.

(iii) Companies reward shareholders through stock split when it continuously perform better than capital market expectations.

(iv) Stock split increases the number of shares a shareholder holds and, thus, makes it convenient for him/her to divide the wealth.

Bonus Shares

Companies capitalise free reserves, share premium and capital redemption reserve by issuing bonus shares to members. Issue of bonus shares does not result in inflow of funds to the company, it results in conversion of reserves into issued, subscribed and paid-up capital.

Section 63 of the Companies Act, 2013 provides that a company can issue fully paid bonus shares to its members, out of:

(i) its free reserves,

(ii) the securities premium account, or

(iii) the capital redemption reserve account.

No issue of bonus shares shall be made by capitalising reserves created by the revaluation of assets.

No company shall capitalise its profit or reserves for the purpose of issuing fully paid-up bonus shares, unless:

(a) it is authorised by its articles,

(b) it has, on the recommendation of the Board, been authorised in the general meeting of the company,

(c) it has not defaulted in payment of interest or principal in respect of fixed deposits or debt securities issued by it,

NOTES

(d) it has not defaulted in respect of payment of statutory dues of the employees, such as, contribution to provident fund, gratuity or bonus,
(e) the partly paid-up shares, if any outstanding on the date of allotment are made fully paid-up,
(f) it complies with such conditions as may be prescribed.

The relevant rules prescribe that the company which has once announced the decision of its Board recommending the bonus issue, shall not subsequently withdraw the same.

The SEBI guidelines require that a listed company can issue bonus shares out of free reserves built out of the genuine profits or share premium collected in cash only. It further provides the following guidelines:

1. Revaluation reserve created on revaluation of fixed assets should not be capitalised.
2. The bonus issue is not made unless the partly paid shares, if any existing, are made fully paid-up.
3. The benefit of bonus issue should be extended to the holders of Fully Convertible Debentures (FCDs)/Partly Convertible Debentures (PCDs), through reservation of shares in proportion to such convertible part of FCDs or PCDs.
4. A company that has defaulted in payment of interest or principal in respect of fixed deposits/debentures should not issue bonus shares.
5. A company that has defaulted in respect of the payment of statutory dues of the employees should not issue bonus shares.
6. There should be a provision in the articles of association of the company for capitalisation of reserves.
7. A company that announces its bonus issue after the approval of the Board of Directors must implement the proposal within a period of six months from the date of such approval and shall not have the option of changing the decision.
8. Consequent to the issue of bonus shares, if the subscribed and paid-up capital exceeds the authorised share capital, a resolution should be passed by the company at its General Body Meeting for increasing the authorised capital.

Usually, companies issue bonus shares to give a positive signal to the capital market and to enhance the feel good factor. Moreover, bonus issue increases the number of floating shares in the market and thus enhances liquidity. Issue of bonus shares should not result in any change in the amount of market capitalisation. However, in practice, market capitalisation increases, because of improvement in market sentiments about the scrip. In most situations, capital markets do not wait for actual issue of bonus shares: they discount the good news immediately on hearing rumours of a possible bonus issue. Therefore, market capitalisation increases even before the actual issue of bonus shares, and the event of actual issue does not further enhance market capitalisation.

CASE STUDY 9.4

A Ltd.: Extract of Balance Sheet as on March 31, 2018

		₹
Authorised capital		
1,00,000	Equity shares of ₹10 each	10,00,000
Issued and subscribed capital		
80,000	Equity shares of ₹10 each, ₹8 paid up	6,40,000
Reserve and surplus		
	General reserve	1,00,000
	Capital reserve	60,000

NOTES

	Share premium	25,000
	Profit and loss a/c	1,50,000
Secured loan		
	12 percent preference shares of ₹10 each fully paid	90,000
	12 percent partly convertible debentures of ₹100 each	5,00,000
		15,65,000

On April 1, 2018, the company called up the balance of ₹2 per share on 80,000 equity shares. The call money was received in full by April 15, 2018. On April 30, 2018, the Board of Directors decided to issue bonus shares at the rate of one share for every four shares held.

Share premium includes a premium of ₹10,000 for shares issued to vendors pursuant to an agreement for which no payment was received in cash. 20 percent of 12 percent debentures are convertible into equity shares of ₹10 each fully paid on July 1, 2018.

Show the necessary journal entries in the books of 'A' Ltd., and prepare the extract of the balance sheet immediately after the bonus issue, but before the conversion of debentures.

Solution

Journal of 'A' Ltd.

Date	**Particulars**		₹		₹
Apr. 1, 2017	Equity share final call a/c	Dr.	1,60,000		
	To equity share capital a/c			Cr.	1,60,000
	(being final call at the rate of ₹2 per share on 80,000 shares, due vide Board of Directors' resolution No. ... dated...)				
Apr. 15, 2017	Bank a/c	Dr.	1,60,000		
	To equity share final call a/c			Cr.	1,60,000
	(being receipt of call money on 80,000 shares in full)				
Apr. 30, 2017	Capital reserve a/c	Dr.	60,000		
	Share premium a/c	Dr.	15,000		
	General reserve a/c	Dr.	1,00,000		
	Profit and loss a/c	Dr.	25,000		
	To bonus to shareholders a/c			Cr.	2,00,000
	(being bonus issue at the rate of one share for every four shares held by utilising various reserves vide Board of Directors' resolution No. ... dated...)				
Apr. 30, 2017	Bonus to shareholders a/c	Dr.	2,00,000		
	To equity share capital a/c			Cr.	2,00,000
	(being capitalisation of profit)				

A Ltd.: Extract of Balance Sheet as on April 30, 2017

Authorised capital			
	1,22,500	Equity shares of ₹10 each	12,25,000
			13,25,000
Issued and subscribed capital			
	1,00,000	Equity shares of ₹10 each, fully paid (Out of above, 20,000 equity shares of ₹10 each were issued by way of bonus)	10,00,000
Reserve and surplus			
		Share premium	10,000
		Profit and loss a/c	1,25,000

NOTES

Secured loan		
	12 percent preference shares of ₹10 each, fully paid	90,000
	12 percent partly convertible debentures of ₹100 each	5,00,000
		17,25,000

Working notes:

1. As per SEBI guidelines, share premium collected in cash can only be utilised for bonus issue. Therefore, only ₹15,000 could be utilised for the bonus issue.
2. Number of equity shares to be issued:

To existing shareholders	20,000
To be reserved for debenture-holders	2,500
	22,500

Key Terms
Stock split, bonus shares

Self-Test Questions

Self-test question 9.8

Indicate whether the following statements are true (T) or false (F):

(i) Bonus shares are shares issued to shareholders free of cost.
(ii) Issue of bonus shares enhances the feel good factor, but not market capitalisation.
(iii) Issue of bonus shares enhances share capital in the balance sheet, but not the equity.
(iv) Issue of bonus shares has exactly the same effect as stock split.

SUMMARY

In stock split, the face value of the shares change. Issue of bonus shares does not change the face value. However, in both the cases, the number of shares in the hand of existing shareholders increases. In both the cases, the fundamental value of the company does not change. On issue of bonus shares, a part of the reserves and surplus is transferred to share capital, while in stock split, there is no transfer from reserves and surplus to share capital.

RIGHTS ISSUE

Section 62 of the Companies Act, 2013, provides a pre-emptive right to existing shareholders to subscribe to further issue of capital by the company. The Companies Act, 2013, requires that where at any time, it is proposed to increase the subscribed capital of the company by allotment of further shares, then such further shares shall be offered to the persons who are holders of equity shares on the date of the offer. The offer is to be made in proportion to the capital paid up on those shares on that date.

Unless the Articles of association of the company otherwise provide, the offer for rights issue is deemed to include a right to renounce the shares in favour of any other person. On expiry of the specified period within which the offer for rights issue is to be accepted or the right to renounce is to be exercised, the Board of Directors may dispose of the shares in such manner as they think most beneficial to the company.

Market value of a share with rights-on contains the value of the right. Therefore, the offer price should be lower than the market price at the expiration date. If the offer price is equal to the market price at the expiration date, the right to subscribe, which is traded in the market, will have zero value. Moreover, a rational investor will only subscribe to the rights offering if the offer price is below the market price at the expiration date.

CASE STUDY 9.5

'A' Ltd. decides to issue right shares at a time when the prevailing market price is ₹48 per share. It decides to issue one right share at ₹37 each for every 10 shares held.

Required

Calculate the value of the right.

Solution

The stock holding before rights issue is ₹48 × 10, or ₹480. If the shareholder subscribes to the rights issue, the value of 11 shares increases to ₹480 + ₹37, or ₹517. The price after the rights issue should be ₹(517/11), or ₹47. The only difference between the old (right-on) share price of ₹48 and the new (ex-rights) share price of ₹47 is that the former carried rights to subscribe to the issue. The difference of ₹1 is the price of one right. Someone who does not hold shares in A Ltd. may acquire ten rights and then exercise them at a further cost of ₹37. The total cost would be (₹1 × 10) + ₹37, or ₹47. The alternative is that he or she can purchase ex-right share from the market at ₹47. It should be appreciated that the rights issue does not enhance the productivity of assets in place, and thus do not change the expected cash flow stream. Therefore, the issue price is irrelevant as long as the rights are exercised.

Self-Test Questions

Self-test question 9.9

Indicate whether the following statements are true (T) or false (F):

(i) Right issue refers pre-emptive right to existing shareholders to subscribe to further issue of capital by the company.

(ii) A shareholder has the option not to subscribe to the righ issue.

(iii) Right to subscribe is traded in the market.

(iv) Logically, Right shares should be issued at a price below the market price at the expiration date.

BUY-BACK OF SHARES

Companies Act, 2013 and SEBI (Buy-Back of Securities) Regulations regulate buy-back of own shares.

Sections 68, 69 and 70 of the Companies Act, 2013, deal with share buy-back. Companies can buy-back their own shares and other specified securities out of:

1. Their free reserves.
2. The securities premium account.
3. The proceeds of any shares or other specified securities.

Provided that no buy-back of any kind of shares or other specified securities shall be made out of the proceeds of an earlier issue of the same kind of shares or same kind of other specified securities. No company can purchase its own shares or other specified securities unless:

1. The buy-back is authorised by the articles of association.
2. A special resolution has been passed in a general meeting of the company authorising the buy-back.
3. The buy-back is 25 percent or less than 25 percent of the total paid-up capital and free reserves of the company.
4. The buy-back of equity shares in any financial year should not exceed 25 percent of its total paid-up equity capital in that financial year.

NOTES

Key Terms
Treasury stock

5. The ratio of the debt owed by the company is not more than twice the capital and its free reserves after such buy-back, unless the Central Government prescribes a higher ratio.
6. All the shares or other specified securities for buy-back are fully paid up.

Listed companies should buy-back shares and other specified securities in accordance with SEBI regulations. Every buy-back should be completed within twelve months from the date of passing the special resolution in the general meeting. The buy-back may be:

(a) from the existing security holders on a proportionate basis,
(b) from the open market,
(c) from odd lots, and
(d) by purchasing the securities issued to employees of the company pursuant to a scheme of stock option or sweat equity.

When a company buys-back its own securities, it will extinguish and physically destroy the securities so bought-back within seven days of the last date of completion of buy-back. If a company completes a buy-back of its shares or other specified securities, it shall not make further issue of the same kind of shares or other specified securities within a period of six months except by way of bonus issue or in the discharge of subsisting obligations, such as conversion of warrants, stock option scheme, sweat equity or conversion of preference shares or debentures into equity shares.

No company can purchase its own shares if a default by the company in repayment of deposit or interest payable thereon, redemption of debentures or preference shares, or payment of dividend to any shareholder, or repayment of any term loan or interest payable thereon to any financial institution or bank is subsisting. Where a company purchases its own shares out of free reserves, or securities premium account, then a sum equal to the nominal value of the share so purchased should be transferred to the capital redemption reserve account and the details of such transfer should be disclosed in the balance sheet. Free reserves means those reserves that are free for distribution as dividend.

Companies buy-back their own shares to distribute surplus cash to shareholders, or to enhance the share price in the capital market by reducing the number of floating shares, or for restructuring their capital by reducing the proportion of share capital in the capital structure or to increase the proportion of promoters holding.

Though, in India, companies are not allowed to hold bought-back shares as *treasury stock* that can be reissued, in the USA, reissue of bought-back shares is permitted under relevant statutes.

Self-Test Questions

Self-test question 9.10

Indicate whether the following statements are true (T) or false (F):

(i) Securities premium reserve can be used to buy-back shares.
(ii) Companies often use share buy-back to distribute excess cash to shareholders.
(iii) Companies can reissue bought back shares.
(iv) Controlling shareholders often do not participate in share buy-back scheme to enhance their holding (as a percentage of total outstanding shares).
(v) The Companies Act, 2013 does not permit a company to hold treasury stock.

SUMMARY

Companies buy-back shares to distribute excess cash to shareholders. Often the controlling shareholder does not participate in the buy-back scheme to strengthen his/her control. Companies Act, 2013 and SEBI (Buy-Back of Securities) Regulations regulate buy-back of own shares. Companies are required to extinguish bought back shares within seven days. They are not permitted to hold bought back shares as treasury stock and reissue the same. Companies are allowed to buy-back shares from (a) their free reserves (b) the securities premium account; and (c) the proceeds of any shares or other specified securities.

NOTES

REDEMPTION OF PREFERENCE SHARES

A company limited by shares, if so authorised by its 'Articles of association', may issue *redeemable preference shares.* These shares can be redeemed only out of profits of the company that would otherwise be available for dividend, or out of proceeds of fresh issue of shares made for the purpose of redemption. When new shares are issued at a premium, the amount received excluding premium should be considered as 'proceeds from the fresh issue'. On the other hand, when shares are issued at par or at a discount, the actual amount received should be considered as 'proceeds from the fresh issue'.

Preference shares cannot be redeemed unless they are fully paid. The premium, if any, payable on redemption must be provided for out of the profits of the company or out of the share premium account before the shares are redeemed.

Where preference shares are redeemed other than from the proceeds of a fresh issue, a sum equal to the nominal amount of the shares redeemed should be transferred from profit to the *capital redemption reserve account.* The capital redemption reserve account can be utilised for the issue of bonus shares. The objective of such transfer is to ensure that the security for creditors is not reduced.

If preference shares are redeemed by converting into some other types of shares, no amount is required to be transferred to the capital redemption reserve account.

CASE STUDY 9.6

Case 1 'A' Ltd. decides to redeem at par ₹2,00,000 of 12 percent preference shares by fresh issue of 8,000 shares of ₹10 each at par.

₹1,20,000 should be transferred to the capital redemption reserve account.

Case 2 'B' Ltd. decides to redeem at par ₹2,00,000 of 12 percent preference shares by fresh issue of 8,000 shares of ₹10 each at 10 percent premium.

₹1,20,000 should be transferred to the capital redemption reserve account.

Case 3 'C' Ltd. decides to redeem at par ₹2,00,000 of 12 percent preference shares by fresh issue of 8,000 shares of ₹10 each at 10 percent discount.

₹1,28,000 should be transferred to the capital redemption reserve account.

Case 4 'D' Ltd. decides to redeem ₹2,00,000 of 12 percent preference shares at a premium of 10 percent by fresh issue of 8,000 shares of ₹10 each at 10 percent discount.

₹128,000 should be transferred to the capital redemption reserve account.

Case 5 'E' Ltd. decides to redeem ₹2,00,000 of 12 percent preference shares at par. The balance sheet shows profit of ₹40,000 and share premium of ₹10,000.

The proceeds from fresh issue of capital should not be less than ₹1,60,000, because premium of ₹10,000 is not available for transfer to the capital redemption reserve account.

Case 6 'F' Ltd. decides to redeem ₹2,00,000 of 12 percent preference shares at 10 percent premium. The balance sheet shows profit of ₹40,000 and share premium of ₹10,000.

The proceeds from fresh issue of capital should not be less than ₹1,70,000, because after adjustment of premium on redemption only ₹30,000 would be available for transfer to the capital redemption reserve account.

Case 7 'G' Ltd. decides to redeem ₹2,00,000 of 12 percent preference shares at 10 percent premium. The balance sheet shows profit of ₹40,000, general reserve ₹20,000, dividend equalisation fund ₹40,000 and share premium ₹10,000.

The proceeds from the fresh issue of capital should not be less than ₹1,10,000, because after adjustment of premium on redemption, only ₹90,000 would be available for transfer to the capital redemption reserve account.

NOTES

CASE STUDY 9.7

The balance sheet of 'A' Ltd. as on December 31, 2017 is as follows:

Liabilities	Amount (₹)	Amount (₹)	Assets	Amount (₹)	Amount (₹)
Share capital:			PP&E		
Issued and fully paid			Land and buildings	1,20,000	
10,000 equity shares of			Plant	50,000	
₹10 each		1,00,000	Furniture	20,000	1,90,000
Reserve surplus:			Current assets:		
Share premium	10,000		Stock	30,000	
General reserve	40,000		Debtors	30,000	
Profit and loss	30,000	80,000	Investments	40,000	
Borrowings			Bank	20,000	1,20,000
1,000 12 percent redeemable preference shares of ₹100 each		1,00,000			
Current liabilities		30,000			
		3,10,000			3,10,000

The company decided to redeem its preference shares at a premium of 5 percent on January 31, 2018. A fresh issue of 5,000 equity shares of ₹10 each was made at ₹12 per share payable in full on January 31, 2018. These were fully subscribed and all monies were duly collected. All investments were sold, realising ₹45,000. The Board of Directors decided that only the minimum reduction should be made in the revenue reserve.

Give the journal entries for the transactions including those relating to bank and draw of the balance sheet as it would appear after redemption of preference shares.

Solution

Journal of 'A' Ltd.

Date	Particulars		₹		₹
2018					
Jan. 31	Bank a/c	Dr.	45,000		
	To profit on sale of investment a/c			Cr.	5,000
	To investment a/c			Cr.	40,000
	(being realisation of profit on sale of investments)				
Jan. 31	Bank a/c	Dr.	60,000		
	To share application and allotment a/c			Cr.	60,000
	(being application money received on 5,000 shares at the rate of ₹12 per share)				
Jan. 31	Share application and allotment a/c	Dr.	60,000		
	To equity share capital a/c			Cr.	50,000
	To share premium a/c			Cr.	10,000
	(being transfer of application money on 5,000 shares on allotment vide Board of Directors' resolution No. ... dated...)				
Jan. 31	Redeemable preference share capital a/c	Dr.	1,00,000		
	Share premium a/c	Dr.	5,000		
	To preference shareholders a/c			Cr.	1,05,000
	(being amount payable on redemption of preference shares at a premium of 5 percent premium debited to the share premium a/c)				
Jan. 31	Preference shareholders a/c	Dr.	1,05,000		
	To bank a/c			Cr.	1,05,000
	(being amount due to preference shareholders paid)				

Jan. 31	General reserve a/c	Dr. 15,000	
	Profit and loss a/c	Dr. 35,000	
	To capital redemption reserve a/c		Cr. 50,000
	(being amount transferred on redemption of preference shares for the difference between the nominal value of preference shares redeemed and the nominal value of new shares issued, that is, ₹1,00,000 – ₹50,000)		

Balance Sheet of 'A' Ltd.
As on January 31, 2018 (After redemption of preference shares)

Liabilities	Amount (₹)	Amount (₹)	Assets	Amount (₹)	Amount (₹)
Share capital:			PP&E		
15,000 equity shares of		1,50,000	Land and buildings	120,000	
₹10 each 1,000 12%			Plant	50,000	
Reserve surplus:			Furniture	20,000	1,90,000
Share premium	15,000		Current assets:		
Capital redemption reserve	50,000		Stock	30,000	
General reserve	25,000	90,000	Debtors	30,000	
Current liabilities		30,000	Bank	20,000	80,000
		2,70,000			2,70,000

Self-Test Questions

Self-test question 9.11

Indicate whether the following statements are true (T) or false (F):

(i) Preference shares cannot be redeemed unless they are fully paid.
(ii) Preference shares must be redeemed within 10 years from the date of issue.
(iii) If preference shares are redeemed by converting into some other types of shares, no amount is required to be transferred to the capital redemption reserve account.
(iv) Capital redemption reserve cannot be used for payment of dividend.

SUMMARY

Companies are not allowed to issue irredeemable preference shares. Redeemable preference shares can be redeemed only out of profits of the company that would otherwise be available for dividend, or out of proceeds of fresh issue of shares made for the purpose of redemption. Where preference shares are redeemed other than from the proceeds of a fresh issue, a sum equal to the nominal amount of the shares redeemed should be transferred from profit to the *capital redemption reserve account*. If preference shares are redeemed by converting into some other types of shares, no amount is required to be transferred to the capital redemption reserve account.

PRESENTATION OF SHARE CAPITAL IN BALANCE SHEET

Schedule III of the Companies Act, 2013, provides the format in which a company should present its balance sheet.

Examples of how share capital is presented in published financial statements in accordance with requirements of the Companies Act, 2013, are given as follows:

NOTES

Extract from the report and accounts of 1999 of Hindustan Lever Ltd.

	March 31, 2017 (₹, crores)	31 March 2016 (₹, Crores)
A Capital		
Authorised		
2,25,00,00,000 equity shares of ₹1 each	225	225
Issued, subscribed and fully paid-up		
2,16,43,49,639 (March 31, 2016: 2,16,39,36,971)		
equity shares of ₹1 each fully called and paid up	216	216

Schedule III (Division II) requires disclosure of following additional information:

Equity Share Capital: For each class of equity share capital:

(a) the number and amount of shares authorised;
(b) the number of shares issued, subscribed and fully paid, and subscribed but not fully paid;
(c) par value per share;
(d) a reconciliation of the number of shares outstanding at the beginning and at the end of the period;
(e) the rights, preferences and restrictions attaching to each class of shares including restrictions on the distribution of dividends and the repayment of capital;
(f) shares in respect of each class in the company held by its holding company or its ultimate holding company including shares held by subsidiaries or associates of the holding company or the ultimate holding company in aggregate;
(g) shares in the company held by each shareholder holding more than five percent shares specifying the number of shares held;
(h) shares reserved for issue under options and contracts or commitments for the sale of shares or disinvestment, including the terms and amounts;
(i) for the period of five years immediately preceding the date at which the Balance Sheet is prepared:
(a) aggregate number and class of shares allotted as fully paid-up pursuant to contract without payment being received in cash; (b) aggregate number and class of shares allotted as fully paid-up by way of bonus shares; (c) aggregate number and class of shares bought back;
(j) terms of any securities convertible into equity shares issued along with the earliest date of conversion in descending order starting from the farthest such date;
(k) calls unpaid (showing aggregate value of calls unpaid by directors and officers);
(l) forfeited shares (amount originally paid up).

OTHER EQUITY

We have discussed components and presentation of Other Equity in Chapter 5.

ACCOUNTING FOR DEBENTURES

Issue of Debentures

Accounting entries for issue of debentures are similar to accounting entries for issue of shares. Sometimes, debentures are issued as additional security against a loan. In such a case, the loan would appear as a liability; the debentures issued would be shown only within brackets below the particulars of loan to indicate the fact that they have been issued only as a security. Thus, debentures would not be recognised as a separate liability. Alternatively, a suspense account may be debited with the amount of debentures issued as an additional security and the amount credited to the debentures account. The entry is reversed on the payment of the loan. No interest is payable on such debentures.

CASE STUDY 9.8

'A' Ltd. secured a bank loan of ₹1,00,000 by issuing 1,200 of 10 percent debentures of ₹100 each as collateral security. Show how the debentures should be shown in the balance sheet of the company.

Solution (First alternative)

A Ltd.: Balance Sheet as on ... (extract)

Liabilities	**Amount (₹)**
Secured loan Bank loan (secured by the issue of 1,200 of 10 percent debentures of ₹100 each as collateral security)	1,00,000

(Second alternative)

Journal Entries of A Ltd.

Particulars	**₹**	**₹**
Debenture suspense a/c	Dr. 1,20,000	
To 10 percent debentures a/c		Cr. 1,20,000
(being issue of 1,200 of 10 percent debentures of ₹100 each as a collateral security for a bank loan of ₹1,00,000 vide Board of Directors' resolution No. ... dated...)		

A Ltd.: Balance Sheet as on ... (extract)

Liabilities	**Amount (₹)**	**Assets**	**Amount (₹)**
Secured loan: 1,200 of 10 percent debentures of ₹100 each (issued as collateral security)	1,20,000	*Miscellaneous expenses* Debenture suspense a/c	1,20,000
Bank loan secured by the issue of 1,200 of 10% debentures of ₹100 each as collateral security	1,00,000		

Issue and Redemption of Debentures at a Premium

Debenture is a liability, which is measured at amortised cost. Therefore, effective interest rate is calculated adjusting the coupon rate by the premium or discount on issue of the debentures and also by premium on redemption of debentures.

We discussed Effective Interest Rate in Chapter 5.

Debentures issued at a premium

Debentures may be issued at a premium, that is, at a price higher than the face value. For example, debenture with face value of ₹1,000 and coupon rate of 12 percent per annum, are issued at ₹1,100. Debentures will be redeemed at face value, that is, at maturity, debenture holders will receive ₹1,000 per debenture. Assume that the transaction cost incurred in issuing the debentures is ₹1 per debenture. The company should initially recognise the liability at ₹1,099 per debenture. Effective interest rate (EIR) will be lower than the coupon rate of 12 percent per annum. EIR method will ensure that at the time of maturity the carrying amount of the liability will be ₹1000 per debenture. Therefore, on redemption, the liability will be derecognised.

Debentures issued at a discount

Debentures may be issued at a discount, that is, at a price lower than the face value. For example, debenture with face value of ₹1,000 and coupon rate of 12 percent per annum, are

NOTES

issued at ₹900. Debentures will be redeemed at face value, that is, at maturity, debenture holders will receive ₹1,000 per debenture. Assume that the transaction cost incurred in issuing the debentures is ₹1 per debenture. The company should initially recognise the liability at ₹899 per debenture. Effective interest rate (EIR) will be higher than the coupon rate of 12 percent per annum. EIR method will ensure that at the time of maturity the carrying amount of the liability will be ₹1000 per debenture. Therefore, on redemption the liability will be derecognised.

Debentures redeemable at premium

The terms and conditions of issue of debentures may commit redemption of debentures at a premium. For example, debenture with face value of ₹1,000 and coupon rate of 12 percent per annum, are issued at ₹1,000. Debentures will be redeemed at 1,100 per debenture, that is, at maturity, debenture holders will receive ₹1,100 per debenture. Assume that the transaction cost incurred in issuing the debentures is ₹1 per debenture. The company should initially recognise the liability at ₹999 per debenture. Effective interest rate (EIR) will be higher than the coupon rate of 12 percent per annum. EIR method will ensure that at the time of maturity the carrying amount of the liability will be ₹1000 per debenture. Therefore, on redemption the liability will be derecognised.

Debenture Redemption Reserve

Companies are allowed to issue only redeemable debentures. Redeemable debentures may be redeemed after a fixed number of years or any time after a certain number of years have elapsed since their issue, on giving a specified notice or by annual drawing.

Companies are required to create a sinking fund called the *debenture redemption reserve fund.*

The Companies Act, 2013 requires every company to create a debenture redemption reserve for redemption of debentures issued. An adequate amount has to be credited to the said reserve from out of the profit every year until such debentures are redeemed. The amount credited to the debenture redemption reserve shall not be utilised by the company except for the purpose of redemption of debentures.

Investment every year equals the aggregate of the amount appropriated out of profit and the interest or dividend, if any, earned on the amount already invested. Investment is sold in the year of redemption of debentures. Any profit or loss on sale of investments is transferred to the debenture redemption reserve fund. An amount equal to the face value of debentures redeemed is transferred from the debenture redemption reserve fund to the general reserve. The balance in the debenture redemption reserve fund represents surplus, that is, excess of fund over amount paid to debenture-holders or deficit. The surplus is transferred to the capital reserve, while the deficit is transferred to the profit and loss appropriation account.

Sometimes, debentures are redeemed at a premium. In such a case, the appropriation to the debenture redemption reserve fund should be sufficient to pay both the amount of debentures and the premium on redemption. In absence of a sinking fund, a provision should be created for the premium payable over the maturity period of debentures.

CASE STUDY 9.9

'A' Ltd. has issued debentures amounting to ₹1,00,000 on January 1, 2013. The debentures are redeemable on December 31, 2017. As per the terms and conditions of issue, 'A' Ltd. should create a debenture redemption reserve fund. The trustee expects to earn a profit of 10 percent on investment. Determine the amount to be appropriated out of profit and show relevant ledger accounts.

Solution The amount to be appropriated out of profit is to be calculated as follows:

₹100 invested at the end of the year will generate interest @ ₹10. At the end of the second year,

₹110 + 100, i.e., ₹210 will be invested. It will generate interest of ₹21. At the end of the third year, ₹210 + 21 + 100, i.e., ₹331 will be invested. It will generate interest of ₹33.10. At the end of the fourth year, ₹331 + 33.10 + 100, i.e., ₹464.10 will be invested. It will generate interest of ₹46.40. Thus, at the end of the fifth year, ₹464.10 + 46.40 + 100, i.e., ₹610.50 will be available. Therefore, ₹1,00,000 ÷ ₹610.50 × 100, i.e., ₹16,380 should be appropriated every year, beginning in the year in which the debentures are issued, to ensure availability of ₹1,00,000 at the end of the fifth year.

Relevant ledger accounts are presented hereinafter:

Debenture Redemption Reserve Fund Account

Dr. Date	Particulars	Amount (₹)	Date	Particulars	Cr. Amount (₹)
Dec. 31, 2013	To balance c/d	16,380.00	Dec. 31, 2013	By profit and loss app. a/c	16,380.00
		16,380.00			16,380.00
Dec. 31, 2014	To balance c/d	34,398.00	Dec. 31, 2014	By balance c/d	16,380.00
				By bank (interest)	1,638.00
				By profit and loss app. a/c	16,380.00
		34,398.00			34,398.00
Dec. 31, 2015	To balance c/d	54,217.80	Jan. 1, 2015	By balance c/d	34,398.00
			Dec. 31, 2015	By bank (interest)	3,439.80
				By profit and loss app. a/c	16,380.00
		54,217.80			54,217.80
Dec. 31, 2016	To balance c/d	76,019.58	Jan. 1, 2016	By balance b/d	54,217.80
				By bank (interest)	5,421.78
				By profit and loss app. a/c	16,380.00
		76,019.58			76,019.58
Dec. 31, 2017	To general reserve	1,00,000.00	Jan. 1, 2017	By balance b/d	76,019.58
	To capital reserve	1.54	Dec. 31, 2017	By bank (interest)	7,601.96
				By profit and loss app. a/c	16,380.00
		1,00,001.54			1,00,001.54

Debenture Redemption Investment Account

Dr. Date	Particulars	Amount (₹)	Date	Particulars	Cr. Amount (₹)
Dec. 31, 2013	To bank	16,380.00	Dec. 31, 2013	By balance c/d	16,380.00
		16,380.00			16,380.00
Jan. 1, 2014	To balance b/d	16,380.00	Dec. 31, 2014	By balance c/d	34,398.00
Dec. 31, 2014	To bank	18,018.00			
		34,398.00			34,398.00
Jan. 1, 2015	To balance b/d	34,398.00	Jan. 1, 2015	By balance c/d	54,217.80
Dec. 31, 2015	To bank	19,819.80			
		54,217.80			54,217.80
Jan. 1, 2016	To balance b/d	54,217.80	Dec. 31, 2016	By balance c/d	76,019.58
Dec. 31, 2016	To bank	21,801.78			
		76,019.58			76,056.71
Jan. 1, 2017	To balance b/d	76,019.58	Dec. 31, 2017	By bank (realisation)	76,019.58
		76,019.58			76,019.58

Debenture Account

Dr. Date	Particulars	Amount (₹)	Date	Particulars	Cr. Amount (₹)
Dec. 31, 2013	To balance c/d	1,00,000	Jan. 1, 2013	By bank	1,00,000
		1,00,000			1,00,000
Dec. 31, 2014	To balance c/d	1,00,000	Jan. 1, 2014	By balance b/d	1,00,000
		1,00,000			1,00,000
Dec. 31, 2015	To balance c/d	1,00,000	Jan. 1, 2015	By balance b/d	1,00,000
		1,00,000			1,00,000
Dec. 31, 2016	To balance c/d	1,00,000	1 Jan. 2016	By balance b/d	1,00,000
		1,00,000			1,00,000
Dec. 31, 2017	To bank	1,00,000	1 Jan. 2017	By balance b/d	1,00,000
		1,00,000			1,00,000

NOTES

Purchase of Debentures in Open Market

A company may purchase its own debentures in the open market either to cancel the same, to keep them alive for issue at a later date, or to hold them as an investment. A company may purchase its own debentures as an investment in a sinking fund.

As regards interest, where there is a sinking fund, the interest on debentures held as a sinking fund investment should be credited to the sinking fund. In the absence of a sinking fund, interest on debentures is charged to the statement of profit and loss as an expense and is credited to the *statement of profit and loss* as an *income*; the statement of profit and loss is debited and credited by the same amount.

On cancellation of debentures, an amount equal to the nominal value of debentures cancelled is transferred from the debenture redemption reserve to the general reserve.

In accounting for investments in own debentures or otherwise, the amount paid on purchase of securities should be segregated into *principal* and *interest*. Usually, debentures are quoted either on *ex-interest basis*, or on *cum-interest basis*. In case the transaction is on ex-interest basis, the purchaser pays to the seller, in addition to the price of the security, the amount of interest accrued till the date of the transaction. In case, the transaction is on cum-interest basis, interest accrued till the date of the transaction is included in the price. In absence of any specific mention, it is assumed that the transaction is on cum-interest basis. The specific mention of the term becomes material only when the interest date is very near to the date of the transaction. When the interest date is far off, the retention of right in interest by the seller is an impractical proposition, as mutation usually does not wait for a very long time.

In the case of equity shares or similar securities, the amount of dividend accruing between the date of the last dividend's payment and the date of purchase cannot be immediately ascertained. However, the principle for accounting for dividend is the same as accounting for interest in the case of interest-bearing securities. The amount of dividend for the period for which the investors did not hold shares is accounted for as part recovery of the cost of investment. Similarly, *dividend received out of pre-acquisition profit is accounted for as part recovery of the cost of investment.* The allocation of dividend between pre-acquisition and post-acquisition is often arbitrary. It is assumed that the dividend received for a particular period has accrued evenly over the period.

CASE STUDY 9.10

'A' Ltd. has issued 10,000 of 12 percent debentures for ₹10,00,000, interest being payable on 30 June and 31 December. The company purchased 500 debentures for ₹96 on ex-interest basis on November 1, 2012. Record the transaction in the journal of 'A' Ltd. Also, show the accounting of interest on debentures paid on December 31, 2012.

Solution

A Ltd.: Journal

Date	Particulars	₹	₹
Nov. 1, 2012	Own debentures a/c	Dr. 48,000	
	Interest on debentures a/c	Dr. 2,000	
	To bank a/c		Cr. 50,000
	(being purchase of 500 own debentures for ₹96 on ex-interest basis vide Board of Directors' resolution No. ... dated...; interest for 4 months debited to interest on debentures a/c)		

NOTES

Date	Particulars	₹	₹
Dec. 31, 2012	Interest on debentures a/c	Dr. 57,000	
	To bank a/c		Cr. 57,000
	(being interest for 6 months paid to holders of 9,500 debentures)		
	Interest on debentures a/c	Dr. 1,000	
	To interest received a/c		Cr. 1,000
	(being interest on own debentures for 2 months saved)		

Subsequent measurement of own debentures

Subsequent to initial measurement, investment in own debentures is to be measured either at amortised cost or at fair value depending on the intention of the company. Debentures usually meet the Solely Payments of the Principal and Interest (SPPI) on principal amount outstanding criterion. If the company intends to hold the investment to collect contractual cash flows, the investment should be measured at amortised cost. On the other hand, if the company holds the investment with the intention to hold it or sell, the investment should be measured at fair value.

Key Terms
cum-interest, ex-interest, sinking fund, SPPI criterion

Self-Test Questions

Self-test question 9.12

Indicate whether the following statements are true (T) or false (F):

(i) Debentures are carried in the balance sheet at amortised cost.

(ii) Under the effective interest rate method the premium or discount on the issue of debentures is accounted for as a part of interest.

(iii) Premium on redemption of debentures is recognised as an expense of the period in which the debentures are redeemed.

(iv) Companies are permitted to hold its own debentures as investment of sinking fund.

(v) Investment in own debentures are carried in the balance sheet at fair value.

SUMMARY

Accounting for issue of debentures is similar to accounting for issue of shares. Debenture is a liability. It is measured at amortised cost. Under the effective interest rate (EIR) method, coupon rate is adjusted for premium or discount on issue of debentures and also for premium on redemption. Companies can buy debentures from the open market either to cancel them or to hold them as an investment. Investment in own debentures is carried in the balance sheet either at amortised cost or at fair value depending on the business model under which the company holds the investment.

ANSWERS TO SELF-TEST QUESTIONS

9.1 (i) T; (ii) F; (iii) F; (iv) T

9.2 (i) T; (ii) T; (iii) T; (iv) F; (v) T

9.3 (i) T; (ii) T; (iii) F; (iv) T; (v) F

9.4 (i) T; (ii) F; (iii) T; (iv) T; (v) T

9.5 (i) T; (ii) F; (iii) T; (iv) T; (v) T

9.6 (i) T; (ii) F; (iii) F; (iv) T

9.7 (i) T; (ii) F; (iii) F; (iv) T

NOTES

9.8 (i) T; (ii) T; (iii) T; (iv) F

9.9 (i) T; (ii) T; (iii) T; (iv) T

9.10 (i) T; (ii) T; (iii) F; (iv)T; (v) T

9.11 (i) T; (ii)F; (iii) T; (iv) T

9.12 (i) T; (ii) T; (iii) F; (iv) T; (v) F

ASSIGNMENTS

Multiple Choice Questions

1. Tick the correct statement.

(i) The liability of a shareholder of a limited liability company is:
  (a) unlimited.
  (b) limited to the face value of his shares.
  (c) limited to the unpaid amount on the shares held by him.
  (d) determined by the Board of Directors.

(ii) A limited company is allowed to issue preference shares that:
  (a) are either redeemable or irredeemable.
  (b) are redeemable after the expiry of a period determined by the management.
  (c) should be redeemed within 20 years from the date of issue.
  (d) should be redeemed within 10 years from the date of issue.

(iii) Debenture-holders of a limited liability company are:
  (a) lenders who have voting rights.
  (b) lenders who have voting rights which they can transfer to others by selling their debentures in the market.
  (c) lenders who do not have any voting rights but can transfer their rights and risks associated with the investment by selling their debentures in the market.
  (d) lenders who can vote in the general meeting on matters relating to their interests.

(iv) 'A' Ltd. forfeited one share of face value of ₹100 that was issued for ₹120 due to failure of the member to pay the final call of ₹40. 'Share forfeited account' should be credited by:
  (a) ₹100. (b) ₹80.
  (c) ₹60. (d) ₹40.

(v) 'B' Ltd. reissued one share of face value of ₹100 for ₹90. The share, originally issued at ₹120, was forfeited due to non-receipt of the final call of ₹50. Reissue of the forfeited share has resulted in:
  (a) loss of ₹10. (b) profit of ₹20.
  (c) profit of ₹40. (d) profit of ₹30.

(vi) 'C' Ltd. reissued one share of face value of ₹100 for ₹80. The share, originally issued at ₹90, was forfeited due to the failure of the member to pay the final call of ₹30. Reissue of the forfeited share resulted in:
  (a) loss of ₹10. (b) profit of ₹50.
  (c) profit of ₹60. (d) profit of ₹20.

(vii) 'D' Ltd. decides to redeem ₹3,00,000 of 12 percent preference shares at a premium of 10 percent by issue of 10,000 shares of ₹10 each at 10 percent discount. The capital redemption reserve account should be credited by:
  (a) ₹2,30,000. (b) ₹2,40,000.
  (c) ₹2,10,000. (d) ₹2,00,000.

(viii) 'E' Ltd. decides to redeem ₹4,00,000 of 12 percent preference shares at a premium of 10 percent by fresh issue of 15,000 shares of ₹10 each at a premium of 20 percent. The capital redemption reserve should be credited by:
  (a) ₹2,60,000. (b) ₹2,20,000.
  (c) ₹2,90,000. (d) ₹2,50,000.

(ix) 'F' Ltd. decides to redeem ₹2,00,000 of 12 percent preference shares at a premium of 20 percent. The balance sheet shows a profit ₹40,000, general reserve of ₹50,000 and share premium of ₹10,000. The proceeds of the fresh issue of capital should not be less than:
  (a) ₹1,40,000. (b) ₹1,30,000.
  (c) ₹1,10,000. (d) ₹1,50,000.

(x) A limited liability company, when purchasing its own debentures:
  (a) should cancel them within seven days of purchase.
  (b) hold these as treasury stock for cancellation at a later date.

(c) hold these as treasury stock for reissue or cancellation at a later date.
(d) hold these as treasury stock for reissue at a later date.

2. Indicate whether the following statements are true (T) or false (F):

(i) A limited liability company cannot issue equity shares with differential voting rights.
(ii) In the absence of any clear provision in the Articles of association of a limited liability company, preference shares issued by it are deemed to be cumulative preference shares.
(iii) A limited liability company cannot issue irredeemable preference shares.
(iv) Applications for shares and debentures cannot be issued unless a prospectus accompanies them.
(v) The face value or par value of share has no economic significance.
(vi) In most situations, the book value of an equity share can be used as a surrogate for the market value of the same.
(vii) Issue of sweat equity shares by a limited liability company does not require prior approval of the Central Government.
(viii) The amount forfeited on shares on which the holder failed to pay an overdue amount is a capital profit.
(ix) Alteration of share capital by a limited liability company usually changes its market capitalisation significantly.
(x) Stock is the consolidation of the share capital into one unit divisible into aliquot parts.
(xi) Issue of bonus shares does not change the amount of equity in the balance sheet.
(xii) Issue of bonus shares is generally perceived as a positive signal by the capital market, so rumours of bonus issue usually increase market capitalisation of the limited liability company, though marginally.
(xiii) In the case of a right issue, the offer price is immaterial.
(xiv) A limited liability company can buy its own shares in the market and can hold them as its investment.
(xv) No interest is payable on debentures issued as collateral security.
(xvi) Creation of a debenture redemption reserve for redemption of debentures is at the discretion of the Board of Directors of the limited liability company.
(xvii) In the absence of any specific mention of the basis of a transaction of purchase and sale of securities, it is assumed to be on cum-interest basis.
(xviii) Dividend received out of pre-acquisition profit is accounted for as part recovery of the cost of investment.

Analytical Question

1. "Sweat equity is an important innovation to provide ownership to technocrats who bring knowledge but not financial capital, but it has the potential for misuse, particularly for expropriation of wealth of shareholders who are not in control of the company." Do you agree? Explain your position on this issue.

Problems

1. Expert Engineers Ltd. with an authorised capital of ₹5,00,000 divided into 50,000 equity shares of ₹10 each, issued 40,000 shares payable ₹3 on application, ₹5 on allotment (including ₹2 premium) and ₹2 each on two calls. Holders of 2,000 shares failed to pay allotment money; further, on 1,000 shares, there were arrears of first call. All these shares were forfeited.

Then the final call was made. There were arrears on 400 shares. All the shares on which only application money was paid and half of the shares on which there was default of first call money were reissued at ₹8 as fully paid shares.

Pass journal entries and show how these will appear in the balance sheet.

(ICWA, Inter.)

2. Beta Ltd. invited applications for 20,000 equity shares of ₹10 each issued at ₹12 payable as follows:

On application on July 1, 2017	₹5 per share
On allotment on July 31, 2017 (including premium)	₹5 per share
On first and final call on August 31, 2017	₹2 per share

Applications were received for 25,000 shares, and it was decided to deal with them as follows in arrangement with the stock exchange authorities to

(a) refuse allotment to an applicant for 1,000 shares.
(b) give full allotment to an applicant for 4,000 shares.
(c) allot the remaining shares pro rata amongst other applicants.
(d) utilise the surplus received on application in part-payment of sums due on allotment.

An applicant, to whom 100 shares were allotted failed to pay the amount due on the first and final call, and his shares were forfeited on December 31, 2017. These shares were reissued on February 15, 2018 as fully paid at ₹9 per share.

Give journal entries, including those relating to the bank to record the above transactions.

3. 'A' Ltd. decided to increase its existing share capital by making a right issue to the existing shareholders in the proportion of two new shares for every 10 shares held. Right shares of face value ₹100 were issued at a premium of ₹60. The market value of the share immediately before the announcement of the right issue was ₹184.

You are required to calculate the price of the right.

4. Alpha Ltd. has issued share capital of 1,000, of 7 percent redeemable preference shares of ₹100 each and 5,000 equity shares of ₹50 each. The preference shares are redeemable at a premium of 10 percent on April 1, 2017.

The company's balance sheet as on March 31, 2017 is as follows:

Liabilities	Amount (₹)	Assets	Amount (₹)
Share capital:		Fixed assets	3,50,000
Issued and subscribed		Investments	70,000
5,000 equity shares of ₹50 each		Balance in bank	40,000
fully paid	2,50,000		
Profit and loss a/c	50,000		
1,000 of 7 percent redeemable			
preference shares of ₹100			
each, fully paid	1,00,000		
Sundry creditors	60,000		
	4,60,000		4,60,000

In order to facilitate the redemption of the preference shares, the company decided to:

(a) sell all the investments for ₹68,000.

(b) finance part of the redemption from company funds, subject to leaving a balance of ₹20,000 in the profit and loss account.

(c) issue sufficient equity shares of ₹50 each at a premium of ₹10 per share to raise the balance of funds required.

The preference shares were redeemed on the due date and the issue of equity shares was fully subscribed.

You are required to prepare:

(a) the necessary journal entries to record the above transactions, including bank transactions

(b) the balance sheet on completion of the redemption of preference shares

5. The summarised balance sheet of Prudent Co. Ltd. on June 30, 1965 was as follows:

Liabilities	Amount (₹)	Assets	Amount (₹)
Share capital:		Sundry assets	49,00,000
Authorised, issued and paid up: 1,00,000		Cash in bank	7,00,000
9 percent redeemable preference			
shares of ₹10 each	10,00,000		
2,50,000 equity shares of ₹10 each	25,00,000		
Current liabilities	15,00,000		
Profit and loss account	6,00,000		
	56,00,000		56,00,000

The conditions of issue of the redeemable preference shares provided for their being redeemed on July 15, 1965 at a premium of 5 percent. The profit available not being sufficient to redeem the whole issue, the company issued 5,000 of 10 percent preference shares of ₹100 each at par on July 1, 1965, which were duly taken up and paid for. The redeemable preference shares were redeemed on the due date.

On September 1, 1965, the company decided to utilise the capital redemption reserve account to issue ₹10 equity shares as bonus shares to the old equity shareholders. Show journal entries to record the above transactions.

(ICWA, Inter.)

6. The summarised balance sheet of Gamma Ltd. as on December 31, 1999 was as follows:

Liabilities	Amount (₹)	Assets	Amount (₹)
Share capital: 5,00,000 equity shares of ₹10 each, fully paid	50,00,000	Fixed assets (at cost less depreciation)	2,00,00,000
General reserve	80,00,000	Debentures redemption Funds investments	48,00,000
Debenture redemption fund	50,00,000	Cash and bank balances	50,00,000
12 percent convertible debentures, 1,00,000 debentures of ₹10 each	1,00,00,000	Other current assets	1,67,00,000
Other loans	60,00,000		
Current liabilities and provisions	1,25,00,000		
	4,65,00,000		4,65,00,000

The debentures are due for redemption on March 31, 2000. The terms of issue of debentures provided that they were redeemable at a premium of 5 percent and also conferred option to the debenture-holders to convert 20 percent of their holding into equity shares at a predetermined price of ₹15 per share, payment to be made in cash.

Assuming that:

(a) except for 100 debenture-holders holding totally 25,000 debentures, the rest of them exercise the option for maximum conversion.

(b) the investment realised is ₹5 million.

(c) all the transactions are put through without any lag on March 31, 2000.

Redraft the balance sheet of the company as on March 31, 2000 after giving effect to the redemption and conversion.

Accounts of Limited Liability Companies
Final Accounts

CHAPTER **10**

LEARNING OBJECTIVES

The objective of this chapter is to provide an understanding of the provisions in the Companies Act, 2013 regarding financial statements. After reading this chapter, you will develop understanding of the following:

- General provisions regarding preparation and presentation of financial statements
- Applicability of accounting standards
- Re-opening of accounts
- Board of director's report
- Directors' responsibility statement
- CEO and CFO certification
- Managerial remuneration and computation of profit for the same
- General provisions regarding divisible profit
- Regulations regarding payment of dividend
- Accounting for Dividend Distribution Tax
- Preparation of balance sheet and the statement of profit and loss

NOTES

GENERAL PROVISIONS

Financial Statements

Section 132 of the Companies Act, 2013 provides that the Central Government may, by notification, constitute a National Financial Reporting Authority (NFRA) to provide for matters relating to accounting and auditing standards. Section 133 of the Companies Act, 2013 provides that The Central Government may prescribe the standards of accounting, as recommended by the Institute of Chartered Accountants of India, in consultation with and after examination of the recommendations made by the NFRA. The government is yet to constitute NFRA. As an interim measure, The Ministry of Corporate Affairs (MCA) issues accounting standards on the recommendations of National Advisory Committee on Accounting Standards (NACAS), a body that is constituted in accordance with the erstwhile Companies Act.

Section 129 of the Companies Act, 2013 prescribes the requirements regarding preparation and presentation of financial statements. It requires that:

(a) Financial statements should comply with applicable accounting standards notified by the Ministry of Corporate Affairs (MCA) and shall be in the forms prescribed in Schedule III [Available at: http://www.mca.gov.in/SearchableActs/Schedule3.htm]. Schedule III has been discussed in Units 4 to 6. Schedule III (Division II) is applicable to non-finance companies, which are required to apply Ind AS, which is the set of Indian Accounting Standards, fully convergent with International Financial Reporting Standards (IFRS). However, the schedule is not applicable to electricity companies to which the Electricity Act, 2003 is applicable. MCA will issue separate forms for non-banking finance companies (NBFC). Accounting standards and forms issued by MCA are not applicable to insurance companies and banking companies. RBI issues accounting standards and forms applicable to banking companies. Similarly, IRDAI issues accounting standards and forms applicable to insurance companies.

(b) At every annual general meeting (AGM) of a company, the Board of Directors of the company should lay before such meeting financial statements for the financial year.

(c) The Board of Directors of a company, which has one or more subsidiaries and/or associate companies and/or joint ventures, should lay before the AGM consolidated financial statements, in addition to separate financial statements.

It should also attach along with its financial statement, a separate statement containing the salient features of the financial statement of its subsidiary or subsidiaries (and associate companies and joint ventures, if any) in such form as may be prescribed.

(d) Where the financial statements of a company do not comply with applicable accounting standards, the company shall disclose in its financial statements, the deviation from the accounting standards, the reasons for such deviation and the financial effects, if any, arising out of such deviation.

(e) If a company contravenes the provisions of Section 129, the MD, the Finance Director, the CFO and in the absence of MD/Finance Director/CFO, all the directors shall be punishable with imprisonment for a term which may extend to one year or with fine which shall not be less than fifty thousand rupees but which may extend to five lakh rupees, or with both.

Self-Test Questions

Self-test question 10.1

Indicate whether the following statements are true (T) or false (F):

(i) Companies are required to apply accounting standards issued by the Institute of Chartered Accountants of India.

(ii) Companies are not allowed to deviate from accounting principles and methods stipulated in accounting standards.

(iii) Only listed companies are required to issue consolidated financial statements.

(iv) RBI issues accounting standards applicable to NBFCs.

(v) Contravention of the requirements of section 129 of the Companies Act, 2013 might lead to imprisonment of directors.

Re-opening of Accounts

(a) Section 130 of the Companies Act, 2013 stipulates that a company shall not re-open its books of account and not recast its financial statements, unless an application in this regard is made by the Central Government, the Income-tax authorities, the Securities and Exchange Board, any other statutory regulatory body or authority or any person concerned and an order is made by a court of competent jurisdiction or the Tribunal to the effect that:

   (i) the relevant earlier accounts were prepared in a fraudulent manner, or

   (ii) the affairs of the company were mismanaged during the relevant period, casting a doubt on the reliability of financial statements:

   The accounts revised or re-cast based on the order of the court or Tribunal shall be final.

(b) Section 131 of the Companies Act, 2013 stipulates that if it appears to the directors of a company that:

   (i) the financial statement of the company, or

   (ii) the report of the Board,

   does not comply with the provisions of Section 129 or Section 134 [see point (6) below], they may prepare revised financial statement or a revised report in respect of any of the three preceding financial years, after obtaining approval of the Tribunal on an application made by the company.

Such revised financial statement or report shall not be prepared or filed more than once in a financial year.

The detailed reasons for revision of such financial statement or report shall also be disclosed in the Board's report in the relevant financial year in which such revision is being made.

Where copies of the previous financial statement or report have been sent out to members or delivered to the Registrar or laid before the company in general meeting, the revisions must be confined to:

(a) the correction in respect of which the previous financial statement or report do not comply with the provisions of Section 129 or Section 134, and

(b) the making of any necessary consequential alternation.

Self-Test Questions

Self-test question 10.2

Indicate whether the following statements are true (T) or false (F):

(i) Central Government, the Income-tax authorities, the Securities and Exchange Board may require companies to re-open the books of accounts and recast financial statements by filing an application to the court or Tribunal.

(ii) Companies are not permitted to revise financial statements voluntarily.

NOTES

Financial Statements and Board Reports

Section 134 of the Companies Act, 2013 provides the following:

(i) The financial statement, including consolidated financial statement, if any, should be approved by the Board of Directors.

(ii) The auditors' report shall be attached to every financial statement.

(iii) There shall be attached to statements laid before a company in general meeting, a report by its Board of Directors, which shall include:

- (a) The extract of the annual return as provided under sub-section (3) of Section 92.
- (b) Number of meetings of the Board.
- (c) Directors' Responsibility Statement.
  - (ca) Details in respect of frauds reported by auditors under sub-section (12) of Section 143 other than those which are reportable to the Central Government.
- (d) A statement on declaration given by independent directors under sub-section (6) of Section 149.
- (e) In case of a company covered under sub-section (1) of Section 178, company's policy on directors' appointment and remuneration including criteria for determining qualifications, positive attributes, independence of a director and other matters provided under sub-section (3) of Section 178.
- (f) Explanations or comments by the Board on every qualification, reservation or adverse remark or disclaimer made:
  - (i) by the auditor in his report, and
  - (ii) by the company secretary in practice in his secretarial audit report.
- (g) Particulars of loans, guarantees or investments under Section 186.
- (h) Particulars of contracts or arrangements with related parties referred to in sub-section (1) of Section 188 in the prescribed form;
- (i) The state of the company's affairs;
- (j) The amounts, if any, which it proposes to carry to any reserves;
- (k) The amount, if any, which it recommends should be paid by way of dividend;
- (l) Material changes and commitments, if any, affecting the financial position of the company which have occurred between the end of the financial year of the company to which the financial statements relate and the date of the report;
- (m) The conservation of energy, technology absorption, foreign exchange earnings and outgo, in such manner as may be prescribed;
- (n) A statement indicating development and implementation of a risk management policy for the company including identification therein of elements of risk, if any, which in the opinion of the Board may threaten the existence of the company;
- (o) The details about the policy developed and implemented by the company on corporate social responsibility initiatives taken during the year;
- (p) In case of a listed company and every other public company having such paid-up share capital as may be prescribed, a statement indicating the manner in which formal annual evaluation has been made by the Board of its own performance and that of its committees and individual directors;
- (q) Such other matters as may be prescribed.

(iv) The report of the Board of Directors should be attached to the financial statement.

(v) The Board's report and any annexures thereto under sub-section (3) shall be signed by its chairperson of the company if he is authorised by the Board and where he

NOTES

is not so authorised, shall be signed by at least two directors, one of whom shall be a managing director, or by the director where there is one director.

(vi) A signed copy of every financial statement, including consolidated financial statement, if any, shall be issued, circulated or published along with a copy each of:

(a) any notes annexed to or forming part of such financial statement;

(b) the auditor's report; and

(c) the Board's report referred to in sub-section (3).

(vii) If a company contravenes the provisions of this section, the company shall be punishable with fine which shall not be less than fifty thousand rupees but which may extend to twenty-five lakh rupees and every officer of the company who is in default shall be punishable with imprisonment for a term which may extend to three years or with fine which shall not be less than fifty thousand rupees but which may extend to five lakh rupees, or with both.

Self-Test Questions

Self-test question 10.3

Indicate whether the following statements are true (T) or false (F):

(i) The board of directors is responsible for approving financial statement, and thus, it is responsible to ensure that financial statements give a true and fair view.

(ii) Companies are required to publish financial statements with auditor's report and the report of the board of directors.

(iii) The board of directors is required to identify and disclose in its report risk, if any, which in its opinion may threaten the existence of the company.

(iv) The board of directors is not required to disclose and comment on material changes and commitments, which have occurred after the balance sheet date.

(v) The board of director's report must disclose particulars of related party transactions.

Directors' Responsibility Statement

Section 134(3) of the Companies Act, 2013 requires that the board's report shall include a Director's Responsibility Statement. It is an instrument to enforce accountability of directors towards shareholders and other stakeholders. It shall state that:

(a) In the preparation of the annual accounts, the applicable accounting standards had been followed along with proper explanation relating to material departures.

(b) The directors had selected such accounting policies and applied them consistently and made judgments and estimates that are reasonable and prudent so as to give a true and fair view of the state of affairs of the company at the end of the financial year and of the profit and loss of the company for that period.

(c) The directors had taken proper and sufficient care for the maintenance of adequate accounting records in accordance with the provisions of the Companies Act, 2013 for safeguarding the assets of the company and for preventing and detecting fraud and other irregularities.

(d) The directors had prepared the annual accounts on a going concern basis.

(e) The directors, in the case of a listed company, had laid down internal financial controls to be followed by the company and that such internal financial controls are adequate and were operating effectively.

(f) The directors had devised proper systems to ensure compliance with the provisions of all applicable laws and that such systems were adequate and operating effectively.

Internal financial controls

The term 'internal financial controls' means the policies and procedures adopted by the company for ensuring the orderly and efficient conduct of its business, including adherence to company's policies, the safeguarding of its assets, the prevention and detection of frauds and errors, the accuracy and completeness of the accounting records, and the timely preparation of reliable financial information.

Self-Test Questions

Self-test question 10.4

Indicate whether the following statements are true (T) or false (F):

(i) Directors' Responsibility Statement is a protection to shareholders and other stakeholders against potential earnings management.

(ii) Directors are responsible for accurate bookkeeping.

(iii) Internal control is a much broader concept than controls for protecting frauds and errors.

CEO/CFO Certification

Clause 17(8) of the SEBI (Listing Agreement and Disclosure Requirements) Regulations 2015, which is applicable to companies that have listed their equity shares in a recognised stock exchange, requires that the chief executive officer and the chief financial officer shall submit the following compliance certificate to the board of directors:

(A) They have reviewed financial statements and the cash flow statement for the year and that to the best of their knowledge and belief:

 (1) these statements do not contain any materially untrue statement or omit any material fact or contain statements that might be misleading;

 (2) these statements together present a true and fair view of the listed entity's affairs and are in compliance with existing accounting standards, applicable laws and regulations.

(B) There are, to the best of their knowledge and belief, no transactions entered into by the listed entity during the year which are fraudulent, illegal or violative of the listed entity's code of conduct.

(C) They accept responsibility for establishing and maintaining internal controls for financial reporting and that they have evaluated the effectiveness of internal control systems of the listed entity pertaining to financial reporting and they have disclosed to the auditors and the audit committee, deficiencies in the design or operation of such internal controls, if any, of which they are aware and the steps they have taken or propose to take to rectify these deficiencies.

(D) They have indicated to the auditors and the Audit committee:

 (1) significant changes in internal control over financial reporting during the year,

 (2) significant changes in accounting policies during the year and that the same have been disclosed in the notes to the financial statements, and

 (3) instances of significant fraud of which they have become aware and the involvement therein, if any, of the management or an employee having a significant role in the listed entity's internal control system over financial reporting.

NOTES

SUMMARY

Companies are required to prepare and place before AGM both stand-alone financial statements and consolidated financial statements. Companies, other than banks and insurance companies, prepare financial statements applying accounting standards issued by MCA. RBI issues accounting standards applicable to banking companies and IRDAI issues accounting standards applicable to insurance companies. Companies, other than banking companies, insurance companies and electricity companies, are required to present financial statements in forms prescribed in Schedule III of the Companies Act, 2013. Only in specified situations, companies are allowed to recast financial statements. Auditor's report and board of director's report should accompany financial statements. Board of director's report should include director's responsibility statement. CEO and CFO should jointly certify to the board of directors that they have reviewed financial statements.

MANAGERIAL REMUNERATION

Statutory Limits

Section 197 of the Companies Act, 2013 stipulates the following:

(1) The total managerial remuneration payable by a public company, to its directors, including managing director and whole-time director, and its manager in respect of any financial year shall not exceed eleven percent of the net profits of that company for that financial year computed in the manner laid down in Section 198 except that the remuneration of the directors shall not be deducted from the gross profits:

Provided that the company in general meeting may, with the approval of the Central Government, authorise the payment of remuneration exceeding eleven percent of the net profits of the company, subject to the provisions of Schedule V: Provided further that, except with the approval of the company in general meeting,

(i) the remuneration payable to any one managing director; or whole-time director or manager shall not exceed five percent of the net profits of the company and if there is more than one such director remuneration shall not exceed ten percent of the net profits to all such directors and manager taken together,

(ii) the remuneration payable to directors who are neither managing directors nor whole-time directors shall not exceed,

(A) one percent of the net profits of the company, if there is a managing or whole-time director or manager;

(B) three percent of the net profits in any other case.

(2) The percentages aforesaid shall be exclusive of any sitting fees payable to directors.

(3) Notwithstanding anything contained in sub-sections (1) and (2), but subject to the provisions of Schedule V, if, in any financial year, a company has no profits or its profits are inadequate, the company shall not pay to its directors, including any managing or whole-time director or manager, by way of remuneration any sum exclusive of any sitting fees payable to directors except in accordance with the provisions of Schedule V and if it is not able to comply with such provisions, with the previous approval of the Central Government.

Schedule V of the Companies Act, 2013 (Extract)

(Schedule V contains detailed provisions for managerial remuneration in different circumstances. The extract provides general provisions. Readers interested to get details should refer to schedule V.)

Where in any financial year during the currency of tenure of a managerial person, a company has no profits or its profits are inadequate, it may, without Central Government approval, pay remuneration to the managerial person not exceeding the higher of the limits under (A) and (B) given below:

NOTES

(A)

(1)	(2)
Where the effective capital is	*Limit of yearly remuneration payable shall not exceed (₹)*
(i) Negative or less than 5 crores	60 lakhs
(ii) 5 crores and above but less than 100 crores	84 lakhs
(iii) 100 crores and above but less than 250 crores	120 lakhs
(iv) 250 crores and above	120 lakhs plus 0.01 percent of the effective capital in excess of ₹250 crores

The above limits shall be doubled if the resolution passed by the shareholders is a special resolution.

For a period less than one year, the limits shall be pro-rated.

'Effective capital' means the aggregate of the paid-up share capital (excluding share application money or advances against shares); amount, if any, for the time being standing to the credit of share premium account; reserves and surplus (excluding revaluation reserve); long-term loans and deposits repayable after one year (excluding working capital loans, over drafts, interest due on loans unless funded, bank guarantee, etc., and other short-term arrangements) as reduced by the aggregate of any investments (except in case of investment by an investment company whose principal business is acquisition of shares, stock, debentures or other securities), accumulated losses and preliminary expenses not written off.

(B) In the case of a managerial person who was not a security holder holding securities of the company of nominal value of rupees five lakh or more or an employee or a director of the company or not related to any director or promoter at any time during the two years prior to his appointment as a managerial person, – 2.5 percent of the current relevant profit:

Provided that if the resolution passed by the shareholders is a special resolution, this limit shall be doubled

"Current relevant profit" means the profit as calculated under Section 198 but without deducting the excess of expenditure over income referred to in sub-section 4(l) thereof in respect of those years during which the managerial person was not an employee, director or shareholder of the company or its holding or subsidiary companies.

Ascertainment of Profit for Managerial Remuneration

Section 198 of the Companies Act, 2013 stipulates the following:

(1) In computing the net profits of a company in any financial year for the purpose of Section 197:
   (a) credit shall be given for the sums specified in sub-section (2), and credit shall not be given for those specified in sub-section (3); and
   (b) the sums specified in sub-section (4) shall be deducted, and those specified in sub-section (5) shall not be deducted.

(2) In making the computation aforesaid, credit shall be given for the bounties and subsidies received from any Government, or any public authority constituted or authorised in this behalf, by any Government, unless and except in so far as the Central Government otherwise directs.

(3) In making the computation aforesaid, credit shall not be given for the following sums, namely:
   (a) profits, by way of premium on shares or debentures of the company, which are issued or sold by the company;

(b) profits on sales by the company of forfeited shares;

(c) profits of a capital nature including profits from the sale of the undertaking or any of the undertakings of the company or of any part thereof;

(d) profits from the sale of any immovable property or fixed assets of a capital nature comprised in the undertaking or any of the undertakings of the company, unless the business of the company consists, whether wholly or partly, of buying and selling any such property or assets:

Provided that where the amount for which any fixed asset is sold exceeds the written-down value thereof, credit shall be given for so much of the excess as is not higher than the difference between the original cost of that fixed asset and its written-down value;

(e) any change in carrying amount of an asset or of a liability recognised in equity reserves including surplus in profit and loss account on measurement of the asset or the liability at fair value.

(4) In making the computation aforesaid, the following sums shall be deducted, namely:

(a) all the usual working charges,

(b) directors remuneration,

(c) bonus or commission paid or payable to any member of the company's staff, or to any engineer, technician or person employed or engaged by the company, whether on a whole-time or on a part-time basis,

(d) any tax notified by the Central Government as being in the nature of a tax on excess or abnormal profits,

(e) any tax on business profits imposed for special reasons or in special circumstances and notified by the Central Government in this behalf,

(f) interest on debentures issued by the company,

(g) interest on mortgages executed by the company and on loans and advances secured by a charge on its fixed or floating assets,

(h) interest on unsecured loans and advances,

(i) expenses on repairs, whether to immovable or to movable property, provided the repairs are not of a capital nature,

(j) outgoings inclusive of contributions made under Section 181,

(k) depreciation to the extent specified in Section 123,

(l) net profits in accordance with this section in any year which begins at or after the commencement of this Act, in so far as such excess has not been deducted in any subsequent year preceding the year in respect of which the net profits have to be ascertained,

(m) any compensation or damages to be paid in virtue of any legal liability including a liability arising from a breach of contract,

(n) any sum paid by way of insurance against the risk of meeting any liability such as is referred to in clause (m),

(o) debts considered bad and written off or adjusted during the year of account.

(5) In making the computation aforesaid, the following sums shall not be deducted, namely:

(a) income-tax and super-tax payable by the company under the Income-tax Act, 1961, or any other tax on the income of the company not falling under clauses (d) and (e) of sub-section (4),

(b) any compensation, damages or payments made voluntarily, that is to say, otherwise than in virtue of a liability such as is referred to in clause (m) of sub-section (4),

(c) loss of a capital nature including loss on sale of the undertaking or any of the undertakings of the company or of any part thereof not including any excess of the written-down value of any asset which is sold, discarded, demolished or destroyed over its sale proceeds or its scrap value,

(d) any change in carrying amount of an asset or of a liability recognised in equity reserves including surplus in profit and loss account on measurement of the asset or the liability at fair value.

Section 123(2) of the Companies Act, 2013 provides that depreciation shall be provided in accordance with the provisions of Schedule II.

NOTES

CASE STUDY 10.1 Managerial Remuneration

The following is the profit and loss account of Delta Ltd. for the year ended March 31, 2017:

Particulars	Amount (₹)	Particulars		Amount (₹)
To administrative, selling and distribution expenses	8,30,000	By balance b/d		5,75,000
To donation to charitable funds	26,000	By gross profit		40,00,000
To directors fees	67,000	By subsidies received from government		2,50,000
To interest on debentures	32,000	By interest on investment		20,000
To compensation for breach of contract	42,000	By transfer fees		1,000
To managerial remuneration	2,85,000	By profit on sale of machinery:		
To depreciation on fixed assets	5,30,000	Amount realised	60,000	
To provision for taxation	12,40,000	Written-down value	30,000	30,000
To general reserve	4,00,000			
To investment revaluation reserve	12,000			
To balance c/d	14,12,000			
	48,76,000			48,76,000

Additional information:

1. Original cost of the machinery sold: ₹40,000.
2. Depreciation as per Schedule II of the Companies Act, 2013, was ₹5,80,000.

You are required to comment on the managerial remuneration in the following situations:

(a) There is only one whole-time director.
(b) There are two whole-time directors.
(c) There are two whole-time directors, a part-time director and a manager.

Solution

	Amount (₹)	Amount (₹)
Balance from trading account		40,00,000
Add:		
Subsidies received from govt.	2,50,000	
Interest on investment	20,000	
Transfer fees	1,000	
Profit on sale of machinery (40,000 – 30,000)	10,000	2,81,000
		42,81,000
Less:		
Administrative, selling and distribution expenses	8,30,000	
Donation to charitable funds	26,000	
Director's fees	67,000	
Interest on debentures	32,000	
Compensation for breach of contract	42,000	
Depreciation on fixed assets as per Schedule XIV	5,80,000	15,77,000
		27,04,000

NOTES

Key Terms
Divisible profit

Situations

(a) There is only one whole-time director:
5 percent of ₹27,04,000 = ₹1,35,200

(b) When there are two whole-time directors:
10 percent of ₹27,04,000 = ₹2,70,400

(c) When there are two whole-time directors, a part-time director and a manager:
11 percent of ₹27,04,000 = ₹2,97,440

Self-Test Questions

Self-test question 10.5

Indicate whether the following statements are true (T) or false (F):

(i) Gain or loss from change in fair values of assets and liabilities, which are measured in fair value, is not included in profit for computing profit for managerial remuneration.

(ii) In effect, profit for calculating managerial remuneration is post-tax profit.

(iii) Capital profits are not included in profit that is used for calculating managerial remuneration.

(iv) Profit on sale of an item of property, plant and equipment, which is in excess of the difference between the sale proceeds and original cost, is capital profit.

(v) A company that has incurred loss has to necessarily take central government's approval for payment of salary to M.D.

SUMMARY

The Companies Act, 2013 prescribes the percentage of profit that can be used to pay remuneration to the M.D. and other directors. In absence of profit or inadequacy of profit, shareholders' approval is required to pay managerial remuneration within the amount provided in Schedule V. The Companies Act, 2013 prescribes the method for calculating profit, which is used to calculate managerial remuneration. Broadly, it is pre-tax profit, excluding gains or losses from fair value changes and capital profit.

DIVISIBLE PROFIT

General Provisions

Section 123 of the Companies Act, 2013 and related rules stipulate as follows:

(1) No dividend shall be declared or paid by a company for any financial year except:

(a) out of the profits of the company for that year arrived at after providing for depreciation in accordance with the provisions of sub-section (2), or out of the profits of the company for any previous financial year or years arrived at after providing for depreciation in accordance with the provisions of that sub-section and remaining undistributed, or out of both, or

(b) out of money provided by the Central Government or a State Government for the payment of dividend by the company in pursuance of a guarantee given by that Government.

Section 123(2) states that depreciation shall be provided in accordance with the provisions of Schedule II, which provides the indicative useful life of different types of assets and stipulates that the residual value should not be more than 5 percent of the original cost. However, Schedule II allows deviation.

No company should declare dividend unless carried over previous losses and depreciation not provided in previous year or years are set off against profit of the company for the current year.

Voluntary transfer to reserve

A company may, before the declaration of any dividend in any financial year, transfer such percentage of its profits for that financial year, as it may consider appropriate, to the reserves of the company.

Declaration of dividend from free reserves

In the event of inadequacy or absence of profits in any year, a company may declare dividend out of free reserves subject to the fulfilment of the following conditions:

(i) The rate of dividend shall not exceed the average of the rates at which dividend was declared by it in the three years immediately preceding that year.

This rule shall not apply to a company, which has not declared any dividend in each of the three preceding financial year.

(ii) The total amount to be drawn from such accumulated profits shall not exceed one-tenth of the sum of its paid-up share capital and free reserves as appearing in the latest audited financial statement.

(iii) The amount so drawn shall first be utilised to set off the losses incurred in the financial year in which dividend is declared before any dividend in respect of equity shares is declared.

(iv) The balance of reserves after such withdrawal shall not fall below fifteen per cent of its paid-up share capital as appearing in the latest audited financial statement.

Provided also that no dividend shall be declared or paid by a company from its reserves other than free reserves.

Key Terms

Interim dividend

Interim dividend

Section 123(3) of the Companies Act, 2013 provides that the Board of Directors of a company may declare interim dividend during any financial year out of the surplus in the profit and loss and out of profits of the financial year in which such interim dividend is sought to be declared:

In case the company has incurred loss during the current financial year up to the end of the quarter immediately preceding the date of declaration of interim dividend, such interim dividend shall not be declared at a rate higher than the average dividends declared by the company during the immediately preceding three financial years.

Payment of dividend

Section 123(4) of the Companies Act, 2013 provides that the amount of the dividend, including interim dividend, shall be deposited in a scheduled bank in a separate account within five days from the date of declaration of such dividend.

Section 123(5) of the Companies Act, 2013 provides that no dividend shall be paid by a company in respect of any share therein except to the registered shareholder of such share or to his order or to his banker and shall not be payable except in cash:

However, there is no prohibition to the capitalisation of profits or reserves of a company for the purpose of issuing fully paid-up bonus shares or paying up any amount for the time being unpaid on any shares held by the members of the company:

Provided further that any dividend payable in cash may be paid by cheque or warrant or in any electronic mode to the shareholder entitled to the payment of the dividend.

Section 123(6) of the Companies Act, 2013 provides that a company, which fails to comply with the provisions of Sections 73 and 74, shall not, so long as such failure continues, declare any dividend on its equity shares. Sections 73 and 74 of the Companies Act, 2013 deal with the acceptance of deposit from public.

NOTES

Transfer to Reserves

Transfer of a part of profit to general reserve, which was mandatory under Section 205(2A) of the Companies Act, 1956 has been dispensed with and made optional for the company under the Companies Act, 2013.

INTEREST ON CAPITAL

Companies Act, 2013 does not have any section corresponding to Section 208 of the Companies Act, 1956, which allowed a company to pay interest on the paid-up capital out of capital in certain specified circumstances. Thus, Companies Act, 2013 does not permit payment of interest on the paid-up capital out of capital in any situation.

Self-Test Questions

Self-test question 10.6

Indicate whether the following statements are true (T) or false (F):

(i) An interim dividend is declared by the Board of Directors at any time before the closure of financial year, whereas a final dividend is declared by the members of a company at its annual general meeting.

(ii) Companies are not permitted to declare dividend in the year in which they have incurred loss.

(iii) Dividend has to be paid only in cash or by cheque or in electronic mode.

(iv) There is a mandatory requirement to transfer a specified percentage of profit to reserve for calculating the profit available for distribution as dividend.

SUMMARY

Divisible profit refers to the amount of profit that is available for distribution to shareholders as dividend. Dividend can be paid from the current year's profit and/or accumulated profit (except capital reserve and other specified reserves) of past years and/or government grant received for the purpose. The board of directors, at its discretion, may decide to transfer a part or whole of the profit to reserves, and thus, determine how much profit is available for distribution as dividend. The Companies Act, 2013 limits the percentage of dividend to the average dividend of previous three years, if dividend is paid, partly or wholly, from reserves.

DIVIDEND

Dividend Declaration Policy

Table F of Schedule I of the Companies Act, 2013 presents Articles of Association of a company limited by shares. It provides the following:

1. The company in general meeting may declare dividends, but no dividend shall exceed the amount recommended by the Board.
2. Subject to the provisions of Section 123, the Board may from time to time pay to the members such interim dividends as appear to it to be justified by the profits of the company.
3. (i) The Board may, before recommending any dividend, set aside out of the profits of the company such sums as it thinks fit as a reserve or reserves which shall, at the discretion of the Board, be applicable for any purpose to which the profits of the company may be properly applied, including provision for meeting contingencies or for equalising dividends; and pending such application, may, at the like discretion, either be employed in the business of the company or be

invested in such investments (other than shares of the company) as the Board may, from time to time, thinks fit.

(ii) The Board may also carry forward any profits, which it may consider necessary not to divide, without setting them aside as a reserve.

4. (i) Subject to the rights of persons, if any, entitled to shares with special rights as to dividends, all dividends shall be declared and paid according to the amounts paid or credited as paid on the shares in respect whereof the dividend is paid, but if and so long as nothing is paid upon any of the shares in the company, dividends may be declared and paid according to the amounts of the shares.

(ii) No amount paid or credited as paid on a share in advance of calls shall be treated for the purposes of this regulation as paid on the share.

(iii) All dividends shall be apportioned and paid proportionately to the amounts paid or credited as paid on the shares during any portion or portions of the period in respect of which the dividend is paid; but if any share is issued on terms providing that it shall rank for dividend as from a particular date such share shall rank for dividend accordingly.

5. The Board may deduct from any dividend payable to any member all sums of money, if any, presently payable by him to the company on account of calls or otherwise in relation to the shares of the company.

6. (i) Any dividend, interest or other monies payable in cash in respect of shares may be paid by cheque or warrant sent through the post directed to the registered address of the holder or, in the case of joint holders, to the registered address of that one of the joint holders who is first named on the register of members, or to such person and to such address as the holder or joint holders may in writing direct.

(ii) Every such cheque or warrant shall be made payable to the order of the person to whom it is sent.

7. Any one of two or more joint holders of a share may give effective receipts for any dividends, bonuses or other monies payable in respect of such share.

8. Notice of any dividend that may have been declared shall be given to the persons entitled to share therein in the manner mentioned in the Act.

9. No dividend shall bear interest against the company.

A company that excludes Table F of Schedule I may pay dividend as per its own Articles of Association. Where the Articles of Association is silent, the amount of dividend should be calculated on the nominal amount of shares.

NOTES

Key Terms
Unpaid dividend

Unpaid Dividend

Section 124 of the Companies Act, 2013 deals with unpaid dividend.

1. Where a dividend has been declared by a company but has not been paid or claimed within thirty days from the date of the declaration to any shareholder entitled to the payment of the dividend, the company shall, within seven days from the date of expiry of the said period of thirty days, transfer the total amount of dividend which remains unpaid or unclaimed to a special account to be opened by the company in that behalf in any scheduled bank to be called the Unpaid Dividend Account.
2. The company shall, within a period of ninety days of making any transfer of an amount to the Unpaid Dividend Account, prepare a statement containing the names, their last known addresses and the unpaid dividend to be paid to each person and place it on the website of the company, if any, and also on any other website approved by the Central Government for this purpose, in such form, manner and other particulars as may be prescribed.

NOTES

Key Terms
Dividend distribution tax (DDT)

3. If any default is made in transferring the total amount or any part thereof to the Unpaid Dividend Account of the company, it shall pay, from the date of such default, interest on so much of the amount as has not been transferred to the said account, at the rate of twelve percent per annum and the interest accruing on such amount shall ensure to the benefit of the members of the company in proportion to the amount remaining unpaid to them.
4. Any person claiming to be entitled to any money transferred to the Unpaid Dividend Account of the company may apply to the company for payment of the money claimed.
5. Any money transferred to the Unpaid Dividend Account of a company which remains unpaid or unclaimed for a period of seven years from the date of such transfer shall be transferred by the company along with interest accrued, if any, thereon to the Investor Education and Protection Fund established under sub-section (1) of Section 125 and the company shall send a statement in the prescribed form of the details of such transfer to the authority which administers the said Fund and that authority shall issue a receipt to the company as evidence of such transfer.

Dividend Distribution Tax

The tax law in India requires companies to pay tax on dividend distributed to shareholders. This is known as Dividend Distribution Tax (DDT). The salient features of DDT are as follows:

- The DDT is in addition to the income tax payable by a domestic company.
- DDT is chargeable on any amount of dividend declared, distributed or paid by a company to shareholders.
- The effective rate of DDT, at present (financial year 2017–18), is 17.304 percent.
- DDT is payable even if no income tax is payable by the domestic company on its total income.
- DDT is treated as the final payment of tax on the dividend and no further credit shall be claimed by the company or by any person in respect of the tax so paid.

Accounting

DDT is recognised in equity for DDT on dividend payable to equity shareholders, as dividend payable to equity shareholders is distribution of profit and not an expense. DDT is recognised in the statement of profit and loss for dividend payable on preference dividend, as preference dividend is recognised as interest in the statement of profit and loss.

Self-Test Questions

Self-test question 10.7

Indicate whether the following statements are true (T) or false (F):

(i) Articles of Association include dividend policy.
(ii) Shareholders may propose and approve payment of dividend without the recommendation of the board of directors.
(iii) That part of profit, which is not appropriated to any reserve, must be paid as dividend.
(iv) Any money transferred to the Unpaid Dividend Account of a company which remains unpaid or unclaimed for a period of seven years from the date of such transfer shall be transferred by the company along with interest accrued, if any, thereon to the Investor Education and Protection Fund.
(v) Dividend distribution tax on dividend payable to equity shareholders is an expense for the period in which the dividend is approved by shareholders in the AGM.

NOTES

SUMMARY

Articles of association include dividend policy. The board of directors can pay interim dividend. On the recommendation of the board of directors, shareholders approve the payment of final dividend in the AGM. Without board of director's recommendation, shareholders cannot propose and approve payment of final dividend. The board of directors, at its discretion, can appropriate a part of or full profit to reserves. Any money transferred to the Unpaid Dividend Account of a company which remains unpaid or unclaimed for a period of seven years from the date of such transfer shall be transferred by the company along with interest accrued, if any, thereon to the Investor Education and Protection Fund. Domestic companies are required to pay dividend distribution tax on dividend paid to shareholders.

DEPRECIATION

Companies Act, 2013 does not prescribe the depreciation method that should be adopted by companies. It also does not prescribe depreciation rates. However, schedule II of the Companies Act, 2013 provides indicative useful life of various assets. It also stipulates that the residual value should not be more than 5 percent of the original cost. Usually companies adopt the useful life indicated in schedule II. However, a company may use useful life different from that indicated in Schedule II, based on technical estimate. If, a company uses useful life that is different from that indicated in Schedule II, it is required to disclose the fact.

FORMS OF FINANCIAL STATEMENTS

The forms of financial statements provided in Schedule III (Division II) of the Companies Act, 2013 have already been discussed in Units 4 to 6. Here, we are presenting some case studies.

CASE STUDY 10.2 Balance Sheet and Statement of Profit and Loss

Silver Pot Limited was registered with a nominal capital of ₹50,000 divided into shares of ₹10 each. The following is the trial balance of the company as at March 31, 2017:

Trial Balance of Silver Pot Limited as at March 31, 2017

Particulars	Dr. (₹)	Cr. (₹)
Buildings	29,000	
Machinery	10,000	
Closing stock	9,000	
Purchase (adjusted)	21,000	
Salaries	6,000	
Directors fees	1,000	
Rent	2,600	
Depreciation	2,000	
Bad debts	600	
Interest accrued on investment	200	
1,200 shares of Y Ltd. of ₹10 each, ₹8 paid up	12,000	
Debenture interest	2,800	
Loose tools	2,300	
Advance tax	6,000	
Sundry expenses	1,800	

NOTES

Particulars	Dr. (₹)	Cr. (₹)
Debtors	12,500	
Bank balance	3,000	
Sales		52,000
Outstanding expenses		200
Provision for doubtful debts (April 1, 2015)		300
Equity share capital		20,000
General reserve		4,000
Profit and loss a/c (April 1, 2015)		2,500
Creditors		9,200
Provision for depreciation—Building		5,000
Provision for depreciation—Machinery		5,500
14 percent Debentures		20,000
Interest on debentures accrued but not due		1,400
Interest on investments		1,200
Unclaimed dividend		500
Total	1,21,800	1,21,800

Additional information/Adjustments

(i) Bills discounted but not yet matured: ₹1,000

(ii) Closing stock is more than opening stock by ₹8,000

(iii) Provide for doubtful debts @4 percent on debtors

(iv) Make a provision for income tax @30 percent.

(v) Depreciation expense includes depreciation of ₹800 on buildings and that of ₹1,200 on machinery.

(vi) The directors recommend a dividend @25 percent and transfer to general reserve @10 percent.

(vii) Assume dividend distribution tax @20 percent.

Silver Pot Limited
Statement of Profit and Loss for the year ended March 31, 2017

Particulars	Note No.	(₹)
I. Revenue from operations		52,000
II. Other income		1,200
III. Total Income		53,200
IV. Expenses		
Purchases (21,000 + 8,000)		29,000
Changes in inventories (1,000 – 9,000)		(8,000)
Employee benefits expenses		6,000
Finance costs		2,800
Depreciation and amortisation expenses		2,000
Other expenses	1	6,200
Total expenses		38,000
V. Profit before tax (III – IV)		15,200
VI. Tax expense @30 percent		(4,560)
VII. Profit for the period (V – VI)		10,640
Basic Earnings Per Equity Share = 10,640/2,000 = ₹5.32		

NOTES

Silver Pot Limited
Balance Sheet as at March 31, 2017

Particulars	₹	₹
I. EQUITY AND LIABILITIES		
(1) Equity		
(a) Share capital	2	20,000
(b) Other Equity: Reserves and surplus	3	17,140
(2) Non-Current Liabilities		
(a) Long-term borrowings (Debentures)		20,000
(3) Current Liabilities		9,200
(a) Trade payables (Sundry creditors)		
(b) Other current liabilities	4	2,100
(c) Short-term Provisions—Provision for tax		4,560
Total		73,000
II. ASSETS		
(1) Non-Current Assets		
(a) Property, Plant and Equipment	5	28,500
(b) Non-current Investments (1,200 shares of Y Ltd. of ₹10 each, ₹8 paid up)		12,000
(2) Current Assets		
(a) Inventories	6	11,300
(b) Trade Receivables	7	12,000
(c) Cash and cash equivalents		3,000
(d) Short-term Loans and Advances (Advance payment of tax)		6,000
(e) Other current assets—interest accrued on investments		200
Total		73,000
Contingent Liabilities and Commitments	8	

NOTES TO ACCOUNTS

1. Other Expenses

	₹
Rent	2,600
Miscellaneous expenses	1,800
Directors' fees	1,000
Bad debts	600
Provision for doubtful debts (4 percent of 12,500 – 300)	200
	6,200

2. Share Capital

	₹
Authorised capital	
5,000 equity shares of ₹10 each	50,000
Issued capital	
2,000 equity shares of ₹10 each	20,000
Subscribed and fully paid up capital	
2,000 equity shares of ₹10 each	20,000

3. Other equity: Reserves and Surplus

	₹	₹
General reserve		
Opening balance	4,000	
Add: Transfer from net profit (10 percent of 10,640)	1,064	5,064
Balance in profit and loss account		
Opening balance	2,500	
Add: Net profit for the period	10,640	
Less: Transfer to general reserve (10 percent of 10,640)	1,064	12,076
		17,140

4. Other Current Liabilities

	₹
Unclaimed dividend	500
Outstanding expenses	200
Interest accrued on borrowings (Debentures)	1,400
	2,100

5. Property, Plant and Equipment

	Cost (₹)	Provision for depreciation (₹)	Closing written down value (₹)
Building	29,000	5,000	24,000
Machinery	10,000	5,500	4,500
	39,000	10,500	28,500

6. Inventories

	₹
Closing stock of finished goods	9,000
Loose tools	2,300
	11,300

7. Trade Receivables

	₹
Sundry debtors	12,500
Less: Provision for doubtful debts	500
	12,000

8. Contingent Liabilities and Commitments (to the extent not provided for)

	₹
I. Contingent liabilities	
Bills discounted but not yet matured	1,000
II. Commitments	
(a) Uncalled liability on partly paid shares (1,200 shares of ₹10, ₹8 paid up)	2,400
(b) Proposed equity dividend (25 percent of ₹20,000)	5,000
(c) Dividend distribution tax (20 percent of ₹5,000)	1,000

NOTES

CASE STUDY 10.3 Balance Sheet and Statement of Profit and Loss

Moon Beam Limited have authorised capital of ₹5 lakhs divided into 50,000 equity shares of ₹10 each. The following is the trial balance of the company as on March 31, 2017:

Particulars	Dr. (₹)	Cr. (₹)
Opening stock	66,500	
Discounts and rebates	3,000	
Carriage inwards	5,750	
Patterns	37,500	
Rates, taxes and insurance	5,500	
Furniture and fixtures	15,000	
Purchases	1,23,250	
Wages	1,36,800	
Freehold land	1,25,000	
Plant and machinery	75,000	
Engineering tools	15,000	
Goodwill	37,500	
Sundry debtors	26,600	
Bills receivables	13,450	
Advertisement	1,500	
Commission and brokerage	6,750	
Business expense	5,600	
Bank current account	2,000	
Cash in hand	800	
Debenture interest paid	1,000	
Interest on bank overdraft	9,100	
Preliminary expenses	1,000	
Calls in arrear @₹2 per share	1,000	
Equity share capital (20,000 shares of ₹10 each)		2,00,000
4 percent Debentures (repayable after 10 years)		50,000
Bank overdraft		75,700
Sundry creditors (for goods)		24,050
Sales		3,61,700
Rent (Cr.)		3,000
Transfer fees received		650
Profit and Loss Account (Cr.)		6,700
Repairs to building	4,650	
Bad debts	2,550	
Total	7,21,800	7,21,800

Additional information:

(i) The stock (valued at cost or market value, whichever is lower) as on March 31, 2016 was ₹70,800

(ii) Outstanding liabilities for wages ₹2,500 and business expenses ₹3,600

(iii) Dividend declared @20 percent on paid-up capital

Adjustments:

(i) Charge depreciation: Plant and machinery @5 percent; Engineering tools @20 percent; Patterns @10 percent; and Furniture and fixture @10 percent

(ii) Provide 10 percent on debtors as doubtful debts after writing off ₹1,600 as bad debts.

(iii) Write off preliminary expenses fully.

(iv) Create debenture redemption reserve @10 percent of debentures.
(v) Transfer to general reserve @2.5 percent.
(vi) Provide for income tax @30 percent; Dividend distribution tax rate @20 percent.

Required

Prepare statement of profit and loss for the year ended March 31, 2017 and balance sheet as on that date.

Solution

Moon Beam Limited
Statement of Profit and Loss for the year ended March 31, 2017

Particulars	Note No.	₹
I. Revenue from operations		3,61,700
II. Other income	1	3,650
III. Total income (I + II)		3,65,350
IV. Expenses		
Cost of purchases		1,23,250
Change in inventories (66,500 – 70,800)		(4,300)
Employee benefit expenses (1,36,800 + 2,500)		1,39,300
Finance costs (2,000 + 9,100)		11,100
Depreciation and amortization expenses	6	12,000
Other expenses	2	44,000
Total expenses		3,25,350
V. Profit before tax (III – IV)		40,000
VI. Tax expenses @30 percent		12,000
VII Profit for the period (V – VI)		28,000

Moon Beam Limited
Balance Sheet as at March 31, 2017

Particulars	Note No.	₹
I. EQUITY AND LIABILITIES		
(1) Equity		
(a) Share capital	3	1,99,000
(b) Other equity: Reserves and surplus	4	34,700
(2) Non-current liabilities		
Long-term borrowings (Debentures)		50,000
(3) Current liabilities		
(a) Trade payables (Sundry creditors)		24,050
(b) Other current liabilities	5	82,800
(c) Short-term provisions – Provision for tax		12,000
Total		4,02,550
II. ASSETS		
(1) Non-current assets		
(a) Property, plant and equipment	6	2,55,500
(b) Goodwill		37,500
(2) Current assets		
(a) Inventories		70,800
(b) Trade receivables	7	35,950
(c) Cash and cash equivalents	8	2,800
Total		4,02,550
Contingent liabilities and commitments	9	

NOTES

NOTES TO ACCOUNTS

1. Other Income

Particulars	₹
Miscellaneous income (Transfer fee)	650
Rental income	3,000
Total	3,650

2. Other Expenses

Particulars	₹
Carriage inward	5,750
Discount and rebates	3,000
Advertisement	1,500
Rent	5,500
Repairs to building	4,650
Preliminary expenses	1,000
Commission and brokerage	6,750
Miscellaneous expenses (5,600 + 3,600)	9,200
Bad debts (2,550 + 1,600)	4,150
Provision for doubtful debts [10 percent of (26,600 – 1,600)	2,500
Total	44,000

3. Share Capital

Authorised capital	₹
50,000 equity shares of ₹10 each	5,00,000
Issued capital	
20,000 equity shares of ₹10 each	2,00,000
Subscribed capital and fully paid	
19,500 equity shares of ₹10 each	1,95,000
Subscribed capital and not fully paid	
500 equity shares of ₹10 each, ₹8 paid up	4,000
	1,99,000

Note: Call unpaid ₹1,000

4. Other Equity: Reserves and Surplus

Particulars	₹	₹
Debenture redemption reserve		5,000
General reserve:		
Opening balance	Nil	
Transfer from profit for the current year	700	700
Surplus (Balance in profit and loss account)		
Opening balance	6,700	
Profit for the period	28,000	
Transfer to General Reserve @2.5 percent	(700)	
Transfer to Debenture redemption reserve	(5,000)	29,000
		34,700

NOTES

5. Other Current Liabilities

Particulars	₹
Bank overdraft	75,700
Outstanding expenses (2,500 + 3,600)	6,100
Interest accrued on borrowings (2,000 – 1,000)	1,000
	82,800

6. Property, Plant and Equipment

Particulars	Value given (₹)	Depreciation charged (₹)	Written down value at the end (₹)
Land	1,25,000	–	1,25,000
Plant and machinery	75,000	3,750	71,250
Furniture and fixtures	15,000	1,500	13,500
Patterns	37,500	3,750	33,750
Engineering tools	15,000	3,000	12,000
	2,67,500	12,000	2,55,500

7. Trade receivables

Particulars	₹
Sundry debtors (26,600 – 1,600)	25,000
Provision for doubtful debts	(2,500)
	22,500
Bills receivables	13,450
	35,950

8. Cash and cash equivalents

Particulars	₹
Cash balance	800
Bank balance	2,000
	2,800

9. Contingent liabilities and commitments

Particulars	₹
Contingent liabilities	Nil
Commitments:	
Proposed equity dividend [12 percent of (2,00,000 – 1,000)]	23,880
Dividend distribution tax (20 percent of 23,880)	4,776

CASE STUDY 10.4 Balance Sheet

On March 31, 2017 Bose and Sen Ltd. provides you the following ledger balances after preparing its Statement of Profit and Loss for the year ended March 31, 2017:

Credit Balances

	₹
Equity share capital, fully paid shares of ₹10 each	70,00,000
General reserve	15,49,100
Loan from State Finance Corporation, secured by hypothecation of Plant and Machinery (repayable within one year ₹2,00,000)	10,50,000
Loans: Unsecured (long-term)	8,47,000
Sundry creditors for goods and expenses (payable within 6 months)	14,00,000
Profit and Loss Account	7,00,000
Provision for taxation	3,25,500
Proposed dividend	4,20,000
Provision for dividend distribution tax	71,400
	1,33,63,000

Debit Balances

	₹
Calls in arrear	7,000
Land	14,00,000
Buildings	20,50,000
Plant and Machinery	36,75,000
Furniture and Fixture	3,50,000
Stock: Finished goods	14,00,000
Stock: Raw materials	3,50,000
Sundry debtors	14,00,000
Advances: Short-term	2,98,900
Cash-in-hand	2,10,000
Balances with banks	17,29,000
Preliminary expenses	93,100
Patents and Trade marks	4,00,000
	1,33,63,000

The following additional information is also provided:

(i) 4,20,000 fully paid equity shares were allotted as consideration for land and buildings.

(ii) Cost of building ₹28,00,000; Cost of Plant and Machinery ₹49,00,000; and Cost of Furniture and Fixture ₹4,37,500.

(iii) Sundry debtors for ₹3,80,000 are due for more than 6 months.

(iv) The amount of balances includes ₹18,000 with a bank, which is not a scheduled bank, and the deposits of ₹5 lakhs are for a period of 9 months.

(v) Unsecured loan includes ₹2,00,000 from a bank and ₹1,00,000 from related parties.

You are not required to give previous year figures. You are required to prepare the Balance Sheet of the company as on March 31, 2017 as required under revised Schedule III of the Companies Act, 2013.

(Adapted, CA, IPC, Nov, 2015)

NOTES

Solution

	Note No.	Figures at the end of current reporting period (₹)
EQUITY AND LIABILITIES		
I. Equity	1	
(a) Share capital	2	69,93,000
(b) Other equity: Reserves and surplus		26,47,400
II. Non-current Liabilities		
(a) Long-term borrowings	3	16,97,000
III. Current Liabilities		
(a) Trade payables		14,00,000
(b) Other current liabilities	4	2,00,000
(c) Short-term provisions	5	3,25,500
		1,32,62,900
ASSETS		
I. Non-current assets		
(a) Fixed assets:		
Property, plant and equipment	6	74,75,000
Intangible assets (Patents and Trademarks)		4,00,000
II. Current assets		
(a) Inventories	7	17,50,000
(b) Trade receivables	8	14,00,000
(c) Cash and cash equivalents	9	19,39,000
(d) Short-term loans and advances		2,98,900
		1,32,62,900

NOTES TO ACCOUNTS

	₹	₹
1. Share capital		
Equity share capital		
Issued subscribed and called up 7,00,000 equity shares of ₹10 each	70,00,000	
(Out of the above, 4,20,000 shares have been issued for consideration other than cash.)		
Less: Calls in arrears	7,000	69,93,000
2. Other equity: Reserves and surplus		
General reserve		20,40,500
Surplus (profit and loss account)	7,00,000	
Less: Preliminary expenses	93100	6,06,900
		26,47,400
3. Long-term borrowings		
Secured		
Loan from State Finance Corporation (10,50,000 – 2,00,000)		8,50,000
(Secured by hypothecation of Plant and Machinery)		
Unsecured		
Bank loan	2,00,000	
Loan from related parties	1,00,000	
Others	5,47,000	8,47,000
		16,97,000

	₹	₹
4. Other current liabilities		
Loan instalment repayable within one year		2,00,000
5. Short-term provisions		
Provision for taxation		3,25,500
		3,25,500
6. Property, plant and equipment		
Land		14,00,000
Buildings	28,00,000	
Less: Depreciation	7,50,000	20,50,000
Plant and machinery	49,00,000	
Less: Depreciation	12,25,000	36,75,000
Furniture and fittings	4,37,500	
Less: Depreciation	87,500	3,50,000
		74,75,000
7. Inventories		
Raw material		3,50,000
Finished goods		14,00,000
		17,50,000
8. Trade receivables		
Debts outstanding for a period exceeding six months		3,80,000
Other debts		10,20,000
		14,00,000
Cash and cash equivalents		
Cash at bank with Scheduled banks including bank deposit for period 9 months amounting ₹5,00,000	17,11,000	
Cash at bank with others	18,000	17,29,000
Cash in hand		2,10,000
		19,39,000

Commitments: Proposed dividend: ₹4,20.000; Dividend distribution tax: ₹71,400

ANSWERS TO SELF-TEST QUESTIONS

10.1 (i) F; (ii) F; (iii) F; (iv) F; (v) T
10.2 (i) T; (ii) F
10.3 (i) T; (ii) T; (iii) T; (iv) F; (v) T
10.4 (i) T; (ii) T; (iii) T
10.5 (i) T; (ii) F; (iii) T; (iv) T; (v) F
10.6 (i) T; (ii) F; (iii) T; (iv) F
10.7 (i) T; (ii) F; (iii) F; (iv) T; (v) F

ASSIGNMENTS

Multiple Choice Questions

1. Tick the right answer:
   (i) Schedule III to the Companies Act, 2013 has
      (a) prescribed the formats for the balance sheet and the profit and loss account.
      (b) prescribed the format for the balance sheet.
      (c) prescribed the format for the profit and loss account.
      (d) prescribed the format for the balance sheet and the requirements for the profit and loss account.

NOTES

(ii) 'A' Ltd. has sold a machine for ₹1,20,000. The cost and accumulated depreciation of the same at the time of sale were ₹1,00,000 and ₹80,000, respectively. In computing profit for managerial remuneration, credit should be taken for:
   (a) ₹1,00,000
   (b) ₹20,000
   (c) ₹80,000
   (d) ₹40,000

(iii) Dividend can be paid only out of
   (a) current year's profit.
   (b) current year's profit and undistributed profits of previous years.
   (c) current year's profit, undistributed profits of previous years, and government grants received for the purpose.
   (d) current year's profit and government grants received for the purpose.

(iv) Where, during any financial year, any asset has been sold
   (a) no depreciation should be provided for that year.
   (b) depreciation should be provided for the full year.
   (c) depreciation should be provided on pro rata basis up to the date on which such asset has been sold.
   (d) management, at its discretion, may or may not provide depreciation for that year.

(v) A limited liability company should provide depreciation using the rates
   (a) specified in the income tax rules.
   (b) specified in the Companies Act, 2013.
   (c) determined with reference to estimated useful lives and residual values of assets.
   (d) using the rates determined with reference to estimated useful lives and residual values of assets, but the amount of depreciation should not be less than the amount calculated using the rates specified in the Companies Act, 2013.

(vi) Share premium account and capital redemption reserve account are
   (a) revenue reserves.
   (b) capital reserves, so should be included in the carrying amount of capital reserves.
   (c) capital reserves, but should be shown separately in the balance sheet.
   (d) neither revenue reserve nor capital reserve, so should be shown separately in the balance sheet.

2. Indicate against each statement whether it is true (T) or false (F):

(a) Statement of profit and loss and balance sheet of a limited liability company should comply with accounting standards issued by the Institute of Chartered Accountants of India.
(b) The Companies Act, 2013, requires that a holding company present consolidated financial statements of the holding company and its subsidiaries.
(c) Contributions made to charitable funds should not be deducted for computing net profit for the purpose of managerial remuneration.
(d) The Companies Act, 2013, does not allow payment of interest on capital.
(e) Under the Companies Act, 2013, there is no requirement for the preparation of a separate profit and loss appropriation account.
(f) Profit prior to incorporation is capital profit.
(g) Provision for doubtful debts represents a liability.

Fund Flow and Cash Flow Statement

CHAPTER

11

LEARNING OBJECTIVES

The objective of this chapter is to provide an understanding of the preparation and use of Fund Flow Statement and Cash Flow Statement. After reading this chapter, you will be able to understand the following:

- The use of Fund Flow Statement and Cash flow Statement
- Impact of transactions related to non-current assets and liabilities on working capital
- Sources and applications of funds
- How to Compute funds from operation
- How to compute fund from sale of items of property, plant and equipment
- How to prepare and present Fund Flow Statement
- Analysing Fund Flow Statement
- Distinction between operating, investing and financing activities
- Direct and indirect methods for preparing and presenting Cash Flow Statement
- How to prepare cash flows from operating activities under indirect method
- How to compute cash flow from sale of items of property, plant and equipment
- How to deal with exchange difference in preparing Cash Flow Statement
- How to present Cash Flow Statement
- Analysing Cash Flow Statement

NOTES

Key Terms
Working capital, working capital gap

INTRODUCTION

The balance sheet and the statement of profit and loss are prepared on 'accrual accounting' basis and, therefore, do not present cash flow for the year directly. The fund flow statement and cash flow statement summarise the fund flow and cash flow outcomes of operating, investing and financing decisions.

Fund flow statement

Entities invest in non-current assets and current assets. Entities are not required to arrange finance to support the total investment in current assets. A part of the investment in current assets is financed by spontaneous (non-interest bearing) credits, such as trade creditors and advances from customers. Therefore, an enterprise is required to finance only the balance of the investment in current assets, known as a *working capital gap*. In practice, investment in non-current assets and resources mobilised through long-term sources of finance in a particular year seldom matches. This gap causes change in investment in working capital. Enterprises prepare and present fund flow statements that focuses on long-term sources of finance and investment in non-current assets. It exhibits the working capital implication of changes in non-current assets and non-current liabilities. The change in working capital is presented as a balancing figure in the fund flow statement. A fund flow statement does not exhibit changes in each component of the working capital. A cash flow statement, which may be viewed as an improved version of the fund flow statement, does not have this limitation.

In a fund flow statement, a fund is defined as *working capital*. Therefore, in a fund flow statement, working capital may be viewed as a reservoir and fund flows in and out of the reservoir on account of transactions and events relating to non-current assets and non-current liabilities. Fund flow statement presents changes in working capital due to changes in non-current assets and non-current liabilities.

Cash flow statement

In a cash flow statement, cash is the 'reservoir' and cash flows in and out of the reservoir on account of transactions and events relating to assets (other than cash) and liabilities. Cash flow statement presents changes in cash during the accounting period due to changes in current and non-current assets (other than cash) and current and non-current liabilities.

Both the statements focus on transactions and events that generate flow, and not on the reservoir. Fund flow statement exhibits 'net changes' rather than 'gross changes' in different types of assets and liabilities. For example, they do not show the amount of money borrowed during the year and the amount repaid during the year separately. They show the net borrowing (repayment).

A cash flow statement forms part of the set of financial statements being issued by companies on yearly basis. Cash flow statement exhibits 'gross changes'.

Self-Test Questions

Self-test question 11.1

Indicate whether the following statements are true (T) or false (F):

(i) Fund flow and cash flow statements add informative value of financial statements, as core financial statements are prepared using accrual method of accounting.

(ii) In Fund Flow statement, working capital is considered as the reservoir.

(iii) Fund flow statement can be used as a tool for managing working capital.

(iv) Cash Flow statement is an improvement over Fund Flow statement.

NOTES

SUMMARY

The balance sheet and the statement of profit and loss are prepared on accrual basis. Therefore, from those statements, it is difficult to evaluate fund flows and cash flows for the year. Therefore, companies prepare fund flow statement and cash flow statement. Fund flow statement presents how the working capital was affected by non-current transactions. Cash flow statement presents cash flows from operating, investing and financing activities. Cash flow statement is an improvement over the fund flow statement. A cash flow statement forms part of the set of financial statements being issued by companies on yearly basis. Cash flow statement exhibits 'gross changes'.

FUND FLOW STATEMENT

The Concept

Key Terms
Fund flow, cash flow

A fund flow statement provides information on how, during the reporting period, decisions relating to capital structure, dividend and investment in non-current assets have changed the amount invested in working capital. *However, it should be clear that there is no cause and effect relationship between investment in non-current assets and financing decisions and the investment in working capital.* Management of working capital is a task that can be examined independently of investment in non-current assets and financing decisions. Table 11.1 provides examples of working capital implications of transactions involving non-current assets and liabilities.

In a fund flow statement, the term 'fund' connotes working capital. A fund flow statement presents sources and application of funds. Sources imply those movements in non-current assets, non-current liabilities and equity that increase the working capital. Applications imply those movements in non-current assets, non-current liabilities and equity that reduce the working capital. Usually the fund flow statement is supported by a 'statement of changes in working capital'.

TABLE 11.1

Working Capital Implications of Transactions Involving Non-current Assets and Non-current Liabilities

S. No.	Transaction details	Change in non-current assets/liabilities and equity	Change in current assets/liabilities	Working capital implications
1.	Martina Limited (ML) purchases a piece of land for ₹10,00,000 on deferred credit that is payable in ten equal installments starting from the next year. Interest is payable separately every year.	Non-current asset (Land): + ₹10,00,000; Non-current liabilities (Deferred credit): + ₹9,00,000	Current liabilities (Installment of deferred credit payable next year): + ₹1,00,000	– ₹1,00,000
2.	Martina Limited (ML) purchases furniture on cash for ₹1,00,000.	Non-current asset (Furniture): + ₹1,00,000	Current assets (Cash): – ₹1,00,000	– ₹1,00,000
3.	Martina Limited (ML) purchases equipment for ₹5,00,000 on credit for three months. The amount will fall due next year.	Non-current asset (equipment): + ₹5,00,000	Current liabilities (Amount payable next year): + ₹5,00,000	– ₹5,00,000
4.	Martina Limited (ML) mobilises ₹20,00,000 by issuing share capital.	Equity: + ₹20,00,000	Current assets (Cash): + ₹20,00,000	+ ₹20,00,000
5.	Martina Limited (ML) borrows ₹10,00,000 payable after 3 years.	Non-current liabilities (Debt): + ₹10,00,000	Current assets (Cash): + ₹10,00,000	+ ₹10,00,000

(Contd.)

NOTES

TABLE 11.1

Working Capital Implications of Transactions Involving
Non-current Assets and Non-current Liabilities (*Contd.*)

S. No.	Transaction details	Change in non-current assets/liabilities and equity	Change in current assets/liabilities	Working capital implications
6.	Martina Limited (ML) repays ₹10,00,000, which was payable after 3 years from the date of borrowing	Non-current liabilities (Debt): – ₹10,00,000	Current assets (Cash): – ₹10,00,000	– ₹10,00,000
7.	Martina Limited (ML) sells an item of property, plant and equipment for ₹20,000.	Non-current asset (equipment): – ₹20,000	Current assets (Cash): + ₹20,000	+ ₹20,000
8.	Martina Limited (ML) exchanges an item of equipment (carrying amount ₹1,00,000) for another item of equipment.	Non-current asset (equipment): Nil	Current assets: Nil	No change in working capital.

Self-Test Questions

Self-test question 11.2

Fill in the blanks: [Where the blank space is not to be filled in by amount, choose between the words 'increased' and decreased'.]

(i) DS Limited purchased equipment by paying ₹100,000 to the vendor immediately by cheque, causing ....in working capital by ₹............ .

(ii) NK Limited borrowed ₹20 lakhs, which is repayable over a period of five years in equal yearly installments starting from the end of the first year. The working capital has....................... by ₹............ .

(iii) UV Limited borrowed ₹20 lakhs, which is repayable at the end of the fifth year. The working capital has....................... by ₹............ .

(iv) SK Limited purchased 20 percent shares of one of its major vendors for ₹5 crores from the market. The working capital has....................... by ₹............ .

(v) PQ Limited issued sweat equity to its promoter-directors, valued at ₹80 Crores, without receiving cash or any other asset, resulting in change in working capital by ₹............ .

Sources and Applications of Funds

1. Sources:
   (a) Funds from business operations
   (b) Sale of non-current assets
   (c) Issue of share capital
   (d) Long-term borrowings
   Total (1)
2. Applications (or uses):
   (a) Purchase of non-current assets
   (b) Redemption of debentures
   (c) Repayment of other long-term liabilities
   (d) Buy-back of shares
   (e) Redemption of preference shares
   (f) Payment of income tax
   (g) Distribution of cash dividend
   Total (2)
3. Change in working capital (1 – 2)

Equity during the reporting period changes on account of:

1. Net profit/(loss) for the period
2. Fresh contribution from shareholders
3. Buy-back of own shares
4. Distribution of cash dividend

Distribution of stock dividend by issue of bonus shares does not change equity. It results in movement between different components of equity, namely, share capital, share premium and retained profit.

A fund flow statement shows changes in different elements of *equity*, rather than an aggregate figure for change in equity.

Preparation of the fund flow statement does not require analyses of individual transactions. It analyses balance sheet figures of assets and liabilities at the commencement and at the close of the year. If movement in non-current assets matches movement in non-current liabilities and equity, there is no movement in the working capital. If movement in non-current assets does not match movement in non-current liabilities, and equity, the movement in the working capital explains the difference. This flows from the fundamental accounting principle that increase or decrease in assets (current and non-current together) should match increase or decrease in liabilities: (current and non-current liabilities) and equity.

Funds from Operations

Profit from operations is considered to be a long-term source of funds, because net profit, unless distributed to owners, enhances the equity. Similarly, net loss reduces the equity. Net profit/(loss) increases/(decreases) the investment in working capital. However, in an accrual accounting system, increase/(decrease) in working capital does not match the reported net profit/(loss). The difference arises, because, the statement of profit and loss is debited by certain expenses which represent non-current amortisations. The most common examples of such amortisations are depreciation and amortisation of intangible assets. If the expenditure was incurred in earlier years, it does not result in outflow of assets or assumption of liabilities in the current reporting period. Therefore, it does not cause any decrease in working capital. If the expenditure is incurred in the current reporting period, it is exhibited as a separate item under 'application of fund' in the fund flow statement. For example, if equipment is purchased for ₹1,00,000 on cash basis, the fund flow statement exhibits the total amount of such expenditure as a separate item, namely, 'purchase of non-current asset, under 'application of funds'. Therefore, even if the expenditure is incurred during the current period, net profit/(loss) should be adjusted for the part allocated to the current period and charged to the profit and loss account as depreciation.

Net profit/(loss) should also be adjusted for income or expenses that do not directly relate to the operation of the business. Those items of income and expenses are exhibited as separate items in the fund flow statement.

The following are the most common items for which net profit/(loss) is adjusted to determine the amount of funds from operations:

1. Depreciation on depreciable assets
2. Amortisation of intangible assets (e.g., goodwill, trademarks and patents)
3. Profit/(loss) on transactions related to non-current assets
4. Non-operating expenses
5. Provision for income tax
6. Non-operating income
7. Subsidy credited to the statement of profit and loss
8. Credit from reserves (e.g., revaluation reserve)

NOTES

CASE STUDY 11.1 Fund from Operation

The statement of profit and loss of Delhi Ltd. for the year 2017 is presented as follows:

		Amount (₹'000)
Sales		5,000
Less: Materials consumed	1,000	
Manufacturing expenses	2,000	
Administration and selling expenses	750	
Depreciation	250	
Amortisation of: Patent	250	
Loss on sale of equipment	50	4,300
Operating profit		700
Add: Dividend received		100
		800
Less: Income tax		200
Net profit		600

Calculate the fund from operation for the year 2017.

Solution

Funds from operation		
Net profit as per statement of profit and loss		600
Add: Loss on sale of equipment (cash flow from sale will be shown as a separate item)	50	
Depreciation (non-current amortisation)	250	
Amortisation of intangible assets (non-current amortisation)	250	550
		1,150
Less: Dividend received (will be shown as a separate item)		100
Fund from operation		1,050

Fund from operation represents increase in working capital due to operating activities of the firm.

In order to determine fund from operations accurately, net profit is adjusted for impairment of current assets charged to the statement of profit and loss. Examples of such charges are bad debt and depreciation of inventory. These represent non-cash expenses. Care should be taken to adjust the difference between the opening and closing balance of the relevant current asset for the impairment loss, to determine the movement in working capital. Let us take an example. The opening and closing balances of trade debtors are ₹1,00,000 and ₹1,50,000, respectively. During the period, ₹20,000 is written off as bad debt.

In order to determine fund from operation accurately, ₹20,000 is added to the net profit reported in the profit and loss account, and in the 'statement of changes in working capital', increase in 'trade debtors' is shown at (₹1,50,000 – ₹1,00,000 + 20,000) or ₹70,000. However, usually no adjustment is made for bad debt written off to determine 'fund from operation', and increase in 'trade debtors' is shown at (₹1,50,000 – ₹1,00,000) or ₹50,000.

Self-Test Questions

Self-test question 11.3

Fill in the blanks:

(i) The statement of profit and loss for the year 2017 reported net profit (after tax) of ₹10,00,000. The net profit includes dividend income ₹50,000, depreciation ₹1,00,000 and income from sale of scrap ₹20,000. Income tax paid was equal to interest expense. Fund from operations for the year was ₹.............................. .

(ii) The statement of profit and loss for the year 2017 reported net profit (after tax) of ₹20,00,000. The net profit includes interest expense ₹2,00,000, bad debt ₹30,000, dividend income ₹60,000, depreciation ₹1,00,000 and income from sale of machinery ₹10,000. Income tax paid was equal to interest expense. Fund from operations for the year was ₹............................ .

NOTES

Fund Flow Related to Non-current Assets

Transactions relating to non-current assets require special consideration. The carrying amount of items of property, plant and equipment and intangible assets reduces due to depreciation (amortisation) even without any fresh transaction relating to those assets. Therefore, adjustment for depreciation (amortisation) is required to determine the amount of fund flow on account of transactions relating to PP&E and intangible assets.

Sale of item of PP&E and intangible assets results in increase in working capital by the amount of cash or other current asset received or receivable as consideration. Therefore, funds from the sale of the depreciable asset are the aggregate of the asset's WDV and the profit/(loss) on sale of the asset. In order to determine the funds from sale of a depreciable asset, we should collect information on its Written-Down Value (WDV). Similarly, outflow of funds on account of acquisition of a depreciable asset is presented in the fund flow statement on gross basis. Therefore, in order to determine the cost of a depreciable asset purchased during the year, the difference in the net book value of the depreciable asset at the end and at the commencement of the reporting period should be adjusted for depreciation for the year.

CASE STUDY 11.2 Fund Flow from Sale of Old Machinery

'A' Ltd. has provided the following information relating to its plant and machinery account.

		(₹'000)
	Year 2016	**Year 2017**
Gross book value at the end of the year	100	140
Accumulated depreciation at the end of the year	20	34

Additional information:

1. Loss on sale of plant and machinery	1
2. Depreciation charged during the year	16
3. Purchase of new machinery during the year	45

Calculate the fund generated in 2017 from the sale of the old item of plant and machinery.

Solution

		(₹'000)
(a) Gross book value of asset sold:		
Balance as on December 31, 2016	₹1,00,000	
Purchases during 2017	45,000	
	₹1,45,000	
Sold during 2017 (balance figure)	5,000	
Balance as on December 31, 2017 (Given)	₹1,40,000	
(b) Accumulated depreciation on the asset sold:		
Balance as on December 31, 2016		₹20,000
Add: Depreciation for the year 2017 (Given) (Reported in the statement of profit and loss)		16,000
		36,000
Less: Accumulated depreciation on the item sold (balancing figure)		2,000
Accumulated depreciation as on December 31, 2017 (Given)		₹34,000
(c) Fund flow from sale of plant and machinery:		
Gross book value of plant sold		₹5,000
Less: Accumulated depreciation		2,000
Written-down value of the item sold		3,000
Less: Loss on sale of plant and machinery		1,000
Fund flow from sale of machinery		₹2,000

NOTES

CASE STUDY 11.3 Fund Flow Statement

Sushmita Limited (SL) provides the following information:

Amount (₹'000)

Non-current assets, non-current liabilities and equity	Amount at the end of the year	Amount at the beginning of the year
Property, plant and equipment, net of depreciation	290	130
Investment in Rani Limited (RL)	580	270
Debentures	150	500
Contributed capital	800	800
Reserves and surplus	820	475

The following additional information is provided by SL:

(a) Dividends paid during the year ₹80,000

(b) A gain on sale of equipment of ₹30,000 has been included in net income. The cost of the equipment and the written down value at the date of sale were ₹1,20,000 and ₹50,000, respectively.

(c) Depreciation on property, plant and equipment charged in the income statement for the year was ₹90,000.

Required

Prepare the fund flow statement for the year covered by the income statement.

Solution

Working notes:

(a) Funds from business operation (Amount in ₹'000)

Increase in reserves and surplus (820 – 475)	345
Add: Dividends paid	80
Add: Depreciation on property, plant and equipment	90
	515
Less: Gain on sale of equipment	30
	485

(b) Sale of equipment (Amount in ₹'000)

Written down value of the equipment	50
Gain on sale of equipment	30
Sale of equipment	80

(c) Purchase of equipment (Amount in ₹'000)

Increase in the net book value of property, plant and equipment	160
Add: Depreciation on property, plant and equipment for the year	90
Add: Written down value of the equipment sold	50
Increase in the gross block (purchase)	300

Fund Flow Statement of SL for the year ended ...

Particulars	Amount (₹'000)
Sources of Funds	
Funds from business operations	485
Sale of equipment	80
Total (A)	565
Application of Funds	
Purchase of equipment	300
Purchase of investment	310
Redemption of debentures	350
Dividends paid	80
Total (B)	1,040
Decrease in Working Capital (B – A)	475

Analysing the Fund Flow Statement

A fund flow statement may be used to address a variety of questions that help to understand the dynamics of working capital management:

1. How strong is the entity's internal fund generation? Is the fund flow from operations positive? If it is negative, what are the reasons?
2. Have long-term sources been adequate to support long-term applications? If not, what are the reasons? Is it a deliberate policy to reduce investment in working capital?
3. Is the investment in working capital adequate?
4. Has the liquidity position of the firm improved?

Answers to these questions provide an insight into the entity's financing strategy and its ability to manage the working capital.

NOTES

CASE STUDY 11.4 Fund Flow Statement

The balance sheets of 'A' Ltd. for a period of three years as on 31 March each year are as follows:

(₹, lakhs)

	Year 2015	Year 2016	Year 2017
Liabilities:			
Share capital, in equity shares of ₹10 each	30	35	35
General reserve	10	15	18
Surplus	5	8	9
13 percent debentures	10	5	10
Bank credit	5	10	15
Trade creditors	10	12	15
Income tax provision for the current year	8	11	14
Proposed dividend	6	10.5	14
	84	106.5	130
Assets:			
Plant and machinery	45	55	70
Investments	10	15	20
Stock	12	15	15
Debtors	14	15	12
Cash and bank	3	6.5	13
	84	106.5	130

Other details:

(i) Depreciation provided in the books:

Year 2015	₹ 6 lakh
Year 2016	₹ 8 lakh
Year 2017	₹ 10 lakh

(ii) A part of the debentures was converted into equity at par in June 2015.

(iii) There was no sale of depreciable asset during the period.

The management seeks your advice on the liquidity position of the company. Use the fund flow statement for the purpose.

Solution

1. Statement of changes in working capital

(₹, lakhs)

	Year 2015	Year 2016	Year 2017
(a) *Current assets:*			
Stock	12.00	15.00	15.00
Debtors	14.00	15.00	12.00
Cash and bank	3.00	6.50	13.00
	29.00	36.50	40.00

NOTES

(₹, lakhs)

	Year 2015	Year 2016	Year 2017
(b) *Current liabilities:*			
Bank credit	5.00	10.00	15.00
Trade creditors	10.00	12.00	15.00
	15.00	22.00	30.00
(c) *Working capital (a – b)*	14.00	14.50	10.00
(d) *Changes in working capital*		0.50	(4.50)

2. Statement of funds from operations		*1992*	*1993*
Increase in retained profit:			
Surplus		3.00	1.00
General reserve		5.00	3.00
		8.00	4.00
Proposed dividend		10.50	14.00
Profit for the year		18.50	18.00
Depreciation (non-current amortisation)		8.00	10.00
Tax provisions (To be shown as a separate line item)		11.00	14.00
Funds from operation		37.50	42.00
3. Funds flow statement			
(a) *Sources:*			
Funds from operations		37.50	42.00
Issue of 13% debentures		—	5.00
		37.50	47.00
(b) *Applications:*			
Purchase of plant and machinery		18.00	25.00
Purchase of investments		5.00	5.00
Income tax paid		8.00	11.00
Dividend paid		6.00	10.50
		37.00	51.50
(c) *Change in working capital (a – b)*		0.50	(4.50)

Working notes:

1. To determine the amount of fund from operations, we have added proposed dividend to the amount of increase in the retained profit. This is because the increase in retained profit represents profit earned during the period reduced by the proposed dividend.
2. The number for purchase of plant and machinery is the total of depreciation for the year and the difference between opening and closing balances of plant and machinery.
3. The balance sheet shows income tax provisions for the current year. It is assumed that the actual tax liability was equal to the provision, and that provision created in one accounting year was paid in the next accounting period.
4. Proposed dividend becomes the liability on approval by shareholders in the annual general meeting. Unpaid dividend is a current liability. In this case, balance sheets do not show unpaid dividend. Therefore, it is assumed that dividend proposed in one accounting year was paid in the next accounting year.

Interpretation:

(a) A large part of funds generated from operations were used to pay tax and dividend. It was 37.33 percent and 51.19 percent for 2016 and 2017, respectively.

(b) The funds generated from operations in 2017 were more than 2016 by 12 percent.

(c) In 2016, 62.67 percent of the funds generated from operations were used in investment activities. Funds generated from operations were adequate to pay tax and dividend, and also to finance acquisition of fixed assets and investment. However, in 2017, the balance (48.81 percent) left after payment of tax and dividend was not adequate to finance investment activities. Investment activities in that year were financed by funds from operations (68.33 percent), proceeds from the issue of 13 percent debentures (16.67 percent), and reduction in working capital (15.00 percent).

(d) Reduction in working capital in 2017 might be the result of the conscious policy of the company to maintain a low current ratio. The current ratio of the company declined from 1.93 in 2015 to 1.33 in 2017. The ratio of 1.33 is usually considered acceptable, and should not adversely affect the performance of the company. However, further investigation is required to understand whether decline in the current ratio is good or bad for the company. A comparison with industry norms and the company's inventory management policy should be examined.

(e) The firm's debt-equity ratio as on December 31, 2017 is 0.31:1. Therefore, the firm has sufficient capacity to borrow, if necessary. It should not worry for liquidity.

NOTES

Self-Test Questions

Self-test question 11.4

Fill in the blanks: [Where the blank space is not to be filled in by amount, choose between the words 'increased' and 'decreased'.]

(i) During the year 2017, SD Limited sold a machine and recognised other income of ₹10,000 from the sale of the machine in the statement of profit and loss. The cost of the machine was ₹5,00,000 and accumulated depreciation of the same up to the date of sale was ₹4,50,000. Fund generated from the sale of the machine was ₹...................... .

(ii) In the Fund Flow statement for the year 2017, Sources of fund show a total of ₹80,00,000 and Applications of fund show a total of ₹85,00,000. During the year the working capital is ....by ₹...................... .

(iii) After preparation of the Fund Flow Statement, the accountant detected an error. Goods-in-transit was omitted from the balance sheet and no liability was provided on this account due to non-receipt of information. Correction of the error will .... Applications of fund by ₹...................... .

(iv) During 2017, MC Limited issued 2,00,000 bonus shares with face value of ₹10 per share. This resulted in ....in Sources of funds by ₹...................... .

(v) On 31 March, 2017, KK Limited invested ₹30 lakhs in 90-day treasury stock. This has increase Application of funds by ₹.......................... .

SUMMARY

A fund flow statement has two segments: 'Sources of fund' and 'Applications of fund'. Sources of funds depict the increase in working capital from transactions and other events related to non-current items, for example, fund from operations, sale of PP&E, issue of fresh equity and long-term borrowings. Similarly, Applications of funds depict the decrease in working capital from transactions and other events related to non-current items, such as redemption of debentures, redemption of preference shares, repayment of long-term loan, and purchase of PP&E. If the total amount of sources of funds exceeds the total amount of applications of funds, the working capital increases. Although the Fund Flow Statement takes working capital as reservoir, it fails to provide insights into working capital management.

CASH FLOW STATEMENT

Users of financial statements evaluate the ability of an entity to generate cash and cash equivalents and the timing and certainty of their generation. Information about the cash flows of an entity is useful in providing users with a basis to assess the ability of the entity to generate cash and cash equivalents and the needs of the entity to utilise those cash flows.

A statement of cash flows, when used in conjunction with the rest of the financial statements, provides information that enables users to evaluate the changes in net assets of an entity, its financial structure (including its liquidity and solvency), and its ability to affect the amounts and timing of cash flows in order to adapt to changing circumstances

NOTES

Key Terms
Operating activities, investing activities, financing activities

and opportunities. The statement of cash flows enhances the comparability of performance of different entities. This is so because it eliminates the effects of using different accounting policies for the same transactions and events. It also helps one examine the relationship between profitability and net cash flow and the impact of changing prices.

Cash and Cash Equivalents

Cash flow statement provides an analysis of changes in cash and cash equivalents; it is important to understand what constitutes cash and cash equivalents.

Bank borrowings are generally considered to be financing activities. However, bank overdrafts, which are repayable on demand, form an integral part of an entity's cash management. In these circumstances, bank overdrafts are included as a component of cash and cash equivalents. A characteristic of such banking arrangements is that the bank balance often fluctuates from being positive to overdrawn.

Cash flows exclude movements between items that constitute cash or cash equivalents because these components are part of the cash management of an entity rather than part of its operating, investing and financing activities. Cash management includes the investment of excess cash in cash equivalents.

Classification of Activities

Cash flows are classified into three categories: cash flow from:

(a) operating activities;
(b) investing activities; and
(c) financing activities.

The classification is presented in Table 11.2.

TABLE 11.2

Classification of Activities

Origin of cash flow	Description
Operating activities	Principal revenue producing activities of an entity. They generally include the transactions and other events that enter into determination of net income.
Investing activities	Activities related to capital expenditure, inter-corporate investments and acquisitions. Receipt of interest and dividend are investment activities. Disposal of non-current assets is included in investment activities.
Financing activities	Financing activities relate to transactions and activities that change the capital structure. In other words, they are transactions with financiers.

Direct and Indirect Methods

Ind AS 7 prescribes two alternative formats—direct method and indirect method—for presentation of cash flow. The key difference in these two methods lies in their presentation of Cash Flows from Operating Activities. In the direct method, operating cash receipts and payments are reported directly. In the indirect method, cash flows from operating activities are reported by way of adjustments of the net profit of the reporting period presented in the statement of profit and loss. Users prefer the indirect method because it establishes linkage between the cash flow statement, the balance sheet, and the statement of profit and loss. SEBI requires companies listed in Indian stock exchanges to use the indirect method to present the statement of cash flows. A firm that uses the direct method in presenting the statement of cash flows provides reconciliation between the reported net profit and the change in cash balance during the reporting period.

CASH FLOWS FROM OPERATING ACTIVITIES

Nature of Operating Cash Flows

Cash flows from operating activities are primarily derived from the principal revenue-producing activities of the firm. Therefore, they generally result from the transactions and other events that enter into the determination of net profit or loss. In other words, cash flow measures the amount of cash generated or used by the firm in producing and selling goods and services.

Examples of cash flows from operating activities are:

(a) Cash receipts from the sale of goods and the rendering of services.
(b) Cash receipts from royalties, fees, commissions and other revenues.
(c) Cash payments to suppliers for goods and services.
(d) Cash payments to and on behalf of employees.
(e) Cash receipts and cash payments of an insurance enterprise for premiums and claims, annuities and other policy benefits.
(f) Cash payments or refunds of income taxes, unless they can be specifically identified with financing and investing activities.
(g) Cash receipts and payments relating to futures contracts, forward contracts, option contracts and swap contracts when the contracts are held for dealing or trading purposes.

Gain or loss from sale of non-current assets

Some transactions (e.g., the sale of an item of non-current assets) give rise to a gain or loss, which is included in the determination of net profit or loss. However, the cash flows relating to such transactions are cash flows from investing activities. An example of such a transaction is the sale of an item of property, plant and equipment.

Purchase and sale of dealing or trading securities

An enterprise may hold securities and loans for dealing or trading purposes, in which case they are similar to inventory acquired specifically for resale. Therefore, cash flows arising from the purchase and sale of dealing or trading securities are classified as *operating activities*. Similarly, cash advances and loans made by financial enterprises are usually classified as operating activities since they relate to the main revenue-producing activity of that enterprise.

Interest and dividends

Interest paid and interest and dividends received are classified as *operating cash flows* for a financial institution.

Interest paid is classified as *financing cash flows* because it represents the cost of obtaining debt capital (financial resource); and interest received is classified as *investing cash flows* because it represents returns on investments.

Dividend received is classified as investing cash flows because it represents returns on investments.

Dividend paid is classified as financing cash flow because it represents transaction with providers of equity capital.

NOTES

Taxes on income

Cash flows arising from taxes on income should be separately disclosed and classified as cash flows from operating activities unless they can be specifically identified with financing and investing activities.

Self-Test Questions

Self-test question 11.5

Indicate whether the following statements are true (T) or false (F):

(i) Increase in bank overdraft is presented as a component of cash flow from financing activities.
(ii) Dividend received is presented as a component of cash flow from investing activities.
(iii) Interest paid is classified as cash flow from operating activities.
(iv) Tax paid on income is presented as a separate line item under cash flow from operating activities.
(iv) Net borrowing (i.e., amount borrowed during the year less amount repaid during the year) is presented as a line item under financing activities.

Method for Calculating Operating Cash Flows

For calculating cash flows from operating activities, we have considered interest and dividends received as cash flows from investment activities and interest and dividends paid as cash flows from financing activities.

CASE STUDY 11.5 Operating Cash Flows

KK Limited (KKL), which is in the merchandising business, commenced its operation on April 1, 2016. The following is the statement of profit and loss for the year ended March 31, 2017:

Statement of Profit and Loss of KKL for the Year Ended March 31, 2017

Expenses	Amount (₹'000)	Income	Amount (₹'000)
To Purchase of goods in trade	8,000	By Sales	10,000
To Operating expenses	2,000	By Closing stock	2,000
To Depreciation	500		
To Income tax expense	600		
To Net profit	900		
	12,000		12,000

The following additional information is provided:

(a) As on March 31, 2017, ₹20,00,000 were due from customers.
(b) As on March 31, 2017, ₹10,00,000 were due to creditors for goods and ₹5,00,000 were due to creditors for services.
(c) Income tax expense includes ₹2,00,000 deferred tax expense, and the total amount of current tax liability has already been paid as advance tax.

Required

Calculate the amount of cash flows from operating activities for the year 2016–1017.

Solution

Direct method

Cash flows from operating activities can be measured directly from the information provided by KKL as follows:

NOTES

		Amount (₹'000)
Cash inflows		
Cash receipts from customers (10,000 – 2,000)		8,000
Cash outflows		
Purchase of goods (8,000 – 1,000)	7,000	
Operating expenses (2,000 – 500)	1,500	
Income tax paid (600 – 200)	400	(8,900)
Net cash flow from operating activities		(900)

Depreciation is a non-cash expense because it is allocation of the cost of PP&E to the current period. Therefore, depreciation has no cash flow implication.

Deferred tax has no cash flow implication. Cash outflow on account of income tax is the amount actually paid to the revenue department during the current period.

Indirect method

The same result should be obtained if indirect method is used to calculate cash flows from the operating activities. The current year (2016–2017), being the first year of operation, there was no opening balance of trade receivables, trade payables and income tax liability. Similarly, there was no opening balance of finished goods (merchandise).

	Remarks	Amount (₹'000)
Profit before taxation (900 + 600)		1,500
Adjustment for depreciation	Non-cash expense	500
		2,000
Increase in trade receivables (2,000 – 0)		(2,000)
Increase in trade creditors (1,500 – 0)		1,500
Increase in inventories (2,000 – 0)		(2,000)
Cash generated from operations		(500)
Income tax paid		(400)
Net cash flows from operating activities		(900)

CASE STUDY 11.6 Operating Cash Flow

NT Limited (NTL) is in the merchandising business. The following are the balance sheets of NTL as at March 31, 2016 and March 31, 2017:

Equity and Liabilities	Amount (₹'000)		Assets	Amount (₹'000)	
	2016/03/31	2017/03/31		2016/03/31	2017/03/31
Share capital	5,000	5,000	PP&E (Net block)	10,000	8,000
Reserves and surplus	23,300	40,100	Inventory of finished goods	10,000	12,000
Deferred tax liability	600	500	Trade receivables	20,000	18,000
Loan	5,000	5,000	Cash and cash equivalents	2,000	21,720
Trade creditors for goods	7,500	8,600			
Trade creditors for services	500	400			
Income tax liability (net of advance tax paid)	500	500			
Total	42,000	59,720	Total	42,000	59,720

NOTES

The following is the statement of profit and loss of NTL for the year ended March 31, 2017:

Expenses	Amount (₹'000)	Income	Amount (₹'000)
To Opening stock	10,000	By Sales	120,000
To Purchase of goods in trade	80,000	By Closing stock	12,000
To Operating expenses	12,000		
To Depreciation	2,000		
To Income tax expense	11,200		
To Net profit	16,800		
	132,000		132,000

Required: Calculate the cash flows from operating activities of NTL for the year 2016–2017.

Solution

Direct method

		Amount (₹'000)
Cash inflows		
Cash receipts from customers (20,000 + 1,20,000 – 18,000)		1,22,000
Cash outflows		
Purchase of goods (7,500 + 80,000 – 8,600)	78,900	
Operating expenses (500 + 12,000 – 400)	12,100	
Income tax paid (100 + 11,300 – 120)	11,280	(1,02,280)
Net cash flow from operating activities		19,720

Note: Deferred tax liability as at March 31, 2017 (₹6,00,000) was lower than the same as at March 31, 2010 (₹5,00,000) by ₹1,00,000. Therefore, the current tax expense for 2016–2017 was the total tax expense (₹1,12,00,000) plus the amount by which the deferred tax liability was reduced. Thus, the current tax expense for 2009–2010 was ₹1,13,00,000 (1,12,00,000 + 1,00,000).

Indirect method

	Remarks	Amount (₹'000)
Profit before taxation (16,800 + 11,200)		28,000
Adjustment for depreciation	Non-cash expense	2,000
		30,000
Decrease in trade receivables (20,000 – 18,000)		2,000
Increase in trade creditors (9,000 – 8,000)		1,000
Increase in inventories (12,000 – 10,000)		(2,000)
Cash generated from operations		31,000
Income tax paid		(11,280)
Net cash flows from operating activities		(19,720)

BOX 11.1 Increase or Decrease in Working Capital

Increase in current assets reduces the cash flow from operations while increase in current liabilities increases the cash flow from operations. Similarly, decrease in current assets increases the cash flow from operations, while decrease in current liabilities decreases the cash flow from operations. Therefore, if a firm earns large profit, but in the process builds large inventories (in an effort to compete on speed) and receivables (with sales to marginal customers), its cash flow from operating activities should be much lower than the net profit reported in the statement of profit and loss. This creates pressure on liquidity and adversely affects the operation of the firm.

Self-Test Questions

Self-test question 11.6

Fill in the blanks: [Where the blank space is not to be filled in by amount, choose between the words 'increased' and decreased'.]

(i) The net profit after tax for the year was ₹60,00,000. There was no change in working capital during the year. Depreciation for the year was ₹10,00,000 and deferred tax expense included in tax expense was ₹2,00,000. Tax paid during the year was equal to current tax expense. Cash flow from operating activities was ....

(ii) The net profit after tax for the year was ₹60,00,000. There was no change in working capital during the year. Depreciation for the year was ₹10,00,000 and tax expense was ₹15,00,000. Amount paid towards income tax based on self-assessment and demand from tax department for earlier years was ₹20,00,000. Cash flow from operating activities was ....

(iii) The net profit after tax for the year was ₹60,00,000. Working capital increased during the year by ₹10,00,000. Depreciation for the year was ₹10,00,000 and tax expense was ₹15,00,000. Amount paid towards income tax based on self-assessment and demand from tax department for earlier years was ₹20,00,000. Cash flow from operating activities was ....

CASH FLOWS FROM INVESTING ACTIVITIES

Nature of Investing Cash Flows

Investing activities are the acquisition and disposal of long-term assets and other investments not included in cash equivalents.

Cash flows from investing activities represent the extent to which expenditures have been made for resources intended to generate future income and cash flows. Only those expenditures that result in a recognised asset in the balance sheet are eligible for classification as investing activities. Examples of cash flows arising from investing activities are:

1. Cash payments to acquire property, plant and equipment and other long-term assets.
2. Cash receipts from sales of property, plant and equipment and other long-term assets.
3. Cash payments to acquire equity or debt instruments of other entities and interests in joint ventures.
4. Cash receipts from sales of equity or debt instruments of other entities and interests in joint ventures.
5. Cash advances and loans made to other parties (other than advances and loans made by a financial institution).
6. Cash receipts from the repayment of advances and loans made to other parties (other than advances and loans of a financial institution).
7. Cash payments for futures contracts, forward contracts, option contracts and swap contracts except when the contracts are held for dealing or trading purposes or payments.
8. Cash receipts from futures contracts, forward contracts, option contracts and swap contracts except when the contracts are held for dealing or trading purposes or receipts.

When a contract is accounted for as a hedge of an identifiable position, the cash flows of the contract are classified in the same manner as the cash flows of the position being hedged.

Discussion on items 7 and 8 (above) is beyond the scope of this book.

NOTES

Nature of Financing Cash Flows

Financing activities are activities that result in changes in the size and composition of the contributed equity and borrowings of the firm.

The separate disclosure of cash flows arising from financing activities is useful in predicting claims on future cash flows by providers of capital to the firm. Examples of cash flows arising from financing activities are:

(a) Cash proceeds from issuing shares or other equity instruments.
(b) Cash payments to owners to acquire or redeem the company's shares.
(c) Cash proceeds from issuing debentures, loans, notes, bonds, mortgages and other short-term or long-term borrowings.
(d) Cash repayments of amounts borrowed.
(e) Cash payments by a lessee for the reduction of the outstanding liability relating to a finance lease.

Self-Test Questions

Self-test question 11.7

Fill in the blanks:

(i) Proceeds from issue of fresh equity are classified as cash flow from .... activities.
(ii) Proceeds from issue of debentures are classified as cash flow from .... activities.
(iii) Cash outflow on acquisition of a business is classified as cash flow from...........activities.
(iv) Cash payment by a lessee for the reduction of the outstanding liability relating to a finance lease is classified as .... activities.
(v) Cash inflow from sale of an item of property, plant and equipment is classified as............. activities.
(vi) Interest payment is classified as..............activities.
(vii) Interest received is classified as..............activities.

SUMMARY

Cash flow statement presents cash flows from operating activities, investing activities and financing activities separately. Cash flow from operating activities can be presented by using either direct method or indirect method. Under indirect method cash flow from operating activities is derived by adjusting reported profit before tax for non-cash items, changes in working capital and cash flows that are presented either as cash flow from investing activities or cash flows from financing activities. Interest and dividend received are considered cash flows from investing activities. Similarly, interest and dividend paid are considered cash flows from financing activities. Gross cash flows are presented, rather than net cash flows. For example, amount borrowed during the year and loan refunded during the year are presented separately. Cash flow statement is analysed to develop a perspective on the company's strategy and ability to generate cash flows in future.

CASE STUDY 11.7 Cash Flow Statement: Indirect Method

Statement of Profit and Loss for 2017 (₹'000)

Sales	700
Cost of goods sold	(520)
Gross margin	180
Operating expenses (including depreciation of ₹38)	(150)
Operating profit	30

NOTES

(v) Repayment of bonds:	
Balance at the commencement of the year	250
Issued during the year (Exchange of equipment)	100
Less Redeemed during the year (Balancing figure)	50
Balance at the end of the year	300

Issue of bond is disclosed in note, because it is a non-cash transaction.

CASE STUDY 11.8 Cash Flow Statement: Indirect Method

The following are the summarized balance sheets of Piyali Limited (PL) as at December 31, 2016 and December 31, 2017:

Balance Sheet of Piyali Limited

	December 31, 2017 Amount (₹'000)	**December 31, 2016 Amount (₹'000)**
ASSETS		
Plant and equipment	2,000	1,030
Land and buildings	1,000	1,000
Short-term investments	560	600
Sundry debtors	2,200	2,500
Inventories	1,500	1,300
Interest receivable	100	60
Cash in hand	300	500
Cash at bank	1,290	780
	8,950	7,770
LIABILITIES		
Contributed capital	2,600	2,200
Reserve and surplus	660	100
15 percent Debentures	2,000	1,800
Deferred tax liability	600	500
Sundry creditors	400	600
Wages outstanding	40	20
Income tax payable	400	450
Accumulated depreciation on property, plant and equipment	900	800
Accumulated depreciation on land and buildings	550	500
Provision for dividend	800	800
	8,950	7,770

Income Statement of PL for Year Ending December 31, 2017

	Amount (₹'000)
Sales revenue	45,500
Less: Cost of sales	38,920
Gross profit	6,580
Less: Depreciation	570
Selling and administration expenses	3,200
Interest expense	300
Add: Interest income	80
Dividend income	100
Insurance settlement received	10
Profit on sale of equipment	20
Profit before tax	2,720
Less: Income tax expenses	600
Net profit	2,120

NOTES

The following additional information is provided by PL (amount, ₹'000) for the year 2017:

(i) 15 percent debentures of ₹200 were issued.

(ii) Equipment costing ₹500 having accumulated depreciation of ₹420 was sold for 100.

(iii) ₹1,560 (including interim dividend of ₹760) were distributed as dividend. Assume that there is no dividend tax.

(iv) All sales and purchases were made on credit basis.

Required: Prepare a statement of cash flows of PL for 2009 using the indirect method.

Solution

Working notes:		**Amount (₹'000)**
Income tax paid		
Income tax liability at the beginning of the year		450
Current income tax expense:		
Income tax expenses in income statement	600	
Less: Increase in deferred tax liability	100	500
		950
Income tax liability at the end of the year		400
Income tax paid during 2009		550
Equipment purchased		
Gross block at the end of the year		2,000
Gross block at the beginning of the year		1,030
		970
Add: Cost of equipment sold		500
Amount of equipment purchased during 2005		1,470
Interest received		
Opening balance of interest receivable		60
Interest income for 2009		80
		140
Less: Closing balance of interest receivable		100
Interest received during 2009		40

Cash Flow Statement of PL for 2017

Particulars	**Amount (₹'000)**
Cash flow from operating activities	
Net profit before taxation	2,720
Adjustments for:	
Depreciation	570
Interest income	(80)
Dividend income	(100)
Interest expense	300
Profit on sale of equipment	(20)
Operating profit before working capital changes	3,390
Decrease in sundry debtors	300
Increase in inventory	(200)
Decrease in sundry creditors	(200)
Increase in wages outstanding	20
Cash generated from operations	3,310
Income tax paid	(550)
Net cash from operating activities	2,760
Cash flow from investing activities	
Purchase of equipment	(1,470)
Proceeds from sale of equipment	100
Proceeds from sale of investment	40
Interest received	40
Dividend received	100
Net cash used in investing activities	(1,190)

Cash flow from financing activities	
Proceeds from issue of share capital	400
Proceeds from issue of debentures	200
Interest paid	(300)
Dividend paid	(1,560)
Net cash used in financing activities	(1,260)
Net increase in cash and cash equivalents	310
Cash and cash equivalents at the beginning	1,280
Cash and cash equivalents at the end	1,590

NOTES

CASE STUDY 11.9 Cash Flow Statement: Indirect Method

From the following information, prepare the cash flow statement for the year ended March 31, 2017:

Balance Sheet as at March 31, 2016 and March 31, 2017

Amount (₹)

Capital and Liabilities	**March 31, 2016**	**March 31, 2017**
Share capital	2,00,000	2,50,000
General reserve	50,000	60,000
Profit and Loss Account	30,500	30,600
Bank loan	70,000	0
Sundry creditors	1,50,000	1,35,200
Provision for taxation	30,000	35,000
	5,30,500	5,10,800
ASSETS		
Land and building	2,00,000	1,90,000
Plant and machinery	1,50,000	1,69,000
Stock	1,00,000	74,000
Sundry debtors	80,000	64,200
Cash	500	600
Bank	0	8,000
Goodwill	0	5,000
	5,30,500	5,10,800

Additional information:

(i) Dividend of ₹23,000 was paid.

(ii) The following assets of another company were purchased for a consideration of ₹50,000 paid for in shares:
Stock ₹20,000, Machinery ₹25,000

(iii) Further machinery was purchased for ₹25,000 during the year.

(iv) Depreciation written off on building ₹10,000, Machinery ₹14,000.

(v) Income tax paid during the year ₹28,000.

Solution

Assumption: There was no profit or loss on sale of machinery. Therefore, sale proceeds were equal to the written down value (WDV) of the machinery sold.

Working notes:

(i) Sales of machinery	₹1,50,000
Opening balance	(14,000)
Depreciation	1,36,000
Purchase	50,000
	1,86,000
Closing balance	1,69,000
WDV of machinery sold	₹17,000

(ii) Income tax expense for 2017

Closing provision for income tax	₹35,000
Income tax paid during the year	28,000
	63,000
Opening provision for income tax	30,000
Income tax expense for the year	₹33,000

(iii) Net profit for 2017

Increase in general reserve	₹10,000
Increase in Profit and Loss Account (in the balance sheet)	100
	10,100
Dividend paid	23,000
	33,100
Income tax expense for the year	33,000
	₹66,100

(iv) Cash implications for change in stock (Increase from cash/credit transactions)

Closing stock balance	₹74,000
Increase due to acquisition without payment of cash	(20,000)
	54,000
Opening balance	(1,00,000)
	₹(46,000)

Cash Flow Statement for 2017

	Amount (₹)
Cash flow from operating activities	
Profit before income tax	66,100
Adjustment for depreciation for the year	24,000
Cash flow before adjustment for changes in working capital	90,000
Adjustments for changes in working capital:	
Decrease in stock	46,000
Decrease in debtors	15,800
Decrease in sundry creditors	(14,800)
	1,37,100
Income tax paid	(28,000)
Net cash flow from operating activities	1,09,100
Cash flow from investing activities	
Purchase of machinery	(25,000)
Sale of machinery	17,000
Net use of cash for investing activities	(8,000)
Cash flow from financing activities	
Repayment of bank loan	(70,000)
Dividend paid	(23,000)
Net use of cash for financing activities	(93,000)
Net increase in cash and cash equivalents	8,100
Opening balance of cash and cash equivalents	500
Closing balance of cash and cash equivalents	8,600

Disclosures

(a) Components of cash and cash equivalents

	31.3.90	31.3.91
Cash	₹500	₹600
Cash at bank	–	–
Total	₹500	₹600

(b) Acquisition of assets with payment of cash

The following assets of another company were purchased for a consideration of ₹50,000 paid in shares:

Stock	₹20,000
Machinery	25,000
Goodwill	5,000
	₹50,000

Points to remember

1. Transactions that have no cash implications are excluded from the cash flow statement. Therefore, the transaction involving acquisition of assets by issue of equity share is excluded from the cash flow statement. Accordingly, increase in stock is calculated after excluding the stock acquired by issue of shares. Similarly, the machinery acquired by issue of equity share is excluded.
2. Disclosures are in accordance with Ind AS 7.

NOTES

EXCHANGE DIFFERENCE

General principle

Cash flows arising from transactions in a foreign currency are recorded in a firm's functional currency by translating the foreign currency amount into the functional currency using the exchange rate *at the date of the cash flow.* Cash flows of a foreign subsidiary should be translated using the exchange rates prevailing *at the date of the cash flows.*

For practical reasons, a company may apply a rate (e.g., weighted average rate for the period) that approximates the actual rate.

Direct method

When a company enters into a transaction denominated in foreign currency, there are no cash flow consequences until payments are received or paid. The receipts and payments are recorded in the accounting records of the company at the exchange rate prevailing at the date of payment and these amounts are reflected in the statement of cash flows.

For preparing the consolidated statement of cash flows using the direct method, cash flows of the subsidiary are measured at its functional currency and then translated at the presentation currency of the company (parent).

Indirect method

Where the exchange differences relate to operating items such as sales or purchases of inventory by the firm, no adjustment is to be made while calculating cash flows from operating activities using the indirect method. For example, if cash settlement of a sale transaction takes place during the period when the transaction occurred, the net profit includes both the amount recorded at the date of sale and the exchange difference on settlement. Therefore, the net profit is based on the cash flow arising from the sale transaction. If the settlement takes place in a period subsequent to the period in which the transaction occurred, net profit includes exchange difference arising from the translation of the receivables at the closing rate. However, no adjustment is required because the increase or decrease in the amount of receivables during the period is adjusted to determine the cash flows from operating activities for the period. The increase or decrease in receivables includes the exchange difference. [Remember the journal entry for exchange difference (gain): Debit Receivables and Credit Exchange Difference.]

Determining the value of non-operating cash flows

Adjustment to net profit is required for exchange difference arising from settlement or translation (at the closing rate) of a transaction relating to non-operating cash flows. An example of non-operating cash flow is cash flow relating to purchase of an item of property, plant and equipment. The adjustment is required because the net profit includes the exchange difference while the amount of investment recorded initially is not adjusted. Therefore, the exchange difference should be taken out of the net profit and should be adjusted to the cash flow relating to the purchase of the item of the PP&E. This cash flow should be included in cash flows from investing activities.

Exchange difference relating to cash and cash equivalents

The effect of exchange rate movements on foreign currency cash and cash equivalents is not a cash flow. However, it is necessary to include those exchange differences in the

NOTES

statement of cash flows in order to reconcile the movement in cash and cash equivalents to the corresponding amounts presented in the balance sheet at the beginning and at the close of the period. The exchange difference is presented as a footnote to the statement of cash flows.

ANALYST'S PERSPECTIVE

The starting point in the analysis is to enquire whether the company has generated positive cash flow from operating activities. Several factors affect a company's ability to generate positive cash flow from operating activities. Usually, a healthy enterprise in a steady state and operating in a mature industry generates positive cash flow. On the other hand, a growing enterprise that invests significantly in research and development, advertising, training and working capital to support its future growth may not be able to generate positive cash flow from operations. Cash flow from operating activities should be analysed from this perspective.

The next question that an analyst asks about a company that generates positive cash flow from operating activities is whether it is self-sufficient. The surplus cash that is available after working capital investment is available for distribution to debt-holders (interest and installment), long-term investment and distribution to shareholders. If the internally generated surplus cash is not sufficient to meet the needs of the company, it resorts to external financing. Analysts analyse the financing policy of the company by examining the different sources that it has used to mobilise additional resources.

Cash flow is analysed from investing activities to understand the company's strategy for long-term growth. A company may achieve growth either through mergers and acquisitions, or through investment in new assets (projects). Analysis of cash flow from investing activities also provides an insight into the company's strategy for spin-off and disinvestment and its ability to manage surplus cash.

Reconciliation of net profit and cash flow from operating activities helps one to understand the *quality of net profit* reported in the profit and loss account. An examination of the gap between the two provides an understanding of the accounting policy of the company regarding non-current amortisations. It also helps one to understand whether increase/decrease in current assets and current liabilities are normal, and whether adequate explanation is available for those changes.

A cash flow statement alone may not provide answers to all questions. An analyst should gather information from the Board of Director's report and the Management Discussion and Analysis presented in the annual report along with annual financial statements. Those two reports provide management's analysis of past performance, management perspective of the business environment, and its projection of future performance. Those reports, to an extent, describe the corporate strategy. A cash flow statement should be analysed in the context of corporate strategy and likely changes in the business environment.

ACTIVITY

Download the cash flow statement of a listed company of your choice and analyse the same.

ANSWERS TO SELF-TEST QUESTIONS

11.1 (i) T; (ii) T; (iii) F; (iv) T

11.2 (i) decreased, ₹1,00,000; (ii) increased, ₹16 lakhs; (iii) increased, ₹20 lakhs; (iv) decreased, ₹5 crores; (v) Zero

11.3 (i) ₹10,50,000; (ii) ₹20,60,000

11.4 (i) ₹60,000; (ii) reduced, ₹5,00,000; (iii) increase/decrease, ₹zero; (iii) increase/decrease, ₹Zero; ₹Zero

11.5 (i) F; (ii) T; (iii) F; (iv) T; (v) F

11.6 (i) ₹72,00,000; (ii) ₹65,00,000; (iii) ₹55,000

11.7 (i) Financing activities; (ii) Financing activities; (iii) Investing activities; (iv) Financing activities; (v) Investing activities; (vi) Financing activities; (vii) Investing activities

ASSIGNMENTS

NOTES

Multiple Choice Questions

1. Fill in the blanks:

(i) The net profit presented in the income statement of Ankit Limited (AL) for 2017 is ₹2,000. Depreciation charged during the year is ₹400. The amounts of working capital in the balance sheet at the beginning and at the end of the year are the same. The cash flow from the operation is ₹............ .

(ii) The net profit presented in the income statement of Kartina Limited (KL) for 2017 is ₹3,000. Depreciation charged during the year is ₹500, and interest expense for the year is ₹100. The net profit includes interest and dividend income of ₹50 and ₹80, respectively. The amount of working capital in the balance sheet at the beginning and at the end of the year is same. The cash flow from the operation is ₹............ .

(iii) The net profit presented in the income statement of Malaika Limited (ML) for 2017 is ₹4,000. Depreciation charged during the year is ₹600, and interest expense for the year is ₹200. The net profit includes interest and dividend income of ₹100 and ₹150, respectively. The amount of working capital in the balance sheet at the beginning and at the end of the year are ₹2,200 and ₹2,500, respectively. The cash flow from the operation is ₹............ .

(iv) The net profit presented in the income statement of Parvinder Limited (PL) for 2017 is ₹3,500. Depreciation charged during the year is ₹550. Interest expense for the year is ₹200. The net profit includes interest and dividend income of ₹100 and ₹200, respectively. The amounts of working capital in the balance sheet at the beginning and at the end of the year are ₹3,000 and ₹2,800, respectively. The cash flow from the operation is ₹............ .

(v) The net profit presented in the income statement of Ananya Limited (AL) for 2017 is ₹5,500. The amounts of accumulated depreciation in the balance sheet at the beginning and at the end of the period are ₹3,300 and ₹3,100, respectively. During the year 2017, AL sold equipment costing ₹750; the written down value of the equipment at the time of sale was ₹200. The net profit presented in the income statement includes a profit of ₹100 from the sale of the equipment. The net profit also includes interest and dividend income of ₹100 and ₹200, respectively. Interest expense for the year is ₹300. The amounts of working capital in the balance sheet at the beginning and at the end of the year are ₹3,500 and ₹3,800, respectively. The cash flow from operation is ₹............ and the proceeds from the sale of the equipment are ₹............ .

(vi) The net profit presented in the income statement of Sunayani Limited (SL) for 2017 is ₹6,000. The amounts of accumulated depreciation in the balance sheet at the beginning and at the end of the period are ₹3,300 and ₹3,500, respectively. During 2017, SL sold equipment costing ₹1,000; the written down value of the equipment at the time of sale was ₹700. The net profit presented in the income statement includes a loss of ₹200 from the sale of the equipment. The net profit also includes interest and dividend income of ₹100 and ₹200, respectively. Interest expense for the year is ₹400. The amounts of working capital in the balance sheet at the beginning and at the end of the year are ₹3,500 and ₹3,200, respectively. The cash flow from operation is ₹............ and the proceeds from the sale of the equipment are ₹............ .

(vii) The net profit presented in the income statement of Tripta Limited (TL) for 2017 is ₹6,500. The amounts of gross block in the balance sheet at the beginning and at the end of the period are ₹4,800 and ₹5,000, respectively. The amounts of accumulated depreciation in the balance sheet at the beginning and at the end of the period are ₹4,000 and ₹4,100, respectively. During 2017, TL sold equipment costing ₹700 at ₹200. The net profit presented in the income statement includes a profit of ₹100 from the sale of the equipment. The net profit also includes interest and dividend income of ₹150 and ₹250, respectively. Interest expense for the year is ₹400. The amounts of working capital in the balance sheet at the beginning and at the end of the year are ₹3,500 and ₹4,000, respectively. The cash flow from operation is ₹............ and the cost of equipment purchased is ₹............ .

NOTES

Analytical Questions

1. "The cash flow statement does not provide any additional information, yet it provides important insights into investment and financing decisions of the enterprise." Explain the statement.
2. "In the fund flow statement, working capital assumes importance, because of the presentation format, otherwise it provides almost no information on working capital management." Do you agree with this view? Write a short note explaining the purpose of presenting a fund flow statement.
3. "Treasury function in an enterprise is mainly concerned with day-to-day cash management. A cash flow statement does not provide any information to assess the effectiveness of the treasury function and, therefore, it is an unnecessary addition to the set of financial statements." Examine the statement critically.
4. "Operating, investment and financing decisions in a business do not centre around cash; there are many other factors that influence such decisions. Undue importance to cash flow statements might drive managers to unduly focus on cash, which might lead to sub-optimal decisions." Write a note explaining the statement.

Problems

1. The profit and loss account of Ludhiana Ltd. for the year 2017 is presented as follows:

			Amount (₹'000)
Sales		8,000	
Less:	Materials consumed	1,600	
	Manufacturing expenses	3,000	
	Administration and selling expenses	1,000	
	Depreciation	400	
	Amortisation of: Patent	100	
	Preliminary expenses	200	
	Loss on sale of fixed assets	50	6,350
	Operating profit		1,650
Add:	Dividend received	350	
			2,000
Less:	Income tax		600
	Net profit		1,400

Required: Calculate the fund from operations for the purpose of preparing the fund flow statement.

2. Nagpur Ltd. has provided the following information relating to its 'plant and machinery account':

Amount (₹'000)

	2016	2017
Gross book value at the end of the year	600	1,000
Accumulated depreciation at the end of the year	200	290
Additional information		
(a) Profit on sale of plant and machinery		20
(b) Depreciation charged during the year		100
(c) Purchase of new machinery during the year		450

Required: Calculate the fund flow for the year 2017 from the sale of the old item of plant and machinery.

3. Dhaka Ltd. has provided the following information relating to its 'plant and machinery account':

Amount (₹'000)

	2016	2017
Written-down value at the end of the year	700	1,000
Additional information		
(a) Depreciation charged during the year		150
(b) Loss on the sale of plant and machinery		20
(c) Written-down value of the item sold		50

Required: Calculate: (a) the fund flow for the year 2017, from the sale of the old item of plant and machinery; (b) the cost of new machinery purchased during the year 2017.

4. The following are the balance sheets of Vasi Ltd.:

Vasi Ltd. Balance Sheet as on December 31, 2017

(₹'000)

Liabilities	2016	2017	Assets	2016	2017
Equity:			*Fixed assets:*		
Share capital	100	100	Goodwill	50	40
Reserve and surplus	200	320	Plant and machinery (WDV)	500	600
Secured loan:			Investment	100	80
6 percent debentures	100	100	*Current assets:*		
Loan from IDBI	95	50	Stock	100	120
Cash credit from SBI	100	80	Debtors	75	100
Current liabilities:			Prepaid expenses	30	20
Trade creditors	250	300	Cash	10	20
Provision for taxation	20	30			
	865	980		865	980

The following is the statement of profit and loss of Vasi Ltd. for the year 2017.

Vasi Ltd.
Statement of Profit and Loss for the year 2017

(₹'000)

Expenses	Amount	Income	Amount
To opening stock	100	By sales	1,500
To purchases	800	By income from dividend	10
To freight inward	40	By profit on sale of machinery	20
To manufacturing expenses	260	By closing stock	120
To administrative and selling expenses	140		
To depreciation	50		
To amortisation of goodwill	10		
To interest paid	50		
To income tax	80		
To net profit	120		
	1,650		1,650

Additional information: The written-down value as on December 31, 2017 of the item of machinery sold was ₹30. No depreciation has been charged on that item for the year 2017.
Required: Prepare the cash flow statement using the indirect method.

5. The following details are taken from the books of 'B' Ltd. as on two dates:

Amount (₹'000)

	March 31, 2016	March 31, 2017
Cash	5,04,090	4,05,350
Debtors	7,71,800	7,31,500
Short-term investments	11,05,000	8,40,000
Prepaid expenses	12,100	11,550
Stock	9,21,540	10,55,380
Cash surrender value of insurance policies on employees	46,070	53,530
Land	2,50,000	2,50,000
Buildings and machinery	14,77,780	18,27,820
Debenture discount	43,050	28,670
	51,31,430	52,03,800
Creditors	10,30,870	9,56,560
Outstanding expenses	1,27,070	2,16,630
4 percent mortgage debentures	8,20,000	6,85,000
Accumulated depreciation	9,66,180	8,16,330
Allowance for stock loss	20,000	85,000
Reserve for contingencies	10,67,310	13,41,780
Surplus in profit and loss account	1,00,000	1,02,500
Share capital	10,00,000	10,00,000
	51,31,430	52,03,800

NOTES

Further, the following information is available:

(a) Premium on life insurance policies was ₹27,730 of which ₹16,270 was charged to the statement of profit and loss of the year.

(b) Net profit for 2016–2017 as per the statement of profit and loss was ₹4,90,970.

(c) A 10 percent dividend was paid during the year.

(d) The allowance for inventory loss was credited by a charge to expense in each year to provide for obsolete items.

(e) A debit to reserve for contingencies of ₹1,14,000 was made during the year. This was in respect of settlement of a past tax liability.

(f) New machinery was purchased for ₹3,13,650, and machinery costing ₹3,26,250 was sold during the year. Depreciation on machinery sold had accumulated to ₹2,91,050 on the date of sale. It was sold as scrap for ₹15,000. The remaining increase in fixed assets resulted from construction of a building.

(g) The mortgage debentures mature at the rate of ₹50,000 per year. In addition to this the company purchased and retired ₹85,000 of the debentures at ₹103.

Both the premium on retirement and the applicable discount were charged to the profit and loss account.

You are required to prepare a statement showing the sources and application of funds for the year 2016–2017.

Note: Schedule of detailed changes in working capital is not required.

(Adapted, *CA Final*)

6. Andaz Ltd. furnishes you with the following information:

(a)

Balance Sheet as on March 31, 2016 and 2017

(₹, crore)

	2017	**2016**
Sources of funds:		
Equity share capital	100	60
Preference share capital	—	20
Share premium	80	—
Other reserves and surplus	160	100
Owners' funds	340	180
Loan funds	10	70
	350	250
Funds employed in:		
Fixed assets:		
Cost	500	350
Less: Depreciation	300	250
	200	100
Investments at cost:		
In subsidiary (wholly owned)	—	60
Net current assets	150	90
	350	250
Details of net current assets:		
Inventory	20	15
Customers dues	135	60
Cash/bank	15	35
Advances	30	60
	200	170
Creditors	40	60
Tax provision in excess of payment	10	20
	50	80
Net current assets	150	90

(b) During the year, the subsidiary merged into Andaz Ltd. The subsidiary had only fixed assets on the date of its merger, and their written-down value was ₹90 crore. These were taken over at ₹90 crore.

(c) Fixed assets costing ₹40 crore and written-down value of ₹15 crore were sold for ₹10 crore.

(d) Andaz Ltd. made a right equity issue of ₹40 crore at an issue price of three times the par value. Preference shares were redeemed at par out of this right issue.

(e) Details of tax assessments:

NOTES

(₹, crore)

		March 31, 2017	March 31, 2016
Net tax provision			
Assessment year	1999–2000	10	—
	1998–99	—	9
	1997–98	—	6
	1996–97	—	5
		10	20

The tax liability for the various assessment years was settled by payment of ₹4 crores for A.Y. 2014–15, ₹4.5 crore for A.Y. 2015–16 and ₹9 crore for A.Y. 2016–17 on receipt of assessment orders. Advance tax and tax deduction at source totalled ₹30 crore.

(f) Preference dividend of ₹3 crore and equity dividend of ₹30 crore were paid. Interest paid on loans amounted to ₹10.5 crore.

You are asked to prepare the following for the year ended March 31, 2017.

(i) Statement of changes in working capital.

(ii) Statement of sources and application of funds.

(iii) Statement of cash flow.

(Adapted, *CA Final*)

Financial Statement Analysis Basics

CHAPTER 12

LEARNING OBJECTIVES

The objective of this chapter is to provide an understanding of the context and environment of Financial Statement Analysis (FSA) and its basic techniques. After reading this chapter, you will be able to understand the following:

- Purpose of financial statement analysis
- Concept of earnings quality
- Earnings management strategy and techniques
- Motivation for earnings management
- Regulatory protection to stakeholders from earnings management
- Red flags, which indicate noise in financial statements
- Basic principles underlying preparation of consolidated financial statements
- Vertical analysis of financial statements
- Horizontal analysis of financial statements

INTRODUCTION

Objective of Financial Statement Analysis

NOTES

Financial statement analysis is a part of business analysis, which is the evaluation of a firm's economic prospect and risks. It starts with an analysis of firm's business environment and strategy. An analyst can draw right conclusions from financial statement analysis only with an understanding of the business environment in which the firm operates and in the context of the firm's strategy.

An analyst should analyse the firm's performance over a reasonably long period to understand the past trend and how structural changes in the business environment and internal restructuring had affected the performance of the firm. The reasonability of the period selected depends on the nature of the industry and the firm. Usually, a period of five to seven years is considered reasonable. Analysts face challenges when the firm changes accounting policy. For example, large Indian companies have adopted Ind AS from 2016–17. Therefore, figures in financial statements of earlier years are not exactly comparable with the figures in financial statements of 2016–17 onwards.

Different stakeholders analyse financial statements from different perspectives. Table 12.1 presents perspectives of different stakeholders.

TABLE 12.1

Different Perspectives of Different Stakeholders

S. No.	Stakeholder group	Perspective
1.	Investors and prospective investors in the equity of the firm	Investors and prospective investors in the equity of the firm are interested in its valuation, in particular, in the valuation of the equity. Therefore, they assess *both the downside risks and upside potential.* In mergers and acquisitions, due diligence includes financial analysis. Analysts with mutual funds, hedge funds, wealth management firms and other financial institutions use financial analysis to identify equity shares, which are trading at below or above the fundamental value.
2.	Creditors	Creditors focuses on credit risk. They primarily evaluate the *downside risk.* Short-term creditors have an interest in the liquidity of the firm, while long-term creditors have interest in the solvency of the firm. Liquidity is the firm's ability to arrange cash in short-term to meet its short-term obligations. Solvency is the firm's long-term viability and ability to honour long-term financial commitments. Banks and other financial institutions determine the terms and conditions of loan, including the rate of interest and collateral based on financial analysis. While considering a troubled loan, banks and financial institutions analyse finance from a broader perspective.
3.	Customers	Before establishing long-term relationship with a supplier, customers analyse the finance of the supplier to assess his financial strength to support his commitment to supply goods on a long-term basis according to the agreed schedule. They assess the risks of relying on the supplier for long-term supply of inputs.
4.	Top management/Board of Directors	The top management of a conglomerate having large number of businesses uses financial analysis as a tool for managing those businesses.
5.	Employees	Immediate earnings (e.g., variable pay) and career development of employees depend on the survival and growth of the firm. Therefore, they use financial analysis to assess the financial position and performance of the firm.

NOTES

Key Terms
Earnings quality, earnings management

S. No.	Stakeholder group	Perspective
6.	Other stakeholders	Stakeholders having an interest in the survival and growth of the firm use financial analysis to protect their interests. For example, the local community has an interest in the survival and growth of a firm that provides employment to the members of the local community and contributes to its development by generating positive externalities. Therefore, the community has an interest in the strategy and performance of the company.

Self-Test Questions

Self-test question 12.1

Indicate whether the following statements are true (T) or false (F):

(i) Financial statement analysis is a part of business analysis.

(ii) Analysing financial statements of a company without understanding its business environment and strategy is a meaningless exercise.

(iii) Investors and potential investors in the equity of a company assess only upside potential of the company.

(iv) Lenders and creditors assess the downside risk of the company.

(v) Same set of information is generally useful for evaluating performance credit risks.

SUMMARY

Financial statement analysis is a part of business analysis. An analysts cannot draw right conclusions from analysing financial statements if he or she does not understand the business environment, strategy and business model of the entity. Different stakeholders analyse financial statements from different perspectives. Investors and potential investors analyse financial statements to assess downside risks and upside potentials in order to value equity of the company. Lenders and other creditors analyse financial statements to assess credit risks of extending credit to the entity.

EARNINGS MANAGEMENT

Earnings Quality

Earnings quality is defined as follows:

"Higher quality earnings provide more information about the features of a firm's financial performance that are relevant to a specific decision made by a specific decision-maker." [Ref: Statement of Financial Accounting Concepts No. 1 (SFAC No. 1) issued by FASB, USA]. In accordance with the definition, earnings quality should be assessed in the specific context and specific information needs of the decision-maker. Primary users of financial statements are investors and potential investors, who are interested in valuing equity of the company, and lenders and other creditors, who evaluate credit risk of extending credit to the company. Therefore, earnings quality of published financial statements is evaluated with reference to predictive and confirmative value of the information. Simply saying, higher earnings quality enables investors, potential investors, lenders and other creditors to predict future cash flows and earning capacity of the firm more accurately; and to evaluate past forecasts better. Earnings quality is discussed in the following paragraph from that perspective.

Earnings quality or, more precisely, accounting quality, means different things to different people. Many believe that the earnings quality of firms that adopt a conservative approach is higher than that of the firms adopting aggressive accounting policy. Many others believe that the consistency (lack of volatility) of reported earnings improves the quality of earnings. Neither of these two propositions is correct. The quality of earnings depends on the ability of the firm to select the appropriate accounting policy and to minimise estimation errors. Noise in reported earnings arises primarily from estimation errors, bias in selection of the accounting policy, and distortions in the application of selected accounting policy.

The quality of earnings is lowered by management's discretionary actions.

NOTES

Self-Test Questions

Self-test question 12.2

Indicate whether the following statements are true (T) or false (F):

(i) If earnings quality is good for a particular user of financial statements, it is good for all.
(ii) More conservative is the accounting policy, better is the quality of earnings.
(iii) Smoothing of income improves the decision-usefulness of information.
(iv) Noise in reported earning reduces the earnings quality.
(v) Strict compliance with accounting standards and minimisation of estimation errors improve earnings quality.

Accounting Policy

Entities have no discretion but to use accrual system of accounting. Choice of accounting policy is inherent in the accounting system because Business Models and environments differ significantly among business enterprises, and therefore, their economic realities are different. Each firm chooses accounting principles and methods that are most appropriate for its business and the environment in which it operates.

Accounting standards regulate the accounting policy of entities. An entity has to choose from alternative accounting principles and methods stipulated in accounting standards. Choice is made in two stages. In the first stage, standard setters select acceptable accounting principles and methods from various accounting practices available at a particular point of time. They tradeoff between the theoretical robustness of a particular accounting method and the level of difficulties in its implementation. In the second stage, the reporting entity selects the accounting principles and methods that are most appropriate for them from the set of accounting principles and methods stipulated in the accounting standards. It is rare that none of the accounting principles and methods stipulated in an accounting standard is appropriate for the entity.

An analyst should go through notes to accounts and audit report to make an assessment of the appropriateness of the accounting policy.

Self-Test Questions

Self-test question 12.3

Indicate whether the following statements are true (T) or false (F):

(i) Accounting policy of companies operating in different industries cannot be similar because their contexts differ.
(ii) By restricting choice of accounting policy by individual companies, accounting standards adversely affect earnings quality.
(iii) Accounting standards are revised and new accounting standards are issued to improve the earnings quality.
(iv) Accounting standards articulate accounting principles and methods and application of those rules in a particular industry evolves over time.
(v) Leader in the industry greatly influences accounting practices in the industry.
(iv) Boiler plate disclosure of accounting policy does not help analysts to assess the appropriateness of the accounting policy.
(v) Disclosure of uncertainties surrounding accounting estimates is not very helpful, as cost of revising estimates by an individual analyst is prohibitive.

NOTES

Meaning of Earnings Management

Research has established that managers have temptations to manage earnings to maximise their own utility and/or the market value of the company. They manage earnings through accounting manipulations, and also, by manipulating cash flow consequences through interventions. For example, managers manipulate cash flow consequences by delaying delivery of goods to customers or by dumping goods on dealers with the arrangement that goods will be taken back in the next accounting year.

There are two points of view on whether earnings management is good or bad from the shareholders' perspective and from the perspectives of lenders and other users of financial statements. The obvious view is that earnings management is bad because it is a device by which managers enhance their utility, and thus, enrich themselves at the cost of shareholders and lenders. However, another view is that a little earnings management is good because of the following reasons:

(i) While entering into contractual arrangements, agents (e.g., lenders) allow for earnings management in deciding the compensation (e.g., interest, employees' compensation). Earnings management brings some flexibility into the system that protects managers and the organisation in the face of uncertainties of unanticipated changes in the internal and external environment. This flexibility is advantageous to all contracting parties.

(ii) Managers have inside information that is not available to other stakeholders. Based on this information, managers manage earnings often to give an impression of smooth earnings or that the earning is growing. Therefore, earnings management may be perceived as a device of communicating inside information.

It is now well-settled that earnings management is bad. Firms should not manage earnings to give a wrong impression to the users of financial statements. Financial statements must present the economic reality of transactions and other events on the performance and financial position of the firm in a fair manner. Information should reflect the business reality. For example, if volatility is inherent in the nature of a business, financial statements should reflect such volatility. It should be left to the users of financial statements to assess the performance and financial position of the company in order to forecast future earning capacity of the firm. The assumption that underlies this well-accepted principle is that the users of financial statements understand the business.

Motivation for Earnings Management

More often than not, employee compensation is linked to current year's earnings. This provides strong motivation to manage current year's earnings. However, in a regulated regime of accounting standards, entities are not allowed to change their accounting policies voluntarily. This effectively restrains earnings management with a short-term perspective. However, there is ample motivation to manage earnings with a long-term perspective. The following are the motivations:

(i) *Reduce tax liability*: Though it is a well-accepted principle that tax laws should not influence the choice of accounting policy, firms often choose accounting policies that minimise tax liabilities.

(ii) *Meet debt covenants*: Firms manage earnings to meet debt-equity ratio, current ratio, net worth and other financial parameters specified in long-term debt covenant, as violations of debt covenants are costly to the entity.

(iii) *Reduce political visibility*: Entities manage earnings in order to avoid public pressure for additional regulations. This is true particularly for large companies that operate in politically sensitive sectors, such as the power sector, the pharmaceutical sector and the healthcare sector.

(iv) *Share price effect*: Companies manage earnings to temporarily boost share price, for example, when managers plan to exercise options. They also prefer smoothen earnings to lower perceived risk of investment in equity of the company in order to reduce the cost of capital.

In addition to the aforesaid motivations for managing earnings with long-term perspective, a variety of motivations exist for managing earnings around the time of Initial Public Offerings (IPO). By definition, no established market price is available at the time of an IPO. As a result, potential investors rely on information in financial statements to value equity. This provides enough motivation to manage earnings.

Motivations for managing earnings also exist around the time of appointment of a new CEO. For example, the retiring CEO would like to enhance his/her retiring benefits that are linked to earnings by managing earnings. Similarly, the new CEO would resort to large write-offs in the name of cleaning the balance sheet so that he/she can report better performance in the subsequent years.

NOTES

Key Terms
Big bath, income smoothing

Self-Test Questions

Self-test question 12.4

Indicate whether the following statements are true (T) or false (F):

(i) Little bit of earnings management is good.
(ii) Earnings management is nothing but window dressing of financial statements.
(iii) Managers have inherent temptation to manage earnings.
(iv) Earnings management to reduce political visibility is good from the perspective of shareholders, but not from the perspectives of other stakeholders.
(v) Managers who do not resort to earnings management, do a disservice to the company, as counterparties (e.g., banks and employees) assume that the company will resort to earnings management and set performance parameters in contracts accordingly.

Strategies and Mechanics for Earnings Management

Earnings Management Strategies

The following are the three typical earnings management strategies:

(i) *Increasing income:* Management follows a strategy to increase a period's reported earnings to present the entity's performance favourably. It increases income in this manner over several periods. Management may reverse accruals more than what is appropriate and report income higher than the actual (estimated) earnings. In the long-term, the strategy busts as happened in the case of WorldCom.

(ii) *Big bath:* Management takes as many write-offs as possible in a period of markedly poor performance. It often uses the *big bath strategy* in conjunction with *increasing income* strategy in other periods. Entities resort to big bath in the period of recession or when it is going through restructuring or when a new CEO joins. Management clears all past distortions, which gives an opportunity to resort to increasing income strategy afresh.

(iii) *Income smoothing:* Management decreases or increases reported earnings in order to reduce the volatility in reported earnings from period to period. Income smoothing involves not reporting income in a year of good performance. For example, banks were allowed to create 'secret reserves' for income smoothing. However, now income smoothing is prohibited.

Mechanics for Earnings Management

The following are the most common mechanics for earnings management:

(i) *Income shifting:* Entities shift revenue and expenses from one period to another in order to smooth earnings. Examples of shifting incomes and expenses are:

NOTES

(a) channel loading by persuading dealers or wholesalers to purchase excess products near the end of the accounting period,
(b) capitalising expenses in order to delay recognition of the same, and
(c) accelerating recognition of expenses by taking large one-time charge, such as impairment loss and restructuring expenses.

(ii) *Classificatory earnings management:* Managers selectively misclassify expenses and revenue in the statement of profit and loss. Analysts, while analysing financial statements, attach less importance to certain line items such as exceptional items, special items (e.g., restructuring expenses and impairment loss) and profit/loss from discontinued operations. Therefore, managers have temptation to include operating expenses in those line items in order to present better operating performance than actual operating performance.

Self-Test Questions

Self-test question 12.5

Indicate whether the following statements are true (T) or false (F):

(i) Under 'big bath' strategy of earnings management, the management takes as many write-offs as possible in a period of markedly poor performance.
(ii) The drive by a new CEO for cleaning the balance sheet might be an earnings management strategy to resort to 'increasing income' strategy of earnings management in future years.
(iii) By creating secret reserve, managers improve the decision-usefulness of information, as they better predict the likely changes in external contexts than investors.
(iv) Classificatory earnings management aims to misguide analysts, who primarily focus on operating profit.
(v) Earnings management refers to accounting manipulations only.

Earnings Management and Accrual System of Accounting

Under accrual accounting, assets and liabilities are carried in the balance sheet at estimated values. In many situations, those estimates depend on the management's perception about uncertainties that surround the inflow or outflow of economic benefits. For example, the carrying amount of receivables in the balance sheet depends on management's estimate of doubtful debts. Moreover, the concepts of 'allocation' or 'accrual' are at the heart of accrual accounting. It is difficult to set out the objective criteria for the selection of the accrual policy. For example, it is difficult to set out the objective criteria to decide the period over which an item of PP&E should be depreciated. Similarly, it is difficult to develop objective criteria to allocate revenue to the current period and future periods (deferred revenue). Users and auditors can seldom question the bases selected by the management for allocations of expenditures and incomes over more than one accounting period. Similarly, often estimation of the fair value of assets and liabilities is judgemental. Consequently, the accrual accounting system provides enough opportunities for managing earnings.

The most common methods for earnings management are

(i) under- or over-valuation of inventory,
(ii) under- or over-provisioning for depreciation,
(iii) amortisation of expenses over a shorter or longer period,
(iv) under- or over-provisioning for doubtful debts,
(v) under- or over-provisioning for liabilities,
(vi) advance recognition of revenue or deferment of revenue recognition,
(vii) derecognition of liabilities on the strength of dubious transactions, and
(viii) recognition of assets on the strength of dubious transactions.

Self-Test Questions

Self-test question 12.6

Indicate whether the following statements are true (T) or false (F):

(i) More intensive use of fair value has increased the scope of earnings management.

(ii) Cash method of accounting is superior to accrual basis of accounting, as cash basis of accounting does not require use of accounting estimates, and thus, narrows down the scope of earnings management significantly.

(iii) Auditors find it difficult to detect under-provisioning, as provisions are measured at the best estimate of the management.

(iv) Analysts should focus on the timing of recognising impairment loss, as management is usually tempted to decide the timing for recognising impairment loss based on the expected performance of the company.

(v) Management's decision to defer discretionary expenses should be perceived as earnings management.

Safeguards against Earnings Management

Accounting Standards

Accounting standards aim at minimising opportunities for earnings management by narrowing down the choice of accounting principles and methods. However, in applying accounting standards, judgement is required for developing perspectives on economic impact of transaction and events. This provides opportunities for earnings management.

Audit Committee

Audit committee is a subcommittee of the Board of Directors of a company. The Companies Act, 2013 requires that the Board of Directors of every listed company, every public company with paid up capital of ₹10 crore or more, every public company having turnover of ₹100 crore or more, and every company having in aggregate outstanding loans or borrowing or debentures or deposits exceeding ₹50 crore must constitute an audit committee. The audit committee should consist of at least three members, and at least two-third of the members of the committee should be independent directors. Independent directors are non-executive directors not having any pecuniary relationship with the company and not having more than two percent shareholding in the company. The brief of the committee includes consideration of accounting policies. The audit committee is expected to take an independent view on accounting policies, adequacy and effectiveness of the internal control system, and reasonability of accounting estimates. Moreover, the committee provides a communication channel to auditors, including the internal auditor, and thus, protects audit independence.

Director's Responsibility Statement

In India, Section 134(5) of the Companies Act, 2013 stipulates that the Board of Director's report should include a director's responsibility statement. The statement should indicate the following:

(a) In the preparation of the annual accounts, the applicable accounting standards had been followed along with proper explanation relating to material departures,

(b) The directors had selected such accounting policies and applied them consistently and made judgements and estimates that are reasonable and prudent so as to give a true and fair view of the state of affairs of the company at the end of the financial year and of the profit and loss of the company for that period,

(c) The directors had taken proper and sufficient care for the maintenance of adequate accounting records in accordance with the provisions of the Companies Act for

NOTES

safeguarding the assets of the company and for preventing and detecting fraud and other irregularities,

(d) The directors had prepared the annual accounts on a going concern basis, and

(e) The directors, in the case of a listed company, had laid down internal financial controls to be followed by the company and that such internal financial controls are adequate and were operating effectively.

Assertions by directors in the responsibility statement provide a kind of safeguard, particularly when the Board of Directors is an independent and balanced board.

Compliance Certificate

The Securities and Exchange Board of India (Listing Obligations and Disclosure Requirements) Regulations, 2015 requires the Chief Executive Officer (CEO) and Chief Financial Officer (CFO) to furnish the following compliance:

A. They have reviewed financial statements and the cash flow statement for the year and that to the best of their knowledge and belief:
   (1) These statements do not contain any materially untrue statement or omit any material fact or contain statements that might be misleading,
   (2) These statements together present a true and fair view of the listed entity's affairs and are in compliance with existing accounting standards, applicable laws and regulations.

B. There are, to the best of their knowledge and belief, no transactions entered into by the listed entity during the year, which are fraudulent, illegal or violative of the listed entity's code of conduct.

C. They accept responsibility for establishing and maintaining internal controls for financial reporting and that they have evaluated the effectiveness of internal control systems of the listed entity pertaining to financial reporting and they have disclosed to the auditors and the audit committee, deficiencies in the design or operation of such internal controls, if any, of which they are aware and the steps they have taken or propose to take to rectify these deficiencies.

D. They have indicated to the auditors and the audit committee:
   (1) significant changes in internal control over financial reporting during the year;
   (2) significant changes in accounting policies during the year and that the same have been disclosed in the notes to the financial statements; and
   (3) instances of significant fraud of which they have become aware and the involvement therein, if any, of the management or an employee having a significant role in the listed entity's internal control system over financial reporting.

External Audit

It is mandatory for limited liability companies and some other types of entities in which public money is invested to get their financial statements audited by a Chartered Accountant or by a firm of Chartered Accountants. It is an important safeguard against earnings management. Auditors provide a reasonable assurance to shareholders that the financial statements provide a true and fair view. They also report on the adequacy and effectiveness of the internal control system. Users of financial statements rely on the judgement of auditors' because of their knowledge, skill and independence. Therefore, regulations jealously protect the independence of auditors and regulators penalise auditors who fail to perform their duties diligently or connive in perpetrating fraud. Moreover, the Institute of Chartered Accountants of India (ICAI) sets ethical standards for its members, mandates continuous professional education and regularly revises the syllabus to provide contemporary knowledge and skills. Financial statements are published along with the audit report.

NOTES

Self-Test Questions

Self-test question 12.7

Indicate whether the following statements are true (T) or false (F):

(i) Protecting independence of independent directors is important to protect stakeholders from earnings management.

(ii) Ingenuity of the CFO makes the audit committee ineffective in protecting stakeholders from earnings management, as accrual accounting provides ample scope for earnings management.

(iii) CEO/CFO Certification is an instrument to enforce accountability.

(iv) Accounting standards have reduced earnings management significantly.

(v) In spite of so many institutions in place to check earnings management, the practice is rampant among listed companies.

Potential Red Flags

An analyst should develop the skill of identifying red flags. The following are some of the common red flags:

(i) Unexplained change in accounting policy;

(ii) Unusual increase in accruals including receivables, inventory, creditors and depreciation;

(iii) An increasing gap between reported earnings and cash flow from operations;

(iv) An increasing gap between a firm's reported income and its taxable income;

(v) Increase in securitization and unusual short-term financing;

(vi) Large fourth-quarter adjustments;

(vii) Qualified audit opinion;

(viii) Change in external or internal auditor; and

(ix) Increase in related party transactions.

An analyst should examine in detail the accounting policy and its implementation to form a judgement on the quality of earnings. Red flags only indicate the potential for noise and distortions in reported earnings.

In case of doubt about the quality of reported earnings, an analyst should examine information provided in the annual report as a part of the financial statements, and also, information provided outside the financial statements. He/she should further investigate any inconsistency noticed in the information provided in different parts of the annual report, and also, in the information provided on the website of the company.

It may be a good idea to adjust reported earning with reference to notes, audit report, and reconciliation between reported earnings and cash flow from the operations presented in the cash flow statement.

SUMMARY

Higher quality earnings provide more information about the features of a firm's financial performance that are relevant to a specific decision made by a specific decision-maker. Earnings quality should be assessed from the perspective of the user of the information and in the context of specific decision. However, in general, earnings quality is discussed from the perspectives of primary users, that is, from the perspectives of investors, potential investors and lenders. Earnings quality is impaired from the discretionary actions of the management. Compliance with accounting standards and elimination of estimation errors improve earnings quality. Managers have inherent temptations to management earnings. They resort to various earnings management techniques for improving their utility, to boost share prices, and also, to lower perceived risks of investing in the company's equity to reduce cost of capital. Regulators have introduced various safeguards to protect stakeholders from earnings management. Analysts should develop skills to identify noises in information presented in financial statements. If noises are present in the information, they should dig deep to identify distortions in the earnings quality due to earnings management.

NOTES

Key Terms
Consolidated financial statement, group, parent, subsidiary, associate, joint venture

ANALYSE CONSOLIDATED FINANCIAL STATEMENTS

Companies having subsidiaries, associates and joint ventures prepare both stand-alone financial statements and consolidated financial statements. Analysts analyse consolidated financial statements of companies, rather than their stand-alone financial statements. Consolidated financial statements provide information on the financial position, performance and cash flows of the group, as a single entity.

Group, Parent, Subsidiary, Associate and Joint Venture

Group consists of the company (the parent), subsidiaries, associates and joint ventures. Subsidiary of a company (investor) is the investee, which is controlled by the company (investor). An investor usually controls the operating and financial policy decisions of its subsidiary (investee) by holding more than 50 percent voting rights of the subsidiary. But, control can be achieved by many other means such as controlling the Board of Directors or through shareholder agreement. An investor is said to have significant influence over its associate (investee), if it has power to participate in the operating and financial policy decisions of the investee, for example, through participation in board meetings. A company does not have the power to control the operating and financial policy decisions of its associate. Usually, a company holds more than 20 percent but less than 50 percent voting rights of its associate. Joint venture of a company is the investee, which the company jointly controls with other shareholders by virtue of an agreement with them, irrespective of the percentage of its shareholding.

Although, a company is called parent only to describe its relation with subsidiaries, we shall use the term parent to refer to a company that has either a subsidiary or an associate or a joint venture. The term 'Group' refers to the group of the parent and subsidiaries. We shall use the term 'Group' to refer to the group of the parent, subsidiaries, associates and joint ventures.

Why Analyse Consolidated Financial Statements

The parent extends its support, financially or otherwise, to a subsidiary or an associate or a joint venture, which is passing through difficult times, to protect the value of its investment. Similarly, when they perform well, the value of its investment in them goes up. In case of subsidiary, it controls the financial and operating decisions, and also, controls the distribution of accumulated profit. Therefore, the value of the parent's equity and credit risks of lending or extending credit to the parent depends significantly on group's performance and financial position. Therefore, investors, potential investors and lenders analyse consolidated financial statements of a company, which has one or more subsidiaries.

Self-Test Questions

Self-test question 12.8

Indicate whether the following statements are true (T) or false (F):

(i) The value of equity of the parent company depends on the forecasted performance of the group.

(ii) The performance of the parent is not affected by the performance of its subsidiaries.

(iii) Usually, the parent provides financial guarantee to the lenders of the subsidiary, and therefore, if the subsidiary fails to honour the commitment, the liability is to be assumed by the parent.

(iv) Usually, the parent provides performance guarantee on behalf of the subsidiary, and therefore, if the subsidiary fails to perform, the parent has to compensate the subsidiary's customer for the loss.

(v) Legally, the parent and subsidiary are two different juridical persons, and therefore, information in the stand-alone financial statements of the parent is more relevant than the information in the consolidated financial statements of the group in assessing the credit risk of lending to the parent.

NOTES

Key Terms
Non-controlling interest

Consolidation Methods

The methods for consolidating financial statements of the parent and its subsidiaries/associates/joint ventures are quite elaborate. We are providing a very brief sketch below to enable you to feel comfortable while analysing consolidated financial statements. Therefore, the discussion is very inadequate for learning the methods for consolidating financial statements.

Consolidation of Parent's Financial Statements with those of Subsidiaries

Financial statements of the subsidiary are incorporated in the financial statements of the parent by using the method, which is called *line-by-line consolidation*. In consolidated financial statements of the parent, the carrying amount each line item in the balance sheet, statement of profit and loss and cash flow statement, is the total of carrying amounts of that item in the financial statements of the parent and subsidiaries. The carrying amount of each item of assets and liabilities in the consolidated balance sheet is the total of the carrying amounts of assets and liabilities in the balance sheets of the parent and its subsidiary. Similarly, revenue and expenses in the consolidated statement of profit and loss is the total of the revenues of the parent and its subsidiaries. However, transactions between the parent and subsidiaries and between subsidiaries within the group are eliminated. For example, inter-company debtors and creditors are eliminated. Similarly, inter-company sales are eliminated and unrealised profit in the assets (e.g., stock-in-trade) that the group holds is also eliminated.

Investment of parent in subsidiary

Investment of the parent in subsidiary does not appear in the consolidated balance sheet. In effect, parent's investment in the subsidiary is taken out and net asset of the subsidiary is incorporated in the parent's balance sheet through line-by-line consolidation of assets and liabilities. Goodwill, if any, is recognised in the consolidated balance sheet.

Non-controlling interest (earlier called minority interest)

The share capital in the consolidated balance sheet is the share capital of the parent. Other equity in the consolidated balance sheet is the total of parent's other equity and parent's share in post-acquisition reserves and surplus of the subsidiary.

Consolidated balance sheet shows 'non-controlling interest' as a separate line item in equity. 'Non-controlling interest' represents the net asset (assets minus liabilities) of the subsidiary that is not attributable, directly or indirectly, to the parent. In other words, it represents the interest of shareholders other than the parent in the net assets of the subsidiary.

In the statement of consolidated profit and loss, the share of non-controlling interest in the net profit and other comprehensive income is presented separately.

Consolidation of Parent's Financial Statements with those of Associates and Joint Ventures

Financial statements of associates and joint ventures are consolidated using the equity method, which is also called *one line consolidation*. Under equity method, the cost of investment in the associate/joint venture is adjusted for change in the net assets of the associate/joint venture and the carrying amount of the investment is reduced by the amount of dividend received from the associate/joint venture. Therefore, carrying amounts of assets and liabilities in the consolidated balance sheet do not include carrying amounts

NOTES

Key Terms
Vertical analysis, horizontal analysis

of those items in the balance sheet of the associate/joint venture. Profit or loss and other comprehensive income of the associates/joint venture are included in the profit or loss and other comprehensive income of the parent and are presented as a separate line item in the statement of consolidated profit and loss. Unrealised profit from transactions between the associate/joint venture and the parent (and its subsidiaries) is eliminated to the extent of parent's share in that profit.

Self-Test Questions

Self-test question 12.9

Indicate whether the following statements are true (T) or false (F):

(i) In the consolidated balance sheet, the amount against each line item is the total of carrying amounts in the balance sheets of subsidiaries, associates and joint ventures.

(ii) Based on the principle that an entity cannot transact with itself, transactions between the subsidiaries within the group and between the subsidiaries within the group and the parent are eliminated.

(iii) Equity method of consolidation that is applied to consolidate the financial statements of the parent (investor) and its associates and joint ventures is called one-line consolidation.

SUMMARY

The value of the equity of the parent largely depends on the forecasted performance and financial position of the group. Similarly, credit risks of lending or extending credit to the parent depend on the forecasted financial position of the group. Therefore, investors, prospective investor, lenders and creditors analyse consolidated financial statements of a company that has one or more subsidiaries. Financial statements of subsidiaries are incorporated in the financial statements of the parent using a method, which is called line-by-line consolidation. Financial statements of associates/joint ventures are incorporated in the financial statements of the parent using a method, which is called one-line consolidation. Non-controlling interests in the net interest of subsidiaries are presented as a separate line item under equity. Similarly, non-controlling interests in the profit or loss of subsidiaries are presented as a separate line item in the statement of consolidated profit and loss.

VERTICAL ANALYSIS (COMMON SIZE FINANCIAL STATEMENTS)

Vertical analysis (also called *common-size analysis*) requires preparation of common-size financial statements, which present each line item as a percentage of some measure of the size of the firm. For a balance sheet, each line item is expressed as a percentage of total amounts of assets, which is equal to the total amounts of liabilities plus equity. For the statement of profit and loss, each line item is expressed as a percentage of the total income. Common-size financial statements provide an insight into the changes in the capital structure of an entity, and also, the changes into relative size of the components of assets, income and expenses. They are prepared as a first step in analysing financial statements of a firm. They are used for trend analysis, and also, to compare the financial statements of two or more companies.

A meaningful analysis of common-size statements requires understanding the business environment in which the entity operates and the strategy of the entity. For example, the capital structure of an entity depends not only on its past performance but also on the financial strategy of the company. Similarly, for an entity, which outsources a significant part of its manufacturing activities, the proportion of Property, Plant and Equipment (PP&E) in total assets should be lower than that of another entity that internally manufactures most of its products. Advertising expense (as a proportion of total expenses) of an entity whose strategy is massive sales promotion through advertisements is likely to be higher than that of another entity that relies more on its salesforce to promote its products.

Comparing common-size financial statements of a company with peers and examining the reasons for the differences in assets, liabilities, income and expenses provide an insight into the strategy of the competitors. However, the limitation of the analysis is that it fails to provide an understanding the impact of differences in the size of the companies on the composition of assets, liabilities, incomes and expenses, as common-size statements do not reflect the size of the company.

CASE STUDY: Vertical Analysis of Balance Sheet

Table 12.2 presents the extract of the consolidated balance sheets of Hindustan Unilever Limited (HUL), Infosys Limited (Infosys) and Suzlon Energy Limited (Suzlon) and Table 12.3 presents the common-size financial statements of those companies.

TABLE 12.2

Extract from Consolidated Balance Sheets as at March 31, 2017

(Amount ₹ in crore)

Particulars	HUL	Infosys	Suzlon
ASSETS			
Non-current assets	5,488	29,650	2,990
Current assets	10,218	53,705	9,170
Total	15,706	83,355	12,160
EQUITY			
Equity share capital	216	1,144	1,005
Other equity	6,528	67,838	(7,846)
Non-controlling interest	22	0	8
Total	6,766	68,982	(6,833)
LIABILITIES			
Non-current liabilities	1,226	360	5,234
Current liabilities	7,714	14,013	13,759
Total	8,940	14,373	18,993
Grand total	15,706	83,355	12,160

TABLE 12.3

Common-size Consolidated Summarised Balance Sheet as at March 31, 2017

Particulars	HUL	Infosys	Suzlon
ASSETS			
Non-current assets	34.94	35.57	24.59
Current assets	65.06	64.43	75.41
Total	100.00	100.00	100.00
EQUITY			
Equity share capital	1.38	1.37	8.26
Other equity	41.56	81.39	(64.52)
Non-controlling interest	0.14	0	.07
Total	43.08	82.76	(56.19)
LIABILITIES			
Non-current liabilities	7.81	0.43	43.04
Current liabilities	49.11	16.81	113.15
Total	56.92	17.24	156.19
Grand total	100.00	100.00	100.00

NOTES

Observations

(i) Table 12.3 is constructed by expressing every line item in the balance sheet as a percentage of total assets. Total of the amounts of equity and liabilities, by accounting rules, always equals the amount of total assets in the balance sheet.

(ii) The table shows that the amount of total liabilities in case of HUL is 56.92 percent of total assets, which is only 17.24 percent in case of Infosys. In case of Suzlon, it is 156.19 percent. Quite clearly, Suzlon's financial position is stressed. How much of the assets should be financed by liabilities depends on the structure of the industry, proportion of fixed expenses in total operating expenses and it is also a matter of judgement.

(iii) The equity (also called net worth) of Suzlon is negative because the amount of total liabilities is more than the amount of total assets. It has accumulated significant losses over its life. The amount of other equity (81.39 percent of the amount of total assets) is very high in case of Infosys. This reflects that it has retained most of profit without distributing to shareholders either by way of dividend or share buy-back. Analysts form opinion whether it is a good or a bad policy by examining the strategy of the company for growth and sustainability. The amount of other equity in case of HUL is significant (41.56 percent of the total assets).

(iv) The amount of current liabilities of Suzlon is 113.15 percent of the total assets and (113.15/75.41) or 150.52 percent of current assets. It implies that the company has to arrange finance to settle its short-term obligations, which are to be settled within 12 months after the balance sheet date. Even by liquidating all its current assets (short-term assets), it will not be able to settle its current liabilities. Liquidation of current assets is an impractical proposition because companies are required to hold current assets to support current operations. In case of Infosys, the amount of current liabilities is much smaller than that of current assets. In case of HUL, the amount of current assets is more than that of current liabilities.

Common-size balance sheet is prepared by expressing all the items on the face of the balance sheet. The technique is simple. Therefore, readers should take the balance sheet of a company and prepare common-size balance sheet, as an exercise.

Common-size balance sheets of the same company for number of years (say, five years) provide insights into the pattern of change, which often reflects the change in Business Model and the external environment.

ACTIVITY I Download the balance sheets of previous five years of a company of your choice and prepare common-size balance sheets and understand the trend.

Common-size statements of non-current assets

Table 12.4 shows that the composition of non-current assets of HUL, which is an FMCG company, and Infosys, which is an Information Technology company, is almost the same. It is little surprising. Therefore, it will be interesting to look into the composition of non-current assets and current assets of the three companies.

The technique that is used to prepare the common-size balance sheet can be applied to analyse the composition of non-current assets and current assets. In case of non-current assets, each component should be expressed as a percentage of total non-current assets. Similarly, in case of current assets, each component should be expressed as a percentage of total current assets.

Table 12.4 presents the composition of non-current assets of HUL, Infosys and Suzlon and Table 12.5 provides the common-size analysis of the same.

NOTES

TABLE 12.4

Composition of Non-current Assets as at March 31, 2017

(Amount ₹ in crores)

Particulars	HUL	Infosys	Suzlon
Property, plant and equipment	3,968	9,751	1,420
Capital-work-in-progress	229	1,365	118
Investment property	0	0	34
Goodwill	0	3,652	8
Other intangible assets	370	776	204
Goodwill on consolidation	81	0	0
Intangible assets under development	0	0	87
Investment in associates and joint ventures	0	71	189
Financial assets:			
Investments	6	6,382	0
Trade receivables			46
Loans	0	29	6
Other financial assets	128	309	712
Non-current tax assets (Net)	461	5,716	0
Deferred tax assets (Net)	170	540	0
Other non-current assets	75	1,059	166
Total	5,488	29,650	2,990

Note: For HUL: Pursuant to the merger of Aquagel Chemicals Private Limited (ACPL) with Lakme Lever Private Limited in the FY 2014–15, the excess of cost to the group of its investment in ACPL over the group's portion of equity in ACPL, amounting to ₹81 crore has been treated as 'goodwill on consolidation'.

TABLE 12.5

Common-size Analysis of the Composition of Non-current Assets as at March 31, 2017

Particulars	HUL	Infosys	Suzlon
Property, plant and equipment	72.30	32.89	47.49
Capital-work-in-progress	4.17	4.60	3.95
Investment property	0	0	1.14
Goodwill	0	12.32	0.27
Other intangible assets	6.74	2.62	6.82
Goodwill on consolidation	1.48	0	0
Intangible assets under development	0	0	2.91
Investment in associates and joint ventures	0	0.24	6.32
Financial assets:			
Investments	0.11	21.52	0
Trade receivables			1.54
Loans	0	0.10	0.20
Other financial assets	2.33	1.04	23.81
Non-current tax assets (Net)	8.40	19.28	0
Deferred tax assets (Net)	3.10	1.82	0
Other non-current assets	1.37	3.57	5.55
Total	100.00	100.00	100.00

From Table 12.5, it is obvious that the composition of 'non-current assets' is different for the three different companies under consideration.

Common-size analysis of property, plant and equipment provides further insight on how the infrastructure requirements of the three companies operating in three different industries are different. Infrastructure requirements also depend on the strategy of the

NOTES

company. For example, a manufacturing company that focuses on in-house manufacturing will require higher investment in infrastructure than a company, which has outsourced manufacturing.

Table 12.6 presents the composition of PP&E of HUL, Infosys and Suzlon as at March 31, 2017 and Table 12.7 presents the common-size analysis of PP&E.

TABLE 12.6

Composition of PP&E (Net Block) as at March 31, 2017

(Amount in ₹ crore)

Particulars	HUL	Infosys	Suzlon
Freehold land	60	1,095	164
Leasehold land	25	644	
Site development			69
Buildings	1,135	4,839	442
Plant and equipment	2,656	748	655
Wind research and measuring equipment			12
Furniture and fixtures	50	601	26
Vehicles	0	14	15
Office equipment	42	323	37
Computer equipment		1,487	
Total	3,968	9,751	1,420

Note: Presumably, in case of HUL and Suzlon, computer equipment is included in office equipment.

TABLE 12.7

Common-size Analysis of the Composition of PP&E (Net Block) as at March 31, 2017

(Amount in ₹ crore)

Particulars	HUL	Infosys	Suzlon
Freehold land	1.51	11.23	11.55
Leasehold land	0.63	6.60	0
Site development	0	0	4.86
Buildings	28.60	49.64	31.12
Plant and equipment	66.94	7.67	46.13
Wind research and measuring equipment	0	0	0.85
Furniture and fixtures	1.26	6.16	1.83
Vehicles	0	0.14	1.06
Office equipment	1.06	3.31	2.60
Computer equipment		15.25	
Total	100.00	100.00	100.00

Observations

(i) The carrying amount of the plant and equipment is 66.94 percent of the PP&E of HUL. The carrying amount of the land and building is 67.57 percent of the PP&E of Infosys.

(ii) The total of the carrying amounts of land, building and plant and machinery is 97.68 percent in case of HUL, 75.14 percent in case of Infosys and 93.66 percent in case of Suzlon.

(iii) In case of Infosys, investment in computer equipment is significant.

Common-size analysis of current assets and current liabilities

Analysts use common-size analysis of current assets and current liabilities to assess the quality of current assets (in terms of liquidity) and quality of current liabilities (in terms of the possibility of rolling over the liabilities) in evaluating the liquidity of the firm. *Liquidity* refers to the ability of the firm to meet short-term commitments.

ACTIVITY 2 Analyse the composition of non-current assets and property, plant and equipment using the vertical analysis technique from the balance sheets downloaded in performing Activity 1.

NOTES

CASE STUDY: Vertical Analysis of the Statement of Profit and Loss

Table 12.8 presents the statement of profit and loss of HUL, Infosys and Suzlon for the period ended on March 31, 2017, and Table 12.9 presents the common-size analysis of the same. Common-size statement of profit and loss is prepared by dividing the amount of each line item by the amount of total income.

TABLE 12.8

Statement of Consolidated Profit and Loss for the Period Ended March 31, 2017

(Amount in ₹ crore, except for EPS)

Particulars	HUL	Infosys	Suzlon
INCOME			
Revenue from operations	35,759	68.484	12,692
Other operating income	0	0	22
Other income	369	3,080	89
Total income	36,128	71,564	12,803
EXPENSES			
Cost of material consumed	11,946	0	8,291
Purchase of stock-in-trade	4,223	0	0
Changes in inventories of finished goods (including stock-in-trade) and work-in-progress	144	0	(749)
Excise duty	2,597	0	0
Employee benefits expenses	1,743	37,659	1,046
Cost of technical sub-contractors	0	3,833	0
Travel expenses		2,235	
Cost of software packages and others	0	1,597	0
Communication expenses	0	549	0
Consultancy and professional charges	0	763	0
Finance costs	35	0	1,288
Depreciation and amortisation expenses	432	1,703	389
Other expenses	8,766	3,244	1,626
Total expenses	29,886	51,583	11,891
Profit before exceptional items and tax	6,242	19,981	912
Exceptional items	237	0	0
Profit before tax	6,479	19,981	912
Share of profit/(loss) from associates and joint ventures	0	(30)	(48)
Profit before tax from continuing operations	6,479	19,951	864
Tax expenses			
Current tax	(1,947)	(5,653)	12
Deferred tax credit/(charge)	(30)	55	0
Profit After Tax From Continuing Operations (A)	4,502	14,353	852
Profit/(Loss) from discontinued operations before tax	(13)	0	0

(Contd.)

NOTES

TABLE 12.8

Statement of Consolidated Profit and Loss for the Period Ended March 31, 2017 (*Contd.*)

Particulars	HUL	Infosys	Suzlon
Tax expenses of discontinued operations	1	0	0
Profit/(Loss) from discontinued operations after tax (B)	(12)	0	0
Profit for the year (A + B)	4,490	14,353	852
OTHER COMPREHENSIVE INCOME			
Items that will not be reclassified subsequently to profit or loss:			
Remeasurement of the net defined benefit plans	(33)	(45)	(16)
Equity instruments through other comprehensive income	0	(5)	
Share of other comprehensive income in jointly controlled entities	0	0	0
Income tax related to items that will not be reclassified subsequently to profit or loss:			
Remeasurement of the net defined benefit plans	11		0
Items that will be reclassified subsequently to profit or loss:			
Fair value changes on cash flow hedges (net)		39	0
Exchange differences on translation of foreign operations		(257)	(230)
Fair value of debt instruments through other comprehensive income	2	(10)	0
Gains/(loss) on dilution of investment in subsidiaries			6
Income tax related to items that will be reclassified subsequently to profit or loss:			0
Fair value of debt instruments through other comprehensive income	0		0
Other comprehensive income, net of tax for the year (C)	(20)	(278)	(240)
Total comprehensive income for the year (A + B + C)	4,470	14,075	612
Profit attributable to:			
Owners of the company	4,476	14,353	858
Non-controlling interests	14	0	(6)
Other comprehensive income attributable to:			
Owners of the company	(20)	(278)	(255)
Non-controlling interests	0	0	15
Total comprehensive income attributable to:			
Owners of the Company	4,456	14,075	603
Non-controlling interests	14	0	9
Earnings per equity share from continuing operations:			
Basic (₹)	20.68	62.80	1.71
Diluted (₹)	20.68	62.77	1.60
Earnings per equity share from discontinued operations:			
Basic (₹)	(0.06)	0	0
Diluted (₹)	(0.06)	0	0
Earnings per equity share from continued and discontinued operations:			
Basic (₹)	20.62	62.80	1.71
Diluted (₹)	20.62	62.77	1.60

TABLE 12.9

Common-size Analysis of Statement of Consolidated Profit and Loss for the Period Ended March 31, 2017

Particulars	HUL	Infosys	Suzlon
INCOME			
Revenue from operations	98.98	95.70	99.13
Other operating income	0	0	0.17
Other income	1.02	4.30	0.70
Total income	100.00	100.00	12,803
EXPENSES			
Cost of material consumed	33.06	0	64.76
Purchase of stock-in-trade	11.69	0	0
Changes in inventories of finished goods (including stock-in-trade) and work-in-progress	0.40	0	(5.85)
Excise duty	7.19	0	0
Employee benefits expenses	4.82	52.63	8.17
Cost of technical sub-contractors	0	5.36	0
Travel expenses		3.12	
Cost of software packages and others	0	2.23	0
Communication expenses	0	0.76	0
Consultancy and professional charges	0	1.07	0
Finance costs	0.10	0	10.06
Depreciation and amortisation expenses	1.20	2.37	3.04
Other expenses	24.26	4.54	12.70
Total expenses	82.72	72.08	92.88
Profit before exceptional items and tax	17.28	27.92	7.12
Exceptional items	0.66	0	0
Profit before tax	17.94	27.92	7.12
Share of profit/(loss) from associates and joint ventures	0	(0.04)	(0.37)
Profit before tax from continuing operations	17.94	27.88	6.75
Tax expenses:			
Current tax	(5.40)	(7.87)	(0.09)
Deferred tax credit/(charge)	(0.08)	0.08	0
Profit after tax from continuing operations (A)	12.46	20.05	6.66

Observations

(i) We have compared companies operating in different industries. Therefore, composition of income and expense are not comparable. Vertical analysis of comparable companies provides significant insights into the difference in the business model and strategies of different companies in the same industry.

(ii) It is obvious from Table 12.9 that profit after tax from continuing operation as a percentage of total income is highest in case of Infosys (20.25 percent) and lowest in case of Suzlon (6.66 percent). It is 12.46 percent in case of HUL. This is indicative of the industry attractiveness. However, a better measure to assess industry attractiveness is to compare average 'return on invested capital' of major players in the industry over a period of five years.

(iii) Published statement of profit and loss present expenses using the 'natural classification' method. In case of Infosys, the employee benefit cost is 52.63 percent of the total income. Major part of this cost must relate to the employees directly engaged in project implementation. In the absence of separate disclosure of employee benefit expense related to those employees, it is difficult to assess the efficiency in rendering services.

NOTES

Self-Test Questions

Self-test question 12.10

Indicate whether the following statements are true (T) or false (F):

(i) Vertical analysis is often referred to as common-size analysis.
(ii) In a common-size balance sheet, each line item is expressed as a percentage of the total amounts of assets.
(iii) In a common-size statement of profit and loss, each line item is expressed as a percentage of the total income.
(iv) Comparing common-size financial statements of companies operating in different industries provides more insights than comparing common-size financial statements of companies operating in the same industry.
(v) An important weakness of common-size financial statements is that they camouflage the size of the company leading to misinterpretation of information, as companies of different sizes are often not comparable.

SUMMARY

Vertical analysis requires preparation of common-size financial statements. It helps in comparing financial statements of comparable companies operating in the same industry. Vertical analysis provides an insight into the strategy and Business Model of competitors. However, the most important weakness of common-size financial statements is that they camouflage the size of the company. The technique of vertical analysis can be used to get an insight into the composition of a particular group of assets and liabilities.

CASE STUDY: HORIZONTAL ANALYSIS (INDEXED FINANCIAL STATEMENTS)

Horizontal analysis, also called *trend analysis*, expresses financial statement items as an index relative to the base year. It provides an understanding of how financial statement items have changed over time. Calculation of index is not possible if the base year amount is zero. Therefore, in order to develop the index, analysts take the amount of ₹1 for the base year. An analyst uses indexed balance sheets and statements of profit and loss to get a feel of the trend in the financial position and performance of the firm, which helps him/her to plan financial analysis.

Table 12.10 presents the summarised consolidated balance sheets of HUL for the year ended March 31, 2017 and two previous years, and Table 12.11 presents indexed summarised consolidated balance sheets of HUL for the year ended March 31, 2017 and two previous years.

TABLE 12.10

Summarised Consolidated Balance Sheets of HUL for the Year Ended March 31, 2017 and Two Previous Years

(*Amount in ₹ crore*)

Particulars	31.03.2017	31.03.2016	31.03.2015
ASSETS			
Non-current assets	5,488	4,449	4,006
Current assets	10,218	10,345	10,025
Total	15,706	14,794	14,031
EQUITY			
Equity share capital	216	216	216
Other equity	6,528	6,357	6,238
Non-controlling interest	22	20	19
Total	6,766	6,593	6,473

NOTES

Particulars	31.03.2017	31.03.2016	31.03.2015
LIABILITIES			
Non-current liabilities	1,226	1,134	902
Current liabilities	7,714	7,067	6,656
Total	8,940	8,201	7,558
Grand total	15,706	14,794	14,031

TABLE 12.11

Indexed Summarised Consolidated Balance Sheets of HUL for the Year Ended March 31, 2017 and Two Previous Years

Particulars	31.03.2017	31.03.2016	31.03.2015
ASSETS			
Non-current assets	136.99	111.06	100.00
Current assets	101.93	103.19	100.00
Total	111.94	105.44	100.00
EQUITY			
Equity share capital	100.00	100.00	100.00
Other equity	104.65	101.91	100.00
Non-controlling interest	115.79	105.26	100.00
Total	104.53	101.85	100.00
LIABILITIES			
Non-current liabilities	135.92	125.72	100.00
Current liabilities	115.90	106.17	100.00
Total	118.29	108.51	100.00
Grand total	111.94	105.44	100.00

In constructing the indexed summarised consolidated balance sheets of HUL for the year ended March 31, 2017 and two previous years, 2014–15 has been considered as the base year. Therefore, carrying amount of each item in the consolidated balance sheet as at March 31, 2015 has been considered as 100. Carrying amount of each line item the balance sheets as at March 31, 2016 and March 31, 2017 is calculated as index numbers. For example, the carrying amount of non-current asset as at March 31, 2016 is calculated as [(4,449/4,406) ×100] or 111.06.

Indexed balance sheet and indexed statement of profit and loss can be constructed using this simple technique. This helps the analysts is understanding the trend. For example, from Table 12.11, it is obvious that in the year 2015–16, non-current assets of HUL had grown by 11.06 percent and in the year 2016–17, it had grown by [(136.99/111.06) ×100] or 23.35 percent.

A better insight is obtained by analysing indexed balance sheet together with indexed statement of profit and loss. For example, analysing growth in assets together with growth in revenue from operations helps in understanding whether growth in assets is commensurate with the growth in revenue from operations.

Analysts use 'vertical analysis' and 'horizontal analysis' just to develop a perspective on the financial health and performance as the starting point for analysing financial statements. They use ratio analysis extensively to develop deep understanding of past performance in order to forecast the future.

ACTIVITY 3 Apply the horizontal analysis technique to analyse financial statements downloaded while performing Activity 1.

NOTES

Self-Test Questions

Self-test question 12.11

Indicate whether the following statements are true (T) or false (F):

(i) Horizontal analysis requires expressing financial statement items as an index relative to the base year.

(ii) Horizontal analysis helps in understanding the trend of changes in assets, liabilities, incomes and expenses of a company.

(iii) Horizontal analysis provides significant insights into the financial position and performance over number of years.

SUMMARY

In horizontal analysis, a base year is selected. The figure against each line item in the balance sheet and the statement of profit and loss of the base year is taken as 100. Figure against each line item in balance sheet and statement of profit and loss of each subsequent year is presented as index number taking the base year figure as 100. The technique of horizontal analysis is used to get an insight into the trend of changes in the assets, liabilities, incomes and expenses of a company over number of years.

ANSWERS TO SELF-TEST QUESTIONS

12.1 (i) T; (ii) T; (iii) F; (iv) T; (v) T
12.2 (i) F; (ii) F; (iii) F; (iv) T; (v) T
12.3 (i) T; (ii) F; (iii) T; (iv) T; (v) T
12.4 (i) F; (ii) T; (iii) T; (iv) T; (v) F
12.5 (i) T; (ii) T; (iii) F; (iv) T; (v) F
12.6 (i) T; (ii) F; (iii) T; (iv) T; (v) T
12.7 (i) T; (ii) T; (iii) T; (iv) T; (v) F
12.8 (i) T; (ii) F; (iii) T; (iv) T; (v) F
12.9 (i) F; (ii) T; (iii) T
12.10 (i) T; (ii) T; (iii) T; (iv) F; (v) T
12.11 (i) T; (ii) T; (iii) F

ASSIGNMENTS

Multiple Choice Questions

1. Which of the following statement are most appropriate:

(i) SET (A)

(a) Earnings quality should be assessed with reference to a specific context and specific information needs for a decision.

(b) Although, earnings quality should be assessed with reference to a specific context and specific information needs for a decision, generally, earnings quality is assessed with reference to the information needs of investors, potential investors, lenders and creditors.

(c) Context and specific need are not relevant in assessing earnings quality.

(d) None of the above.

(ii) SET (B)

(a) Conservative accounting policy improves earnings quality.

(b) Consistency (less volatility) in reported earnings from year to year improves earnings quality.

(c) Compliance with accounting standards and minimization of estimation errors improve earnings quality.

(d) None of the above.

(iii) SET (C)

(a) Earning management refers to bending accounting rules to present better financial position and better performance than what they actually are.

(b) Managers manage earnings through accounting manipulations and also by manipulating cash flow consequences through interventions.

(c) Managers manage earnings by manipulating cash flow consequences through interventions.

(d) None of the above.

(iv) SET (D)

(a) Estimation is central to accrual accounting, and therefore, accrual accounting provides enough scope for earnings management.

(b) Cash basis of accounting is better than accrual accounting because it provides less scope for earnings management.

(c) Irrespective of the accounting method being used, unscrupulous managers are able to manage earnings through cash flow intervention.
(d) None of the above.

(v) SET (E)
(a) Protecting audit independence is the best protection against earnings management.
(b) Protecting audit independence and independence of independent directors is the best protection against earnings management.
(c) Accruals and provisions are measured at the best estimate of the management and, therefore, independent auditor and independent board of directors cannot protect stakeholders from earnings management.
(d) None of the above.

(vi) SET (F)
(a) Standalone financial statements, rather than consolidated financial statements of a company having subsidiaries should be analysed to forecast future earning capacity of the company.
(b) Consolidated financial statements, rather than stand-alone financial statements of a company having subsidiaries should be analysed to forecast future earning capacity of the company.
(c) Both consolidated financial statements and stand-alone financial statements of a company having subsidiaries should be analysed to forecast future earning capacity of the company.
(d) None of the above.

(vii) SET (G)
(a) Vertical analysis is used to analyse the trend in changes in assets, liabilities, incomes and expenses over past few years.
(b) Analysing common size financial statements carefully, one can get insights into the strategy and business model of competitors.
(c) Analysing common size financial statements carefully, one can get insights into the strategy and business model of competitors, only if comparable companies are selected before preparing common size financial statements.
(d) None of the above.

(viii) SET (H)
(a) Banks generate Non-performing Assets (NPA) because they lack skills in analysing financial statements.
(b) Banks generate Non-performing Assets (NPA) because they lend companies for long-term and assess the intention and capacity of the borrower to repay the loan.
(c) Banks generate Non-performing Assets (NPA) because they lend companies for long-term and fails to predict changes in business environment in which the borrower operates.
(d) None of the above.

(ix) SET (I)
(a) In order to analyse financial statements one does not require accounting knowledge.
(b) In order to analyse financial statements one does not requires understanding strategy and business model.
(c) In order to analyse financial statements one requires knowledge of basic arithmetic only, as it involves calculating rations from figures available in published financial statements.
(d) None of the above

(x) SET (J)
(a) Natural classification of expenses in the statement of profit and loss provides more information, which is required for analysing financial statements, than the functional classification.
(b) Functional classification of expenses in the statement of profit and loss provides more information, which is required for analysing financial statements, than the natural classification.
(c) Functional classification of expenses in the statement of profit and loss provides more information, which is required for analysing financial statements, than the natural classification, but functional classification lacks objectivity.
(d) None of the above.

NOTES

CHAPTER

13

Ratio Analysis
Reorganising Financial Statements

Learning Objectives

The objective of this chapter is to provide an understanding of the methods for reorganising balance sheet and the statement of profit and loss for the purpose of calculating and analysing financial ratios. After reading this chapter, you will be able to understand the following:

- Limitations of accounting measures
- General principles for calculating and analysing financial ratios
- Concept of trend analysis and cross-sectional analysis
- Principles for reorganising balance sheet and statement of profit and loss
- Operating and non-operating assets, liabilities, incomes and expenses
- Concept of net operating assets
- Concept of net financial obligations
- Methods for capitalising operating lease

NOTES

RATIO ANALYSIS—INTRODUCTION

Ratio analysis is an important tool for financial statement analysis. Although accounting measures have many limitations, analysts use them extensively in a number of metrics that measure the financial position and performance of a firm. For a meaningful analysis, financial ratios should be used in conjunction with non-financial ratios or other non-financial measures of performance in different activities of the firm.

Limitations of Accounting Measures

The following are the important limitations of accounting measures:

(i) *Accounting has a bias towards conservatism:* Conservatism often results in understatement of assets. For example, most internally generated intangible assets are not recognised in the balance sheet. Therefore, 'intellectual capital' does not find a place in the balance sheet, although companies achieve growth and survive by creating and managing the same effectively. Core competence of a company does not come from tangible assets or individual knowledge and skills of employees; it comes from unique processes integrated with each other, and institutional knowledge.

(ii) *Different measurement bases are used to measure different classes of assets:* Different asset classes are measured using different attributes. For example, most firms use the 'cost model' to measure property plant and equipment and intangible assets, while current assets are carried at an amount closer to the current value and investments in equity instruments are measured at fair value. Usually, accounting figures that represent historical cost are not adjusted for inflation. This causes inconsistency among different figures that appear in financial statements.

However, in reality, the effect of inflation may not be significant. Usually, firms invest an amount at least equal to depreciation to maintain the existing production capacity. If it is so, the denominator in a ratio that uses the carrying amount of PP&E in the denominator (e.g., revenue/PP&E) does not change. Moreover, in most of the situations, due to inflationary effects on the prices of capital goods, firms invest more than depreciation. This further reduces the distortion, even in the 'stable state' of a firm. During the growth phase, investment in PP&E is much more than depreciation. Thus, a part of the PP&E is presented at the current value. Therefore, inconsistency or distortion is much lower at the growth phase of the firm.

The impact of inflation is much less on those ratios that use 'total invested capital' as the denominator. A significant portion of invested capital is represented by current assets, which are measured at a value close to their current value. This reduces the impact of inflation. There is almost no impact of inflation on those ratios that use current assets or working capital as denominator (e.g., revenue/current assets). Similarly, when a ratio uses numbers from the statement of profit and loss, the distortion is insignificant. However, while interpreting ratios, analysts should keep in mind that inflation does not have any uniform effect on all items in financial statements.

(iii) *Accrual system of accounting*: The accrual system of accounting relies much on management's perspective and judgement on the economic impact of transactions and other events. Those perceptions and judgements are taken into account in determining the carrying amounts of assets and liabilities. In most situations, no straightjacket objective criteria can be established for deciding the carrying amount of those items. For example, in most situations, the choice of the depreciation method for allocating costs of items of PP&E over their useful life reflects the firm's preference, rather than the pattern of cash flow that those assets will generate.

A meaningful analysis of financial statements requires adjustments of accounting figures to overcome these limitations. However, care should be taken to ensure that such adjustments do not make computations so complex that the interpretation of results becomes difficult. Care should also be taken that adjustments to figures presented in the financial statements are not arbitrary. They should be based on clear understanding of the business and the environment (e.g., political, economic, social and technological) in which the firm operates.

NOTES

Key Terms
Trend analysis, cross-sectional analysis

Self-Test Questions

Self-test question 13.1

Indicate whether the following statements are true (T) or false (F):

(i) Conservatism in preparing and presenting financial statements benefits creditors, but reduces the relevance of information in the context of equity valuation.

(ii) Use of different measurement bases for different classes of assets and liabilities reduces the value of information in financial statements.

(iii) Historical cost, which is used for measuring assets and liabilities, is not adjusted for inflation.

(iv) Accrual basis of accounting brings a lot of subjectivity in measuring assets and liabilities, and therefore, chances of bias creeping in cannot be ruled out.

(v) Adjusting financial statements using some thumb rule should be avoided.

Ratio Analysis Guidelines

Trend Analysis and Cross-Sectional Analysis

Financial ratios are used for both trend analysis and cross-sectional analysis.

Trend analysis

Trend analysis refers to the use of financial ratios to understand the trend, if any, in the financial position and performance of a firm. Ratios based on annual financial results of a particular firm covering more than one accounting year are analysed to understand the trend.

Cross-sectional analysis

'Cross-sectional analysis' refers to the analysis of the financial position and performance of a firm in comparison to the performance of its peers. Cross-sectional analysis may cover a single period or it may cover more than one period.

Guidelines

The following guidelines may be helpful in analysing financial ratios:

(i) Ratios by themselves do not provide any insight into the financial position or performance of a firm. For example, in the absence of any context, it is difficult to comment on the current ratio (current assets divided by current liabilities), which is used to measure liquidity. A current ratio of 2:1 is generally considered good from the perspective of vendors, who provide short-term credit to the firm, while it is bad from manager's perspective. Even from creditors' perspective, a lower ratio may be adequate if the firm has adequate capacity to borrow at a short notice.

(ii) No inference can be drawn in the absence of a *benchmark ratio*. Trend analysis does not require comparison of actual ratios with benchmark ratios. Selection of appropriate benchmark ratios is important for cross-sectional analysis. Benchmark ratios may be the industry average, or ratios of the firm's immediate competitor or standard ratios set by some industry association or other similar institution. Benchmark ratios should be established carefully. For example, the industry average cannot be used as a benchmark ratio in analysing financial position and performance of a firm, which is the industry leader. Top management uses budget ratios as benchmark ratios to evaluate performance of the firm against the budget.

(iii) Analysts draw meaningful inferences by comparing ratios of the firm with those of comparable firms. However, it is difficult to define 'comparability'. Comparability between two firms can be established by using a number of parameters. Examples of such parameters are nature of the business, size of the firm, the environment in which the firm operates, and strategy of the firm. Care should be taken to ensure that the criteria established are appropriate in the given situation and for the given purpose. For example, operating ratios (an item of expense divided by net sales) of a firm, which has outsourced its manufacturing process, are not comparable with those of a firm, which manufactures products inside, although both the firms operate in the same industry. However, Return On Invested Capital (ROIC) of those two firms is comparable if, both the firms pursue the objective of creating shareholder value.

(iv) Consistency should be maintained in selecting the numerator and the denominator of each ratio. For example, in calculating the ROIC, if an item of other income is excluded from profit, it is important that the assets, which generate that other income, are excluded from the invested capital. Similarly, consistency should be maintained in the definition of the accounting figures used as the numerator and denominator of each ratio. For example, in calculating the ROIC, the invested capital may be either the invested capital at the end of the period, or the invested capital at the beginning of the period, or the average of the invested capital at the beginning and at the end of the period. Once one of these three alternatives is chosen, it should be used consistently in calculating the return on investment for different periods or for different firms. In the absence of such consistencies, ratios will not be comparable, and consequently, the comparison of those ratios will be misleading. Usually, average of the opening and closing figures is used, when information from the balance sheet is used for calculating ratios.

(v) The purpose of financial statement analysis is to develop a *historical perspective* of the operation of the firm. This historical perspective is used to forecast the future performance of the firm. In order to develop the correct historical perspective, non-financial ratios and non-financial information should be used to supplement the financial ratios. Moreover, financial and non-financial ratios should be integrated with the analyses of the firm's strategy and its environment, both internal and external. Correct historical perspective cannot be developed without such integration.

(vi) Meaningful results will be obtained only if the performance is analysed over a sufficiently long period. Abnormal years should be excluded from the analysis. The selected period should cover at least a complete business cycle for firms that operate in cyclical industries (e.g., cement and steel). As a thumb rule, the selected period should cover at least 5 years.

Self-Test Questions

Self-test question 13.2

Indicate whether the following statements are true (T) or false (F):

(i) In the context of cross-sectional analysis, companies that are operating in the same industry are comparable companies.

(ii) Industry average ratios should always be used as benchmark ratios for evaluation of financial position and performance of a company.

(iii) Financial ratios help in asking right questions, but do not provide answers.

(iv) ROIC calculated using year-end figure of invested capital is misleading because the whole of the capital was not available for use in the operation throughout the year.

(v) Abnormal years should not be excluded for trend analysis, as in most of the cases, it is difficult to identify abnormal years.

NOTES

SUMMARY

Accounting has some serious limitations. Its bias towards conservatism leads to understatement of assets and holding gains. Different measurement attributes are used to measure assets and liabilities. This might result in inconsistencies. Most companies use the cost model to measure the items of property, plant and equipment. They use historical cost, not adjusted for inflation, to measure those items. Accrual method of accounting is judgemental and lack objectivity. In spite of those limitations, analysts use financial ratios extensively to evaluate the financial position and performance of the company, to forecast future cash flows for valuing equity and to assess credit risks of lending the entity. Ratios by themselves do not provide meaningful insights. Ratios when compared with benchmark ratios prompt right questions and enquiry to find answers to those questions provide insights. Consistency should be maintained in defining ratios, which are used for trend analysis and cross-sectional analysis.

REORGANISING FINANCIAL STATEMENTS

The formats in which companies present financial statements (e.g., forms specified in schedule III of the Companies Act, 2013) are not conducive for analysis. Analysts reorganised financial statements for analysis. Some important adjustments are presented in this section.

Analysis of balance sheet and statement of profit and loss is discussed with reference to consolidated balance sheets as at March 31, 2016 and March 31, 2017 and statement of profit and loss for the year 2016–17 of HUL, Infosys and Suzlon (Tables (13.1–13.9). Those are reproduced below for ready reference.

TABLE 13.1

Extract of Consolidated Balance Sheets of HUL, Infosys and Suzlon as at March 31, 2017

(Amount in ₹ crore)

Particulars	HUL	Infosys	Suzlon
ASSETS			
Non-current assets	5,488	29,650	2,990
Current assets	10,218	53,705	9,170
Total	15,706	83,355	12,160
EQUITY			
Equity share capital	216	1,144	1,005
Other equity	6,528	67,838	(7,846)
Non-controlling interest	22	0	8
Total	6,766	68,982	(6,833)
LIABILITIES			
Non-current liabilities	1,226	360	5,234
Current liabilities	7,714	14,013	13,759
Total	8,940	14,373	18,993
Grand total	15,706	83,355	12,160

TABLE 13.2

Extract of Consolidated Balance Sheets of HUL, Infosys and Suzlon as at March 31, 2016

(Amount in ₹ crore)

Particulars	HUL	Infosys	Suzlon
ASSETS			
Non-current assets	4,449	23,597	2,892
Current assets	10,345	51,753	6,831
Total	14,794	75,350	9,723
EQUITY			
Equity share capital	216	1,144	1,004

NOTES

Particulars	HUL	Infosys	Suzlon
Other equity	6,357	60,600	(8,537)
Non-controlling interest	20	0	0
Total	6,593	61,744	(7,533)
LIABILITIES			
Non-current liabilities	1,134	367	9,595
Current liabilities	7,067	13,239	7,661
Total	8,201	13,606	17,256
Grand total	14,794	75,350	9,723

TABLE 13.3

Composition of Non-current Assets in the Consolidated Balance Sheets of HUL, Infosys and Suzlon as at March 31, 2017

(Amount in ₹ crore)

Particulars	HUL	Infosys	Suzlon
Property, plant and equipment	3,968	9,751	1,420
Capital-work-in-progress	229	1,365	118
Investment property	0	0	34
Goodwill	0	3,652	8
Other intangible assets	370	776	204
Goodwill on consolidation	81	0	0
Intangible assets under development	0	0	87
Investment in associates and joint ventures	0	71	189
Financial assets:			
Investments	6	6,382	0
Trade receivables	0	0	46
Loans	0	29	6
Other financial assets	128	309	712
Non-current tax assets (net)	461	5,716	0
Deferred tax assets (net)	170	540	0
Other non-current assets	75	1,059	166
Total	5,488	29,650	2,990

Note: (i) Other financial assets of Suzlon include bank balance of ₹377 crores.

TABLE 13.4

Composition of Non-current Assets in the Consolidated Balance Sheets of HUL, Infosys and Suzlon as at March 31, 2016

(Amount in ₹ crore)

Particulars	HUL	Infosys	Suzlon
Property, plant and equipment	3,165	8,637	1,235
Capital-work-in-progress	408	960	197
Investment property	0	0	33
Goodwill	0	3,764	8
Other intangible assets	12	985	331
Goodwill on consolidation	81	0	0
Intangible assets under development	0	0	35
Investment in associates and joint ventures	26	103	93
Financial assets:			
Investments	6	1,714	0
Trade receivables	0	0	78
Loans	0	25	2
Other financial assets	147	286	775
Non-current tax assets (net)	381	5,230	0
Deferred tax assets (net)	168	536	0
Other non-current assets	55	1,357	105
Total	4,449	23,597	2,892

Note: (i) Other financial assets of Suzlon include bank balance of ₹260 crores.

NOTES

TABLE 13.5

Composition of Current Assets in the Consolidated Balance Sheets of HUL, Infosys and Suzlon as at March 31, 2017

(Amount in ₹ crore)

Particulars	HUL	Infosys	Suzlon
Inventories	2,541	0	3,469
Financial assets:			
Investment	3,788	9,970	481
Trade receivables	1,085	12,322	3,627
Cash and cash equivalents	628	22,625	336
Bank balances other than cash and cash equivalents mentioned above	1,200	0	0
Loans	0	272	49
Other financial assets	331	5,980	149
Current tax assets (net)			45
Other current assets	598	2,536	1,014
Assets held for sale	47	0	0
Total	10,218	53,705	9,170

Notes:

(i) Current investments of HUL include investments in treasury bills amounting to ₹1,459 crore.

(ii) Other financial assets of Infosys include 'unbilled revenue' amounting to ₹3,648 crores and 'restricted deposits' amounting to ₹1,416 crore. Restricted deposits represent deposits with financial institutions to settle employee-obligations as and when they arise during the normal course of business.

(iii) Other financial assets of Suzlon includes interest accrued on deposits, loan and advances amounting to ₹9 crore.

TABLE 13.6

Composition of Current Assets in the Consolidated Balance Sheets of HUL, Infosys and Suzlon as at March 31, 2016

(Amount in ₹ crores)

Particulars	HUL	Infosys	Suzlon
Inventories	2,726	0	2,524
Financial assets:			
Investment	2,560	75	267
Trade receivables	1,264	11,330	2,515
Cash and cash equivalents	830	32,697	627
Bank balances other than cash and cash equivalents mentioned above	2,179	0	0
Loans	0	303	96
Other financial assets	239	5,190	112
Current tax assets (net)			32
Other current assets	525	2,158	658
Assets held for sale	22	0	0
Total	10,345	51,753	6,831

Notes:

(i) Current investments of HUL include investments in treasury bills amounting to ₹1,264 crore.

(ii) Other financial assets of Infosys include 'unbilled revenue' amounting to ₹3,029 crore and 'restricted deposits' amounting to ₹1,238 crore. Restricted deposits represent deposits with financial institutions to settle employee-obligations as and when they arise during the normal course of business.

(iii) Other financial assets of Suzlon include interest accrued on deposits, loan and advances amounting to ₹9 crore.

NOTES

TABLE 13.7

Composition of Liabilities in the Consolidated Balance Sheets of HUL, Infosys and Suzlon as at March 31, 2017

(Amount in ₹ crore)

Particulars	HUL	Infosys	Suzlon
Non-current Liabilities			
Financial liabilities:			
Borrowings	0	0	4,841
Other financial liabilities	73	70	226
Provisions	514	0	127
Non-current tax liabilities (net)	432	0	0
Deferred tax liabilities (net)	0	207	0
Other non-current liabilities	207	83	40
Total (A)	1,226	360	5,234
Current Liabilities			
Financial liabilities:			
Borrowings	277	0	2,076
Trade payables	6,186	367	4,812
Other financial liabilities	195	6,349	4,927
Other current liabilities	664	3,007	1,122
Provisions	392	405	822
Current tax liabilities (net)	0	3,885	0
Total (B)	7,714	14,013	13,759
Total liabilities (A + B)	8,940	14,373	18,993

Notes:

(i) Other current financial liabilities include (a) current maturities of long-term borrowings: HUL: Zero: Infosys: Zero; and Suzlon: ₹4,197 crore; (b) Interest accrued on borrowings: HUL: Infosys: Zero: Suzlon: ₹48 crore; (c) Unpaid dividend: HUL ₹116 crore; Infosys ₹17 crore.

(ii) Long-term provision of HUL includes post-employment employee benefit liabilities amounting to ₹106 crore.

(iii) Long-term provision of Suzlon includes post-employment employee benefit liabilities amounting to ₹38 crore.

TABLE 13.8

Composition of Liabilities in the Consolidated Balance Sheets of HUL, Infosys and Suzlon as at March 31, 2016

(Amount in ₹ crore)

Particulars	HUL	Infosys	Suzlon
Non-current Liabilities			
Financial liabilities:			
Borrowings	0	0	9,225
Other financial liabilities	20	69	129
Provisions	623	0	219
Non-current tax liabilities (net)	306	0	0
Deferred tax liabilities (net)	1	252	
Other non-current liabilities	184	46	22
Total (A)	1,134	367	9,595
Current Liabilities			
Financial liabilities:			
Borrowings	177	0	1,895
Trade payables	5,685	386	2,970
Other financial liabilities	258	6,302	741
Other current liabilities	654	2,629	1,497
Provisions	293	512	558
Current tax liabilities (net)	0	3,410	0
Total (B)	7,067	13,239	7661
Total liabilities (A + B)	8,201	13,606	17,256

NOTES

Notes:

(i) Other current financial liabilities include (a) current maturities of long-term borrowings: HUL: Zero; Infosys: Zero; and Suzlon: ₹295 crore; (b) Interest accrued on borrowings: HUL: Infosys: Zero: Suzlon: ₹16 crore; (c) Unpaid dividend: HUL ₹106 crore; Infosys ₹5 crore.

(ii) Long-term provision for HUL includes post-employment employee benefit liabilities amounting to ₹203 crore.

(iii) Long-term provision of Suzlon includes post-employment employee benefit liabilities amounting to ₹58 crore.

TABLE 13.9

Statement of Consolidated Profit and Loss for the Period Ended March 31, 2017

(Amount in ₹ crore, except for EPS)

Particulars	HUL	Infosys	Suzlon
INCOME			
Revenue from operations	35,759	68.484	12,692
Other operating income	0	0	22
Other income	369	3,080	89
Total income	36,128	71,564	12,803
EXPENSES			
Cost of material consumed	11,946	0	8,291
Purchase of stock-in-trade	4,223	0	0
Changes in inventories of finished goods (including stock-in-trade) and work-in-progress	144	0	(749)
Excise duty	2,597	0	0
Employee benefits expenses	1,743	37,659	1,046
Cost of technical sub-contractors	0	3,833	0
Travel expenses		2,235	
Cost of software packages and others	0	1,597	0
Communication expenses	0	549	0
Consultancy and professional charges	0	763	0
Finance costs	35	0	1,288
Depreciation and amortisation expenses	432	1,703	389
Other expenses	8,766	3,244	1,626
Total expenses	29,886	51,583	11,891
Profit before exceptional items and tax	6,242	19,981	912
Exceptional items	237	0	0
Profit before tax	6,479	19,981	912
Share of profit/(loss) from associates and joint ventures	0	(30)	(48)
Profit before tax from continuing operations	6,479	19,951	864
Tax expenses:			
Current tax	(1,947)	(5,653)	12
Deferred tax credit/(charge)	(30)	55	0
Profit after tax from continuing operations (A)	4,502	14,353	852
Profit/(Loss) from discontinued operations before tax	(13)	0	0
Tax expenses of discontinued operations	1	0	0
Profit/(Loss) from discontinued operations after tax (B)	(12)	0	0
Profit for the year (A + B)	4,490	14,353	852
OTHER COMPREHENSIVE INCOME			
Items that will not be reclassified subsequently to profit or loss:			
Remeasurement of the net defined benefit plans	(33)	(45)	(16)
Equity instruments through other comprehensive income*	0	(5)	
Share of other comprehensive income in jointly controlled entities	0	0	0
Income tax related to items that will not be reclassified subsequently to profit or loss:			
Remeasurement of the net defined benefit plans	11		0
Items that will be reclassified subsequently to profit or loss:			
Fair value changes on cash flow hedges (net)		39	0
Exchange differences on translation of foreign operations		(257)	(230)

NOTES

Particulars	HUL	Infosys	Suzlon
Fair value of debt instruments through other comprehensive income*	2	(10)	0
Gains/(loss) on dilution of investment in subsidiaries			6
Income tax related to Items that will be reclassified subsequently to profit or loss:			0
Fair value of debt instruments through other comprehensive income	0		0
Other comprehensive income, net of tax for the year (C)	(20)	(278)	(240)
Total comprehensive income for the year (A + B + C)	4,470	14,075	612
Profit attributable to:			
Owners of the company	4,476	14,353	858
Non-controlling interests	14	0	(6)
Other comprehensive income attributable to:			
Owners of the company	(20)	(278)	(255)
Non-controlling interests	0	0	15
Total comprehensive income attributable to:			
Owners of the company	4,456	14,075	603
Non-controlling interests	14	0	9
Earnings per equity share from continuing operations:			
Basic (₹)	20.68	62.80	1.71
Diluted (₹)	20.68	62.77	1.60
Earnings per equity share from discontinued operations:			
Basic (₹)	(0.06)	0	0
Diluted (₹)	(0.06)	0	0
Earnings per equity share from continued and discontinued operations:			
Basic (₹)	20.62	62.80	1.71
Diluted (₹)	20.62	62.77	1.60

Notes:

(i) Other incomes of HUL are interest income, dividend income and fair value gain on investments measured at fair value.

(ii) Other incomes of Infosys are interest income, dividend income, fair value gain on investments measured at fair value and foreign exchange gains (₹232 crore).

(iii) Other incomes of Suzlon are interest income, dividend income and fair value gain on investments measured at fair value.

Balance Sheet Reorganisation and Analysis

Operating and Non-Operating Assets and Liabilities

In presenting assets and liabilities in the balance sheet, companies do not classify assets and liabilities into operating and non-operating categories. However, is classification is necessary to analyse financial statements, as forecasting future earning capacity of the company requires evaluating the productivity of operating net assets (measured at the amount of operating assets less the amount of operating liabilities). This also requires classifying incomes and expenses into operating and non-operating categories. Analysts apply judgement and thumb rule to classify assets and liabilities into operating and non-operating categories.

Non-operating assets

Assets, which are not used to carry on the operation of the company or which do not support the same, are non-operating assets. The following are the examples of non-operating assets:

(i) ***Excess cash:*** Cash in excess of the amount that is required to support the operation is a non-operating asset. Companies do not present the amount of excess cash separately in the balance sheet. Analysts estimate the excess cash by deducting

NOTES

the amount of cash required to support the operation from the cash that the company holds. The amount of cash required to support the operation depends on various factors such as the relative bargaining power of the firm vis-à-vis its customers and suppliers, the number of geographical locations in which customers and assets are located, and the efficiency of the financial system of the countries in which the firm operates. Analysts apply their judgement in estimating the excess cash. They often use a thumb rule derived based on industry norm to estimate the cash required to support operation. For example, cash equal to 5 percent of the revenue from operations may be considered as operating asset and the excess may be considered as excess cash (non-operating asset). For example, revenue from operations of Infosys for the year 2016–17 was ₹68,484 crore. Applying the thumb rule, the operating cash was (0.05 × 68,484) or ₹3,424 crore and excess cash was (₹22,625 – 3,424) or ₹19,201 crore.

(ii) ***Investments:*** For firms operating in trading, manufacturing and service sectors, investments are non-operating assets.

(iii) ***Trade investments:*** The assumption that all investments are non-operating assets is simplistic because certain investments in equity instruments issued by another entity might be driven by the objective to earn trade benefits. For example, investments of less than 20 percent of the equity share capital in companies, which are customers or vendors, are trade investments. Financial statements of those companies in which investment of the investor is less than 20 percent of the share capital of the investee are not incorporated in the consolidated financial statements of the investor unless it is established that the investor controls the investee or the investor has significant control over the investee, which is not very common. Companies disclose trade investments in notes to accounts. Although conceptually trade investments are operating assets, in practice, they are treated as non-operating assets, as the statement of profit and loss does not present income (e.g., dividend) from those investments separately to enable the analyst take the income out of other income and add it to operating profit.

(iv) ***Investment in associates and joint ventures:*** Financial statements of associates and joint ventures are consolidated with the financial investment of the investors using the equity method. The investment in an associate or joint venture is carried in the consolidated balance sheet at the cost of investment, adjusted for change in the net assets of the investee post-investment and reduced by the dividend received from the investee. The statement of consolidated statement of profit and loss presents the profit or loss of the investee in a single line item. Therefore, line items in the statement of consolidated profit and loss do not include incomes and expenses of the investee (associate/joint venture). As a result, ratios like profit margin and asset turnover get distorted. Therefore, investments in associates and joint ventures are treated as non-operating assets for ratio analysis. However, investments in associates and joint ventures are strategic in nature. Therefore, analysts calculate return on invested capital by including them in operating assets and including income from those investments in operating profit.

(v) ***Investments as a part of treasury management:*** A company, which does not hold excess cash, invests in short-term debt securities or mutual funds (e.g., liquid funds) as a part of treasury function. Therefore, current investments should be analysed to form a judgement whether those investments arise from normal treasury function of the company. For example, the revenue from operations of HUL for the year 2016–17 was ₹35,759 crore and cash as at March 31, 2017, was ₹628 crore. If we apply the thumb rules 2 percent of revenue, the operating cash is estimated at ₹715 crore. Therefore, the company was not holding excess cash. Details of current investments of HUL show that as at March 31, 2017, ₹1,459 crore was invested in treasury bills. Therefore, conceptually, it is appropriate to assume that investments in treasury bills is a part of treasury function, and therefore, is also a part of operating assets. However, the statement of profit and loss does not present interest and other income from treasury bills and other debt instruments separately. Therefore, in practice, even those investments are treated as non-operating assets.

(vi) ***Investment property:*** Except for firms that are in the business of leasing out properties to earn rent, investment property forms part of non-operating assets. They are non-operating non-financial assets. In analysing financial statements, analysts work with 'net financial obligations', which are measured by deducting the amount of non-operating financial assets from non-operating financial liabilities. Therefore, non-operating non-financial assets and liabilities are to be treated differently for the purpose of capital structure analysis. Accordingly, for the purpose of capital structure analysis, it is appropriate to deduct the amount of investment properties from equity. Income (adjusted for income tax) from investment properties should be excluded from income recognised in the reorganised statement of profit and loss.

NOTES

Key Terms

Operating assets, operating liabilities, operating lease

Operating assets

Assets other than non-operating assets are operating assets. Examples of operating assets are property, plant and equipment, intangible assets, cash, trade receivables, deposits with other entities and loans.

Operating liabilities

Liabilities arising from operating activities are operating liabilities. Usually, liabilities other than borrowings are treated as operating liabilities.

Uncovered pension obligations

In the balance sheet, companies present the liability arising from defined benefit schemes for post-retirement benefits to employees. Under such schemes, the company's obligation is to pay defined benefits to employees. Examples of defined benefit obligation are pensions and gratuity payable to employees after retirement. Employees earn post-retirement benefits as they render service. Therefore, company's obligation increases every year. Obligation is reduced on account of payment of benefits to retired employees. The liability is measured at the difference between the defined benefit obligation and the fair value of the plan assets. Define benefit obligations are measured using the actuarial method. Plan assets are the assets that are created for settling the defined benefit obligations, when due. If the fair value of plan assets is higher than the obligation, an asset is recognised.

Uncovered pension liability refers to the excess of the pension and other post-retirement defined benefit obligations over the fair value of plan assets.

In reorganising the balance sheet, some analysts consider uncovered pension liability as 'debt equivalent' because if the firm had to cover the excess amount of the pension liability, it would have to borrow that much amount for transfer to the plan asset created for the purpose. There are others who consider uncovered pension liability as operating liability. If the amount is significant relative to the total liabilities, it is preferable to consider it as debt. In order to keep the computation of financial ratios simple, if, the uncovered liability is not significant, it should be treated as operating liability.

Deferred Tax Liability (Asset)

Analysts adopt two alternative approaches in treating deferred tax liability (net of deferred tax assets) in the reorganised balance sheet. Deferred tax liability may be considered as 'equity equivalent' or as an operating liability. In this text deferred tax liability (net of deferred tax asset) is considered as an operating liability.

Those who treat deferred tax liability as equity equivalent argue that the timing of reversal of deferred tax liability is significantly uncertain and there is no cost associated with it. Hence, the amount is invested in the business for the benefit of equity shareholders. Therefore, it is appropriate to add deferred tax liability to equity. To be consistent, deferred

NOTES

tax expense should be excluded from tax expense recognised in the statement of profit and loss. In effect, the accounting for the deferred tax liability is reversed. The net effect is that profit after tax reported in the statement of profit and loss is increased by the amount of deferred tax expense, and equity is increased by the amount of deferred tax liability recognised in the balance sheet.

Those who prefer to treat deferred tax liability as operating liability argue that deferred tax expense is similar to operating expenses, and therefore, the corresponding deferred tax liability should be considered as an operating liability. They also argue that usually operating liabilities (e.g., trade credit) are interest-free credits, and therefore, it is not a unique feature of deferred tax liability that no cost is associated with it. If deferred tax liability is considered as an operating liability, no adjustment is required in the statement of profit and loss.

An analyst should be consistent in his approach while reorganising financial statements of the same firm for different years or while restructuring financial statements of different firms for cross-sectional analysis.

Operating Lease

At present, in accordance with Ind AS 37, Leases, lessee classifies leases into operating lease and finance lease. In the case of operating lease, the lease rent is recognised as an expense in the statement of profit and loss. In the case of finance lease, the leased asset is recognised in the balance sheet at fair value and a corresponding liability (borrowing) is also recognised at the inception of the lease. Lease rent paid or payable under a finance lease is allocated to notional interest on the debt and repayment of the principal.

In cross-sectional analysis, analysts compare the financial position and performance of the firm with those of other firms operating in the same industry. In order to bring comparability among firms, analysts capitalise the lease rent paid or payable under operating lease. For example, in the airlines industry, companies own some aircrafts and obtain the remaining aircrafts under lease arrangements. Some lease arrangements are classified as *finance lease,* while others are classified as *operating lease*. Therefore, in order to bring comparability of financial statements, lease rent paid or payable under operating lease is *capitalised*. Capitalisation requires allocation of the lease rent into two components—*interest expense* and *depreciation*. We have discussed two methods, which are commonly used, for capitalising lease rent. It should be appreciated that the methods do not result in precise estimates of lease assets, corresponding liabilities, interest and depreciation. They only provide rough estimates.

Method 1: It is explained below:

$$\text{Rental expense}_t = \text{Asset value}_{t-1} \times [k_d + (1/\text{Asset life})]$$

$$\text{Asset value}_{t-1} = [\text{Rental expense}_t] \div [k_d + (1/\text{Asset life})]$$

Assume that during the current year, lease rent of ₹1,000 was recognised in the statement of profit and loss. Further, assume that the appropriate interest rate is 15 percent per annum and the useful life of the asset is 10 years. Then, the opening balance of the asset should be measured at [1,000/(0.15 + 1/10)] or ₹4,000. In effect, the lease rent of ₹1,000 is allocated as follows: Interest: (4,000 × 0.15) or ₹600; and Depreciation: (4,000/10) or ₹400.

The implied interest payment should be recognised in the statement of profit and loss while reorganising the same, and correspondingly, the tax expense should also be adjusted.

Method 2: The extant Ind AS 37, Leases, requires disclosing the following information regarding operating leases: The future minimum lease payments under non-cancellable operating leases in the aggregate and for each of the following periods:

(i) not later than one year.
(ii) later than one year and not later than five years.
(iii) later than five years.

Some analysts use thumb rule to allocate the total lease payment to each year covered over the estimated lease period. For example, the aggregate lease rent, which is payable later than one year and not later than five years, is divided by 4 to calculate average lease rent per year. The aggregate lease rent, which is payable later than five years, is divided by the average lease rent per year to calculate the lease term. Then, they calculate the present value of the cash outflows on account of payment of lease rent using an appropriate discounting rate (e.g., long-term borrowing rate). The leased asset and the corresponding liability are recognised at the present value of lease payments in the reorganised balance sheet.

ILLUSTRATION 13.1 Capitalisation of Operating Lease

SK Limited (SKL) provides the following information about non-cancellable operating leases:

(i) Lease rent payable not later than one year: ₹500.
(ii) Later than one year and not later than five years: ₹2,400.
(iii) Later than five years: ₹2,600.

The statement of profit and loss for the current year shows the lease rent for the current year is ₹500.

Required

Convert the operating lease into financial lease.

Solution

Average lease rent per year from year 2 to year 5: (₹2,400/4) or ₹600.
Number of years left after the fifth year: (₹2600/600) or 4.33 years.
Remaining lease-term, at the beginning of the current year: (1 + 1 + 4 + 4.33) or 10.33 years.
Estimated long-term borrowing rate: 12 percent per annum.
Estimated cash outflows: Current year: ₹500; Year 1: ₹500; Year 2 to Year 9.33: ₹600 per annum.

The present value of the cash outflow on account of lease rent using the discount rate of 12 percent per annum is: ₹3,293.

In the reorganised balance sheet as at the beginning of the year, the leased asset and the corresponding liability should be recognised at ₹3,793.

In the statement of profit and loss, the lease rent should be allocated between interest and depreciation.

Interest will be 12 percent on ₹3,793 or ₹455.

Assuming straight-line method of depreciation and remaining useful life at the beginning of the year (equal to the remaining lease term) is 10.33 years, the estimated depreciation is (3,793/10.33) or 367.

Therefore, total expenses in the reorganised current year's statement of profit and loss will be (455 + 367) or ₹822 against the lease rent of ₹500.

Managers are tempted to classify leases into operating leases; such classification results in:

(i) understatement of liabilities,
(ii) understatement of assets,
(iii) delaying recognition of expenses,
(iv) understatement of current liabilities (e.g., current portion of long-term lease liability), and
(v) understatement of interest and understatement of operating profit, which is profit before tax.

Ind AS 16, Leases, which will replace Ind AS 37 and expected to come into effect from April 1, 2019, requires entities to recognise the leased asset and corresponding liability (borrowing) in the balance sheet for all leases. Only in case of short-term lease (lease period of one year or less) and small items, entities shall have option to recognise the lease payment as an expense in the statement of profit and loss and not to recognise the leased asset and corresponding liability in the balance sheet. Ind AS 16 will not provide the opportunity to classify long-term leases into operating leases.

Non-Controlling Interest

Non-controlling interest (also called *minority interest*) represents outsiders' interest in the net assets of subsidiaries. It is a part of equity. However, for certain purposes (e.g., valuation of equity shares of the parent company), it is considered as debt. If it is included in borrowings, to be consistent, an amount of notional interest (without tax shield) should be recognised in the reorganised statement of profit and loss. For capital structure analysis, non-controlling interest is considered as a part of equity, as the measurement concentrates on mandatory payment aspects of liabilities.

NOTES

Redeemable Preference Shares

Redeemable preference shares are treated as debt instruments and companies present those in the balance sheet as a part of borrowings.

Key Terms
economic profit,
permanent profit,
operating profit

Self-Test Questions

Self-test question 13.3

Indicate whether the following statements are true (T) or false (F):

(i) Classification of assets and liabilities into operating and non-operating categories is not as important as it is made out to be, otherwise regulators would have mandated that classification for presentation in balance sheet.

(ii) Excess cash should not be treated as non-operating asset, as that is a very rough estimate and does not earn any return.

(iii) In analysing financial statements, trade investments are treated like other investments in financial assets due to lack of separate information on dividend from trade investments.

(iv) Amount invested in investment property is deducted from equity to evaluate the capital structure of the company.

(v) Uncovered pension liability, if material, should be treated as debt.

(vi) Deferred tax liability is often treated as quasi equity.

(vii) Redeemable preference shares are included in equity to evaluate capital structure of the company.

(viii) Non-controlling interest is included in debt to evaluate capital structure of the company.

Reorganisation of Statement of Profit and Loss and Analysis

Reorganisation of the statement of profit and loss should be consistent with reorganisation of the balance sheet.

Economic Profit, Permanent Profit, and Operating Profit

Economic profit

Economic profit measures the change in the shareholder value.

Economic profit is typically determined as cash flow during the period plus the change in the present value of expected future cash flows, represented by the change in the market value of the net assets of the company. Thus, economic profit includes both realised profit (cash flows) and unrealised profit (holding gain or loss). It is similar to measuring return on investment in equity, which is the total of realised gain (dividend) and unrealised gain (change in the fair value of the investment). Economic profit includes both recurring and no-recurring incomes and expenses. Therefore, it is not very useful in forecasting future earning capacity of the entity.

Permanent profit

Permanent profit is the profit that the business is expected to sustain over its life, given the current state of business conditions.

Permanent profit does not include non-recurring items of incomes and expenses. It is the stable average profit. It has long-term connotation. However, it can change on account of structural changes in the internal and external environments. For a going concern, permanent income is divided by the cost of capital to estimate the value of the business. It is also used to value the business using multiples.

Operating profit

Operating profit is the profit that arises from the operating activities of the firm.

Operating profit excludes finance costs and non-operating income (e.g., income from investments in financial assets). It also excludes net profit from discontinued operations. However, it includes non-recurring items like restructuring charges.

Operating profit is measured as Net Operating Profit After Taxes (NOPAT).

$$\text{NOPAT} = \text{Net profit from continuing operations} + \text{Interest expense} \times (1 - \text{Tax rate}) - \text{Non-operating income} \times (1 - \text{Tax rate})$$

Marginal tax rate is used to calculate the NOPAT when tax rates are different for different taxable income slab. If, as it is in India, a single corporate tax rate is applicable, the same is used.

Adjustments in Statement of Profit and Loss

Interest on uncovered pension obligation

If uncovered pension obligation is considered as debt, an amount of notional interest should be recognised in the reorganised statement of profit and loss. If uncovered pension obligation is considered as an operating liability, no adjustment is required in the statement of profit and loss.

Deferred tax expense

If deferred tax liability (net of deferred tax asset) is considered as equity equivalent, income tax expense should be reduced by deferred tax expense (income). If deferred tax liability (net of deferred tax asset) is considered as an operating liability, no adjustment is required in tax expense recognised in the statement of profit and loss.

In this text, deferred tax liability (net of deferred tax asset) is considered as an operating liability.

Preference dividend

Preference dividend on redeemable preference shares is presented in the statement of profit and loss as a part of finance cost. In analysing financial statements, preference dividend, whether paid or not, should be recognised as interest (without tax shield).

Operating lease rent

In reorganising the balance sheet, long-term operating lease is converted into finance lease. Therefore, operating lease rent should be allocated between depreciation and interest. Depending on the method of conversion, the total amount of interest and deprecation might be different from the amount of lease rent [*See* Illustration 13.1]

Income from investment property

When the carrying amount of the investment property is deducted from equity, income (adjusted for income tax) from investment properties should be excluded from income recognised in the reorganised statement of profit and loss. However, income from investment property is not disclosed separately in the notes to accounts unless the income is material. Therefore, if the information is not available, this adjustment is not required.

Comprehensive Income

Comprehensive income is the total of net profit and other comprehensive income. Comprehensive income is closer to economic income, but it is not economic income. This is so because many components of assets and liabilities are not measured at fair value. For example, most companies use the cost model to measure items of property, plant and equipment and liabilities are usually measured at amortised cost. Disclosure of other comprehensive income and comprehensive income in the statement of profit and loss is a recent phenomenon. Relevance of other comprehensive income is not yet established.

Some analysts argue that components of other comprehensive income are not relevant because they do not persist. Some researches find that some of the components of other comprehensive income are relevant for equity valuation. However, many believe that permanent profit is more relevant for equity valuation than the comprehensive income.

NOTES

In general, other comprehensive income may have some relevance in equity valuation, but are not relevant in performance evaluation.

Self-Test Questions

Self-test question 13.4

Indicate whether the following statements are true (T) or false (F):

(i) Computation of economic profit requires valuation of assets and liabilities at market value.
(ii) Permanent profit is a misnomer as the state of business environment seldom remains the same over a long period.
(iii) Operating profit is pre-tax profit.
(iv) Adjustments in the statement of profit and loss should be consistent with the adjustments in the balance sheet.
(v) Comprehensive income is considered relevant for performance evaluation and not for equity valuation.

SUMMARY

Analysts reorganise balance sheet and the statement of profit and loss for calculating financial ratios. They classify assets, liabilities, income and expenses into operating and non-operating categories. Published financial statements do not provide enough information required for precisely correct classification. Therefore, analysts often use judgement and apply thumb rule for roughly correct classification because in the absence of that categorisation, it is difficult to calculate meaningful financial ratios. In addition to classifying assets, liabilities, incomes and expenses into operating and non-operating categories, certain items require adjustments. They are uncovered pension obligation, deferred tax liability, non-controlling interest, investment in associates and joint ventures, lease classified as operating lease by the lessee and investment property. Adjustments in the statement of profit and loss should be consistent with adjustments in the balance sheet.

CASE STUDY: REORGANISED BALANCE SHEETS AND STATEMENT OF PROFIT AND LOSS

Reorganised Balance Sheet

The following are the explanations for reorganised consolidated balance sheets:

(i) Excess cash is calculated only for Infosys as it had large cash balances as at March 31, 2016 and March 31, 2017. For HUL and Suzlon, total cash balance has been considered as operating asset. To be conservative and keeping in view that most clients of Infosys and some of its assets are located outside India, five percent of operating revenue is considered operating cash. It is calculated as follows:

Revenue from operations: 2015–16: ₹62,441 crore, 2016–17: ₹68,484 crore; Operating cash balance: March 31, 2016: (62,441 × 0.05) or ₹3,122 crore; March 31, 2017: (₹68,484 × 0.05) or ₹3,424 crore; Excess cash: March 31, 2016: (₹32,697 – 3,122) or 29,575 crore; March 31, 2017: (₹22,625 – 3,424) or ₹19,201 crore.

(ii) (a) Investments, other than investments in associates and joint ventures, are considered as non-operating financial assets. (b) Bank balances other than those included in cash and cash equivalents are considered as non-operating financial assets. (c) Excess cash is considered as non-operating financial assets.

(iii) There is no investment property in the balance sheets of HUL and Infosys. In case of Suzlon, the carrying amount of the investment property is not material. Therefore, no adjustment is carried out in equity. It is included in operating assets.

(iv) Assets held for sale are included neither in non-operating assets nor in operating assets, as in profitability calculations, only profit or loss from continuing operations is included.

(v) Uncovered 'post-employment benefit liability' is considered as operating liability, as the amount is not significant.

TABLE 13.10

Reorganised Extract of Consolidated Balance Sheet of HUL, Infosys and Suzlon as at March 31, 2017

(Amount in ₹ crore)

Particulars	HUL	Infosys	Suzlon
ASSETS			
Operating Assets			
Non-current assets			
Non-financial	5,354	22,859	2,037
Financial	128	338	387
Total (A)	5,482	23,197	2,424
Current assets			
Non-financial	3,139	2,536	4,528
Financial	2,044	20,582	4161
Total (B)	5,183	23,118	8,689
Total operating assets (A + B) (C)	10,665	46,315	11,113
Non-operating Assets			
Non-current assets			
Non-financial	0	71	189
Financial	6	6,382	377
Total (D)	6	6,453	566
Current assets			
Non-financial	0	0	0
Financial	4,988	30,587	481
Total (E)	4,988	30,587	481
Total non-operating assets (D + E) (F)	4,994	37,040	1,047
Other Assets			
Assets held for sale (G)	47	0	0
Total Assets (C + F + G)	15,706	83,355	12,160
EQUITY			
Equity share capital	216	1,144	1,005
Other equity	6,528	67,838	(7,846)
Non-controlling interest	22	0	8
Total (Adjusted Equity)	6,766	68,982	(6,833)
LIABILITIES			
Operating Liabilities			
Non-current liabilities			
Non-financial	1,153	290	167
Financial	73	70	226
Total (A)	1,226	360	393
Current liabilities			
Non-financial	1,056	7,297	1,944
Financial	6,265	6,699	5,494
Total (B)	7,321	13,996	7,438
Total operating liabilities (A + B) (C)	8,547	14,356	7,831

(Contd.)

NOTES

TABLE 13.10

Reorganised Extract of Consolidated Balance Sheet of HUL, Infosys and Suzlon as at March 31, 2017 (*Contd.*)

Particulars	HUL	Infosys	Suzlon
Non-operating Liabilities			
Non-current liabilities			
Non-financial	0	0	0
Financial	0	0	4,841
Total (D)	0	0	4,841
Current liabilities			
Non-financial	0	0	0
Financial	277	0	6,321
Total (E)	277	0	6,321
Total non-operating liabilities (D + E) (F)	277		11,162
Other liabilities			
Non-financial	0	0	0
Financial	116	17	0
Total other liabilities (G)	116	17	0
Total liabilities (C + F + G)	8,940	14,373	18,993
Total equity plus liabilities	15,706	83,355	12,160

Notes:

(i) Other financial liability is unpaid dividend. This is a non-operating liability, but not in the nature of borrowings.

(ii) Non-operating non-financial non-current assets include investments in associates and joint ventures: HUL: Zero; Infosys: ₹71 crore; and Suzlon: ₹189 crore.

TABLE 13.11

Reorganised Extract of Consolidated Balance Sheet of HUL, Infosys and Suzlon as at March 31, 2016

(*Amount in ₹ crore*)

Particulars	HUL	Infosys	Suzlon
ASSETS			
Operating Assets			
Non-current assets			
Non-financial	4,270	21,469	1,944
Financial	147	311	595
Total (A)	4,417	21,780	2,539
Current assets			
Non-financial	3,251	2,158	3,214
Financial	2,333	18,707	3,350
Total (B)	5,584	20,865	6,564
Total operating assets (A + B) (C)	10,001	42,645	9,103
Non-operating Assets			
Non-current assets			
Non-financial	26	103	93
Financial	6	1,714	260
Total (D)	32	1,817	353
Current assets			
Non-financial	0	0	0
Financial	4,739	30,888	267
Total (E)	4,739	30,888	267
Total non-operating assets (D + E) (F)	4,771	32,705	620
Other Assets			
Assets held for sale (G)	22	0	0
Total Assets (C + F +G)	14,794	75,350	9,723

Particulars	HUL	Infosys	Suzlon
EQUITY			
Equity share capital	216	1,144	1,004
Other equity	6,357	60,600	(8,537)
Non-controlling interest	20	0	0
Total (Adjusted Equity)	6,593	61,744	(7,533)
LIABILITIES			
Operating Liabilities			
Non-current liabilities			
Non-financial	1,114	298	241
Financial	20	69	129
Total (A)	1,134	367	370
Current liabilities			
Non-financial	947	6,551	2,055
Financial	5,837	6,683	3,400
Total (B)	6,784	13,234	5,455
Total operating liabilities (A + B) (C)	7,918	13,601	5,825
Non-operating Liabilities			
Non-current liabilities			
Non-financial	0	0	0
Financial	0	0	9,225
Total (D)	0		9,225
Current liabilities			
Non-financial	0	0	0
Financial	177	0	2,206
Total liabilities (E)	177	0	2,206
Total non-operating liabilities (D + E) (F)	177		11,431
Other liabilities			
Non-financial	0	0	0
Financial	106	5	0
Total other liabilities (G)	106	5	0
Total liabilities (C + F + G)	8,201	13,606	17,256
Total equity plus liabilities	15,706	75,350	9,723

Notes:

(i) Other financial liability is unpaid dividend. This is a non-operating liability, but not in the nature of borrowings.

(ii) Non-operating non-financial non-current assets include investments in associates and joint ventures HUL: ₹26 crore; Infosys: ₹103 crore; Suzlon: ₹93 crore.

NOTES

Key Terms

Trend analysis, net financial obligation (NFO)

In order to facilitate analysing financial statements, reorganised balance sheet may be summarised as presented in Tables 13.12 and 13.13.

The following definitions are used to summarise reorganised balance sheets:

1. ***Net Financial Obligations and Net financial Assets (NFA):*** The NFO is measured as the difference between the amount of non-operating financial liabilities and non-operating financial assets. If the amount of financial assets exceeds the amount of financial obligations, the difference is Net Financial Assets (NFA).
2. ***Net Operating Assets (NOA) or Invested Capital:*** The amount of net operating assets is measured by deducting operating liabilities from operating assets. This should be equal to the total of the amount of equity and NFO reduced by assets that are included neither in operating assets nor in non-operating assets.

NOTES

TABLE 13.12

Summarised Reorganised Balance Sheets as at March 31, 2017

(Amount in ₹ crore)

Particulars	HUL	Infosys	Suzlon
NET OPERATING ASSETS			
Operating assets (A)	10,665	46,315	11,113
Operating liabilities (B)	8,547	14,356	7,831
Net operating assets (A – B)	2,118	31,959	3,282
NET FINANCIAL OBLIGATIONS			
Non-operating financial liabilities (C)	277	0	11,162
Unpaid dividend (D)	116	17	0
Non-operating financial assets (E)	4,994	36,969	858
Net financial obligations/(Net financial assets) (C + D – E) (F)	(4,601)	(36,952)	10,304
EQUITY (G)	6,766	68,982	(6,833)
OTHER ASSETS			
Investments in associates and joint ventures	0	71	189
Assets held for sale	47	0	0
Total other assets (H)	47	71	189
NET OPERATING ASSETS (F + G – H)	2,118	31,959	3,282

Notes:

(i) Unpaid dividend is not an operating liability, as it does not arise from operating transactions/events. For analysing financial statements, it is considered as interest-free borrowing.

(ii) Investment in associates and joint ventures is excluded from operating assets.

(iii) Asset held for sale is excluded from operating assets, as profit/(loss) from discontinued operations is excluded from profit that is considered for evaluating margin etc.

TABLE 13.13

Summarised Reorganised Balance Sheets as at March 31, 2016

(Amount in ₹ crore)

Particulars	HUL	Infosys	Suzlon
NET OPERATING ASSETS			
Operating assets (A)	10,001	42,645	9,103
Operating liabilities (B)	7,918	13,601	5,825
Net operating assets (A – B)	2,083	29,044	3,278
NET FINANCIAL OBLIGATIONS			
Non-operating financial liabilities (C)	177	0	11,431
Unpaid dividend (D)	106	5	0
Non-operating financial assets (E)	4,745	32,602	527
Net financial obligations/(Net financial assets) (C + D – E)(F)	(4,462)	(32,597)	10,904
EQUITY (G)	6,593	61,744	(7,533)
OTHER ASSETS			
Investments in associates and joint ventures	26	103	93
Assets held for sale	22	0	0
Total other assets (H)	48	103	93
Net operating assets (F + G – H)	2,083	29,044	3,278

Note: Same as under Table 13.12

Reorganised Statement of Consolidated Profit and Loss

Table 13.14 presents the reorganised statement of consolidated profit and loss of HUL, Infosys and Suzlon for the year ended on March 31, 2017. Table 13.9 presents the statement of consolidated profit and loss of those companies for year ended March 31, 2017 in the format (Schedule III, Division II) prescribed under the Companies Act, 2013.

NOTES

TABLE 13.14

Reorganised Statement of Consolidated Profit and Loss of HUL, Infosys and Suzlon for the Year Ended on March 31, 2017

(Amount in ₹ crore, except for EPS)

Particulars	**HUL**	**Infosys**	**Suzlon**
OPERATING INCOME			
Revenue from operations	35,759	68.484	12,692
Other operating income	0	0	22
Total (A)	35,759	68,484	12,714
COST OF SALES			
Cost of material consumed	11,946	0	8,291
Purchase of stock-in-trade	4,223	0	0
Changes in inventories of finished goods (including stock-in-trade) and work-in-progress	144	0	(749)
Excise duty	2,597	0	0
Total (B)	18,910	0	7,542
Gross profit (A – B) (C)	16,849	68,484	5,172
OPERATING EXPENSES			
Employee benefits expenses	1,743	37,659	1,046
Cost of technical sub-contractors	0	3,833	0
Travel expenses		2,235	
Cost of software packages and others	0	1,597	0
Communication expenses	0	549	0
Consultancy and professional charges	0	763	0
Depreciation and amortisation expenses	432	1,703	389
Foreign exchange loss/(gain)	0	(232)	0
Other expenses	8,766	3,244	1,626
Total (D)	10,941	51,351	3,061
Net operating profit before exceptional items and tax (C – D) (E)	5,908	17,133	2,111
Tax expense on operating profit before exceptional items	1,779	4,612	427
Net operating profit after tax before exceptional items (F)	4,129	12,521	1,684
Exceptional items after tax @34.61% (G)	155	0	0
Net operating profit after tax (F + G) (H)	4,284	12,521	1,684
Share of profit/(loss) from associates and joint ventures (I)	0	(30)	(48)
Profit after tax but before financial expenses from continuing operations (H + I) (J)	4,284	12,491	1,636
NET FINANCIAL EXPENSES			
Finance cost after tax @34.61%	23	0	842
Income from non-operating financial assets @34.61 (L)	241	1,862	58
Net financial expenses after tax (K)	(218)	(1,862)	784
Profit after tax and financing expenses from continuing operations (J–K) (L)	4,502	14,353	852
Profit/(Loss) from discontinued operations before tax	(13)	0	0
Tax expenses of discontinued operations	1	0	0
Profit/(Loss) from discontinued operations after tax (M)	(12)	0	0
Profit for the year (L + M) (N)	4,490	14,353	852
OTHER COMPREHENSIVE INCOME			
Items that will not be reclassified subsequently to profit or loss:			
Remeasurement of the net defined benefit plans	(33)	(45)	(16)
Equity instruments through other comprehensive income*	0	(5)	
Share of other comprehensive income in jointly controlled entities	0	0	0
Income tax related to items that will not be reclassified subsequently to profit or loss:			
Remeasurement of the net defined benefit plans	11		0
Items that will be reclassified subsequently to profit or loss:			
Fair value changes on cash flow hedges (net)		39	0
Exchange differences on translation of foreign operations		(257)	(230)

(*Contd.*)

NOTES

TABLE 13.14

Reorganised Statement of Consolidated Profit and Loss of HUL, Infosys and Suzlon for the Year Ended on March 31, 2017 (*Contd.*)

(Amount in ₹ crore, except for EPS)

Particulars	HUL	Infosys	Suzlon
Fair value of debt instruments through other comprehensive income*	2	(10)	0
Gains/(loss) on dilution of investment in subsidiaries			6
Income tax related to items that will be reclassified subsequently to profit or loss:			0
Fair value of debt instruments through other comprehensive income	0		0
Other comprehensive income, net of tax for the year (O)	(20)	(278)	(240)
Total comprehensive income for the year (N + O)	4,470	14,075	612
Profit attributable to:			
Owners of the company	4,476	14,353	858
Non-controlling interests	14	0	(6)
Other comprehensive income attributable to:			
Owners of the company	(20)	(278)	(255)
Non-controlling interests	0	0	15
Total comprehensive income attributable to:			
Owners of the company	4,456	14,075	603
Non-controlling interests	14	0	9
Earnings per equity share from continuing operations:			
Basic (₹)	20.68	62.80	1.71
Diluted (₹)	20.68	62.77	1.60
Earnings per equity share from discontinued operations:			
Basic (₹)	(0.06)	0	0
Diluted (₹)	(0.06)	0	0
Earnings per equity share from continued and discontinued operations:			
Basic (₹)	20.62	62.80	1.71
Diluted (₹)	20.62	62.77	1.60

Notes:

(i) (a) Gross profit is measured by deducting cost of sales (also called cost of goods sold) from operating income. In the absence of functional classification of expenses, it is not possible to calculate cost of sales precisely. For example, there is no information on how much of employee benefit expenses and depreciation and amortisation are attributable to manufacturing activities. However, a rough estimate of gross profit also provides some insights, particularly when we compare performance of the same entity over number of years or we compare performance of comparable companies.

(b) Gross profit figure for Infosys is meaningless. In the absence of information, it is not possible to estimate how much of employee benefits expense is attributable to employees directly engaged in software projects.

(ii) Income tax on 'operating profit before exceptional items and tax' is calculated by deducting from tax expense: (a) income tax on exceptional items; (b) income tax on income from non-operating financial assets; and adding income tax on finance cost. Income tax rate of 34.61 percent applicable to domestic companies is applied.

(a) HUL: 1,977 – (0.3461 × 237) – (0.3461 × 369) + (0.3461 × 35) = ₹1,779 crore

(b) Infosys: 5,598 – 0 – ((0.3461 × (3,080 – 232)) + 0 = ₹4,612 crore

(c) Suzlon: 12 – 0 – (0.3461 × 89) + (0.3461 × 1,288) = ₹427 crore

Other income of Infosys includes foreign exchange gain of ₹232, which is deducted from other income to calculate income from non-operating financial assets.

(iii) For the sake of keeping calculations simple for easy understanding of the method, corporate tax rate of 34.61 percent is applied to income from non-operating financial assets. Income tax on capital gain on sale of investments is calculated using different rates based on the nature of investment (e.g., equity or debt) and the holding period. Similarly dividend is not taxable in the hands of the recipient, subject to exceptions.

Observations

(i) Share of profit/(loss) from associates and joint ventures is not included in operating profit because investments in associates and joint ventures are considered as non-operating assets.

NOTES

(ii) Net Operating Profit After Tax (NOPAT) before exceptional items is closer to the concept of permanent profit. It is appropriate to take the average of 'NOPAT before exceptional items' for three years or a complete business cycle (in case of a company operating in cyclical industry like cement and steel) in order to measure permanent profit.

(iii) In this text, in ratios that use NOPAT as numerator or denominator, 'NOPAT before exceptional items' is used, as it is logical to exclude non-recurring incomes and expenses from operating profit that is used to measure performance.

EBITDA

Analysts calculate some ratios using 'Earnings Before Interest, Tax, Depreciation and Amortisation (EBITDA)' as numerator. It can be calculated from the information available in the reorganised statement of consolidated profit and loss.

$$\text{EBITDA} = \text{Net operating profit before exceptional items and tax} + \text{Depreciation and amortisation} \tag{13.1}$$

EBITDA for the year 2016–17:

HUL: ₹5,908 crore + 432 = ₹6,340 crore; Infosys: ₹17,133 + 1,703 = ₹18,836 crore; and Suzlon: ₹2,111 crore + 389 = ₹2,500 crore

ANSWERS TO SELF-TEST QUESTIONS

13.1 (i) T; (ii) T; (iii) T; (iv) T; (v) T

13.2 (i) F; (ii) F; (iii) T; (iv) T; (v) F

13.3 (i) F; (ii) F; (iii) T; (iv) T; (v) T; (vi) T; (vii) F; (viii) F

13.4 (i) T; (ii) T; (iii) F; (iv) T; (v) F

ASSIGNMENTS

Multiple Choice Questions

1. Tick the correct answer:

(i) Bias towards conservatism:

(a) Result in overstatement of assets.

(b) Result in understatement of assets and overstatement of liabilities.

(c) Result in understatement of assets and profit and overstatement of liabilities.

(d) None of the above.

(ii) The principle of conservatism aims to:

(a) protect users of financial statements from the inherent temptation of managers to disclose good news early and delay bad news.

(b) protect, primarily lenders and creditors, from the inherent temptation of managers to disclose good news early and delay bad news.

(c) protect users of financial statements from the inherent temptation of managers to disclose good news early and delay bad news, but it help lenders and creditors more than investors and potential investors and sometimes hurt the interests of investors and potential investors in equity.

(d) None of the above.

(iii) In analysing financial statements:

(a) Abnormal years should be excluded.

(b) In principle, abnormal years should be excluded, but in practice it is difficult to identify abnormal years, because every business goes through bad and good phases, particularly on the face of fast changing business environment.

(c) In principle, abnormal years should be excluded, but abnormal year should be narrowly defined in order to exclude those years in which business was adversely affected due to internal disruptions.

(d) None of the above.

(iv) Classification of assets, liabilities, incomes and expenses into operating and non-operating categories is important, because:
 (a) Analysts focus on operating performance.
 (b) Analysts focus on operating performance and the classification helps to calculate net financial obligations, which is useful in understanding the drivers of return on equity (ROE).
 (c) In cross-sectional analysis, it helps to compare apple with apple and even in trend analysis the focus is on understanding the trend in operating performance.
 (d) None of the above.

(v) Permanent profit:
 (a) Excludes non-recurring incomes and expenses.
 (b) Includes non-recurring incomes and expenses, but excluded non-operating incomes and expenses.
 (c) Excludes both non-recurring and non-operating incomes and expenses.
 (d) None of the above.

(vi) Uncovered pension obligation:
 (a) Should be considered as debt.
 (b) Should be considered as debt, only if the amount is material, otherwise it should be considered as operating liability.
 (c) Should be considered as debt, only if the amount is material, otherwise it should be considered as non-operating liability.
 (d) None of the above.

(vii) Non-controlling interest is:
 (a) Interest of shareholders, other than the parent, in the net assets of the subsidiary and it is treated as debt in analysing consolidated financial statements.
 (b) Interest of shareholders, other than the parent, in the net assets of the subsidiary and it is treated as equity in analysing consolidated financial statements.
 (c) Interest of shareholders, other than the parent, in the net assets of the subsidiary and it is treated as equity in analysing consolidated financial statements, but it is treated as debt for the purpose of equity valuation.
 (d) None of the above.

(viii) Investments in Associates and joint ventures are:
 (a) Considered as non-operating assets.
 (b) Considered as operating assets.
 (c) Considered as non-operating assets for calculating operating efficiency, but is considered as operating assets for calculating return on invested capital (ROIC).
 (d) None of the above.

(ix) Investments, which are a part of, treasury function:
 (a) Are considered as operating assets.
 (b) Are considered as non-operating assets.
 (c) Should be considered as operating assets, but due to lack of information are considered as non-operating assets.
 (d) None of the above.

(x) Investment property is:
 (a) A non-operating asset.
 (b) An operating asset.
 (c) A non-operating asset, but as it can be included neither in 'net operating assets' nor in 'net financial obligations', it is deducted from equity for analysing financial statements.
 (d) None of the above.

Ratio Analysis Computation and Interpretation

CHAPTER

14

Learning Objectives

The objective of this chapter is to provide an understanding of the techniques for calculating commonly used financial ratios and their interpretations. After reading this chapter, you will be able to understand the following:

- Return on invested capital (ROIC) and decomposition of ROIC
- Operating liability leverage (OLLEV) and its impact on ROIC
- Return on equity (ROE) and decomposition of ROE
- Gross profit ratio, operating profit ratio, and EBITDA ratio
- Turnover ratios
- DuPont model
- Liquidity and solvency
- Current ratio, working capital cycle and conversion cycle
- Gearing ratio, interest coverage ratio, fixed charge coverage ratio and debt service coverage ratio
- Economic value added (EVA)
- Segment analysis
- Market-to-book ratio, P/E ratio and PEG ratio

NOTES

Key Terms
NOPAT, invested capital

CASE STUDY: RETURN ON INVESTMENT AND PROFITABILITY ANALYSIS

Two widely used measures of Return on Investment (ROI) are 'Return On Invested Capital (ROIC)'; and 'Return on Equity (ROE)'. Some analysts use the term 'capital employed' to refer to invested capital, and thus, ROCE to refer to ROIC. That is little confusing, as traditionally, capital employed measures long-term investment in the company, and consequently excludes short-term borrowings.

ROIC measures return on total investment in the firm, while ROE measures return on investment in the equity capital of the firm.

Return on Invested Capital

Return On Invested Capital (ROIC) is also called Return on Net Operating Assets (RNOA). We shall use the term interchangeably.

Importance of ROIC

The ROIC is widely used to measure profitability, managerial effectiveness and planning and control.

The ROIC is the most important summary measure of profitability. It uses information from both the statement of profit and loss and the balance sheet. Therefore, it is much superior than measures that use information available either in the statement of profit and loss or balance sheet. For example, measuring growth in revenue or net profit fails to provide insights into profitability.

The ROIC depends on the effectiveness of managing resources. It depends on the manager's ability to formulate right strategy and execute the same effectively. In other words, it depends on the operating and financing decisions. Therefore, the ROIC computed over a year or longer helps in assessing the managerial effectiveness.

Managers use the ROIC in measuring profitability of different business segments. They estimate expected ROIC from alternative uses of resources, establish target ROIC for the chosen alternative and compare actuals with the target for taking corrective actions. Therefore, the ROIC is relevant for planning and control.

Measuring profitability using the ROIC has the following advantages:

(i) It allows analysts to compare success of comparable companies with invested capital; and

(ii) It allows analysts to compare ROIC of a company with its cost of capital.

A company creates shareholder value only when it earns ROIC higher than its cost of capital. It destroys value when ROIC is lower than the cost of capital. It neither creates nor destroys value when ROIC equals cost of capital.

Computation of ROIC

ROIC is computed as:

$$\text{ROIC} = (\text{NOPAT})/(\text{Average NOA})$$

Table 13.12 and Table 13.13 present the computation of 'Net Operating Assets (NOA)'. The NOA measure the invested capital. Table 13.14 presents the computation of NOPAT. For the computation of the ROIC, NOPAT before exceptional items is used, as it is preferable to exclude non-recurring items from the computation of ROIC.

Table 14.1 presents the computation of ROIC of HUL, Infosys and Suzlon for the year 2016–17.

TABLE 14.1

ROIC for the Year 2016–17

(Amount in ₹ crore, except ROIC)

Particulars	HUL	Infosys	Suzlon
NOA as at March 31, 2017 (A)	2,118	31,959	3,282
NOA as at March 31, 2016 (B)	2,083	29,044	3,278
Average NOA [(A+B)/2] (C)	2,101	30,502	3,280
NOPAT before exceptional items (D)	4,129	12,521	1,684
ROIC [(D/C)×100]	196.53%	41.05%	51.34%

Note: (i) NOA is abbreviation of 'Net Operating Assets'; NOPAT is abbreviation of 'Net Operating Profit After Tax'.

ROIC considering investment in associates and joint ventures as operating asset

Investments in associates and joint ventures are strategic investments. Although inclusion of those investments in operating assets included in invested capital makes further analysis difficult, analysts calculate ROIC, including those in operating assets to understand the impact of those investments on ROIC. When those investments are included in operating assets, share profit or loss of associates and joint ventures are also included in the operating income (Table 14.2).

TABLE 14.2

ROIC (Including Investments in Associates and Joint Ventures in Operating Assets) for the Year 2016–17

(Amount in ₹ crore, except ROIC)

Particulars	HUL	Infosys	Suzlon
NOA as at March 31, 2017 (A)	2,118	31,959	3,282
Investments in associates and joint ventures as at March 31, 2017 (B)	0	71	189
NOA as at March 31, 2016 (C)	2,083	29,044	3,278
Investments in associates and joint ventures as at March 31, 2016 (D)	26	103	93
Average NOA [(A + B + C + D)/2] (E)	2,114	30,589	3,421
NOPAT before exceptional items (F)	4,129	12,521	1,684
Share of profit/(loss) of associates and joint ventures (G)	0	(30)	(48)
NOPAT, including share of profit/(loss) of associates and joint ventures but before exceptional items (H)	4,129	12,491	1,636
ROIC [(H/E)×100]	195.32%	40.83%	47.76%

Note: (i) NOA is the abbreviation of 'Net Operating Assets'; NOPAT is the abbreviation of 'Net Operating Profit After Tax'.

Decomposition of ROIC

The ROIC calculated in Table 14.1 is decomposed into its components. In Table 14.1, the ROIC is calculated without including 'investment in associates and joint ventures' in invested capital and 'share of profit or loss of associates and joint ventures' in operating profit. This is because inclusion of 'share of profit or loss of associates and joint ventures' in operating profit distorts the calculation of margin, as 'total operating income' does not include the share of the parent in the operating income of associates and joint ventures.

$$\text{ROIC} = \text{Net Operating Margin} \times \text{Operating Asset Turnover} \times \text{Adjustment for tax}$$

$$\text{ROIC} = \frac{\text{NOPAT}}{\text{Average NOA}} = \frac{\text{Operating profit before tax}}{\text{Total Operating Income}} \times \frac{\text{Total Operating Income}}{\text{Average NOA}} \times \frac{\text{NOPAT}}{\text{Operating profit before tax}}$$

NOTES

Key Terms
Operating liability leverage

Table 14.3 presents Decomposition of ROIC

TABLE 14.3

Decomposition of ROIC

(Amount in ₹ crore, except ROIC)

Particulars	HUL	Infosys	Suzlon
Average NOA (A) [See Table 14.1]	2,101	30,502	3,280
Net operating profit before exceptional items and tax (B)	5,908	17,133	2,111
NOPAT before exceptional items (C)	4,129	12,521	1,684
Total operating income (D)	35,759	68,484	12,714
Operating margin [(B/D)×100] (E)	16.522%	25.018%	16.604%
Net operating asset turnover (D/A) (E)	17.02×	2.245×	3.876×
Tax adjustment (C/B)	0.699	0.715	0.798
ROIC (D×E)	196.53%	41.05%	51.34%

Notes:

(i) While margin is expressed in percentage, turnover is expressed in 'number of times' (shorthand, ×).

(ii) Some analysts calculate the margin by using the formula: Margin = (NOPAT/Total Operating Income). In that case, ROIC is decomposed as, ROIC = Margin × Turnover

(iii) Some analysts use the term 'sales' instead of 'total operating income'. However, it is preferable to use the term 'total operating income', as the term is appropriate for companies operating in both manufacturing and service sectors. It is also appropriate for finance companies.

Observations

(i) Decomposition of ROIC helps us in carrying out simple sensitivity analysis. For example, if Infosys feel pressure on margin and the operating margin reduces by 2 percent, ROIC will come down to (23.08 × 2.245 × 0.715) or 37.05 percent from 41.05 percent. If HUL's operating margin reduces by 2 percent, ROIC will come down to (14.522 × 17.02 × 0.699) or 172.77 percent from 196.53 percent.

(ii) The drivers of value of an entity (Equity + Debt) are ROIC, growth and Weighted Average Cost of Capital (WACC). Therefore, the challenge before the management is how to achieve growth without reducing ROIC. It is challenging to balance between growth and operating margin. WACC does not change significantly unless the industry structure and business environment change significantly, unless the risk-free interest rate changes.

Effect of Operating Liability Leverage

Operating Liability Leverage (OLLEV) is measured as follows:

$$\text{OLLEV} = \frac{\text{Average operating liabilities}}{\text{Average net operating assets}}$$

The relationship between ROIC and OLLEV is as follows:

$$\text{ROIC} = \frac{\text{NOPAT}}{\text{Total operating revenue}} \times \frac{\text{Total operating revenue}}{\text{Average operating assets}} \times (1 + \text{OLLEV})$$

Table 14.4 presents the effect of Operating Liability Leverage (OLLEV)

TABLE 14.4

Effect of Operating Liability Leverage

(Amount in ₹ crore, except ROIC)

Particulars	HUL	Infosys	Suzlon
Average NOA (A) [*See* Table 14.1]	2,101	30,502	3,280
NOPAT before exceptional items (B)	4,129	12,521	1,684
Total operating income (C)	35,759	68,484	12,714
Operating assets as at March 31, 2016 (D)	10,001	42,645	9,103

NOTES

Particulars	HUL	Infosys	Suzlon
Operating assets as at March 31, 2017 (E)	10,665	46,315	11,113
Average operating assets [(E+F)/2] (F)	10,333	44,480	10,108
Operating liabilities as at March 31, 2016 (G)	7,918	13,601	5,825
Operating liabilities as at March 31, 2017 (H)	8,547	14,356	7,831
Average operating liabilities [(H+I)/2] (I)	8,233	13,979	6,828
OLLEV (I/A) (J)	3.918×	0.458×	2.082×
NOPAT/Total Op. Rev (B/C) (K)	11.547%	18.283%	13.245%
Total Op. Rev/Av. Op. Assets (C/F) (L)	3.461×	1.540×	1.258×
ROIC [K×L× (1+J)]	196.53%	41.05%	51.34%

Observations

(i) The NOA is the difference between the amount of operating assets and the amount of operating liabilities. Therefore, increase in operating liabilities reduces NOA. This is advantageous so long as the NOPAT is not affected by increase in operating liabilities. The NOPAT is affected if vendors increase the price of inputs to cover interest on outstanding credit to the company.

(ii) Operating Liability Leverage (OLLEV) depends on the bargaining power of the company vis-à-vis its suppliers. For example, OLLEV for HUL is 3.918, while it is 2.082 in case of Suzlon. In case of Infosys, it is quite low at 0.458 because, Infosys being a service company, trade payables constitute a very insignificant part of its operating liabilities.

(iii) It is interesting to compare turnover of net operating assets and turnover of gross operating assets. HUL: Turnover of net operating assets: 17.02, Turnover of gross operating assets: 3.461; Infosys: Turnover of net operating assets: 2.245, Turnover of gross operating assets: 1.540; and Suzlon: Turnover of net operating assets: 3.876, Turnover of gross operating assets: 1.258. Managers endeavour to increase the turnover of gross operating assets because OLLEV has no bearing on the productivity of gross operating leverage.

Self-Test Questions

Self-test question 14.1

Indicate whether the following statements are true (T) or false (F):

(i) The terms 'invested capital' and 'net operating assets' are used interchangeably.

(ii) ROIC is relevant for planning and control, and also, for measuring managerial efficiency.

(iii) Investments in associates and joint ventures are strategic investments.

(iv) ROIC is driven solely by margin earned by the company on its operating income.

(v) It is not true always true that higher the OLLEV, better is the ROIC.

SUMMARY

Return on invested capital (ROIC) is used widely to measure profitability, managerial effectiveness and planning and control. The ROIC is the most important summary measure of profitability. It ROIC is not affected by the capital structure decision. Therefore, ROIC of companies operating in the same industry are comparable, irrespective of different financing strategies. The drivers of ROIC are operating margin, Net Operating Assets (NOA) turnover and tax adjustment. Managers strive to balance margin and turnover to improve ROIC. Higher Operating Liability Leverage (OLLEV) improves the ROIC so long as it do not affect the operating margin.

Return on Equity

Importance of Return on Equity

Return On Equity (ROE) is relevant from the perspective of investors in the equity capital of the company (hereafter, shareholders). It is compared with the cost of equity to the company. Cost of equity measures the expected return on investment by shareholders. The ROE is used in valuation of equity of a company.

Computation of Return on Equity

The following is the formula for computation of return on equity:

$$\text{ROE} = [(\text{Net profit})/(\text{Average equity})] \times 100$$

Net profit is presented in the statement of profit and loss after deducting dividend on redeemable preference shares. Dividend on redeemable preference shares is a component of finance cost. In India, companies are not permitted to issue preference shares other than redeemable preference shares. If preference shares are not redeemable, preference dividend, whether paid or not, is deducted from the net profit and adjusted net profit is used for the computation of the ROE.

Reported net profit should be adjusted for 'profit or loss from discontinued operations after tax', as that is a transitory component of net profit. To achieve consistency, equity should be reduced by the carrying amount of the 'asset held for sale'.

Table 14.5 presents the computation of ROE.

TABLE 14.5

ROE for the Year 2016–17

(Amount in ₹ crore, except for ROE)

Particulars	HUL	Infosys	Suzlon
Equity as at March 31, 2017 (A)	6,766	68,982	(6,833)
Asset held for sale as at March 31, 2017 (B)	47	0	0
Equity as at March 31, 2016 (C)	6,593	61,744	(7,533)
Asset held for sale as at March 31, 2016 (D)	22	0	0
Average equity adjusted for assets held for sale [(A – B + C – D)/2] (E)	6,645	65,363	(7,183)
Net profit for the year 2016–17 (F)	4,490	14,353	852
Profit/(loss) after tax from discontinued operations (G)	(12)	0	0
Exceptional items after tax (H)	155	0	
Net profit adjusted for profit/(loss) after tax from discontinued operations (F – G – H) (I)	4,347	14,353	852
ROE [(I/E)×100]	65.418%	21.959%	Not applicable

Notes

(i) Profit/(loss) after tax from discontinued operations and exceptional items after tax have been excluded from net profit for computing the ROE because of their transitory nature. Those were also excluded in computing net operating profit after tax (NOPAT) for computing return on invested capital (ROIC).

(ii) Negative equity (in case of Suzlon) shows that equity investment, which represents owners' capital, is less than zero. Therefore, the question of the ROE does not arise. The number for the ROE that will be obtained by applying the formula will be meaningless.

Decomposition of Return on Equity

The relationship between Return On Equity (ROE), Return On Invested Capital (ROIC), Financial Leverage (FINLEV), and Net Borrowing Cost (NBC) can be illustrated as follows:

$$\text{ROE} = \text{ROIC} + \text{FLEV} \times \text{Spread}$$

where spread is the difference between ROIC and NBC.

ROIC is also called Return On Net Operating Assets (RNOA).

Financial leverage (FLEV) is the ratio of net financial obligations to equity. For example, if invested capital is ₹100, of which ₹25 is financed by equity and ₹75 is net financial obligations. Therefore, FLEV is (75/25) or 3.

Trading in equity

The relationship provides an insight into the effect of financial leverage on return on equity (ROE). If the net borrowing cost (NBC) is lower than ROIC, the spread is positive and higher leverage results in higher ROE. This is called *trading in equity.*

Key Terms
Financial leverage, trading in equity

ILLUSTRATION 14.1 Effect of Financial Leverage on ROE

The average return on invested capital of SM Limited (SML) is 50 percent. Its net borrowing cost (after tax) is 10 percent. SML has not invested any amount in non-operating financial assets. 75 percent of its invested capital is financed by equity.

Required

(i) Calculate the ROE of SML; and
(ii) Calculate the ROE of SML, assuming that it reduces the proportion of its investment in equity to 50 percent.

Solution

(i) Spread = (50% – 10%) or 40%; FLEV = (25/75) or 0.3333; ROIC = 50%
Therefore, ROE = 50% + (0.3333 × 40%) = (50% + 13.33%) = 63.33%
(ii) If investment in equity is reduced to 50%, FLEV will be (50/50) or 1.

Assuming that ROIC and borrowing cost remain the same,

ROE = 50% + (1 × 40%) = (50% + 40%) = 90%

Increase in financial leverage, increases the return on equity, if the entity is able to borrow at a rate (after tax) lower than the return on invested capital. However, it should not be concluded that higher financial leverage (FLEV) benefits equity shareholders. This is so because increase in the proportion of net financial obligation (NFO) in the capital structure beyond a limit increases the risk of equity investment and increase in ROE may not be commensurated with the increase in financial risk. What should be the borrowing limit is a matter of judgement. Moreover, there are other costs of debt, which cannot be quantified. For example, debt covenants do not allow the company to take risks, which are acceptable to equity shareholder, who have, by definition, higher risk-appetite than lenders. This is the reason that prosperous companies do not like to have debt in their capital structure.

Net Borrowing Cost (NBC)

Net borrowing cost is calculated by dividing Net Financial Expense (NFE) by average Net Financial Obligation (NFO). If NFE is negative, it is appropriate to calculate return on Net Financial Asset (NFA).

Table 14.6 presents the computation of net borrowing cost (NBC).

TABLE 14.6

Computation of Net Borrowing Cost (NBC) for the Year 2016–17

(Amount in ₹ crore, except for NBC)

Particulars	HUL	Infosys	Suzlon
Net financial obligations/(net financial assets) as at March 31, 2017 (A)	(4,601)	(36,952)	10,304
Net financial obligations/(net financial assets) as at March 31, 2016 (B)	(4,462)	(32,597)	10,904
Average net financial obligations/(net financial assets) [(A+B)/2] (C)	(4,531.5)	(34,774.5)	10,604
Net financial expenses after tax/(net financial income after tax) for the year 2016–17 (D)	(218)	(1,862)	784
Net borrowing cost/Return on net financial assets (D/C)	4.811%*	5.354%*	7.393%**

*Return on net financial assets; **Net borrowing cost

NOTES

Financial Leverage (FLEV)

Net financial leverage, or simply Financial Leverage (FLEV), is calculated by dividing Net Financial Obligations (NFO) by equity, i.e., FLEV = (NFO/E).

Gross Financial Leverage (GFLEV) is calculated by dividing 'net operating assets' (NOA) by equity, i.e., GFLEV = (NOA/E).

The calculation of average FLEV at the end of March 31, 2017 is shown in Table 14.7.

TABLE 14.7

Average Financial Leverage (FLEV) as at March 31, 2017

(Amount in ₹ crore)

Particulars	HUL	Infosys	Suzlon
Equity as at March 31, 2017 (A)	6,766	68,982	(6,833)
Asset held for sale as at March 31, 2017 (B)	47	0	0
Equity as at March 31, 2016 (C)	6,593	61,744	(7,533)
Asset held for sale as at March 31, 2016 (D)	22	0	0
Average equity adjusted for assets held for sale [(A–B+C–D)/2] (E)	6,645	65,363	(7,183)
Net financial obligations as at March 31, 2017 (F)	(4,601)	(36,952)	10,304
Net financial obligations as at March 31, 2016 (G)	(4,462)	(32,597)	10,904
Average net financial obligations [(F+G)/2]	(4,531.5)	(34,774.5)	10,604
Average financial leverage (FLEV)	–0.6819	–0.5320	Not applicable*

*Equity being negative, FLEV cannot be calculated.

Return on invested capital (ROIC) is calculated taking into account investment in associates and joint ventures to present the relationship between ROIC, financial leverage, and net borrowing cost. The relationship is presented in Table 14.8:

TABLE 14.8

Relationship between ROIC, FLEV and NBC

(Amount in ₹ crore, except ROIC, NBC, spread and ROE)

Particulars	HUL	Infosys	Suzlon
ROIC (A)	195.32%	40.83%	47.76%
Financial leverage (B)	–0.6819	–0.5320	Not applicable
Net borrowing cost (C)	4.81%	5.35%	7.39%
Spread (A – C)(D)	190.51%	35.48%	40.37%
ROE [A + B × D]	65.41%	21.96%	Not applicable

For intuitive understanding, when the amount of non-operating financial assets exceeds the amount of non-operating financial obligations, the following formula, i.e.,

ROE = ROIC + FLEV × Spread

can be rewritten as

ROE = ROIC – [(Net financial assets/Equity) × (ROIC – Return on net financial assets)]

The ratio [(Net financial assets/Equity) is the same as financial leverage in Table 14.8, except that it is positive, while financial leverage is negative. Similarly, spread in Table 14.8 is (ROIC – Return on net financial assets). Therefore, we may calculate the ROE as follows:

ROE of HUL = [195.32 – (0.6819 × 190.51)] or 65.41%

ROE of HUL = [40.83 – (0.5320 × 35.48)] or 21.96%.

Observations

(i) Our sensitivity analysis (*see* observations under Table 14.3) shows that 2 percent reduction in operating margin would reduce ROIC, in case of HUL, to 172.77 percent and in case of Infosys, to 37.05 percent. Consequently, in case of HUL,

ROE would be reduced to [172.77 + (–0.6819 × 167.96)] or 56.56 percent from 65.41 percent. Similarly, in case of Infosys, ROE would be reduced to [37.05 +(–0.5320 × 31.70)] or 20.19 percent from 21.96 percent.

(ii) Infosys is holding significant amount of excess cash, which earns no return. Therefore, if Infosys returns excess cash through share buy-back, its return on net financial assets will improve from current 5.35 percent and ROE will improve. In fact, in December 2017, Infosys has returned ₹13,000 crore to shareholders through share buy-back.

Self-Test Questions

Self-test question 14.2

Indicate whether the following statements are true (T) or false (F):

(i) The ROE is used for valuation of equity.

(ii) Trading in equity is always beneficial to shareholders.

(iii) When a prosperous company holds excess cash, the ROE is affected adversely.

(iv) ROE for a company having negative net worth is negative.

(v) Companies without debt in the capital structure may not be considered too conservative as borrower often restricts companies from taking legitimate risks, which adversely affects the ROIC.

SUMMARY

Return on equity (ROE) is relevant from the perspective of investors in the equity capital of the company It is compared with the cost of equity to the company and is used in valuation of equity of a company. The ROE depends on three variables—ROIC, financial leverage and spread, which is the difference between the ROIC and net borrowing cost. If a company is able to borrow at a cost (net of tax) that is lower than the ROIC, the ROE will improve with higher proportion of borrowing in the capital structure. This is called *trading in equity*. However, excessive borrowings hurt shareholders. If the company's investment in financial assets exceeds borrowing, and the net return (Return on investments – Finance cost) on net investment (Investments – Financial obligations) is lower than the ROIC, the ROE is lower than the ROIC.

Profitability and Operating Ratios

Return on invested capital is driven by three factors—net operating margin, invested capital turnover (often called asset turnover) and income tax adjustment. Operating margin is measured by Operating Profit Before Tax (OPBT). Analysts use various profitability ratios and operating ratios to understand the drivers of net operating margin. In this section, we shall discuss those profitability measures and operating ratios.

OPBT Margin

The OPBT margin is calculated by dividing the OPBT by total operating income for the period. It is the appropriate metric for the measurement of operational efficiency of entities (Table 14.9).

TABLE 14.9

OPBT Margin for the Year 2016–17

(Amount in ₹ crore, except EBITDA Margin)

Particulars	HUL	Infosys	Suzlon
Total operating income (A)	35,759	68,484	12,714
Net operating profit before exceptional items and tax (OPBT) (B)	5,908	17,133	2,111
OPBT margin [(B/A)×100] (E)	16.525%	25.018%	16.604%

NOTES

Key Terms
Gross profit, EBITDA

Observations

(i) Operating margin often is determined by the industry structure and competitive position of the company. Therefore, the operating margins of HUL, Infosys and Suzlon are not comparable.

(ii) Analysis of trend in operating margin of a company provides significant insight into the changing strategy of the company and increasing or decreasing attractiveness of the industry. A company may change product portfolio through diversification, enhance focus on a particular business segment or adopt a different business model to improve operating margin.

(iii) Comparing operating margin of comparable companies one can get an insight into the competitive positions of companies.

Earnings Before Interest and Tax (EBIT) Margin

Some analysts consider that EBIT is the measure of operating profit. This is not correct, as EBIT includes other income (e.g., income from investments in financial assets). However, if the non-operating income is insignificant, the EBIT may be used as a proxy for the OPBT.

Operating Margin (NOPAT/Total operating income)

Some analysts measure operating margin by using NOPAT in the numerator. They are of the view that income tax is an operating expense like any other operating expense. It is not worth debating the issue whether (NOPAT/Total operating income) is a better measure of operating profit margin than (OPBT/Total operating income) ratio. What is important is that one should be consistent in selecting the ratio for measuring operating profit margin.

We should keep in mind that in calculating return on invested capital, the NOPAT should be used as numerator of the ratio. Table 14.10 presents operating margin using the formula (NOPAT/Total operating income) of HUL, Infosys and Suzlon for the year 2016–17.

TABLE 14.10

Operating Margin (NOPAT/Total Operating Income) for the Year 2016–17

(Amount in ₹ crore, except EBITDA margin)

Particulars	HUL	Infosys	Suzlon
Total operating income (A)	35,759	68,484	12,714
Net Operating Profit After Tax (NOPAT) before exceptional items (F)	4,129	12,521	1,684
Operating (NOPAT) margin [(D/A)×100] (E)	11.547%	18.282%	13.245%

Gross Profit Margin

Gross profit is the difference between the amount of operating income and cost of sales. *Cost of sales* is the total of the amount of purchase price or manufacturing cost, logistic expenses and other costs incurred to bring the goods to the location and condition of sale. Cost of sales does not include operating expenses, including expenses incurred on brand promotion and advertisement. Gross profit is a good metric for measuring procurement, manufacturing and logistics efficiency. This is an important ratio for companies, such as merchandising companies, the overall profitability of which depends largely on their gross profit. However, we should use the gross profit ratio cautiously. A company may improve gross profit by increasing the operating revenue through sales promotion activities without actually improving the operating result, because sales promotion expense is an operating expense and is not included in the cost of sales.

Published statement of profit and loss does not provide enough information for calculating gross profit. Therefore, an external financial analyst cannot calculate the gross profit ratio precisely.

EBITDA Margin

Earnings Before Interest, Tax Depreciation, and Amortisation (EBITDA) is a proxy for pre-tax cash operating profit. Depreciation and amortisation are non-cash expenses. Other expenses are paid in cash immediately or within a short period. Therefore, the EBITDA is considered to be the proxy for pre-tax cash operating profit. The EBITDA to 'total operating revenue' is a good metric to assess the profitability of companies operating in capital-intensive industries (e.g., companies providing mobile telephone services and power distribution companies). These companies are not required to invest in facilities on a continuous basis for replacement or for balancing facilities. Therefore, they focus on improving the cash margin in order to improve the ROIC. When a company goes through a bad phase, it endeavours to earn at least positive EBITDA.

The EBITDA margins of companies operating in the same industry, but who have created facilities at different points in time, are comparable. Table 14.11 presents the EBITDA margin of HUL, Infosys and Suzlon for the year 2016–17.

TABLE 14.11

EBITDA Margin for the Year 2016–17

(Amount in ₹ crore, except EBITDA Margin)

Particulars	HUL	Infosys	Suzlon
Total operating income (A)	35,759	68,484	12,714
Net operating profit before exceptional items and tax (B)	5,908	17,133	2,111
Depreciation and amortisation expenses (C)	432	1,703	389
EBITDA (B+C) (D)	6,340	18,836	2,500
EBITDA margin [(D/A)×100] (E)	17.730%	27.504%	19.663%

Operating Ratios

Operating ratio is calculated by dividing each operating expense by total operating income. This ratio is used to evaluate operating efficiency. Usually, lower the operating ratio, better is the operating efficiency. Higher gross profit ratio compared to earlier years shows improvement in procurement and manufacturing efficiency in terms of cost management. Lower operating ratios as compared to earlier years reflect improvement in operating efficiency and effective cost management in administration, marketing and sales functions. One should be careful in interpreting operating ratios related to discretionary expenses. In case of discretionary expenses, lower operating ratio might not reflect improved efficiency. For example, lower operating ratio for research expense may need deeper investigation, as the management might have cut the research expense to improve profit, which is not desirable.

Comparing gross profit ratio and operating ratios of the entity with those of competitors helps in understanding competitors' business strategy and drivers of competitive advantage.

Table 14.12 presents operating ratios of HUL, Infosys and Suzlon for the year 2016–17.

TABLE 14.12

Operating Ratios for the Year 2016–17

(Amount in ₹ crore, except ratios in bracket)

Particulars	HUL	Infosys	Suzlon
Total operating income (A)	35,759	68,484	12,714
Employee benefits expenses	1,743 (4.874%)	37,659 (54.989%)	1,046 (8.592%)
Cost of technical sub-contractors	0	3,833 (5.597%)	0
Travel expenses	0	2,235 (3.264%)	0
Cost of software packages and others	0	1,597 (2.332%)	0
Communication expenses	0	549 (0.802%)	0

(Contd.)

NOTES

TABLE 14.12

Operating Ratios for the Year 2016–17 (*Contd.*)

Particulars	HUL	Infosys	Suzlon
Consultancy and professional charges	0	763 (1.114%)	0
Depreciation and amortisation expenses	432 (1.208%)	1,703 (2.487%)	389 (3.195%)
Foreign exchange loss/(gain)	0	(232) (0.339%)	0
Other expenses	8,766 (24.514%)	3,244 (4.737%)	1,626 (13.356%)
Total operating expenses	10,941 (30.596%)	51,351 (74.982%)	3,061 (25.414%)

Note: Figure in bracket below the expense amount shows the operating ratio.

Other expenses form significant portion of total operating expenses. Therefore, it is necessary to analyse operating ratios for items included in 'other expenses'. Companies provide details in notes to accounts.

Table 14.13 presents additional operating ratios of HUL, Infosys and Suzlon for the year 2016–17.

TABLE 14.13

Additional Operating Ratios (Not Included in Table 14.12) for the Year 2016–17

(*Amount in ₹ crore, except ratios in bracket*)

Particulars	HUL	Infosys	Suzlon
Total operating income (A)	35,759	68,484	12,714
Advertising and promotion/brand and marketing	3,542 (9.905%)	342 (0.499%)	19 (0.156%)
Carriage and freight	1,516 (4.239%)		
Royalty	1,069 (2.989%)		
Power, fuel, light, water	295 (0.825%)	228 (0.033%)	71 (0.583%)
Rent	267 (0.747%)		78 (0.641%)
Processing charges	193 (0.540%)		
Travelling and motor car expenses	179 (0.501%)		133 (1.092%)
Repairs and maintenance	131 (0.367%)	1,242 (1.814%)	48 (0.394%)
Rates and taxes (excluding income tax)	116 (0.324%)	148 (0.216%)	31 (0.255%)
Corporate social responsibility expense	107 (0.299%)	230 (0.336%)	17 (0.140%)
Operating lease payment	0	491 (0.717%)	
Impairment recognised (reversed)	0	140 (0.204%)	
Stores and spares consumed			182 (1.495%)
Factory and site expenses			90 (0.739%)
Performance guarantee expenditure			158 (1.298%)
Liquidated damages expenditure			151 (1.240%)

Particulars	HUL	Infosys	Suzlon
Operations and maintenance warranty expenditure			121 (0.994%)
Freight outward and packing expenses			332 (2.727%)
Consultancy charges			105 (0.862%)
Exchange difference loss (gain)			(297) (2.440%)
Miscellaneous expenses	1,351 (3.778%)	423 (0.618%)	387 (3.179%)
Total other operating expenses	8,766 (24.514%)	3,244 (4.737%)	1,626 (13.356%)

Note: We have added some expenses, details of which are provided by the companies, with miscellaneous expenses.

Observations

(i) There is no uniformity of practice as to which expenses should be included under the heading 'other expenses' on the face of the statement of profit and loss. For example, Infosys has presented exchange gain on the face of the statement of profit and loss, while Suzlon has included it in 'other expenses'. Therefore, it is important to analyse the details of other expenses presented in the notes.

(ii) Some material and important expense items are included in 'other expenses'. Examples are advertisement and promotion expenses, carriage and freight and royalty in case of HUL; impairment loss in case of Infosys; and performance guarantee expenses, liquidated damages expenses and operations and maintenance warranty expenses in case of Suzlon.

(iii) Nature and amount of operating expenses differ among companies operating in different industries. They also differ among companies operating in the same industry, but adopted different Business Models. Therefore, it is important to think through why nature and magnitude of operating expenses different among otherwise comparable companies.

Self-Test Questions

Self-test question 14.3

Indicate whether the following statements are true (T) or false (F):

(i) Gross profit cannot be calculated accurately from the information presented in statement of profit and loss, as Indian companies present expenses using 'natural classification'.
(ii) Improved gross profit ratio always results in improving operating margin.
(iii) The maxim, 'lower is better' cannot be applied to all operating ratios.
(iv) EBIT can always be used as a proxy for operating profit before tax.
(v) EBITDA measures operating cash flow.

SUMMARY

It is a widespread belief that the EBIT measures operating profit. But, that is incorrect, as the EBIT includes other income. Gross profit margin is useful for evaluating the manufacturing and procurement efficiency. However, gross profit cannot be calculated precisely from information provided in the statement of profit and loss because expenses are presented using 'natural classification' method. The EBITDA is used as a proxy for cash profit. The EBITDA ratio is used to measure the cash margin earned by the company. It is a very useful measure for companies operating in capital-intensive industry and is comparable across companies operating in the same industry irrespective of differences in their age. Operating ratios are used to evaluate operating efficiency. Usually, lower ratio shows better efficiency. However, we should be careful in interpreting operating ratios related to discretionary expenses because lower spending might improve the current year's profit, but likely to affect long-term earning capacity adversely.

Activity Ratios (Turnover Ratios)

NOTES

Operating asset turnover provides an insight into the efficiency of using resources. Property, plant and equipment, and intangible assets turnover show the efficiency in utilisation of capacity. A low ratio shows underutilisation of capacity either because of idle capacity or because of use of the capacity for producing low value-added products or services. Working capital, which is measured at net (operating) current assets, supports the current operation. Working capital turnover measures the efficiency in managing working capital. Analysts usually examine inventories turnover (for a manufacturing company) and receivables turnover separately because these two items together constitute a significant portion of total current assets.

Inventories turnover

Analysts use the following formulas to calculate turnovers of various components of inventories:

(i) Raw materials turnover = $\dfrac{\text{RM consumed}}{\text{Average stock of RM}}$

(ii) Work-in-progress turnover = $\dfrac{\text{Cost of production}}{\text{Average stock of WIP}}$

(iii) Finished goods turnover = $\dfrac{\text{Cost of sales}}{\text{Average stock of FG}}$

where RM stands for Raw Material, WIP is work-in-progress, and FG is finished goods.

Some analysts use the term 'cost of goods sold' instead of cost of sales to emphasise that cost of sales includes only those costs, which are included in the cost of finished goods.

It is difficult to calculate the cost of production and cost of sales directly from published financial statements because expenses are presented in the statement of profit and loss account based on natural classification. Indian GAAP does not permit use of functional classification in analysing expenses in the statement of profit and loss.

Table 14.14 presents key turnover ratios of HUL, Infosys and Suzlon for the year 2016–17.

TABLE 14.14

Key Turnover Ratios for the Year 2016–17

(Amount in ₹ crore, except the turnover ratios)

Particulars	HUL	Infosys	Suzlon
Total operating income (A)	35,759	68,484	12,714
NET OPERATING ASSETS TURNOVER			
NOA as at March 31, 2017 (B)	2,118	31,959	3,282
NOA as at March 31, 2016 (C)	2,083	29,044	3,278
Average NOA [(B+C)/2] (D)	2,101	30,502	3,280
NOA turnover (D/A) (E)	17.02×	2.245×	3.876×
PP&E TURNOVER			
PP&E as at March 31, 2017 (F)	3,968	9,751	1,420
PP&E as at March 31, 2016 (G)	3,165	8,637	1,235
Average PP&E [(F+G)/2] (H)	3,567	9,194	1,328
PP&E turnover (A/H) (I)	10.03×	7.45×	9.17×
TRADE RECEIVABLES TURNOVER			
Trade receivables as at March 31, 2017 (J)	1,085	12,322	3,627
Trade receivables as at March 31, 2016 (K)	1,264	11,330	2,515
Average trade receivables [(J+K)/2] (L)	1,175	11,826	3,071

NOTES

Particulars	HUL	Infosys	Suzlon
Trade receivables turnover (A/L) (M)	30.45×	5.79×	3.96×
Number of days of trade receivables (365/M)	11.99	63.03	90.07
INVENTORY TURNOVER			
Inventory as at March 31, 2017 (N)	2,541	0	3,469
Inventory as at March 31, 2016 (O)	2,726	0	2,524
Average inventory [(N+O)/2] (P)	2,634	0	2,997
Inventory turnover (A/P) (Q)	13.58×	NA	4.06×
Number of days of inventory (365/Q)	26.88	NA	89.84

Acronyms used: NOA: Net Operating Assets; PP&E: Property, Plant and Equipment.

Observations

(i) In analysing the trend in PP&E turnover, one must be cautious that in a company operating in a stable state, the carrying amount of PP&E reduces every subsequent year resulting in increase in the PP&E turnover without any increase in the total operating income.

(ii) In cross-sectional analysis, the PP&E turnover of otherwise comparable companies might not be comparable because the cost of building similar capacity might differ based on the difference in the age of companies.

(iii) PP&E turnover also depends on the Business Model of the company. For example, PP&E turnover of a company that has outsourced manufacturing and focuses only on brand management should be much higher than a company that manufactures products internally.

(iv) It is important to analyse the composition of total operating assets. For example, operating assets of Infosys includes—capital WIP (average carrying amount, ₹1,163 crore), goodwill (₹3,708 crore), intangible assets, other than goodwill (₹881 crore) and non-current tax assets (₹5,473 crore). It may be interesting to look at turnover of net operating assets, excluding those assets.

Self-Test Questions

Self-test question 14.4

Indicate whether the following statements are true (T) or false (F):

(i) It is tricky to balance between operating margin and operating assets turnover.

(ii) PP&E turnovers of companies operating in the same industry are always comparable.

(iii) It is easier to understand trade receivables and inventories turnover expressed in terms of number of days.

(iv) Companies, which follow differentiation strategy, expect to have high asset turnover and low operating profit margin.

(v) Low current assets turnover and high working capital turnover is desirable for any company irrespective of the industry in which it operates.

SUMMARY

Asset turnover ratios provide insights into the productivity of assets. Higher the turnover, better is the productivity. Usually, analysts calculate turnover of different classes of assets to measure the productivity of each individual class of assets. Turnovers of trade receivables and inventories are generally expressed in terms of number of days. Inventories turnover is decomposed into raw materials turnover, work-in-progress turnover and finished goods turnover.

NOTES

Key Terms
Liquidity, solvency

DuPont Model

DuPont Model (also known as the *DuPont analysis*) breaks down the return on equity into three parts, as presented in Exhibit 14.1.

The name comes from the DuPoint Corporation of the USA, which invented and started using this formula in the 1920s.

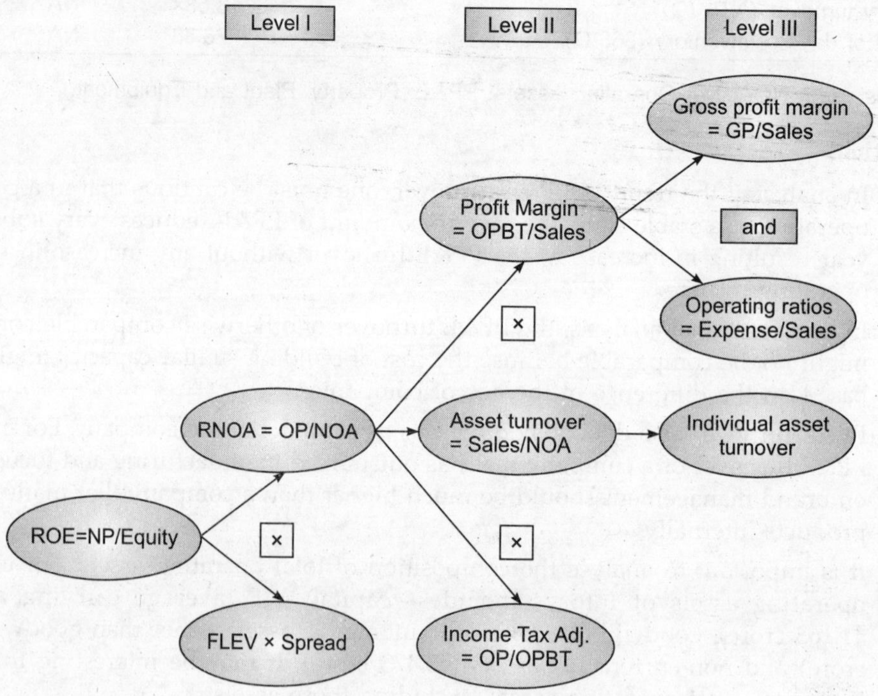

EXHIBIT 14.1 DuPont Model.

This model helps managers and investors is analysing what is causing the current ROE. It helps in pinpointing the problem area whether it is a lower profit margin, asset turnover, or poor financial leveraging. The drivers of ROE flows from the strategy, Business Model and operating efficiency. For example, a company that follows differentiation strategy, earns high margin, but achieves low asset turnover. On the other hand, a company that follows low cost strategy focuses on high asset turnover and work with low margin. Improvement in operating efficiency improves gross profit and operating ratios, and consequently, improves the ROIC and the ROE.

We have discussed computation of all the ratios that are used in the DuPont Model in earlier sections of this chapter.

CASE STUDY: CREDIT ANALYSIS

Lenders and creditors have interest in analysing the liquidity and solvency of the company. *Liquidity* refers to the ability of the company to meet short-term commitments. *Solvency* refers to the long-term viability of the company. In this section, we shall discuss financial ratios and other tools that are commonly used to measure liquidity and solvency.

Liquidity

Liquidity of company depends on its ability to convert assets into cash or to generate cash through operations in a short period to meet short-term obligations. When a company finds it difficult to arrange enough cash to meet short-term obligations, we say that it is facing liquidity problem. A company that continually faces liquidity problem might face closure, as its supply chain may get choked due to non-payment to supply chain partners and employees, and failure to meet terms and conditions of debt covenant. Therefore, its liquidity is vital for the survival of a company.

One-year period may be considered as short-term.

Working capital

Working capital is a measure of liquidity. It is the excess of the amount of current assets over the amount of current liabilities. For example, if the amount of current assets is ₹3,00,000 and the amount of current liabilities is ₹1,00,000, the amount of working capital is (₹3,00,000 – 1,00,000) or ₹2,00,000. Working capital provides safety cushion to creditors. It is also a measure of liquid reserve to meet contingencies and uncertainties surrounding company's future cash inflows and outflows.

Absolute amount of working capital fails to provide insights into the adequacy of working capital.

ILLUSTRATION 14.2 Measure of Working Capital

Company M has current assets amounting to ₹10,00,000 and current liabilities amounting to ₹9,00,000 and thus, working capital of ₹1,00,000. Company N's working capital is also measured at ₹1,00,000, which is constituted of current assets of ₹2,00,000 and current liabilities of ₹1,00,000. Can we say that both the companies have equally comfortable liquidity position?

Solution

We cannot say that both the companies have equally comfortable liquidity position. This is because their relative working capital positions are different. In case of company M, the ratio of the amount of current assets to the amount of current liabilities is (10,00,000/9,00,000) or 1.11. The same for N is (2,00,000/1,00,000) or 2. Therefore, we can say that company N's liquidity position is much better than that of company M.

Calculation of Current Ratio

Current ratio, which is calculated by dividing current assets by current liabilities, is widely used to assess liquidity. It measures the following:

(i) *Current liability coverage:* Higher the current ratio, greater is the assurance that current liabilities will be met.

(ii) *Safety margin:* Higher the current ratio, larger is the buffer against the risk that carrying amount of a non-cash current asset may not be realised in full.

(iii) *Reserve of liquid funds:* Higher the current ratio, larger is the reserve of liquid funds, which is required to sail through difficult cash flow situations.

TABLE 14.15

Current Ratio as at March 31, 2017

(Amount in ₹ crore, except the current ratio)

Particulars	HUL	Infosys	Suzlon
Current assets as at March 31, 2017 (A)	10,218	53,705	9,170
Current liabilities as at March 31, 2016 (B)	7,714	14,013	13,759
Current ratio (A/B) (C)	1.325	3.833	0.666

Observations

(i) It is difficult to establish what the optimal current ratio is. A thumb rule of 2 is widely used. However, the use of the thumb rule might misguide us. For example, if we apply the thumb rule, we shall conclude that HUL's liquidity position is not satisfactory, because its current ratio is 1.325 (Table 14.15). But, in reality it is not so because it is a prosperous company and has never faced liquidity problem.

(ii) Managers manage working capital to achieve higher working capital turnover, which is measured by dividing the total operating income by average working capital. Adequacy of working capital from managerial perspective differs from the same from creditors' perspective. We should be careful in interpreting current ratio.

(iii) We should be cautious about the limitations of current ratio.

Limitations of Current Ratio

Failure to predict future cash flows

Assessing liquidity is about assessing the ability of the company to generate adequate cash inflows in the short-term. Unfortunately, current ratio does not help us either in predicting future cash flows or in measuring the adequacy of future cash flows.

Less relevant for a going concern

Investments in most current assets do not get unlocked except in liquidation. For example, investments in trade receivables and inventories do not get unlocked, except in liquidation. A going concern does not use or liquidate current assets to settle current liabilities. This is evident from the nature of current assets. Table 14.16 presents the important components of current assets and current liabilities and their characteristics.

Exclusion of prospective cash outlays from current liabilities

Current liabilities do not include some prospective cash outlays. For example, a firm commitment to purchase equipment might result in cash outflow within twelve months after the balance sheet date, but the same is not included in current liabilities. Companies disclose commitments in notes to accounts. Analysts may adjust current liabilities for commitments for the purpose of calculating current ratio.

Exclusion of prospective cash inflows from current assets

Prospective cash inflows are not included in current assets. For example, unused portion of an open-credit arrangement (e.g., pre-approved revolving credit like cash credit limit or credit limit on credit cards) with banks are not included in current assets. Companies can always use open-credit arrangements to draw cash in order to settle current liabilities.

TABLE 14.16

Elements of Current Assets and Current Liabilities

Components	Characteristics
A. CURRENT ASSETS	
Cash and cash equivalent	Cash is a non-earning asset. Although there are exceptions like Infosys, which holds excess cash, managers do not prefer to hold cash in excess of what is required as precautionary reserves against cash imbalances that might occur in future. It is rare that a company uses the available cash to settle current obligations. Cash does not help us in predicting future cash flows, as cash balance has little relevance to the existing level of operations.
Marketable securities (Investments in financial assets held for trading)	A part of 'investments in financial assets held for trading' represents precautionary reserve. The balance, which represents cash in excess of precautionary reserve, is available to settle current obligations. Investments in financial assets held for trading are measured at fair value. We should remember that as we move away from the balance sheet date, the chance that the current fair value is different from the fair value at the balance sheet date increases. Investments in financial assets held for trading do not help us to predict future cash flows, as the volume of these investments has little relevance to the existing level of operations.

Components	Characteristics
Trade receivables	Trade receivables are not available for settling current obligations because of their revolving nature. Realisation of current receivables is succeeded by new credits to customers. Therefore, investment in trade receivables never gets unlocked, except in liquidation. Trade receivables, to some extent, helps us in predicting future cash flows, as the current level of operations drives their volume. However, the amount of 'trade receivables' does not vary in direct proportion to the total operating income, as it is determined by credit policy and efficiency in collecting amount from customers.
Inventories	As in the case of trade receivables, investment in inventories does not get unlocked, except in liquidation, as management always holds inventories to keep the production going and to serve customers with speed. The inventory level is determined by the company's strategy and the nature of the items that the company use as raw materials, and components and items that it produce as finished goods. Inventories, to some extent, help us in predicting future cash flows, as the current level of operations drives their volume.
Prepaid expenses	Prepaid expenses never get converted into cash. Therefore, often analysts exclude the same from current assets for calculating current ratio. However, usually, the amount of prepaid expenses is not significant. Therefore, inclusion of the same in current assets does not distort the current ratio.
CURRENT LIABILITIES	
Trade payables	The payment of trade payables is a refunding activity. Trade payables arise from sale of goods and services. When sales remain stable or grow, new trade payables replace old trade payables, which are settled, when due. Therefore, using current trade payables in the denominator does not provide valuable insights.

Use of Current Ratio

Bankers' perspective

Bankers use current ratio to evaluate the ability of the company to settle current liabilities in the worst situation, which is when the company will stop generating future cash inflows. Therefore, they always include current ratio in debt covenant and use the ratio in deciding the limit for short-term credit (e.g., working capital loan and cash credit limit).

Quality of current assets and current liabilities

From banker's perspective, it is interesting to look into the quality of current assets and current liabilities. Quality of current assets is assessed in terms of liquidity of the assets included in current assets. For example, 'trade receivable' is a better quality current asset than inventories because trade receivable can be converted into cash faster than converting inventories into cash. Quality of current liabilities is assessed in terms of urgency to settle the liability. For example, 'trade payable' is a better quality current liability than statutory dues. This is so because payment to suppliers of goods and services can be deferred through negotiation with them and because of long-term relationship, but settlement of statutory dues (e.g., income tax deducted at source and employees' provident fund contribution) cannot be deferred, as delay in payment of statutory dues attracts penalty, damages reputation (e.g., attachment of bank accounts by statutory authorities) and causes business disruption.

Perspective of other creditors

Current ratio is not useful in assessing liquidity of a going concern. Creditors, other than bankers such as suppliers of goods and services, are interested in understanding the ability of the company to generate future cash inflows in the short-term. Therefore, they assess liquidity with reference to the forecasted future performance of the company and its financial flexibility.

NOTES

Key Terms
Working capital cycle

Perspective of investors and prospective investors in equity, and managers

Investors, prospective investors and managers use current ratio to evaluate the effectiveness in managing working capital. Trend analysis and cross-sectional analysis provide significant insights into the effectiveness in managing working capital. From their perspective, lower the current ratio, better is working capital management. However, too low current ratio signals danger of slowing down operations in future due to non-availability of raw materials and components, or losing in competition due to delay in supplying finished goods to customers.

Acid-test Ratio (Quick Ratio)

Acid-test ratio, also called *quick ratio,* is a more stringent test of liquidity. In the numerator, the total amounts of only those current assets, which are readily convertible into cash, are included.

It may be computed as follows:,

Quick ratio = Current assets − inventories − prepaid expenses ÷ Current liabilities

Inventories are excluded, because they are the least liquid current assets. Pre-paid expenses are excluded because they do not get converted into cash. We must be cautious that in some industries (e.g., oil industry), inventories are more liquid than trade receivables.

The acid-test ratio suffers from the similar limitations as the limitations of the current ratio. Therefore, the ratio should be interpreted carefully.

Cash-based Ratios

Some analysts use cash-based ratios for assessing liquidity.

Cash-to-current asset ratio

It is calculated as follows

Cash + Cash equivalents + Marketable securities ÷ Current assets

Larger the ratio, more liquid are the current assets.

Cash-to-current liabilities ratio

It is calculated as follows:

Cash + Cash equivalents + Marketable securities ÷ Current liabilities

It is more severe test than quick ratio. It emphasises that ultimately cash is required to settle current liabilities. It is often used as a ratio supplementary to the 'cash-to-current asset' ratio.

Working Capital Cycle

Working capital cycle is measured in number of days. It comprises the inventory holding period, receivable days and payable days. For example, if the 'receivable days' are 30 days, 'inventory holding period' is 60 days and 'payable period' is 45 days, the working capital cycle is (30 + 60 − 45) days or 45 days.

An analysis of working capital cycle provides significant insights into the company's efficiency in managing working capital. Managers endeavour to reduce the working capital cycle. The shorter the working capital cycle, the faster the company is able to free up its cash stuck in working capital.

Receivable days are calculated by dividing average trade receivables by total operating income per day. Inventory holding period is calculated by dividing average inventories by total operating income per day. Payable days are calculated by dividing average trade payables by purchases per day. Usually, the figure for purchase is not available directly from the statement of profit and loss. However, it can be derived from the information available in that statement.

To calculate inventory holding period more precisely, the holding periods of raw materials, work-in-progress and finished goods should be calculated separately. Raw material holding period is calculated with reference to consumption of raw material per day.

NOTES

Work-in-progress holding period is calculated with reference to cost of production per day. Finished goods holding period is calculated with reference to cost of sales per day.

The working capital cycle does not take into account locking of funds in loans and advances, and current assets other than receivables and inventories. Similarly, it does not take into account operating current liabilities (including provisions and advance from customers).

Conversion Cycle (Operating Cycle)

Conversion cycle, also called operating cycle, is the total of receivable days and inventory holding period. For example, if the receivable days are 30 days and inventory holding period is 60 days, the conversion cycle is (30 + 60) or 90 days. Conversion cycle measures how many days the company takes to both sell its inventories and to collect the receivables. It is a useful inventory liquidity measure.

Key Terms
Conversion cycle, financial flexibility

Financial Flexibility

Financial flexibility refers to the ability of the company to quickly respond to unexpected interruptions in cash inflows. Financial flexibility has a bearing on liquidity of the company. Assessing financial flexibility requires evaluation of qualitative factors.

A company has financial flexibility if

(i) it can borrow at a short notice;
(ii) it can sell and redeploy assets quickly; and
(iii) it can quickly adjust the direction of its operations to respond to the changes in the business environment.

A company's financial flexibility depends on,

(i) the extent of debt in the capital structure and availability of open-line of credit,
(ii) current rating of its bonds,
(iii) restrictions on the sale of assets,
(iv) the extent to which the expenses are discretionary, and
(v) ability to negotiate favourably with employees and supply chain partners to adjust to the change in direction of operations.

Self-Test Questions

Self-test question 14.5

Indicate whether the following statements are true (T) or false (F):

(i) Current ratio is not a useful measure of liquidity for a going concern.
(ii) Creditors, other than banks and financial institutions, are more interested in the ability to generate cash inflows in future rather than the current ratio.
(iii) Current ratio below 2 indicates poor liquidity of a company.
(iv) Current ratio is useful to bankers because they are worried about 'what if' if the company goes into liquidation.
(v) Cash outflows requirement arising from firm commitments is not included in current liabilities.

SUMMARY

Liquidity refers to the ability of the company to meet short-term commitments. Current ratio is used widely to evaluate liquidity. However, it is not a useful measure for assessing the liquidity of a going concern because of the very nature of current assets and current liabilities, and also, because companies do not liquidate current assets to pay current liabilities. Managers manage working capital to support operations and not to provide buffer to creditors. Therefore, they endeavour to work with low current ratio. Creditors assess financial flexibility and forecasted future performance of the company to assess liquidity because they are interested in the ability of the company to generate future cash inflows. Acid-test ratio and cash-based measures are more stringent measures than current ratio, but they suffer from the similar limitation as the limitations of current ratio. Working capital cycle and conversion cycle are used to measure efficiency of working capital management.

NOTES

Key Terms
Solvency, gearing

Solvency

Solvency refers to the long-term viability of the company. Analysis of solvency involves analysing the capital structure of the company and adequacy of earning to honour long-term financial commitments. In liquidity analysis, the time horizon is fairly short. In solvency analysis, the time horizon is fairly long. Long-term forecasts are less reliable than short-term forecasts. Therefore, solvency analysis is less precise than liquidity analysis.

Capital Structure Analysis

The following capital structure measures are used to analyse solvency.

Financial leverage

It is calculated as follows:

$$\text{Financial leverage} = \frac{\text{Net financial obligation}}{\text{Equity}}$$

Gearing ratio

The gearing ratio measures the proportion of a company's borrowed funds to its equity. Book value of equity is used in calculating the gearing ratio. Gearing is expressed as a percentage.

The following are the various formulas used to measure gearing:

Net gearing

It is calculated as follows:

$$\text{Net gearing} = \frac{\text{Total debt} - \text{Cash and Cash equivalents}}{\text{Equity}} \times 100$$

Total debt should include all liabilities, including current liabilities. Some analysts deduct cash and cash equivalents and marketable securities from total debt to calculate net debt, which is used in the numerator.

Gross gearing

Alternative formulas, which are used for calculating gross gearing, are as follows:

$$\text{Gross gearing} = \frac{\text{Total debt}}{\text{Equity}} \times 100$$

The following formula is also used to calculate gearing:

$$\text{Gross gearing} = \frac{\text{Total debt}}{\text{Total assets}} \times 100$$

Some analysts prefer to use long-term debt in the numerator and use the following formula:

$$\text{Debt-equity ratio} = \frac{\text{Total long-term debt}}{\text{Equity}} \times 100$$

The above ratio is also called *debt-equity ratio*.

It is a good idea to calculate the percentage of short-term debt in the total debt. If the proportion of short-term debt is high, it is a matter to worry. The company will have to repay short-term debts within the next financial year.

The ratio roughly measures the financial risk to which a business is subjected, as excessive debt can lead to financial difficulties. In a business downturn, a company with high gearing ratio (often called highly leveraged company) may have trouble in meeting its debt repayment schedules, and could risk bankruptcy. A low gearing ratio may be indicative of conservative financial management. However, companies operating in highly cyclical industries cannot afford to have high debt in its capital structure in the face of an inevitable downturn in operating income and profits. Prosperous companies usually work with very low debt.

Appropriate gearing ratio

The appropriate gearing ratio depends on the nature of the industry. It depends on the proportion of fixed costs in the total cost of delivering products or services to customers. If the proportion of fixed costs is high, the firm prefers low debt in its capital structure. If the proportion of fixed costs is low, the firm has the flexibility to have high debt in its capital structure. Gearing ratio also depends on the volatility in input prices or supply of inputs, and also, on volatility in demand for the products or services of the firm. Low debt in the capital structure provides the desired flexibility that helps the firm to manage difficult situations.

Generally, investors and creditors should worry if net gearing is 50 percent or above. Net gearing of 100 percent and above is dangerous.

Operating leverage

The proportion of fixed costs in the cost structure is measured by *operating leverage,* which is calculated as follows:

$$\text{Operating leverage} = \frac{\text{Total contribution}}{\text{EBIT}}$$

Operating leverage is also called *operational gearing.*

'Contribution' is the difference between sales and variable costs of sales. For example, if the sale value is ₹10 lakh and variable cost of sales is ₹6 lakh, contribution is (₹10 lakh – 6 lakh) or ₹4 lakh. EBIT is the difference between total contribution and fixed costs. For example, if contribution is ₹4 lakh and fixed cost is ₹1 lakh, the EBIT is (₹4 lakhs –1 lakh) or ₹3 lakhs. In that case, operating leverage is (4/3) or 1.33. On the other hand, if 'sales' is ₹10 lakh, variable cost is ₹4 lakh, and fixed cost is ₹3 lakh, operating leverage is (6/3) or 2. In both the cases sales and EBIT are ₹10 lakh and ₹3 lakh, respectively, but the operating leverage is higher in the second case, as the fixed cost is higher than that in the first case. Higher operating leverage signifies higher fixed cost in the cost structure. The use of EBIT in the denominator assumes that the firm has no income other than revenue income.

Table 14.17 presents the gearing ratio of Suzlon Limited.

TABLE 14.17

Gearing Ratio of Suzlon Limited

(Amount in ₹ crores, except the gearing ratio)

Particulars	March 31, 2017	March 31, 2016	March 31, 2015
Total assets (A)	12,160	9,723	21,542
Cash and cash equivalent (B)	336	627	2,540
Current liabilities (C)	13,760	7,661	17,472
Non-current liabilities (D)	5,234	9,595	11,708
Short-term borrowing (E)	2,076	1,895	4,556
Long-term borrowing (F)	4,841	9,225	10,748
Equity (G)	(6,824)	(7,533)	(7,639)
Total debt (C+D) (H)	18,994	17,256	29,180
Net debt (H–B) (I)	18,658	16,629	26,640
Net gearing [(I/G) × 100]	NA	NA	NA
Gross gearing [(H/A) × 100]	156.201%	177.476%	135.456%
ST debt/T debt [(C/H) × 100]	72.444%	44.396%	59.877%
Total borrowings/T assets [((E+F)/A) × 100]	56.883%	114.368%	71.043%

Note: Figures have been taken from the consolidated balance sheet presented in the annual report for the year 2016–17.

Observations

(i) We are unable to calculate any ratio with denominator as equity, as the amount of equity is negative. A negative number in the denominator gives a negative percentage, which is meaningless.

(ii) Gross gearing shows an alarming position. It is more than 150 percent. This implies that the company does not have enough assets to pay its liabilities. A company with negative equity will always have gross gearing of more than 100 percent.

(iii) 'Short-term liabilities' as a percentage of 'total liabilities' has increased from 44.396 percent as at March 31, 2016 to 72.444 percent. This is also alarming, as the company has to arrange funds in 2017–18 to pay short-term liabilities. It is quite likely that its operation will be affected due to fund crunch.

(iv) If we use borrowings only in the numerators, we get a misleading picture. 'Borrowings' to 'total assets' ratio has improved from 114.368 percent on March 31, 2016 to 56.883 percent on March 31, 2017. This ratio camouflages the fact that the company has resorted to other types of credit. Therefore, we should always consider total liabilities as total debt.

Earnings Coverage

Analysts use capital structure for screening purpose, that is, to understand whether debt is high in the capital structure, and thus, require further investigation. Assessing the earning capacity provides greater insights, as a leveraged company do not face difficulties if it generates enough cash inflow to meet its commitments to pay interest on borrowings and to repay the principal as per schedule.

Interest coverage

$$\text{Interest coverage} = \frac{\text{EBIT}}{\text{Interest Expense}}$$

Interest expense to be used in calculating the interest coverage ratio should not be adjusted for interest income. Moreover, the interest amount capitalised should be added to the interest expense recognised in the statement of profit and loss. Interest coverage of 3 and above is considered good because empirically, it is established that firms having interest coverage ratio of 3 do not file bankruptcy petition.

Fixed charge coverage ratio

$$\text{Fixed charge coverage ratio} = \frac{\text{EBIT + Fixed charge}}{\text{Interest expense + Fixed charge}}$$

Usually lease rent is considered to be the fixed charge.

Debt service coverage ratio (DSCR)

$$\text{Debt service coverage ratio} = \frac{\text{EBITDA – Current Tax}}{\text{Instalment fo principal + Interest + Lease rent}}$$

Usually, financial institutions use DSCR to evaluate loan applications. Each financial institution establishes its own benchmark DSCR. However, usually, less than 1 is not acceptable, as it indicates that the company may not be able to generate enough cash inflows to meet its commitment to pay interest and instalment of principal due during the year.

Table 14.18 presents the interest coverage ratio of Suzlon.

TABLE 14.18

Interest Coverage Ratio of Suzlon

(Amounts are in ₹ crore, except the interest coverage ratio)

Particulars	2016–17	2015–16
Profit before tax (A)	912	584
Finance costs (B)	1,288	1,304
EBIT (A+B)(C)	2,200	1,888
Interest coverage (C/B)	1.71×	1.45×

NOTES

Observations

(i) Interest coverage has improved from 1.45 to 1.71. It is positive sign. But, it is still much below 3, which we should worry about.

(ii) We should be careful in interpreting the ratio. Finance cost is the cost of interest bearing credits, primarily, borrowings. The company has financed a large part of its assets by interest-free credit. This credit line may dry if the company fails to pay to creditors in time. In that situation, the company has to borrow further and because of the high gearing ratio and low interest coverage, incremental interest rate is likely to be much higher. This will adversely affect the interest coverage ratio.

Self-Test Questions

Self-test question 14.6

Indicate whether the following statements are true (T) or false (F):

(i) Capital structure ratios are more useful in assessing solvency than earnings ratios.

(ii) In calculating gearing ratios, total debt should exclude current liabilities.

(iii) If gearing ratio is moderately high, but the interest coverage ratio is low, there is nothing much to worry about the solvency of the company.

(iv) If gearing ratio is very high, but the interest coverage ratio is much above 3, there is nothing much to worry about the solvency of the company.

(v) Gearing ratio will always be higher than 100 percent for a company having negative net worth.

SUMMARY

Solvency refers to the long-term viability of the company. Long-term forecasting being less accurate, solvency measures are also less precise. Ratios related to capital structure and earnings coverage are used to measure solvency. Gearing ratios measure the extent of debt in the capital structure. How much debt in the capital structure is optimum depends on the industry in which the company is operating. However, excessive debt is not desirable. Highly leveraged companies find survival difficult during recession or when the industry faces downturn. Gearing ratio is an effective tool for screening. If the gearing ratio is high, one looks into whether the company generates sufficient cash to pay interest and to pay loan instalments when they fall due. Interest coverage ratio measures the same. Usually, coverage of 3 is considered adequate.

ACTIVITY

Collect information from the website of Suzlon and scan through the news items related to Suzlon to understand the financial strategy of the company to sail through this difficult time.

SEGMENT ANALYSIS

Companies disclose segment information in financial statements. They disclose segment revenue, segment result (operating profit), segment assets and segment liabilities. Analysts can use this information to analyse profitability and asset turnover of different segments.

The business segments are identified considering:

(i) The nature of products and services,

(ii) The differing risks and returns,

(iii) The internal organisation and management structure, and

(iv) The internal financial reporting systems.

ECONOMIC VALUE ADDED (EVA)

Economic Value Added (EVA) = Net Operating Profit after Taxes (NOPAT) – Cost of Capital Employed (COCE)

where,

COCE = Weighted Average Cost of Capital (WACC) × Average Invested Capital

We may write the formula as follows:

EVA = Average invested capital × (ROIC – WACC)

EVA is residual income after charging the company for the cost of capital provided by lenders and shareholders. It represents the value added to the shareholders by generating operating profits in excess of the cost of capital employed in the business.

A company creates value when its ROIC is greater than WACC, so the factor, (ROIC – WACC) is positive. A company destroys value when its ROIC is lower than WACC, so the factor, (ROIC – WACC) is negative. A company neither creates nor destroys value when its ROIC is equal to WACC, so the factor, (ROIC – WACC) is equal to zero.

Key Terms
Economic value added (EVA)

Managers endeavour to increase EVA by:

(i) Improving operating efficiency resulting in growth in operating profits without additional capital,
(ii) Investing in projects that return more than the cost of obtaining new capital additional capitals, or
(iii) Liquidating unproductive capital by curtailing activities that do not cover the cost of capital.

MARKET-BASED RATIOS

Two market-based ratios, which are used for equity valuation, are the following:

(i) Market value to book-value ratio, and
(ii) Price-to-Earnings (PE) ratio.

A ratio that is being used by traders in the capital market to identify undervalued and overvalued shares is the PE Growth (PEG) ratio.

Market Value to Book Value Ratio (PB Ratio)

The ratio is often called Price-to-Book (PB) ratio. It is calculated as follows:

PB ratio = Market value of equity ÷ Book value of equity

The ratio is often used as a multiple to estimate the market value of equity. For example, if the book value of equity is ₹100 crore and average PB ratio of comparable companies is 1.5, the estimated market value of the company's equity is (₹100 crore × 1.5) or ₹150 crore.

Price-to-Earnings (PE) Ratio

PE ratio is calculated as follows:

PE ratio = Market price per share ÷ EPS

EPS stands for 'Earnings per share'.

PE ratio is often used as a multiple to estimate the market price per share. For example, if the EPS is 100 and the average PE of comparable companies is 16, the estimated market price per share is (₹100 × 16) or ₹160.

PE ratio is called *trailing P/E,* when annual EPS used in the ratio is calculated based on earnings of past four quarters.

PE ratio is called *forward P/E* or *leading P/E,* when annual EPS used in the ratio is calculated based on expected earnings for next twelve months.

PE ratio cannot be calculated for companies having no earnings or having negative earnings.

PE to growth ratio (PEG Ratio)

PEG ratio is widely used as a stock-screening matrix. It is calculated as follows:

$$\text{PEG ratio} = \text{P/E} \div \text{(Estimated short-term earnings growth rate)}$$

For example, if the PE ratio is 20 and expected short-term growth rate is 20 percent, PEG is (20/20) or 1. Proponents of this ratio classify a share as overvalued if PEG is more than 1, and undervalued if PEG is less than 1.

The validity of PEG ratio is yet to be demonstrated empirically.

ALTMAN'S Z-SCORE

The most well-known model of financial distress is Altman's Z-Score. Altman's Z-Score uses a statistical technique (multiple discriminant analysis) to produce a predictor that is a linear function of several explanatory variables. This predictor classifies or predicts the likelihood of bankruptcy or non-bankruptcy.

Five financial ratios are included in the Z-Score:

- X_1 = Working capital/Total assets [Signifies liquidity]
- X_2 = Retained earnings/Total assets [Signifies age of the firm and cumulative profitability]
- X_3 = EBIT/Total assets [Signifies profitability]
- X_4 = Equity/Total liabilities [Signifies financial structure]
- X_5 = Sales/Total assets [Signifies capital turnover rate]

The Altman Z-Score is computed as follows:

$$Z = 0.717X_1 + 0.847X_2 + 3.107X_3 + 0.420X_4 + 0.998X_5$$

A score of less than 1.20 suggests a high probability of bankruptcy. Z-score above 2.90 implies a low probability of bankruptcy. Scores between 1.20 and 2.90 are in grey area.

Z-Score is a useful screening, monitoring and attention-directing tool. However, integrated analysis of ratios discussed in this chapter also help in predicting financial distress.

ANSWERS TO SELF-TEST QUESTIONS

14.1 (i) T; (ii) T; (iii) T; (iv) F; (v) T

14.2 (i) T; (ii) F; (iii) T; (iv) F; (v) T

14.3 (i) T; (ii) F; (iii) T; (iv) F; (v) F

14.4 (i) T; (ii) F; (iii) T; (iv) F; (v) F

14.5 (i) T; (ii) T; (iii) F; (iv) T; (v) T

14.6 (i) F; (ii) F; (iii) F; (iv) T; (v) T

ASSIGNMENTS

Multiple Choice Questions

1. Tick the correct answer:

(i) SET (A)

(a) Return on invested capital (ROIC) improves with revenue growth without further investment.

(b) Return on invested capital (ROIC) improves with revenue growth with same margin and without further investment.

(c) Return on invested capital (ROIC) improves with improvement in margin.

(d) None of the above.

(ii) SET (B)

(a) Return on equity (ROE) can be improved by borrowing at a cost lower than ROIC.

(b) Return on equity (ROE) improves if net borrowing cost is lower than ROIC.

(c) Return on equity (ROE) is greater than ROIC, if net borrowing cost is lower than ROIC, but is lower than ROIC if return on net investments in financial assets is lower than ROIC.

(d) None of the above.

(iii) SET (C)

(a) ROIC depends on industry attractiveness and not on capital structure of the company.

NOTES

(b) ROIC depends on industry attractiveness and on capital structure of the company.
(c) ROIC depends on industry attractiveness and competitive position of the company and not on capital structure of the company.
(d) None of the above.

(iv) SET (D)
(a) ROIC increases with increase in the operating liability leverage (OLLEV).
(b) ROIC is not affected by the operating liability leverage (OLLEV)
(c) ROIC increases with increase in the operating liability leverage (OLLEV) only if net operating profit after tax (NOPAT) is not reduced due to higher priced charged by suppliers due to delayed payments.
(d) None of the above.

(v) SET (E)
(a) EBITDA is a proxy for cash profit, but not a measure of cash flows from operating activities.
(b) EBITDA measures of cash flows from operating activities.
(c) EBITDA is a proxy for cash profit and EBITDA to Operating revenue ratio provides meaningful insights than those provided by operating margin when the industry is facing down turn.
(d) None of the above.

(vi) SET (F)
(a) Gross profit ratio is useful in measuring the procurement and production efficiency.
(b) Gross profit ratio is useful in measuring the procurement and production efficiency, but it may improve without improvement in procurement and production efficiency.
(c) Gross profit ratio is useful in measuring the procurement efficiency of a merchandising company and not useful for a manufacturing company.
(d) None of the above.

(vii) SET (G)
(a) Pressure on price affects operating margin only and not assets turnover.
(b) Pressure on price affects both operating margin and assets turnover if the company fails to increase quantity (in terms of units) sold.
(c) Pressure on price necessarily affects ROIC and ROE adversely.
(d) None of the above.

(viii) SET (H)
(a) Managers aim to work with high current assets turnover.
(b) Managers aim to work with high current assets turnover, while creditors are comfortable with low current assets turnover.
(c) Managers aim to work with high current assets turnover, while creditors are comfortable with low current assets turnover, but sudden increase or decrease in current assets turnover should be taken as a red flag.
(d) None of the above.

(ix) SET (I)
(a) Current ratio is useful in assessing liquidity of a firm.
(b) Current ratio is not at all useful in assessing liquidity of a firm.
(c) Current ratio is not at all useful in assessing liquidity of a going concern.
(d) None of the above.

(x) SET (J)
(a) Gearing ratio does not help in assessing solvency of a company.
(b) Gearing ratio does not help in assessing solvency of a company, but helps in screening to decide whether further investigation is required.
(c) Gearing ratio and interest coverage ratio should be used together for assessing solvency of a company.
(d) None of the above.

(xi) SET (K)
(a) Economic value added (EVA) measures the value created by the company during the accounting period.
(b) Economic value added (EVA) measures the value created by the company during the accounting period, but improves without managerial efforts if, the bench mark interest rate reduces.
(c) Economic value added (EVA) can be used to measure managerial efficiency, because it can be improved only through managerial efforts.
(d) None of the above.

Fixed Assets and Investment Property

CHAPTER

15

LEARNING OBJECTIVES

Fixed assets are long-lived assets, which an entity uses for producing goods and services or for administration. Fixed assets can be tangible assets or intangible assets. Tangible fixed assets are called 'Property, Plant and Equipment (PP&E)'. Investment property is a property that the entity holds as investment and not for producing goods and services or for administration. This chapter discusses the accounting fixed assets and investment property.

After reading this chapter, you will develop understanding of the following:

- Nature of property, plant and equipment, intangible assets and investment property
- Accounting principles for recognising items of property, plant and equipment
- Accounting principles for measuring items of property, plant and equipment
- The concept of component accounting
- Accounting principles for recognising and measuring items of intangible assets
- Nature of investment property
- Accounting principles for recognising and measuring investment property

NOTES

PROPERTY, PLANT AND EQUIPMENT (PP&E)

Applicable Ind AS

Accounting principles for the accounting for PP&E are primarily laid down in Ind AS 16, Property, Plant and Equipment. Accounting principles stipulated in Ind AS 23, Borrowing Costs, and Ind AS 20, Accounting for Government Grants and Disclosure of Government Assistance are also applicable in accounting for PP&E.

Depreciation and impairment of items of property, plant and equipment are discussed in Chapter 13.

Nature of PP&E

Key Terms
Fixed assets

PP&E are tangible assets. An entity holds them for use in the production or supply of goods or services, for rental to others, or for administrative purposes. It expects to use them during more than one period. PP&E are classified as non-current assets.

In practice, period for this definition is considered to be a full accounting period of one year.

It is not necessary that the asset should be directly used in the production or for administrative purposes. Therefore, assets that are acquired for research activities are classified as PP&E if they meet the definition of PP&E. Such assets support the ongoing supply of goods and services in the long term. Similarly, assets that are acquired for safety or environmental reasons and meet the definition of PP&E qualify for recognition as PP&E. They enable the entity to derive future economic benefits from related assets in excess of what could be derived had those items not been acquired.

Examples of different classes of PP&E are

(i) land;
(ii) land and buildings;
(iii) machinery;
(iv) ships;
(v) aircraft;
(vi) motor vehicles;
(vii) furniture and fixtures;
(viii) office equipment; and
(ix) bearer plants.

Bearer plants

A biological asset is defined to be a living animal or plant and includes produce growing on bearer plants.

A bearer plant is a living plant that:

(i) is used in the production or supply of agricultural produce;
(ii) is expected to bear produce for more than one period; and
(iii) has a remote likelihood of being sold as agricultural produce, except for incidental scrap sales.

Examples are trees in timber plantation, cotton plants, tobacco plants, tea bushes, grape vines, rubber trees and fruit trees.

Bearer plants are classified as PP&E. Therefore, accounting principles for recognition and measurement of PP&E are applicable for recognition and measurement of bearer plants.

Livestock (living animals) is not a bearer plant. They are usually classified as non-current assets and are measured at fair value.

Spare parts, stand-by equipment and servicing equipment

Items such as spare parts, stand-by equipment and servicing equipment are classified as PP&E or inventory. They are recognised as PP&E when they meet the definition of PP&E, including the requirement that the entity expects to use them during more than one period. There is no requirement that those items to be used only in connection with an item of PP&E.

NOTES

SUMMARY

PP&E are tangible assets. An entity holds them for use in the production or supply of goods or services, for rental to others, or for administrative purposes. It expects to use them during more than one period. Bearer plants are treated as PP&E. Spare parts, stand-by equipment and servicing equipment are classified as PP&E when they meet the definition of PP&E.

Self-Test Questions

Self-test question 15.1

Indicate whether the following statements are true (T) or false (F):

(i) Assets that are classified as property, plant and equipment are tangible assets.

(ii) Assets that an entity holds for use in the production or supply of goods or services, for rental to others, or for administrative purposes are classified as PP&E irrespective of the period over which the entity intends to use the same.

(iii) Bearer plant and livestock are classified as PP&E.

(iv) Stores and spare parts are always classified as inventories.

(v) Stand-by equipment and servicing equipment are classified as PP&E only when management intends to use those only in connection with an item of PP&E.

Recognition

Recognition principle

The cost of an item of property, plant and equipment should be recognised as an asset if and only if (i) it is probable that future economic benefits associated with the item will flow to the entity; and (ii) the cost of the item can be measured reliably.

Unit for measure for recognition

This standard does not prescribe the unit of measure for recognition, that is, what constitutes an item of PP&E. Thus, judgement is required in applying the recognition criteria to an entity's specific circumstances.

It may be appropriate to aggregate individually insignificant items such as moulds, tools and dies, and to apply the criteria to the aggregate value. However, dissimilar items should not be aggregated. Similarly, items that are separately identifiable and individually significant should be recognised separately.

Component accounting

An item of PP&E is often composed of various parts with varying useful lives and consumption patterns. These parts are individually replaced during the useful life of the asset. In order to achieve more appropriate calculation of depreciation and derecognition of parts replaced, entities allocate the amount initially recognised in respect of an item of PP&E to its significant parts. Deciding whether a part is significant or not is a matter of judgement.

A significant part of an item of PP&E may have a useful life and a depreciation method that are the same as the useful life and the depreciation method of another significant part of the same item. Such parts may be grouped in determining the depreciation charge.

For example, it may be appropriate to recognise and depreciate separately the airframe and engines of an aircraft. Similarly, it may be appropriate to recognise and depreciate separately structural design, elevators, heating system, water system and electrical system of a building.

NOTES

Repair and maintenance costs

Costs of day-to-day servicing are not recognised in the carrying amount of the item of PP&E. They are primarily the costs of labour and consumables, and may include the cost of small parts.

> **BOX 15.1 Carrying Amount**
>
> Carrying amount of an item of PP&E is the amount at which an asset is recognised after deducting any accumulated depreciation (amortisation) and accumulated impairment losses thereon. For example, if the cost (fair value) of the asset is ₹1,000 and accumulated depreciation is ₹500, and accumulated impairment loss is ₹100, the carrying amount of the asset is ₹400.

Parts replacement

In the carrying amount of an item of PP&E, an entity recognises the cost of replacing part of such an item if the recognition criteria are met. The carrying amount of those parts that are replaced is derecognised.

For example, the cost of relining an electrical furnace is added to the carrying amount of the furnace and the carrying amount, if any, of the existing lining is derecognised. Similarly, costs of replacing seats and galleries are added to the carrying cost of the airframe and the carrying amount of the existing seats and galleries is derecognised.

Major inspection and overhaul

When each major inspection or overhaul is performed, its cost is recognised in the carrying amount of the item of PP&E as a replacement if the recognition criteria are satisfied. Any remaining carrying amount of the cost of the previous inspection (as distinct from physical parts) is derecognised. In order to apply this principle, it might be necessary to estimate what was the cost of the existing inspection component when the item was acquired or constructed. The estimated cost of a future similar inspection may be used as an indication for such estimate.

For example, a regulatory condition for continuing to operate an aircraft may be performing major inspection at regular intervals. The cost of such an inspection is recognised in the carrying amount of the aircraft or as a separate component of the aircraft.

Key Terms
Carrying amount, component accounting

SUMMARY

The cost of an item of property, plant and equipment should be recognised as an asset if and only if

(i) it is probable that future economic benefits associated with the item will flow to the entity; and
(ii) the cost of the item can be measured reliably.

Significant parts of an asset are recognised as separate items in order to improve depreciation accounting and replacement accounting. At initial recognition, the total cost of an item is allocated to these parts. Costs of day-to-day servicing are not recognised in the carrying amount of the item of PP&E. When each major inspection or overhaul is performed, its cost is recognised in the carrying amount of the item of PP&E as a replacement if the recognition criteria are satisfied.

Self-Test Questions

Self-test question 15.2

Indicate whether the following statements are true (T) or false (F):

(i) If the cost of an item of PP&E cannot be measured reliably, it is not recognised in the balance sheet.

(ii) All the components of an item of PP&E that are separately identifiable and individually significant should be recognised separately.
(iii) Component accounting aims at improving depreciation accounting and accounting for replacement of parts.
(iv) Costs of day-to-day servicing are not recognised in the carrying amount of the item of PP&E.
(v) An entity should estimate the cost of the existing major inspection component of an item of PP&E when the item was acquired or constructed.

MEASUREMENT AT RECOGNITION

Measurement principle

At initial recognition, an item of PP&E is measured at its cost.

Elements of cost

The cost of an item of PP&E comprises:

(i) its purchase price, including import duties and non-refundable purchase taxes, after deducting trade discounts and rebates;
(ii) any costs directly attributable to bringing the asset to the location and condition necessary for it to be capable of operating in the manner intended by management; and
(iii) the initial estimate of the costs of dismantling and removing the item and restoring the site on which it is located, the obligation for which an entity incurs either when the item is acquired or as a consequence of having used the item during a particular period for purposes other than to produce inventories during that period.

Cessation of Accumulating costs

Recognition of costs in the carrying amount of an item of property, plant and equipment ceases when the item lies in the location and is in the condition necessary for it to be capable of operating in the manner intended by management. Therefore, costs, which incurred in using or redeploying an item, are not included in the carrying amount of that item.

Directly attributable costs

Deciding which costs are directly attributable to bring the asset to the location and in the condition of intended use is a matter of judgement.

Table 15.1 provides examples of directly attributable costs.

TABLE 15.1

Directly Attributable Costs

Nature of cost	Directly attributable	Not directly attributable
Employee benefit expenses attributable to employees directly engaged in the construction or acquisition of the item of PP&E	√	
Costs of site preparation	√	
Initial delivery and handling costs	√	
Costs (net of income) of testing whether the asset is functioning properly	√	

(Contd.)

NOTES

TABLE 15.1

Directly Attributable Costs (*Contd.*)

Nature of cost	Directly attributable	Not directly attributable
Start-up and commissioning cost[1]	√	
Cost incurred to make an asset ready for use[2]	√	
Professional fees (e.g., fees paid to architect and supervisor)	√	
Preliminary stage costs[3]		√
Pre-acquisition stage costs[4]		√
Costs of opening a new facility		√
Costs of introducing a new product or service (including costs of advertising and promotional activities)		√
Costs of conducting business in a new location or with a new class of customer (including costs of staff training)		√
Administration and other general overhead costs		√
Costs incurred while an item is ready for use, but yet to be brought into use or is operated at less than full capacity		√
Initial operating losses such as those incurred while demand for the item's output builds up		√
Costs of relocating or reorganising part or all of an entity's operations		√

[1] The cost associated with a start-up or commissioning should be included in the cost of PP&E only when the asset is available for use, but is incapable of operating at normal levels without such a start-up or commissioning period.

[2] Expenditure incurred to bring the fixed asset to its working condition is capitalised, provided the same was contemplated at the time of acquisition of the asset. The underlying principle is that if the purchase price assumes that an additional expenditure would be incurred to make the asset ready for use, the additional expenditure should be a part of the acquisition cost.

[3] Preliminary stage costs, which are in the nature of research expenses, should be charged to the statement of profit and loss for the period in which they are incurred. Examples of preliminary stage costs are costs of exploration of opportunities for acquisition or construction of an asset, costs of feasibility studies, costs of engineering studies, and costs of design layouts.

[4] The preliminary stage ends and the pre-acquisition stage begins when the acquisition of the asset is *probable* as evidenced by management's authorisation and allocation of fund. Internal and external costs incurred in the pre-acquisition stage are charged to the statement of profit and loss account for the period in which they are incurred unless these are *directly attributable* to the specific asset.

CASE STUDY 15.1 Directly Attributable Cost

In the beginning of the year 2018, SK Limited (SKL) purchased equipment to produce a new product, which it believed would complete the portfolio of skin care products and, thus, would help achieve the target market share in skin care products. The purchase price of the equipment was ₹1 crore (10 million). In addition, it incurred the following expenditure:

(i)	Cost for transporting the equipment to the site:	₹50,000
(ii)	Labour charges for loading and unloading the equipment:	₹5,000
(iii)	Transit insurance:	₹2,00,000
(iv)	Cost of preparing the site:	₹1,00,000
(v)	Cost to train employees in operating the equipment:	₹2,00,000
(vi)	Cost to promote the new product:	₹10,00,000

Question

The CEO of SKL seeks your advice on which of the above costs are not directly attributable to the acquisition of the asset.

NOTES

Solution

Costs at (v) and (vi) are not directly attributable to the acquisition of the asset. Cost to train employees in operating the equipment was not necessarily to be incurred for acquiring and installing the equipment. Similarly, cost to promote the new product was not necessarily to be incurred for acquiring and installing the equipment. All other costs listed above were necessarily to be incurred for acquiring and installing the equipment.

CASE STUDY 15.2 Allocation of Cost to Land and Building and Directly Attributable Costs

BN Limited (BNL) has purchased a building for ₹2 crore (20 million). It incurred the following additional expenditures to make the building ready for the intended use:

(i) Amount paid to an advocate to search the title of the land and building: ₹20,000
(ii) Amount paid towards registration charges: ₹20 lakh (2 million)
(iii) Amount paid to 'vastu' expert to suggest modifications in the building: ₹1,00,000
(iv) Amount paid to an architect to design and supervise modifications: ₹10,00,000
(v) Cost of demolishing a part of the building for reconstruction: ₹1,00,000
(vi) Cost of modifications: ₹40,00,000

The fair value (at the date of acquisition) of the land on which the building is constructed is estimated at ₹1.2 crore (12 million).

Question

The CFO of BNL requires you to help her in calculating the cost of the building.

Solution

Land and building should be recorded as separate items of PP&E because land is not a depreciable asset while building is depreciated over its useful life. The composite cost should be allocated to these two items in the ratio of their respective fair values. It may be assumed that the composite cost of ₹2 crore (20 million) is the fair value of the land and building together. The fair value of the land is ₹12 million or 60 percent of the composite value. Balance 40 percent or ₹8 million should be allocated to the building. It is appropriate to allocate 60 percent of the cost related to searching the title and registration to the land.

All costs are directly attributable to the acquisition of the building. Dismantling cost is directly attributable because the activity was necessary to make the building ready for intended use. Many in India believe that a vastu compliant building brings fortune to the owner/user of the building. Many others do not share that belief. It is a business decision to make the building *vastu* compliant. Accounting does not depend on the efficacy or otherwise of a business decision. Therefore, it is irrelevant to debate whether the amount paid to the vastu specialists adds to the service potential of the asset.

The cost of the building is (80,00,000 + 8,000 + 8,00,000 + 1,00,000 + 10,00,000 + 1,00,000 + 40,00,000) or ₹14.008 million.

CASE STUDY 15.3 Allocation of Cost Between Land and Building

CD Limited (CDL) has purchased 200 square metres of space in a 26-storey tower (total available space 4,00,000 square metres) constructed for commercial use in the central business district in Kolkata. The price paid is ₹10 million. As per the sale deed, the land in the precincts of the tower is allocated to all the buyers of commercial space in the tower.

Question

Discuss whether the price paid should be allocated to land and building and whether these should be recorded separately.

Solution

The fair value of the share of land allocated to CDL is not material. Therefore, there is no need to recognise land and building separately. Consequently, it is not necessary to allocate the price between land and building. CDL should disclose the accounting policy, as the information is relevant to the users of financial statements. Whether the fair value of the land is material or not is a matter of judgement.

CASE STUDY 15.4 Relocation Costs

LP Limited (LPL) is engaged in manufacturing leather products. LPL's factory is located at Topsia in Kolkata. Over the year, Topsia has developed as a residential area, and with the extension of the city, it has emerged as a posh locality. The State Government, as a policy, has decided to shift leather units to the outskirts of the city and has created a leather complex. It is now mandatory for all leather companies to shift their manufacturing facilities to the leather complex. Accordingly, LPL has decided to shift its manufacturing facility to the leather complex.

Question

The company proposes to allocate relocation cost to items of PP&E in proportion to their respective carrying amount. However, it is also open to the alternative accounting of capitalising the relocation cost as a separate item of intangible assets. The CFO of LPL seeks your advice on which is the appropriate accounting.

Solution

Relocation cost is not directly attributable to the acquisition of the items of PP&E. Therefore, carrying amounts of the items of PP&E should not be adjusted by relocation cost. The relocation cost is expected to benefit the company in future because if the entity decides not to incur the expenditure, it will not be allowed to continue the business. Therefore, an intangible asset is created. But, the value of the same cannot be measured reliably. Consequently, the intangible asset should not be recognised in the balance sheet. Relocation costs should be recognised as expense in the period in which they are incurred.

CASE STUDY 15.5 Commencement of Commercial Production

N Cables Limited (NCL) imported equipment to produce cables. After installation, the equipment could not produce cables of intended quality and size. NCL started negotiating with the supplier to rectify or replace the equipment. This turned into a long-drawn dispute. In order to mitigate the financial loss, the firm started producing and marketing sub-quality cables, until a settlement with the supplier could be reached. However, the production and sale of sub-standard wires resulted in loss because the direct cost of production was higher than the sales realisation.

Question

Explain accounting for the loss caused by selling sub-standard product.

Solution

NCL started commercial production when it started production and sale of sub-quality cables because it had produced quantity much higher than what is usually produced during the test run. Expenses incurred after the commencement of commercial production should not be capitalised. Therefore, the loss incurred on sale of low quality cables should not be included in the cost of the equipment. It should be recognised in the statement of profit and loss for the period in which the cables are sold.

CASE STUDY 15.6 Start-up Cost

L Hotels Limited (LHL) has constructed a hotel in a newly developed township called Kolkata Riverside. The hotel has 200 rooms and 50 service apartments. The construction of the hotel was complete in time. However, the township project is yet to be ready, and the industrial park has been delayed by three years. As a result, the occupancy rate of the hotel is abysmally low. The hotel has incurred considerable loss during the current year.

Question

Explain whether the loss incurred during the current year should be included in the cost of the hotel building.

Solution

The loss incurred by the hotel cannot be classified as start-up cost and has not arisen from activities that are necessary to make the hotel ready for use. Therefore, the loss should not be included in the cost of the hotel building.

CASE STUDY 15.7 Cost of Demolishing Existing Building

H Limited (HL) purchased a land with a building for ₹5 million. Mr. Salim, the Chartered Engineer appointed by HL to value the property, allocated ₹4.8 million to the land and ₹0.20 million to the building. The management of HL had considered the building unusable and decided to demolish it and construct a new building for company use. It incurred ₹0.5 million to demolish the building.

Question

Explain how the purchase price and the cost of demolishing the existing building should be recorded in the books.

Solution

The total purchase price should be recorded as the cost of the land since the management of HL considered the building unusable. The cost of demolishing the existing building should be capitalised. It is not clear whether it should be added to the cost of land or to the cost of the building. One view is that it should be included in the cost of the land, as that was incurred to make the land ready for the construction of the new building. The other view is that it should be included in the cost of the building because demolition is a direct result of the decision to construct a new building.

CASE STUDY 15.8 Demolition Cost

EP Limited (EPL) purchased a land with a building for ₹5 million. Ms. Ranjita, the Chartered Engineer appointed by EL to value the property, allocated ₹4.5 million to the land and ₹0.50 million to the building. The management of EL had considered the building unsuitable for its intended use. However, it decided to demolish the building only after two years because of the current liquidity crunch. During the intervening period, it would use the building as dumping yard for disposable items. The demolition cost is estimated at ₹0.5 million.

Question

Explain how the purchase price and the estimated cost of demolishing the existing building should be recorded in the books.

NOTES

Solution

Although the building is unsuitable for intended use, it would provide benefits to EPL, as it would be used as dumping yard for disposable item. The land should be measured at ₹4.5 million. The building should be measured at ₹0.50 million, which should be depreciated to nil over a period of two years. The demolishing of the building can be considered as an activity to make the land ready for use because the activity would be undertaken after two years from the date of acquisition. It cannot be attributed to the construction of the new building. Therefore, the actual cost of demolishing the existing building will be recognised as an expense in the statement of profit and loss for the period in which the demolition will occur.

CASE STUDY 15.9 Cost of Relocating the Community

VF Limited (VFL) has decided to construct a golf course in Greater Noida, located in the National Capital Region (NCR), primarily for use by its employees. However, membership would be allowed to outsiders. Construction of the golf course will require relocating the community settled on the ground identified for the construction of the golf course. The relocating cost will be significant.

Question

The CFO of VFL seeks your advice on whether costs to be incurred for relocating the community should be included in the cost of the golf course.

Solution

Costs to be incurred for relocating the community should be included in the cost of the golf course because they are directly attributable to the construction of the same.

CASE STUDY 15.10 Cost of Modification of Building

V Limited (VL) had purchased an old building for ₹10,00,000. The company intended to use it as a training centre. It incurred ₹4,00,000 to modify the building to make it suitable for the intended use.

Question

Advise VL how it should account for the cost incurred for the modification of the building.

Solution

Assuming that the modification of the building was contemplated at the time of acquisition, we advise VL to include the cost of modification in the cost of the asset. Accordingly, VL should record the asset at (₹10,00,000 + ₹4,00,000) or ₹14,00,000.

CASE STUDY 15.11 Demolition Cost

P P Limited (PPL) had purchased a building with land for ₹25,00,000. It allocated the cost between land and building using appraisal method. The company recognised land at ₹15,00,000 and building at ₹10,00,000. Immediately after purchase, it received a notice from the Ahmedabad Municipal Corporation (AMC) advising the company to demolish the unauthorised extension. PPL incurred an expenditure of ₹50,000 to demolish the unauthorised portion. The cost of the unauthorised portion is estimated at ₹1,00,000.

NOTES

Question

Explain how PPL should account for the cost incurred to demolish the unauthorised portion and whether it should write off the cost of the portion of the building demolished.

Solution

The demolition was not contemplated at the time of acquisition. Therefore, PPL should recognise the cost of demolition as an expense in the statement of profit and loss for the year in which the expenditure is incurred. In addition, it should write down the carrying amount of the building by the carrying amount attributable to the portion demolished. Assuming that the demolition was carried out in the year of acquisition, the cost of the demolished portion (₹1,00,000) should be written off as a loss and the cost of the building should be written down by that amount.

CASE STUDY 15.12 Cost of Repairing a used Car Acquired Through Purchase

S Limited (SL) purchased a used car for office use. At the time of purchase, the company estimated that it would incur an additional expenditure of ₹1,00,000 to make the car ready for use. The actual expenditure incurred was ₹2,50,000. The details of repair bill showed that ₹1,30,000 were incurred to repair an accidental damage, which was camouflaged so well that it was not detected during the pre-purchase inspection.

Question

Advise SL how it should account for the cost of repair and modifications to make the car ready for use.

Solution

The repair of the accidental damage was not contemplated at the time of the purchase of the used car. Therefore, an expenditure of ₹1,30,000 attributed to repair the accidental damage should be recognised as an expense in the statement of profit and loss for the period in which the expenditure was incurred. The balance amount of ₹1,20,000 should be included in the cost of the car as it was incurred for repair and modifications contemplated at the time of purchase of the car. The estimated cost of ₹1,00,000 had no bearing on the accounting for the actual expenditure although that had a bearing on the decision to purchase the car.

CASE STUDY 15.13 Cost of Changing Plant Layout

IK Limited (IKL) has incurred an expenditure of ₹5 million to change the plant layout. The objective is to improve the flow of material from one workstation to another. It is expected that the modification will reduce the synthetic time (number of hours to produce one unit of the product) of production and will also reduce the material handling cost.

Question

Explain how IKL should account for the expenditure incurred to change the layout.

Solution

The expenditure should be recognised as expense in the statement of profit and loss for the period in which the expenditure is incurred. The expenditure is not expected to increase economic benefits embedded in items of PP&E, which are relocated. It is difficult to measure the benefits that will flow in future, and consequently, no intangible asset should be recognised from the expenditure.

NOTES

CASE STUDY 15.14 Cost of Relocating Assets

The manufacturing facility of S Limited (SL) was located in an area, which is a victim of flood every year. As a result, the facility could be used only for ten months in a year. In the current year, SL has relocated the factory in another district to ensure that the facility can be used for all the twelve months of the year. It has incurred an expenditure of ₹4 million (excluding the cost of land and building in the new location) to relocate the factory.

Question

Explain how SL should account for the expenditure incurred to relocate the manufacturing facility.

Solution

The expenditure should be recognised as expense in the statement of profit and loss for the period in which the expenditure is incurred. The expenditure is not expected to increase economic benefits embedded in the items of PP&E, which are relocated. It is difficult to measure the benefits that will flow in future due to increase in the use of the items of PP&E, and consequently, no intangible asset should be recognised from expenditure to relocate the factory.

Asset retirement obligation

Cost of dismantling and removing the item and restoring the site after retirement of the asset from use (called *asset retirement obligation*) should be included in the cost of the item of PP&E. An entity estimates the asset retirement obligation and recognises a liability (provision) in the balance sheet and includes the same in the acquisition cost of the asset. The provision is recognised at the *present value of the estimated amount* that will be required to settle the obligation. Usually, the probability-weighted expected value of the amount to be spent is discounted by the risk-free rate, which is the yield-to-maturity of government bond of maturity that matches with the useful life of the asset. In India, yield-to-maturity of 10-year bond is used if the useful life of the asset is ten years or more.

If the liability arises while operating the equipment, the amount of liability is included in the cost of inventory. For example, if the production site gets damaged on production of goods using the equipment, the liability is to be recognised only when the equipment is operated, and the amount of the liability should be included in computing the cost of the goods included in the inventory.

Change in provision due to unwinding of discount

The carrying amount of the provision increases in each period due to unwinding of discount rate. This increase is recognised as borrowing cost in the statement of profit and loss.

ILLUSTRATION 15.1 Change in Provision Due to Unwinding of Discount

The liability as at March 31, 2017 was recognised at ₹10,000, which is the PV of the estimated amount that would be required to fulfill the asset retirement obligation. The PV was calculated using the discount rate of 8 percent. The amount was included in the cost of the asset.

Question

Calculate the carrying amount of liability in the balance sheet as at March 31, 2018, and how the difference will be accounted for in the financial statements for the year 2017-18. Assume that there is no change in the estimated amount that would be required to fulfill the asset retirement obligation.

Solution

The liability should be carried at the balance sheet at (₹10,000 ×1.08) or ₹10,800. The increase of ₹800, being an increase due to unwinding of discount, should be recognised as borrowing cost in the statement of profit and loss for the year 2017–18.

Change in provision due to reasons other than unwinding of discount

Changes in the measurement of an existing decommissioning, restoration and similar liability might result from changes in the estimated timing or amount of the outflow of resources required to settle the obligation, or a change in the discount rate.

Cost model: If the entity uses the cost model for measuring the asset, the carrying amount of the asset is the acquisition cost less accumulated depreciation and accumulated impairment loss. If the entity uses the cost model, increase (decrease) in the liability should be added to (deducted from) the cost of the related asset in the current period. However, if a decrease in the liability exceeds the carrying amount of the asset, the excess shall be recognised immediately in profit or loss.

Revaluation model: If the entity uses the revaluation model for measuring the asset, the asset is revalued periodically and the carrying amount of the asset represents its fair value at the balance sheet date. The revaluation gain is accumulated under revaluation reserve, which is a component of other equity. Revaluation loss is recognised in the statement of profit and loss.

If the entity uses the revaluation model:

(i) Changes in the liability alter the revaluation surplus or deficit previously recognised on that asset, so that:
  (a) a decrease in the liability should (subject to (ii)) be recognised in other comprehensive income and increase the revaluation surplus within equity, except that it shall be recognised in profit or loss to the extent that it reverses a revaluation deficit on the asset that was previously recognised in profit or loss;
  (b) an increase in the liability shall be recognised in profit or loss, except that it shall be recognised in other comprehensive income and reduce the revaluation surplus within equity to the extent of any credit balance existing in the revaluation surplus in respect of that asset.

(ii) In the event that a decrease in the liability exceeds the carrying amount that would have been recognised had the asset been carried under the cost model, the excess shall be recognised immediately in profit or loss.

Change in liability at the end of the useful life: Once the related asset has reached the end of its useful life, all subsequent changes in the liability shall be recognised in profit or loss.

Cost of self-constructed asset

The cost of a self-constructed asset is determined using the same principles as for an acquired asset. If an entity makes similar assets for sale in the normal course of business, the cost of the asset is usually the same as the cost of constructing an asset for sale. Therefore, any internal profits are eliminated in arriving at such costs. Similarly, the cost of abnormal amounts of wasted material, labour, or other resources incurred in self-constructing an asset is not included in the cost of the asset.

Capitalisation of borrowing costs

An entity should capitalise borrowing costs that are directly attributable to the acquisition, construction or production of a 'qualifying asset' as part of the cost of that asset. *Qualifying asset* is defined as an asset that necessarily takes a substantial period of time to get ready for its intended use or sale. Usually, a self-constructed item of PP&E is a qualifying asset. Therefore, directly attributable borrowing costs are recognised in the carrying amount of the item. It is not necessary that the entity should specifically borrow to finance the construction of the asset. An entity may borrow funds generally and use them to finance the construction of the asset.

An entity begins capitalising borrowing costs when it first meets all of the following conditions:

(i) It incurs expenditures for the asset;
(ii) It incurs borrowing costs; and

NOTES

(iii) It undertakes activities that are necessary to prepare the asset for its intended use or sale.

Activities that are necessary to prepare the asset for its intended use or sale include technical and administrative work prior to the commencement of physical construction such as the activities associated with obtaining permits prior to the commencement of the physical construction.

An entity should suspend capitalisation of borrowing costs during extended periods in which it suspends active development of the asset.

An entity should cease capitalising borrowing costs when substantially all the activities necessary to prepare the qualifying asset for its intended use or sale are complete. An asset is normally ready for its intended use or sale when the physical construction of the asset is complete even though routine administrative work might still continue. If minor modifications such as the decoration of a property to the user's specification are all that are outstanding, this indicates that substantially all the activities are complete.

Expenditure during construction period

Entities usually incur indirect expenditures during the construction of a project. Indirect expenditures are those, which cannot be assigned directly to those items of PP&E that have been constructed at the construction site. However, those expenditures are essential to the construction activity. They are allocated to the items of PP&E constructed during the construction period.

Expenditures that are capitalised include the following:

(i) General administration and office expenditure at the construction site;
(ii) Expenditure on running of vehicles;
(iii) Expenditure in connection with temporary structures and service facilities; and
(iv) Depreciation of items of PP&E used.

Accumulation of costs against a specific project should commence from the date the management authorises and commits fund for the project. In a large project, often expenditures that are in the nature of preliminary-stage expenditure are incurred in the pre-acquisition stage. For example, after approval of the project, the project team prepares the detailed project report, conducts surveys and preliminary studies, and negotiates with collaborators on the terms and conditions of collaboration. Those expenditures are directly attributable to the project. They are capitalised as part of the project cost.

However, expenditures that are not attributable to the construction activity should not be capitalised. Examples of such expenditure are expenditure on staff training, expenditure related to work for preparing for production activities, advance publicity campaign, costs involved in borrowing for the purpose of working capital, preliminary corporate expenditure and corporate expenses.

Sometimes, the same group of people, who are supervising current operations, supervises a new project of an existing entity. In that situation, it is difficult to attribute any part of the general administrative and similar expenditure incurred by the entity for its current operations to construction activities. However, if the entity incurs certain additional expenditure that could be avoided had it not taken up the new project, that expenditure might be capitalised. For example, if the firm pays incentive for the additional work involved in supervising the project, the same should be capitalised.

Indirect costs incurred during the construction period are allocated to different items of property, plant and equipment in proportion to the costs of items of PP&E that constitute the project.

Commercial substance: An exchange transaction has commercial substance if the configuration (risk, timing and amount) of the cash flows of the asset received differs from the configuration of the cash flows of the asset transferred; and the difference is significant relative to the fair value of the assets exchanged.

If the cash flows of the asset cannot be identified independently of other assets, the exchange transaction has commercial substance if entity-specific value of the portion of the entity's operations affected by the transaction changes as a result of the exchange; and is significant relative to the fair value of the assets exchanged.

Acquisition through government grant

If government grant is received to subsidise the acquisition of an item of PP&E, the asset is recognised at cost and the grant is recognised as deferred income. An item of PP&E acquired through government grant is measured at its fair value and the amount is recognised as deferred income. The deferred income is recognised in profit or loss on a systematic basis over the useful life of the asset. If it is non-depreciable asset, deferred revenue should be recognised in profit or loss over the life of any obligation attached to that asset. For example, if the grant of a land is conditional on construction of a building over it, deferred revenue may be recognised over the life of the building. If there is no obligation attached to the grant of a non-depreciable asset, the government grant is recognised as other income in the statement of profit or loss for the period in which the asset is received.

NOTES

Key Terms
Asset retirement obligation, commercial substance, directly attributable costs, government grant, unwinding of discount

SUMMARY

At initial recognition, an item of PP&E is measured at its cost. The cost includes purchase price, costs that are directly attributable in bringing the asset in the location and condition of use and the present value of the asset retirement obligation. Recognition of costs in the carrying amount of an item of PP&E ceases when the item is in the location and condition necessary for intended use. The carrying amount of the provision for asset retirement obligation increases in each period due to unwinding of discount rate. This increase is recognised as borrowing cost in the statement of profit and loss. When a company uses the cost model to measure an item of PP&E subsequent to initial recognition, changes in the provision for asset retirement obligation for reasons other than unwinding of discount are adjusted in the carrying amount of the asset. However, if a decrease in the liability exceeds the carrying amount of the asset, the excess shall be recognised immediately in profit or loss. If the entity uses the revaluation model for measuring the asset, such changes in the provision for retirement obligation is adjusted in 'Revaluation Reserve', if any, or in the statement of profit or loss.

The cost of a self-constructed asset is determined using the same principles as for an acquired asset. An entity should capitalise borrowing costs that are directly attributable to the acquisition, construction or production of a 'qualifying asset' as part of the cost of that asset. Usually, a self-constructed item of PP&E is a qualifying asset. Indirect costs, which are incurred during the construction period and are directly attributable to a specific project, are allocated to different items of PP&E in proportion to the costs of items of PP&E that constitute the project. The income and related expenses of incidental operations relating to construction of a project should be recognised in profit or loss for the period. However, income from operations that are necessary for construction activities should be deducted from construction cost.

The cost of an item of PP&E is the cash price equivalent at the recognition date. If payment is deferred beyond normal credit terms, the difference between the cash price equivalent and the total payment is recognised as interest over the credit period. However, such interest is capitalised in accordance with principles for capitalisation of borrowing costs. The cost of such an item of PP&E that is acquired in exchange of a non-monetary asset is measured at its fair value unless (i) the exchange transaction lacks commercial substance or (ii) the fair value of neither the asset received nor the asset given up is reliably measurable. If the acquired item is not measured at fair value, its cost is measured at the carrying amount of the asset given up.

NOTES

Government grant received to subsidise the acquisition of an item of PP&E is recognised as deferred income and is not adjusted to the cost of the asset. An item of PP&E acquired through government grant is measured at its fair value and the amount is recognised as deferred income. The deferred income is recognised in profit or loss on a systematic basis over the useful life of the asset. If it is non-depreciable asset, deferred revenue should be recognised in profit or loss over the life of any obligation attached to that asset. If there is no obligation attached to the grant of a non-depreciable asset, the government grant is recognised as other income in the statement of profit or loss for the period in which the asset is received.

Self-Test Questions

Self-test question 15.3

Indicate whether the following statements are true (T) or false (F):

(i) The purchase price of an item of PP&E is the cash price equivalent at the recognition date.

(ii) Only those costs that are directly attributable to the acquisition or construction of an item of PP&E are included in the acquisition cost of that asset.

(iii) If land and building are acquired in a single transaction, it is not necessary to allocate the purchase price into land and building because land and building belong to the same class of asset.

(iv) Present value of estimated asset retirement obligation is included in the cost of the asset.

(v) The cost of an item of PP&E that is acquired in exchange of a non-monetary asset is usually measured at its fair value.

(vi) Government grant received to subsidise the acquisition of an item of PP&E is initially recognised as deferred revenue.

(vii) Indirect expenditure incurred during the construction of a project is recognised in the statement of profit and loss for the period in which the expenditure is incurred.

(viii) Income earned during construction period is always recognised as income in the statement of profit and loss.

(ix) Borrowing costs directly attributable to the acquisition of an item of PP&E are capitalised.

(x) The additional expenditure incurred to make an item of PP&E ready for use should be a part of the acquisition cost only if the purchase price assumes that the additional expenditure would be incurred to make the asset ready for use.

Subsequent Measurement

Accounting policy choice

An entity has the option to choose either the 'cost model' or the 'revaluation model' as its accounting policy. The choice has to be made for each class of PP&E. For example, it can choose to apply revaluation model for measuring land and cost model for measuring plant and machinery. If it chooses to apply revaluation model to land, it has to apply that model for measuring pieces of land located in different geographic locations. In other words, the accounting policy should be applied to the entire class of PP&E.

Cost model

After recognition as an asset, an item of PP&E is carried at its cost less any accumulated depreciation and any accumulated impairment losses.

Revaluation of items of PP&E is not permitted.

Revaluation model

After recognition as an asset, an item of property, plant and equipment whose fair value can be measured reliably should be carried at a revalued amount, being its fair value at the date of the revaluation less any subsequent accumulated depreciation and subsequent accumulated impairment losses.

Frequency of revaluation: Revaluations should be made with sufficient regularity to ensure that the carrying amount does not differ materially from that, which would be determined using fair value at the end of the reporting period. The frequency of revaluation depends on the changes in fair values of the items of PP&E being revalued. If an item of property, plant and equipment is revalued, the entire class of property, plant and equipment to which that asset belongs should be revalued.

When an item of property, plant and equipment is revalued, the carrying amount of that asset is adjusted to the revalued amount.

Accounting for revaluation gain or loss: If the carrying amount of an asset is increased as a result of a revaluation, the increase is recognised in other comprehensive income and accumulated in other equity under the heading of 'Revaluation Reserve'. The revaluation gain is recognised in profit or loss to the extent that it reverses a revaluation decrease (of the same asset) that was previously recognised in profit or loss.

If the carrying amount of an asset is decreased as a result of a revaluation, the decrease is recognised in profit or loss. However, the decrease is recognised in other comprehensive income to the extent of any credit balance existing in the revaluation surplus in respect of that asset. The decrease recognised in other comprehensive income reduces the amount accumulated in equity under the heading of 'Revaluation Reserve'.

ILLUSTRATION 15.4 Revaluation Gain

A machine with carrying amount (book value) of ₹1,000 is revalued at ₹1,500 on March 31, 2018.

Required

Explain how the revaluation should be accounted for.

Solution

The asset's carrying amount in the balance sheet as at March 31, 2018 should be restated at ₹1,500 and revaluation gain of ₹500 should be recognised in other comprehensive income. The revaluation gain of ₹500 is a part of other equity. It should be presented as a separate line item as "revaluation reserve".

ILLUSTRATION 15.5 Revaluation Loss and Subsequent Revaluation Gain

A machine, whose book value was ₹1000, was revalued at ₹800 on March 31, 2016. It was further revaluated on March 31, 2018 at ₹750. The depreciation charged for 2016–17 and 2017–18 was ₹150 per annum.

Required

Explain how the revaluation should be accounted for.

Solution

The revaluation loss of ₹200 should be recognised in the statement of profit and loss for the year 2015–16. The carrying amount of the asset as at March 31, 2018 is (₹800 minus depreciation accumulated after revaluation) ₹500. The asset is revalued at ₹750. The revaluation gain is ₹250. Out of this, ₹200 should be recognised in the statement of profit and loss to reverse the earlier recognition of revaluation loss of ₹200. The balance ₹50 is to be recognised in other comprehensive income and shall be presented in the balance sheet as revaluation reserve.

ILLUSTRATION 15.6 Revaluation Gain and Subsequent Revaluation Loss

A piece of land with carrying amount of ₹1,000 was revalued at ₹1,500 on March 31, 2017. The same piece of land is revalued at ₹1,200 on March 31, 2018.

Required

Explain how the revaluation should be accounted for.

NOTES

Solution

The revaluation gain of ₹500 arising from revaluation of the asset on March 31, 2017 was accumulated in other equity and it was presented in the balance sheet as at March 31, 2017 as revaluation reserve. The revaluation loss of ₹300 arising from revaluation of the asset on March 31, 2018 should be recognised in other comprehensive income and not in the statement of profit and loss, and consequently, the 'revaluation reserve' in the balance sheet as at March 31, 2018 shall be ₹200.

Transfer of accumulated revaluation gain to retained earnings

The revaluation reserve included in other equity in respect of an item of property, plant and equipment may be transferred directly to retained earnings when the asset is derecognised. This may involve transferring the whole of the revaluation reserve to retained earnings when the asset is retired or disposed of. However, some of the revaluation reserve may be transferred as the asset is used by an entity. In such a case, the amount of the surplus transferred would be the difference between depreciation based on the revalued carrying amount of the asset and the depreciation based on the asset's original cost. Transfers from revaluation surplus to retained earnings are not made through profit or loss. The effects of taxes on income, if any, resulting from the revaluation of property, plant and equipment are recognised and disclosed in accordance with Ind AS 12, Income Taxes.

SUMMARY

An entity has the option to choose either the 'cost model' or the 'revaluation model' as its accounting policy. The choice has to be made for each class of PP&E. If an entity decides using the revaluation model, it should revalue the asset with sufficient regularity to ensure that the carrying amount does not differ materially from that, which would be determined using fair value at the end of the reporting period. Revaluation gain is accumulated in other equity through other comprehensive income and is transferred to retained earnings when the asset is derecognised or periodically as the asset is used. Revaluation loss is adjusted to 'revaluation reserve', if any, and if revaluation reserve is inadequate or does not exist, it is recognised in profit or loss.

Self-Test Questions

Self-test question 15.4

Indicate whether the following statements are true (T) or false (F):

(i) An entity that uses the cost model for measuring a class of PP&E is allowed to revalue the asset, but not as frequently as is required if the entity uses the revaluation model for measuring items in that class of assets.
(ii) If an entity decides to use the revaluation model for measuring land, it should necessarily use the same for measuring building.
(iii) Under the revaluation model, items of PP&E are measured at fair value.
(iv) No depreciation is charged on an item of PP&E that is measured using the revaluation model.
(v) Revaluation gain and loss are accumulated under equity in the balance sheet through other comprehensive income.
(vi) Revaluation reserve is transferred to retained earnings only when the asset is derecognised.

Derecognition

An entity derecognises the carrying amount of an item of property, plant and equipment on disposal; or when no future economic benefits are expected from its use or disposal.

Disposal

The disposal of an item of property, plant and equipment may occur in a variety of ways (e.g., by sale, by entering into a finance lease or by donation). The date of disposal is the date the recipient obtains control when the performance obligation is satisfied.

PP&E held for sale

An entity classifies an item of property, plant and equipment as held for sale if its carrying amount will be recovered principally through a sale transaction rather than through continuing use. It is measured at the lower of its carrying amount (at the point of classifying the asset as held for sale) and fair value less costs to sell. Gain or loss on sale or change in the carrying amount is recognised in profit or loss.

Gain or loss on disposal

The gain or loss arising from the derecognition of an item of property, plant and equipment is determined as the difference between the net disposal proceeds, if any, and the carrying amount of the item. For example, if the sale proceeds is ₹1,00,000 and the carrying amount at the date of sale is ₹80,000, gain will be ₹20,000.

The gain or loss that arises from derecognition of an item of property, plant and equipment is included in profit or loss when the item is derecognised (unless Ind AS 17 requires otherwise on a sale and leaseback). Gains are not be classified as revenue.

Transfer to inventory on derecognition

An entity that, in the course of its ordinary activities, routinely sells items of property, plant and equipment that it has held for rental to others, transfers such assets to inventories at their carrying amount when they cease to be rented and become held for sale. The proceeds from the sale of such assets are recognised as revenue.

CASE STUDY 15.17 Transfer to Inventory

EF Limited (EFL) is located in Delhi. It is in the business of renting out high-class modern furniture to individuals, customers and companies. Its customer base includes corporate executives, who plan to stay in National Capital Region (NCR) temporarily during their posting in NCR, and the companies, which hire contemporary furniture for their offices and guesthouses. EFL rents out new furniture only. It regularly sells furniture after two years from the date of purchase.

Question

The CFO of EFL seeks your advice on the accounting for furniture.

Solution

EFL's primary business is to rent out furniture. Therefore, furniture meets the definition of property, plant and equipment (PP&E). It should record new furniture as PP&E. It should apply the GAAP for recording for disposal of items of PP&E. Furniture, as items of PP&E, are disposed of when they are retired from the primary business of renting out furniture. According to the GAAP, an entity that is in the business of renting out items of PP&E and regularly sells those items after retirement should transfer the items, after retirement, to inventory. Therefore, after two years, furniture should be classified as inventory.

Important Disclosures

The GAAP lists out the information that entities should disclose in financial statements. For each class of PP&E, financial statements should disclose:

NOTES

(i) The measurement bases used for determining the gross carrying amount;
(ii) The depreciation methods used;
(iii) The useful lives or the depreciation rates used;
(iv) The gross carrying amount and the accumulated depreciation (aggregated with accumulated impairment losses) at the beginning and end of the period; and
(v) A reconciliation of the carrying amount at the beginning and end of the period

The financial statements shall also disclose:

(i) The existence and amounts of restrictions on title, and property, plant and equipment pledged as security for liabilities;
(ii) The amount of expenditures recognised in the carrying amount of an item of property, plant and equipment in the course of its construction;
(iii) The amount of contractual commitments for the acquisition of property, plant and equipment; and
(iv) If it is not disclosed separately in the statement of profit and loss, the amount of compensation from third parties for items of property, plant and equipment that were impaired, lost or given up that is included in profit or loss.

If items of property, plant and equipment are stated at revalued amounts, the entity should disclose the following:

(i) The effective date of the revaluation;
(ii) Whether an independent valuer was involved;
(iii) For each revalued class of property, plant and equipment, the carrying amount that would have been recognised had the assets been carried under the cost model; and
(iv) The revaluation surplus, indicating the change for the period and any restrictions on the distribution of the balance to shareholders.

INTANGIBLE ASSETS

Accounting principles for the accounting for intangible assets are laid down in Ind AS 39, Intangible Assets.

Depreciation and impairment of intangible assets are discussed in Chapter 13.

Nature of Intangible Assets

Intangible resources

Entities frequently acquire, develop, maintain or enhance intangible resources such as scientific or technical knowledge, design and implementation of new processes or systems, licenses, intellectual property, market knowledge and trademarks (including brand names and publishing titles). Common examples of items encompassed by these broad headings are computer software, patents, copyrights, motion pictures, customer lists, mortgage servicing rights, fishing licenses, import quotas, franchises, customer or supplier relationships, customer loyalty, market share, and marketing rights.

All the items described above may not meet the definition of an intangible asset. If an item does not meet the definition of an intangible asset, expenditure to acquire it or generate it internally is recognised as an expense when it is incurred. However, if the item is acquired in a business combination, it forms part of the goodwill recognised at the acquisition date.

Goodwill

Goodwill is an amorphous asset that an entity creates in the course of its operation. It arises from business connections, trade name, regular customers, good reputation, and efficient management. It subsumes intangibles like corporate brand (e.g. highly respected company), product brand, organisation culture, knowledge, high employee morale, and customer

NOTES

relationship. It is the *pre-eminent unidentifiable* intangible asset. Internally generated goodwill is not recognised in the balance sheet because of valuation uncertainty.

In a business combination, the acquirer acquires items of PP&E and intangible assets and it assumes liabilities. If it pays more than the fair value of net assets (assets – liabilities), it is assumed that it has paid for intangible asset that could not be identified separately. Therefore, the excess of the purchase consideration over the fair value of net assets is recognised as goodwill. For example, if the purchase consideration is ₹1,00,000 and fair value of net assets is ₹80,000, the goodwill is measured at (₹1,00,000 – 80,000) or ₹20,000.

If the amount of the purchase consideration is less than the fair value of net assets, the acquirer recognises the excess of the fair value over the purchase consideration in the balance sheet as capital reserve.

Definition of Intangible Asset

An intangible asset is an identifiable non-monetary asset without physical substance.

Identifiability

An asset is identifiable if it either:

(i) is separable, that is, it is capable of being separated or divided from the entity and sold, transferred, licensed, rented or exchanged, either individually or together with a related contract, identifiable asset or liability, regardless of whether the entity intends to do so; or

(ii) arises from contractual or other legal rights, regardless of whether these rights are transferable or separable from the entity or from other rights and obligations.

Control

An economic resource is an asset if the entity controls it. Therefore, an intangible resource meets the definition of asset, if the entity controls it. Usually, control stems from legal rights enforceable in the court of law. For example, an entity controls copyright, patent, and trade mark. But, it has no control over the institutional knowledge of processes developed by it or specific technical knowledge, unless these are protected by patent or copyright. It has insufficient control over employees and the knowledge that resides in them.

Future economic benefits

The future economic benefits flowing from an intangible asset may include revenue from the sale of products or services, cost savings, or other benefits resulting from the use of the asset by the entity. For example, the use of intellectual property in a production process may reduce future production costs rather than increase future revenues.

Intangible asset contained in or on a physical substance

Some intangible assets may be contained in or on a physical substance, but the cost of the physical substance containing the intangible asset is usually not significant. Therefore, the cost is commonly treated as a part of the intangible asset. Examples are compact disk, legal documentation or a film.

In case an intangible asset is an integral part of an item of PP&E, *judgement is required* on whether such an asset should be accounted for as an item of PP&E or as an intangible asset taking into account *which element is predominant*. For example, software used in a numerically controlled machine is an integral part of the machine, and therefore, is accounted for as a component of the machine. On the other hand, the operating platform (software) of a computer is accounted for as an intangible asset, separate from the computer hardware. Similarly, hardware of a website developed for internal use is accounted for as an item of PP&E, while the software is accounted for as an intangible asset.

SUMMARY

An intangible asset is an identifiable non-monetary asset without physical substance. Goodwill is an amorphous asset that an entity creates in the course of its operation. It is the *preeminently unidentifiable* intangible asset. Internally generated goodwill is not recognised in the balance sheet. Goodwill is recognised in a business combination. Some intangible assets may be contained in or on a physical substance, but the cost of the physical substance containing the intangible asset is usually not significant. Therefore, the cost is commonly treated as a part of the intangible asset. In case an intangible asset is an integral part of a tangible fixed asset, *judgement is required* on whether such an asset should be accounted for as an item of property, plant and equipment or as an intangible asset.

Self-Test Questions

Self-test question 15.5

Indicate whether the following statements are true (T) or false (F):

(i) The terms 'intangible asset' and 'fictitious asset' are used interchangeably.
(ii) An intangible asset that is contained in or on a tangible asset is always classified as PP&E.
(iii) An intangible asset that is not separable from goodwill is subsumed in goodwill, unless it arises from contractual or other legal rights.
(iv) An entity derives competitive advantage from the entity's unique institutional knowledge, and therefore, that knowledge is an intangible asset.

Recognition

An intangible asset should be recognised if and only if:

(i) It is probable that the future economic benefits that are attributable to the asset will flow to the enterprise; and
(ii) The cost of the asset can be measured reliably.

An entity shall assess the probability of expected future economic benefits using reasonable and supportable assumptions that represent management's best estimate of the set of economic conditions that will exist over the useful life of the asset. An entity should be extra careful in assessing the probability that future economic benefits will flow to the enterprise. It should give greater *weight to external evidence.*

Measurement

Initial measurement

On initial recognition, an intangible asset is measured at cost.

Cost of an intangible asset acquired separately is determined applying the accounting principles, which are used in determining the cost of an item of PP&E.

The cost of that intangible asset that is acquired in a business combination is its *fair value* at the acquisition date.

Assets acquired by way of government grant

The principles for accounting for items of PP&E that are received as government grant are applicable in accounting for intangible assets that are received as government grant. Any expenditure that is directly attributable to making the asset ready for its intended use should be included in the cost of the asset.

Examples of intangible assets, which an enterprise might receive by way of government grant, are airport landing right, licenses to operate radio or television station, import licenses or quotas, or right to access other restricted resources.

Subsequent measurement

An entity has the option to choose either the cost model or the revaluation model to measure an intangible asset after initial recognition.

If the enterprise chooses to account for an intangible asset using the revaluation model, all the other assets in the class of that intangible asset should be accounted for using the same model unless there is no active market for those assets. The revalued amount is the fair value of the intangible asset at the date of revaluation. *The fair value should be determined by reference to an active market.* As most intangible assets do not have active markets, entities usually use the *cost model* to measure an intangible asset after initial recognition.

The accounting principles applicable for measuring intangible assets using the revaluation model are the same as those applicable for measuring PP&E using the revaluation model.

Subsequent expenditure

Accounting principles are the same as those applicable for the accounting of subsequent expenditure related to an item of PP&E. However, in most situations, subsequent expenditure on an intangible asset is not capitalised because it is difficult (i) to attribute such expenditure directly to a particular intangible asset rather than to the business as a whole; and (ii) to determine whether subsequent expenditure will enhance or maintain the economic benefits that will flow to the enterprise from those assets.

SUMMARY

Control is an important element in the definition of an asset. In many situations, control over assets that could otherwise be classified as intangible assets is insufficient. Therefore, many intangibles do not find a place in the balance sheet as assets. Intangible assets are initially measured at cost. Fair value of intangible assets acquired in a business combination is considered as cost for initial measurement. An entity has the option to choose either the cost model or the revaluation model to measure an intangible asset after initial recognition. As most intangible assets do not have active markets, entities usually use the cost model to measure an intangible asset after initial recognition. Subsequent expenditures on an intangible asset is usually recognise as an expense for the period in which the expenditure is incurred.

Self-Test Questions

Self-test question 15.6

Indicate whether the following statements are true (T) or false (F):

(i) On initial recognition, an intangible asset is measured at fair value.

(ii) The cost of that intangible asset that is acquired in a business combination is its fair value at the acquisition date.

(iii) In most situations, subsequent expenditure on an intangible asset is not capitalised.

Internally Generated Intangible Assets

Internally generated goodwill

The GAAP does not allow recognition of internally generated goodwill due to valuation uncertainties.

Research and development expenditure

Innovation is key to business success. Therefore, research and development are important activities for most business entities. Research and development are two different phases in developing intangible assets internally. Development phase begins when research phase ends. Examples of activities during the development phase are as follows:

(i) The design, construction and testing of pre-production or pre-use prototypes and models;
(ii) The design of tools, jigs, moulds and dies involving new technology;
(iii) The design, construction and operation of a pilot plant that is not of a scale economically feasible for commercial production; and
(iv) The design, construction and testing of a chosen alternative for new or improved materials, devices, products, processes, systems or services.

If an entity cannot distinguish the research phase from the development phase of a project, it should treat the expenditure on the project as if it were incurred in the research phase only.

Expenditure during research phase

The GAAP does not permit recognition of an asset from expenditure incurred during the research phase. Entities recognise expenditure incurred during the research phase as an expense for the period in which the expenditure is incurred.

Expenditure during development phase

An entity recognises an asset from development phase expenditure only if it demonstrates the following:

(i) The technical feasibility of completing the intangible asset;
(ii) Its intention to complete the intangible asset and use or sell it;
(iii) Its ability to use or sell the intangible asset;
(iv) The commercial viability of the intangible asset;
(v) The availability of adequate technical, financial and other resources to complete the development and to use or sell the intangible asset; and
(vi) Its ability to reliably measure the expenditure attributable to the intangible asset during its development.

The accumulation of cost of an asset from the expenditure during the development phase should commence *from the time when the intangible asset first meets the recognition criteria.* Development expenditure that was initially recognised as an expense in previous *annual financial statements* or *interim financial reports* should not be recognised as part of the cost of an intangible asset later.

Usually, entities do not recognise an asset from the development expenditure because it is often quite difficult to demonstrate that the expenditure meets the recognition criteria.

PP&E related to R&D activities

If an item of property, plant and equipment that is purchased and used for research has alternative uses, it is accounted for as any other item of PP&E. For example, a building in which research facilities are located should be accounted for an item of PP&E if the building has alternative use.

Internally generated intangible assets other than goodwill

Brands, mastheads and similar assets

The GAAP does not permit recognition of internally generated brands, mastheads, publishing titles, customers' list, and items similar in substance as intangible assets because expenditure on those items cannot be distinguished from the cost of developing the business as a whole.

Entities recognise in the balance sheet brands and similar assets acquired either individually or with other assets.

Recognition of an expense

The GAAP does not permit recognition of intangible assets from the following and similar expenditures:

(i) Expenditure on start-up activities (i.e., start-up cost), unless it is included in the cost of an item of PP&E. Start-up cost may consist of establishment cost such as legal and secretarial cost incurred in establishing a legal entity and pre-operating costs;
(ii) Expenditure on training activities;
(iii) Expenditure on advertising and promotional activities;
(iv) Expenditure on relocating or reorganising part or all of an entity; and
(v) Expenditure on Voluntary Retirement Schemes (VRSs).

SUMMARY

The GAAP does not permit recognition of internally generated goodwill. It does not permit recognition of an intangible asset from expenditure incurred during the research phase. It permits recognition of an intangible asset from expenditure incurred during the development phase only if it meets some stringent criteria. Entities usually do not recognise an asset from expenditure incurred during the development phase. If an item of property, plant and equipment that is purchased and used in research has alternative uses, it is accounted for as any other item of PP&E. The GAAP does not permit recognition of internally generated brands, mastheads, publishing titles, customers-list and items similar in substance. Brands and similar assets acquired either individually or with other assets should be recognised in the balance sheet. It does not permit recognition of assets from expenditures on start-up activities, training, and advertising and product promotion.

Self-Test Questions

Self-test question 15.7

Indicate whether the following statements are true (T) or false (F):

(i) The GAAP does not allow recognition of internally generated goodwill due to valuation uncertainties.
(ii) An entity can recognise an intangible asset from expenditure incurred during the research phase provided it demonstrates its financial and other capabilities to complete the research and development and economic viability of the new product or process.
(iii) An entity recognises an asset from expenditure on advertisement and sales promotion if the management estimates that the expenditure will benefit the entity for more than one year.
(iv) Product brands acquired from a third party are recognised in the balance sheet.
(v) If an item of property, plant and equipment, which is purchased and used for research has alternative uses, it is accounted for as any other item of PP&E.

Software and Website

Software for internal use

Preliminary stage costs should be recognised as expenses for the period in which these costs are incurred. Cost capitalisation commences when an entity has completed the conceptual formulation, design, and testing of possible project alternatives, including the process of vendor selection for purchased software. Costs incurred subsequent to the preliminary project stage are capitalised if they are expected to provide economic benefits over a number of periods. Costs incurred during the application development stage of the software development process are also capitalised. These include coding and testing activities and various implementation costs. These costs are limited to:

(i) External direct costs of materials and services consumed in developing or obtaining internal-use computer software.
(ii) Payroll and payroll-related costs of employees who are directly associated with the company and who devote time to the internal-use software project to the extent of time directly spent on the project.
(iii) Interest costs incurred while developing internal-use software.

General and administrative costs, overheads and training costs are expensed as incurred.

Website costs

An entity's own Website, which is created for internal or external access, is an internally generated intangible asset. A Website which is an outgrowth of development should be recognised as an intangible asset if and only if an entity can demonstrate how its Website will generate probable future economic benefits. For example, it may demonstrate that the website is capable of generating revenues, including direct revenues from enabling customers to place orders. An entity, when it is not able to demonstrate how a Website developed solely or primarily for promoting and advertising its own products and services will generate probable future economic benefits, all expenditure on developing such a Website should be recognised as an expense when incurred.

Any expenditure which is incurred internally on the development and operation of an entity's own Website should be accounted for in accordance with the accounting principles for the accounting for expenditure incurred during the development phase. An entity should evaluate the nature of each activity for which expenditure is incurred (e.g., training employees and maintaining the Website) and the Website's stage of development or post-development to determine the appropriate accounting treatment. The following general guidelines may be followed:

(i) Expenditure incurred in the planning stage should be recognised as an expense when it is incurred.
(ii) The application and infrastructure development stage, the graphical design stage and the content development stage, to the extent that the content is developed for purposes other than to advertise and promote an entity's own products and services, are similar in nature to the development phase. Expenditure incurred in these stages shall be included in the cost of a Website recognised as an intangible asset when the expenditure can be directly attributable to and is necessary to create, produce or prepare the Website for it to be capable of operating in the manner intended by the management. For example, expenditure on purchasing or creating content (other than content that advertises and promotes an entity's own products and services) specifically for a Website, or expenditure to enable use of the content (e.g., a fee for acquiring a license to reproduce) on the Website, should be included in the cost of development.
(iii) Expenditure incurred in the content development stage, to the extent that the content is developed to advertise and promote an entity's own products and services (e.g., digital photographs of products), should be recognised as an expense when incurred.
(iv) The operating stage begins once development of a Website is complete. Expenditure incurred in this stage should be recognised as an expense when it is incurred.

INVESTMENT PROPERTY

Accounting principles for the accounting for investment property is laid down in Ind AS 40, Investment Property.

NOTES

Nature of Investment Property

Property, in the context of investment property, is land or a building. An entity holds investment property to earn rentals or capital appreciation or both. In contrast, an entity holds 'owner-occupied property' for use in the production or supply of goods or services or for administrative purposes. An owner-occupied property is classified as property, plant and equipment.

The distinguishing feature of an investment property is that it generates cash flows largely independently of the other assets held by an entity. An owner-occupied property generates cash flows that are attributable not only to the property but also to other assets used in the production or supply process.

Dual-use property

An entity may hold a portion of the property to earn rentals or for capital appreciation, and hold another portion for use in the production or supply of goods or services or for administrative purposes. It classifies the portion the property, which it holds to earn rentals or for capital appreciation, as an investment property only if it can sell that portion separately (or can lease out that portion separately under a finance lease). If the entity cannot sell the portion separately, it classifies the whole property as an investment property, only when it holds an insignificant portion of the property for use in the production or supply of goods or services or for administrative purposes.

Classifying a dual-use property either as an investment property or as an item of PP&E is a matter of judgement, if the entity cannot sell the portion that it holds for rental or capital appreciation separately.

Entity providing ancillary services

In some cases, an entity provides ancillary services to the occupants of a property it holds. The classification of such a property depends on whether the services that the entity provides are significant or insignificant. The property is classified as an investment property if the services are insignificant to the arrangement as a whole.

It may be difficult to determine whether ancillary services being provided by the entity are significant or insignificant. Entities develop criteria for assessing whether ancillary services are significant and apply the same consistently.

Property under construction

An entity classifies a property under construction as an investment property or as an item of PP&E based on the intended use of the property.

Property held for a currently undetermined future use

Property held for a currently undetermined future use should be classified as an investment property.

CASE STUDY 15.18 Classification of Property

N D Limited (NDL) specialises in constructing multi-level car parking. It uses different business models for earning income from car parks constructed by it. The following are the business models:

(i) **Business model 1:** The company constructs car parks adjacent to apartments owned by it and which it holds solely to earn rental income. Designated space in each car park is allotted to each resident of the apartment adjacent to which the car park is located. The rent of the car park space is included in the rent of the apartment. Only residents of the apartments have the right to use the car park. The company operates those car parks.

(ii) **Business model 2:** The company constructs car parks adjacent to apartments, which it does not own. It sells the designated spaces in the cark park to owners of the apartments adjacent to which the car park is located. It operates those car parks.

(iii) **Business model 3:** The company constructs car parks in municipal markets. Anyone can use the car park located in a market. The company charges fees on hourly basis for using the car park facilities. The company operates those car parks.

Question

The CFO of NDL seeks you advice on how the car parks already constructed and car parks under construction are to be classified for presentation in the balance sheet. Should they be classified as property, plant and equipment (PP&E), investment property or inventory?

Solution

(i) **Business model 1:** Car parks, which have been constructed or which are under construction, should be classified as investment property because they are part of the apartments, which the company holds to earn rent. The service provided by operating the car park is insignificant as compared to the services that apartment owners require for a decent living.

(ii) **Business model 2:** The company does not own the apartments adjacent to which car parks are constructed. It constructs the car parks to sell designated spaces. Therefore, it should classify car parks, which are already constructed, and those under construction as inventory.

(iii) **Business model 3:** The company neither sells the designated space in car parks nor rent out designated spaces. Therefore, it is inappropriate to classify the car parks either as inventory or as investment property. The company uses the car parks for providing car-parking service. Therefore, it should classify car parks, which are already constructed, and those under construction as PP&E.

CASE STUDY 15.19 Classification of Property

FG Hotels Limited (FGHL) is a hotel chain in India. It runs three-star and five-star hotels to cater to different customer segments. It has around 50 hotels in the country. The following are the business models:

Model 1: The company owns the property and manages the hotel. It outsources operating activities to an outsourcing partner. The cash flow risk is born by the company.

Model 2: The company owns the property and leases out to an entity to manage the hotel. The lease rent includes the royalty for using the brand and logo owned by the company. The cash flow risk is born by the lessee.

Question

The CFO requests you to advise her on how the hotel properties should be classified for presentation in the financial statements.

Solution

Model 1: The company bears the cash flow risk, although it has outsourced operating services to an outsourcing partner. It does not hold the property to earn rent or for capital appreciation. Therefore, it is inappropriate to classify the property as an investment property. The property should be classified as PP&E.

Model 2: The company does not bear the cash flow risk. Its earning from the property is lease rent. Therefore, it is appropriate to classify the property as an investment property.

Recognition and Measurement

Recognition

Investment property should be recognised as an asset when, and only when:

(a) It is probable that the future economic benefits that are associated with the investment property will flow to the entity; and
(b) The cost of the investment property can be measured reliably.

Measurement

The accounting principles for the initial measurement of an investment property are the same as those for the initial measurement of PP&E.

The GAAP allows use of the cost model only for the subsequent measurement of an investment property. The accounting principles for measuring an investment property using the cost model are the same for measuring PP&E using the cost model.

Measurement for disclosure

The GAAP requires all entities to measure the fair value of investment property for the purpose of disclosure even though they are required to follow the cost model. An entity is encouraged, but not required, to measure the fair value of investment property on the basis of a valuation by an independent valuer who holds a recognised and relevant professional qualification and has recent experience in the location and category of the investment property being valued.

SUMMARY

An entity holds investment property (land and building) to earn rentals or capital appreciation or both. The distinguishing feature of an investment property is that it generates cash flows largely independently of the other assets held by an entity. An entity classifies the portion of a dual-use property, which it holds to earn rentals or for capital appreciation, as an investment property, only if it can sell that portion separately (or can lease out that portion separately under a finance lease). The accounting principles for the initial measurement of an investment property are the same as those for the initial measurement of PP&E. The GAAP requires all entities to measure the fair value of investment property for the purpose of disclosure even though they are required to follow the cost model.

Self-Test Questions

Self-test question 15.8

Indicate whether the following statements are true (T) or false (F):

(i) The distinguishing feature of an investment property is that it generates cash flows largely independently of the other assets held by an entity.
(ii) Employee quarters are classified as investment property if the entity recovers rent from employees.
(iii) An entity has the choice either to use the cost model or to use the revaluation model to measure investment properties subsequent to initial recognition.
(iv) An entity should mandatorily disclose the fair value of investment properties.
(v) An entity that runs hotel business necessarily classifies a property, which it has leased out to a third party for use as a hotel, as investment property.

NOTES

ANSWERS TO SELF-TEST QUESTIONS

15.1 (i) T; (ii) F; (iii) F; (iv) F; (v) F

15.2 (i) T; (ii) F; (iii) T; (iv) T; (v) T

15.3 (i) T; (ii) T; (iii) F; (iv) T; (v) T; (vi) T; (vii) F; (viii) F; (ix) F; (x) T

15.4 (i) F; (ii) F; (iii) T; (iv) F; (v) F; (vi) F

15.5 (i) F; (ii) F; (iii) T; (iv) F

15.6 (i) F; (ii) T; (iii) T

15.7 (i) T; (ii) F; (iii) F; (iv) T; (v) T

15.8 (i) T; (ii) F; (iii) F; (iv) T; (v) F

ASSIGNMENTS

Quiz

1. Tick the most appropriate statement:

   (i) Events other than transactions entered into by an enterprise
   - (a) do not result in recognition or derecognition of assets or liabilities.
   - (b) might result in recognition or derecognition of assets or liabilities or change in their carrying amount.
   - (c) might result in recognition or derecognition of assets, but never result in recognition or derecognition of liabilities.
   - (d) might result in recognition or derecognition of liabilities.

   (ii) Evidence that supports recognition of an asset or a liability
   - (a) should necessarily be external evidence.
   - (b) should not necessarily be external evidence, but external evidence is considered superior to internal evidence.
   - (c) should necessarily be internal evidence.
   - (d) can either be an external evidence or internal evidence.

   (iii) Control of the enterprise over a resource is an essential requirement for recognising it as an asset, and such control
   - (a) should necessarily be supported by legal protection.
   - (b) should not be supported by any evidence—that management's perception is enough for recognising the asset.
   - (c) should not necessarily be supported by legal protection, though legal protection provides a strong evidence of control.
   - (d) comes from ownership rights only.

   (iv) Recognition of an asset or liability requires resolution of uncertainties as to the future inflow or outflow of economic benefits to or from the enterprise. The uncertainty gets resolved at an acceptable level
   - (a) for both asset and liability, if it is probable (more likely than not) that economic benefit will flow *to* or *from* the enterprise.
   - (b) for both asset and liability, if it is sufficiently certain that economic benefit will flow *to* or *from* the enterprise.
   - (c) for the asset, if it is sufficiently certain that economic benefit will flow *to* the enterprise, and for the liability, if it is probable that the economic benefit will flow *from* the enterprise.
   - (d) for both asset and liability, if there is any possibility that economic benefit will flow *to* or *from* the enterprise.

   (v) In recognising assets or liabilities, accountants
   - (a) balance relevance and reliability.
   - (b) assign greater importance to relevance than reliability.

(c) assign greater importance to reliability than relevance.
(d) place importance on reliability and ignore relevance.

(vi) Under historical cost basis of measurement, an item of property, plant and equipment
(a) is always carried at acquisition cost.
(b) is carried at fair value as on the balance sheet's date.
(c) is carried at fair value on the date of acquisition, adjusted for depreciation and impairment loss.
(d) is carried at acquisition cost, adjusted for depreciation and impairment loss.

(vii) In selecting the appropriate basis for measuring assets and liabilities, the thumb rule is
(a) if both the historical cost measure and the current value measure are reliable, historical cost is the better measure.
(b) if both the historical cost measure and the current value measure are reliable, current value measure is the better measure.
(c) if both the historical cost measure and the current value measure are reliable, the better measure to use will be the one that is the most relevant.
(d) if only one of the measures available is reliable, that should be used even if it is not relevant.

(viii) As a general rule, the cost of an item of property, plant and equipment
(a) always includes expenditure on start-up and commissioning.
(b) does not include expenditure on start-up and commissioning.
(c) includes only the expenditure on commissioning.
(d) includes expenditure on start-up and commissioning *only* if the asset is incapable of operating at normal level without such a start-up or commissioning period.

(ix) Under Ind AS, goodwill
(a) should not be recognised in the balance sheet.
(b) should be recognised in the balance sheet.
(c) except internally generated goodwill, may be recognised in the balance sheet and should be amortised over a period to be decided by the management.
(d) except internally generated goodwill, may be recognised in the balance sheet and should be tested for impairment annually.

2. Indicate against each statement whether it is true (T) or false (F)

(i) The concept of deferred revenue expenditure is not relevant in the asset-liability measurement approach.
(ii) In accounting, external evidence is considered superior to internal evidence.
(iii) Historical cost is always a better measure as compared to the fair value measure.
(iv) An attribute cannot be considered unreliable, solely because it is subjective.
(v) The estimated cost of dismantling and removing an asset and restoring the site should not be included in the cost of tangible fixed assets.
(vi) Borrowing costs should not be included in the cost of an item of property, plant and equipment unless the fund is borrowed specifically for the asset.
(vii) The cost of an item of property, plant and equipment should be adjusted for change in the carrying amount of the related liability, denominated in foreign currency, due to change in exchange rates.
(viii) It is the management's discretion to decide the periodicity of subsequent revaluation of the revalued fixed assets.
(ix) Revaluation reserve is not available for distribution to shareholders either as dividend or as bonus shares.
(x) An item of property, plant and equipment temporarily retired from active use should be stated at the lower of its net book value and net realisable value.
(xi) An item of property, plant and equipment, classified as 'held for sale', should be carried at the lower of its net book value and fair value less costs to sell.
(xii) Acquisition of a group of assets purchased from another enterprise might result in recognition of goodwill.
(xiii) An enterprise is usually precluded from recognising an intangible asset purchased as a part of business acquisition if it is not traded in an active market.
(xiv) Major stores and spare parts may qualify for recognition as items of PP&E.

(xv) The cost of an item of property, plant and equipment is the cash price equivalent at the recognition date.

(xvi) The carrying amount of the fixed asset should be adjusted for exchange difference arising on settlement or restatement of a liability, denominated in a foreign currency, assumed on acquisition of the item of PP&E.

(xvii) Administration and other general overhead costs allocated to activities related to the construction of a building internally by an entity are directly attributable to the construction of the building and should be included in its acquisition cost.

(xviii) Borrowing costs incurred on borrowings, which are directly attributable to the construction of a project, up to the commencement of commercial use of the facility should be capitalised.

(xix) Increase in the provision for asset retirement obligation during a particular period should be adjusted to the carrying amount of the asset.

(xx) Expenditure incurred to bring the fixed asset to its working condition should not be capitalised if the same was not contemplated at the time of acquisition of the asset.

3. Tick the most appropriate answer:

(i) Mallika Limited (ML) purchased a machine for ₹20,00,000 for its manufacturing operation and paid transportation charge of ₹10,000. In addition, ML spent ₹50,000 towards testing and preparing the machine for use. The cost of the machine should be recorded at

(a) ₹20,60,000 (b) ₹20,10,000

(c) ₹20,50,000 (d) ₹20,00,000

(ii) On December 1, 2006, Shipra Limited (SL) purchased a piece of land for ₹40,00,000 for a factory site. SL razed an old structure and sold the material salvaged from the old structure. The company incurred additional costs and realised salvage proceeds during December 2006 as follows:

Demolition of old building	₹70,000
Legal fees	₹50,000
Registration charges	₹4,00,000
Proceeds from sale of salvaged material	₹15,000

In its balance sheet on December 31, 2006, SL should carry the land at

(a) ₹44,50,000 (b) ₹45,20,000

(c) ₹45,05,000 (d) ₹40,00,000

(iii) In 2006, Anuj Limited (AL) had purchased an old building on a free hold land for ₹80,00,000. The fair value of the land was estimated at ₹40,00,000. AL paid ₹10,00,000 towards registration charges and it incurred ₹50,000 towards legal expenses for documentation and registration. When renovation of the building was in progress, AL received a notice from the local municipal corporation for demolition of the building as the building plan was not approved by the municipality. AL appointed a lawyer to deal with the issue. A settlement was reached, according to which AL had to pay penalty of ₹5,00,000 and it had to demolish a part of the building. The cost of demolition was ₹1,00,000. The lawyer was paid ₹20,000. An architect estimated that the part demolished constituted 5 percent of the original building in terms of its value. The building should be carried (gross block) in the balance sheet as at December 31, 2006 at

(a) ₹45,25,000 (b) ₹51,45,000

(c) ₹42,98,750 (d) ₹48,87,750

(iv) Nisha Limited (NL) began constructing a building for its own use in January 2006. During 2006, NL incurred an interest of ₹60,000 on the amount specifically borrowed for construction of the building, and ₹20,000 on other borrowings. Interest computed on the weighted average amount of accumulated expenditures for the building during the year 2006 was ₹35,000. NL should capitalise interest amounting to

(a) ₹60,000 (b) ₹35,000

(c) ₹80,000 (d) ₹20,000

(v) On April 20, 2007, Preeti Limited (PL) exchanges a car for 1,000 equity shares of Indian Oil Corporation Limited (IOCL). On that date, the written down value of the car was ₹3,50,000 and its fair value was ₹4,50,000. On that date, the share price of IOCL in the Bombay Stock exchange (BSE) was ₹395 per share. PL intends to hold the share for long term. PL should record the cost of investment at

NOTES

(a) ₹3,50,000 (b) ₹3,95,000
(c) ₹4,50,000 (d) ₹4,00,000

(vi) Omkara Limited (OL) participated in an auction of a 'haveli' (manson) which was put on auction by the revenue department of the government. OL purchased the haveli for ₹2 crore. The most popular and respected business 'daily' reported that the government could not realise the fair value of the property as Mr. Omkara participated in the auction. The daily estimates the fair value at ₹4 crore. The newspaper daily alleges that the reserve price was set at ₹2 crore to facilitate OL's acquisition of the property at a discount. OL should record the haveli as an asset at

(a) ₹2 crore (b) ₹4 crore
(c) ₹3 crore (d) None of the above

4. Fill in the blanks:

(i) A piece of equipment imported from the USA on deferred credit basis during the reporting period (calendar year) was recorded at ₹4,00,000 ($1 = ₹40). On the balance sheet's date, the exchange rate is $1 = ₹45. Under Ind AS, the asset should be carried in the balance sheet at ₹________ (ignore depreciation).

(ii) The carrying amount of a machine as on January 1, 2006 was ₹1,00,000. The enterprise revalues the asset on that date at ₹1,40,000. The asset was first revalued in 2003, and a revaluation loss of ₹10,000 was recognised. Revaluation reserve should be recognised at ₹________.

(iii) The gross book value and accumulated depreciation of an asset as on January 1, 2006 are ₹1,50,000 and ₹90,000, respectively. On June 30, 2006, the asset is sold at Rs 70,000. The profit/(loss) on sale of the asset is ₹________ (ignore depreciation for 2006).

(iv) During the reporting period (calendar year) 2005, an enterprise incurred an expenditure of ₹4,00,000 on development of a new product. Out of the total expenditure, ₹3,50,000 were incurred till November 30, 2005. The expenditure met the criteria for recognition of an intangible asset on December 1, 2005. The recoverable amount of the know-how is estimated at ₹1,00,000. During 2006, expenditure incurred is ₹10,00,000. On the balance sheet's date, the recoverable amount is estimated at ₹9,50,000. In the balance sheet as at December 13, 2005, the intangible asset was recognised at ₹________. The cost of the intangible asset till December 13, 2006 is ₹________. The intangible asset should be recognised in the balance sheet as at December 31, 2006 at ₹________.

Analytical Questions

1. The factory of Aman Limited, located at Naini near Allahabad, faced a hailstorm in 2005, causing serious damage to the roof of the factory building. The company incurred an expenditure of ₹1 million to put a new roof on the building. Should the expenditure be capitalised?

2. Sania Limited (SL) borrows funds to finance large projects. The lending institution releases funds in agreed instalments. Usually, funds are released at the interval of six months to meet the requirements for the next six months. SL parks the funds released by the lending institution in treasury bills of different maturity.

   Should the interest earned on investments in treasury bills be deducted from the amount of interest paid to the lending institution to arrive at the borrowing cost to be capitalised?

3. Charlie Limited purchased a '*BMW*' for use by its Chief Executive Officer (CEO). The car met with an accident while driving to the factory immediately after taking delivery from the showroom. The car had no insurance cover.

   The firm incurred an expenditure of ₹0.3 million to repair the car, which includes the cost of a new engine to replace the engine damaged in the accident. Should the expenditure be capitalised?

Problem

1. India Cables Limited commissioned a plant imported from Germany at a cost of ₹50 million on January 1, 2005. Initially, due to a technical snag, the output produced by the machine did not meet the specifications and the quality guaranteed by the supplier. It could produce cables shorter than the standard length and of low quality. A team of engineers from the firm that supplied the machine visited the plant on January 31, 2005 but could not rectify the defect. Another team visited the plant on March 30, 2005. They could not fully rectify the defect, but they could make the machine capable of producing high-quality cable although of shorter length.

NOTES

The company decided to continue to operate the plant.

From April 15, 2005, India Cables Limited, in order to reduce losses, produced and sold sub-quality shorter length cables as seconds. After prolonged negotiations, the supplier firm agreed to refund ₹15 million.

India Cables Limited proposes to capitalise ₹40 million of expenditure incurred by it on salaries, wages and other overhead expenses during the period January 1, 2005 to April 14, 2005, which constitute start-up and commissioning costs.

Advise whether the company should capitalise the expenditure. Also, advise whether the amount refunded by the supplier should be deducted from the cost of the machine.

CHAPTER 16

Inventories

Learning Objectives

This chapter discusses the accounting principles for the measurement of inventories.

After reading this chapter, you will develop understanding of the following:

- Nature of inventories
- Measurement of finished goods, work-in-progress, raw materials and components
- Measurement of cost of finished goods, work-in-progress, raw materials and components
- Principles for assigning fixed production overheads to inventories
- Concept of net realisable value
- Concept of FIFO and weighted-average cost
- Retail method for measuring inventories

Accounting principles for the accounting for investment property are laid down in Ind AS 2, Inventories. The accounting principles discussed in this section are not applicable to inventories of financial instruments, and biological assets related to agricultural activity and agricultural produce at the point of harvest.

NATURE OF INVENTORIES

Inventories are the assets

(i) held for sale in the ordinary course of business;
(ii) in the process of production for such sale; or
(iii) in the form of materials or supplies to be consumed in the production process or in the rendering of services.

Inventories encompass goods purchased and held for resale, including, merchandise purchased by a retailer and held for resale, or land and other property held for resale. Inventories also encompass finished goods produced or work-in-progress being produced by the entity and materials and supplies awaiting use in the production process.

Stores and spares, which cannot be classified as PP&E, are classified as inventory.

MEASUREMENT PRINCIPLE

General Principle

Entities should measure inventories at the lower of cost and net realisable value.

The practice of writing inventories down below cost to net realisable value is consistent with the view that assets should not be carried in excess of amounts that the entity expects to realise from their sale or use.

Inventories are usually written down to net realisable value item by item. In some circumstances, however, it may be appropriate to group similar or related items. This may be the case with items of inventory relating to the same product line that have similar purposes or end uses, are produced and marketed in the same geographical area, and cannot be practicably evaluated separately from other items in that product line.

Table 16.1 presents an example of the principle for comparing cost and NRV.

TABLE 16.1

Comparison of Costs and NRVs

Item of stock	Cost (₹)	NRV (₹)	Carrying amount of inventory (₹)
Cricket bat	1,00,000	1,10,000	1,00,000
Cricket ball	1,00,000	90,000	90,000
Tennis racket	1,00,000	1,05,000	1,00,000
Tennis ball	1,00,000	95,000	95,000
Total	4,00,000	4,00,000	3,85,000

Observation

The aggregate of production cost equals the aggregate realisable value, and therefore, if global comparison is allowed, the inventory should be valued at ₹4,00,000. However, global comparison is not permitted; hence, the inventory should be measured at ₹3,85,000.

Table 16.2 presents measurement principles applicable to different types of inventories.

NOTES

TABLE 16.2

Measurement Principles Applicable to Different Types of Inventories

S. No.	Inventory type	Comments	Measurement principle
1.	Service provider's inventory (work-in-progress)	Ind AS 2 is not applicable. Ind AS 115, Revenue from Contract with Customers, is applicable.	Costs to fulfill a contract, which relate directly to a contract or anticipated contract and are recoverable.
2.	Construction contractor's inventory (work-in-progress)	Ind AS 2 is not applicable. Ind AS 115, Revenue from Contract with Customers, is applicable.	Costs to fulfill a contract, which relate directly to a contract or anticipated contract and are recoverable.
3.	Producer's inventories of commodities (minerals and mineral products).	Ind AS 2 is not applicable. Measurement at NRV is in accordance with well-established practice.	NRV
4.	Broker-trader's inventories of commodities.	Ind AS 2 is not applicable. Broker-traders acquire them for selling in the near future and generate profit from fluctuations in price or broker-trader's margin.	Fair value less costs to sell
5.	Inventories of financial instruments held by a stock broker	Ind AS 2 is not applicable. Ind AS 32, Financial Instruments: Presentation, and Ind AS 109, Financial Instruments, are applicable.	Fair value
6.	Inventories of biological assets (i.e., living animals or plants) related to agricultural activity and agricultural produce at the point of harvest	Ind AS 2 is not applicable. Ind AS 41, Agriculture, is applicable	Fair value less costs to sell
7.	Producer's inventories of agricultural and forest produce	Ind AS 2 is not applicable. Measurement at NRV is in accordance with well-established practice.	NRV
8.	Producer's inventories of agricultural produce after harvest	Ind AS 2 is not applicable. Measurement at NRV is in accordance with well-established practice.	NRV
9.	Inventory of 'agricultural produce after harvest' held by an entity other than the producer	Ind AS 2 is applicable.	Lower of cost and NRV
10.	Real estate developer's inventories of apartments and buildings and those under construction	Ind AS 2 is applicable.	Lower of cost and NRV
11.	Merchandiser's inventories of goods	Ind AS 2 is applicable.	Lower of cost and NRV
12.	Manufacturer's inventory of finished goods and work-in-progress	Ind AS 2 is applicable.	Lower of cost and NRV

(*Contd.*)

NOTES

TABLE 16.2

Measurement Principles Applicable to Different Types of Inventories (*Contd.*)

S. No.	Inventory type	Comments	Measurement principle
13.	Inventories of raw materials and components	Ind AS 2 is applicable.	Usually, at cost. At replacement cost, a decline in the price of materials indicates that the cost of the finished products exceeds NRV.
14.	Inventories of stores and spare parts	Ind AS 2 is applicable.	Cost, adjusted for decline in value
15.	Inventories of loose tools	Ind AS 2 is applicable.	Cost, adjusted for decline in value

COST

The cost of inventories shall comprise all costs of purchase, costs of conversion and other costs incurred in bringing the inventories to their present location and condition.

Cost of agricultural produce harvested from biological assets

The GAAP requires that inventories comprising agricultural produce that an entity has harvested from its biological assets should be measured on initial recognition at their fair value less costs to sell at the point of harvest. This is the cost of the inventories at that date.

Cost of purchase

The cost of purchase of inventories comprises the purchase price, import duties and other taxes (other than those subsequently recoverable by the entity from the taxing authorities), and transport, handling and other costs directly attributable to the acquisition of finished goods, materials and services. Trade discounts, rebates and other similar items are deducted in determining the cost of purchase.

Discounts

Cash, trade or volume discounts and rebates received are deducted from the cost of purchase. If it is probable that the rebate or volume discount will be earned and the amount can be estimated reliably, then the discount or rebate should be recognised as a reduction in the purchase price when the inventory is bought. If the discount or rebate is recognised subsequent to when the item is sold, then the proportionate amount of discount attributable to items sold should be recognised in profit or loss.

Demurrage charge

Demurrage charge is the charge for storage in a warehouse (e.g., custom authority's warehouse, warehouse of a shipping line or airline, and warehouse of railway), which accrues after a given time, for consignments not collected. Demurrage charge is not a cost that is necessarily incurred to bring the goods to the location and condition of sale. Therefore, demurrage charge should not be included in the cost of purchase, and consequently, in the cost of inventories.

Purchase on deferred settlement

An entity may purchase inventories on deferred settlement terms. Such an arrangement effectively contains a financing element. For example, the difference between the purchase price under normal credit terms and the purchase price under deferred settlement represents the finance element, which is recognised as interest expense over the period of financing.

Cost of conversion

The cost of conversion of inventories includes costs directly related to the units of production such as direct labour. It also includes a systematic allocation of fixed and variable production overheads that are incurred in converting materials into finished goods.

Fixed production overheads

Fixed production overheads are those indirect costs of production that remain relatively constant regardless of the volume of production, such as depreciation and maintenance of factory buildings and equipment, and the cost of factory management and administration.

Entities should allocate fixed production overheads to the costs of conversion based on the normal capacity of the production facilities. In periods of abnormally high production, the amount of fixed production allocated to conversion cost based on the normal capacity is decreased so that inventories are not measured above cost.

Normal capacity

Normal capacity is the production that the entity expects to achieve on average over a number of periods or seasons under normal circumstances, taking into account the loss of capacity resulting from planned maintenance. The actual level of production may be used if it approximates normal capacity. The following factors should be considered in determining the normal capacity:

(i) The nature of business, economic factors, the status of product life cycles, and the reliability of forecasts;
(ii) Installed (maximum) capacity and planned maintenance shut down; and
(iii) Expected average utilisation of capacity over the number of periods, adjusted for unusual fluctuations or circumstances.

Determination of normal capacity is a matter of judgement.

CASE STUDY 16.1 Determination of Normal Capacity

N Limited (NL) is in the business of manufacturing fountain pens. It operates on single shift basis. The company used to produce fountain pens for use by college students and office employees. However, in view of sliding demand for its product, a few years back, it had decided to produce premium fountain pens for use by senior executives and diplomats. Its designer fountain pens have caught the fancy of the market, and NL is earning a decent return on its investment. It could also make a mark in the export market after first penetration in 2016.

Installed capacity on single shift basis:	10,00,000 units
Loss of capacity resulting from planned maintenance:	1,00,000 units
Production and sales achieved in the previous three years:	
For 2015:	3,00,000 units
For 2016:	3,50,000 units
For 2017:	4,20,000 units
Budget for 2018:	5,00,000 units
Actual production and sales achieved in 2018:	4,95,000 units
Forecasted production and sales for the next three years:	
For 2019:	5,10,000
For 2020:	5,30,000
For 2021:	5,60,000

Question

The CFO of NL seeks your advice on determining the normal capacity for 2018.

NOTES

Solution

Installed capacity adjusted for loss of capacity resulting from planned maintenance is 9,00,000 units. It is much higher than the capacity utilised in the recent past. Therefore, it is inappropriate to establish the normal capacity at 9,00,000 numbers. Capacity utilisation is showing an increasing trend. Therefore, it is not appropriate to consider the average of capacity utilisation for the past three years as normal capacity. Most auditors will prefer to take the budgeted production for 2018 at 5,00,000 units as the normal capacity. Alternatively, the average of target production for 2018 and forecasted production for the next three years may be considered as normal capacity. The average comes to 5,25,000 units.

Variable production overheads

Variable production overheads are those indirect costs of production that vary directly, or nearly directly, with the volume of production, such as indirect materials and indirect labour. Variable production overheads are allocated to each unit of production on the basis of the actual use of the production facilities.

Joint and by products

A production process may result in more than one product being produced simultaneously. This is the case, for example, when joint products are produced or when there is a main product and a by-product. When the costs of conversion of each product are not separately identifiable, they are allocated between the products on a rational and consistent basis. The allocation may be based, for example, on the relative sales value of each product either at the stage in the production process when the products become separately identifiable, or at the completion of production. Most by-products, by their nature, are immaterial. When this is the case, they are often measured at net realisable value and this value is deducted from the cost of the main product. As a result, the carrying amount of the main product is not materially different from its cost.

ILLUSTRATION 16.1 Cost of Joint Products

B Limited (BL) produces a variety of chemicals for industrial use. The core process produces three joint products A, B, and C. These products are further processed to produce a variety of chemicals required by the rubber industry. The cost of operating the core process in the year 2017 was ₹10,20,000. Realisation from sale of by-products was ₹20,000. The net realisable values (NRVs) of A, B, and C at the point of separation were ₹3,00,000, ₹2,50,000 and ₹1,50,000 respectively. The NRV at the point of separation is calculated by deducting from the final sales value the total of the cost of further processing and estimated profit on the further processing cost.

Required

Allocate the joint cost incurred in the year 2009 to the three joint products.

Solution

The amount of joint cost, net of realisation from the sale of by-products, should be allocated to A, B, and C in proportion to their respective NRV at the separation point. The net joint cost was ₹10,00,000. This amount should be allocated as follows:

A: 10,00,000 × (300/700) = ₹4,28,571

B: 10,00,000 × (250/700) = ₹3,57,143

C: 10,00,000 × (150/700) = ₹2,14,286

Other costs

Other costs are included in the cost of inventories only to the extent that they are incurred in bringing the inventories to their present location and condition. For example, it may be appropriate to include non-production overheads or the costs of designing products for specific customers in the cost of inventories.

NOTES

Costs that are excluded from cost of inventories

Examples of costs excluded from the cost of inventories and recognised as expenses in the period in which they are incurred are:

(i) Abnormal amounts of wasted materials, labour or other production costs;

(ii) Storage costs, unless those costs are necessary in the production process before a further production stage;

(iii) Administrative overheads that do not contribute to bringing inventories to their present location and condition; and

(iv) Selling costs.

Costs of designing products

Non-production overheads and costs of designing products for specific customers are included in the cost of inventory. For example, development costs related to a specific product or process are amortised and assigned to inventories.

Borrowing costs

Borrowing costs are included in the cost of inventories only in special circumstances. For example, borrowing costs may be included in the cost of wine and timber, which involves processing for a long period.

Distribution, packaging and transport costs

Distribution costs and costs of transporting goods to customers are not allocated to inventories. They are recognised as expenses for the period in which they are incurred.

Transport or distribution costs that are necessary to bring the inventory to its present location and condition for sale form part of the cost of inventory. For example, following costs are allocated to inventory:

(i) Distribution or transport costs that are incurred at the intermediate stage of the production process; and

(ii) Distribution or transport costs that are incurred to get the inventory from the central warehouse to the point of sale.

Packaging costs that are incurred to prepare inventory for sale are part of the cost of inventory.

CASE STUDY 16.2 Valuation of Inventories—Retail Business

K Limited (KL) is a retailer. It has several retail stores across the country. The company negotiates prices with suppliers and places orders centrally. Suppliers deliver goods at central warehouses. Each city, which has more than one retail store, has a central warehouse. Stores in a city place order on the central warehouse for replenishment of stock twice a week.

It provides the following information about an item, which is one among the fast moving items:

Average purchase price per unit:	₹100
Average transportation cost per unit charged by suppliers:	₹2
Average transportation cost per unit charged by local transporters for transporting goods from the central warehouse:	₹2
Average warehousing cost per unit:	₹3
Average lease rent (of the retail store) per unit	₹4

Question

The CFO of KL seeks your advice on how to calculate the cost of inventories in different stores at the balance sheet date.

Solution

The cost of inventories comprises the purchase price and other costs incurred to bring the items to the location and condition of sale. Therefore, warehousing cost and lease rent should be excluded from the cost of inventories. The cost of the item to be used for inventory valuation is ₹104.

CASE STUDY 16.3 Valuation of Inventories—Grocer

A Limited (AL) is a small retailer. It operates only one grocery store in New Market in Kolkata. It sells only its private brand. The company is hugely popular for its high-quality products, high-quality service, and innovative packaging. Another reason for the popularity of the store is its excellence in managing customer relationship.

AL maintains a warehouse in the outskirts of Kolkata. The warehouse receives goods purchased in bulk. Goods received in the warehouse are cleaned through a simple automated process established in the warehouse. The packaging is also carried out in the warehouse through an automated process.

Question

The CFO of AL seeks your advice on whether warehousing costs should be included in the cost of inventories. She also seeks your advice on whether the cost of transporting goods from the warehouse to the store should be included in the cost of inventories in the store.

Solution

AL should include warehousing costs, including fixed costs (e.g., depreciation on PP&E), in the cost of inventories because goods are stored in the warehouse primarily to carry out further processing in order to bring the goods to saleable condition. Similarly, costs of transporting goods from the warehouse should be included in the cost of inventories in the store because those costs are incurred to bring the items to the location of sale.

CASE STUDY 16.4 Valuation of Inventories—Large Retailer

G Limited (GL) is the largest retailer globally. The company is known for its ability to sell high-quality products at prices lower than that of its competitors. There are many factors that help GL to procure goods at a price lower than that of its competitors and to sell them at low prices. The most important factor is the efficiency in logistics management. GL prides for its unique logistics management system. It is a model that presents how innovations in technology and management can be combined to establish competitive advantage over other players in the market. The highly efficient logistic system provides GL the flexibility to choose suppliers from any corner of the world. This flexibility puts GL in a strong bargaining position vis-à-vis its suppliers.

GL operates the logistics system internally.

Question

The auditor of GL seeks your advice on whether fixed cost (e.g., depreciation of PP&E and compensation to employees) of operating the logistics system should be allocated to items of goods for determining the cost of sales and cost of inventories.

Solution

Costs of operating the logistics system, including fixed costs, are incurred to bring the goods to the location and condition of sale. Therefore, these should be included in the cost of sale and in the cost of inventories. However, the assignment of fixed costs should be based on the normal capacity of the logistics system.

Techniques for the measurement of the cost

Techniques for the measurement of the cost of inventories, such as the standard cost method or the retail method, may be used for convenience if the results approximate cost.

NOTES

Standard costs

Standard costs take into account normal levels of materials and supplies, labour, efficiency and capacity utilisation. They are regularly reviewed and, if necessary, revised in the light of current conditions.

Retail method

The retail method is often used in the retail industry for measuring inventories of large numbers of rapidly changing items with similar margins for which it is impracticable to use other costing methods. The cost of the inventory is determined by reducing the sales value of the inventory by the appropriate percentage gross margin. The percentage used takes into consideration inventory that has been marked down to below its original selling price. An average percentage for each retail department is often used.

ILLUSTRATION 16.2 Retail Method

N Retails Limited (NRL) provides the following information for the year 2017–18:

Opening inventory:	(Cost: ₹6,000; Retail price: ₹8,000)
Purchases:	(Cost: ₹20,000, Retail price: ₹32,000)
Inventory on hand:	(Retail price: ₹24,000)

Required

Determine the cost of the closing inventory.

Solution

Cost:	(₹6,000 + 20,000) or ₹26,000
Retail price:	(₹8,000 + 32,000) or ₹40,000
Cost percentage of retail price:	(26,000/40,000) × 100 or 65%
Cost of closing inventory:	(₹24,000 × 0.65) or ₹15,600

Cost formulas

An entity should use the same cost formula for all inventories having a similar nature and use to the entity. For inventories with a different nature or use, different cost formulas may be justified.

The cost of inventories of items that are not ordinarily interchangeable and goods or services produced and segregated for specific projects shall be assigned by using specific identification of their individual costs. The cost of inventories, which are ordinarily interchangeable or which have not been produced and segregated for specific projects, shall be assigned by using the First-In, First-Out (FIFO) or weighted average cost formula.

Specific identification method

Specific identification of cost means that specific costs are attributed to specifically identified items of inventory. This is the appropriate treatment for items that are segregated for a specific project, regardless of whether they have been bought or produced.

FIFO formula

The FIFO formula assumes that the items of inventory that were purchased or produced first are sold first, and consequently, the items remaining in inventory at the end of the period are those most recently purchased or produced.

NOTES

Weighted average cost formula

Under the weighted average cost formula, the cost of each item is determined from the weighted average of the cost of similar items in the beginning of a period and the cost of similar items purchased or produced during the period. The average may be calculated on a periodic basis, or as each additional shipment is received, depending on the circumstances of the entity.

NET REALISABLE VALUE (NRV)

The NRV is the estimated selling price in the ordinary course of business less the estimated costs of completion and the estimated costs necessary to make the sale.

ILLUSTRATION 16.3 NRV of WIP

Job No. E-101 was incomplete at the balance sheet date. The cost incurred on that job till that date was ₹5,50,000. The entity estimates that it will incur a further amount of ₹1,00,000 to complete the job. The contract price is ₹8,00,000 and the estimated selling expense is ₹10,000.

Required

Calculate the NRV of the WIP.

Solution

The net realisable value is (₹8,00,000 – 10,000 – 1,00,000) or ₹6,90,000. The NRV being higher than the cost, the job E-101 should be carried in the balance sheet at ₹5,50,000, as a part of the inventory.

NRV of finished goods, work-in-process and merchandise included in inventories

An entity should estimate the NRV based on the most reliable evidence available of the amount the inventories are expected to realise. It takes into consideration fluctuations of price or cost occurring after the balance sheet date, to the extent they provide evidence of conditions existing at the balance sheet date.

CASE STUDY 16.5 NRV—Events After the Balance Sheet Date

N Limited (NL) deals in medical products. In preparing the financial statements for the period 2016–17, it estimated the NRV of Bare Metal Stents (BMSs) at ₹45,000 per unit for estimating the carrying amount of the inventory of BMS in the balance sheet as at March 31, 2017. Before approval of financial statements by Board of Directors, on April 30, 2017, the government announced maximum price for BMS at ₹7,623. From April 1, 2017 to April 30, 2017, NL sold 30 percent of the stock of BMS that it held as at March 31, 2017 at ₹45,000 per unit.

The auditor is insisting that the carrying amount of 70 percent of the inventory as at March 31, 2017, which was in stock as at April 30, 2017, should be determined considering the NRV at ₹7,623. The CFO does not agree with the auditor. According to her, the event after the balance sheet date (government order fixing the maximum price of BMS at ₹7,623) does not provide additional evidence of conditions existing at the balance sheet date.

Question

The CFO of NL seeks your advice on what should be NRV of BMS for estimating the carrying amount of the inventory in the balance sheet as at March 31, 2017.

Solution

In this situation, NRV estimation is judgemental. The CFO's argument cannot be ignored. However, the fact is that because of the government's order, NL would not be able to sell the balance 70 percent of the inventory at a price higher than ₹7,623 per unit. Therefore, if that 70 percent of the inventory of BMS as at March 31, 2017 is carried in the balance sheet at an amount higher than ₹7,623 per unit, financial statements will fail to provide the true and fair view. Therefore, it is appropriate to consider the NRV at ₹7,623 per unit for estimating the

NOTES

carrying amount of 70 percent of the inventory that remained unsold as at April 30, 2017. For determining the carrying amount of 30 percent of the inventory that was sold between April 1, 2017 and April 30, 2017, NRV should be considered at ₹45,000. This is also consistent with the principle that estimates of net realisable value should be based on the most reliable evidence available at the time the estimates are made.

In estimating the NRV, an entity also takes into consideration the purpose for which the inventory is held. For example, the NRV of the quantity of inventory held to satisfy firm's sales or service contracts is based on the contract price. If the sales contracts are for less than the inventory quantities held, the net realisable value of the excess is based on general selling prices.

NRV of raw materials, components and other supplies

Materials and other supplies held for use in the production of inventories are not written down below cost if the entity expects that the finished products in which they will be incorporated will be sold at or above cost. However, a decline in the price of materials indicates that the cost of the finished products exceeds NRV, the materials are written down to NRV. In such circumstances, the replacement cost of the materials may be the best available measure of their net realisable value.

Table 16.3 presents the application of the able rules.

TABLE 16.3

NRV of Raw Materials

Assumption: One unit of raw material is required to produced one unit of the finished product.

S. No.	Cost and replacement Cost of raw material per unit (₹)	Cost and NRV of finished product per unit (₹)	Comments	Carrying amount of raw material per unit (₹)
1.	Cost: 20 Replacement cost: 25	Not relevant	Replacement cost is higher than acquisition cost	20
2.	Cost: 20 Replacement cost: 15	Cost: 100 NRV: 120	NRV of finished product is higher than cost	20
3.	Cost: 20 Replacement cost: 15	Cost: 100 NRV: 98	NRV of finished product is lower than cost	15
4.	Cost: 20 Replacement cost: 15	Cost: 100 NRV: 78	NRV of finished product is lower than cost	15

Estimated loss of finished product is not a factor to be considered in estimating the carrying amount of raw material, component and other supplies.

Reassessment of NRV

A new assessment is made of NRV in each subsequent period.

When the circumstances that previously caused inventories to be written down below cost no longer exist or when there is clear evidence of an increase in net realisable value because of the changed economic circumstances, the amount of the write-down is reversed (i.e., the reversal is limited to the amount of the original write-down) so that the new carrying amount is the lower of the cost and the revised NRV. This occurs, for example, when an item of inventory that is carried at NRV (because its selling price has declined) is still on hand in a subsequent period and its selling price has increased.

SUMMARY

Inventories encompass goods purchased and held for resale, including merchandise purchased by a retailer and held for resale, or land and other property held for resale. Inventories also encompass finished goods produced or work-in-progress being produced by the entity and

NOTES

SUMMARY

materials and supplies awaiting use in the production process. Inventories include stores and spares that cannot be classified as PP&E. Inventories are measured at the lower of cost and net realisable value.

The cost of inventories comprises all costs of purchase; costs of conversion; and other costs incurred in bringing the inventories to their present location and condition.

The cost of inventories of finished goods and the WIP of an entity engaged in manufacturing includes conversion costs. The allocation of fixed production overheads to the costs of conversion is based on the normal capacity of the production facilities. In a period of abnormally high production, average fixed production overhead per unit is calculated by dividing the amount of overheads by actual production. Normal capacity is the production that the management expects to achieve on average over a number of periods or seasons under normal circumstances, taking into account the loss of capacity resulting from planned maintenance. The actual level of production may be used if it approximates normal capacity.

When the costs of conversion of each joint product are not separately identifiable, they are allocated between the products on a rational and consistent basis.

Interest and other borrowing costs are usually not included in the cost of inventory.

Techniques for the measurement of the cost of inventories such as the standard cost method or the retail method may be used for convenience if the results approximate cost. An entity should use a specific identification method for determining the cost of items that are not ordinarily interchangeable or for items that have been segregated for specific projects. It should use the First-In-First-Out (FIFO) rule or the weighted average cost formula for determining the cost of items that are ordinarily interchangeable.

Net Realisable Value (NRV) is the estimated selling price ***in the ordinary course of business*** less the estimated costs of completion and the estimated costs necessary to make the sale. Estimates of net realisable value are based on the most reliable evidence available at the time the estimates are made. The comparison of net realisable value with cost should, in principle, be carried out on an item-by-item basis.

Self-Test Questions

Self-test question 16.1

Indicate whether the following statements are true (T) or false (F):

(i) Inventories include capital work-in-progress.
(ii) Inventories should be measured at lower of cost and net realisable value.
(iii) Volume discount, which is usually allowed by the vendors at the end of the year based on the total procurement during the year, should not be considered in determining the purchase price.
(iv) Entities should allocate fixed production overheads to the costs of conversion based on the normal capacity of the production facilities, even in the period when capacity utilisation is significantly higher than the normal capacity.
(v) Distribution or transport costs that are incurred to get the inventory from the central warehouse to the point of sale are not included in the cost of inventories.
(vi) An entity is not permitted to use Last-In, First-Out (LIFO) method for estimating the cost of inventories.
(vii) Cost of warehousing merchandise at a central warehouse before distribution to retail stores in the city should be included in the cost of inventories.
(viii) Events after the balance sheet date should not be considered in estimating the net realisable value.
(ix) Raw materials and components are usually measured at replacement cost.
(x) Stores and spares are measured at cost.

NOTES

ANSWERS TO SELF-TEST QUESTIONS

16.1 (i) F; (ii) T; (iii) F; (iv) F; (v) F; (vi) T; (vii) F; (viii) F; (ix) F; (x) T

ASSIGNMENTS

Quiz

1. Prema Departmental Stores (PDS) started operations on January 1, 2007. It was engaged in the following transactions during January. Identify the amount that the company should include in the valuation of the merchandise inventory.
   (i) Purchases of merchandise on account during January: ₹50,00,000
   (ii) Freight cost to transport merchandise to the warehouse of PDS: ₹20,000
   (iii) Salary of the purchase manager: ₹50,000
   (iv) Depreciation, taxes, insurance and utilities for the warehouse: ₹30,000
   (v) Salary of the warehouse manager: ₹20,000
   (vi) Cost of merchandise that PDS purchased in part (a) and that was returned to the supplier ₹10,000
   (vii) Cash discount taken by PDS from purchases on account in part (i) ₹5,000
2. On December 20, 2006, Sanjukta Limited (SL) purchased goods costing ₹5,00,000. The terms were 'Free on board' (FOB) destination. The following costs were incurred in connection with the delivery of goods:

Packaging and shipment	₹6,000
Shipping	₹4,000
Special handling charges	₹2,000

   These goods are included in inventory. What cost should be considered for the purpose of inventory valuation?
   (i) ₹5,12,000 (ii) ₹5,10,000
   (iii) ₹5,06,000 (iv) ₹5,00,000
3. On September 1, 2006, Mrinalini Limited (ML) purchased material from Ketan Limited (KL). The list price of the material was ₹1,00,000. KL allowed trade discount and quantity discount of 30 percent and 20 percent, respectively. Credit terms were 2/15, *n*/40 and the sale was made FOB shipping point. The shipping cost was ₹5,000. ML paid the amount due to KL on September 12, 2006. The cost at which the material was recorded in the books of ML is:
   (i) ₹68,880 (ii) ₹54,880
   (iii) ₹61,000 (iv) ₹59,880
4. What is considered to be the normal capacity?
   (i) The average production over the previous five-year period
   (ii) Budgeted production for the period
   (iii) Actual production for the period plus the loss of capacity for planned maintenance
   (iv) Estimated average production during next 3 to 5 years determined after taking into account planned maintenance, and business and industry factors
5. Indicate against each statement whether it is True (T) or False (F):
   (i) Inventories are necessarily classified as current assets.
   (ii) Goods, which are held for sale, are classified as current assets even if they are expected to be sold after 12 months after the balance sheet date.
   (iii) A firm should determine a single normal operating cycle for a particular business.
   (iv) If a firm cannot estimate the normal operating cycle, it is assumed that the normal operating cycle is of 12 months.
   (v) Core inventory of crude oil in an oil refinery should be classified as PP&E.
   (vi) Demurrage charge should be included in the cost of the items in the inventory.
   (vii) By-products are often measured at net realisable value.
   (viii) Cash discount should be deducted in calculating the purchase price.
   (ix) Interest and other borrowing costs are usually not included in the inventory cost.
   (x) In estimating the cost of items in inventory, an entity may use any one of the three cost formulas—FIFO, LIFO, and weighted average.
   (xi) In estimating the NRV, transactions between the balance sheet date and the date of approval of the same by the Board of Directors should be taken into account.
   (xii) A firm, which is engaged in merchandising business and follows the practice of home delivery, should deduct the estimated home delivery cost from the estimated selling price to determine the NRV.

NOTES

6. Fill in the blanks:

   (i) The installed capacity of the production facility of a firm manufacturing a luxury fountain pen is 100,000 units. The attainable capacity, which is calculated as installed capacity less loss of capacity due to shut down on account of normal maintenance, is 90,000 units. The practical capacity, which is the capacity that the firm intended to use at the time of acquisition of the facility, is 85,000 units. At the beginning of the year 2010–11, the firm, after taking into account estimated market demand for its product for the next five years, estimates the average use of the capacity over the next five years at 70,000 units. The normal capacity is .... units.

   (ii) The normal capacity of a production facility owned by Sunayana Limited (SL) is 80,000 units of table fans. During 2010–11, it incurred ₹10,00,000 towards fixed factory overheads and produced 70,000 units of table fans. The amount of fixed factory overheads to be included in the conversion cost of table fans in the year-end inventory is ₹...... per unit.

   (iii) The normal capacity of a production facility owned by Sunayana Limited (SL) is 80,000 units of table fans. During 2010–11, it incurred ₹10,00,000 towards fixed factory overheads and produced 90,000 units of table fans. The amount of fixed factory overheads to be included in the conversion cost of table fans in the year-end inventory is ₹...... per unit.

   (iv) Kaveri Limited (KL) produces machine tools against confirmed orders from customers. The work-in-progress inventory as at the end of the year includes a job order on which cost accumulated till the end of the year was ₹10,00,000. The management estimates that it has to incur ₹5,00,000 to complete the job. The selling price of the job as per the contract is ₹18,00,000. Thus, the estimated gross profit on the job is 20 percent of the total cost of production. The net realisable value at the balance sheet date was ₹......

   (v) Natasha Limited (NL) uses raw material X to produce an electronic safety device that is used by the Railways. One unit of the material is used to produce one unit of the finished product. With the increase in budget allocation for safety items, a large player in the electronic industry has included in its product portfolio a product similar to that is being produced by NL. In order to penetrate the market, it has quoted a price lower than the price at which NL secured orders from Railways in the past. NL has secured a fresh order after matching its price with that of the new player which quoted the lowest price. NL estimates that it will incur a loss of ₹5,000 per unit. The cost of production is estimated at ₹160,000. The book value of the material A is ₹25,000 per unit and its replacement cost is ₹28,000 per unit. The year-end inventory of the material X should be valued at ₹...... per unit.

   (vi) Manshi Limited (ML) uses raw material Y to produce an electronic choke that is used by Railways. One unit of the material is used to produce one unit of the finished product. With the increase in budget allocation for coach maintenance, a large player in the electronic industry has included in its product portfolio a product similar to that is being produced by ML. In order to penetrate the market, it has quoted a price lower than the price at which ML secured orders from the Railways in past. ML has secured a fresh order after matching its price with that of the new player which quoted the lowest price. ML estimates that it will incur a loss of ₹5,000 per unit. The cost of production is estimated at ₹1,50,000. The book value of the material A is ₹24,000 per unit and its replacement cost is ₹20,000 per unit. The year-end inventory of the material X should be valued at ₹...... per unit.

   (vii) Sugandha Limited (SL) is in the business of manufacturing potato flakes. The manufacturing facility is located in Dhanekhali in Nadia district of West Bengal. It purchases potato directly from farmers in West Bengal. The quality and the cost of potato flakes depend on the ability of the company to deliver fresh potatoes to the manufacturing facility. The key is speed of delivery to factory after collection from the farmers and maintenance of appropriate temperature inside the container during transportation. SL manages the inward logistics internally. The fixed overhead of the logistic department is ₹500 million. The fixed overhead of the logistic department .... forms part of the cost of inventories of potatoes. (Select the right word from the two words 'should' and 'should not'.)

   (viii) Aparajita Limited (AL) sold goods to Bidisha Limited (BL) for ₹10,00,000. As per the agreement, BL will pay the amount due to AL after 12 months from the transaction date. AL could borrow the amount for one year at an interest rate of 12 percent per annum and BL could borrow the amount for one year at an interest rate of 15 percent per annum. AL should recognise the revenue and receivable at ₹.........

Depreciation and Impairment of Fixed Assets

CHAPTER 17

Learning Objectives

This chapter aims to provide an understanding of depreciation and impairment of non-financial assets.

After reading this chapter, you will develop understanding of the following:

- Concept of depreciation
- Accounting principles for recognising depreciation
- Estimation of useful life and residual value of assets
- Useful life and residual value under the Companies Act, 2013
- Difference between technical life, economic life and useful life of assets
- Depreciation methods
- Concept of impairment and accounting principles for testing impairment
- Identification of Cash Generating Units (CGUs)
- Principles and methods for estimating 'value-in-use'
- Principles for estimating 'fair value less costs of disposal'
- Impairment test of goodwill
- Allocation of impairment loss of CGU to assets that constitute the CGU
- Reversal of impairment loss recognised in earlier periods

Applicable Ind AS: *Discussion in this chapter is primarily based on Ind AS 36, Impairment of assets.*

DEPRECIATION

Accounting Principle

Nature of depreciation

Except land, items of PP&E have limited useful life. Therefore, after initial recognition, items of PP&E are depreciated on a systematic basis over their useful life. Each part of an item of PP&E with a cost that is significant in relation to the total cost of the items is depreciated separately. The purpose of depreciation is not the recognition of decrease in the value of PP&E. The purpose is to allocate the cost or revalued amount of an asset over its useful life on a systematic basis. Therefore, depreciation is charged even on an asset that is being maintained through regular repairs and maintenance.

Depreciation in 'cost model' of measurement

The net cost of an item of PP&E is the acquisition cost reduced by the amount that the entity expects to receive from disposal of the asset at the end of its useful life (called residual value). For example, if the acquisition cost of the asset is ₹1,00,000 and residual value is ₹5,000, the net cost of the asset to the entity is (₹1,00,000 – 5,000) or ₹95,000. The net cost is called depreciable amount. When an entity adopts the cost model for the accounting of a class of PP&E, it systematically allocates the 'depreciable amount' of items in that class of PP&E over the useful life of the asset. The amount allocated to a particular accounting period is the amount of 'depreciation' for that accounting period. Depreciation is an expense. The depreciation for a period is usually recognised in profit or loss. However, if an item of PP&E is used in producing other asset, the depreciation constitutes part of the cost of the other asset and is included in its carrying amount.

Land

With some exceptions such as quarries and sites used for landfill, land has an unlimited useful life. Therefore, it is usually considered to be a non-depreciable asset and it is not depreciated. However, sometimes, the cost of land includes the costs of site dismantlement, removal and restoration. The part of the land, which represents those costs, is depreciated over the period over which the entity expects to benefit by incurring those costs. In some cases, the land itself may have a limited useful life, and this condition, it is depreciated in a manner that reflects the benefits to be derived from it.

Depreciation under revaluation model of measurement

An entity, which opts for the revaluation model for measurement of PP&E after initial recognition, provides depreciation based on (i) the revalued amount, and (ii) the estimate of the remaining useful life of the asset from the date of revaluation.

Commencement and cessation of depreciation

Depreciation of an asset begins when it is available for intended use, that is, it is in the location and condition necessary for intended use. It is immaterial whether the asset is actually put to use or not.

Depreciation of an asset ceases at the earlier of the date that the asset is classified as 'held for sale' and the date that the asset is derecognised. Depreciation does not cease when the asset becomes idle or is retired from active use, unless the asset is fully depreciated. However, under usage methods of depreciation, the depreciation charge can be zero while there is no production.

SUMMARY

After initial recognition, items of PP&E are depreciated on a systematic basis over their useful life. Each part of an item of PP&E with a cost that is significant in relation to the total cost of the items is depreciated separately. Generally, land is considered a non-depreciable asset. The purpose of depreciation is to allocate the cost or revalued amount of an asset over its useful life on a systematic basis. Depreciation of an asset begins when it is available for intended use and ceases at the earlier of the date that the asset is classified as 'held for sale' and the date that the asset is derecognised.

Self-Test Questions

Self-test question 17.1

Indicate whether the following statements are true (T) or false (F):

(i) Assets that are covered under preventive maintenance plan are not depreciated.
(ii) No depreciation should be charged on an asset that has remained idle during the financial year.
(iii) Land is not a depreciable asset.
(iv) No depreciation is charged on an item of PP&E classified as 'held for sale'.
(v) No depreciation is charged on classes of assets that are measured using the 're-evaluation model'.

Useful Life

Definition

Useful life is the period over which an asset is expected to be available for use by an entity; or the number of production or similar units expected to be obtained from the asset by an entity.

Thus, useful life is usually expressed in terms of number of years (e.g., 10 years) or production units (1,00,000 units of production) or production hours (e.g., 20,000 hours of use).

Useful life under the Companies Act, 2013

Part C of Schedule II of the Companies Act, 2013 provides indicative useful life of different types of assets. The useful life of an asset should not ordinarily be different from the indicative useful life specified in Schedule II. However, a company can estimate useful life of an asset that differs from the indicative useful life in Schedule II. In that case, the financial statements must disclose such difference and must provide justification in this behalf duly supported by technical advice.

The useful lives of assets working on shift basis have been specified in the Schedule II based on their single shift working. Except for assets in respect of which no extra shift depreciation is permitted (indicated by NESD in Part C of Schedule II), if an asset is used for any time during the year for double shift, the depreciation will increase by 50 percent for that period, and in case of the triple shift, the depreciation shall be calculated on the basis of 100 percent for that period.

It is appropriate to consider 365 days in a year to calculate extra-shift depreciation.

Factors to be considered in estimating useful life

An entity should consider all the following factors in determining the useful life of an asset:

(i) Expected usage of the asset;
(ii) Expected physical wear and tear, which depends on operational factors such as the

number of shifts for which the asset is to be used and the repair and maintenance programme, and the care and maintenance of the asset while idle;

(iii) Technical or commercial obsolescence; and

(iv) Legal or similar limits on the use of the asset such as the expiry dates of related leases.

Review of useful life

An entity should review the useful life of an asset at least at each financial year-end. Change in the estimated useful life, if any, should be accounted for as a change in an accounting estimate. Accordingly, the remaining depreciable amount of the asset, at the commencement of the current year, is allocated to the current year and subsequent years based on the remaining useful life of the asset.

For example, if at the end of the fifth year (before charging depreciation for the fifth year), the entity revises the estimated useful life of an item of PP&E to 8 years from the original estimate of 10 years, it will allocate the remaining depreciable amount at the beginning of the fifth year over remaining (8 years – 4 years) or 4 years, that is, to the current year and the subsequent three years.

Technical life, economic life and useful life of assets

Technical life

The technical or physical life is the period over which the asset is expected to produce the intended result. The manufacturer of the asset estimates the technical life of an asset. The technical life is asset-specific.

Economic life

Economic life is the period over which the use of the asset makes economic sense. In a way, this is also specific to the asset. Economic life may be shorter than the technical life of the asset.

Useful life

The useful life is entity-specific and not asset-specific. It may be shorter than the economic life. The useful life of an asset is defined in terms of the asset's expected utility to the entity. Based on its strategy, an entity may decide to dispose of the asset after a specified time or after consumption of a specified proportion of the future economic benefits embodied in the asset. Estimating useful life is a matter of judgement. For example, a travel house serving high-end customers, as a policy, disposes cars after three years from the date of purchase, while another travel house serving mid-segment customers disposes cars after six years from the date of purchase. Both the travel houses use the same car model. The technical life and the economic life of cars are the same for both the travel houses. However, useful life of cars is three years for the first travel house and the same is six years for the second travel house.

Residual Value

Definition

The residual value of an asset is the estimated amount that an entity would currently obtain from disposal of the asset after deducting the estimated costs of disposal, if the asset were already of the age and in the condition expected at the end of its useful life.

For example, the residual value, as at March 31, 2018, of a car having a useful life of 10 years, is the price as at March 31, 2018 of a 10-year old used car, which is of the same model and which was put to similar use.

In practice, the residual value of an asset is often insignificant, and therefore, immaterial in the calculation of the depreciable amount.

The residual value of an asset may increase to an amount equal to or greater than the asset's carrying amount. If it does, the asset's depreciation charge is zero unless and until its residual value subsequently decreases to an amount below the asset's carrying amount.

Residual value under the Companies Act, 2013

Schedule II of the Companies Act, 2013 stipulates that the residual value of an asset should not be more than 5 percent of the original cost of the asset.

Where a company uses a residual value, which is higher than the ceiling (5 percent) specified in Schedule II, the financial statements must disclose such difference and must provide justification in this behalf duly supported by technical advice.

Review of residual value

An entity should review the residual value of an asset at least at each financial year-end. Change in the estimated residual value, if any, should be accounted for as a change in an accounting estimate. Therefore, the entity should revise the remaining depreciable amount and allocate the same over the remaining useful life of the asset.

SUMMARY

Useful life is the period over which the management intends to use the asset. It may be equal to or shorter than the technical life. The Companies Act, 2013 provides indicative useful lives of different types of assets. A company may use useful life that is different from the indicative useful life of the asset, with proper disclosure.

The residual value of an asset is the estimated amount that an entity would currently obtain from disposal of the asset after deducting the estimated costs of disposal, if the asset were already of the age and in the condition expected at the end of its useful life. The Companies Act, 2013 stipulates that the residual value of an asset should not be more than 5 percent of the original cost of the asset. A company may estimate residual value higher than the ceiling, with proper disclosure.

An entity should review the useful life and residual value of an asset at least at each financial year-end. Any change should be accounted for as a change in an accounting estimate.

Self-Test Questions

Self-test question 17.2

Indicate whether the following statements are true (T) or false (F):

(i) Useful life depends, among other factors, on the entity's strategy.
(ii) Useful life cannot be longer than the economic life of the asset.
(iii) Both useful life and economic life are entity-specific.
(iv) Residual value of an asset should be estimated at least once every year.
(v) Companies are not permitted to use useful life other than the indicative useful life provided in the Companies Act, 2013.

Depreciation Methods

Depreciation method—Guiding principle

An entity should choose a depreciation method based on the pattern in which the entity expects to consume the asset's future economic benefits. Deciding the most appropriate depreciation method is a matter of judgement. Most entities apply the straight-line method of depreciation, as in practice, it is difficult to match depreciation with the pattern of consumption of benefits embedded in the asset.

Change in depreciation method is considered a change in estimate.

NOTES

Depreciation method under the Companies Act, 2013

The Companies Act, 2013 does not prescribe use of any particular depreciation method.

Review of depreciation method

An entity should review the depreciation method applied to an asset at least at each financial year-end. If there has been a significant change in the expected pattern of consumption of the future economic benefits embodied in the asset, the method should be changed to reflect the changed pattern. Such a change shall be accounted for as a change in an accounting estimate.

Straight-line time method

The straight-line time method of depreciation divides the depreciable amount by the number of years of useful life for calculating annual depreciation.

ILLUSTRATION 17.1 Straight-line Time Depreciation Method

The following are the details of a machine acquired in 2018:

Acquisition cost	₹1,10,000
Estimated useful life	10 years
Estimated residual value	₹10,000
No. of units estimated to be produced over the useful life	1,00,000 units

The entity uses the straight-line time method of depreciation.

Required

Calculate the depreciation rate and the amount of depreciation per annum.

Solution

Depreciation should be charged @ 10 percent per annum to allocate the cost reduced by the estimated residual value over the useful life of the machine, which is 10 years. The amount of depreciation is to be charged uniformly over the useful life of the asset. The depreciation per annum will be

$$\frac{(1,10,000-10,000)}{10} = ₹\,10,000$$

Straight-line use method

The straight-line use method allocates the depreciable amount of the asset over its useful life in terms of the number of units estimated to be produced, or the machine hours estimated to be used during the asset's useful life. This method is superior to the straight-line time method or reducing balance method because it matches costs with revenue more accurately. However, the precision depends on the accuracy with which the total output during the useful life of the asset can be estimated.

Under this method, a rate per unit is calculated by dividing the depreciable amount by the estimated number of units that the entity expects to produce over the estimated useful life of the asset. Depreciation for a particular period is calculated by multiplying the actual number of units produced by the depreciation rate per unit.

ILLUSTRATION 17.2 Straight-line Use Depreciation Method

Assume the information provided in the Illustration 17.1. The production for 2018 was 9,000 units.

Required

Calculate the depreciation rate if the entity uses the straight-line use method of depreciation and the amount of depreciation to be charged in 2018.

Solution

Depreciation rate will be

$$\frac{(1{,}10{,}000 - 10{,}000)}{1{,}00{,}000} = ₹\,1 \text{ per unit}$$

The depreciation to be charged each year would be calculated by multiplying the number of units produced during the year by the rate per unit. Depreciation for 2018 would be 9,000 × ₹1 = ₹9,000.

Reducing balance method

Under the reducing balance method, the amount of depreciation reduces over the years. In the initial year, the amount of depreciation is high and then it reduces exponentially. Under this method, a fixed percentage is applied on the reducing balance, popularly known as Written-Down Value (WDV). The formula for calculating that fixed rate can be derived as follows:

Let r be the rate of depreciation. If C represents the cost of acquisition, R the residual value, and n the useful life, then

$$C \times (1 - r)^n = R$$

or

$$(1 - r) = \sqrt[n]{\frac{R}{C}}$$

or

$$r = 1 - \sqrt[n]{\frac{R}{C}}$$

Some accountants prefer the reducing balance method of depreciation to the straight-line method on the ground that it equitably allocates the total cost of maintaining an asset over its useful life. The total cost of maintaining an asset is the total of the cost of its acquisition and the maintenance cost. The maintenance cost usually increases as the machine gets old. Therefore, a method of depreciation that results in reduction in the amount of depreciation, as the asset grows old, is more appropriate. It is argued that use of the reducing balance method of depreciation results in expending almost an equal amount, taking depreciation and maintenance costs together, per annum, over the useful life of the asset. However, the argument is not flawless because with preventive maintenance, maintenance cost per year for the most part of the useful life of an asset remains the same.

ILLUSTRATION 17.3 Reducing Balance Method of Depreciation

Assume the same information that has been provided in Illustration 17.1.

Required

Calculate the depreciation rate for using the reducing balance method of depreciation.

Solution

The rate of depreciation under the reducing balance method is

$$r = 1 - \sqrt[10]{\frac{10{,}000}{1{,}10{,}000}} = 1 - 0.787 = 0.213$$

Thus, the rate of depreciation is 21.3 percent against the straight-line method of 10 percent.

NOTES

TABLE 17.1

Reducing Balance Method of Depreciation

Year	Written Down Value (₹)	Rate (percent)	Depreciation (₹)	Cumulative depreciation reducing balance method@21.3 percent (₹)	Cumulative depreciation straight line time method@21.3 percent (₹)
2018	1,10,000	21.3	23,430	23,430	10,000
2019	86,570	21.3	18,439	41,869	20,000
2020	68,131	21.3	14,512	56,381	30,000
2021	53,619	21.3	11,421	67,802	40,000
2022	42,198	21.3	8,988	76,790	50,000
2023	33,210	21.3	7,074	83,864	60,000
2024	26,136	21.3	5,567	89,431	70,000
2025	20,569	21.3	4,381	93,812	80,000
2026	16,188	21.3	3,448	97,260	90,000
2027	12,740	21.3	2,740	1,00,000	1,00,000

The amount of depreciation for 2027 is calculated as the difference between WDV at the beginning of the year and the residual value. Applying 21.3 percent on ₹12,740, we get ₹2,714. The difference of ₹26 has arisen due to accumulation of rounding-off errors (Table 17.1).

Under the reducing balance method, ₹67,622 or 68 percent of the depreciable amount will be written off in the first four years. Under the straight-line method, only 40 percent will be written off in the first four years. It may be noted that the rate of depreciation under the reducing balance method depends on the estimated residual value.

For example, if the residual value is estimated at 0.00001 percent of the cost, the rate will be $r = 1 - 0.200 = 0.80$ or 80 percent per annum.

Thus, if the residual value is estimated at close to zero, 80 percent of the cost will be written off in the very first year. If the residual value is estimated at 5 percent of cost, the rate of depreciation rate will be $r = 1 - 0.741 = 0.259$ or 25.9 percent per annum.

Schedule II to the Companies Act, 2013, which provides tentative useful life, stipulates that the residual value cannot be more than 5 percent of the original cost.

Sum-of-the-years' digits method

Under sum-of-the-years' digits method, the amount of depreciation is calculated by multiplying the depreciable amount by the factor (k/s). If n be the estimated useful life of the asset, then k for year 1 is n. It is $(n - 1)$ for the year 2, $(n - 2)$ for the year 3, and so on. Thus, for the nth year, k is 1. S is the sum of the numbers 1 to n. Thus, if the useful life is estimated at 10 years, $S = 55$. Thus, (k/s) for the year 1 is (10/55). If the depreciable amount is ₹1,00,000, depreciation for the first year is ₹1,00,000 × (10/55) or ₹18,182. Depreciation for the 10th year is ₹1,00,000 × (1/55) or ₹1,818.

SUMMARY

An entity should choose a depreciation method based on the pattern in which the entity expects to consume the asset's future economic benefits. Deciding the most appropriate depreciation method is a matter of judgement. The Companies Act, 2013 does not prescribe depreciation methods. The most commonly used depreciation methods are straight-line time depreciation method, straight-line use depreciation method and reducing balance method.

Self-Test Questions

Self-test question 17.3

Indicate whether the following statements are true (T) or false (F):

(i) If residual value remains the same, under straight-line time depreciation method, a uniform amount of depreciation is charged every year.
(ii) If residual value remains the same, under straight-line use depreciation method, a uniform amount of depreciation is charged every year.
(iii) Under the reducing balance depreciation method, the amount of depreciation reduces in every subsequent year.
(iv) Even if the residual value is estimated at zero, under the reducing balance depreciation method, the carrying amount of the asset is never reduced to zero.
(v) Under straight-line use depreciation method, no depreciation is charged in the accounting year in which the asset remained idle.

IMPAIRMENT OF PROPERTY, PLANT AND EQUIPMENT

Concept of Impairment

The carrying amount of an asset in the balance sheet should not exceed its recoverable amount. Therefore, if at the balance sheet date, the carrying amount exceeds its recoverable amount, the carrying amount is written down to the recoverable amount and impairment loss is recognised. For example, if the carrying amount of an asset as at March 31, 2018 is ₹1,000 (after charging depreciation for 2017–18) and the management estimates the recoverable amount at ₹800, the entity recognises the asset in the balance sheet as at March 31, 2018 at ₹800 and recognises impairment loss of ₹200 in the statement of profit and loss for the year 2017–18.

Recoverable amount

Recoverable amount is the higher of 'value-in-use' and 'fair value less costs of disposal'. 'Value-in-use' is the present value of cash flows that the entity expects to derive from the use of the asset over its useful life. 'Fair value less costs of disposal' is the price that the entity expects to receive by selling the asset in an orderly transaction with market participants at the measurement date. Costs of disposal are incremental costs directly attributable to the disposal of the asset, excluding finance costs and income tax expense.

For example, the recoverable amount of an asset is ₹1,500 if the value-in-use is ₹1,200 and 'fair value less costs of disposal' is ₹1,500.

General Principles

Identifying levels at which assets are tested for impairment

Whenever possible, individual assets should be tested for impairment. For example, an investment property can be tested for impairment on stand-alone basis, as it generates cash flows independent of cash flows from other assets. However, most assets generate cash flows together with other assets in the group. Therefore, in most cases, impairment is tested at the group (called cash generating unit) level. Cash Generating Unit (CGU) is the smallest group of assets that generates cash flows from continuing use largely independent of cash flows generated by other assets or CGUs.

Indicator-based impairment testing

An entity should assess at the end of each reporting period whether there is any indication that an asset may be impaired. If any such indication exists, the entity should estimate the

NOTES

recoverable amount of the asset. An entity's assessment is based on internal and external information.

Internal indications

The following are the examples of internal indications:

(i) Obsolescence or physical damage of an asset;
(ii) Significant changes in the extent to which, or manner in which, an asset is used or is expected to be used;
(iii) A plan to dispose of an asset before the previously expected date of disposal;
(iv) Internal reporting indicates that the economic performance of an asset is, or will be, worse than expected; and
(v) Cash flows for acquiring the asset, operating or maintaining it that are significantly higher than originally budgeted.

External indications

The following are the examples of external indications:

(i) The asset's value has declined during the period significantly more than what would be expected as a result of the passage of time or normal use.
(ii) Significant changes with an adverse effect on the entity have taken place during the period, or will take place in the near future, in the technological, market, economic or legal environment in which the entity operates or in the market to which an asset is dedicated.
(iii) Market interest rates or other market rates of return on investments have increased during the period, and those increases are likely to affect the discount rate used in calculating an asset's 'value-in-use' and decrease the asset's recoverable amount materially.
(iv) The carrying amount of the net assets of the entity is more than its market capitalisation.

CASE STUDY 17.1 Impairment Indicators of CGU

NM Limited (NML) is a listed company. It has three CGUs. All the CGUs are operating profitably, although margins earned by them have come down. The average share price over last twelve month is significantly lower than the book value (carrying amount of net assets per share). The auditor is insisting the management to test all the three CGUs for impairment.

Question

The CFO of NML seeks your expert opinion on whether all the three CGUs should be tested for impairment.

Solution

The carrying amount of net assets more than market capitalisation is an impairment indicator. Therefore, in accordance with the GAAP, NML should test its assets for impairment. However, as all the three CGUs are operating profitably, it is difficult to identify the drivers for low market capitalisation. Therefore, all the three CGUs should be tested for impairment.

CASE STUDY 17.2 Impairment Indicators of CGU

KP Limited (KPL) is in the retailing business. It has three CGUs—X, Y and Z. Division X deals in fashion garments. Division Y deals in fashion accessories. Division Z deals in toys. Divisions X and Y are profitable. Division Z has incurred operating loss in the year 2017–18 due to competition from low-quality toys (in terms of materials used and in-built safety mechanism) that are cheaper. The top management of KPL and the Divisional Manager of the Division Z believes that the division will return to profit after a couple of years because it will be able to cut costs, and also, due to increasing awareness of health hazards from toys that are selling cheap in the market and increase in purchasing power of young parents.

Question

The CFO of KPL seeks your advice whether the company should test the division Z for impairment while preparing financial statements for the year 2017–18.

Solution

The fact that the division Z has incurred operating loss indicates impairment. Therefore, the company should test division Z for impairment.

Review of useful life, depreciation method and residual value

If there is an indication that an asset might have been impaired, the entity should review the asset's estimated remaining useful life, depreciation method, and residual value. The entity should review those irrespective of whether or not it recognises impairment loss.

Mandatory annual impairment testing

An entity is required to test the following assets for impairment annually:

(i) Intangible assets with indefinite useful lives and intangible assets not yet available for use; and

(ii) CGUs to which goodwill has been allocated.

The assets which are required to be tested annually should be tested for impairment whenever there is any indication for impairment.

SUMMARY

When the carrying amount of an asset is higher than the estimated recoverable amount, impairment loss is recognised in the statement of profit and loss and the asset is written down to the recoverable amount. Recoverable amount is the higher of 'value-in-use' and 'fair value less costs of disposal'. Whenever possible, individual assets should be tested for impairment. However, most assets generate cash flows together with other assets in the group called the cash generating unit (CGU). Therefore, in most of the cases, impairment is tested at CGU level, which is the smallest group of assets that generates cash flows from continuing use largely independent of cash flows generated by other assets or CGUs. Intangible assets with indefinite useful lives, intangible assets not yet available for use, and CGUs to which goodwill has been allocated are tested for impairment annually. Other assets are tested for impairment if internal or external information indicates that the asset or the CGU to which the asset belongs might have been impaired.

Self-Test Questions

Self-test question 17.4

Indicate whether the following statements are true (T) or false (F):

(i) An asset is impaired if the 'value-in-use' is lower than its carrying amount.

(ii) An investment property can be tested for impairment on stand-alone basis if it generates cash flows independently from cash flows being generated by other assets.

(iii) A CGU should be tested for impairment if the available information suggests that future technological changes would adversely impact the performance of the CGU.

(iv) If the carrying amount of the net assets of the entity is more than its market capitalisation, all the CGUs should be tested for impairment unless the entity is able to identify which CGUs have been impaired.

(v) Physical damage of an essential asset of a CGU indicates that the CGU might have been impaired.

NOTES

Cash Generating Unit (CGU)

A CGU is the smallest group of assets that generates cash flows from continuing use largely independent of cash flows generated by other assets or CGUs. Identification of CGU at a higher level might camouflage the impairment loss of certain assets.

Identification of CGU

Identification of CGU is a matter of judgement. The management asks the following two questions while identifying CGUs:

(i) Are these groups of assets generating revenue streams that are independent of one another?

(ii) Are these groups of assets operated together to such an extent that they do not generate independent revenue streams?

The assets referred in (ii) do not include corporate assets. Entities should consider only the operating assets.

CASE STUDY 17.3 Identifying CGU

The government has issued license to KL Airlines Plc. (KLAP), which is an International airline, to operate in India, subject to fulfillment of certain conditions. The conditions include providing minimum services to specified sectors in India. The company has allocated aircraft and other resources to each sector. The management manages and monitors performance of each sector separately.

Question

The CFO seeks your advice on whether each sector should be identified as a CGU.

Solution

Separate sectors fail the revenue test. KLAP cannot close down operations in unprofitable sectors and continue its operations in other sectors. It is inappropriate to conclude that each sector in India generates revenue independently of revenues being generated by the other sectors.

Therefore, different sectors cannot be identified as separate CGUs. CGU is the Indian operation as a whole.

CASE STUDY 17.4 Identifying CGU

Century Bazar Limited (CBL) is a retail stores chain, which has large number of retail stores across India. Each retail store serves one or more residential areas in the city. CBL decides the number of stores to be operated in a city depending on the population density of the city, distance between different residential areas and the average family income of residents of each residential area or cluster of residential areas. CBL maintains a central warehouse in each city, which caters to the needs of all the stores. The purchasing activity is located centrally at its headquarters in Mumbai. Each retail store has to follow the pricing policy decided centrally by the corporate office. Each store enjoys volume discount of 10 percent on purchases based on the volume of goods purchased centrally. The management evaluates the performance of each store separately.

Question

The CEO of CBL seeks your advice on whether each store can be identified as a CGU.

Solution

Each retail store generates revenue separately from other stores, although the pricing policy is formulated centrally. The volume discount of 10 percent constitutes a very small part of the

NOTES

total cash flow. All the stores have separate operating assets. The central warehouse is the only common asset that is used by all the stores in the city. The cost of warehouse, if notionally allocated to each store, would constitute an insignificant part of the total cost of operating assets of each store. For the purpose of identifying CGU, the warehouse may be considered as a corporate asset. Therefore, it would be incorrect to conclude that all the operating assets belonging to different stores in a city are operated together.

Each store should be identified as a separate CGU.

CASE STUDY 17.5 Identifying CGU

New India Pumps Limited (NIPL) manufactures small agricultural pumps in its three factories located in Joka (West Bengal), Thane (Maharashtra) and Noida (Uttar Pradesh). All the three factories have separate operating assets and they operate independently. Each has developed local vendors for important components and manages its own supply chain. All the three factories serve the demand across the country and support execution of export orders. The company receives orders centrally and allocates them to three manufacturing units depending on their capacity and backlog of orders. The top management has identified each factory as a cost centre and evaluates its performance based on performance metrics that focus on manufacturing excellence.

Question

The CFO of NIPL seeks your advice on whether each factory can be considered as a CGU.

Solution

All three factories meet the operating asset test, as they have separate operating assets. However, they fail to meet the revenue test. The capacity utilisation of factories depends on the allocation of orders by the corporate office. Therefore, it would be incorrect to conclude that they generate revenue streams that are independent of each other. Therefore, each factory should not be identified as a separate CGU. The company as a whole is the CGU.

CASE STUDY 17.6 Identifying CGU

FG Limited (FGL) manufactures and sells electronic consumer durables such as refrigerators and air conditioners. It has two factories. One factory, located in Manesar in Haryana, produces the final product and sells them in the market. The second factory, located in Noida in Uttar Pradesh, produces components. The Noida factory supplies components to the Manesar factory and also sells spare parts directly in the market. Almost all the customers that buy the final products buy the spare parts. The pricing policy is decided at the corporate office. The transfer price charged to the Manesar factory is lower than the market price of the same component. Pricing decision is a strategic decision, and often margins for final products are kept low and margins for spare parts are kept high.

Question

The CFO of FGL proposes to consider the company as the CGU. The auditor differs. She proposes to consider the two factories as separate CGUs because their operating assets are separate, and they generate revenue separately.

Solution

The operating assets of the two factories are separate. Therefore, if we apply the 'separate assets' test, those should be considered as separate CGUs. But, they do not pass the 'separate revenue' test. The customer base is the same for the two factories and the pricing of final products and spare parts are linked. Therefore, we cannot conclude that those two factories are generating revenue separately. Consequently, the two factories cannot be considered as separate CGUs. The company should be considered as the CGU.

Vertically integrated organisation

If an active market exists for the output produced by an asset or group of assets, that asset or group of assets is identified as a CGU even if some or all of the output are used internally.

SUMMARY

A CGU is the smallest group of assets that generates cash flows from continuing use largely independent of cash flows generated by other assets or CGUs. Identification of CGU is a matter of judgement. The two key criteria in identifying CGUs are that the groups (of assets) generate revenue independently of each other and they do not operate together to such an extent that they do not generate independent revenue streams. If an active market exists for the output produced by an asset or group of assets, that asset or group of assets is identified as a CGU even if some or all of the outputs are used internally.

Self-Test Questions

Self-test question 17.5

Indicate whether the following statements are true (T) or false (F):

(i) Two stores (of a retail chain) in the same city cannot be identified as separate CGUs if the central warehouse in the city for stocking goods is used by both the stores.

(ii) If two production units share common facilities (operating assets), which form significant part of operating assets, it is unlikely that they can be identified as separate CGUs.

(iii) Identification of CGUs at higher level results in camouflaging impairment loss of some of the assets.

(iv) If an entity manages order book position centrally and allocates customer orders to different factories, the factories cannot be identified as different CGUs.

(v) A strategic business unit (SBU) that produces goods for use by other SBUs of the entity cannot be identified as a CGU.

Value-In-Use

'Value-in-use' is the present value of future cash flows that the entity expects to derive from the asset or the CGU over its remaining useful life.

Useful life of a CGU and forecast period

The forecast period for forecasting cash flows is the useful life of the CGU. Usually, entities consider the useful life of the asset that is central (essential) to the operation of the CGU in estimating the useful life of the CGU. This involves judgement. For example, in a manufacturing facility that is producing gas cylinders, the useful life of the electric heating furnace may be deemed to be the useful life of the CGU.

It is not necessary that the essential asset should be one that is recognised in the balance sheet. For example, an entity may conclude that the unrecognised brand or the right to use land under an operating lease is the essential asset.

Cash flow estimation

An entity should use *pre-tax* cash flow for estimating value-in-use.

Composition of cash flows

Cash flows include:

(i) Cash inflows from continuing use;
(ii) Cash inflows necessary to generate the cash inflows (including overheads); and
(iii) Net cash flows from the ultimate disposal of the asset.

Proposed capital expenditure

An entity does not take into account the effect of proposed capital expenditure in projecting the cash outflow and cash inflow. It considers the capital expenditure and its effect on the cash flow in case the CGU is in the development stage because in the absence of that expenditure, the CGU will not be complete and will not generate cash flows.

Future capital expenditure that will maintain the CGU's/asset's performance is included in the projected cash flows.

CASE STUDY 17.7 Future Capital Expenditure

BC Limited (BCL) has a CGU that includes a factory. The useful life of the essential asset is 30 years. The useful lives of other assets are 10 years.

Question

The CFO of BCL seeks your advice on whether future capital expenditure, which will be required to replace assets with useful lives shorter than the useful life of the essential asset, should be included in the forecasted cash flows that will be used to estimate the value-in-use.

Solution

The forecast period is determined by the useful life of the essential asset. Therefore, the forecast period in this case is 30 years. Future capital expenditures to replace assets with shorter useful lives will be required tc maintain the CGU's performance. Those capital expenditures should be considered part of expenditure for day-to-day servicing of the CGU and should be included in projected cash flows.

Restructuring

An entity tests the CGU for impairment in its present condition. Therefore, in projecting future cash inflows and outflows, it does not take into account the effect of proposed restructuring, if any. The entity takes into account the effect of proposed restructuring only if it is so close to implementation that the entity has practically no option to withdraw the proposal.

Cash flow forecast

Projection based on approved budgets or forecasts should cover a maximum period of five years unless a longer period can be justified. Cash flow projection beyond the period covered by approved budgets/forecasts should be estimated by extrapolating the projection based on the budgets/forecasts. A steady or declining growth rate should be considered for subsequent years unless an increasing rate can be justified. The growth rate should not exceed the long-term average growth rates for the products, industries, or country (or countries) in which the entity operates, or for the market in which the asset is used. However, an entity may justify use of a higher growth rate.

Discount rate

An entity should use pre-tax discount rate, as the cash flow to be discounted is the pre-tax cash flow.

The discounting rate should be consistent with the projection of cash flow. Risk-free rate should be used if the projected cash flow is the 'expected cash flow' (as the term is used in statistics), as it represents 'risk-free equivalent cash flow'. If the cash flow is not the expected cash flow, the entity should use the discounting rate, which incorporates the time value of money, and also, the risks surrounding the cash flow. The discount rate should reflect the *market assessment* of the time value of money and the risk that the future cash flows will differ in amount or timing from estimates.

The Weighted Average Cost of Capital (WACC) is the appropriate discount rate, only if the risk to the CGU under consideration is the average risk of the entity. In case the risk to which the CGU is exposed is significantly different from the average risk of the entity, the entity should use a discount rate different from the WACC.

Foreign currency cash flow

At the first stage, the entity estimates future cash flows in the currency in which they will be generated. At the second stage, it discounts the forecasted cash flows using a discount rate appropriate for that currency. Finally, it translates the present value using the exchange rate at the balance sheet date.

Cash flow of a CGU that does not sell output

In case the production of a CGU is being used internally by the entity, management's best estimate of future price that could be achieved at arm's length transactions should be used in estimating the value-in-use of the CGU when measuring (i) the *future cash inflows* that relate to the internal use of the output by another CGU, and (ii) the *future cash outflows* that relate to the internal use of the output supplied by another CGU.

An entity should not use internal transfer price in estimating cash flows of the CGU.

Fair Value Less Costs to Sell

Fair value less costs to sell is the amount that the entity expects to receive from the sale of an asset in an arm's length transaction between knowledgeable and willing parties, less the costs of disposal.

The best evidence of an asset's net selling price is *a price in a binding sale agreement* in an arm's length transaction, reduced by costs of disposal. If there is no binding sale agreement, the net selling price is the asset's market price (*current bid price*) in an active market, reduced by costs of disposal. In case current bid prices are unavailable, the price of the most recent transaction should be used to estimate the net selling price. However, the same should be adjusted for significant changes in the economic circumstances between the transaction date and the date at which the estimate is made.

There might be situations in which neither a binding sale agreement nor an active market for an asset is available. In such a situation, the net selling price should be based on the best information available to reflect the amount that the entity could obtain at the balance sheet date for the disposal of the asset. *Outcome of recent transactions for similar assets within the same industry should be used as the basis for estimating the amount.*

Usually, an entity does not sell a going concern piecemeal. In most of the situations, it determines the net selling price of a CGU, for which no active market exists. Therefore, in the absence of bid price in an active market or recent transactions involving similar assets, established valuation models may be used to determine the fair value less costs to sell, unless there is a binding sale agreement. However, use of valuation models may result in an estimate that is close to the value-in-use unless additional benefits that are expected to accrue to the buyer are incorporated in the model. Usually, buyers agree to pay a price higher than the value-in-use. They expect higher cash flows than the estimated cash flows from the present use of the asset by the present owner due to synergy or higher market share or some other economic benefits.

Appraisal method

An enterprise may determine the realisable value of its assets by using the *appraisal method*. The value determined through the appraisal method may be used as a substitute measure of the net selling price.

SUMMARY

'Value-in-use' is the present value of cash flows that the CGU is expected to generate over its useful life and on disposal of assets. The useful life of a CGU is the useful life of the central (essential) asset. The CGU is tested for impairment in its current position. Therefore, future capital expenditure and its impact is not included in projected cash flows. However, future capital expenditure that is aimed at maintaining the CGU's/asset's performance is included in projected cash flows. Similarly, effect of proposed restructuring is considered in projecting cash flows only if it is so close to implementation that the entity has practically no option to withdraw the proposal. Pre-tax cash flows are discounted by an appropriate pre-tax discounting rate to estimate the 'value-in-use'.

Fair value less costs to sell is the amount that the entity expects to receive from the sale of an asset in an arm's length transaction between knowledgeable and willing parties, less the costs of disposal. The best evidence of an asset's net selling price is ***a price in a binding sale agreement*** in an arm's length transaction, reduced by costs of disposal.

Self-Test Questions

Self-test question 17.6

Indicate whether the following statements are true (T) or false (F):

(i) In estimating the 'value-in-use', 'expected cash flows' (as the term is used in statistics) should be discounted by risk-free interest rate.

(ii) 'Value-in-use' is entity-specific measure, while fair value is a market-determined measure.

(iii) Cash flows should be projected based on reasonable assumptions, and therefore, year-to-year cash flows cannot be projected for a very long period (say, more than five years).

(iv) Often 'value-in-use' of a CGU is close to the 'fair value less cost of disposal' unless the entity is not putting the CGU in its best use.

(v) In the absence of a binding contract, the 'fair value less cost of disposal' cannot be estimated.

Testing Goodwill for Impairment

If the goodwill is allocated to an individual CGU, the CGU (including goodwill) is tested for impairment.

If the goodwill could not be allocated to an individual CGU, but is allocated to a group of CGUs, then the impairment testing is performed in the following two stages:

(i) The first impairment test is performed at the individual CGU level (without goodwill), and any impairment loss is recognised. This is called *bottom-up test.*

(ii) The second impairment test is applied to the group of CGUs to which goodwill relates. This is called *top-down test.*

ILLUSTRATION 17.4 Testing Goodwill for Impairment)

NB Limited (NBL) determines that there are indications that CGU T might have been impaired. The carrying amount (without goodwill) of the CGU T is ₹1,000. Goodwill with carrying amount of ₹500 could not be allocated to individual CGUs. It relates to CGU T and other two CGUs—M and P. The carrying amount of M is ₹600 and that of P is ₹400. The recoverable amount of the CGU T is estimated at ₹800. The recoverable amounts of CGUs M and P are ₹650 and ₹450 respectively.

Required

Explain how the goodwill should be tested for impairment.

Solution

(i) ***Bottom-up test:*** The carrying amount (₹1,000) of CGU T is higher than the recoverable amount (₹800) by ₹200. Therefore, impairment loss of ₹200 is to be recognised.

(ii) The carrying amount of the group of three CGUs (T, M and P), after recognising the impairment loss of the CGU T, is (₹800 + 600 + 400) or ₹1,800. The recoverable amount of the group of CGUs is (₹800 + 650 + 450) or ₹1,900. The recoverable amount is higher than the carrying amount of the group of CGUs to which the goodwill relates. Therefore, there is no impairment of goodwill.

Impairment of Corporate Assets

The key characteristic of corporate assets is that they do not generate cash inflows independently from other assets or groups of assets. Examples of corporate assets are building of the corporate headquarters, EDP equipment, and research centre. The carrying amount of those assets cannot be attributed to a particular CGU under review except on an arbitrary basis. The recoverable amount of an individual corporate asset cannot be determined unless the management decides to dispose of the asset. Therefore, if there is any indication that a corporate asset is impaired, the recoverable amount is determined for the CGU to which the corporate asset belongs. It is compared with the carrying amount of the CGU to determine the impairment loss. Usually, the CGU for corporate assets is the entity as a whole.

Allocation of Impairment Loss of a CGU

The impairment loss of a CGU should be allocated to reduce the carrying amount of assets of the CGU in the following order:

First, to goodwill, if any, allocated to the CGU, and then, to other assets of the unit on a pro-rata basis based on the carrying amount of each asset in the unit.

In allocating an impairment loss, the carrying amount of an asset should not be reduced below the highest of:

(i) its net selling price (if determinable)
(ii) its value-in-use (if determinable), and
(iii) zero.

The amount of the impairment loss that would otherwise have been allocated to the asset should be allocated to other assets of the unit on a pro-rata basis. For example, if a CGU has a piece of land among other assets and the net selling price of the land is higher than its carrying amount, no part of the impairment loss estimated for the CGU should be allocated to the piece of land.

Reversal of Impairment Loss

Ind AS 36 does not allow reversal of impairment loss of goodwill recognised in earlier periods. It stipulates principles for the reversal of impairment loss of other assets recognised in earlier periods.

General principle

An impairment loss recognised for an asset in prior accounting periods should be reversed if there has been a *change in the estimates of cash inflows, cash outflows*, or *discount rates* used to determine the asset's recoverable amount since the last impairment loss was recognised.

An asset's value-in-use may become greater than the assets carrying amount simply because the PV of future cash inflows increases as they become closer although there is no increase in the service potential of the asset. The impairment loss is not reversed just because of unwinding of the discount.

Indications of reversal

An entity should assess at each balance sheet date whether there is any indication that an impairment loss recognised for an asset in prior accounting periods may no longer exist or may have decreased. If there is any such indication, the entity should estimate the recoverable amount of that asset.

Accounting for reversal

A reversal of an impairment loss should be recognised as income in the statement of profit and loss for the period in which the impairment loss is reversed.

In the case of a revalued asset, the reversal of the impairment loss should be considered as revaluation increases. However, if a portion of the impairment loss recognised in prior period was charged in the statement of profit and loss, the reversal to that extent should be recognised as income in the statement of profit and loss.

Words of caution

The increased carrying amount of an asset due to a reversal of an impairment loss should not exceed the carrying amount that would have been determined had no impairment loss been recognised for the asset in prior accounting periods.

Reversal of impairment loss of a CGU

A reversal of an impairment loss for a CGU should be allocated to the assets of the unit, except for goodwill, pro rata with the carrying amounts of those assets. These increases in carrying amounts shall be treated as reversals of impairment losses for individual assets and will be accounted for in accordance with the rules applicable for reversal of impairment loss related to an individual asset.

The carrying amount of an asset should not be increased above the lower of:

(i) Its recoverable amount, if determinable, and
(ii) The carrying amount that would have been determined had no impairment loss been recognised for the asset in prior accounting periods.

SUMMARY

If goodwill cannot be allocated to a specific CGU and it relates to more than one CGU, bottom-up and top-down tests are performed to test impairment of the goodwill. Usually, the CGU for corporate assets is the entity as a whole. The impairment loss of a CGU should be allocated to reduce the carrying amount of assets of the CGU in the following order:

First, to goodwill, if any, allocated to the CGU, and then, to other assets of the unit on a pro-rata basis based on the carrying amount of each asset in the unit.

In allocating an impairment loss, the carrying amount of an asset should not be reduced below the highest of (i) its net selling price (if determinable), (ii) its value in use (if determinable), and (iii) zero.

Reversal of impairment loss of goodwill recognised in earlier periods is not permitted. An entity can reverse the impairment loss of other assets if there has been a ***change in the estimates of cash inflows, cash outflows,*** or ***discount rates*** used to determine the asset's recoverable amount since the last impairment loss was recognised. The carrying amount of an asset should not be increased above the lower of (i) Its recoverable amount, if determinable, and (ii) the carrying amount that would have been determined had no impairment loss been recognised for the asset in prior accounting periods.

Self-Test Questions

Self-test question 17.7

Indicate whether the following statements are true (T) or false (F):

(i) Goodwill should be tested for impairment only if the available information indicates that at least one of the CGUs to which it relates might have been impaired.

(ii) Testing impairment of goodwill is always a two-step process.

(iii) Goodwill of a CGU is written down to zero if the impairment loss of the CGU is higher than the carrying amount of the goodwill.

(iv) Impairment loss of goodwill recognised in earlier periods cannot be reversed.

(v) Impairment loss recognised in earlier periods cannot be reversed if the 'value-in-use' has increased only due to unwinding of discount.

ANSWERS TO SELF-TEST QUESTIONS

17.1 (i) F; (ii) F; (iii) T; (iv) T; (v) F

17.2 (i) T; (ii) T; (iii) F; (iv) T; (v) F

17.3 (i) T; (ii) F; (iii) T; (iv) T; (v) T

17.4 (i) F; (ii) T; (iii) T; (iv) T; (v) T

17.5 (i) F; (ii) T; (iii) T; (iv) T; (v) F

17.6 (i) T; (ii) T; (iii) T; (iv) T; (v) F

17.7 (i) F; (ii) F; (iii) T; (iv) T; (v) F

ASSIGNMENTS

Quiz

1. Indicate against each statement whether it is True (T) or False (F):
   (i) Depreciation measures wear and tear of fixed assets.
   (ii) Residual value of intangible assets is usually taken as zero.
   (iii) Useful life of an asset is the period over which the asset is expected to produce the intended output/result.
   (iv) The economic life of an asset is specific to the asset and useful life of an asset is specific to the entity.
   (v) Impairment of an asset necessarily leads to reduction in its useful life.
   (vi) Usually, no depreciation is charged on land because there is a general assumption that land has indefinite useful life.
2. Tick the correct answer:
   (i) In which of the following situations is the unit of production method of depreciation most appropriate?
      (a) A service potential of an asset's declines with use.
      (b) A service potential of an asset's declines with the passage of time.
      (c) An asset is subject to rapid obsolescence.
      (d) An asset is subject to increasing repairs and maintenance with increasing use.
   (ii) On January 1, 2003, Naina Limited (NL) purchased a machine for ₹3,00,000 and depreciated it by the straight-line method using an estimated useful life of 10 years with no salvage value. On January 1, 2006, NL determined that the machine had a useful life of six years from the date of acquisition and would have a salvage value of ₹30,000. An accounting change was made in 2006 to reflect the additional data. The

accumulated depreciation for this machine should have a balance at December 31, 2006, of

(a) ₹1,50,000
(b) ₹1,80,000
(c) ₹1,44,000
(d) None of the above

(iii) Rumki Limited (RL) acquired an asset on January 1, 2003. It estimated the useful life of the asset at five years and residual value at 5% of the cost of the asset. On December 31, 2006, accumulated depreciation, using the sum-of-the years' digits method would be

(a) (Original cost less salvage value) multiplied by 14/15
(b) (Original cost less salvage value) multiplied by 1/15
(c) Original cost multiplied by 14/15
(d) Original cost multiplied by 1/15

3. Fill in the blanks:

(i) The acquisition cost of equipment, acquired during the reporting period, is ₹1,20,000. On the balance sheet date, the PV of the future cash flow to be generated by the equipment is estimated at ₹90,000 and the 'fair value less costs to sell' is estimated at ₹1,00,000. The impairment loss should be reçognised at ₹__________ (ignore depreciation for the reporting period).

(ii) The carrying amount of a fixed asset as on December 31, 2005 was ₹2,00,000. During 2006, ₹40,000 had to be charged towards depreciation. On December 31, 2006, the PV of the future cash flow from the asset, its immediate realisable value, and its replacement cost had been estimated at ₹1,70,000, ₹1,20,000 and ₹1,50,000, respectively. The deprived value is ₹__________ and the current value is ₹__________. The fixed asset should be carried in the balance sheet at__________ if the company is using the cost model.

(iii) The acquisition cost of a machine acquired on January 1, 2000 is ₹2,00,000. The residual value and useful life of the machine were estimated at zero and 10 years. The enterprise uses the straight-line method of depreciation for depreciating this type of machine. On December 31, 2004, the enterprise revalued the machine at ₹1,60,000. Depreciation to be charged to the profit and loss account for 2005 was ₹______, and the amount to be transferred to the general reserve from revaluation reserve was ₹______. (Please note that this situation does not arise in Ind AS regime, as an entity, as the accounting policy, has to choose between cost model and revaluation model.)

Problems

1. Jose Limited (JL) has three divisions, one of which produces chemicals. The factory producing chemicals emits chemical waste to the nearby canal. The company has recognised a liability of ₹10,00,000 towards the estimated cost of cleaning the canal, as required by a newly enacted environmental law. The assets of JL, which are subject to impairment test, are carried at ₹10,00,00,000. The chemical factory is a CGU. The company can sell the chemical factory as a whole, and the buyer will have to take over the liability for restoration of the environment. The net selling price (fair value less costs to sell) of the factory is estimated at ₹89,00,000. The value in use, considering the present value of expenditure to be incurred for restoration of the environment, is estimated at ₹85,00,000.

   Required: Calculate the impairment loss, if any.

2. On January 1, 2005, Mallika Limited (ML) acquired Shabnam Limited (SL). ML is in the business of retailing. It has a highly reputed retail stores in the up-markets. SL is in the textile business. It has two divisions—cloth division and readymade garments division. ML pays ₹1,200 million to the shareholders of SL towards purchase consideration. The estimated fair value of identifiable tangible and intangible assets is ₹900 million. ML recognises goodwill in its balance sheet at ₹300 million. After acquisition, ML has three CGUs—retail division, cloth division, and readymade garments division.

   ML expects that its retail business will also benefit from this acquisition. Assume the following two situations separately:

   (i) ML allocates the goodwill of ₹300 million as follows:

   (a) Retail division (Division A): ₹30 million

(b) Cloth division (Division B): ₹120 million

(c) Readymade garment division (Division C): ₹150 million

(ii) ML is unable to allocate goodwill to individual CGUs.

The carrying amounts of assets (excluding goodwill) of the three divisions are as follows:

Division A: ₹400 million; Division B: ₹350 million; Division C: ₹500 million. Assume the recoverable amounts of the three divisions as follows:

Division A: ₹450 million; Division B: ₹440 million; Division C: ₹700 million

Required: Estimate the impairment loss of goodwill, taking each situation separately.

Revenue from Contracts with Customers

CHAPTER

18

Learning Objectives

Customers of an entity are those who buy goods or services, which are the outputs of entity's ordinary activities. Income from supplying goods or services to the customers is recognised as revenue. The timing of recognising revenue and the amount at which revenue is recognised depend on terms and conditions of contracts with customers. This chapter discusses the accounting principles for the recognition of revenue. After reading this chapter, you will develop understanding of the following:

- The concept of revenue
- General principles for recognising of revenue
- General principles for measuring revenue
- Five steps revenue model
- Performance for identifying contracts with customers
- Principles for identifying performance obligations in a contract
- Principles for determining transaction price in a contract
- The concept of constrained variable consideration
- Principles for allocating the transaction price to the performance obligations in a contract
- Concept of control
- Principles for satisfying performance obligation over time and recognising revenue at a point in time
- Accounting for sales with a right to return, warranties, customer loyalty programmes, and bill-and-hold arrangement
- Accounting for licensing arrangements and sale- and production-based royalties

Applicable accounting standards: *Ind AS 115, Revenue from contracts with customers; and Ind AS 109, Financial instruments.*

NOTES

CORE PRINCIPLES

Revenue

In the statement of profit and loss, income is grouped into three categories—revenue, other operating income and other income. Revenue arises in the course of an entity's ordinary activities, primarily from selling goods or services to customers. Other operating income arises from activities incidental to core activities such as sale of scrap generated during manufacturing activities. Other income includes incomes that cannot be classified either as revenue or as other operating income. For example, for a non-finance company, other income includes income from investments. For financial institutions, income from investments is revenue.

Contract with customers

An entity enters into contracts with customers, which purchases output (goods and services) of the entity's ordinary activities. An entity that purchases items other than the output from the entity's ordinary activities (e.g., used items of property, plant and equipment) is not a customer. A contract with a customer creates enforceable rights and obligations. The entity's obligation is to deliver promised goods and services and its right is to receive consideration promised by the customer. The customer's right is to receive promised goods and services and its obligation is to pay promised consideration. It is not necessary that the contract should be in writing. For example, a retailer, which sells goods over the counter, usually does not enter into a written contract with customers. Some terms of the contract are often implicit and established by customs and practices of the industry and the entity.

The terms and conditions of the contract with the customer determine the timing of revenue recognition and the amount at which it is recognised.

Importance of timing of revenue recognition and measurement

Timing of recognising revenue and the amount at which it is recognised are key in presenting true and fair view of economic performance and financial position of the entity. The timing determines the accounting period in which the gross profit (or loss) from sale of goods or services is recognised. The amount at which the revenue is recognised is important, as it determines the amount of gross profit and the amount at which trade receivables is measured in the balance sheet.

Example

An entity has entered into a contract to supply goods for ₹1,00,000. On March 31, 2018, the goods were ready for delivery, but the control of the goods was not transferred to the customer by that date. The entity has incurred cost of ₹70,000 to produce the goods. It does recognise revenue in the financial year 2017–18 and in the balance sheet as at March 31, 2018, it recognises cost incurred as an asset (inventory). On April 1, 2018, it delivers the goods to the customer. It recognises the revenue in the financial year 2018–19. Consequently, the asset is derecognised and the cost (₹70,000) is recognised as expense (cost of goods sold) in the statement of profit and loss for the year 2018–19. Thus, the entity recognises the gross profit of ₹30,000 in the financial year 2018–19 and not in the financial year 2017–18.

Analysts use the amount of revenue in analysing the performance of the entity. For example, they often use revenue growth to measure the growth in the size of the entity. The amount of revenue is used as a denominator in calculating the asset turnover ratio (revenue divided by average net operating assets), which is used to measure the efficiency and effectiveness in utilising assets. 'Trade receivable' is usually a part of current asset, and therefore, overstatement or understatement of trade receivables distorts the current ratio (current assets divided by current liabilities), which is commonly used to assess liquidity of the entity. Therefore, the timing of revenue recognition and revenue measurement is important in presenting the performance and financial position of the entity fairly.

Recognition principle

An entity recognises revenue when it transfers the promised goods and services to the customer and expects receiving the promised consideration. Depending on the nature of goods or services, entities recognise revenue over a period of time to depict performance or at a point in time, when control of the goods or services is transferred to the customer. For example, usually, in case of a construction or service contract, obligation to deliver promised services is satisfied over a period of time, and accordingly, revenue is recognised over time. In a merchandising business, the obligation to deliver the promised merchandise is satisfied at a particular point in time, and accordingly, the merchandiser recognises the revenue at a point in time.

Measurement

An entity measures revenue at an amount that reflects the consideration which the entity expects to be entitled in exchange for goods or services. For example, if the entity expects to receive ₹10,000 as consideration against the contract price of ₹12,000, the entity should recognise the revenue at ₹10,000 and not at ₹12,000.

Five Steps in Revenue Model

The following are the five steps in the revenue model:

Stage 1: Identify the contract;

Stage 2: Identify the performance obligation in the contract;

Stage 3: Determine the transaction price;

Stage 4: Allocate the transaction price to the performance obligations in the contract; and

Stage 5: Recognise revenue.

SUMMARY

Revenue is the income resulting from satisfying performance obligations arising from contracts with customers, who purchase entity's output (goods or services) from the entity's ordinary activities. A contract that establishes enforceable rights and obligations of the parties (the entity and the customer) in the contract is not necessarily to be in writing. The timing for recognising revenue and the amount at which the revenue is recognised are important, as they affect the profit reported by the entity, and also, the evaluation of entity's performance. An entity recognises revenue when it transfers the promised goods and services to the customer and expects receiving the promised consideration. It measures revenue at an amount that reflects the consideration which the entity expects to be entitled in exchange for goods or services.

Self-Test Questions

Self-test question 18.1

Indicate whether the following statements are true (T) or false (F):

(i) An entity that regularly purchases the scrap generated during the manufacturing process of the company is a customer of the company.

(ii) Revenue is measured when the performance obligation is satisfied and control over goods or services is transferred to the customer.

(iii) An entity measures revenue at the amount of consideration stipulated in the contract with the customer.

(iv) No entity is permitted to recognise revenue over time, as revenue should be recognised at a point in time.

(v) Income from a contract that is not enforceable in the court of law should not be recognised as revenue.

NOTES

IDENTIFYING A CONTRACT

An entity recognises revenue only when a contract with the customer exists.

Existence of a contract

A contract comes into existence only when *all* of the following criteria are met:

(i) The parties to the contract (the entity and the customer) have approved the contract and are committed to perform their respective obligations;
(ii) The entity can identify each party's rights regarding the goods or services to be transferred;
(iii) The entity can identify the payment terms for the goods or services to be transferred;
(iv) The contract has commercial substance, in the sense that the risk or timing or amount of the entity's future cash flows is expected to change as a result of the contract; and
(v) The customer has the *ability* and *intention* to pay the consideration, and thus, it is probable that the entity will collect the same.

Consideration received before the contract comes into existence

When an entity receives consideration from the customer before the contract comes into existence, the entity should recognise the consideration received as a liability. For example, an entity recognises the amount received before finalisation of all the terms of the contract as a liability.

However, the entity should recognise the consideration received as revenue only when either of the following events has occurred:

(i) The entity has no remaining obligations to transfer goods or services to the customer and all, or substantially all, of the consideration promised by the customer has been received by the entity and is non-refundable; or
(ii) The contract has been terminated and the consideration received from the customer is non-refundable.

For example, if the entity has the right to forfeit the advance received from the customer and the customer decides not to take the negotiation forward and not to finalise the contract, the advance should be recognised as revenue when the customer finally informs the entity that it withdraws from the negotiation and is not interested to purchase the goods or services from the entity.

CASE STUDY 18.1 Existence of Contract

AB Infra Tech Limited (ABITL) is a real estate developer. It has entered into a contract with Ms. Sujatha for the sale of a building for ₹5 crore in a Vasant Kunj in Delhi. Vasant Kunj is the most preferred residential area for upper middle-class families. Sujatha intends to open a fine dining restaurant in the building. In Vasant Kunj, restaurant business faces high level of competition and Sujatha is a fresh MBA graduate without any experience in business. As per the contract, Sujatha has paid ₹75 lakh at the inception of the contract and the balance 85 percent is payable over a period of ten years. Sujatha intends to pay the balance from her income from the restaurant business. The financing arrangement is provided on a non-recourse basis, which means that if Sujatha defaults, the ABITL can repossess the building, but cannot seek further compensation from her, even if the collateral does not cover the full value of the amount owed. ABITL's cost of the building is ₹3.5 crore. Sujatha obtains control of the building at contract inception.

Question

The CFO of ABITL seeks your advice on whether the contract meets the criterion specified in

NOTES

Ind AS 115 to assess whether a contract exists for the purpose of revenue recognition and how to account for the amount received from Sujatha.

Solution

The contract does not meet the criterion of probability of collecting the consideration to which ABITL is entitled in exchange for the transfer of the building, as the customer's ability and intention to pay may be in doubt because of the following factors:

(i) Sujatha intends to repay the loan (which has a significant balance) primarily from income derived from her restaurant business (which is a business facing significant risks because of high competition in the business and the Sujatha's limited experience);

(ii) She lacks other income or assets that could be used to repay the loan; and

(iii) Sujatha's liability under the loan is limited because the loan is non-recourse.

The amount received from Sujatha at the inception of the contract should be recognised as liability. The management should periodically assess the 'probability of collecting the consideration'. ABITL should recognise the revenue as and when the contract meets the criterion.

[Adapted from Example (1) of the Basis of Conclusion for IFRS 15.]

Combining contracts

Sometimes, appropriate accounting requires combining two or more contracts. Contracts entered into at or near the same time with the same customer (or related parties) should be combined if one or more of the following criteria are met:

(i) The contracts are negotiated as a package with a single commercial objective;

(ii) The consideration in one contract depends on the price or performance of the other contract; or

(iii) The goods and services promised in the contracts (or some of the goods and services promised in each of the contracts) are a single performance obligation.

For example, an entity enters into two separate contracts, one for designing the building and getting necessary approvals and another to construct the building, it may be appropriate to combine the two contracts. The entity should evaluate whether the conditions for combining two or more contracts are met.

Portfolio approach

Ind AS 115 stipulates accounting principles for accounting for revenue from individual contracts. However, as a practical expedient, it allows an entity to apply those principles to a portfolio of contracts (or performance obligations) with similar characteristics if the entity reasonably expects that the financial statement effect of applying the principles to the portfolio or to individual contracts (or performance obligations) within the portfolio would not be materially different.

SUMMARY

An entity recognises revenue only when a contract with the customer exists. A contract comes into existence when specified criteria are met. When an entity receives consideration from the customer before the contract comes into existence, the entity should recognise the consideration received as a liability. However, the entity recognises the amount received before the contract comes into existence as revenue if the contract is terminated before it meets all the criteria and the amount is non-refundable. Sometimes, appropriate accounting requires combining two or more contracts. The accounting principles stipulated in Ind AS 115 should be applied to each individual contract (or a combined contract) separately. However, as a practical expedient, an entity may apply those principles to a portfolio of similar contracts.

NOTES

Self-Test Questions

Self-test question 18.2

Indicate whether the following statements are true (T) or false (F):

(i) A contract to exchange similar goods or services does not result in revenue recognition, as it lacks commercial substance.

(ii) If there is significant uncertainty about the customer's *ability* and *intention* to pay the consideration, no revenue should be recognised from the sale of goods or services to that customer.

(iii) Amount received from a customer before the transaction price is agreed should be recognised as a liability and not as revenue.

(iv) It might be appropriate to combine two contracts, one for the supply of equipment and another to supply spare parts, if those are entered at the same time as a package.

(v) Amount forfeited on cancellation of a contract may be recognised as revenue.

IDENTIFYING PERFORMANCE OBLIGATIONS

Performance obligation is a unit of account

A performance obligation is a promise in a contract with a customer to transfer goods or services to the customer. It is the unit of account for revenue recognition. An entity recognises revenue when the performance obligation is satisfied, provided it expects to collect the consideration.

The key question is when to *unbundle* 'performance obligations' in a contract or when to bundle apparently separate performance obligations in a contract. For example, in telecom industry, free goods and services as well as options for additional goods and services for a discounted price might be separate performance obligations. Similarly, a technology company providing integrated solutions, should analyse whether the promises in the contract should be unbundled for recognising revenue and the outcome of that analysis mostly depends on the degree of customisation and integration of components as well as on the right to payment.

A contract may have more than one performance obligation

A contract may have more than one performance obligations. Therefore, it is important to identify each performance obligation separately. For example, in a contract with a customer, an automobile dealer promises to deliver the car and provide free maintenance services for one year. In this contract, there are two performance obligations—one is to deliver the car, and the other to provide maintenance services. The dealer recognises revenue from the delivery of the car when it transfers control of the car to the customer and revenue from providing the maintenance services as and when the services are rendered. If the contract specifies a single price for both the performance obligations, the dealer allocates the price between two distinct performance obligations.

Identification of performance obligation

An entity should identify as a performance obligation *each promise* to transfer to the customer either:

(i) a good or service (or a bundle of goods or services) that is distinct; or

(ii) a series of distinct goods or services that are substantially the same and that have the same pattern of transfer to the customer.

We shall discuss the nature of 'distinct goods or services' and 'a series of distinct goods and services' in the following paragraphs.

Examples of goods and services

Examples of different types of goods and services are provided in Table 18.1:

TABLE 18.1

Examples of Common Goods and Services

S. No.	Types of goods and services	Examples
1.	Sale of goods produced by an entity	Home appliances being sold by LG Electronics India (Private) Limited
2.	Resale of goods purchased by an entity	Groceries being sold by Big Bazaar
3.	Resale of rights to goods or services purchased by an entity	An entity purchases tickets of an entertainment show in bulk on its own account and resells the same
4.	Performing a contractually agreed-upon task (or tasks) for a customer	Wilson Fleming providing catering services in wedding parties
5.	Providing a service of standing ready to provide goods or services	Promise of entity manufacturing and selling computer software to provide unspecified updates to software on a when-and-if-available basis
6.	Providing a service of arranging for another party to transfer goods or services to a customer	Services being provided by shipping agents, who act on behalf of ship owners
7.	Granting rights to goods or services to be provided in the future that a customer can resell or provide to its customer	An entity selling a product to a retailer promises to transfer an additional good or service to an individual who purchases the product from the retailer
8.	Constructing, manufacturing or developing an asset on behalf of a customer	Hindustan Construction Limited constructs infrastructures and civil projects like the tunnel, nuclear power plants, hydropower plants, highways, expressways, and bridges
9.	Granting licences	Licenses for intellectual properties such as licenses for software and technology, motion pictures, and franchises
10.	Granting options to purchase additional goods or services	Sales incentives, customer-award credits (or points), contract renewal options or other discounts on future goods or services.

Distinct good or service

A good or service that is promised to a customer is distinct if *both* of the following criteria are met:

(i) The customer can benefit from the good or service; and
(ii) The entity's promise to transfer the good or service to the customer is separately identifiable from other promises in the contract.

Criterion 1—A customer can benefit from a good or service

A customer can benefit from a good or service if the good or service could be used, consumed, sold for an amount that is greater than scrap value or otherwise held in a way that generates economic benefits.

For some goods or services, a customer may be able to benefit from a good or service on its own. For other goods or services, a customer may be able to benefit from the good or service only in conjunction with other readily available resources.

A *readily available resource* is a good or service that is sold separately by the entity or another entity. Similarly, a readily available resource is that resource which the customer has already obtained from the entity or from other transactions or events. Various factors may provide evidence that the customer can benefit from a good or service either on its own or in conjunction with other readily available resources.

NOTES

Criterion 2—Goods and services are separately identifiable from other promises

Factors that indicate that an entity's promise to transfer a good or service to a customer is separately identifiable include, but are not limited to, the following:

(i) The entity does not provide a significant service of integrating the good or service with other goods or services promised in the contract into a bundle of goods or services that represent the *combined output* for which the customer has contracted. In other words, the entity is not using the good or service as an input to produce or deliver the combined output specified by the customer.

For example, an entity enters into a contract with a hosing society to install 75 CCTV cameras. The contract specifies the specification and brand of cameras and other equipment, and also, mentions the delivery date of cameras and other equipment and the date for completion of the installation. The turnkey contract is to deliver combined output, and therefore, the promises to provide goods and services, which are used as inputs, are not separately identifiable.

(ii) The good or service does not significantly modify or customise another good or service promised in the contract.

For example, an entity enters into a contract to furnish an office space with wooden furniture. The contract requires the entity to deliver branded furniture and customise those according the structure of the office space and needs of the customer. Promise to deliver branded furniture and promise to provide installation service are not separately identifiable, as installation service significantly modifies and customise the furniture.

(iii) The good or service is not highly dependent on, or highly interrelated with, other goods or services promised in the contract. For example, the fact that a customer could decide to not purchase the good or service without significantly affecting the other promised goods or services in the contract might indicate that the good or service is not highly dependent on, or highly interrelated with, those other promised goods or services.

CASE STUDY 18.2 Significant Integration Service

P Construction Limited (PCL) is a leading player in the construction industry. It enters into a contract to build a hospital for M Hospitals Limited (MHL). Under the contract, PCL is responsible for the overall management of the project. It will identify various promised goods and services, including engineering, site clearance, foundation, procurement, construction of the structure, piping and wiring, installation of equipment and finishing. PCL normally undertakes Engineering, Procurement and Construction (EPC) contracts, and also provides those services separately.

Question

The CFO of PCL seeks your advice on what the distinct performance obligations included in the contract are.

Solution

Many of the goods and services that PCL will provide to MHL are readily available resources because PCL and its competitors regularly sell those goods and services separately to other customers. In addition, the customer could generate economic benefit from the individual goods and services by using, consuming, selling or holding those goods or services. Therefore, those goods and services meet the criterion that 'the customer can benefit from those goods and services'.

Those goods and services fail to meet the criterion that 'goods and services are separately identifiable from other promises' because PCL uses those as inputs and provides significant integrating services in constructing the hotel (combined output) for which it is contracted. Thus, the goods and services meet only one criterion. In order to be identified as distinct performance obligations, separate goods and services to be provided by PCL should meet both the criteria.

Therefore, we conclude that ACL should account for all the goods and services as a single performance obligation.

[Adapted from Example (10A) of the Basis of Conclusion for IFRS 15.]

NOTES

CASE STUDY 18.3 Distinct Goods or Services

K Info Tech Limited (KITL) is a software developer. It enters into a contract with P Electricals Limited (PEL) to transfer a software licence, perform an installation service and provide unspecified software updates and technical support (online and telephone) for a two-year period. KITL sells the licence, installation service and technical support separately. The installation is not complex and does not require significant modification of the software. Other entities provide installation service. The software remains functional without the updates and the technical support.

Question

The CFO of KITL seeks your advice on which goods and services included in the contract are distinct and whether promises for delivering each item of goods and services are distinct performance obligations.

Solution

KITL promises to deliver the following goods and services:

(i) Software licence, (ii) installation service, (iii) updates, and (iv) technical support.

KITL delivers the software licence before providing other services. PEL can get the software installed by some other party, as installation is a routine activity and is not complex. The software remains functional without updates and technical support. Therefore, PEL can benefit from the software even before the other services are provided by KITL. It can benefit from the updates together with the software licence transferred at the start of the contract. Therefore, each item of goods and services meets the first criterion, that is, 'a customer can benefit from the good or service'.

The installation services to be provided by the entity do not significantly affect the customer's ability to use and benefit from the software licence because the installation services are routine and can be obtained from alternative providers. The software updates do not significantly affect the customer's ability to use and benefit from the software licence during the licence period. None of the promised goods or services significantly modify or customise one another. The software and the services do not significantly affect each other, and therefore, are not highly interdependent or highly interrelated because the entity would be able to fulfil its promise to transfer the initial software licence independently from its promise to subsequently provide the installation service, software updates or technical support. Therefore, each good or service meets the second criterion, that is, 'promise to transfer each good and service to the customer is separately identifiable from each of the other promises'.

On the basis of this assessment, we can conclude that the contract has the following four performances obligations, that are distinct from each other:

(i) The software licence; (ii) an installation service; (iii) software updates; and (iv) technical support.

[Adapted from Example (11A) of the Basis of Conclusion for IFRS 15.]

Bundle of goods and services that is distinct

If a promised good or service is not distinct, an entity shall combine that good or service with other promised goods or services until it identifies a bundle of goods or services that is distinct. In some cases, that would result in the entity accounting for all the goods or services promised in a contract as a single performance obligation. For example, promise to

NOTES

deliver CCTV cameras and other equipment and promise to install those are to be bundled into a single performance obligation.

Series of distinct goods or services

An entity treats a series of goods and services as a single performance obligation if goods and services are *substantially the same* and both the following criteria are met:

(i) Each distinct good or service is a performance obligation satisfied over time; and
(ii) The same method is used to measure progress towards satisfaction of each distinct good or service in the series.

CASE STUDY 18.4 Series Guidance

VB Limited (VBL) enters into contracts for cleaning green office buildings. Usually, contracts cover a two-year period. Under the contract, VBL cleans the specified office buildings weekly once. The fee for the cleaning service is fixed based on per square feet rate negotiated with the customer and is stipulated in the contract.

Question

The CFO of VBL seeks your advice on whether the series guidance is applicable to cleaning contracts.

Solution

The performance of the cleaning service is satisfied over time because the customer benefits from the cleaning services as VBL performs. Each increment of weekly service is distinct, as the customer benefits from that period of service on its own and each increment of service is separable from those preceding and following it. Service in one period does not significantly affect, modify or customise the service of another period.

In view of the above, the contract with the customer is a single performance obligation to provide two years of cleaning service, as it meets the following criteria:

(i) Each distinct increment of services is satisfied over time; and
(ii) A consistent measure of progress to recognise revenue is used.

SUMMARY

A performance obligation is a promise in a contract with a customer to transfer a good or service to the customer. An entity recognises revenue when a performance obligation is satisfied. The key question is when to *unbundle* performance obligations in a contract or when to bundle apparently separate performance obligations in a contract. An entity should identify as a performance obligation ***each promise*** to transfer to the customer either: (i) a good or service (or a bundle of goods or services) that is distinct; or (ii) a series of distinct goods or services that are substantially the same and that have the same pattern of transfer to the customer.

A good or service that is promised to a customer is distinct if *both* of the following criteria are met:

(i) The customer can benefit from the good or service; and
(ii) The entity's promise to transfer the good or service to the customer is separately identifiable from other promises in the contract.

If a promised good or service is not distinct, an entity shall combine that good or service with other promised goods or services until it identifies a bundle of goods or services that is distinct. In some cases, that would result in the entity accounting for all the goods or services promised in a contract as a single performance obligation.

An entity treats a series of goods and services as a single performance obligation if goods and services are ***substantially the same*** and both the following criteria are met:

(i) Each distinct good or service is a performance obligation satisfied over time; and
(ii) The same method is used to measure progress towards satisfaction of each distinct good or service in the series.

NOTES

Self-Test Questions

Self-test question 18.3

Indicate whether the following statements are true (T) or false (F):

(i) A contract can have only one performance obligation.

(ii) A contract with a customer that promises delivery of a good and a right for additional good for a discounted price might be separate performance obligations.

(iii) A turnkey contract with a customer, which promises installation of a complex system with inputs procured from different manufactures of those inputs has two distinct performance obligations—one for supply of inputs, and the other for integrating the inputs to install the system.

(iv) A contract to sell a heritage building and converting it into resort as per the design prepared by the entity's architect has two distinct performance obligations.

(v) An annual contract to administer pesticides in an agricultural farm every week has 52 performance obligations.

TRANSACTION PRICE

Transaction price is the amount of consideration to which an entity expects to be entitled in exchange for transferring promised goods or services to a customer, excluding amounts collected on behalf of third parties. Accordingly, revenue recognised in the statement of profit and loss excludes goods and service tax and other indirect taxes collected on behalf of the government. Similarly, the transaction price of an agent is its commission because the transaction price excludes the amount payable to the principal.

Determining the Transaction Price

An entity measures revenue at the transaction price. It estimates the transaction price at contract inception. In determining the transaction price, it should assume that the goods or services will be transferred to the customer as promised in accordance with the existing contract and that the contract will not be cancelled, renewed or modified.

Components of Transaction Price

The consideration promised in a contract with a customer may include fixed amounts, variable amounts, or both. In determining the transaction price, an entity considers the effect of the following:

(i) Variable consideration;

(ii) Time value of money;

(iii) Consideration payable to the customer; and

(iv) Non-cash consideration.

Variable consideration

Variable consideration encompasses any amount that is variable under the contract. For example, an amount of consideration can vary because of discounts, rebates, refunds, credits, price concessions, incentives, performance bonuses, penalties or customer's right of return.

An example of variable consideration is performance bonus receivable by the entity (a construction company) of ₹10,00,000 if the building is finished more than 30 days before the promised date and ₹20,00,000 if the building is finished more than 60 days before the promised date.

NOTES

Variability in the consideration may be stated explicitly in the contract. It may even be implied from the entity's customary practice. For example, the entity's customary practice might create a valid expectation among customers that the entity will accept an amount lower than that stated in the contract, or there is an intention to offer a price concession to a customer.

Constraining estimate of variable consideration

An entity includes some or all of the estimated amount of variable consideration in the transaction price, but only to the extent that it is *highly probable* that a significant reversal in the amount of cumulative revenue recognised will not occur when the uncertainty associated with the variable consideration is subsequently resolved.

In assessing whether the variable consideration should be included in the transaction price, an entity considers both the likelihood of revenue reversal and the potential magnitude of revenue reversal when the uncertainty related to the variable consideration has been resolved. The assessment of the magnitude should be relative to the transaction price of the contract.

Reassessment of variable consideration

At each reporting date, an entity reassesses the estimated transaction price, including its assessment of whether its estimate of variable consideration is constrained. It should take into consideration the circumstances present at the reporting date and changes in circumstances that occurred during the reporting period.

Estimating the amount of variable consideration

An entity uses either the 'expected value' method (probability-weighted amount) or the 'most likely amount' method, depending on which method is more appropriate to predict the amount of consideration to which it is entitled.

The 'expected value' method is more appropriate when the entity has a large number of contracts with similar characteristics. For example, an entity has large number of similar contracts, which include terms for performance bonus. According to the terms of such contracts, the entity receives either 100 percent of the bonus amount or does not receive any bonus. In past, the entity earned bonus in 70 percent of contracts. Based on this experience, the entity uses the 'expected value' method to estimate the variable consideration and estimates that the probability of earning bonus is 70 percent. In the contract under consideration, the performance bonus is ₹1,00,000. The entity estimates that (₹1,00,000 × 0.70) or ₹70,000 of the variable consideration is not constrained and includes the same in the transaction price.

The 'most likely method' is appropriate when the entity does not have large number of similar contracts and the contract has only two possible outcomes. For example, if the entity does not have large number of similar contracts, and as per terms of the contract under consideration, the entity receives either 100 percent of the bonus amount or does not receive any bonus, the entity should assess the most likely amount. If it assesses that it will earn the bonus, it includes the amount of bonus in the transaction price.

CASE STUDY 18.5 Variable Consideration—Volume Discount

On January 1, 2018, KL Limited (KLL) has entered into a contract with a customer for the sale of a product for total consideration of ₹100/unit for a one-year period. As per the terms of the contract, if the customer purchases more than 75 units of the product, the total consideration will be ₹80/unit applied retrospectively, that is, all the purchases will be at ₹80/unit. Based on past history (that has predictive value) with this particular product and the customer, KLL assess, at the contract inception, that the customer will not meet the target required to avail the volume discount. During the year 2017–18, that is up to March 2018, the customer purchased 15 units of the product. At the balance sheet date (March 31, 2018), KLL assesses that the customer will not be able to meet the target. During the period from April 1 to June 30, 2018, the customer purchased additional 30 units. While preparing the financial statement for the quarter ending June 30, 3018, KLL assesses that the customer will achieve the target to avail the volume discount.

Question

The CFO of KLL seeks your advice on how to estimate the transaction price for recognising revenue for the financial year 2017–18 and for the quarter ending June 30, 2018 of the financial year 2018–19.

Solution

The transaction price has two components—Fixed consideration: ₹80/unit, and variable consideration: ₹20/unit. At the inception of the contract, KLL assesses that the customer will not buy more than 75 units during the contractual period and it is ***highly probable*** that a significant reversal in the amount of cumulative revenue recognised will not occur when the uncertainty associated with the variable consideration is subsequently resolved. Therefore, it includes the variable consideration in the transaction price. Accordingly, it should record the sales at the rate of ₹100/unit. At the close of the year 2017–18, KLL reassesses the variable consideration and does not change the conclusion arrived at the inception of the contract. Therefore, in the statement of profit and loss for the year 2017–18, it recognises the revenue at (15 × ₹100) or ₹1,500.

At the end of the June quarter of the year 2018–19, KLL reassesses the variable consideration and concludes that it is likely that the customer will purchase more than 75 units of the product during the contractual period. Therefore, it considers the variable consideration as constrained and decides to exclude the same from the transaction price. Therefore, revenue will have to be retrospectively adjusted to the rate of ₹80/unit. This adjustment will be recorded in the current period, meaning in the quarter ending June 30, 2018. The cumulative sale under the contract up to June 30, 2018 is 45 units. Cumulative revenue up to June 30, 2018 is, (45 × ₹80) or ₹3,600. Revenue to be recognised in the statement of profit and loss for the quarter ending June 30, 2018 is (₹3,600 – 1,500) or ₹2,100.

CASE STUDY 18.6 Variable Consideration—Performance-based Incentive

On April 1, 2017, F Securities Limited (FSL) enters into a two-year contract with a customer to provide investment management services. The customers invest their wealth in equity instruments issued by large listed companies. As per the contract, FSL receives:

(i) A quarterly management fee of 2 percent per quarter for assets under management, measured at fair value, at the end of the quarter.

(ii) A performance-based incentive fee of 20 percent of the total return (over the contract period) in excess of observable return on NIFTY 50 index over the contract period.

Question

The CFO of FSL seeks your advice on how to determine the transaction price for recognising revenue for the year 2017–18.

Solution

Both the management fee and performance-based incentive fee are variable consideration.

The cumulative amount of the management fee to which FSL is entitled at the end of the accounting period 2017–18 is not constrained because it is calculated based on asset values at the end of each quarter. Therefore, the amount of fee for each quarter is known at the end of the quarter and it is ***highly probable*** that a significant reversal in the amount of cumulative revenue recognised will not occur in future.

The performance-based incentive fee is constrained because it is ***highly probable*** that a significant reversal in the amount of cumulative revenue recognised might occur in future. The

NOTES

assessment is based on the fact that: (i) the incentive fee has high variability and the probability of downward adjustment is significant; (ii) the experience of FSL on similar contracts is not predictive of the outcome of the current contract; and (iii) there is large number of possible outcomes.

In view of the above, the transaction price for the calculation of revenue for the year 2017–18 should include only the management fee.

Time value of money

An entity considers the time value of money in estimating the transaction price in a contract when the contract contains a significant financing component. The objective is to recognise revenue at an amount that reflects what the cash selling price would have been if the customer had paid cash for the promised goods and services at the point when they are transferred to the customer.

As a practical expedient, an entity is not required to adjust the promised amount of consideration for the effects of a significant financing component if the entity expects, at contract inception, that the period between when the entity transfers a promised good or service to a customer and when the customer pays for that good or service will be one year or less.

Discount rate

An entity should use the discount rate that would be reflected in a separate financing transaction between the entity and its customer at the contract inception. The discount rate should be the market interest rate for financing with similar terms and credit risks. Usually, an entity determines that rate by identifying the rate that discounts the nominal amount of the promised consideration to the price that the customer would pay in cash for the goods and services when the entity transfers them to the customer. The entity should not update the rate for change in circumstances.

Accounting for interest

An entity should present the effects of financing (interest revenue or interest expense) separately from revenue from contracts with customers in the statement of profit and loss.

ILLUSTRATION 18.1 Time Value of Money

On April 1, 2017, VB Limited (VBL) enters into a contract with MN Limited (MNL) to construct and deliver a piece of equipment. The construction is expected to take two years and the delivery date is March 31, 2019. As per the contract, the customer pays the selling price of the equipment, which is ₹100 lakh, in advance on April 1, 2017. VBL determines the discount rate for computing the present value of the consideration, based on credit characteristics, to be 12 percent per annum.

Required

Calculate the transaction price and the show the accounting for interest expense.

Solution

(i) The transaction price is ₹100 lakh × $(1.12)^2$ or ₹125.44 lakh. VBL should recognise the revenue at ₹125.44 lakh when it will transfer control of the piece of equipment to the customer.

(ii) Interest expense to be recognised in the statement of profit and loss for the year 2017–18: ₹100 lakh × (0.12) or ₹12 lakh. Interest expense (₹12 lakh) to be debited and advance from MNL account will be credited. In the balance sheet as at March 31, 2018, the balance in advance from MNL account will be (₹100 lakh + 12) or ₹112 lakh. In the statement of profit and loss for the year 2017–18, financing cost will include interest expense of ₹12 lakh on advance received from the customer.

(iii) Interest expense to be recognised in the statement of profit and loss for the year 2018–19: ₹112 lakh × (0.12) or ₹13.44 lakh. Interest expense (₹13.44 lakh) to be debited and Advance from MNL Account will be credited. After recording the interest expense, as at March 31, 2019, the balance in advance from MNL account will be (₹112 lakh + 13.44) or ₹125.44 lakh. Assuming that the control on the equipment is transferred on March 31, 2019, sales will be credited by ₹125.44 lakh and Advance from MNL account will be debited by the same amount, resulting in derecognition of the liability (advance from MNL). Thus, in the statement of profit and loss for the year 2018–19, revenue will be recognised at ₹125.44 lakh and financing cost including interest expense will be recognised at ₹13.44 lakh.

Consideration payable to a customer

An entity reduces the transaction price by the consideration paid or payable to a customer or customer's customer, other than the consideration paid or payable for distinct goods or services from the customer or customer's customer. A customer should account for the reduction in revenue when later of either of the following events occur:

(i) The entity recognises the revenue for the transfer of related goods or services to the customer; and

(ii) The entity pays or promises to pay the consideration; this promise might be implied by the entity's customary business practices.

Consideration paid or payable to the customer includes credit or other items, such as a coupon or a voucher, that can be applied against amount owed to the entity or to other parties that purchase the entity's goods and services from the customer.

Non-cash consideration

An entity should measure the non-cash consideration (or promise of non-cash consideration) at fair value. If an entity cannot reasonably estimate the fair value of the non-cash consideration, the entity should measure the consideration indirectly by reference to the stand-alone selling price of the goods or services promised to the customer in exchange for the consideration.

If the fair value of the non-cash consideration promised by a customer varies for reasons other than only the form of the consideration, an entity should apply the guidance for assessing whether the variable consideration is constrained. For example, if the consideration is in the form of equity shares, the change in fair value due to change in the price per share should be considered as change in fair value due to the form of consideration. If the consideration is in the form of corporate bond, the change in the fair value due to change in the benchmark interest rate, should be considered as due to the form of the consideration. However, change in the fair value of the bond because of entity's performance (e.g., downgrading the rating by a credit rating agency) is considered as a change for a reason other than the form of the consideration.

If a customer contributes goods or services (e.g., materials, equipment or labour) to facilitate an entity's fulfilment of the contract, the entity should assess whether it obtains control of those contributed goods or services. If so, the entity should account for the contributed goods or services as non-cash consideration received from the customer.

SUMMARY

An entity measures revenue at the transaction price. It estimates the transaction price at contract inception. Transaction price is the amount of consideration to which an entity expects to be entitled in exchange for transferring promised goods or services to a customer, excluding amounts collected on behalf of third parties (e.g., goods and service tax). In determining the transaction price, an entity considers the effect of the following:

(i) Variable consideration;

(ii) time value of money;

NOTES

(iii) consideration payable to the customer; and
(iv) non-cash consideration.

An entity includes some or all of the estimated amount of variable consideration in the transaction price, but only to the extent that it is ***highly probable*** that a significant reversal in the amount of cumulative revenue recognised will not occur when the uncertainty associated with the variable consideration is subsequently resolved. An entity considers the time value of money in estimating the transaction price in a contract when the contract contains a significant financing component. An entity reduces the transaction price by the consideration paid or payable to a customer or customer's customer, other than the consideration paid or payable for distinct goods or services from the customer or customer's customer. An entity should measure the non-cash consideration (or promise of non-cash consideration) at fair value.

Self-Test Questions

Self-test question 18.4

Indicate whether the following statements are true (T) or false (F):

(i) Transaction price that is used to measure revenue includes GST.
(ii) Transaction price estimated at the inception of the contract should be net of volume discount, which is allowed to the customer if it purchases a minimum quantity of the product over the contract period.
(iii) An entity, which is in the construction business, should recognise performance bonus stipulated in the contract as revenue only when the performance bonus becomes payable on achieving the target.
(iv) In estimating the transaction price, an entity should not consider time value of money if the entity expects to realise the consideration within one year from the date when the entity transfers a promised good or service to a customer.
(v) If an entity, as a strategy, allows two-year credit to an important customer while charging cash selling price, it should measure the revenue at cash selling price.
(vi) Points being awarded by airlines under their Frequent Flyer Programme should be accounted for as 'consideration payable to a customer'.
(vii) Non-cash consideration should be measured at fair value.

ALLOCATING TRANSACTION PRICE TO THE PERFORMANCE OBLIGATIONS IN THE CONTRACT

General principle

At contract inception, an entity allocates the transaction price to each performance obligation on the basis of relative stand-alone prices. However, when specified criteria are met, a discount or variable consideration may be allocated to one or more, but not all, performance obligations in the contract.

Stand-alone selling price

The 'stand-alone selling price' is the price at which an entity would sell a promised good or service separately to a customer.

When observable selling price is not available, an entity considers all information that is reasonably available when estimating a stand-alone selling price. Ind AS 115 mentions the following three methods for estimating 'stand-alone selling price':

(i) ***Adjusted market assessment approach***: An entity evaluates the market in which it sells goods or services and estimates the price that a customer in that market would be willing to pay for those goods or services. For example, the entity may use the prices for similar goods or services from competitors as the starting point and adjust the same to reflect the entity's costs and margins.

NOTES

(ii) ***Expected cost plus a margin approach***: An entity could forecast its expected costs of satisfying a performance obligation and then add an appropriate margin for that good or service.

(iii) ***Residual approach:*** An entity may estimate the stand-alone selling price by reference to the total transaction price less the sum of the observable stand-alone selling prices of other goods or services promised in the contract.

An entity should apply the 'residual approach' only if the stand-alone selling price of one or more goods or services is highly variable or uncertain. The stand-alone selling price of a good or service is highly variable or uncertain if the entity sells the same to different customers for a broad range of amounts or the entity is yet to establish the selling price of that good or service.

If two or more goods or services in a contract have highly variable or uncertain stand-alone selling prices, then an entity needs to use a combination of methods to estimate the stand-alone selling prices of the performance obligations in the contract. For example, if two performance obligations have highly variable or uncertain stand-alone selling prices, at the first stage, the aggregate selling price of those performance obligations may be estimated using the 'residual approach'. At the second stage, the aggregate selling price may be allocated to those two products using 'expected cost plus a margin approach'.

ILLUSTRATION 18.2 Allocation of Transaction Price

FG Limited (FGL) offers one-year mobile contract to its customers. Under the contract, FGL provides the customer a mobile phone and a data/calls/texts plan for a price of ₹500 per month. The phone can be purchased from the manufacturer's website at a price of ₹3,200. FGL provides a one-year plan without a mobile phone which includes the same level of data/calls/texts at ₹400 per month.

Required

Explain if there is a need to allocate the transaction price, and if so, how to allocate the transaction price.

Solution

There are two distinct performance obligations in the contract being offered by FGL. They are mobile phone and the wireless (data/calls/texts) plan. Therefore, there is a need to allocate the transaction price of ₹500 per month to those two distinct performance obligations.

Observable stand-alone selling prices are available for both the performance obligations. The price of the stand-alone mobile phone is ₹3,200 and the stand-alone selling price for wireless services is (₹400 × 12) or ₹4,800 for one year. The aggregate of the stand-alone selling prices of those goods and services is (₹3,200 + 4,800) or ₹8,000. Thus, the price of the mobile phone is (3,200/8,000) × 100 or 40 percent of the aggregate selling price and the price of the wireless is 60 percent of the aggregate selling price. Therefore, the contract price of (₹500 × 12) or ₹6,000 for one year should be allocated as follows:

(i) Mobile phone: ₹6,000 × 0.40 or ₹2,400; and

(ii) Wireless: ₹6,000 × 0.60 or ₹3,600

Allocating discount

A customer receives a discount for purchasing a bundle of goods or services if the sum of the stand-alone selling prices of those promised goods or services in the contract exceeds the promised consideration in a contract. For example, if the sum of stand-alone selling prices of the goods or services in the bundle is ₹1,000 and the contract price is ₹900, the customer receives a discount of ₹100. Usually, an entity allocates the contract price (₹900 in the example) to goods or services in the bundle. In the process, it allocates the discount proportionately to all the goods or services in the bundle. However, if there is observable evidence that the entire discount relates to only one or more goods or services, but not all, then the entity allocates the discount to that or those goods or services to which the discount relates. For example, if the entity sells one of the goods or services in the bundle regularly at a discount over its stand-alone price and the amount of discount in the contract is substantially the same, then it can be said that the discount in the contract is attributable to that good or service.

NOTES

If a discount is allocated entirely to one or more performance obligations in the contract, an entity should allocate the discount before using the residual approach to estimate the stand-alone selling price of a good or service.

Allocating variable consideration

Variable consideration that is promised in a contract may be attributable to the entire contract or to a specific part of the contract. For example, a bonus may be contingent on an entity transferring a promised good or service within a specified period of time. An entity should allocate a variable amount (and subsequent changes to that amount) entirely to a performance obligation or to a distinct good or service that forms part of a single performance obligation, if it is attributable to that part of the contract.

If a contract contains both variable consideration and discount, the variable consideration is allocated before allocating the discount.

Changes in transaction price

After initial allocation, changes in the transaction price are generally allocated to performance obligations on the same basis as at contract inception.

SUMMARY

At contract inception, an entity allocates the transaction price to each performance obligation on the basis of relative stand-alone prices. If observable selling prices are not available, an entity may adopt one of the following approaches:

(i) adjusted market assessment approach;
(ii) expected cost plus a margin approach; and
(iii) residual approach.

An entity allocates the discount proportionately to all the goods or services in the bundle. However, if there is observable evidence that the entire discount relates to only one or more goods or services, but not all, then the entity allocates the discount to that or those goods or services to which the discount relates. An entity should allocate a variable amount (and subsequent changes to that amount) entirely to a performance obligation or to a distinct good or service that forms part of a single performance obligation, if it is attributable to that part of the contract.

Self-Test Questions

Self-test question 18.5

Indicate whether the following statements are true (T) or false (F):

(i) At contract inception, an entity allocates the transaction price to each performance obligation on the basis of relative stand-alone prices.
(ii) Residual approach in estimating the stand-alone price of a performance obligation in the bundle of performance obligations can be used only if other approaches fail.
(iii) When an entity introduces a new product in the bundle of goods or services, it estimates the stand-alone selling price of that product, for the purpose of allocating the transaction price of the contract, with reference to the price of similar products in the market.
(iv) Discount allowed to a customer in a bundle of products offered to a customer is the difference between the total of stand-alone selling prices of products included in the contract and the transaction price.
(v) Variable consideration that is promised in a contract must be allocated to all the products included in the contract.

RECOGNISING REVENUE

General principles

An entity recognises revenue when the entity satisfies a performance obligation by transferring a promised good or service to the customer. Goods and services are assets, even if only momentarily, when they are received and used (as in the case of many services). An asset is transferred when the customer obtains control of that asset.

Control

Control of an asset refers to the ability to direct the use of, and obtain substantially all of the remaining benefits from, the asset. Control includes the ability to prevent other entities from directing the use of, and obtaining the benefits from, an asset. The entity should assess when it has transferred control of the asset to the customer.

The following are the indicators of transfer of control:

(i) The customer is presently obliged to pay for the asset and the entity has a present right to payment for the asset that may indicate that the customer has obtained control of the asset;

(ii) The transfer of legal right of an asset may indicate that the customer has obtained control of the asset;

(iii) Although in some cases, transfer of physical possession does not coincide with control of an asset, generally customer's physical possession of an asset may indicate that the customer has control over the asset;

(iv) The transfer of the significant risks and rewards of ownership of an asset to the customer may indicate that the customer has obtained the control of the asset; and

(v) The customer's acceptance of an asset may indicate that it has obtained the control of the asset.

Performance Obligation Satisfied Over Time: Criteria

Table 18.2 provides criteria, one or more of which should be met for recognising revenue over time.

TABLE 18.2

Criteria for Recognising Revenue Over Time

S. No.	Criterion	Example
1	The customer simultaneously receives and consumes the benefits provided by the entity's performance as the entity performs.	Routine or recurring services (e.g., cleaning service)
2	The entity's performance creates or enhances an asset (for example, work-in-progress) that the customer controls as the asset is created or enhanced.	Building an asset at customer's site (e.g., construction of building or an elevated road)
3	The entity's performance does not create an asset with an alternative use to the entity and the entity has an enforceable right to payment for performance completed to date (e.g., the contract stipulates progress payments, as the work on producing the asset progresses).	Building a specialised asset (e.g., missile) that only the customer can use or building an asset to a customer order (e.g., ship with special features or an office building or a customised software)

NOTES

CASE STUDY 18.7 Recognising Revenue Over Time

GB Consultants (GBC) has entered into a contract to provide consultancy service to MC Limited (MCL). The consultancy service involves providing professional opinion based on facts and circumstances specific to MCL. As per the contract, if MCL decides to terminate the contract for reasons other than non-performance by GBC, then MCL will compensate GBC for costs incurred and 20 percent margin, which GBC normally earns on similar contracts.

Required

The CFO of GBC requests you to examine whether the contract meets any of the criteria for recognising revenue over time.

Solution

Criterion 1: The contract does not meet criterion 1, which is 'the customer simultaneously receives and consumes the benefits provided by the entity's performance as the entity performs'. The conclusion is based on the fact that if GBC does not issue the professional opinion, another professional firm will not benefit from the work-in-progress performed by GBC and it will have to substantially reperform the work completed by GBC.

Criterion 2: The contract does not meet criterion 2, which is 'the entity's performance creates or enhances an asset (for example, work-in-progress) that the customer controls as the asset is created or enhanced'. The conclusion is based on the fact that GBC will submit the professional opinion to MCL only on completion.

Criterion 3: The contract meets criterion 3, which is 'the entity's performance does not create an asset with an alternative use to the entity and the entity has an enforceable right to payment for performance completed to date'. The conclusion is based on the fact that (i) GBC delivers the professional opinion only on completion, and therefore, its performance does not create and enhance an asset; (ii) The asset (professional opinion) has no alternative use to GBC because it relates to specific fact and circumstances specific to MCL, and therefore, there is a practical limitation of GBC's ability to readily direct the asset to another customer; and (iii) GBC has an enforceable right to payment for performance completed to date.

As criterion 3 is met, GBC should recognise revenue from the contract over time.

Performance Obligation Satisfied Over Time: Measuring Revenue

For each performance obligation satisfied over time, an entity recognises revenue over time by measuring the progress towards complete satisfaction of that performance obligation. The objective when measuring progress is to depict an entity's performance in transferring control of goods or services promised to a customer (i.e., the satisfaction of an entity's performance obligation).

ILLUSTRATION 18.3 Measuring Revenue from Construction Contract

An entity has obtained a contract to construct an elevated road on April 1, 2017. The construction is to be completed by March 31, 2020. The transaction price is `1,000 crore. As at March 31, 2018, the entity estimates that it has completed 30 percent of the work to the satisfaction of the customer. As at March 31, 2019, the entity estimates that it has completed 70 percent of the work to the satisfaction of the customer.

Required

Determine the amount of revenue that the entity should recognise in the years 2017–18 and 2018–19.

NOTES

Solution

As at March 31, 2018, the entity estimates that it has completed 30 percent of the work to the satisfaction of the customer. Therefore, it should recognise (₹1,000 crore × 0.30) or ₹300 crore revenue in the year 2017–18. As at March 31, 2019, the entity estimates that it has completed 70 percent of the work to the satisfaction of the customer. Therefore, the cumulative revenue up to March 31, 2019 is (₹1,000 crore × 0.70) or ₹700 crore. The entity should recognise (– ₹700 crore – 300 crore) or ₹400 crore revenue in the year 2018–19..

In some circumstances (for example, in the early stages of a contract), an entity may not be able to reasonably measure the outcome of a performance obligation, but the entity expects to recover the costs incurred in satisfying the performance obligation. In those circumstances, the entity should recognise revenue only to the extent of the costs incurred until such time that it can reasonably measure the outcome of the performance obligation. Application of this accounting principle results in not recognising profit from a contract until the entity is able to reasonably measure the outcome of a performance obligation. For example, the transaction price is ₹1,000 and 20 percent work is complete by the end of the financial year and cost incurred is ₹160. If the entity recognises the revenue bases on progress, it should recognise revenue of (₹1,000 × 0.20) or ₹200. This results in recognising gross profit of (₹200 – 160) or ₹40 for the year. However, contract being in the early stage of completion, the entity recognises revenue at ₹160 only and does not recognise gross profit for the year.

Although the accounting standard (Ind AS 115) does not stipulate a bright line, usually entities do not recognise profit until it completes at least 25 percent of the work required to satisfy the performance obligation.

Performance Obligation Satisfied Over Time: Measuring Progress

An entity uses either an input method or an output method to measure the progress. It selects the appropriate method considering the nature of the goods and services being delivered.

When applying a method for measuring progress, an entity should exclude from the measure of progress any goods or services for which the entity does not transfer control to a customer. Conversely, an entity should include in the measure of progress any goods or services for which the entity does transfer control to a customer when satisfying that performance obligation.

Output methods

Output methods recognise revenue on the basis of direct measurements of the value to the customer of the goods or services transferred to date relative to the remaining goods or services promised under the contract. Output methods include methods such as surveys of performance completed to date, appraisals of results achieved, milestones reached, time elapsed and units produced or units delivered.

As a practical expedient, if an entity has a right to consideration from a customer in an amount that corresponds directly with the value to the customer of the entity's performance completed to date, the entity may recognise revenue in the amount to which the entity has a right to invoice. For example, if as per a service contract, an entity bills a fixed amount for each hour of service provided, it recognises revenue at the amount for which invoice is preferred on the customer.

The disadvantages of output methods are that the outputs used to measure progress may not be directly observable and the information required to apply them may not be available to an entity without undue cost. Therefore, an input method may be necessary.

Input methods

Under input methods, an entity recognises revenue on the basis of the entity's efforts or inputs to the satisfaction of a performance obligation (for example, resources consumed, labour hours expended, costs incurred, time elapsed or machine hours used) relative to the total expected inputs to the satisfaction of that performance obligation. For example, if an entity estimates that it would incur ₹1,000 towards costs directly attributable to the performance obligation (direct costs) to satisfy the same and at the end of the accounting period, it has incurred ₹400 towards direct costs, it estimates that at the end of the accounting period (400/1,000) or 40 percent of the work is complete.

The cost incurred to date should be reduced by the cost of resources wasted due to entity's inefficiency.

If the entity's efforts or inputs are expended evenly throughout the performance period, it may be appropriate for the entity to recognise revenue on a straight-line basis. For example, it might be appropriate to recognise revenue on a straight-line basis in a contract for unspecified software upgrade or health club contract because the pattern of benefits to the customer and the entity's efforts to satisfy the performance obligation are generally even throughout the period. However, it may not be appropriate to recognise revenue on a straight-line basis in an annual contract for administering pesticide in an agricultural farm because pesticide requirement varies from season to season, and also, depends on vagaries of the weather.

For uninstalled materials, in order to depict the entity's performance in transferring control of goods or services to the customer, it might be appropriate for the entity to recognise revenue only to the extent of the cost incurred, if the entity expects at contract inception that all of the following conditions would be met:

(i) The good is not distinct;

(ii) The customer is expected to obtain control of the good significantly before receiving services related to the good;

(iii) The cost of the transferred good is significant relative to the total expected costs to completely satisfy the performance obligation; and

(iv) The entity procures the good from a third party and is not significantly involved in designing and manufacturing the good, but the entity is acting as a principal.

For example, an entity enters into a turnkey project to develop 15 classrooms (already constructed) in a school into smart digital classrooms by installing appropriate furniture and state-of-the-art technological devices. The entity procures furniture and equipment from third parties and delivers those to schools, and then, takes up the installation work. Although delivery of goods is not a distinct performance obligation, as the contract is a turnkey contract, the entity transfers the control of the goods to the customer. In this contract, it might not be appropriate to book profit before the completion of the installation work because cost incurred on procurement of inputs is not proportionate to the entity's progress in satisfying the performance obligation. Therefore, the entity should recognise revenue to the extent of the cost incurred.

Performance Obligation Satisfied at a Point in Time

If a performance obligation is not satisfied over time, an entity satisfies the performance obligation at a point in time. The point in time when the good or service is transferred depends on the terms of the contact. An entity must evaluate the indicators of transfer of control. For example, delivery of goods to an agent of the customer results in transferring the control of the asset. When the contract term is Free On Rail (FOR), once the goods are put on board on rail, the buyer gets the control of the goods. When the contract term is 'Free On Board (FOB) Destination', control of the good remains with the seller until the good reaches the buyer.

NOTES

SUMMARY

An entity recognises revenue when the entity satisfies a performance obligation by transferring a promised good or service to the customer. An asset (good or service) is transferred when the customer obtains control of that asset. An entity measures revenue over time if any one of the following criteria is meet:

(i) The customer simultaneously receives and consumes the benefits provided by the entity's performance as the entity performs;
(ii) The entity's performance creates or enhances an asset (for example, work-in-progress) that the customer controls as the asset is created or enhanced; or
(iii) The entity's performance does not create an asset with an alternative use to the entity and the entity has an enforceable right to payment for performance completed to date.

For each performance obligation satisfied over time, an entity recognises revenue over time by measuring the progress towards complete satisfaction of that performance obligation. In some circumstances (for example, in the early stages of a contract), when an entity is not able to reasonably measure the outcome of a performance obligation, but it expects to recover the costs incurred in satisfying the performance obligation, it should recognise revenue only to the extent of the costs incurred until such time that it can reasonably measure the outcome of the performance obligation. An entity uses either an input method or an output method to measure the progress of a performance obligation to be satisfied over time. It selects the appropriate method considering the nature of the goods and services being delivered.

If a performance obligation is not satisfied over time, an entity satisfies the performance obligation at a point in time.

Self-Test Questions

Self-test question 18.6

Indicate whether the following statements are true or false:

(i) Transfer of the possession of the good to the customer does not necessarily indicate transfer of control.
(ii) The customer's acceptance of an asset may indicate that it has obtained the control of the asset.
(iii) An entity should recognise revenue over time from a contract for manufacturing and delivering a piece of a standard equipment, which is in high demand, but the manufacturing of which takes two years.
(iv) A civil contractor, which measures progress of performance obligation using the input method, should not include in 'cost incurred to date' those costs that are attributable to that part of the completed construction work, which is yet to be accepted by the customer.
(v) When the contract term is 'Free On Board (FOB) Destination', control of the good remains with the seller until the good reaches the buyer.

APPLICATION ISSUES

Sales with a right to return

A *sale with a right to return* is a transaction in which the entity transfers control of a product to a customer, and also, grants the customer the right to return the product for various reasons.

Accounting for 'sale with a right to return' requires an entity to estimate the expected level of return considering the historical experience of similar contracts. The entity recognises:

(i) Revenue, initially measured at the amount of consideration to which the entity expects to be entitled, based on the expected level of return;

(ii) A refund liability, initially measured at the amount of consideration received or receivable to which the entity does not expect to be entitled; and

(iii) An asset (and a corresponding adjustment to the cost of sales) for the right to recover the products from the customer, initially measured with reference to the carrying amount of the products transferred, less expected recovery cost.

An entity updates the measurement of the refund liability at each reporting date. It recognises:

(i) Adjustments to the refund liability as revenue; and

(ii) Adjustments to the refund assets as expense

ILLUSTRATION 18.4 Sales with a Right to Return)

BN Publishers Limited (BNPL) sold 100 copies of a particular book in the month of March 2018. It received ₹10,000 towards sales consideration. Under the contract, customers are allowed to return any undamaged book within 30 days and to receive the full refund in cash. The cost of each book is ₹50. The date by which the customers can return the book will expire on April 10, 2018. BNPL estimates that 5 percent of the books are returned by the customers and the returned books can be sold at a profit. The cost of recovering the books is insignificant.

Required

Explain the accounting for the transaction.

Solution

The entity should pass the following accounting entries:

Entry 1:

Cash	Dr. ₹10,000	
To Refund Liability		Cr. ₹500
To Revenue		Cr. ₹9,500

Entry 2:

Asset (Right to recover) (5 × ₹50)	Dr. ₹250	
Cost of Sales	Dr. ₹4,750	
To Inventory		Cr. ₹5,000

Warranties

Assurance warranty

Assurance warranty provides an assurance that the product complies with the agreed specifications. It is not a separate performance obligation. A liability (provision) is recognised in the balance sheet based on the management's best estimate of the cost that the entity will incur to support the warranty.

Service warranty

Service warranty provides a customer with services in addition to an assurance that the product complies with the agreed specifications. Extended warranty that the customer can purchase separately is a service warranty. Service warranty is a separate performance obligation.

An entity should consider the following factors in assessing whether the warranty or a part of the warranty is a service warranty:

(i) Whether the warranty is required by law: The warranty that is required by law, usually to protect customers from risk of purchasing defective product, is likely to be an assurance warranty;

(ii) The length of the warranty coverage period: The longer the coverage period, the more likely that it is a service warranty; and

(iii) The nature of the tasks that the entity promises to perform: If it is necessary for an entity to perform specified tasks to provide the assurance that a product complies with the agreed-upon specifications (for example, a return shipping service for a defective product), then it is likely that those tasks do not give rise to a performance obligation.

Customer loyalty programmes and other incentives

A customer loyalty programme that provides the customer with a material right is accounted for a separate performance obligation. The transaction price allocated to the customer loyalty programme at the inception is not revised later.

Generally, customer loyalty programmes do not include a significant financing component because the use of loyalty points is at the discretion of the customer.

ILLUSTRATION 18.5 Customer Loyalty Programme

AB Limited (ABL), which has a number of stores selling readymade garments, operates a customer loyalty programme. A customer earns 1 point (equivalent to ₹1) for purchase of every ₹10. Points earned during a financial year are redeemable on future purchases during the following three financial years. ABL does not offer any other discount or rebate to customers.

During the financial year 2015–16, customers purchased goods for ₹1,00,000 and thus, earned 10,000 points. The management, on the basis of the past experience, which it assesses as predictive, expects that 90 percent of the points would be redeemed. The stand-alone selling price of the goods sold to customers without points is ₹1,00,000.

During the year 2016–17, 4,500 points are redeemed; 2017–18, 4,000 points are redeemed and the management has revised estimates of the percentage of points to be redeemed to 95 percent.

Required

Explain the accounting for the revenue for the year 2015–16 and accounting for points earned by customers (in 2015–16) for the years 2015–16, 2016–17 and 2017–18.

Solution

Year 2015–16

(i) Stand-alone selling prices: Goods: ₹1,00,000; Points: (₹1,00,000 × 0.90) or ₹9,000

(ii) Total stand-alone selling prices: (₹1,00,000 + 9,000) or ₹1,09,000

(iii) Selling price ratio: Goods: (1,00,000 /1,09,000) or 91.74 percent; Points: 8.26 percent

(iv) Price allocation: Goods: (₹1,00,000 × 0.9174) or ₹91,740; Points: ₹8,260

Thus, in the statement of profit and loss for the year 2015–16, 'revenue' should be recognised at ₹91,740 and in the balance sheet as at March 31, 2016, 'deferred revenue' (contract liability) should be recognised at ₹8,260.

Year 2016–17

4,500 points are redeemed and the management expects that 9,000 points would be redeemed in total. Accordingly, the entity should recognise (4,500/9,000) × ₹8,260 or ₹4,130 out of the deferred revenue and reduce the deferred liability by the same amount. Thus, revenue recognised in the statement of profit and loss for the year 2016–17 should include ₹4,130 and the deferred revenue in the balance sheet dated March 31, 2017, should include deferred revenue of (₹8,260 – 4,130) or ₹4,130 pertaining to the year 2015–16.

Year 2017–18

4,000 points are redeemed in 2017–18 resulting in cumulative redemption of 8,500 points. Now, the management expects that 9,500 points would be redeemed in total. Accordingly, the entity should recognise cumulative revenue of (8,500/9,500) × ₹8,260 or ₹7,391 out of the deferred revenue and reduce the deferred revenue (liability) by the same amount. Thus, revenue recognised in the statement of profit and loss for the year 2017–18 should include (₹7,391 – 4,130) or ₹3,261 and the deferred revenue in the balance sheet dated March 31, 2018 should include deferred revenue of (₹8,260 – 7,391) or ₹869 pertaining to the year 2015–16.

Principal vs agent

An entity is a principal if it controls the specified good or service, more than momentarily, before that good or service is transferred to a customer. An entity that is a principal may satisfy its performance obligation to provide the specified good or service itself or it may engage another party (for example, a subcontractor) to satisfy some or all of the performance obligation on its behalf.

An entity is an agent if the entity's performance obligation is to arrange for the provision of the specified good or service by another party. An entity that is an agent does not control the specified good or service provided by another party before that good or service is transferred to the customer.

Revenue recognition

If the entity is a principal, it recognises revenue on a gross basis—corresponding to the consideration to which the entity expects to be entitled.

If the entity is an agent, it recognises revenue at the amount of any fee or commission to which it expects to be entitled in exchange for arranging for the specified goods or services to be provided by the other party. An entity's fee or commission might be the net amount of consideration that the entity retains after paying the other party the consideration received in exchange for the goods or services to be provided by that party.

For example, 'BookMyShow' acts as an agent of entertainment providers (e.g., theatres) and its revenue stream includes commission earned from entertainment providers. It does not recognise the gross selling price of tickets as revenue. PVR Cinemas recognises the gross selling price of tickets sold by it directly as revenue because it is a principal.

Consignment arrangements

In a consignment arrangement, an entity delivers the product to another party (such as a dealer or a distributor), which holds the product, but does not obtain control of the product. Accordingly, the entity does not recognise revenue upon delivery of a product to another party if the delivered product is held on consignment. It recognises revenue when that other party sells the product to the end customer.

The following are the indicators that an arrangement is a consignment arrangement:

(a) The product is controlled by the entity until a specified event occurs such as the sale of the product to a customer of the dealer or until a specified period expires;
(b) The entity is able to require the return of the product or transfer the product to a third party (such as another dealer); and
(c) The dealer does not have an unconditional obligation to pay for the product (although it might be required to pay a deposit).

Bill-and-hold arrangement

A bill-and-hold arrangement is a contract under which an entity bills a customer for a product, but the entity retains physical possession of the product until it is transferred to the customer at a point in time in the future. For example, the entity holds the goods, because of the customer's lack of available space for the product or because of delays in the customer's production schedules.

An entity determines when it has satisfied its performance obligation to transfer a product by evaluating when a customer obtains control of that product.

For a customer to have obtained control of a product in a bill-and-hold arrangement, all of the following criteria must be met:

(i) the reason for the bill-and-hold arrangement must be substantive (for example, the customer has requested the arrangement);
(ii) the product must be identified separately as belonging to the customer;
(iii) the product currently must be ready for physical transfer to the customer; and
(iv) the entity cannot have the ability to use the product or to direct it to another customer.

An entity may recognise revenue for the sale of a product on a bill-and-hold basis before the product is shipped, when the customer obtains control of the product. If it recognises revenue before the product is shipped, it assesses whether it is providing custodial service, which is a distinct performance obligation.

Non-refundable up-front fees

In some contracts, an entity charges a customer a non-refundable upfront fee at or near contract inception. Examples include joining fees in health club membership contracts, activation fees in telecommunication contracts, setup fees in some services contracts and initial fees in some supply contracts. In most cases, an entity does not recognise the non-refundable up-front fee as revenue when it is received or receivable.

An entity should assess whether the fee relates to the transfer of a promised good or service. Usually, the upfront fee is an advance payment for future goods or services, and therefore, it is recognised as revenue when those future goods or services are provided. The revenue recognition period extends beyond the initial contractual period if the entity grants the customer the option to renew the contract and that option provides the customer with a material right to acquire future goods or services.

If the non-refundable upfront fee relates to a good or service, the entity should evaluate whether to account for the good or service as a separate performance obligation.

Repurchase arrangement

Repurchase arrangement generally comes in the following three forms:

(i) A forward contract—an entity's obligation to repurchase the asset;
(ii) A call option—an entity's right to repurchase the asset; and
(iii) A put option—an entity's obligation to repurchase the asset at the customer's request

A forward or a call option

If an entity has an obligation or a right to repurchase the asset (a forward or a call option), it does not transfer control of the asset to the customer because the customer is limited in its ability to direct the use of the asset and obtain substantially all of the remaining benefits from it. Consequently, the entity accounts for the contract as either of the following:

(i) A lease, if the entity can or must repurchase the asset for an amount that is less than the original selling price of the asset; or
(ii) A financing arrangement, if the entity can or must repurchase the asset for an amount that is equal to or more than the original selling price of the asset.

When comparing the repurchase price with the selling price, an entity should consider the time value of money.

If the repurchase agreement is a financing arrangement, the entity shall continue to recognise the asset as well as a financial liability for any consideration received from the customer. The entity shall recognise the difference between the amount of consideration received from the customer and the amount of consideration to be paid to the customer as interest.

If the option lapses unexercised, an entity derecognises the liability and recognises revenue.

A put option

If an entity has an obligation to repurchase the asset at the customer's request (put option), the entity accounts for the contract as one of the following:

(i) If the repurchase price is lower than the original selling price of the asset, the entity evaluates, at contract inception, whether the customer has a significant economic incentive to exercise that right. The customer's exercise of that right results in the customer effectively paying the entity consideration for the right to use a specified asset for a period of time. Therefore, if the customer has a significant economic incentive to exercise that right, the entity accounts for the agreement as a lease.

NOTES

To determine whether a customer has a significant economic incentive to exercise its right, an entity shall consider various factors, including the relationship of the repurchase price to the expected market value of the asset at the date of the repurchase and the amount of time until the right expires. For example, if the repurchase price is expected to significantly exceed the market value of the asset, this may indicate that the customer has a significant economic incentive to exercise the put option.

(ii) If the customer does not have a significant economic incentive to exercise its right at a price that is lower than the original selling price of the asset, the entity shall account for the agreement as if it were the sale of a product with a right of return.

(iii) If the repurchase price of the asset is equal to or greater than the original selling price and is more than the expected market value of the asset, the contract is in effect a financing arrangement.

(iv) If the repurchase price of the asset is equal to or greater than the original selling price and is less than or equal to the expected market value of the asset, and the customer does not have a significant economic incentive to exercise its right, then the entity accounts for the agreement as if it were the sale of a product with a right of return.

Licensing

A licence establishes a customer's rights to the intellectual property of an entity. For example,

(i) software and technology;
(ii) motion pictures, music and other forms of media and entertainment;
(iii) franchises; and
(iv) patents, trademarks and copyrights.

A licence may not be a distinct performance obligation. For example, a licence that forms a component of a tangible good (e.g., equipment) and that is integral to the functionality of the good is not a distinct performance obligation. Similarly, a licence that the customer can benefit from only in conjunction with a related service (e.g., licence to access an online service) is not a distinct performance obligation.

If the promise to grant the licence is a separate performance obligation, an entity evaluates the nature of the licence.

If the licence grants to the customer a right to access the entity's intellectual property as it exists throughout the licence period, the entity recognises the revenue over a period of time because the customer simultaneously receives and consumes the benefit from the entity's performance of providing access to its intellectual property as the performance occurs. This is the case when the activities of the entity significantly change the form or functionality of the intellectual property. For example, form or functionality of a product brand changes with the entity's activities directed to maintain and enhance the brand.

If the licence grants to the customer a right to use the entity's intellectual property as it exists (in form and functionality) at the point in time at which the licence is granted, the entity recognises the revenue at a point in time. Examples of intellectual property, which does not get significantly affected by the activities of the entity, and therefore, the customer uses it as it exists, are software, biological compounds or drug formulas, and completed media content (for example, films, television shows and music recordings). An entity should not recognise revenue for a licence that provides a right to use the entity's intellectual property before the beginning of the period during which the customer is able to use and benefit from the licence. For example, if a software licence period begins on March 1, 2018 and the entity provides to the customer a code (which enables the customer to immediately use the software) on April 15, 2018, the entity should recognise revenue on April 15, 2018 and not before.

CASE STUDY 18.8 Franchise Agreement

Sigma Public School Society (SPS Society) manages a highly reputed school (SPS) offering education from playway standard to class XII standard. It licences the right to open a school in a specified location to Narmada Education Society (NES). SPS Society is the franchisor and NES is the franchisee. SPS Society grants licence for a period of ten years on payment of up-front fixed fee of ₹5 crore. NES gets the right to use the name SPS for its school and to use the proprietary pedagogy being used by SPS. The agreement requires SPS Society to maintain the brand through product improvement and publicity.

Question

The CFO of the SPS Society seeks your advice on how to account for the up-front fixed fee of ₹5 crore.

Solution

The licence grants to the customer a right to access the entity's intellectual property as it exists throughout the licence period, and therefore, SPS Society should recognise the up-front fixed fee of ₹5 crore over a period of ten years on straight-line basis. The conclusion is based on the following facts:

(i) SPS Society has to undertake activities to maintain and improve the brand and pedagogy, and those activities will significantly affect the form and functionality of the intellectual property;

(ii) Any action by SPS Society may have a positive or negative effect on NES; and

(iii) Activities do no transfer goods and services to NES.

CASE STUDY 18.9 Software Licence

DS Infotech Limited (DSIL) grants licence to use its econometrics software to educational institutions, on a non-exclusive basis, for a period of three years on payment of up-front fixed fee. As per the agreement, the customer does not receive any upgrade to the software during the licence period.

Question

The CFO of DSIL seeks your advice on how to account for the up-front fixed fee that DSIL receives on granting license.

Solution

DSIL should recognise the up-front fixed fee as revenue at the point in time when customer is able to use and benefit from the licence. The conclusion is based on the fact that customers use the software in its existing form and functionality, and customers do not expect DSIL to undertake activities to change the form or functionality of the software significantly during the licence period.

Sales- or usage-based royalties

Sales- or usage-based royalty is a variable consideration. Ind AS 115 provides for an exception to the normal rules for accounting for variable consideration if the sales- or usage-based royalty relates solely to or predominantly to the intellectual property (IP) licence. According to this exception, an entity should recognise revenue for a sales- based or usage-based royalty promised in exchange for a licence of intellectual property only when the later of the following events occurs:

(i) The subsequent sale or usage occurs; and

NOTES

(ii) The performance obligation to which some or all of the sales-based or usage-based royalty has been allocated has been satisfied (or partially satisfied).

The second test is required, as the agreement might require the entity to undertake activities that might significantly impact the form and functionality of IP or the agreement may include other goods or services. For example, entities may sell franchisee license with consultancy and training services or with supply of equipment and the fees payable by the franchisee is in the form of sales-based or usage-based royalties.

A contract to licence IP may include a fixed element (e.g., minimum royalty guarantee) and a sales-based royalty payment plan. The minimum royalty guarantee element in the transaction price is not a variable consideration, and therefore, normal revenue recognition principles are to be applied in accounting for that part of the consideration. Any additional sales-based or usage-based royalties, in excess of the guaranteed amount, should be recognised using the royalty exception.

SUMMARY

If the contract provides the customer with a right to return products, the entity recognises revenue, a refund liability and an asset for the right to recover the products. An entity updates the measurement of the refund liability at each reporting date.

Assurance warranty is not a separate performance obligation. Service warranty, including extended warranty, is a separate performance obligation.

A customer loyalty programme that provides the customer with a material right is accounted for a separate performance obligation. The transaction price allocated to the customer loyalty programme at the inception is not revised later.

An entity is a principal if it controls the specified good or service, more than momentarily, before that good or service is transferred to a customer. An entity is an agent if the entity's performance obligation is to arrange for the provision of the specified good or service by another party. If the entity is a principal, it recognises revenue on a gross basis—corresponding to the consideration to which the entity expects to be entitled. If the entity is an agent, it recognises revenue in the amount of any fee or commission to which it expects to be entitled in exchange for arranging for the specified goods or services to be provided by the other party.

An entity does not recognise revenue upon delivery of a product to another party if the delivered product is held on consignment. It recognises revenue when that other party sells the product to the end customer.

An entity may recognise revenue for the sale of a product on a bill-and-hold basis before the product is shipped, when the customer obtains control of the product. If it recognises revenue before the product is shipped, it assesses whether it is providing custodial service, which is a distinct performance obligation.

In most cases, an entity does not recognise the non-refundable up-front fee as revenue when it is received or receivable.

In a contract with repurchase arrangement, the entity accounts for the contract as a lease or a financial arrangement or a sale with right to return depending on the terms of the contract, and (in case of put option) entity's assessment of whether the customer has a significant economic interest in returning the product.

If the promise to grant the licence is a separate performance obligation, an entity evaluates the nature of the licence. If the licence grants to the customer a right to access the entity's intellectual property as it exists throughout the licence period, the entity recognises the revenue over a period of time. If the licence grants to the customer a right to use the entity's intellectual property as it exists (in form and functionality) at the point in time at which the licence is granted, the entity recognises the revenue at a point in time.

An entity should recognise revenue for a sales-based or usage-based royalty promised in exchange for a licence of intellectual property only when the later of the following events occurs: (i) the subsequent sale or usage occurs; and (ii) the performance obligation to which some or all of the sales-based or usage-based royalty has been allocated has been satisfied (or partially satisfied).

Self-Test Questions

Self-test question 18.7

Indicate whether the following statements are true (T) or false (F):

(i) Right to return goods sold is a performance obligation separate from the promise to deliver the goods.

(ii) A product warranty that is required by law is likely to be an assurance warranty and it is not a performance obligation separate from the promise to deliver the goods.

(iii) An extended warranty is a performance obligation separate from the promise to deliver the goods.

(iv) Customer loyalty programmes might include a significant financing component depending on the period over which the award points can be used.

(v) An entity is likely to be an agent if it controls the specified good or service only momentarily, before that good or service is transferred to a customer.

(vi) In a bill-and-hold arrangement, the entity recognises revenue even before the control of the product is transferred to the customer.

(vii) An entity should recognise non-refundable up-front fee as revenue immediately when it is received or becomes receivable.

(viii) A contract with a customer in which the entity is obliged to repurchase the product is generally accounted for as a financing transaction.

(ix) An entity should recognise license fee as revenue immediately when it is received or becomes receivable.

(x) The normal rules for accounting for variable consideration are not applicable if the sales- or usage-based royalty relates solely to or predominantly to the intellectual property license.

CONTRACT COSTS

Costs to obtain a contract

An entity should recognise as an asset the incremental costs of obtaining a contract with a customer if the entity expects to recover those costs. However, as a practical expedient, an entity may recognise the incremental costs of obtaining a contract as an expense when incurred if the amortisation period of the asset that the entity otherwise would have recognised is one year or less.

Costs to fulfil a contract

If the costs incurred in fulfilling a contract with a customer are not within the scope of another Standard (for example, Ind AS 2, *Inventories*, Ind AS 16, *Property, Plant and Equipment* or Ind AS 38, *Intangible Assets*), an entity should recognise an asset from the costs incurred to fulfil a contract only if those costs meet all of the following criteria:

(i) the costs relate directly to a contract or to an anticipated contract that the entity can specifically identify (for example, costs relating to services to be provided under renewal of an existing contract or costs of designing an asset to be transferred under a specific contract that has not yet been approved);

(ii) the costs generate or enhance resources of the entity that will be used in satisfying (or in continuing to satisfy) performance obligations in the future; and

(iii) the costs are expected to be recovered.

The following are the examples of costs that may be included in costs to fulfil a contract:

(i) Direct labour (for example, salaries and wages of employees who provide the promised services directly to the customer);

(ii) Direct materials (for example, supplies used in providing the promised services to a customer);

(iii) Allocations of costs that relate directly to the contract or to contract activities (for example, costs of contract management and supervision, insurance and depreciation of tools and equipment used in fulfilling the contract);
(iv) Costs that are explicitly chargeable to the customer under the contract; and
(v) Other costs that are incurred only because an entity entered into the contract (for example, payments to subcontractors).

The following are the examples of costs that should not be included in costs to fulfil a contract and should be expensed when incurred:

(i) General and administrative costs (unless those costs are explicitly chargeable to the customer under the contract);
(ii) Costs of wasted materials, labour or other resources to fulfil the contract that were not reflected in the price of the contract;
(iii) Costs that relate to satisfied performance obligations (or partially satisfied performance obligations) in the contract (i.e., costs that relate to past performance); and
(iv) Costs for which an entity cannot distinguish whether the costs relate to unsatisfied performance obligations or to satisfied performance obligations (or partially satisfied performance obligations).

Amortisation

Capitalised costs to obtain or fulfil a contract are amortised on a systematic basis, consistent with the pattern of transfer of good or service to which the asset relates. The straight-line basis may not be appropriate in all cases. For example, if the contract contains multiple performance obligations to be satisfied at different points in time, the straight-line basis will not be appropriate for amortising capitalised costs to obtain or fulfil the contract.

Impairment

Impairment loss is recognised in profit or loss when the carrying amount of the asset exceeds the recoverable amount. The recoverable amount is the remaining expected amount of consideration less the costs that relate directly to providing goods and services under the contract and that have not been recognised as expense. In estimating the expected amount of consideration, the entity should take into consideration the effect of customer's credit risks.

TRADE RECEIVABLES AND CONTRACT ASSETS

Trade receivable

Trade receivable is the right to payment (for goods and services already transferred to a customer) that is unconditional, except for the passage of time.

Contract asset

A contract asset is an entity's right to payment for goods and services already transferred to a customer if that right to payment is conditional on something other than the passage of time. For example, an entity recognises a contract asset when it has fulfilled a contract obligation, but must perform other obligations before being entitled to payment.

The following is an example of contract asset:

An entity enters into a contract to transfer Products A and B to a customer in exchange for ₹1,000. The contract requires Product A to be delivered first and states that payment for the delivery of Product A is conditional on the delivery of Product B.

The entity identifies the promises to transfer Products A and B as performance obligations and allocates ₹400 to the performance obligation to transfer Product A and ₹600 to the performance obligation to transfer Product B on the basis of their relative stand-alone selling prices. The entity recognises revenue for each respective performance obligation when control of the product transfers to the customer. After performance against the performance obligation of delivering product A, it recognises contract asset for ₹400, as its right to receive ₹400 from the customer is conditional on supply of Product B.

Impairment

Ind AS 109, Financial Instruments, does not permit estimation of doubtful debts applying an estimated loss percentage (e.g., 5%) on the gross amount of trade receivables/contract asset.

The following are the principles for measuring loss allowance for trade receivables and contract assets, both of which represent amount receivable from customers:

(i) Trade receivables and contract assets that do not have a significant financing component: Loss allowance is measured based on 'life-time expected credit losses'; and

(ii) Trade receivables and contract assets that have a significant financing component: Loss allowance is measured either using the general approach or based on 'life-time expected credit losses', depending on the accounting policy elected by the entity.

The general principle is that at the inception, loss allowance is recognised at '12-month credit losses'. If credit risk increases subsequently, loss allowance is recognised at 'life-time credit losses'. '12-month credit losses' are estimated losses over the life of an asset from loss events expected to occur in next 12 months. 'Life-time credit losses' are estimated losses over the life of an asset from loss events expected to occur over the life of the asset.

Usually, trade receivables that do not have significant financing component are short-duration (typically less than 12 months) financial assets. Therefore, 'life-time expected credit losses' generally do not differ from '12-month expected credit losses'. They are usually measured at the transaction cost and the implied effective interest rate is zero. Therefore, discounting of cash shortfall for measuring cash losses is not required.

Ind AS 109, Financial Instruments, allows the use of practical expedients when measuring life-time expected credit losses. Entities can use a provision matrix for measuring the impairment allowance.

Table 18.3 presents an example of provision matrix.

TABLE 18.3

Example of Provision Matrix

	Expected credit loss (%)	Trade receivables (₹)	Impairment allowance
Current	0.2	50,000	100
1–30 days past due	2.0	30,000	600
31–60 days past due	4.0	10,000	400
61–90 days past due	6.0	5,000	300
Over 90 days past due	10.0	1,000	100
Total			1,500

Entities should consider developing different provision matrices for different customer segments based on past loss patterns for different customer segments. For example, customers may be segmented based on geographic location, product type, customer rating, collateral, and type of customer (e.g., wholesalers and retailers).

In developing provision matrix, entities use historical loss experience on its trade receivables, and adjust historical loss rates to reflect information about current conditions, and reasonable and supportable forecasts of future economic conditions.

NOTES

ANSWERS TO SELF-TEST QUESTIONS

18.1 (i) F; (ii) T; (iii) F; (iv) F; (v) T
18.2 (i) T; (ii) T; (iii) T; (iv) T; (v) T
18.3 (i) F; (ii) T; (iii) T; (iv) F; (v) F
18.4 (i) F; (ii) F; (iii) F; (iv) T; (v) F; (vi) T; (vii) T
18.5 (i) T; (ii) T; (iii) T; (iv) T; (v) F
18.6 (i) T; (ii) T; (iii) F; (iv) T; (v) T
18.7 (i) T; (ii) T; (iii) T; (iv) F; (v) T; (vi) F; (vii) F; (viii) F; (ix) F; (x) T

ASSIGNMENTS

Quiz

1. Indicate against each statement whether it is True (T) or False (F):
   (i) There is no significant difference between revenue and 'other operating income'.
   (ii) Any entity that purchases an asset or a service from the entity is entity's customer.
   (iii) In order to be enforceable in the court law, a contract must be in writing.
   (iv) An entity recognises revenue and trade receivables (or cash) simultaneously.
   (v) An entity recognises revenue from sale of goods when it transfers the possession of promised goods and services to the customer and expects receiving the promised consideration.
   (vi) An entity measures revenue at the amount that is specified as consideration (price) in the contract with the customer.
   (vii) An entity recognises revenue when all the distinct performance obligations in the contract are satisfied.
   (viii) A contract to install a system with free maintenance for two years might have three distinct performance obligations.
   (ix) An entity that promises delivery and installation of television should not recognise until the installation is complete, although installation is a routine and simple activity.
   (x) If an entity promises to deliver a combined output (e.g., hospital), it cannot separate other promises (e.g., supply of inputs specified in the contract) from that promise.
   (xi) If the entity, which regularly sells building materials in a competitive market, promises to deliver a commercial space as designed by the customer, it allocates the transaction price to the performance obligation to supply building materials and the performance obligation to integrate inputs to deliver the combined output, which is the commercial space.
   (xii) If an entity expects that the customer will avail cash discount, the transaction price that is used to measure revenue should be net of cash discount.
   (xiii) An entity should not include variable consideration (e.g., performance bonus) in the transaction price.
   (xiv) As a practical expedient, an entity is not required to adjust the promised amount of consideration for the effects of a significant financing component if the entity expects, at contract inception, that it will collect money within one year from the date when it transfers a promised good or service to a customer.
   (xv) Accounting for customer's loyalty programme is an application of the accounting principle that requires an entity to reduce the transaction price by the consideration paid or payable to a customer or customer's customer.
   (xvi) An entity allocates the purchase consideration of a bundle of products to each individual product in the bundle in proportion to their fair values.
   (xvii) An entity recognises revenue over time if the customer simultaneously receives and consumes the benefits provided by the entity's performance as the entity performs.
   (xviii) In measuring revenue over time, most entities use the input method to measure the progress of the performance obligation satisfied.
   (xix) An entity should not recognise revenue from a 'sale with a right to return' until the time allowed to return the goods expires.
   (xx) Extended warranty is a separate performance obligation
2. Tick the most appropriate statement:
   (i) A promise to supply inputs as per customer's specification, which are readily available in the market, and a promise to integrate those into a complex system in a contract with

a customer cannot be identified as two distinct performance obligations because

(a) the customer cannot benefit from the inputs.

(b) the entity's promise to transfer the good or service to the customer is not separately identifiable from other promise in the contract.

(c) the customer cannot benefit from the inputs and the entity's promise to transfer the goods to the customer is not separately identifiable from other promise in the contract.

(d) the customer can benefit from the inputs, but the entity's promise to transfer the goods to the customer is not separately identifiable from other promise in the contract.

(ii) An entity, at the contract inception, decides not be recognised as revenue performance bonus receivable by the entity for early completion of the construction, in a contract to construct an office complex because

(a) the performance bonus is a variable consideration.

(b) this is the first contract secured by the entity in which 'performance bonus' clause is included.

(c) in past, in similar contracts, only in 70 percent of cases, the entity earned performance bonus.

(d) the entity assesses that it is highly probable that a significant reversal in the amount of cumulative revenue recognised will occur, if it recognises revenue before it earns the performance bonus.

(iii) An entity uses the price payable by customers to recognise revenue immediately on sale of the new model of refrigerator introduced by it, although, as a part of sales promotion, it allows credit of 12 months (zero interest) on this model, while it sells other models on cash basis only because

(a) there are many customers, who do not avail the credit facility, pay the full price.

(b) the credit period does not exceed 12 months from the date of sale.

(c) assessing credit risk for each customer (in order to determine the appropriate discount rate) is difficult because the entity is selling the product to large number of retail customers.

(d) the credit allowed is a part of sales promotion for a limited period.

(iv) An entity, which sells products in bundle, has included a new product, which it does not sell on stand-alone basis, in the bundle without increasing the selling price of the bundle for promoting the new product, decides, as the appropriate accounting policy:

(a) not to allocate the transaction price to the new product because the selling price of the bundle remains the same.

(b) not to allocate the transaction price to the new product, because the product is unique and similar products are not available in the market.

(c) not to allocate the transaction price to the new product because inclusion of the product in the bundle is similar to distribution of samples to the existing customers.

(d) to allocate the transaction price to the new product estimating its stand-alone price using the 'cost plus a margin' approach.

3. Fill in the blanks:

(i) A real estate developer, who creates residential complexes, constructs apartments, sells them as it receives clearances from regulators and transfers them to customers by getting them registered on completion of the construction, should recognise revenue .... (Choose between 'over a period of time' and 'at a point in time'.)

(ii) A construction contractor who constructs apartments for a real estate developer should recognise revenue .... (Choose between 'over a period of time' and 'at a point in time'.)

(iii) Cash discount should .... from transaction price. (Choose between 'be deducted' and 'not be deducted'.)

(iv) In measuring the progress of construction work for the purpose of recognising revenue, an entity should ....cost of materials procured specifically for the project but not issued to the site. (Choose between 'include' and 'not include'.)

(v) An entity has sold 100 pieces of a product at a price of ₹1,000 per piece with a right to return within 30 days. The cost per piece is ₹600 and the entity expects that 10 percent of the goods sold will return. The entity should recognise: (a) revenue at ₹.................. (b) refund liability at ₹..................; and (c) right to return at ₹..................

(vi) A warranty that is required by law is likely to be .... (Choose between 'assurance' and 'service'.)

(vii) An entity that produces industrial boilers (of standard specifications) ....

NOTES

recognise revenue when the product is ready for dispatch, if the customer defers the delivery after paying full price and provides a right to the entity to divert the boiler to another customer and deliver it a boiler to be produced later. (Choose between 'should' and 'should not'.)

(viii) An entity that provides health club services, usually, ... the non-refundable joining fee as revenue immediately when it is received or receivable. (Choose between 'recognises' and 'does not recognise'.)

(ix) A contract with a customer under which the entity has an obligation to repurchase the product at a price lower than the selling price should be recognised a ....

(x) Contract asset is a ....asset. (Choose between 'financial' and 'non-financial'.)

Financial Instruments

CHAPTER 19

LEARNING OBJECTIVES

This chapter provides an overview of the accounting for financial instruments.

After reading this chapter, you will develop understanding of the following:

- Nature of financial instruments, financial assets and financial liabilities
- Difference between equity and liability
- Accounting for compound financial instruments
- Classification of financial assets and liabilities into measured at amortised cost, measured at Fair Value Through Other Comprehensive Incomes (FVOCI) and measured at FCTPL
- The concept of FVTPL and business model tests in classifying financial assets
- Principles for recognition and derecognition of financial assets and financial liabilities
- The concept of 'pass through arrangement'
- Principles for measuring various types of financial assets and financial liabilities
- Concept of 12 months expected credit losses and life-time credit losses in testing financial assets for impairment
- Concepts of fair value hedge and cash flow hedge; and
- Accounting for fair value hedge, cash flow hedge and net investment hedge

Applicable Ind AS: *Accounting for financial instruments is covered by the following three accounting standards:*

(i) Ind AS 32, Financial Instruments: Presentation; (ii) Ind AS 107, Financial Instruments: Disclosures; and (iii) Ind AS 109, Financial Instruments.

NOTES

FINANCIAL INSTRUMENTS: DEFINITIONS

Financial Instrument

Financial instrument is defined as follows:

> "A financial instrument is any *contract* that gives rise to a financial asset of one entity and a financial liability or equity instrument of another entity."

The essential features of a financial instrument are given below:

(i) It arises from a contractual arrangement between two or more parties.
(ii) The contract gives rise to a right (financial asset) of one party and obligation (financial liability or equity) of another party.

Contractual arrangement

It is not necessary that the contract should be in writing. However, it is essential that the contract should be enforceable in the court of law.

A right that meets the definition of financial asset is not a financial instrument if it does not arise from a contractual arrangement. Similarly, an obligation that meets the definition of financial liability is not a financial instrument if it does not arise from a contractual arrangement. For example, tax liability, which is an obligation to pay cash to the government, is not a financial instrument because it does not arise from a contractual arrangement, although the obligation is settled by paying cash. For the purpose of accounting, the tax liability is not considered a financial liability because it does not arise from a contractual arrangement.

Financial assets and liabilities

Assets that do not meet the definition of financial asset, and liabilities that do not meet the definition of financial liability are not financial instruments. For example, prepaid expense, which is settled by receipt of goods or services, is not a financial instrument, as it does not meet the definition of financial asset. Similarly, deferred revenue and advance from customers, which are settled by delivery of goods or services, are not financial instruments because they do not meet the definition of financial liability. Assets like pre-paid expenses are not financial assets, and liabilities like deferred revenue are not financial liabilities.

Bundle of rights and obligations

A financial instrument may be viewed as a bundle of rights and obligations. Accounting for financial instruments often require unbundling those rights and obligations and to account for each right and obligation separately. This makes the accounting for financial instruments complex. Moreover, continuous innovation in structuring financial instruments often makes it difficult to understand the nature of rights and obligations embedded in a financial instrument. This further complicates the accounting for financial instruments. In this chapter, we shall provide an overview of the accounting principles for the accounting for financial instruments. We shall not discuss accounting for complex financial instruments and application issues.

Contingent rights and obligations

The ability to exercise a contractual right or the requirement to satisfy a contractual obligation may be absolute, or it may be contingent on the occurrence of a future event. For example, the contractual right of the holder of a financial guarantee (for example, lender) and a corresponding contractual obligation of the issuer of the financial guarantee (guarantor) to pay the lender, are contingent because the right and corresponding obligation arise only if the debtor (for example, borrower) defaults.

A contingent right and obligation meet the definition of financial asset and financial liability, even though such assets and liabilities are not always recognised in the financial statements.

NOTES

SUMMARY

A financial instrument is any ***contract*** that gives rise to a financial asset of one entity and a financial liability or equity instrument of another entity. The contractual arrangement is the essential characteristic of a financial instrument. A right that meets the definition of financial assets is not a financial instrument unless that right arises from a contractual arrangement. Similarly, an obligation that meets the definition of financial liability is not a financial instrument unless that obligation arises from a contractual arrangement. A contingent right and obligation meet the definition of financial asset and financial liability, even though such assets and liabilities are not always recognised in the financial statements. An asset is classified as financial asset if it is a financial instrument. A liability is classified as a financial liability if it is a financial instrument. For example, income tax liability is not classified as financial liability.

Self-Test Questions

Self-test question 19.1

Indicate whether the following statements are true (T) or false (F):

(i) Statutory dues that are to be settled by depositing cash in the government exchequer is a financial instrument.

(ii) A financial instrument arises from a written contract between two or more parties.

(iii) A financial instrument arises from a contract that is enforceable in the court of law.

(iv) A contractual obligation, performance of which is contingent on the occurrence of a future event, is not a financial instrument, even if the obligation meets the definition of a financial liability.

(v) Financial instruments may be viewed as a bundle of rights and obligations.

Financial Asset—Definition

A financial asset is any asset that is:

(a) cash;

(b) an equity instrument of another entity;

(c) a contractual right:

  (i) to receive cash or another financial asset from another entity; or

  (ii) to exchange financial assets or financial liabilities with another entity under conditions that are potentially favourable to the entity; or

(d) A contract that will or may be settled in the entity's own equity instruments and is:

  (i) a non-derivative for which the entity is or may be obliged to receive a *variable number* of the entity's own equity instruments; or

  (ii) a derivative that will or may be settled *other than* by the exchange of a fixed amount of cash or another financial asset for a fixed number of the entity's own equity instruments.

For this purpose, the entity's own equity instruments *do not* include puttable financial instruments or instruments that impose on the entity an obligation to deliver to another party a pro rata share of the net assets of the entity only on liquidation, which do not meet the definition of equity, but are classified as equity instruments; or instruments that are contracts for the future receipt or delivery of the entity's own equity instruments.

NOTES

Puttable instrument

A puttable instrument is a financial instrument that gives the holder the right to put the instrument back to the issuer for cash or another financial asset or is automatically put back to the issuer on the occurrence of an uncertain future event or the death or retirement of the instrument holder. For example, units of a mutual fund are puttable instruments. A puttable instrument is classified as equity if it meets certain specified criteria.

Examples of financial assets

(i) Cash is a financial asset because it represents the medium of exchange and is, therefore, the basis on which all transactions are measured and recognised in financial statements.

(ii) A deposit of cash with a bank or similar financial institution is a financial asset because it represents the contractual right to obtain cash from the institution or to draw a cheque or similar instrument against the balance in favour of a creditor in payment of a financial liability.

(iii) Assets that arise from contracts to receive cash such as trade receivables, loan repayable by the borrower and corporate bond issued by another entity.

(iv) Another type of financial instrument is one for which the economic benefit to be received is a financial asset other than cash. For example, in a contract with a customer, the customer will settle the amount due to the entity by transferring government bonds in favour of the entity. Government bond is a financial asset, as the holder of the government bond has the right to receive cash from the issuer of the government bond. A trade receivable representing the amount due from the customer is a financial asset. Although the customer will not pay cash, the issuer of the government bond will pay cash on maturity and the entity will ultimately receive cash against the amount due from the customer.

(v) Another type of financial instrument is one for which the economic benefit to be received is the variable number of equity shares of the entity other than cash. For example, V Limited (VL) has a contract with a customer, according to which the customer will settle the amount due (say, ₹1,00,000) to VL by delivering variable number of VL's equity shares. The number of equity shares will depend on the market price of the shares on the settlement date. If share price on the settlement date is ₹100, the customer will deliver 1,000 shares of VL. If it is ₹200, the customer will transfer 500 shares of VL. A trade receivable representing the amount due from the customer is a financial asset. The example is hypothetical because the contract results in buying back shares and a company has to comply with the requirement of the Companies Act and SEBI regulations to buy-back shares.

In the above example, if, as per the contract, the customer will settle the amount due to VL by transferring a fixed number of VL's shares stipulated in the contract, 'trade receivable' is not a financial asset.

(vi) Derivative contracts are financial instruments. A derivative contract is recognised as an asset when the change in the condition is favourable to the entity and is recognised as a liability when the change in the condition is unfavourable to the entity. [We shall discuss derivative contracts later in this chapter.]

ILLUSTRATION 19.1 Derivative—Asset

On March 1, 2018, BC Limited (BCL) had sold goods to a customer in the USA for US$ 50,000. It allowed the customer three months credit. BCL, in order to protect itself against variability of exchange rate, had entered into a forward contract to sell US$ 50,000 on May 31, 2018. The forward contract is a derivative instrument. The US$/INR forward rate for May 31, 2018, as at March 1, 2018 and March 31, 2018 were US$ 1 = INR 65 and US$ 1 = INR 64, respectively. On the settlement date (May 31, 2018), the spot rate was US$ 1 = INR 62.

Required

Explain the accounting for the forward contract.

NOTES

Solution

The movement in the forward rate is favourable to BCL. At the balance sheet date, the counter party notionally owes (₹65- 64) × 50,000 or ₹50,000 to BCL. Therefore, in the balance sheet dated March 31, 2018, the derivative (forward contract) should be recognised as an asset, measured at ₹50,000.

On the settlement date (May 31, 2018), the spot rate was US$ 1 = INR 62. On that date, BCL would recognise the forward contract as an asset at (₹64 – 62) × 50,000 or ₹1,00,000. Thus, the total value of the forward contract asset at the settlement date was (₹50,000 + 1,00,000) or ₹1,50,000. The asset (forward contract) would be derecognised on receiving ₹1,50,000 from the counterparty in the forward contract on settlement.

BCL by selling US$ 50,000, which it had received from the customer, at the spot rate, realised ₹62 × 50,000 or ₹31,00,000. Its total realisation, including ₹1,50,000 received from the counterparty in the forward contract was (₹31,00,000 + 1,50,000) or ₹32,50,000. It is equal to the amount that it would have received by selling US$ 50,000 at the forward rate of US$ 1 = INR 65.

Financial Liability—Definition

A financial liability is any liability that is:

(a) a contractual obligation:
   (i) To deliver cash or another financial asset to another entity; or
   (ii) To exchange financial assets or financial liabilities with another entity under conditions that are potentially unfavourable to the entity; or

(b) a contract that will or may be settled in the entity's own equity instruments and is:
   (i) a non-derivative for which the entity is or may be obliged to deliver a *variable number* of the entity's own equity instruments; or
   (ii) a derivative that will or may be settled *other than by* the exchange of a fixed amount of cash or another financial asset for a fixed number of the entity's own equity instruments.

For this purpose, rights, options or warrants to acquire a fixed number of the entity's own equity instruments for a fixed amount of any currency are equity instruments if the entity offers the rights, options or warrants pro rata to all of its existing owners of the same class of its own non-derivative equity instruments. Apart from the aforesaid, the equity conversion option embedded in a convertible bond denominated in foreign currency to acquire a fixed number of the entity's own equity instruments is an equity instrument if the exercise price is fixed in any currency. Also, for this purpose, the entity's own equity instruments *do not* include puttable financial instruments or instruments that impose on the entity an obligation to deliver to another party a pro rata share of the net assets of the entity only on liquidation, which do not meet the definition of equity, but are classified as equity instruments; or instruments that are contracts for the future receipt or delivery of the entity's own equity instruments.

Examples of financial liabilities

(i) Financial instruments give rise to a financial asset for one party and financial liability for another party. Examples are corresponding liability for 'trade receivable' is 'trade payable'; corporate bond is an asset for the investor and a liability for the issuer of the bond; and 'loan receivable' is an asset of the financial institution that has disbursed the loan and the corresponding liability for the borrower is 'loan payable'. In each of the above examples, the financial instrument has given a right to one party to receive cash and an obligation of the counterparty to pay cash.

(ii) As in the case of financial assets, if the contract results in an obligation to deliver a financial asset (e.g., government bond), other than cash, the obligation is a financial liability.

NOTES

(iii) A derivative contract is recognised as a liability when the change in condition is unfavourable to the entity.

(iv) As in the case of financial assets, if the contract gives rise to an obligation to deliver variable number of its own shares to settle a specified amount of liability (e.g., trade payable), the liability is a financial liability.

Financial guarantee contract

A 'financial guarantee contract' is a contract that requires the issuer to make specified payments to reimburse the holder for a loss that it incurs because a specified debtor fails to make payment when it is due in accordance with the original or modified terms of debt instrument.

A contract is classified as a financial guarantee contract only if all the following conditions are satisfied:

(i) The reference obligation is a debt instrument;

(ii) The holder is compensated *only for* a loss that it incurs; and

(iii) The contract does not compensate the holder for more than the actual loss that it incurs.

ILLUSTRATION 19.2 Financial Guarantee Contract

K Limited (KL) borrows money from a bank. M Limited (ML) issues a guarantee to the bank. Under the guarantee contract, ML will make payment to the bank on behalf of KL if KL fails to make payment within 30 days from the date it falls due for payment. As per the contract terms, if the bank subsequently recovers payment from KL, it will immediately reimburse ML for the amount received from KL.

Required

Explain whether the contract meets the definition of financial guarantee contract.

Solution

The contract meets the definition of financial guarantee contract because the reference obligation is a debt instrument and ML will compensate the bank only for actual loss that might arise if KL fails to make the payment to the bank.

ILLUSTRATION 19.3 Financial Guarantee Contract

K Limited (KL) borrows money from a bank. M Limited (ML) issues a guarantee to the bank. Under the guarantee contract, ML will make payment to the bank if the credit rating agency downgrades the credit rating of KL even if the bank does not incur loss.

Required

Explain whether the contract meets the definition of financial guarantee contract.

Solution

The contract cannot be classified as a financial guarantee contract. Although the reference obligation is a debt instrument, but it is not about compensating the bank for actual loss. The contract should be accounted for as a derivative instrument.

SUMMARY

Cash is a financial asset. Investment in an equity instrument of another entity is a financial asset. A contractual right to receive cash or another financial asset from another entity is a financial asset. Examples of such right are trade receivables and investment in a bond issued by another entity. A contractual right to exchange financial assets or financial liabilities with another entity under conditions that are potentially favourable to the entity is a financial asset.

NOTES

Example of such a right is right under options and other derivatives. A contract that will or may be settled in the entity's own equity instruments and is a non-derivative for which the entity is or may be obliged to receive a ***variable number*** of the entity's own equity instruments is a financial asset. Similarly, A contract that will or may be settled in the entity's own equity instruments and is a derivative that will or may be settled ***other than*** by the exchange of a fixed amount of cash or another financial asset for a fixed number of the entity's own equity instruments is a financial asset.

A contractual obligation to deliver cash or another financial asset to another entity is financial liability. Examples are trade payables and bond issued by an entity. A contractual obligation to exchange financial assets or financial liabilities with another entity under conditions that are potentially unfavourable to the entity is a financial liability. Examples of such obligations are options and other derivatives. A contract that will or may be settled in the entity's own equity instruments and is a non-derivative for which the entity is or may be obliged to deliver a ***variable number*** of the entity's own equity instruments is a financial liability. A contract that will or may be settled in the entity's own equity instruments and is a derivative that will or may be settled ***other than by*** the exchange of a fixed amount of cash or another financial asset for a fixed number of the entity's own equity instruments is a financial liability.

Self-Test Questions

Self-test question 19.2

Indicate whether the following statements are true (T) or false (F):

(i) Deferred revenue is a financial liability.

(ii) The obligation of N Limited (NL) to issue 1,000 of its own shares to a vendor to whom it owes ₹1,00,000 is a financial liability.

(iii) A derivative contract is recognised as a financial asset or a financial liability depending on whether the conditions are favourable or unfavourable to the entity.

(iv) Trade receivables that will be settled by the customer by endorsing government bonds in favour of the entity is a financial asset.

(v) Debenture issued by a company is a financial liability.

Equity—Definition

An equity instrument is any contract that evidences a residual interest in the assets of an entity after deducting all of its liabilities.

Equity and Liability—Classification

Both equity and liability represent claims on the assets of an entity. Equity represents owners' claim, while liabilities represent the claim of outsiders (non-owners). Although the distinction between equity and liability is conceptually simple, it is often difficult to apply the principles in practice because of the complex nature of financial instruments. Classification often requires judgement.

Liability

An instrument that creates an obligation is a financial liability if the entity *does not have the unconditional right to avoid* delivering cash or another financial asset in settlement of that obligation.

A contractual obligation is not negated merely because of the inability of the entity to settle the contractual obligation, for example, due to lack of funds, statutory restrictions or insufficient profit or reserve. For example, an issuer of debentures does not have the

NOTES

unconditional right to avoid redemption of the debentures. The entity may not have sufficient funds to redeem the debentures, but that does not negate the obligation and the issuer recognises the outstanding amount against the debentures as liability in the balance sheet.

Equity

An instrument is equity if the entity has *unconditional right* to avoid delivering cash or another financial asset in settlement of the claim.

Fixed for fixed criteria

A contract that will be settled by the entity receiving or delivering a fixed number of its own equity instruments in exchange for a fixed amount of cash, or another financial asset, is an equity instrument. This is called the *fixed for fixed* requirement. However, if there is any variability in the amount of cash or own equity instruments that will be delivered or received, then such a contract is a financial asset or liability, as applicable.

For example, compulsorily convertible debentures or preference shares, where there is no contractual obligation to pay cash and the number of equity shares to be issued on conversion is fixed upfront, are classified as equity.

Substance over form

In deciding the classification of a financial instrument, economic substance rather than the legal form should be considered. For example, redeemable preference shares are classified as liability, as the company does not have the unconditional right to avoid redeeming the preference shares.

CASE STUDY 19.1 Equity and Liability Classification

BV Limited (BVL) issues a non-redeemable financial instrument (base instrument). The dividend on the base instrument is payable if interest on another instrument (linked instrument) is paid. AVL is required to pay interest on the linked instrument.

Question

Classify the base instrument.

Solution

BVL is under contractual obligation to pay dividend on the base instrument, as it is contractually obligated to pay interest on the linked instrument. Therefore, the base instrument should be classified as liability.

Compound instruments—Split accounting

Some instruments are structured to contain elements of both a liability and equity in a single instrument. Such instruments are known as *compound instruments*. Equity and liability components are accounted for separately. *Split accounting* is used to measure the liability and the equity components upon initial recognition of the instrument. The fair value of the consideration for the compound instrument is allocated to its liability and equity components.

An example of compound instrument is optionally convertible debenture that is convertible into fixed number of equity shares and carry interest. Under split accounting, the fair value of the consideration in respect of the liability component is measured at the fair value of a similar liability that does not have any associated equity conversion option. The equity component is assigned the residual amount.

NOTES

ILLUSTRATION 19.4 Compound Financial Instrument—Split Accounting

On April 1, 2017, KK Limited issued 2,000 convertible bonds at the face value of ₹1000. The bonds will mature on March 31, 2020. The coupon rate is 5% and interest is payable annually. The holder of the bonds can convert the bonds at any time before maturity into 1 equity shares, per bond, that is, 2,000 equity shares.

The prevailing market interest rate for similar liability without conversion option, as at April 1, 2017, is 8% per annum.

Required

Explain the accounting for the convertible bond.

Solution

The present value (PV) of cash flows arising from repayment of principal on maturity and payment of interest annually for three years, using the market interest rate (8% per annum) as discount rate, comes to:

PV of the principal: ₹15,87,664 and PV of interest: ₹2,57,710; PV of total cash flow: ₹18,45,374.

At the inception, the liability should be recognised at ₹18,45,374 and equity should be recognised at (₹20,00,000 – 18,45,374) or ₹1,54,626.

Importance of classification

Correct classification is important because it determines whether any interest, dividend, losses and gains related to the instrument are recognised as income or expense in profit or loss. If the instrument is classified as liability, all those items are recognised in profit or loss. If the instrument is classified as equity, all those items are recognised in equity. For example, dividend on redeemable preference shares is included in finance cost that is recognised in profit or loss because redeemable preference shares are classified as liabilities. Dividend on equity shares is not recognised as expense in profit or loss and is directly reduced from equity (e.g., retained earnings or free reserve).

SUMMARY

An instrument that creates an obligation is a financial liability if the entity ***does not have the unconditional right to avoid*** delivering cash or another financial asset in settlement of that obligation. An instrument is equity if the entity has ***unconditional right*** to avoid delivering cash or another financial asset in settlement of the claim. A contract that will be settled by the entity receiving or delivering a fixed number of its own equity instruments in exchange for a fixed amount of cash, or another financial asset, is an equity instrument. This is called the 'fixed for fixed' requirement. Some instruments are structured to contain elements of both a liability and equity in a single instrument. Such instruments are known as compound instruments. Equity and liability components are accounted for separately. 'Split accounting' is used to measure the liability and the equity components upon initial recognition of the instrument.

Self-Test Questions

Self-test question 19.3

Indicate whether the following statements are true (T) or false (F):

(i) A compulsorily convertible debenture, where there is no contractual obligation to pay cash and the number of equity shares to be issued on conversion is fixed upfront, should be classified as equity.

(ii) An optionally convertible debenture where the number of equity shares to be issued on conversion is fixed upfront, should be classified as liability.

NOTES

(iii) Option premium received on a call option, which is written on own shares and gives the holder the right to buy specified number of shares for a specified price, should be recognised as equity.
(iv) Redeemable preference share should be classified as liability.
(v) Trade payables, which will be settled by issuing fixed number of equity shares of the entity, should be classified as a liability.

Derivatives

Ind AS 109 defines 'derivative' as follows:

A financial instrument or other contract within the scope of Ind AS 109, with all three following characteristics is 'derivative':

(a) its value changes in response to the change in one or more underlying;
(b) it requires either no initial net investment or an initial net investment that is smaller than would be required for other types of contracts that would be expected to have a similar response to changes in market factors, and
(c) it is settled at a future date.

Underlying

The underlying variable on which the fair value of a derivative instrument is based may be that of:

(i) The price of a financial instrument (e.g., bond or equity shares);
(ii) The price of a commodity (e.g., gold, oil or wheat);
(iii) The rate (e.g., an interest rate or foreign exchange rate);
(iv) The index of prices (e.g., a stock exchange index); or
(v) Some other variables that have measurable value (e.g., a climate, geological or other physical variable).

Non-financial variable

The standard stipulates that in the case of a non-financial variable, the variable should not be specific to a party to the contract in order to classify the contract as a derivative. This definition is primarily intended to exclude insurance contracts. For example, in a contract in which the issuer of the contract guarantees residual value of the vehicle to the holder and compensates him/her for the decline of the market value and the condition of the car, is not a derivative contract because the variable is specific to the holder of the contract.

No or smaller net investment

The standard requires that the initial net investment should be less than the investment needed to acquire the underlying non-derivative financial instrument. The 'less than' does not necessarily mean insignificant.

Derivatives come in many form. The endeavour of the accounting standard setters was to provide a broad definition that would cover emerging exotic derivatives. We shall discuss some common derivatives in brief to understand the accounting definition. *Discussion on all derivatives is outside the scope of this book.*

The most common derivatives are future and forward contracts, call option and put option, interest rate swap and currency swap.

Forward and future contracts

A forward contract is an agreement to buy or sell an asset at a certain future time for a certain price. One of the parties take a *long position* and agrees to buy the underlying asset and the other party assumes the *short position* and agrees to sell the asset.

NOTES

Future contract is similar to the forward contract. The difference between forward contract and future contract is that forward contracts are traded over the counter, while future contracts are traded on an exchange.

Forward contract in foreign exchange is very popular. In Illustration 10.1, we have given an example of an exporter who has taken a short position in a forward contract to sell US$ 50,000, which it will receive from the customer at a later date. The bank, which is the counterparty, takes the long position in the forward contract to buy the US$ 50,000. In a forward contract in foreign exchange, the importer takes the long position to purchase the foreign exchange at a future date, when the payment to the supplier will fall due, and the bank takes the short position.

The price of the forward contract at the time when it is entered is zero. The forward rate depends on the following factors:

(i) Time until delivery date in the forward contract;
(ii) Price of the underlying asset (e.g., US$) today (spot price); and
(iii) Risk-free rate of interest.

The value of the forward contract changes with the change in the forward rate. At a later stage, it may have a positive or negative value. For example, if the forward rate specified in a long forward contract is ₹60 and the forward rate with the same specified date today is ₹62, the value of the long forward contract is (₹62 – 60) or ₹2.

Forward and future contracts meet the accounting definition of derivative. As there is no initial investment, the value of the contracts varies with the price of the underlying asset (spot price) and the contracts are settled in future.

Call option and put option

A *call option* is an option to buy an asset (called underlying) at a certain price (called strike price) by a certain date (called, exercise date). A *put option* is an option to sell an asset at the strike price by the exercise date. The holder of the option has the right to exercise the option, but has no obligation. The writer (issuer) of the option has the obligation to deliver the asset, in case of call option, and buy the asset, in case of put option, if the holder exercises the option. The holder purchases the right at a price, which is called *option premium*.

For example, on March 22, 2018, when the share price of Infosys Limited (Infy.) is ₹1,161.30, call option on the shares with strike price of ₹1,300 and exercise date of May 31, 2018 is quoted at the price (called option premium) of ₹24. The investor will exercise the option only if the share price moves upward and exceeds ₹1,300. He/she will exercise the right to purchase the shares at ₹1,300 and will sell those in the market to gain from the difference between the then prevailing market price and ₹1,300. For example, if the share price moves to ₹1,500, his/her net gain will be (₹1,500 – 1,300 – 24) or ₹176 per share.

The investor has two options either to buy the call option or to buy the shares on March 22, 2018 and hold it till May 31, 2018. If the share price goes up to ₹1,500, he/she will gain (₹1,500 – 1,161.30) or ₹338.70, which is more than the gain from investing in the call option. But, the risk is that if the share price goes down, he/she loses.

The option price depends on the following factors:

(i) The current price of the share;
(ii) The strike price;
(iii) The time to expiration;
(iv) The volatility of the share price;
(v) The risk-free interest rate; and
(vi) The dividend expected over the life of the option.

If factors other than the share price do not change, the value of the option changes with the change in the price of the underlying share. In case of call option, the option value increases with the increase in share price and decreases with the decrease in share price. In case of put option, the option value decreases with the increase in share price and increases with the decrease in share price.

Call option and put option meet the accounting definition of derivative. The value changes with the change in the price of the underlying; the initial investment (option premium) is lower than the price of the underlying and is settled at a future date.

Interest rate swap

A single currency interest rate swap is a contractual agreement between two parties to exchange interest payments at regular intervals. The most common form of interest rate swap is a 'plain vanilla' type. A company agrees to pay cash flows equal to interest at a predetermined fixed rate on a notional principal for a number of years. In return, it receives interest at a floating rate on the same notional principal for the same period of time. The floating rate is tied to a reference rate, usually Mumbai Interbank Offered Rate (MIBOR). Principal payments are not exchanged in an interest rate swap.

Interest rate swaps provide a way for businesses to hedge their exposure to the changes in interest rates. If a company believes long-term interest rates are likely to rise, it can hedge its exposure to the interest rate changes by exchanging its floating rate payments for fixed rate payments.

For example, under the terms of their contract, A agrees to pay B MIBOR + 1% per month on principal amount (called the notional principal or notional amount) of ₹10,00,000, and B agrees to pay A 1.5% per month on the same notional amount.

An interest swap is worth zero, or close to zero, when it is first initiated. After it is in existence for some time, its value may become positive or negative. The value of the swap changes due to changes in the underlying interest rates. Thus, interest rate swap meets the accounting definition of derivative, as the initial investment is zero, the value changes with the change in the underlying variable (interest rates) and is settled at a future date.

Currency swap

Currency swap (also called cross-currency swap), in its simplest form, involves exchanging principal and interest payments in one currency for principal and interest payment in another. At the inception of the swap, the principal amounts in each currency are exchanged. Equivalent principal amounts are determined using the spot rate. During the length of the swap, each party pays the interest on the swapped principal amount. At the end of the swap, the principal amounts are swapped back at either the prevailing spot rate or a pre-agreed rate such as the rate of the original exchange of principals.

The purpose of a currency swap is to hedge exposure to exchange rate risk or reduce the cost of borrowing a foreign currency.

The value of currency swap at initiation is zero. Subsequently, valuation changes with the changes in forward exchange rate. Thus, currency rate swap meets the accounting definition of derivative; as the initial investment is zero, the value changes with the change in underlying variables (exchange rate) and is settled at a future date.

Embedded Derivatives

A derivative instrument that falls within the scope of Ind AS 109 need not be free-standing. Terms and conditions, which behave like a free-standing derivative, may be embedded in a financial instrument or non-financial contract, which is called the host contract. These derivatives are referred to as *embedded derivatives*. The combination of the host contract and the embedded derivative is a 'hybrid instrument'. An embedded derivative can modify the cash flows of the host contract because the derivative can be related to an exchange rate, commodity price or some other variable that frequently changes.

For example, any contract for the sale or purchase of a non-financial item that is denominated in a foreign currency (i.e., a currency other than the functional currency of the reporting entity) is likely to contain an embedded derivative. Another example of hybrid instrument is convertible bond, which is convertible into equity shares of the issuing company. In case of a convertible bond, the host contract is the bond liability and the embedded derivative is the convertible option.

NOTES

Separation of embedded derivative

Embedded derivatives in financial assets

Embedded derivatives in the host contract, which is a financial asset, is not separated and the entire hybrid (combined) contract is classified based on the accounting principles for classifying financial assets.

Embedded derivatives in financial liabilities

Embedded derivatives that are not closely related to the host contract, which is a financial liability, are separated and accounted for as stand-alone derivatives (i.e., measured at fair value, with changes in fair value recognised in profit or loss). An embedded derivative is not closely related if its economic characteristics and risks are different from those of the rest of the contract. Ind AS 109 sets out many examples to help determine when this test is (and is not) met.

The embedded derivative in a sale and purchase contract denominated in foreign currency is considered to be closely related to the host contract if and only if the contract is denominated in (i) the functional currency of any substantial party to the contract—usually the buyer and the seller; or (ii) the currency in which the related non-financial item is routinely denominated in the world; or (iii) a currency that is commonly used in contracts to purchase or sell non-financial items in the economic environment in which the transaction takes place.

ILLUSTRATION 19.5 Embedded Derivative—Import Order

On April 1, 2018, S Limited (SL), in Indian company (currency, INR) has entered into a contract to import goods from K Limited (KL), an UK company (currency, UK £) for US$ 1,00,000. The goods will be delivered on June 30, 2018.

Assume the following exchange rates:

Exchange rate on April 1, 2018: INR 65.12/US$

Three-month forward rate as at April 1, 2018: INR 65.82/US$

Spot rate at June 30, 2018: INR 65.70/US$

Required

Explain the embedded derivative in the purchase contract.

Solution

The embedded derivative is not closely related to the host contract, as the contract is denominated in US$, which is not the functional currency of either of the parties. The contract should be separated using three-month INR/Dollar forward exchange rate, as at the date of the contract (INR 65.82/US$). The two components of the contract are as follows:

(i) Purchase contract (Host): (1,00,000 × ₹65.82) or ₹65,82,000.

(ii) A three-month currency forward to sell US$ 1,00,000 at the forward rate of INR 65.82/US$.

The forward contract is a derivate contract and its value will change with the forward rate for selling US$ on June 30, 2018. At the maturity date of the forward contract, i.e., on June 30, 2018, the forward rate will be equal to the spot rate. As per the assumptions, it will be INR 65.70/US$. Therefore, on the maturity date, the derivative is an asset, and the cumulative gain is (₹65,82,000 – 65,70,000) or ₹12,000.

NOTES

SUMMARY

A financial instrument or other contract within the scope of Ind AS 109, with all three following characteristics is 'derivative':

(i) Its value changes in response to the change in one or more underlying;
(ii) It requires no initial net investment or an initial net investment that is smaller than would be required for other types of contracts that would be expected to have a similar response to the changes in market factors.
(iii) It is settled at a future date.

In the case of a non-financial variable, the variable should not be specific to a party to the contract in order to classify the contract as a derivative.

Commonly used derivatives fit into the accounting definition of derivative. Terms and conditions, which behave like a free-standing derivative, may be embedded in a financial instrument or non-financial contract, and it is called the host contract. These derivatives are referred to as embedded derivatives. The combination of the host contract and the embedded derivative is a 'hybrid instrument'. Embedded derivatives in the host contract, which is a financial asset, is not separated. Embedded derivatives in the host contract, which is a financial liability, is separated if it is not closely related to the host contract.

Self-Test Questions

Self-test question 19.4

Indicate whether the following statements are true (T) or false (F):

(i) Initial investment in a derivative instrument is insignificant.
(ii) A derivative instrument should necessarily be settled in cash.
(iii) Embedded derivative in a host contract, which is a financial asset, is not separated even if it is not closely related to the host contract.
(iv) Embedded derivative in a host contract, which is a financial liability, is not separated only if it is closely related to the host contract.
(v) Derivative contracts are always measured at fair value and gain or loss arising from the change in fair value is recognised in profit or loss.

CLASSIFICATION OF FINANCIAL ASSETS

Basic Categories

On initial recognition, a financial asset is classified into one of the three primary measurement categories:

(i) Measured at amortised cost;
(ii) Measured at fair value and changes in fair value recognised in other comprehensive income, in short, 'Fair Value through Other Comprehensive Income' (FVOCI); or
(iii) Measured at fair value and changes in fair value recognised in profit or loss, in short, 'Fair Value Through Profit or Loss' (FVTPL).

Financial assets measured at amortised cost

A financial asset is measured at amortised cost only if it meets both of the following conditions:

(i) The asset is held within a business model whose objective is to hold assets to collect contractual cash flows (Held-to-collect business model); and
(ii) The contractual terms of the financial asset give rise on specified dates to cash flows that are solely payment of principal and interest on the principal amount outstanding (SPPI criterion).

NOTES

Financial assets measured at FVOCI

A debt instrument is measured at FVOCI only if it meets both the following conditions:

(i) The asset is held within a business model whose objective is achieved by both collecting contractual cash flows and selling financial assets (both held-to collect and sale business model); and

(ii) The contractual terms of the financial asset meet the SPPI criterion.

Financial assets measured at FVTPL

Financial assets, which do not meet the criteria for classification as subsequently measured at either amortised cost or FVOCI, are classified as subsequently measured at fair value, with changes in fair value recognised in profit or loss.

Exceptions

In addition, Ind AS 109 provides options allowing an entity to, on initial recognition only, irrevocably designate:

(i) Financial assets, which would otherwise be classified at 'amortised cost' or FVOCI based on the general principles, at FVTPL if this designation would reduce or eliminate a so-called 'accounting mismatch';

(ii) Equity instruments, which would otherwise be classified at, FVTPL based on the general principles, at FVOCI category.

SUMMARY

Financial assets, which meet the SPPI criterion and are held within a business model whose objective is to hold assets to collect contractual cash flows, are classified as 'measured at amortised cost'. Financial assets, which meet the SPPI criterion and are held within a business model whose objective is achieved by both collecting contractual cash flows and selling financial assets are classified as 'measured at FVOCI'. All other financial assets are classified as 'measured at FVTPL'. Therefore, investment in equity should necessarily be classified as 'measured at FVTPL'. However, an entity has a choice to designate an investment in equity as 'measured at FVOCI'. The choice has to be made at the inception and irrevocably. The choice is not available to investment in equity held for trading.

Self-Test Questions

Self-test question 19.5

Indicate whether the following statements are true (T) or false (F):

(i) Investments in debt instruments, which satisfy the SPPI criterion and are held within the 'Held-to-collect business model' can be measured at amortised cost.

(ii) Investments in equity instruments cannot meet the SPPI criterion.

(iii) An entity has an option to classify investment in equity held for trading as 'measured at FVOCI'.

(iv) Investment in debt instruments held for trading should necessarily be classified as 'measured at FVTPL'.

(v) An entity may irrevocably designate financial assets, which would otherwise be classified at 'amortised cost' or FVOCI based on the general principles, at FVTPL if this designation would reduce or eliminate a so-called 'accounting mismatch'.

SPPI Criterion

SPPI stands for 'solely payments of principal and interest on principal amount outstanding'.

Contractual cash flows that meet the SPPI criterion are consistent with a *basic lending arrangement*. In such arrangements, consideration for the time value of money and credit risks are typically the most significant elements of interest.

Principal

'Principal' is the fair value of the financial asset on initial recognition. However, the principal may change over time, for example, on repayment of a part of the principal. The definition of principal suggests that the holder of the financial asset should assess SPPI criterion with reference to the contractual cash flows to the amount that it actually invested.

Interest

'Interest' is consideration for time value of money, for the credit risk associated with the principal amount outstanding during a particular period of time and for other basic lending risks (e.g., liquidity risk) and costs (e.g., administrative costs) as well as profit margin that is consistent with a basic lending arrangement. A bond or a loan with variable rate of interest meets the SPPI criterion if the interest rate is established taking into consideration only the above factors.

In extreme economic circumstances, interest can be negative. Negative interest rates have been a real phenomenon in some jurisdictions in recent years.

Modified time value of money

In some cases, the 'time value of money' element in establishing the interest rate is modified in a way that it does not reflect a normal relationship between the time value element and the time period (or maturity) of the instrument. One example of a modified time value element is a loan or bond in which the interest rate resets periodically, but based on a market rate that reflects a longer or shorter time period (e.g., a monthly reset based on a benchmark interest rate for a 12-month loan). In those cases, analysis to assess whether the financial asset meets the SPPI criterion is complicated. The holder of the financial asset is required to assess how different the contractual (undiscounted) cash flows could be from the (undiscounted) cash flows that would arise if the time value of money element was not modified (the benchmark cash flows).

Hybrid instrument

A loan or a bond may not meet the SPPI criterion if it is a hybrid instrument with embedded derivatives. However, it is not necessarily so. Cash flows from bonds or loans with additional features should be examined carefully to assess whether the financial asset meets the SPPI criterion.

Prepayment option

A bond or loan with prepayment option meets the SPPI criterion if the prepayment feature permits the issuer (i.e., debtor) to prepay the debt instrument or permits the holder (i.e., creditor) to put the instrument back to the issuer before maturity; and whose prepayment amount substantially represents unpaid amount of principal and interest on the principal amount outstanding, which may include reasonable additional compensation for the early termination of the contract. For example, home loan with prepayment option, which is a financial asset for the bank that has disbursed the loan (creditor), usually meets the SPPI criterion. In the home loan arrangement, the borrower (the debtor) has the option to prepay the loan before maturity and the prepayment amount is principal and interest on the principal amount outstanding.

Term extension feature

A bond or loan with term extension feature meets the SPPI criterion if the term extension feature permits the issuer (i.e., debtor) or the holder (i.e., creditor) to extend the term of the debt instrument; and results in contractual cash flows during the extension period that are 'solely payments of principal and interest on principal amount outstanding', which may include reasonable additional compensation for the extension of the contract.

NOTES

CASE STUDY 19.2 SPPI Criterion — Mandatory Prepayment Terms

C D Limited (CDL) issued a bond to G H Limited (GHL). As per the terms of the contract, CDL will mandatorily redeem the bond at par in the event of covenant violation or a downgrade. The prepayment amount substantially represents unpaid amounts of principal and interest on the principal amount outstanding.

Question

The CFO of GHL seeks your advice on whether the financial asset (bond issued by CDL) that it holds meets the SPPI criterion.

Solution

The financial asset (bond) meets the SPPI criterion because the mandatory redemption feature protects the holder (GHL) against credit deterioration of the issuer (CDL) and the prepayment amount substantially represents unpaid amounts of principal and interest on the principal amount outstanding.

CASE STUDY 19.3 SPPI Criterion — Prepayment at Fair Value

N K Limited (NKL) acquires a bond at par. The bond contains a put option. The put option gives the issuer the right to redeem the bond before maturity at the fair value of the bond on the date of redemption. Fair value will be determined by discounting future contractual cash flows (principal and interest) at the current market rate.

Question

The CFO of NKL seeks your advice on whether the bond meets the SPPI criterion.

Solution

The bond does not meet the SPPI criterion, as the prepayment amount does not represent unpaid amount of principal and interest. For example, the fair value of the bond may fall due to deterioration in the creditworthiness of the issuer. In that case, the holder (NKL) will suffer a loss and will not be compensated for the time value of money and credit risk during the period the bond is in issue.

Leverage

Leverage enhances the volatility in return on investment and is often used to enlarge the potential return on investment. Financial assets fail to meet the SPPI criterion if the contractual terms introduce exposures to risks or volatility in the contractual cash flows that are unrelated to a basic lending arrangement such as exposure to changes in equity prices or commodity prices. For example, a bond fails to meet the SPPI criterion if interest resets periodically to an amount as fixed margin plus twice the published rate of MIBOR, as the interest is leveraged.

CASE STUDY 19.4 SPPI Criterion — Change In Payment Terms

On April 1, 2018, F S Limited (FSL) acquired a bond, which is issued by D K Limited (DKL), with coupon rate of 10% per annum. The interest is payable on March 31 every year. The bond will mature after five years. As per the terms of the contract, the coupon rate will increase to 20% per annum if the issuer (DKL) defaults in annual interest payment.

NOTES

Question

The CFO of FSL seeks your advice on whether the bond meets the SPPI criterion.

Solution

The contingent event that will give rise to increase in the interest rate is the failure of DKL to pay annual interest, which reflects the increase in the credit risk associated with the financial instrument. As the credit risk associated with the principle amount outstanding during a particular period of time is one of the components of interest, the nature of the contingent event is consistent with the SPPI criterion. The contingent event does not provide evidence of leverage or other feature that will make the bond to fail the test for SPPI criterion.

The bond meets the SPPI criterion.

Equity investments

Investments in equity instruments always 'fail' to meet the SPPI criterion. They must be classified at FVTPL category. However, as an exception, the accounting standard provides a choice to entities to classify those investments at FVOCI category at the inception and irrevocably. However, the choice is not available for investments held for trading.

Contractually linked instruments

The payments on some financial assets are contractually linked to the payments received on a pool of other instruments. These are referred to as *contractually linked instruments*. Unit of mutual funds is an example of contractually linked instruments. Another example is units issued by special purpose entities (SPEs) in various tranches, with the more senior tranches being repaid in priority to the more junior ones.

In order to assess whether the contractually linked instrument meets the SPPI criterion, the investors should take 'look through' approach. This approach looks at the terms of the instrument itself, as well as through to the pool of underlying instruments to assess both the characteristics of these underlying instruments and the tranche's exposure to credit risk relative to the pool of underlying instruments.

To measure an individual tranche at amortised cost, the following conditions must be fulfilled:

(i) The tranche itself (without looking through to the pool of underlying instruments) meets the SPPI criterion;

(ii) The underlying pool must contain one or more instruments which have contractual cash flows that are SPPI and the pool may contain instruments such as derivatives that reduce the cash flow variability of the instruments; and

(iii) The credit risk of the tranche must be equal to or lower than the weighted average credit risk of the underlying pool of financial instruments.

CASE STUDY 19.5 SPPI Criterion—Close-Ended Debt Mutual Fund

UV Limited (UVL) has invested in units issued by a close-ended mutual fund. The fund holds only debt instruments that themselves would qualify for amortised cost classification under Ind AS 109 had these instruments been directly held by the unit holder. The objective of the fund is to hold the assets to maturity rather than to realise fair value changes.

Question

The CFO of UVL seeks your advice on whether the company can measure the investment at amortised cost.

Solution

The investment is in close-ended debt fund. Therefore, cash flows from the unit to the holder meets the SPPI criterion and the investment is held in 'held to collect' business model (see Table 19.1). UVL may be able to measure its investment at amortised cost. However, if the fund

NOTES

does not hold debt instruments, UVL will not be able to measure its investment at amortised cost.

TABLE 19.1

Key Features of Business Models

Business model	Key features	Classification
Held to collect	(i) The objective is to collect contractual cash flows over the life of the instrument; (ii) Sales are incidental; and (iii) It involves lowest level of sales (in frequency and volume) than sales in other business models.	Measured at amortised cost, provided the SPPI criterion is met
Both held to collect and for sale	(i) Financial assets are managed to achieve a particular objective by both collecting contractual cash flows and selling the assets; and (ii) It involves more sales (in frequency and volume) than sales in 'held to collect' business model.	Measured at FVOCI, provided the SPPI criterion is met
Other Business models	The collection of contractual cash flows is incidental. Examples of such business models are: (i) trading; (ii) managing assets on a fair value basis; and (iii) maximising cash flows through sale	Measured at FVTPL; SPPI criterion is irrelevant

Investment in mutual funds

Investments in open-ended mutual funds, including debt funds and liquid funds, and close-ended equity mutual funds always 'fail' to meet the SPPI criterion. They must be classified at FVTPL category. The choice available to classify investments in equity at FVOCI category is not available in case of investment in mutual fund.

Derivatives

Stand-alone option, forward and swap contracts include leverage, and therefore, always 'fail' to meet the SPPI criterion. They must be classified at FVTPL category.

SUMMARY

Contractual cash flows that meet the SPPI criterion are consistent with a ***basic lending arrangement***. In such an arrangement, consideration for the time value of money and credit risks are typically the most significant elements of interest. 'Interest' is consideration for time value of money, for the credit risk associated with the principal amount outstanding during a particular period of time and for other basic lending risks (e.g., liquidity risk) and costs (e.g., administrative costs) as well as profit margin that is consistent with a basic lending arrangement. A bond or a loan with variable rate of interest meets the SPPI criterion if the interest rate is established taking into consideration only the above factors. A loan or a bond may not meet the SPPI criterion if it is a hybrid instrument with embedded derivatives. However, it is not necessarily so. A bond or loan with prepayment option meets the SPPI criterion if prepayment amount substantially represents unpaid amount of principal and interest on the principal amount outstanding, which may include reasonable additional compensation for the early termination of the contract. A bond or loan with term extension feature meets the SPPI criterion if the contractual cash flows during the extension period meet the SPPI criterion. Financial assets fail to meet the SPPI criterion if the contractual terms introduce exposures to risks or volatility in the contractual cash flows that are unrelated to a basic lending arrangement such as exposure to changes in equity prices or commodity prices.

Self-Test Questions

Self-test question 19.6

Indicate whether the following statements are true (T) or false (F):

(i) In basic lending arrangements, consideration for the time value of money and credit risks are typically the most significant elements of interest.

(ii) Debt instruments with floating rate of interest do not meet the SPPI criterion.

(iii) Home loan with prepayment option may or may not meet the SPPI criterion.

(iv) Close-ended equity mutual funds always 'fail' to meet the SPPI criterion.

(v) Financial assets fail to meet the SPPI criterion if the contractual terms introduce exposures to risks or volatility in the contractual cash flows that are unrelated to a basic lending arrangement.

Business Model Test

The classification of debt instruments (e.g., bond and loan) that meets SPPI criterion are based on the Business model for managing those instruments. Debt instruments that do not meet the SPPI criterion are classified at FVTPL, irrespective of the Business model.

Business model refers to how the entity manages its financial assets in order to generate cash flows. Table 19.1 presents the key features of each type of business model and the resultant classification.

Generally, an entity's Business model is a matter of fact that can be observed from the way in which the entity is managed, and from the information provided to the management. When an entity assesses the Business model for newly originated or newly purchased financial assets, it must consider information about how cash flows were realised in the past, along with all other relevant information.

Not an instrument-by-instrument approach

An entity's Business model does not depend on management's intentions for an individual instrument. It is determined at a level that reflects how groups of financial assets are managed together to achieve a particular business objective. Accordingly, the 'Business model' condition is not an instrument-by-instrument approach to classification and should be determined on a higher level of aggregation.

Not at the reporting entity level

A single entity may have more than one Business model for managing its financial instruments. Consequently, classification need not be determined at the reporting entity level.

Objective evidence

The top management determines the Business model by considering all relevant and objective evidence. It includes:

(i) how performance is evaluated and reported to the entity's key management personnel;

(ii) the risks affecting performance of the Business model and how those risks are managed; and

(iii) how managers of the business are compensated (e.g., whether compensation is based on fair value of assets managed or on contractual cash flows collected).

'Worst-case' or 'stressed case scenarios' not to be considered

Business model assessment is not performed on the basis of scenarios that the entity does not reasonably expect to occur, such as so-called 'worst case' or 'stress case' scenarios. For

NOTES

example, if an entity expects that it will sell a particular portfolio of financial assets only in a stress case scenario, that scenario would not affect the assessment of the Business model for those assets if the entity reasonably expects that such a scenario will not occur.

Realisation of cash flows different from expectations

If cash flows are realised in a way that is different from the entity's expectations at the date that the entity assessed the Business model (for example, if the entity sells more or fewer financial assets than it expected when it classified the assets), that does not give rise to a prior period error in the entity's financial statements nor does it change the classification of the remaining financial assets held in that Business model (i.e., those assets that the entity recognised in prior periods and still holds) as long as the entity considered all relevant information that was available at the time it made the Business model assessment.

Reclassification

Reclassification of financial assets is required when and only when an entity changes its Business model for managing the assets. In such a case, the entity is required to reclassify all affected financial assets. Such changes are expected to be very infrequent and are determined by senior management as a result of external or internal changes. The changes must be significant to the entity's operations and demonstrable to external parties. In order for this to be the case, an entity will need to either begin or terminate an activity that is significant to its operations.

Examples of change in Business model

The following are the examples of change in Business model:

(i) An entity holds a portfolio of commercial loans for sale. Subsequently, it acquires an entity whose Business model is to hold similar loans in order to collect contractual cash flows. The commercial loans originally held for sale are transferred to the acquired entity to be managed together with the entity's other loans.

(ii) An entity decides to shut down a part of its business.

Examples of changes that do not represent change in business model

(i) Change in intention related to particular financial assets (even in circumstances of significant changes in market conditions)

(ii) The temporary disappearance of a particular market for financial assets

(iii) A transfer of financial assets between parts of the entity with different Business models.

Reclassification date

When an entity reclassifies financial assets, the reclassification is to be prospective from the reclassification date, which is the first day of the first reporting period following the applicable change in Business model.

Previously recognised gains or losses (including ones relating to impairment) and interest are not to be restated.

Financial Assets held for Trading

Financial assets held for trading are classified at FVTPL category. A financial asset or financial liability is 'held or trading' if it:

(i) is acquired or incurred principally for the purpose of selling or repurchasing it in the near term;

(ii) on initial recognition is part of a portfolio of identified financial instruments that are managed together and for which there is evidence of a recent actual pattern of short-term profit-taking; or

(iii) is a derivative (except for a derivative that is a financial guarantee contract or a designated and effective hedging instrument).

Entities, as a part of treasury management, hold financial assets for trading. Stock brokers hold financial assets for trading. Shares borrowed for short-selling is an example of liability held for trading.

SUMMARY

Business model refers to how the entity manages its financial assets in order to generate cash flows. There are three types of Business model—Held to collect; both held to collect and for sale; and other Business models where collection of cash is incidental such as trading, managing assets on a fair value basis, and maximising cash flows through sale. The 'Business model' condition is not an instrument-by-instrument approach to classification and should be determined on a higher level of aggregation. However, classification need not be determined at the reporting entity level. Business model assessment is not performed on the basis of scenarios that the entity does not reasonably expect to occur such as so-called 'worst case' or 'stress case' scenarios. Changes in business model which requires reclassification are expected to be very infrequent and are determined by senior management as a result of external or internal changes.

Self-Test Questions

Self-test question 19.7

Indicate whether the following statements are true (T) or false (F):

(i) An entity is not permitted to sell a financial instrument held within the 'held to collect' Business model.

(ii) An entity cannot have more than one Business model for managing financial assets.

(iii) If the entity sells more or fewer financial assets than it expected when it classified the assets, it is required to reclassify the remaining financial assets in the Business model.

(iv) Generally, an entity's Business model is a matter of fact that can be observed from the way in which the entity is managed, and from the information provided to the management.

(v) A derivative instrument is always classified as 'held for trading'.

MEASUREMENT OF FINANCIAL ASSETS

Initial Measurement

Financial assets that are classified as FVTPL are initially measured at fair value. Financial assets that are classified at 'amortised cost' or at FVOCI are initially measured at fair value plus transaction costs that are directly attributable to the acquisition. Normally, the transaction price is the best evidence of fair value.

Day one gain or loss

If the transaction price differs from fair value, the difference is recognised immediately as a gain or loss ('day one gain or loss') when the fair value is estimated based on observable inputs. If the fair value is measured using inputs that are not observable, the difference is deferred by way of adjustments to the carrying amount of the financial asset. The deferred difference is subsequently recognised as a gain or loss only to the extent that it arises from a change in a factor (including time) that market participants would consider in setting a price.

In practice, the difference between the fair value and transaction price is recognised in profit or loss.

Trade receivables

Trade receivables that do not have a significant financing component are measured at initial recognition at their transaction price.

Trade receivables with significant financing component are measured at fair value. Therefore, difference may arise between the initial amount of revenue recognised (cash selling price) and the fair value of trade receivables recognised at the date of initial recognition. The difference is recognised as expense (e.g., impairment loss).

If at contract inception, the entity expects that the period between when the entity transfers a promised good or service to a customer and when the customer pays for that good or service will be one year or less, as a practical expedient, it need not adjust the promised amount of consideration for the effects of a significant financing component. If the entity applies the practical expedient, then the trade receivable is measured at the initial recognition at the transaction price.

Subsequent Measurement

The recognition and presentation of gain and losses for each measurement category is presented in Table 19.2:

TABLE 19.2

Subsequent Measurement of Financial Assets

Measurement Category	Recognition and Presentation of Income, Gains and Losses
Amortised cost	*Recognition in the statement of profit and loss:* (i) Interest revenue using the effective interest rate method; (ii) Impairment losses (expected credit losses) and reversals; and (iii) Foreign exchange gain and losses. When the financial asset is derecognised, the gain or loss is recognised in profit or loss.
FVOCI (Debt instruments)	(A) *Recognition in other comprehensive income and accumulation under other equity in the balance sheet:* (i) Gains and losses from changes in fair value When the financial asset is derecognised, the cumulative gains and losses accumulated under 'other equity' are reclassified to profit or loss. (B) *Recognition in profit or loss:* (i) Interest revenue using the effective interest method; (ii) Impairment losses (expected credit losses) and reversals; and (iii) Foreign exchange gain and losses
FVOCI (Equity instruments)	(A) *Recognition in other comprehensive income and accumulation under other equity in the balance sheet:* (i) Gains and losses from changes in fair value The cumulative gains and losses accumulated under 'other equity' are *not reclassified* to profit or loss under any circumstances. When the financial asset is derecognised, the amount may be transferred to other components of 'other equity' (e.g., general reserve). (B) *Recognition in profit or loss:* (i) Dividend incomes unless they clearly represent a repayment of part of the cost of the investment.
FVTPL	*Recognition in profit or loss:* (i) Gains and losses from changes in fair value When the financial asset is derecognised, the gain or loss is recognised in profit or loss.

NOTES

Effective interest rate method

Effective interest rate method is a method of calculating the amortised cost of a financial asset or financial liability and allocating the interest income and expense over the relevant period.

The effective interest rate is calculated on initial recognition of a financial asset or financial liability.

Effective interest rate is the rate that exactly discounts future cash flows through the expected life of the financial instrument to:

(i) the gross carrying amount of the financial asset; or
(ii) the amortised cost of the financial liability.

On initial recognition, the gross carrying amount of a financial asset, or the amortised cost of a financial liability, is generally equal to the fair value of the instrument, adjusted for transaction costs. In case of financial asset, transaction costs are added to the fair value. In case of financial liability, transaction costs are deducted from the fair value.

Calculation of the effective interest rate includes:

(i) All fees paid or received between parties to the contract that are integral part of the effective interest rate.
(ii) Transaction costs; and
(iii) All other premiums and discounts.

The following are the examples of fees, which relate to a financial asset recognised in the balance sheet and are adjusted to effective interest rate:

(i) Origination and commitment fee, when it is probable that the entity will enter into a specific lending agreement;
(ii) Compensation from the borrower for transaction costs incurred by the lender; and
(iii) Appraisal fee for evaluating collateral.

The difference between the effective interest for a given period and the coupon rate is amortisation (or accretion) during that period of the difference between the initial measurement of the instrument and the maturity amount.

ILLUSTRATION 19.6 Effective Interest Rate Calculation

K Bank Limited (KBL) has granted ₹50,000 loan to S D Limited (SDL) on April 1, 2017. SDL has paid an up-front fee of ₹1,000. The net loan proceeds is ₹49,000. The coupon rate is 10% per annum, payable on March 31 every year, starting from March 31, 2018. The loan is repayable at the end of the fifth year.

Required

Calculate the effective interest rate and the gross carrying amount of the instrument.

Solution

Cash flows associated with the financial instruments are ₹5,000 at the end of first four years and ₹55,000 at the end of the fifth year. The Internal Rate of Return (IRR) is 10.53482% per annum, which equates the present value (PV) of cash flows to ₹49,000. Therefore, the effective interest rate is 10.53482% per annum.

(Amount in ₹)

Date	Interest (10.53482%)	Cash flows	Gross carrying amount
April 1, 2017			49,000
March 31, 2018	5,162	5,000	49,162
March 31, 2019	5,179	5,000	49,341
March 31, 2020	5,198	5,000	49,539
March 31, 2021	5,219	5,000	49.758
March 31, 2022	5,242	55,000	—
Total	20,000	75,000	

NOTES

ILLUSTRATION 19.7 Effective Interest Rate Calculation—Prepayment—Recognition of Revenue/Expense

K Bank Limited (KBL) has granted ₹50,000 loan to S D Limited (SDL) on April 1, 2017. SDL has paid an up-front fee of ₹1,000. The net loan proceeds is ₹49,000. The coupon rate is 10% per annum, payable on March 31 every year, starting from March 31, 2018. The loan is repayable at the end of the fifth year. SDL has the option of prepaying the loan. Based on discussion between KBL and SDL on March 31, 2018, it is estimated that SDL will pay ₹20,000 towards the principal amount on March 31, 2019 and the balance ₹30,000 on maturity.

Required

Calculate the effective interest rate, interest income/interest expense and the gross carrying amount of the instrument.

Solution

The effective interest rate is calculated at the inception. It is 10.53482% per annum, which equates the PV of estimated cash flows (as per contract) to ₹49,000.

The gross carrying amount as at March 31, 2018 is the PV as at March 31, 2018 of estimated future cash flows by the effective interest rate of 10.53482% per annum. The estimated cash flows are ₹25,000 on March 31, 2019, ₹3,000 on March 31, 2020 and on March 31, 2021 and ₹3,300 on March 31, 2022.

The interest amount should be recognised as revenue by KBL and as expense by SDL.

(Amount in ₹)

Date	Interest (10.53482%)	Cash flows	Gross carrying amount
April 1, 2017			49,000
March 31, 2018	5,162	5,000	49,400
March 31, 2019	5,204	20,000 + 5,000	29,604
March 31, 2020	3,119	3,000	29,723
March 31, 2021	3,131	3,000	29,854
March 31, 2022	3,145	30,000 + 3,000	—
Total	19,761	69,000	

SUMMARY

Financial assets that are classified as FVTPL are initially measured at fair value. Financial assets that are classified at 'amortised cost' or at FVOCI are initially measured at fair value plus transaction costs that are directly attributable to the acquisition. Normally, the transaction price is the best evidence of fair value. In case of financial assets that are classified as 'measured at amortised cost', the following are recognised in profit or loss:

Interest revenue using the effective interest method; impairment losses (expected credit losses) and reversals; and foreign exchange gain and losses. When the financial asset is derecognised, the gain or loss is recognised in the profit or loss.

In case of financial assets, other than investments in equity, that are classified as 'measured at FVOCI', gains and losses arising from the change in fair value are recognised in OCI and accumulated under 'other equity' in the balance sheet. When the financial asset is derecognised, the cumulative gains and losses accumulated under 'other equity' are reclassified to profit or loss. The following are recognised in profit or loss:

Interest revenue using the effective interest method; impairment losses (expected credit losses) and reversals; and foreign exchange gain and losses.

In case of investments in equity, that are classified as 'measured at FVOCI', gains and losses arising from the change in fair value are recognised in OCI and accumulated under 'other equity' in the balance sheet. The cumulative gains and losses accumulated under 'other equity' are *not reclassified* to profit or loss under any circumstances. When the financial asset is derecognised, the amount may be transferred to other components of 'other equity' (e.g., general reserve). Dividend incomes unless they clearly represent a repayment of part of the cost of the investment are recognised in profit or loss.

In case of financial assets, that are classified as 'measured at FVTPL' gains and losses from changes in fair value are recognised in profit or loss. When the financial asset is derecognised, the gain or loss is recognised in profit or loss.

Self-Test Questions

Self-test question 19.8

Indicate whether the following statements are true (T) or false (F):

(i) Effective interest rate is established at the inception of recognising a financial asset classified as 'measured at amortised cost' or recognising a financial liability that is not classified as 'measured at FVOCI'.

(ii) Use of effective interest rate method results in amortisation of premium, discount and fees over the life of the financial asset or financial liability, as the case may be.

(iii) Effective interest rate on an investment acquired at a discount over the face value is higher than the coupon rate.

(iv) Effective interest rate established at the inception is changed if the asset that is classified as 'measured at amortised cost' is impaired.

(v) Effective interest rate established at the inception is changed when the borrower prepays a part of the amount outstanding against borrowing.

RECOGNITION AND DERECOGNITION OF FINANCIAL INSTRUMENTS

Recognition

An entity recognises a financial instrument in the balance sheet when it becomes a party to contract that is a financial instrument.

An entity becomes a party to the contract when it commits to purchase securities or agrees to enter into derivatives. On the other hand, an entity does not become a party to the contract when it plans (but not commits) purchase of securities, even if it is highly probable that it will commit purchase of those securities.

An entity does not become a party to the contract until its offer to buy or sell financial instruments is accepted by the counterparty.

Applying the above recognition principle, transactions in regulated markets (e.g., stock exchanges) should be accounted for on the trade date. However, in practice, many financial institutions and other entities use settlement date accounting for financial assets.

Derecognition

Ind AS 109 contains specific provisions for the derecognition of financial assets. Application of those provisions requires understanding the cash flows associated with the financial asset and involves judgement. Detailed discussion of the provisions and application issues is outside the scope of this text. In this section, we provide a brief overview of the principles for derecognising financial assets.

Determining the financial asset subject to derecognition

A financial asset or a group of similar financial assets can be broken down into various parts that can be segregated. For example, cash flows from a debt instrument can be segregated

NOTES

into principal and interest. Those can be transferred separately to other parties. The term *'interest only strip'* is used to refer to a security where the holder receives the non-principal portion of the monthly payments on the underlying mortgages, treasury bonds or other bonds. *'Principal only strip'* is a fixed-income security where the holder receives the non-interest portion of the monthly payments on the underlying loan pool.

The first step in applying the derecognition principle is to identify the financial asset subject to possible derecognition. It could be the entire financial asset or a group of similar financial assets or the following cash flows from the financial asset or a group of similar financial assets:

(i) Specifically identified, for example, interest only strip;

(ii) Fully proportionate (pro rata) share, for example, when an entity enters into an arrangement whereby the counterparty obtains the rights to a 90% share of all cash flows of a debt instrument; or

(iii) Fully proportionate share of specifically identified cash flows, for example, when an entity enters into an arrangement whereby the counterparty obtains the rights to 90% share of the interest cash flows from a financial asset.

In subsequent references to 'the financial asset' in this section, it refers to a financial asset, a part of a financial asset, a portfolio of financial assets or a part of portfolio of financial assets.

Derecognition criteria

A financial asset qualifies for derecognition either if the contractual rights to cash flows from the financial asset expire or if an entity transfers a financial asset in a transfer that meets the criteria for derecognition specified in the standard (Ind AS 109).

Contractual rights to cash flows have expired

When the contractual rights to cash flows from the asset have expired, that asset is derecognised.

Modification of terms

A financial asset may be modified or replaced as a part of transaction with the same counterparty. For example, in case of restructuring of loan by a bank, the contract terms are modified. In that situation, the holder of the financial asset (bank in case of loan) performs a quantitative and qualitative evaluation of whether the cash flows of the original financial asset and the modified or replacement financial asset are substantially different. If the cash flows are substantially different, the contractual right to cash flows from the original financial asset should be deemed to have expired.

Quantitative assessment

Terms are considered to have been substantially modified when the net present value of the cash flows under the new terms, including the fees received net of fees paid and discounted using the original effective interest rate (of the original debt instrument) differs by at least 10% from the value of the remaining cash flows under the original terms.

Qualitative assessment

Modification in financial asset may result in the modified cash flows not meeting the SPPI criterion even though the original cash flows did so, or vice versa.

Evaluating whether there is a transfer

An entity transfers a financial asset if and only if it transfers the contractual rights to receive the cash flows of the financial asset or it enters into a qualifying pass-through arrangement.

Transfer of contractual rights

The transfer of legal title, without additional restrictions being imposed as a result of the transfer, should result in transfer of the existing rights associated with the financial asset. The assessment is generally straightforward. For example, sale of an investment in a corporate bond or equity issued by another entity results in transfer of legal title. Sale of loan by a bank to an Asset Reconstruction Company (ARC) without additional restrictions results in transfer of the existing rights associated with the financial asset.

A transferor may continue to administer or provide servicing of assets that it has previously transferred to another entity. For example, a transferor, as an agent of the transferee, may continue to collect the cash flows of receivables that it has transferred.

Pass-through arrangement

In a 'pass-through arrangement' an entity retains the contractual rights to the cash flows of a financial asset and also, assumes a contractual obligation to pay the cash flows to the transferee. A typical situation in which a pass-through arrangement may exist is in a securitisation involving structured entities.

Securitisation is the process of conversion of the existing assets (e.g., car loans and housing loans) or future cash flows (e.g., ticket sales and credit card payments) into marketable securities. The conversion of the existing assets into marketable securities is known as *asset-backed securitisation*, and the conversion of future cash flows into marketable securities is known as *future-flows securitisation*. The 'originator' (e.g., bank) transfers the assets to a Special Purpose Vehicle (SPV). The SPV is a separate entity formed exclusively for the facilitation of the securitisation process and providing funds to the originator. The SPV acts as an intermediary. It divides the assets transferred by the originator into marketable securities. The SPV issues these securities, which are known as Pass-Through Certificates (PTCs). The cash flows received from the obligors (e.g., borrowers) are passed onto the investors, who have invested in the PTCs, on a pro rata basis once the service fees has been deducted.

A 'pass-through arrangement' is considered a transfer if and only if:

(i) The entity has no obligation to pay amounts to the transferee unless the entity collects equivalent amounts from the original financial asset;

(ii) The entity is prohibited from selling or pledging the original financial asset under the terms of the pass-through arrangement; and

(iii) The entity is obliged to remit all the cash flows that it collects without material delay.

Risks and rewards evaluation

The entity that transfers a financial asset evaluates whether it has transferred or retained risks and rewards of ownership of the financial asset. The entity derecognises the financial asset if it has transferred substantially all the risks and rewards of ownership of the financial asset. The entity continues to recognise the financial asset if it has retained substantially all the risks and rewards of ownership of the financial asset.

In case of the transferred financial asset for which it has neither transferred nor retained substantially all the risks and rewards of ownership, the entity evaluates whether it has retained control of that asset. The entity derecognises the asset if it has not retained control of the asset. If the entity has retained control, then it continues to recognise the asset to the extent of its continuing involvement in the asset.

Analysis of risks and rewards

The risks and rewards analysis is performed by comparing the entity's exposure, before and after the transfer, to the variability in the Present Value (PV) of the future cash flows from the financial asset.

Ind AS 109 does not provide any quantitative guidance on what constitutes 'substantially all' of the risks and rewards of the financial asset.

NOTES

CASE STUDY 19.6 Transfer of Risks and Rewards

PP Limited (PPL) transfers short-term receivables of ₹1,000 crore to JJ Limited (JJL) for ₹950 crore. The only significant risk associated with the financial asset is credit risk. The default rates are as follows:

(i) Expected credit loss: 5% of the receivables (₹1,000 crore); and

(ii) Likely range of losses: 4.5% to 6% at the 99.9% confidence interval.

PPL provides a guarantee to reimburse JJL for losses exceeding 6%.

Question

The CFO of PPL seeks your advice on whether PPL has transferred risks and rewards associated with the financial asset substantially to JJL.

Solution

PPL has transferred the reward associated with the financial asset, as actual credit losses may be less than the expected credit losses of 5%. PPL has transferred the risk to JJL, as it will compensate JJL for actual credit losses exceeding 6%, which is unlikely. PPL has transferred the risks and rewards substantially, as after transfer, it is not exposed to variability in cash flows within the range of reasonably possible outcomes.

CASE STUDY 19.7 Transfer of Risks and Rewards

PP Limited (PPL) transfers short-term receivables of ₹1,000 crore to JJ Limited (JJL) for ₹950 crore. The only significant risk associated with the financial asset is credit risk. The default rates are as follows:

(i) Expected credit loss: 5% of the receivables (₹1,000 crore); and

(ii) Likely range of losses: 4.5% to 6% at the 99.9% confidence interval.

PPL provides a guarantee to reimburse JJL for any loss it will suffer due to non-recovery of receivables.

Question

The CFO of PPL seeks your advice on whether PPL has transferred risks and rewards associated with the financial asset substantially to JJL.

Solution

PPL has transferred the reward associated with the financial asset, as actual credit losses may be less than the expected credit losses of 5%. However, PPL has not transferred the risk to JJL, as it will compensate JJL for actual credit losses. PPL has not transferred the risks and rewards substantially.

CASE STUDY 19.8 Transfer of Risks and Rewards

NM Limited (NML) transfers long-term mortgage receivables to KL Limited (KLL). It transfers prepayment/late-payment and interest rate risks while retaining the credit risk. Both the credit risk and combined prepayment/late-payment and interest rate risks are significant.

Question

The CFO of NML seeks your advice on whether NML has transferred risks and rewards associated with the financial asset substantially to KLL.

Solution

NML has not transferred risk to KLL substantially, as it has retained the credit risk that is considered significant. It has transferred prepayment/late-payment and interest rate risks, which together constitute significant risk. Therefore, it is concluded that NML has neither retained nor transferred rewards and risks associated with the financial asset substantially to KLL.

Control

The entity looses controll in a transferred financial asset if the transferee has the practical ability to sell unilaterally the transferred financial asset in its entirety to an unrelated third party without needing to impose additional restrictions on sale.

If there is an active market for the financial asset, usually, the transferee has the practical ability to sell the asset. In the absence of an active market, the transferee does not have the practical ability to sell the asset if it may have to return the asset to the transferor.

CASE STUDY 19.9 Transfer of Control

NM Limited (NML) transfers long-term mortgage receivables to KL Limited (KLL). It transfers prepayment/late-payment and interest rate risks while retaining the credit risk. Both the credit risk and combined prepayment/late-payment and interest rate risks are significant. In order to maintain customer relationship, NML has imposed a condition that KLL will not sell the asset to a third party.

Question

The CFO of NML seeks your advice on whether NML has transferred risks and rewards associated with the financial asset substantially to KLL and whether NML has transferred control on the asset to KLL.

Solution

NML has neither retained nor transferred rewards and risks associated with the financial asset substantially to KLL. It has retained control on the asset, as it has imposed a condition preventing KLL from selling the asset to a third party.

CASE STUDY 19.10 Transfer of Control

GF Limited (GFL) sells a portfolio of corporate loan to TF Limited (TFL) without any condition, but with a call option, which gives GFL the right to repurchase the financial asset after five years.

Question

The CFO of GFL seeks your advice on whether GFL has transferred control of the financial asset sold to TFL.

Solution

There is no condition preventing TFL from selling the asset unilaterally. However, if GFL exercises the option, TFL will have to return the asset to GFL. Usually, there is no active market for portfolio of corporate loans. Therefore, it is not practical for TFL to sell the asset and repurchase the same if GFL exercises the option. Consequently, if TFL decides to sell the asset, it has to sell it with call option similar to that is written by GFL. Therefore, TFL cannot sell the asset to an unrelated third party without needing to impose additional restrictions on sale. In conclusion, GFL has retained its control on the asset.

Continuing involvement

If an entity retains control of a financial asset for which some but not substantially all of the risks and rewards have been transferred, then the entity continues to recognise the financial asset to the extent of its continuing involvement in the financial asset. The extent of the entity's continuing involvement in the transferred asset is the extent to which it is exposed to changes in the value of the transferred asset. For example:

(i) When the entity's continuing involvement takes the form of guaranteeing the transferred asset, the extent of the entity's continuing involvement is the lower of

NOTES

(a) the amount of the asset, and (b) the maximum amount of the consideration received that the entity could be required to repay ('the guarantee amount').

(ii) When the entity's continuing involvement takes the form of a written or purchased option (or both) on the transferred asset, the extent of the entity's continuing involvement is the amount of the transferred asset that the entity may repurchase. However, in the case of a written put option on an asset that is measured at fair value, the extent of the entity's continuing involvement is limited to the lower of the fair value of the transferred asset and the option exercise price.

CASE STUDY 19.11 Continuing Involvement

UY Limited (UYL) transfers short term receivables of ₹1,000 crore to KP Limited (KPL). UYL provides credit loss guarantee of 2% of the receivables (₹1,000 crore). The expected credit losses are 4% and historically credit losses of similar receivables varied between 1% to 5%. As per the contract, KPL is prohibited from selling or pledging the receivables. There is no active market for the receivables.

Question

The CFO of UYL seeks your advice on whether UYL has transferred reward and risks substantially and whether it has retained control on the asset. She also seeks your advice on the continuing involvement of UYL in the asset.

Solution

The expected credit loss is 4%, and historically, credit losses of similar receivables varied between 1% to 5%. UYL has retained some but not substantially all the risks, as it has provided credit loss guarantee of 2% of the receivables against the expected credit loss of 4% and historical trend of credit losses of similar receivables, which varied between 1% to 5%. UYL has retained control on the asset, as there is no active market and the transferee (KPL) is prohibited from selling or pledging the asset.

The maximum extent of UYL's continuing involvement is ₹20 crore (the amount of the guarantee). Therefore, UYL should derecognise ₹980 crore and continue to recognise ₹20 crore, which is lower of (i) the amount of the asset and (ii) the maximum amount of the consideration received that the entity could be required to repay ('the guarantee amount').

Accounting for transfers that do not meet the derecognition criteria

When a transfer does not meet the derecognition criteria, the entity continues to recognise the financial asset and recognise a liability for the consideration received.

A measurement based on continuing involvement requires the entity to recognise the rights and obligations retained by the entity, and measure those, depending on the measurement basis of the financial asset, either at the amortised cost or the fair value.

SUMMARY

An entity recognises a financial instrument in the balance sheet when it becomes a party to contract that is a financial instrument.

A financial asset or a group of similar financial assets can be broken down into various parts that can be segregated, and each part can be transferred separately to other parties.

The first step in applying the derecognition principle is to identify the financial asset subject to possible derecognition. It could be the entire financial asset or a group of similar financial assets or the following cash flows from the financial asset or a group of similar financial assets—specifically identified; fully proportionate (pro rata, e.g., 90%) share; or fully proportionate share of specifically identified cash flows.

A financial asset qualifies for derecognition either if the contractual rights to cash flows from the financial asset expire or if an entity transfers a financial asset in a transfer that meets the criteria for derecognition specified in the standard (Ind AS 109). A financial asset may be modified or replaced as a part of transaction with the same counterparty. If the cash flows, after modification, are substantially different, the contractual right to cash flows from the original financial asset should be deemed to have expired.

An entity transfers a financial asset if and only if it transfers the contractual rights to receive the cash flows of the financial asset or it enters into a qualifying pass-through arrangement. A 'pass-through arrangement' is considered a transfer if and only if:

(i) The entity has no obligation to pay amounts to the transferee unless the entity collects equivalent amounts from the original financial asset; (ii) the entity is prohibited from selling or pledging the original financial asset under the terms of the pass-through arrangement; and (iii) the entity is obliged to remit all the cash flows that it collects without material delay.

The entity derecognises the financial asset if it has transferred substantially all the risks and rewards of ownership of the financial asset. The entity continues to recognise the financial asset if it has retained substantially all the risks and rewards of ownership of the financial asset. In case of the transferred financial asset for which it has neither transferred nor retained substantially all the risks and rewards of ownership, the entity evaluates whether it has retained control of that asset. The entity derecognises the asset if it has not retained control of the asset. If the entity has retained control, then it continues to recognise the asset to the extent of its continuing involvement in the asset.

Self-Test Questions

Self-test question 19.9

Indicate whether the following statements are true (T) or false (F):

(i) An entity derecognises a financial asset when it sells the asset.

(ii) An entity cannot sell or transfer only a specified proportion of cash flows of the entire financial asset or a part of the financial asset.

(iii) An entity should not derecognise investment in shares of a closely held company when it sells the asset with buy-back condition.

(iv) Securitisation is an example of 'pass-through arrangement'.

(v) When a bank restructures an outstanding loan given to a borrower, the bank must derecognise the original loan and recognise the modified loan.

IMPAIRMENT OF FINANCIAL ASSETS

Under Ind AS 109, the impairment model is the 'Expected Credit Loss' model. It is not necessary for a loss event to occur before an impairment loss is recognised. As a result, all financial assets generally carry a loss allowance.

Earlier, the 'incurred loss model' was used for recognising impairment loss. The 'incurred loss model' assumes that all loans will be repaid until evidence to the contrary is identified. Under this model, a financial asset is impaired and impairment losses are incurred only if a loss event has occurred and this loss event had a reliably measurable impact on the future cash flows.

Applicability

Investments in equity instruments

Investments in equity instruments are not tested for impairment because they are accounted for either at FVTPL or at FVOCI, without no reclassification of fair value gains or losses to profit or loss.

Financial instruments measured at FVTPL

Financial instruments measured at FVTPL are not tested for impairment.

Debt instruments measured at amortised cost

Debt instruments measured at amortised cost (e.g., loans, trade receivables and debt securities) are tested for impairment.

Loan commitments

Loan commitments that are not measured at FVTPL are tested for impairment.

Loan commitment is a firm commitment to provide credit under pre-specified terms and conditions. Revolving cash credit facility offered to a customer by a bank is an example of loan commitment. Similarly, credit card issued by a bank is a loan commitment.

Financial guarantee contracts

Financial guarantee contracts that are within the scope of Ind AS 109 and are not measured at FVTPL are tested for impairment.

Lease receivables

Lease receivables are tested for impairment.

Contract assets

Contract assets are tested for impairment.

A contract asset is an entity's right to payment for goods and services already transferred to a customer if that right to payment is conditional on something other than the passage of time. For example, an entity recognises a contract asset when it has fulfilled a contract obligation, but must perform other obligations before being entitled to payment. This is in contrast to a receivable, which is the right to payment that is unconditional, except for the passage of time. Therefore, a receivable is not a contract asset.

The following is an example of contract asset:

An entity enters into a contract to transfer products A and B to a customer in exchange for ₹1,000. The contract requires product A to be delivered first and states that payment for the delivery of product A is conditional on the delivery of product B.

The entity identifies the promises to transfer products A and B as performance obligations and allocates ₹400 to the performance obligation to transfer product A and ₹600 to the performance obligation to transfer product B on the basis of their relative stand-alone selling prices. The entity recognises revenue for each respective performance obligation when control of the product transfers to the customer. After performance against the performance obligation of delivering product A, it recognises contract asset for ₹400, as its right to receive ₹400 from the customer is conditional on supply of product B.

Credit Loss

Credit loss is the difference between all contractual cash flows that are due to an entity in accordance with the contract and all the cash flows that the entity expects to receive (i.e., all cash shortfalls), discounted at the original effective interest rate. Credit losses are discounted to the reporting date.

For Purchased or Originated Credit-Impaired (POCI) financial assets, the cash shortfalls are discounted by credit-adjusted effective interest rate.

NOTES

Credit-adjusted effective interest rate is the interest rate that exactly discounts estimated future cash payments or receipts through the expected life of the financial asset to the amortised cost of that financial asset that is POCI financial asset.

Expected credit loss

Expected credit loss is the weighted average of credit losses with the respective risks of a default occurring as the weights.

The period over which to estimate expected credit losses

An entity should estimate the expected credit losses over the maximum contractual period over which it is exposed to credit risk. Contractual period should include any borrower's option for extension. It should not include lender's option.

Information to be used

The estimate of expected credit losses should reflect reasonable and supportable information that is available without undue cost or effort. Information may include past events and current conditions, and forecasts of future conditions. Estimates of future cash flows may depend on the entity's approach to managing impaired loans. For example, collection policies, work-out strategies, forbearance practice, anticipated debt restructuring, and foreclosure practices should be taken into account in estimating expected credit losses.

Forbearance refers to the temporary relief granted by a lender (e.g., bank) to a borrower who is in difficulties by not exercising its legal right of foreclosure. For example, a bank may allow extra time for repayment of the loan.

ILLUSTRATION 19.8 Cash Shortfall and Credit Loss

On April 30, 2017, VC Limited (VCL) originates a two-year loan with a principal of ₹100 and 12% coupon payable annually. Effective interest rate is also 12% per annum. On March 31, 2018, VCL estimates that there is a significant increase in credit risk on the loan. It estimates that if the borrower defaults, then the estimated future cash flows will be as follows:

April 30, 2018: ₹8

June 30, 2018: ₹4

April 30, 2019: ₹70

June 30: ₹30

Required

Calculate the credit loss.

Solution

Date	Contractual cash flows (₹)	Expected cash flows (₹)	Short fall (₹)	Credit loss (PV discounted at 12% per annum) (₹)
April 30, 2018	12	8	4	3.96
June 30, 2018	—	4	(4)	(3.88)
April 30, 2019	112	70	42	37.16
June 30, 2019	—	30	(30)	(26.04)
Total				11.20

NOTES

ILLUSTRATION 19.9 Expected Credit Loss

GH Limited (GHL) measures expected losses on a portfolio of loans and formulates the following forward looking scenarios:

Scenario 1: Unemployment rate: 3.5%; Expected credit loss: ₹30: Likelihood of occurring: 30%;

Scenario 2: Unemployment rate: 3.6%; Expected credit loss: ₹50: Likelihood of occurring: 50%; and

Scenario 3: Unemployment rate: 3.7%; Expected credit loss: ₹100: Likelihood of occurring: 20%.

Required

Calculate the expected credit losses.

Solution

Scenario	Unemployment rate (%)	Credit loss expected for each scenario (₹)	Likelihood of occurring (%)	Probability-weighted expected credit losses (₹)
Scenario 1	3.5	30	30	9
Scenario 2	3.6	50	50	25
Scenario 3	3.6	100	20	20
Expected credit losses recognised				54

12-month expected credit losses

12-month expected credit losses measure the credit losses that are expected to arise over the life-time of the financial asset resulting from default events occurring within 12 months after the reporting date (or a shorter period if the expected life of a financial instrument is less than 12 months).

Life-time expected credit losses

Life-time credit losses measure the credit losses that result from all possible default events occurring over the expected life of the financial assets.

Default

Ind AS 109 does not define default. Each entity is required to define default. The definition of default should be consistent with that used for internal credit risk management purposes for the relevant financial instrument. An entity should consider qualitative factors such as breaches of covenants, when appropriate. It can use regulatory definition (e.g., definition by the RBI for banks) if it considers qualitative indicators and is consistent with its credit risk management practices.

Examples of default

Contractual payment is not made when it is due, breach of loan covenant.

There is rebuttable presumption that default does not occur later than when a financial asset is 90 days past due. Past due is a loan payment that has not been made as of its due date.

General Approach

Credit risk

A loss allowance equal to 12-month expected credit losses is recognised for a financial instrument whose credit risk has not increased significantly since initial recognition. Life-time credit losses are recognised for financial instruments whose credit risk has increased significantly since initial recognition.

If credit risk on a financial instrument, for which life-time credit losses have been recognised, subsequently improves so that the requirement for recognising life-time credit losses is no longer met, then the loss allowance is measured at an amount equal to 12-month expected credit losses.

Low risk

As an exception to the general requirements, an entity may assume that the credit risk has not increased significantly since initial recognition if credit risk on the financial instrument is low at the reporting date. An entity can choose to apply this simplification on an instrument-by-instrument basis.

The credit risk of a financial instrument is low if:

(i) The instrument has a low risk of default;

(ii) The borrower has a strong capacity to meet its contractual cash flow obligations in the near term; and

(iii) Adverse changes in economic and business conditions in the longer term may, but will not necessarily, reduce the borrower's ability to fulfil its obligations.

Table 19.3 summarises the general approach:

TABLE 19.3

General Approach to Impairment Provisioning

	Deterioration in credit quality		
	Stage 1 (Performing)	**Stage 2 (Under-performing)**	**Stage 3 (Non-performing)**
Credit quality	The credit risk of the financial asset has not increased significantly since initial recognition or the financial asset has low credit risk at the reporting date.	The credit risk of the financial asset has increased significantly since initial recognition, but there is no objective evidence of credit loss event.	Financial asset that has objective evidence of impairment at the reporting date.
Recognition of expected credit losses	12-month expected credit losses are recognised.	Life-time expected credit losses are recognised.	Life-time expected credit losses are recognised.
Recognition of interest	Interest revenue is calculated on the gross carrying amount of the asset.	Interest revenue is calculated on the gross carrying amount of the asset.	Interest revenue is calculated on the net carrying amount of the asset (gross carrying amount less expected credit losses).
Practical expedient	Low credit risk	Credit risk > Low	

Significant increase in credit risk

At each reporting date, an entity assesses whether the credit risk on a financial instrument has increased significantly since initial recognition. In assessing whether the credit risk has increased, the entity considers changes in the risk of default instead of change in the amount of expected credit losses.

The reference point is the credit risk at initial recognition.

A given increase in credit risk is more likely to be significant for a financial instrument with a lower credit risk at initial recognition. For example, 2% increase in the Probability of Default (PD) is more significant for an asset with an initial PD of 5% than an asset with 20% PD.

The risk of a default occurring on financial instruments that have comparable credit risk is higher, the longer the expected life of the instrument. For example, the risk of a default occurring on an asset with an expected life of 20 years is higher than that on an otherwise identical asset that has an expected life of 10 years.

NOTES

Relative concept

Different measurement bases may be required for loans with same credit rating. For example, as per internal credit rating system of a bank, in a scale of 1 (low)–10 (high), loan granted to J had initial credit rating of 2, while loan granted to K had initial credit rating of 4. At the reporting date, credit rating for both the loans is 5. In case of loan to J, the credit risk has increased significantly (from rating of 2 to 5), while in case of loan to K, the credit risk has not increased significantly (from rating of 4 to 5). Therefore, loss allowance equal to 'life-time credit losses' should be recognised for loan to J and loss allowance equal to '12-month credit losses' should be recognised for loan to K.

Rebuttable presumption 30 days past due

There is a rebuttable presumption that credit risk on a financial instrument has increased significantly since initial recognition when contractual payments are more than 30 days past due. However, delinquency is a lagging indicator. Therefore, forward looking data is used to assess the increase in credit risk.

Loss Allowance for Trade Receivables, and Lease Receivables

The following are the principles for measuring loss allowance for trade receivables and contract assets, both of which represent amount receivable from customers:

(i) Trade receivables and contract assets that do not have a significant financing component: Loss allowance is measured based on 'life-time expected credit losses'; and

(ii) Trade receivables and contract assets that have a significant financing component, and lease receivables: Loss allowance is measured either using the general approach or based on 'life-time expected credit losses', depending on the accounting policy elected by the entity'.

Trade receivables

Usually, trade receivables that do not have significant financing component are short-duration (typically less than 12 months) financial assets. Therefore, 'life-time expected credit losses' generally do not differ from '12-month expected credit losses'. They are usually measured at the transaction cost and the implied effective interest rate is zero. Therefore, discounting of cash shortfall for measuring cash losses is not required.

Ind AS 109 allows the use of practical expedients when measuring life-time expected credit losses. Entities can use a provision matrix for measuring the impairment allowance.

Table 19.4 presents an example of provision matrix:

TABLE 19.4

Example of Provision Matrix

	Expected credit loss (%)	Trade receivables (₹)	Impairment allowance
Current	0.2	50,000	100
1–30 days past due	2.0	30,000	600
31–60 days past due	4.0	10,000	400
61–90 days past due	6.0	5,000	300
Over 90 days past due	10.0	1,000	100
Total			1,500

Entities should consider developing different provision matrices for different customer segments based on past loss patterns for different customer segments. For example,

NOTES

customers may be segmented based on geographic location, product type, customer rating, collateral, and type of customer (e.g., wholesalers and retailers).

In developing provision matrix, entities use historical loss experience on their trade receivables, and adjust historical loss rates to reflect information about current conditions, and reasonable and supportable forecasts of future economic conditions.

Lease receivables

When measuring expected credit losses on lease receivable, an entity uses:

(i) cash flows that are consistent with the cash flows used in measuring the lease receivable under Ind AS 17; and
(ii) the discount rate used in measuring the lease receivable under Ind AS 17.

Presentation

Financial assets measured at amortised cost

In case of financial assets measured at amortised cost in the balance sheet, the loss allowance is presented in the balance sheet as deduction from the gross carrying amount of the asset.

In the event of a 'write-off', the entity directly reduces the asset's gross carrying amount. If the amount of loss on write-off is greater than the accumulated loss allowance, the difference represents an additional impairment loss.

Investment in debt instruments measured at FVOCI

Investments in debt instruments designated as measured at FVOCI are measured in the balance sheet at fair value. Therefore, the loss allowance is not presented in the balance sheet as deduction from the gross carrying amount (fair value) of the asset. It is adjusted against the change in fair value (gain or loss) recognised in the Other Comprehensive Income (OCI) and accumulated in the balance sheet under 'other equity' with corresponding charge in the statement of profit and loss.

ILLUSTRATION 19.10 Impairment Loss of a Debt Instrument Measured at FVOCI

CC Limited (CCL) has purchased a debt instrument on July 1, 2018 at ₹10,000, which is the fair value on that date. The coupon rate and effective interest rate are 10% per annum. The instrument has a contractual term of 10 years. CCL has classified the investment as measured at FVOCI. The fair value of the bond on March 31, 2019 (the balance sheet date) is ₹8,000. CCL has assessed that the risk of the bond has not increased significantly and estimated the '12-month expected credit loss' at ₹1,000. On April 1, 2019, it sells the investment at ₹8,000.

Required

Explain the accounting entries for the transactions. Accounting for interest is not required.

Solution

(Amount in ₹)

July 1, 2018 (Purchase of bond)		
Investment in Bond A/C	Dr. 10,000	
To Cash A/C		Cr. 10,000
March 31, 2019 (Recognition of impairment and change in fair value)		
Impairment Loss A/C (expense)	Dr. 1,000	
OCI (Change in fair value, adjusted for impairment)	Dr. 1,000	
To Investment in Bond A/C		Cr. 2,000
April 1, 2019 (Sale of the investment in bond)		
Cash A/C	Dr. 8,000	
Loss on sale of investment A/C (loss)	Dr. 1,000	
To Investment in Bond A/C		Cr. 8,000
To OCI		Cr. 1,000

NOTES

SUMMARY

Investments in equity instruments are not tested for impairment.

Credit loss is the difference between all contractual cash flows that are due to an entity in accordance with the contract and all the cash flows that the entity expects to receive (i.e., all cash shortfalls), discounted at the original effective interest rate. Credit losses are discounted to the reporting date. Expected credit loss is the weighted average of credit losses with the respective risks of a default occurring as the weights. 12-month expected credit losses measure the credit losses that are expected to arise over the life-time of the financial asset resulting from default events occurring within 12 months after the reporting date (or a shorter period if the expected life of a financial instrument is less than 12 months). Life-time credit losses measure the credit losses that result from all possible default events occurring over the expected life of the financial assets.

A loss allowance equal to 12-month expected credit losses is recognised for a financial instrument whose credit risk has not increased significantly since initial recognition. Life-time credit losses are recognised for financial instruments whose credit risk has increased significantly since initial recognition.

If credit risk on a financial instrument, for which life-time credit losses have been recognised, subsequently improves so that the requirement for recognising life-time credit losses is no longer met, then the loss allowance is measured at an amount equal to 12-month expected credit losses. As an exception to the general requirements, an entity may assume that the credit risk has not increased significantly since initial recognition if credit risk on the financial instrument is low at the reporting date. An entity can choose to apply this simplification on an instrument-by-instrument basis. There is a rebuttable presumption that credit risk on a financial instrument has increased significantly since initial recognition when contractual payments are more than 30 days past due. However, delinquency is a lagging indicator. Therefore, forward looking data is used to assess the increase in credit risk.

In case of trade receivables and contract assets that do not have a significant financing component, loss allowance is measured based on 'life-time expected credit losses'. In case of trade receivables and contract assets that have a significant financing component, and lease receivables, loss allowance is measured either using the general approach or based on 'life-time expected credit losses', depending on the accounting policy elected by the entity'. Ind AS 109 allows the use of practical expedients when measuring life-time expected credit losses for trade receivables. Entities can use a provision matrix for measuring the impairment allowance.

Self-Test Questions

Self-test question 19.10

Indicate whether the following statements are true (T) or false (F):

(i) 12-month credit loss is the estimated credit loss that might occur within 12 months after the balance sheet date.

(ii) Life-time credit loss is the estimate of credit loss that might occur over the life-time of the financial asset from loss events that are expected to occur during that period.

(iii) In case of trade receivables that do not have a significant financing component, an entity might estimate the life-time expected credit loss by applying a specified percentage (established based on past pattern) on the total gross amount of trade receivables.

(iv) In case of debt instrument designated as 'measured at FVOCI', the loss allowance is recognised in profit or loss and adjusted against change in fair value accumulated under 'other equity' in the balance sheet.

(v) If the credit risk of two different financial instruments are measured at 6, in a scale of 1 (low) to 10 (very high), at the balance sheet date, after the initial recognition, loss allowance for both the assets should be based on 'life-time credit losses'.

ACCOUNTING FOR FINANCIAL LIABILITIES

Classification

On initial recognition, financial liabilities are classified as subsequently measured at amortised cost. However, there are certain exceptions.

Financial liabilities held for trading

Financial liabilities held for trading are subsequently measured at fair value. Examples of such liabilities are as follows:

(i) Derivatives with a negative fair value;
(ii) Obligations to deliver financial assets borrowed by a short seller; and
(iii) Financial liabilities that are incurred with an intention to repurchasing them in the near term.

Option to designate financial liabilities as at FVTPL

An entity has an option to designate irrevocably on initial recognition a financial liability as measured at Fair Value through Profit and Loss (FVTPL), provided:

(i) The designation eliminates or significantly reduces 'accounting mismatch'; or
(ii) A group of financial liabilities, or financial assets and financial liabilities is managed and its performance is evaluated on a fair value basis, in accordance with documented risk management or investment strategy.

Accounting mismatch

Accounting mismatch refers to measurement or recognition inconsistency that would otherwise arise from measuring assets or liabilities. For example, an entity has financial assets and financial liabilities that share a particular risk, such that their fair values change in opposite directions. However, only some of the instruments are measured at FVTPL. This results in accounting mismatch.

Liabilities with one or more embedded derivatives

If contract, which is a financial liability, contains one or more embedded derivatives, then an entity may designate the entire hybrid (combined) contract as at FVTPL. However, that option is not available if the embedded derivative is insignificant, or if it is obvious that separation of the embedded derivative would be prohibited.

It is generally presumed that a call, put or prepayment option is closely related to the host contract if the exercise price is approximately equal to the amortised cost of the host financial liability at each exercise date. Therefore, separation of such embedded derivatives is prohibited. An example of an embedded derivative for which it is clear that separation would be prohibited is a mortgage loan that is prepayable at an amount approximating at its amortised cost. Therefore, no option is available to designate such a contract as measured at FVTPL.

Measurement

Initial recognition

Initially, all financial liabilities are measured at fair value, adjusted for transaction costs. However, liabilities that are designated as measured at fair value, fair value is not adjusted for transaction costs.

Subsequent measurement

Subsequent to initial recognition, financial liabilities are measured at amortised cost calculated under the effective interest rate method, except for:

NOTES

(i) Liabilities measured at FVTPL;
(ii) Liabilities that arise when transfer of a financial asset does not qualify for derecognition or is accounted for using the continuing involvement approach;
(iii) Liabilities that are commitments to provide a loan at a below-market rate of interest and not measured at fair value through profit or loss; and
(iv) Liabilities that are financial guarantee contracts.

Subsequent measurement of liabilities designated as measured at FVTPL

Liabilities that the entity designates as measured at FVTPL are measured at fair value.

The gain or loss due to change in fair value are split into:

(i) gain or loss that is attributable due to change in the credit risks;
(ii) the remaining amount of gain or loss.

The gain or loss that is attributable due to change in the credit risks is recognised in Other Comprehensive Income (OCI) and accumulated under other equity in the balance sheet. The gain or loss accumulated under other equity is never reclassified to profit or loss. For example, the fair value of a corporate bond reduces even without any change in the market rate of interest if the bond is downgraded by the credit rating agency. Reduction in the fair value of the liability (corporate bond issued by the entity) results in gain. This gain is due to increase in the credit risks.

The remaining amount of the gain or loss is recognised in the statement of profit and loss.

Subsequent measurement of commitments to provide a loan at a below-market interest rate

An issuer of such a commitment, subject to some exceptions, subsequently measures it at the higher of:

(i) the amount of the Expected Credit Loss (ECL) allowance; and
(ii) the amount initially recognised (i.e., fair value) less, when appropriate, the cumulative amount of income recognised.

Subsequent measurement of financial guarantee contracts

An issuer of the financial guarantee contract measures it at the 'higher of':

(i) ECL allowance; and
(ii) The amount initially recognised (i.e., fair value) less any cumulative amount of income/amortisation recognised.

The upfront premium received from the beneficiary is recognised over the period of the loan. For example, company X issues a financial guarantee on April 1, 2016 against loan drawn from bank B by the company Y. The loan is repayable over a period of four years. Company X receives premium of ₹400 against the issuance of the financial guarantee. The fair value of the financial guarantee may be assumed to be ₹400. Therefore, ₹400 received in cash is recognised as a financial liability. Every year, for four years starting from 2016–17, X recognises revenue of (₹400/4) or ₹100 as income in the statement of profit and loss reducing the liability by that amount. Therefore, as at March 31, 2018, company X assesses that loan granted by bank B is impaired and the expected credit loss is estimated at ₹350. In its balance sheet dated March 31, 2018, Company X should measure the liability at higher of (i) ₹200, and (ii) ₹350. Therefore, in the balance sheet, the liability will be recognised at ₹350. In the statement of profit and loss for the year 2017–18, fee income should be recognised at ₹100 and expense for additional credit risk against the financial guarantee at (₹350 – 200) or ₹150. In the subsequent two years, ₹350 would be amortised and each year ₹175 will be recognised as income, provided there is no default and expected credit loss is not increased.

Derecognition

A financial liability is derecognised when it is extinguished.

A financial liability is extinguished when:

(i) payment is made to the lender (e.g., redeemable preference shares are redeemed);

(ii) the borrower is legally released from primary responsibility for the financial liability (e.g., bank has waived the payment of interest accrued on loan); or

(iii) the terms are modified, that is, existing debt instrument is exchanged with a new debt instrument with substantially different terms or the terms of the existing debt instrument are modified substantially (e.g., restructuring or refinancing of an existing loan by bank).

Modification

In order to assess whether the terms of an existing financial instrument has been modified substantially, the entity apply both quantitative and qualitative tests.

Quantitative assessment

The terms of an existing financial instrument are considered modified substantially if the NPV of the cash flows under the new terms, including fees paid net of any fees received differs by at least 10% from the present value of the remaining cash flows under the original terms. The effective interest rate of the original debt instrument is used to discount the cash flows.

Qualitative assessment

Usually, modification is not substantial if the difference in the present values of cash flows is less than 10%. However, if quantitative test does not indicate substantial modification of the financial instruments, the entity performs qualitative assessment. For example, it examines changes in principal amounts, maturities, interest rates, prepayment options and other contingent payment terms.

Accounting for a substantial modification of terms

If modification of terms leads to derecognition of the liability, then the new liability is recognised at fair value and the difference between the carrying amount of the original liability and the total of the fair value of new liability and the additional consideration paid is recognised in profit or loss. For example, if the carrying amount of the original liability is ₹1,00,000, the fair value of the new liability is ₹80,000 and additional consideration paid is ₹8,000, (₹1,00,000 – 80,000 – 8,000) or ₹12,000 is recognised as income in the statement of profit and loss.

Accounting for non-substantial modification of terms

When a financial liability measured at amortised cost is modified without this resulting in derecognition, a gain or loss should be recognised in profit or loss. The gain or loss is calculated as the difference between the original contractual cash flows and the modified cash flows discounted at the original effective interest rate.

SUMMARY

On initial recognition, financial liabilities are classified as subsequently measured at amortised cost, subject to certain exceptions. Initially, all financial liabilities are measured at fair value, adjusted for transaction costs. However, liabilities that are designated as measured at fair value, fair value is not adjusted for transaction costs. Subsequent to initial recognition, financial liabilities are measured at amortised cost calculated under the effective interest rate method, except for (i) liabilities measured at FVTPL; (ii) liabilities that arise when transfer of a financial asset does not qualify for derecognition or is accounted for using the continuing involvement approach; (iii) liabilities that are commitments to provide a loan at a below-market rate of interest and not measured at fair value through profit or loss; and (iv) liabilities that are financial guarantee contracts. A financial liability is derecognised when it is extinguished.

NOTES

Self-Test Questions

Self-test question 19.11

Indicate whether the following statements are true (T) or false (F):

(i) Most financial liabilities are measured at amortised cost using the effective interest rate method.

(ii) Performance guarantee issued by an entity in favour of its subsidiary is recognised as a liability in the balance sheet.

(iii) If modification of terms does not lead to derecognition of the liability, then the carrying amount of the liability is adjusted for fees and transaction costs incurred which are amortised over the remaining life of the modified liability.

(iv) At the initial recognition, financial liabilities are measured at fair value less transaction cost.

(v) If a borrower pays a processing fee of ₹10,000 for a loan of ₹5,00,000 to the bank, at initial recognition, the borrower should measure the liability (loan) at ₹4,90,000 and the bank should measure the asset (loan) at the same amount.

HEDGING AND HEDGE ACCOUNTING

Hedging

Entities are exposed to financial risks arising from their Business models. For example, entities might be exposed to credit risk or risk of changes in exchange rates, interest rates or commodity prices based on their Business models. Entities formulate and implement different risk management strategies to manage their risk exposures, often by using financial instruments. They either reduce or transfer risks through hedging. For example, an exporter may take a short position (position to sell the foreign currency) in a forward contract on foreign exchange to hedge against the risk of change in exchange rate between the date of export and receipt of proceeds in foreign currency.

Hedge accounting

Hedge accounting is optional.

Hedge accounting is a technique that modifies the normal basis for recognising gains and losses (or revenues and expenses) on hedged items and associated hedging instruments, so that both are recognised in profit or loss (or other comprehensive income) in the same accounting period. This eliminates or reduces the volatility in the statement of profit and loss that would arise if the hedged item and the hedging instrument were accounted for separately as per the accounting principles stipulated in Ind AS 109.

Hedged item

A hedged item is an asset, liability, firm commitment, highly probable transaction, or investment in a foreign operation that exposes an entity to changes in fair value or cash flows, and is designated as being hedged.

The hedged item can be a single item, or a group of items.

Hedging instrument

Hedging instrument is a designated derivative (e.g., forward contracts, future contracts, options, interest swap and foreign currency swap) whose fair value or cash flows are expected to offset changes in the fair value or cash flows of a designated hedged item. For a hedge of the risk of changes in foreign currency exchange rates, a non-derivative financial asset or non-derivative financial liability may be designated as hedging instrument.

Types of hedging relationship

The following are three types of hedging relationships— (i) fair value hedge; (ii) cash flow hedge; and (iii) net investment hedge.

NOTES

Fair value hedge

Fair value hedge is a hedge against the risk to a change in the fair value of an asset or liability or an unrecognised firm commitment, that is attributable to a particular risk and could affect profit or loss. Changes in fair value might arise through changes in interest rates (for fixed-rate loans), foreign exchange rates, equity prices or commodity prices.

Firm commitment: A firm commitment is a binding agreement for the exchange of a specified quantity of resources at a specified price on a specified future date or dates. For example, a binding contract entered by an entity with a counterparty for the supply of equipment at a fixed price is an example of firm commitment. The firm commitment is not recognised in the balance sheet as none of the parties has acted on its obligations. The purchaser recognises the equipment and corresponding liability when the control over the equipment is passed on to it.

Examples of fair value hedge: The following are the examples of fair value hedge:

(i) using a forward contract to hedge the commodity price risk or foreign exchange risk of a firm commitment to purchase an asset or incur a liability.

(ii) using an interest rate swap to hedge the interest rate risk of a fixed-rate interest-bearing asset or liability.

Accounting for fair value hedge: The hedging instrument is measured at fair value with changes in the fair value recognised in profit or loss. However, if the hedging instrument hedges an investment in equity instrument designated as measured at FVOCI, the change in the fair value is recognised in other comprehensive income (OCI) and accumulated under other equity in the balance sheet. The amount accumulated in other equity is never recycled to profit or loss.

The hedged item is remeasured to fair value in respect of the hedged risk during the period of hedging relationship. Any resulting adjustment to the carrying amount of the hedged item related to the hedged risk is recognised in profit or loss. However, if the hedged item is an investment in equity instrument designated as measured at FVOCI, then those amounts remain in OCI and never recycled to profit or loss.

A firm commitment (hedged item) is not recognised in the balance sheet. Therefore, the change in the fair value of the firm commitment attributable to the hedged risk during the period of hedging relationship is being recognised as an asset or liability in the balance sheet, with a corresponding gain or loss recognised in profit or loss. When the asset is acquired or a liability is assumed against the firm commitment, the initial carrying amount of the asset or liability is adjusted to include the cumulative change in fair value of the hedged item that was recognised in the balance sheet.

ILLUSTRATION 19.11 Fair Value Hedge-Firm Commitment

On March 1, 2018, BC Limited (BCL) has placed a firm order to purchase equipment on a supplier located in the USA for US$ 50,000. The equipment will be delivered on May 31, 2018 and payment has to be made immediately on delivery. BCL, in order to protect the fair value of the equipment at the inception of the contract against variability of exchange rate, has entered into a forward contract to buy US$ 50,000 on May 31, 2018. It has designated the forward contract as the hedging instrument. The hedged item is the firm commitment to procure the equipment. Assume that the US$/INR forward rate for May 31, 2018, as at March 1, 2018 is INR 65/US$ and on March 31, 2018, it will be INR 64/US$. The spot rates as at March 1, 2018 is INR 67/US$ and on March 31, 2018, it will be INR 66/US$. On the settlement date (May 31, 2018), the spot rate will be INR 62/US$.

Required

Explain the objective of hedging and accounting for the fair value hedge.

Solution

In the solution, we have ignored time value of money in determining the fair value of the derivative instrument and hedged item.

NOTES

BSC enters into the forward contract to buy US$ 50,000 that will be paid to the supplier on May 31, 2018 by locking in (₹65 × 50,000) or ₹32,50,000, for a machine valued at (₹67 × 50,000) or ₹33,50,00 on March 1, 2018. In other words, using a hedging instrument or a derivative—the forward contract, BSC has hedged the fair value exposure of the unrecorded firm commitment (equipment)—the hedged item, to a value fixed at ₹33,50,000 and expected a total gain of [(₹67 – 65) × 50,000] or ₹1,00,000 when the transactions would be completed on May 31, 2018.

Financial year ending on March 31, 2018

The movement in the forward rate is unfavourable to BCL. At the balance sheet date, BCL notionally owes [(₹65 – 64) × 50,000] or ₹50,000 to the counter party. Therefore, in the balance sheet dated March 31, 2018, the derivative (forward contract) should be recognised as a liability, measured at ₹50,000, with corresponding recognition of 'loss on forward contract' in profit or loss for the year 2017–18. The fair value of the firm commitment, calculated using the spot exchange rate is (₹67 × 50,000) or ₹33,50,000 on March 1, 2018. The same as at balance sheet date is (₹66 × 50,000) or ₹33,00,000. The reduction in fair value of the firm commitment (liability assumed to procure the equipment) is a gain. It is recognised as an asset in the balance sheet dated March 31, 2018 and as income in profit or loss for the year 2017–18. The net effect of loss on change in fair value of hedging instrument (₹50,000) and gain on hedged item (₹50,000) is nil.

Settlement date

On the settlement date (May 31, 2018), the spot rate is INR 62/US$. On that date, BCL should recognise the forward contract as liability at [(₹64 – 62) × 50,000] or ₹1,00,000. The 'loss on forward contract' of ₹1,00,000 will be recognised in profit or loss for the year 2018–19. Thus, the value of the forward contract liability at the settlement date is (₹50,000 + 1,00,000) or ₹1,50,000. At the first step, the accretion to the value of the liability should be recognised by debiting the 'loss on forward contract' by ₹1,00,000. The loss will be recognised in the profit or loss for the year 2018–19.

The liability (forward contract) is derecognised on settlement date by paying ₹1,50,000 to the counterparty in the forward contract.

The fair value of the firm commitment on May 31, 2018 is (₹62 × 50,000) or ₹31,00,000. The difference in the fair value as at March 31, 2018 and settlement date (which is the same when the transaction for acquiring the equipment is completed) is (₹33,00,000 – ₹31,00,000) or ₹2,00,000. The value of asset, representing change in the fair value of the firm commitment, increases by ₹2,00,000 and 'gain on change in the fair value of hedged item' is recorded. The gain will be recognised as income in profit or loss for the year 2018–19. The cumulative loss on hedging instrument over the period of the hedge is ₹1,50,000, whereas cumulative gain due to the change in fair value of the hedged item over the hedging period is ₹2,50,000. The net effect is a gain of (₹2,50,000 – 1,50,000) or ₹1,00,000, which BCL expected when it entered into the forward contract.

On initial recognition, BCL should measure the equipment at the amount payable to the vendor converted at the spot rate on the date of payment (₹62 × 50,000) or ₹31,00,000, plus the amount (₹2,50,000) of cumulative change in the fair value of hedged item (firm commitment) recognised as an asset. Thus, on initial recognition, the equipment is measured at (₹31,00,000 + 2,50,000) or ₹33,50,000. Thus, at initial recognition, the carrying amount of the equipment is its fair value at the inception of the contract.

Actual cash outflow on account of purchase of the equipment is (₹62 × 50,000) or ₹31,00,000, plus the amount [(₹65 – 62) × 50,000] or ₹1,50,000 paid to the counterparty in the forward contract, that is, ₹32,50,000. The amount is equal to the amount payable to the vendor in US$ converted at the forward rate of INR 65/US$.

Cash flow hedge

Cash flow hedge aims to hedge risk of variability in cash flows that is attributable to a particular risk associated with a recognised asset or liability, an unrecognised firm commitment (currency risk only) or a *highly probable* forecast transaction, and could affect profit or loss.

Future cash flows might relate to existing assets and liabilities, such as future interest payments or receipts on floating rate debt. Future cash flows can also relate to forecast sales or purchases in a foreign currency. Volatility in future cash flows might result from changes in interest rates, exchange rates, equity prices or commodity prices.

Highly probable forecast transaction: Forecast transaction is an uncommitted but anticipated future transaction. For example, an exporter does not have a binding contract for export of goods, but based on past trend, it is highly probable that in the next two months, it will export goods worth US$ 1,00,000 to the customers located in the USA. This is a highly probable forecast transaction. In a highly probable forecast transaction, the entity may not know the exact goods or the names of counterparties in the transaction.

Example: The following are the examples of cash flow hedges:

(i) Using an interest swap to hedge the interest rate risk of a floating-rate interest bearing asset or liability;

(ii) Using a forward contract to hedge the foreign currency risk of foreign currency denominated future operating lease or payroll payments; and

(iii) Using a forward contract to hedge the commodity price risk of highly probable forecast purchase or sale transaction.

Accounting: Provided the hedge is effective, effective portion of changes in the fair value of the hedging instrument is initially recognised in OCI. The ineffective portion of the change in the fair value of the hedging instrument (if any) is recognised directly in P&L.

The amount recognised in OCI (*cash flow hedge reserve*) should be the lower of:

(i) the cumulative gain or loss on the hedging instrument from the inception of the hedge, and

(ii) the cumulative change in the fair value (present value) of the expected cash flows on the hedged item from the inception of the hedge.

If the cumulative change in the hedging instrument exceeds the change in the hedged item, ineffectiveness should be recognised. If the cumulative change in the hedging instrument is less than the change in the hedged item, no ineffectiveness should be recognised. For example, if the cumulative change in the fair value of the hedging instrument is ₹1,000 and the same for hedged item is ₹800, the cash flow hedge reserve should be recognised in OCI and accumulated under 'other equity' in the balance sheet at ₹800 (effective portion) and ₹200 (ineffective portion) should be recognised in current period's profit or loss. On the other hand, if the cumulative change in the fair value of the hedging instrument is ₹1,000 and the same for hedged item is ₹1,200, the 'cash flow hedge reserve' should be recognised in OCI and accumulated under 'other equity' in the balance sheet at ₹1,000 and the ineffective portion (₹200) should not be recognised in current year's profit or loss. It may be noted that unlike 'fair value hedge', in 'cash flow hedge', the change in the fair value of the hedged item is not recorded in books/financial statements.

For cash flow hedges of a forecast transaction which result in the recognition of a financial asset or liability, the accumulated gains and losses recorded in equity (cash flow hedge reserve) should be reclassified to profit or loss in the same period or periods during which the hedged expected future cash flows affect the profit or loss.

If a hedged forecast transaction subsequently results in the recognition of a non-financial asset or non-financial liability, or a hedged forecast transaction for a non-financial asset or a non-financial liability becomes a firm commitment for which fair value hedge accounting is applied, the entity should remove that amount from the cash flow hedge reserve and include it directly in the initial cost or other carrying amount of the asset or the liability.

NOTES

ILLUSTRATION 19.12 Cash Flow Hedge—Firm Commitment

Assume the same fact pattern as presented in Illustration 10.11 above.

Required

Explain the objective of hedging and accounting for the cash flow hedge.

Solution

In the solution, we have ignored time value of money in determining the fair value of the derivative instrument and hedged item.

BSC enters into the forward contract, to buy US$ 50,000 that will be paid to the supplier on May 31, 2018 by locking in (₹65 × 50,000) or ₹32,50,000. In other words, using a hedging instrument (forward contract), BSC has hedged its cash flow exposure on account of the unrecorded firm commitment at ₹32,50,000. Note that under the fair value hedge, the objective is to hedge the fair value of the equipment at the inception of the contract and not the cash flow. The locking of the cash flow at ₹32,50,000 is incidental.

Financial year ending on March 31, 2018

The change in the fair value of the hedging instrument, which is unfavourable, is ₹50,000, and the change in the fair value of the firm commitment (in the opposite direction) is ₹50,000. Therefore, the change in fair value of the hedging instrument is effective. Accordingly, the hedging instrument is recorded in the balance sheet as a liability (measured at ₹50,000), and correspondingly, the 'loss on the forward contract' is accumulated under 'other equity' as 'cash flow hedge reserve'. The 'cash flow hedge reserve' shows debit balance (negative), as to record the change in the fair value of the hedging instrument, the 'cash flow hedge reserve' is debited and 'forward contract' is credited. Note that the fair value change in the hedged item is not recorded in the financial statement.

Settlement date

On settlement date, the cumulative change (unfavourable) in the fair value of the hedging instrument is ₹1,50,000 and the cumulative change in the fair value of the hedged item is ₹2,50,000. Therefore, the balance in the 'cash flow hedge reserve' should be maintained at ₹1,50,000, as it is lower than the cumulative change in the fair value of the hedged item. As explained earlier, the 'cash flow hedge reserve' shows a debit balance.

At the time of initial recognition, the equipment should be recorded at the amount (US$ 50,000) payable to the vendor converted at the spot rate when the transaction is completed (May 31, 2018), adjusted for the balance in the 'cash flow hedge reserve'. Thus, it is measured at (₹62 × 50,000) or ₹31,00,000 plus ₹1,50,000, that is, at ₹32,50,000.

Actual cash outflow on account of purchase of the equipment is (₹62 × 50,000) or ₹31,00,000, plus the amount [(₹65 – 62) × 50,000] or ₹1,50,000 paid to the counterparty in the forward contract, that is, ₹32,50,000. The amount is equal to the amount payable to the vendor in US$ converted at the forward rate of 1 US$ = INR 65. The cash flow arising from the firm commitment is protected from changes in the exchange rate.

Difference between fair value hedge and cash flow hedge

The following are the fundamental differences between fair value hedge and cash flow hedge:

(i) The objective of fair value hedge is to mitigate the risk of changes in the fair value of a recognised asset or liability or of an unrecognised firm

NOTES

commitment from a specified risk that affects the fair value of the item. For example, fair value hedge mitigates the risk of change in fair value of fixed interest loan, fixed interest bond, inventories and unrecognised firm commitment to purchase inventories.

Entities use cash flow hedge to manage the risk associated with cash flows rather than the fair value of assets, liabilities or unrecognised firm commitment. For example, cash flow hedge mitigates the risk of change in cash flows arising from variable items such as variable-interest loan, variable-interest bond, unrecognised firm commitment or highly probable forecast transaction, from a specified risk that affects future cash flows.

(ii) In fair value hedge accounting, there is no requirement to split the change in the fair value of the hedging instrument into effective and ineffective portion.

In cash flow hedge accounting, the accounting treatment of effective portion of the change in the fair value of the hedging instrument is different from the accounting treatment of the ineffective portion. Effective portion is that part of the cumulative change in the fair value of the hedging instrument that is lower than or equal to the cumulative change in the fair value of the hedged item.

(iii) In accounting for fair value hedge, both the change in the fair value of the hedging instrument and that of the hedge item are included in the current period's profit or loss with one exception. If the hedged item is an investment in equity instrument designated as measured at FVOCI, the change in the fair value of the hedged item is recognised in other comprehensive income and accumulated in other equity in the balance sheet. The amount accumulated in other equity is never recycled to profit or loss. The fair value of the hedging instrument is recognised as asset or liability in the balance sheet depending on whether the movement in the fair value is favourable or unfavourable for the entity. Similarly, the cumulative change in the fair value of the hedged item is recognised as an asset or liability depending on whether the movement in the fair value is favourable or unfavourable for the entity.

In cash flow hedge, only the ineffective portion of the fair value change of the hedging instrument is included in the current period's profit or loss and the effective portion of the change in fair value is accumulated in other equity under the heading 'cash flow hedge reserve', through other comprehensive income. The fair value of the hedging instrument is recognised as asset or liability in the balance sheet. The fair value change of the hedged item is not recorded in the books/financial statements.

(iii) In case of fair value hedge, the balance in the asset or liability recognised from the change in the fair value of the hedged item is adjusted to the carrying amount of the asset or liability on initial recognition.

In case of cash flow hedge, the accumulated amount in the 'cash flow hedge reserve' is included in profit or loss when the hedged expected future cash flows affect the profit or loss, or when the hedged forecast transaction occurs. When the hedged item is a firm commitment or a highly probable forecast transaction, the initial carrying amount of the non-financial asset or non-financial liability is adjusted with the balance in the 'cash flow hedge reserve'.

(iv) As in the case of normal accounting for derivative instruments, the asset or liability representing the fair value of the derivative instrument is extinguished by receiving cash from or paying cash to the counterparty in the derivative contract.

NOTES

Net investment hedge

An entity might have overseas subsidiaries, associates, joint ventures or branches (foreign operations). As per Ind AS 21, the amount of a net investment in a foreign operation is the reporting entity's interest in the net assets of that operation, including any recognised goodwill. Exchange differences arising on the incorporation of these net assets in the financial statements of the reporting entity are recognised in other comprehensive income and accumulated in the balance sheet under 'other equity'. The exchange difference accumulated under 'other equity' is recognised in profit or loss, on disposal or liquidation of the foreign operation, as part of the gain or loss on disposal.

An entity might hedge the currency risk associated with the translation of the net assets of these foreign operations into the parent entity's functional currency. Often the exposure to the risk of changes in exchange rate arising from net investment in a foreign operation is hedged through borrowings denominated in foreign operation's functional currency, or in more limited circumstances, derivative currency contracts.

Accounting: The foreign currency gains or losses on the hedging instrument are deferred in OCI to the extent that the hedge is effective, until the foreign operation is disposed of or liquidated, when they become part of the gain or loss on disposal.

Qualifying criteria for hedge accounting

Hedge accounting is an exception to the normal accounting rules. Therefore, Ind AS 109 stipulates certain qualifying criteria and an entity is allowed to apply hedge accounting only if it meets the specified qualifying criteria. The following are the criteria:

(i) Formal designation and documentation of the hedging relationship and the entity's risk management objective and strategy for undertaking the hedge must be in place at the inception of the hedge relationship;

(ii) The hedging relationship should consist only of eligible hedging instruments and hedged items stipulated in Ind AS 109; and

(iii) The hedging relationship should meet the hedge effectiveness requirements.

Hedge effectiveness

Hedge effectiveness is defined as the extent to which changes in the fair value or cash flows of the hedging instrument offset changes in the fair value or cash flows of the hedged item. In order to be effective, the following criteria should be met:

(i) An economic relationship should exist between the hedged item and the hedging instrument so that the value of the hedging instrument and the value of the hedged item move in the opposite directions as a result of the common underlying or hedged risk;

(ii) A change in the credit risk of the hedging instrument or the hedged item must not be of such magnitude that it dominates the value changes that result from that economic relationship; and

(iii) The hedge ratio, which is the relationship between the quantity of the hedging instrument and the quantity of the hedged item in terms of their relative weighting, used for hedge accounting purposes should be the same as that used for risk management purposes.

An entity assesses the hedge effectiveness at the inception of the hedging relationship and on an ongoing basis—at a minimum at each reporting date or on a significant change in the circumstances affecting the hedge effectiveness requirements. Entities use both quantitative and qualitative methods to assess hedge effectiveness.

NOTES

SUMMARY

Hedge accounting is optional. An entity can opt for hedge accounting for hedges that meet the qualifying criteria. One of the qualifying criteria is that the hedge should meet the hedge effectiveness test at the inception and throughout the hedging period.

Hedge accounting is a technique that modifies the normal basis for recognising gains and losses (or revenues and expenses) on hedged items and associated hedging instruments, so that both are recognised in profit or loss (or other comprehensive income) in the same accounting period. This eliminates or reduces the volatility in the profit or loss that would arise if the hedged item and the hedging instrument were accounted for separately as per the accounting principles stipulated in Ind AS 109.

Fair value hedge is a hedge against the risk to a change in the fair value of an asset or liability or an unrecognised firm commitment that is attributable to a particular risk and could affect profit or loss. Entities use cash flow hedge to manage the risk associated with cash flows rather than the fair value of assets, liabilities or unrecognised firm commitment. For example, cash flow hedge mitigates the risk of change in cash flows arising from variable items such as variable-interest loan, variable-interest bond, unrecognised firm commitment or highly probable forecast transaction, from a specified risk that affects future cash flows. Net investment hedge aims to hedge the currency risk associated with the translation of the net assets of foreign operations into the parent entity's functional currency.

Self-Test Questions

Self-test question 19.12

Indicate whether the following statements are true (T) or false (F):

(i) Hedge accounting is optional.

(ii) Only derivative instruments can be used as hedging instruments.

(iii) There is no difference between unrecognised firm commitment and highly probable forecast transaction.

(iv) Hedge accounting reduces the volatility in profit or loss due to mismatch arising from normal accounting of hedging instruments and other assets and liabilities.

(v). Fair value hedge is not applicable to hedge risk of change in fair value of an asset or liability that might arise from a forecast transaction.

(vi) Hedge of a firm commitment can be accounted for either using fair value hedge accounting or cash flow hedge accounting depending on the objective of hedging.

ANSWERS TO SELF-TEST QUESTIONS

19.1 (i) F; (ii) F; (iii) T; (iv) F; (v) T
19.2 (i) F; (ii) F; (iii) T; (iv) T; (v) T
19.3 (i) T; (ii) F; (iii) T; (iv) T; (v) F
19.4 (i) F; (ii) F; (iii) T; (iv) T; (v) T
19.5 (i) T; (ii) T; (iii) F; (iv) T; (v) T
19.6 (i) T; (ii) F; (iii) T; (iv) T; (v) T
19.7 (i) F; (ii) F; (iii) F; (iv) T; (v) T
19.8 (i) T; (ii) T; (iii) F; (iv) F; (v) F
19.9 (i) T; (ii) F; (iii) T; (iv) T; (v) F
19.10 (i) F; (ii) T; (iii) F; (iv) T; (v) F
19.11 (i) T; (ii) F; (iii) T; (iv) T; (v) T
19.12 (i) T; (ii) F; (iii) F; (iv) T; (v) T; (vi) T

ASSIGNMENTS

Multiple Choice Questions

1. Provide brief answers to the following questions:
   (i) Why advance paid to a vendor is not a financial asset?
   (ii) Why income tax liability is not a financial liability?
   (iii) Why the premium earned by a company by writing a call or put option on own shares is not recognised as income?
   (iv) Why a derivative instrument is classified as a financial instrument?
   (v) Why a guarantee issued by an entity on behalf of a borrower, which requires the guarantor to pay to the lender a specified amount if a credit rating agency downgrades the borrowing is not a financial guarantee?
   (vi) Why compulsorily convertible debentures are classified as equity?
   (vii) Why the amount received against optionally convertible debentures, which gives the option to the holder to convert or not to convert the debentures into equity, is split into equity and liability?
   (viii) Why redeemable preference shares are classified as liability?
   (ix) Why investment in equity instrument cannot be measured at amortised cost?
   (x) Why open-ended debt mutual funds should always be classified as FVTPL category?
   (xi) Why derivative instruments fail to meet the SPPI criterion?
   (xii) Why investment in a close-ended equity mutual fund fails to meet the SPPI criterion?
   (xiii) Why application of expected credit loss concept might result in higher provision for impairment of financial assets than the amount of impairment provision that is to be created based on estimated future credit losses?

2. The contractual arrangement between the company and the supplier of equipment is that the amount due to the supplier against the delivery of the equipment will be paid by issue of company's equity shares and the number of shares will depend on the market price of the share on the date when the payment will fall due.

   Required: Explain how the amount due to the supplier on the date of the delivery of the equipment will be recognised in the balance sheet, which is prepared on the date on which the equipment is delivered.

3. A non-banking financial institution grants and disburses loan to home buyers. The interest rate varies between 10% to 13.5% depending on the loan amount, the tenure of the loan and the credit risk assessed by the bank. Borrowers have the option to close the loan account by prepaying the outstanding amount of the loan, the amount of interest outstanding on the loan and a penalty of 2% on the outstanding amount of the loan.

   Required: Explain whether the home loan granted to home buyers, which is a financial asset for the financial institution, meets the SPPI criterion.

4. An entity acquires a corporate bond with the coupon rate of 13% per annum at par. The bond contains a put option. The put option gives the issuer the right to redeem the bond before maturity at the fair value of the bond on the date of redemption. Fair value will be determined by discounting future contractual cash flows (principal and interest) at the current market rate.

   Required: Explain whether the bond, which is an asset for the investor, meets the SPPI criterion.

5. On April 1, 2019, an investor acquired a corporate bond with coupon rate of 10% per annum. The interest is payable on March 31 every year. The bond will mature after five years. As per the terms of the contract, the coupon rate will increase to 20% per annum if the issuer (DKL) defaults in annual interest payment.

   Required: Explain whether the bond, which is an asset of the investor, meets the SPPI criterion.

6. On April 1, 2019 KK Limited issued 2,000 convertible bonds at the face value of ₹1000. The bonds will mature on March 31, 2022. The coupon rate is 5% and interest is payable annually. The holder of the bonds can convert the bonds at any time before maturity into 1 equity shares per bond, that is, 2,000 equity shares.

   The prevailing market interest rate for similar liability without conversion option, as at April 1, 2019, is 8% per annum.

   Required: Explain the accounting for the convertible bond.

NOTES

7. K Limited (KL) holds a portfolio of investments in open-ended debt mutual funds as a part of treasury management. It sells units of mutual funds as and when cash is required to support the working capital.

   Required: Explain how the investments included in the portfolio of investments should be classified for subsequent measurement.

8. Q Limited (QL) holds a portfolio of investments, which includes investments in corporate bonds and equity shares issued by other companies. The performance bonus that the investment manager earns every year depends on the total return on investment during the year. In computing the total return QL takes into account interest and dividend earned, profit or loss on sale of investments and gain or loss from the change in the fair value of the investments held in the portfolio at the balance sheet date.

   Required: Explain how the investments included in the portfolio of investments should be classified for subsequent measurement.

9. M Bank Limited (MBL) has granted ₹50,000 loan to U V Limited (UVL) on April 1, 2017. The UVL has paid an up-front fee of ₹1,000. The net loan proceeds is ₹49,000. The coupon rate is 10 percent per annum, payable on March 31 every year, starting from March 31, 2018. The loan is repayable at the end of the fifth year. UVL has the option of prepaying the loan. Based on discussion between MBL and UVL on March 31, 2018, it is estimated that SDL will pay ₹25,000 towards the principal amount on March 31, 2019 and the balance ₹25,000 on maturity.

   Required: Calculate the effective interest rate, interest income/interest expense and the gross carrying amount of the instrument.

CHAPTER

20

Non-Financial Liabilities

LEARNING OBJECTIVES

This chapter aims to provide an understanding of liabilities and accounting for provision and contingent liabilities. It also discusses the liabilities arising from employers' obligations to provide post-retirement benefits to employees under employment contracts.

After reading this chapter, you will develop understanding of the following:

- Nature of liabilities
- The concept of constructive obligation
- Nature of provision and distinction between provision and accrual
- Recognition and measurement of provision
- Nature and accounting for executory contracts and onerous contracts
- Accounting for reimbursement against settlement of provision
- Recognition of liabilities arising from restructuring plan
- Nature and disclosure of contingent liabilities and commitments
- Nature and classification of post-retirement benefits plans
- Recognition and measurement of liabilities arising from defined contribution plan and
- Recognition and measurement of liabilities arising from defined benefit plan

Applicable Ind AS: *Discussion in this chapter is primarily based on Ind AS 37, Provisions, Contingent Liabilities, and Contingent Assets; and Ind AS 19, Employee Benefits.*

NOTES

DEFINITIONS

Financial Instrument

Liability

Liability is defined as follows:

> *"A liability is a present obligation of the entity arising from past events, the settlement of which is expected to result in an outflow from the entity of resources embodying economic benefits."*

Present obligation

The obligation should be present at the balance sheet date in the sense that the entity has practically no option but to settle the obligation. In most situations, it is clear whether an obligation is present at the balance sheet date. Only in certain situations, for example, in case of a law suit, the entity has to develop a perspective of the situation to formulate a view on whether an obligation is present at the balance sheet date.

Past event (obligating event)

An obligating event is an event that creates a legal or constructive obligation, which results in an entity having no realistic alternative to settling that obligation.

Financial statements present economic effect of transactions and events occurred during the reporting period. Balance sheet presents the financial position of the entity at the balance sheet date. It does not present the possible financial position in future. Therefore, obligations that might arise in future from likely future events are not recognised in the balance sheet.

Outflow of resources

A present obligation is recognised as a liability in the balance sheet only if it is probable that economic resources embodying economic benefits will flow out of the entity in settling the obligation and the management can estimate the amount of that outflow. If it is less than probable that economic resources embodying economic benefits will flow out of the entity, the obligation is disclosed under the heading "Contingent Liability". If the possibility of an outflow of resources embodying economic benefits is remote, the possible obligation is not disclosed.

Legal obligation

A legal obligation is an obligation that derives from:

(i) a contract (through its explicit or implicit terms);
(ii) legislation; or
(iii) other operation of law.

Examples of legal obligations are borrowings, trade creditors, advance from customers, GST collected from customers and payable to the government, and income tax liability. Among the examples, borrowings and trade creditors are financial liabilities and others are non-financial liabilities.

Constructive obligation

A constructive obligation is an obligation that derives from an entity's actions where:

(i) by an established pattern of past practice, published policies or a sufficiently specific current statement, the entity has indicated to other parties that it will accept certain responsibilities; and
(ii) as a result, the entity has created a valid expectation on the part of those other parties that it will discharge those responsibilities.

Example of constructive obligation is obligation arising from the practice of ex-gratia payment to retiring employees.

An obligation always involves a commitment to another party. Therefore, a management or board's decision does not give rise to a constructive obligation at the end of the reporting period unless the decision has been communicated before the end of the reporting period to those affected by it in a sufficiently specific manner to raise a valid expectation in them that the entity will discharge its responsibilities.

NOTES

CASE STUDY 20.1 Constructive Obligation—VRS

On March 31, 2018, the board of SV Limited (SVL) has approved a Voluntary Retirement Scheme (VRS) for employees. The decision will be communicated to employees on April 15, 2018. A window of three months will be allowed for employees to submit their offer for voluntary retirement under the scheme. It is expected that the management accept offers by September 30, 2018.

Question

The CFO of SVL seeks your advice on whether a liability for VRS should be recognised in the balance sheet dated March 31, 2018, and if the liability is not recognised in the balance sheet dated March 31, 2018, whether the entity should recognise the liability in balance sheet dated June 30, 2018.

Solution

No constructive obligation has arisen on March 31, 2018 because the VRS was not communicated to the target employees in the financial year 2017–2018. A constructive obligation will arise when the VRS will be communicated to the target employees. Legal obligation will arise when the management will accept offers from employees for the VRS. The liability should be recognised in the balance sheet dated June 30, 2018 as the management has communicated the VRS to the target employees on April 15, 2018, although legal obligation will arise later when the management will accept offers from employees for voluntary retirement under the scheme.

Key Terms
Constructive obligation, Legal obligation, Liability, Obligating event

SUMMARY

A liability is a present obligation of the entity arising from past events, the settlement of which is expected to result in an outflow from the entity of resources embodying economic benefits.

A legal obligation is an obligation that derives from (i) a contract (through its explicit or implicit terms); (ii) legislation; or (iii) other operation of law.

A constructive obligation is an obligation that derives from an entity's actions where:

(i) by an established pattern of past practice, published policies or a sufficiently specific current statement, the entity has indicated to other parties that it will accept certain responsibilities; and

(ii) as a result, the entity has created a valid expectation on the part of those other parties that it will discharge those responsibilities.

Self-Test Questions

Self-test question 20.1

Indicate whether the following statements are true (T) or false (F):

(i) If an entity has realistic alternative to settling an obligation, then that obligation is not a liability.

NOTES

(ii) Application of the principle of conservatism requires that an entity should recognise in the balance sheet obligations that might arise in future from likely future events.
(iii) A constructive obligation does not arise from a decision of the Board of Directors unless that decision is communicated to those who will be benefitted from that decision.
(iv) Liability arising from a voluntary retirement scheme is not recognised until the management accepts offers from employees for voluntary retirement under the VRS.
(v) A liability is recognised only if the entity is able to estimate the amount with reasonable accuracy.

PROVISION

Nature of Provision

A provision is defined as follows:

"A provision is a liability of uncertain timing or amount."

Examples of provision are obligations for:

(i) income tax liability until it is finally assessed by the Income Tax Department;
(ii) product warranty;
(iii) dismantling of assets and environment restoration;
(iv) post-retirement employee benefits;
(v) disputed claim by customers; and
(vi) disputed claim by the revenue department of the government.

In all these examples, the time is uncertain, or the amount is uncertain, or both are uncertain.

Distinction between provisions and trade payables

Provisions can be distinguished from trade payables. Trade payables are the liabilities to pay for goods or services that have been received or supplied and have been invoiced or formally agreed with the supplier. Therefore, there is no uncertainty about the amount and timing of settlement.

Distinction between provisions and accruals

Provisions can also be distinguished from accruals (also called outstanding liabilities). Accruals are the liabilities to pay for goods or services that have been received or supplied but have not been paid, invoiced or formally agreed with the supplier, including amounts due to employees (for example, amounts relating to accrued vacation pay). Although estimation is required to measure accruals, estimation uncertainty is much lower than that in estimating provision. Similarly, uncertainty about timing of settlement of accruals is much lower than the same in case of provisions.

Accruals are often reported as part of trade and other payables, whereas provisions are reported separately.

Use of Provision

A provision should be used only for expenditure for which it was originally recognised. For example, a provision for *product warranty* should be used only to meet expenses related to it.

Recognition

A provision shall be recognised when:

(i) an entity has a present obligation (legal or constructive) as a result of a past event;

NOTES

(ii) it is probable that an outflow of resources embodying economic benefits will be required to settle the obligation; and

(iii) a reliable estimate can be made of the amount of the obligation.

If these conditions are not met, no provision shall be recognised.

Financial statements deal with the financial position of an entity at the end of its reporting period and not its possible position in the future. Therefore, an entity should not recognise a provision for costs that need to be incurred to operate in the future. It is only those obligations arising from past events existing independently of an entity's future actions (i.e., the future conduct of its business) that are recognised as provisions.

An obligation always involves another party to whom the obligation is owed. It is not necessary, however, to know the identity of the party to whom the obligation is owed—indeed the obligation may be to the public at large. For example, a company provides liability for product warranty arising from the past event (sale of goods) without knowing which of the customers would seek replacement or repair of the defective goods.

CASE STUDY 20.2 Recognition of Provision

FG Limited (FGL), which manufactures ferrochrome by melting chrome ore in electrical furnace, has received a notice from the Pollution Control Department to reduce pollution level within and outside the plant. The board of the company in its meeting dated March 31, 2018 decided to install pollution control equipment to bring down the pollution level. The estimated cost of the equipment is ₹1 crore.

Question

The CFO of FGL seeks your advice on whether the company should provide a liability, measured at the cost of the equipment in its balance sheet dated March 31, 2018.

Solution

The company should not provide liability in the balance sheet dated March 31, 2018, as it can avoid the future expenditure by its future actions, for example, by changing its method of operation. It has no present obligation for that future expenditure and no provision is recognised.

CASE STUDY 20.3 Recognition of Provision—Enactment of Law—Virtual Certainty

ABC Limited (ABCL) produces several chemicals. The emission of chemical waste from the factory pollutes the adjacent field. The Board of Directors met on May 31, 2018 to approve financial statements for the year 2017–18, and decided to enact an environmental law shortly, which will put an obligation on the entity to clean the field from chemical pollution.

Question

The CFO of ABCL seeks your advice on whether ABCL should provide liability that will arise on the enactment of the law for cleaning the field, which has been polluted due to its operations in 2017–18 and earlier years.

Solution

The company should recognise the provision only if there is virtual certainty that the law will be enacted as drafted and it is able to estimate the cost that it will incur to clean the field. For example, if the law has been passed by both the houses of the Parliament (Lok Sabha and Rajya Sabha) and it is waiting for the President's assent, it may be said that it is virtually certain that the law will be enacted as drafted. Only in that case a provision should be recognised in the balance sheet dated March 31, 2018.

NOTES

Measurement

Best estimate

A provision is measured at the *best estimate* of the expenditure required to settle the obligation as on the balance sheet date.

The best estimate is the amount that the entity would *rationally pay* to settle the obligation at the balance sheet date or to transfer to a third party at that time. The estimates of outcome and financial effects are determined by the judgement of the management of the entity. The management takes into consideration its own and others' experience of similar transactions in estimating the provision. In some cases, it obtains reports from independent experts. For example, the management obtains an expert's opinion in estimating the liability for cleaning the water body adjacent to its plant polluted by flow of contaminated water from its plant due to failure of its pollution control equipment.

Risks and uncertainties

The management takes into account risk and uncertainties that surround many events and circumstances in estimating the provision. Similarly, it takes into account future events that may affect the amount required to settle an obligation if there is sufficient *objective evidence* that those events will occur. For example, the liability to clean up the site when the operation will cease should be measured at an amount that reflects the expected technological changes having a bearing on cleaning costs. However, in the absence of objective evidence, the management should not anticipate a future event.

Gains

The management should not take into account gains on expected disposal of assets in estimating the provision, even if the expected disposal is closely linked to the event giving rise to the provision.

Effect of time value of money

The management should measure the provision at the present value of estimated cash outflows, where the effect of time value of money is material. The discount rate should be a *pre-tax rate* that reflects the *current market assessments* of the time value of money and the risk specific to the liability. The discount rate should not reflect the risks for which future cash flow estimates have been adjusted.

Method for estimating the liability

The method of estimating the amount of provision depends on the circumstances. For example, where the provision being measured involves a large population, the liability is measured at the *expected value,* calculated using subjective probabilities.

Where a single obligation is being measured, the most likely individual outcome may be the best estimate of the liability.

ILLUSTRATION 20.1 Provision—Large Population

S Limited (SL) sells television sets with a warranty for one year. In 2017–18, it sold 1,00,000 units. Under the warranty, SL repairs defects that surface during the warranty period. It estimates that 80% of the units sold will have no defects, 15% will have minor defects, and 5% will have major defects. It further estimates that repair of a major defect will cost ₹5,000 per unit, while repair of a minor defect will cost ₹1,000 per unit. The warranty covers one year from the date of purchase by the customer.

Required

Calculate the amount at which the provision for the product warranty should be recognised in the balance sheet dated March 31, 2018.

NOTES

Solution

The expected value of the cost of repair is

(0.80 × Nil) + (0.05 × 1,00,000 × ₹5,000) + (0.15 × 1,00,000 × ₹1,000)

= ₹2,50,00,000 + ₹1,50,00,000

= ₹4,00,00,000

A provision of ₹4,00,00,000 should be recognised in the balance sheet dated March 31, 2018 towards product warranty. The amount is not discounted, as the time value of money is not material.

ILLUSTRATION 20.2 Provision—Single Obligation

A customer complaint about a major defect in the plant installed by S Transformers Limited (STL) is yet to be attended on the date when financial statements for 2017–18 are approved by the Board of Directors. STL expects to repair the defect at the first attempt, and in that case, it will cost ₹5,000. However, if the defect cannot be removed at the first attempt, the cost will be much higher. The management of the STL proposes to recognise a provision towards the obligation in the balance sheet as at March 31, 2018 at ₹20,000 because it is quite probable that more than one attempt will be necessary.

Required

Explain if it is appropriate to recognise a provision at the amount suggested by the management.

Solution

Where a single obligation is being measured, the most likely individual outcome may be the best estimate of the liability. We may assume that the management's proposal is based on its best estimate which is formulated on the basis of experience and available evidence. Therefore, it is appropriate to recognise the provision at ₹20,000 towards the cost for rectification of the defect.

Reimbursement

An entity may expect reimbursement of some or all of the expenditure that it will incur to settle the provision. It should recognise the same as a separate asset if and only if it is *virtually certain* that the reimbursement will be received. The amount recognised for the reimbursement should not exceed the amount of the provision. In the statement of profit and loss, expense relating to a provision may be presented *net of the amount* recognised for a reimbursement.

ILLUSTRATION 20.3 Reimbursement

The Pollution Control Department of the Union Government reimburses 25% of the environment remedial costs incurred by a manufacturing enterprise, subject to fulfillment of certain conditions. One of the environmental laws requires manufacturing firms to remedy the damage caused to the environment through its manufacturing process. Z Limited (ZL) estimates that it will incur an expenditure of ₹2 million towards remediation of environment due to damage caused by its manufacturing process during 2017–18.

Required

Explain the accounting for the expected reimbursement.

Solution

ZL should recognise the reimbursement as a separate asset at ₹0.5 million in the balance sheet as at March 31, 2018 provided it is *virtually certain* that the reimbursement will be received. It will recognise in the balance sheet dated March 31, 2018, provision of ₹2 million towards the obligation. The reimbursement should be considered virtually certain only if it is sectioned and only disbursement is pending.

In the statement of profit and loss account for 2017–18, it will recognise environment remediation expense at the net amount of ₹1.5 million if it recognises an asset towards reimbursement from the pollution control department. In case the reimbursement is not virtually certain, it will not recognise the asset and it will recognise the expense at ₹2 million.

NOTES

Executory Contracts and Onerous Contracts

As a general principle, a liability is recognised only if the obligation arises from one or more past events. No provision should be recognised for future operating losses. However, as an exception to this rule, the management is required to provide for estimated loss that will arise from onerous contracts.

Executory contract

Executory contract is a contract under which neither party has performed any of its obligations or both parties have partially performed their obligations to an equal extent.

Onerous contract

An executory contract is onerous if the unavoidable costs of meeting the obligations under the contract exceed the expected economic benefits.

Provision

An entity should provide for estimated loss that will arise from an onerous contract.

CASE STUDY 20.4 Recognition of Provision—Onerous Contract

In March 2018, L Limited (LL) entered into a contract with S Limited (SL) for construction of a plant. It was a fixed-price contract for ₹500 crores with a penalty clause. LL would have to pay SL ₹50 crore if it failed to execute the contract. LL would have to import several items of equipment from the USA for executing the contract. Immediately after the contract was signed, the supplier of materials and components significantly increased the price. LL estimated that due to increase in costs of materials and components, execution of the contract would result in a loss of ₹70 crore. Therefore, the management decided to place before the Board of Directors a proposal to exit the contract in the board meeting scheduled in April 2018.

Question

The CFO of LL seeks your advice on whether it should provide for the estimated loss in the balance sheet dated March 31, 2018.

Solution

As a general rule, no liability should be provided for future operating losses. However, there is an exception. A liability for estimated loss from an onerous contract should be recognised in the balance sheet, and consequently, the estimated loss is recognised in the statement of profit and loss. The contract with SL is an executory contract because neither LL nor SL has performed its obligations under the contract. The contract is onerous, as LL will incur loss if it executes the contract. Therefore, LL should recognise liability for the estimated loss in its balance sheet dated March 31, 2018.

If the board approves the proposal of exiting the contract, the liability should be measured at ₹50 crore, which is the amount of the penalty that LL will have to pay to SL for cancellation of the contract. If the board decides the contract should be executed to protect the credibility and reputation of the company, liability should be measured at ₹70 crore, which is the amount of estimated loss that the company will incur on executing the contract.

Restructuring

IAS 37 defines *restructuring* as a programme that is planned and controlled by the management, and materially changes either the scope of a business undertaken by an entity or changes the manner in which the business is conducted.

Restructuring may involve:

(i) sale or closures of a line of business;
(ii) closure of a location or relocation of business activities;
(iii) changes in management structure; and
(iv) changes in the nature or focus of an existing business.

A constructive obligation for restructuring arises when the entity (i) has drawn a detailed formal plan for the restructuring; and (ii) has aroused a valid expectation among the people or entity affected by the plan that the plan will be carried out.

An enterprise generates a valid expectation either by initiating the implementation of the plan or by announcing its main features, with sufficient detail, to those who will be affected by the plan. A restructuring plan gives rise to a constructive obligation when it is communicated to those who will be affected by it, and its implementation is to start as soon as possible and to be completed in a timeframe that makes significant changes to the plan unlikely.

A restructuring provision includes only the direct expenditure arising from restructuring. The expenditure should arise necessarily from restructuring and should not be associated with the ongoing activities of the entity. A restructuring provision does not include some costs such as (i) retraining or redeployment of continuing employees, (ii) marketing, and (iii) investment in new systems or distribution networks.

NOTES

Key Terms
Accrual, Provision

SUMMARY

Provision is a liability of uncertain timing or amount. It is measured at the management's ***best estimate*** of the expenditure required to settle the obligation. The best estimate is the amount that the entity would ***rationally pay*** to settle the obligation at the balance sheet date or to transfer to a third party at that time. Provision is measured at the Present Value (PV) of the estimated cash flows, where the effect of time value of money is material. Gains on expected disposal of assets are not taken into account in measuring the provision even if the expected disposal is closely linked to the event giving rise to the provision.

As a general principle, a liability is recognised only if the obligation arises from one or more past events. No provision should be recognised for future operating losses. An exception to this rule is the provision for onerous contracts.

A restructuring plan gives rise to a constructive obligation when it is communicated to those who will be affected by it, and its implementation is to start as soon as possible and to be completed in a timeframe that makes significant changes to the plan unlikely. A restructuring provision includes only the direct expenditure arising from the restructuring. The expenditure should arise necessarily from restructuring and should not be associated with the ongoing activities of the entity.

An entity should recognise reimbursement as a separate asset if and only if it is ***virtually certain*** that the reimbursement will be received.

Self-Test Questions

Self-test question 20.2

Indicate whether the following statements are true (T) or false (F):

(i) There is no estimation uncertainty in measuring accruals, while estimation uncertainty is high in measuring provisions.
(ii) No provision is recognised if the management fails to estimate the amount reliably.
(iii) No provision is recognised if the entity is unable to identify entities to whom it owes the money or some other economic benefits.
(iv) If an entity expects reimbursement of some or all of the expenditure that it will incur to settle the provision, it recognises the reimbursement as a separate asset only if it is reasonably certain that it will receive the reimbursement.
(v) No provision is recognised for liabilities that will arise from implementation of a restructuring plan in future, even if the plan is communicated to those who will be affected by the plan.

NOTES

CONTINGENT LIABILITIES

Entities do not recognise contingent liabilities in the balance sheet. They disclose contingent liabilities by way of a note below the balance sheet.

A contingent liability is a liability the existence of which will be confirmed only by the occurrence or non-occurrence of one or more uncertain future events not wholly within the control of the entity. Often the term 'possible obligation' is used for such a liability. For example, the liability on account of performance guarantee issued in favour of another party will arise only if that other party fails to perform. Therefore, that liability is a 'possible obligation' and is not recognised in the balance sheet.

'Contingent liability' also refers to that liability that does not meet the recognition criteria because either it is not probable that an outflow of resources embodying economic benefits will be required to settle the obligation, or a sufficiently reliable estimate of the amount of the obligation cannot be made. Examples are claims (e.g., from employees, customers and suppliers) not acknowledged as debt, claims under arbitration, claims under pending law suits, and claims by income tax and other revenue departments, which are under appeal before appellate authorities.

Contingent liability and provision

Provisions are recognised as liabilities (assuming that a reliable estimate can be made) because they are present obligations and it is probable that an outflow of resources embodying economic benefits will be required to settle the obligations. There is a thin difference between contingent liabilities and provision. For example, a provision is recognised against a claim by a customer (under arbitration) if legal opinion suggests that the entity will be required to settle the claim by paying money to the customer. On the other hand, the claim is disclosed as a contingent liability if the legal opinion suggests that it is less than probable that payment to the customer will be required to settle the claim.

Disclosure

Contingent liabilities are disclosed by way of notes below the balance sheet. An entity discloses for each class of contingent liability at the end of the reporting period a brief description of the nature of the contingent liability and, where practicable, (i) an estimate of its financial effect; (ii) an indication of the uncertainties relating to the amount or timing of any outflow; and (iii) the possibility of any reimbursement.

Commitments

Commitments are not contingent liabilities. For example, commitment to purchase equipment is not a contingent liability. Liability will arise when the other party will execute the contract to supply the equipment. Most regulators require entities to disclose commitments under the heading "Contingent Liabilities".

SUMMARY

Possible obligations are disclosed as contingent liabilities. In case it is less than probable that economic benefits will flow out of the entity in settling an obligation, then that obligation is disclosed as a contingent liability. Contingent liabilities also include liabilities for which the entity is unable to reliably estimate that amount of economic benefits that will outflow for settling those liabilities. Commitments are not contingent liabilities. However, usually, regulators require entities to disclose the same.

NOTES

Self-Test Questions

Self-test question 20.3

Indicate whether the following statements are true (T) or false (F):

(i) Management is not required to disclose the financial effects of contingent liabilities.

(ii) There is a thin difference between contingent liability and provision.

(iii) A contingent liability is not disclosed if there is only a remote possibility that economic benefits will flow out of the entity to settle the possible obligation.

(iv) A firm commitment to purchase equipment is a contingent liability.

LIABILITIES FOR POST-RETIREMENT EMPLOYEE BENEFITS

Employers' rights and obligations under employee benefit plans are financial assets and financial liabilities, respectively, as they arise from contracts that are settled in cash. However, those are not within the scope of Ind AS 109, Financial Instruments. They are accounted for in accordance with the principles and methods stipulated in Ind AS 19, Employee Benefits.

Nature and Classification Post-Retirement Benefit Plans

Nature of post-retirement employee benefits

Post-employment benefits include the following:

- Retirement benefits, e.g., gratuity and pension
- Other benefits, e.g., post-employment life insurance and post-employment medical care

Post-employment benefit plans are deferred payment plans. An employee earns those benefits when he/she renders service. The amount of those benefits increases as the employee continues to render the service. However, after a certain length of service, additional service does not result in increase in the amount of benefits. For example, under a pension scheme, an employee earns full pension on completion of 20 years of service. Therefore, if an employee serves for more than 20 years, she does not get pension more than what an employee who has completed just 20 years of service would get, provided other things are equal.

Classification

Post-employment benefit plans are classified into two types—

(i) defined contribution plans, and (ii) defined benefit plans.

(i) Defined contribution plan

A defined contribution plan is one in which the employer pays a fixed contribution (e.g., 10% of basic salary) into a separate entity or fund and its obligation is limited to that contribution. The employer is not required to contribute further if the fund does not hold sufficient assets to pay all the employee expected benefits relating to employee service on the current and prior periods. In defined contribution plan, the financial risks are borne by the employee. The amount of benefit depends on the performance of plan assets. Examples of the defined contribution plan is the provident fund and the contributory pension plan.

(ii) Defined benefit plan

A defined benefit plan is a post-employment benefit plan other than defined contribution plans. As the name implies, under a defined benefit plan, the benefit to employees is defined. Therefore, under such a plan, the employer has the obligation to provide the agreed benefits to the current and former employees. An example of defined benefit plans

NOTES

is the gratuity scheme under which the amount of gratuity payable to an employee is determined based on the period of service and last pay drawn. It is not linked to the contributions by the employer over the period of employment or on the plan performance of the assets.

Measurement of Liabilities

Defined contribution plan

An enterprise recognises contributions payable as an expense in the profit and loss account for the period in which the employee has rendered the service. If the amount of contribution paid is less than the amount payable, the difference is recognised as a liability (accrued expense) in the balance sheet as at the end of the period. Similarly, any amount paid in excess of the amount due is recognised as an asset (prepaid expense) in the balance sheet as at the end of the period.

Defined benefit plan

Defined benefit plans may be (i) unfunded, or (ii) wholly or partly funded by contributions by an enterprise, and sometimes by its employees.

When a defined benefit plan is funded, the enterprise contributes to an entity (e.g., insurance company) or fund that is legally separate from the reporting enterprise. That entity or fund is called plan asset. Employee benefits are paid out of the plan asset. However, the amount payable does not depend on the financial position and the performance of the plan asset. Employee benefits are defined in the plan. The entity, in reality, underwrites the actuarial and investment risks associated with the plan. Thus, the expense recognised in a defined benefit plan is not necessarily the amount of the contribution due for the period.

Entities use actuarial valuation to estimate the present value of defined benefit obligations at the balance sheet date. They use the "projected unit credit method" to estimate the present value of the defined benefit obligations of an enterprise.

Presentation of the liability under the defined benefit plan

The liability is carried in the balance sheet at the difference between the amount of the obligation and the fair value of the plan asset. For example, if the amount of the obligation is ₹1,000 and the fair value of the plan asset is ₹900, the liability recognised in the balance sheet is (₹1,000 – 900) or ₹100.

If the fair value of the plan asset is higher than the amount of the obligation, then the surplus is recognised as an asset, subject to the asset ceiling. The *asset ceiling* is the present value of any economic benefits available to the entity in the form of:

(i) a refund, to which the entity has unconditional right; or
(ii) a reduction in future contributions.

For example, if the fair value of the plan asset is ₹20,000 and the amount of the obligation is 18,000, the asset should be recognised subject to the asset ceiling. If the asset ceiling is ₹1,500, the asset is measured at ₹1,500, although the fair value of the plan asset is higher than the present value of the obligation by ₹2,000.

Projected unit credit method for estimating the obligation under the defined benefit plan

The projected unit credit method considers each period of service as giving rise to an additional unit of benefit entitlement and measures each unit separately to build up the final obligation. In short, the projected unit cost method estimates obligations for services already rendered by employees up to the valuation date. However, in estimating the obligations, it makes many assumptions, including the assumption about the rate at which benefits will be payable to the employee. Let us take an example. An employee, who has completed 10 years of service at the balance sheet date and is expected to work for another 10 years before retirement, is entitled to gratuity on retirement. The entitlement is determined by a formula that takes into consideration the period of service and the last pay drawn. The projected unit credit method will estimate the obligation on the balance sheet date taking into consideration, among other things, the period of service completed by the employee at the balance sheet date and the estimated salary that he will draw immediately before retirement.

NOTES

ILLUSTRATION 20.4 Unit Credit Method

JJ Limited (JJL) operates a defined benefit plan that provides an annual pension of 1/40th of the final salary for each year of service. The total expected annual salary on retirement of employees covered by the plan is ₹40,00,000. All the employees are expected to retire in 10 years and have worked for five years to date (March 31, 2018). After retirement, the employees are expected to live for 20 years.

Required

Explain how the unit credit method will be applied to calculate the defined benefit obligation as at March 31, 2018 and the employee cost for the accounting year 2017–18.

Solution

The defined benefit obligation is the present value of the expected payment to employees over a period of 15 years. Up to March 31, 2018, employees have rendered service for five years. Therefore, they have earned pension of (₹40,00,000 × 1/40 × 5) or ₹5,00,000 per annum. They are expected to live for 15 years. Therefore, the total pension payable is (₹5,00,000 × 15) or ₹75,00,000. The defined benefit obligation as at March 31, 2018 is the present value of ₹75,00,000 calculated using the appropriate discount rate.

The employee cost for the accounting year 2017–18 is equal to the present value of (₹40,00,000 × 1/40 × 15) or ₹15,00,000, adjusted for the actuarially determined probability of outcome.

Discount rate for estimating obligation under the defined benefit plan

Discount rate has a material effect on the measurement of defined benefit obligation. It reflects the time value of money, but not the actuarial or investment risk. Furthermore, it does not reflect the entity-specific credit risk borne by the entity's creditors, nor does it reflect the risk that future experience may differ from actuarial assumptions.

Entities should use the discount rate determined by reference to market yields at the end of the reporting period on government bonds. However, subsidiaries, associates, joint ventures and branches domiciled outside India should use the discount rate determined by reference to market yields at the end of the reporting period on high quality corporate bonds.

Key Terms
Asset ceiling, Defined benefit plan, Defined contribution plan, Projected unit credit method

SUMMARY

Post-employment benefits include (i) retirement benefits, e.g. gratuity and pension, and (ii) other benefits, e.g. post-employment life insurance and post-employment medical care. Post-employment benefit plans are classified into (i) defined contribution plan, and (ii) defined benefit plan. In defined contribution plan, the financial risks are borne by employees. The amount of benefit depends on the performance of plan assets. Under a defined benefit plan, the benefit to employees is defined. Therefore, under such a plan, the employer has the obligation to provide the agreed benefits to the current and former employees. An enterprise uses actuarial valuation to determine the defined benefit obligations at the balance sheet date. Projected unit credit method is used to estimate the defined benefit obligation. The liability under a defined benefit plan is recognised in the balance sheet at the amount, which is the difference between the estimated amount of the obligation and the fair value of the plan asset. If the fair value of the plan asset exceeds the estimated amount of the obligation, an asset is recognised measured at the difference between the fair value of the plan asset and the obligation, subject to asset ceiling.

NOTES

Self-Test Questions

Self-test question 20.4

Indicate whether the following statements are true (T) or false (F):

(i) Gratuity payable under the Payment of Gratuity Act should be classified as a benefit under 'defined benefit plan'.

(ii) Contributory pension scheme should be classified as a 'defined benefit plan'.

(iii) The defined benefit obligation is presented as a liability in the balance sheet and the fair value of the plan asset is presented as an asset in the balance sheet.

(iv) The liability under a defined benefit scheme is recognised as and when employees render service and not when the benefits are payable.

(v) Discount rate used to estimate the defined benefit obligation should reflect only the time value of money.

ANSWERS TO SELF-TEST QUESTIONS

20.1 (i) T; (ii) F; (iii) T; (iv) F; (v) T

20.2 (i) F; (ii) T; (iii) F; (iv) F; (v) F

20.3 (i) F; (ii) T; (iii) T; (iv) F

20.4 (i) T; (ii) F; (iii) F; (iv) T; (v) T

ASSIGNMENTS

MCQ

1. Write brief answers to the following questions:

   (i) How disclosure of information on contingent liabilities help in analysing financial statements?

   (ii) Why does recognition of constructive obligations lead to early recognition of contractual obligations?

   (iii) Why it is said that there is a thin difference between provision and contingent liability?

   (iv) How do information on commitments help in analysing financial statements?

   (v) Why should liability not be recognised future operating expenses or losses?

   (vi) Which is the underlying accounting convention of the accounting principle that requires provision should be recognised for estimated loss from an executory contract that is onerous?

   (vii) Which is the underlying accounting convention of the accounting principle that requires provision should be recognised for estimated liability for post-retirement employee benefits under-defined benefit schemes every year during the period when employees remain in service?

   (viii) What is 'uncovered pension liability'?

   (ix) Why it is that in determining the discount rate, which is used for estimating the liability for post-retirement employee benefits under the defined benefit scheme, the benchmark rate in India is the market yield of government bonds, while in advanced economies, it is the market yield of high-quality corporate bonds?

   (x) What is the difference between 'reasonable certainty' and 'virtual certainty'?

2. K Limited (KL) has received a notice from the government to shift its leather processing plant in the outskirts of Kolkata, where a leather complex has been established by the government. The board of the company in its meeting dated March 31, 2019 decided to shift the plant to the land allocated to the company in the leather complex before June 30, 2019. The estimated cost of constructing the factory building and shifting the plant is ₹1 crore.

   Required: Explain whether the company should recognise a provision for the expenditure in its balance sheet dated March 31, 2019.

3. The Pollution Control Department of the Union Government reimburses 25% of the environment remedial costs incurred by a manufacturing enterprise, subject to fulfillment of certain conditions. One of the environmental laws, which is recently promulgated, requires manufacturing firms to remedy the damage caused to the environment through its manufacturing process. Y Limited (YL) estimates that it will incur an expenditure of ₹50 lakhs towards remediation of environment due to damage caused by its manufacturing process during 2017–18 and earlier years. Government reimburses 20% of the expenditure only after the expenditure is incurred.

   Required: Explain what are the assets and liabilities to be recognised in the balance sheet dated March 31, 2018 and at what amounts?

Business Combination and Consolidated Financial Statements

CHAPTER 21

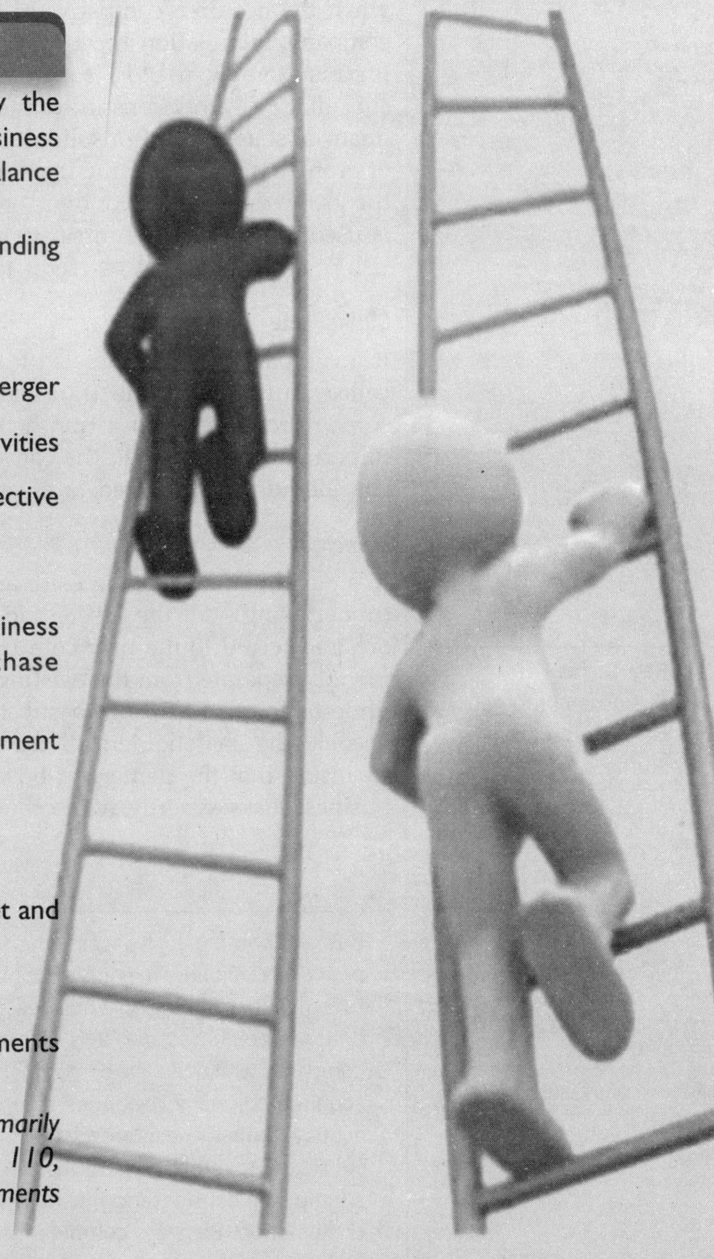

LEARNING OBJECTIVES

This chapter aims to provide understanding of only the basic principles and methods of accounting for business combination and for the preparation of consolidated balance sheet and consolidated statement of profit and loss.

After reading this chapter, you will develop understanding of the following:

- Nature of business combination
- The concepts of business, slump sale and demerger
- The concept of control, power and relevant activities
- The concept of potential voting rights and protective rights
- The concept of variability of return
- Acquisition method of accounting for business combination, reverse acquisition, purchase consideration and valuation
- Non-controlling interest (NCI) and its measurement
- Acquisition in stages
- Measurement of goodwill and capital reserve
- Method for preparing consolidated balance sheet and consolidated statement of profit and loss
- Concept of associates and joint ventures
- Equity method for consolidating financial statements of associates and joint ventures

Applicable Ind AS: *Discussion in this chapter is primarily based on Ind AS 103, Business Combination; Ind AS 110, Consolidated financial statements; and Ind AS 28, Investments in Associates and Joint Ventures.*

INTRODUCTION

Business combination occurs when one company or any other entity acquires control of another entity or company. We shall discuss business combination in the context of companies.

It is quite common that in a business combination two companies merge together to combine the businesses and continue as a single entity. For example, X Ltd. and Y Ltd. combine and decide to form Z Ltd., which will run the combined business. But emergence of a new entity is not necessary. For example, X Ltd. and Y Ltd. combine and decide to run the combined business as X Ltd.

It is also quite common that a company acquires control of another company, while the other company continues to operate as a separate company. For example, X Ltd. acquires control of Y Ltd. and both the companies continue to operate as separate entities. The company that controls the other company (in this example, X Ltd.) is called *parent* and that other company (in this example, Y Ltd.) is called *subsidiary*. In other words, when the acquiree company (in this example, Y Ltd.) continues to operate as a separate company, the relationship between the acquirer (in this example, X Ltd.) and the acquiree (in this example, Y Ltd.) is said to have the parent-subsidiary relationship. The parent and subsidiary together constitutes the *Group*. The parent is required to present the consolidated financial statements. Consolidated financial statements present the balance sheet, statement of profit, cash flow statement and statement of changes in equity of the group assuming that the group is a single economic entity. Information in the consolidated financial statements is used to estimate the intrinsic value of the equity of the parent and to assess the credit risk of extending loan or credit to the parent.

Slump sale

If a company acquires assets of another company for a lump sum consideration (usually called slump sale), the transaction does not result in business combination. Business combination occurs in a transaction involving acquisition of a 'business'. Therefore, it is important to understand the concept of 'control' and 'business'. In slump sale the purchase consideration is allocated to assets acquired. Goodwill does not arise in slump sale.

Demerger

In a demerger, an existing company forms a new company to hive off one of its businesses (undertaking). All the assets and liabilities of the undertaking of the demerged business are transferred to the new company. The new company, which has an economic and legal identity separate from the existing company, issues shares to shareholders of the demerged undertaking. As a result, a substantial number of shareholders of the existing company become the shareholders of the new company. Usually, companies demerge a business to ensure that the demerged business get the required attention and when the demerged business lacks synergy with other businesses of the company.

Key Terms
Business combination, Demerger, Parent, Slump sale, Subsidiary

SUMMARY

Business combination occurs when one company or any other entity acquires control of another entity or company. It is quite common that in a business combination two companies merge together to combine the businesses and continue as a single entity. But emergence of a new entity is not necessary. It is also quite common that a company acquires control of another company, while the other company continues to operate as a separate company. When the acquiree company continues to operate as a separate company, the relationship between the acquirer and the acquiree is said to have the parent-subsidiary relationship. The parent and subsidiary together constitutes the Group. If a company acquires assets of another company for a lump sum consideration (usually called *slump sale*), the transaction does not result in business combination. Business combination occurs in a transaction involving acquisition of a 'business'.

In a demerger, an existing company forms a new company to hive off one of its businesses (undertaking).

Self-Test Questions

Self-test question 21.1

Indicate whether the following statements are true (T) or false (F):

(i) When two existing companies combine a new company comes into existence.

(ii) Business combination might not occur when one company acquires all the assets and assumes all the liabilities of another company.

(iii) A holding-subsidiary relationship arises only when the investor acquires less than 100% shares of the transferee company.

(iv) When an existing company hives off a part of its undertaking, it is called demerger.

(v) A Group consists of the holding company and its subsidiaries.

CONTROL

Ind AS 10, Consolidated Financial Statements, defines control as follows:

> "An investor controls an investee when it is exposed, or has rights, to variable returns from its involvement with the investee and has the ability to affect those returns through its power over the investee."

The definition of control is very wide to bring into net all kind of relationships of the investor with the investee, which give the investor substantive right to control the relevant activities of the investee.

A right is substantive if the investor can exercise it when investee takes decisions. Simply saying, the investor's right is substantive if it has the current ability to exercise the right. For example, Y holds 100% voting rights of Z Ltd. However, the government, due to some reason, has taken over the management of Z Ltd. and prohibited Y from exercising its voting rights. The voting right of Y is not substantive, as it cannot exercise the right at present.

Components of control

Control requires power, exposure to variability of returns and a linkage between the two.

In some situations, it is quite complex to assess whether the investor has control over the investee. In the following sections, we shall explain fundamental principles wih simple examples.

Power and Relevant Activities

The investor has power if it has the current ability to direct relevant activities of the investee.

Protective rights

An investor does not consider its protective rights in assessing whether it has power to direct the relevant activities. Protective rights are related to fundamental changes in the activities of an investee, or rights that apply only in exceptional circumstances. Examples of protective rights are rights that can be exercised when the entity decides changing the constitution or selling an undertaking or commencing bankruptcy proceedings. Sometimes, protective rights become exercisable in exceptional circumstances. For example, a lender can exercise protective rights when the borrower breaches the borrowing covenants.

Relevant activities

Relevant activities are the activities which significantly affect the investee's return.

A range of operating and financing activities significantly affect the investee's return. Examples of relevant activities of a business enterprise are: sales of goods, acquisition and

NOTES

disposal of operating assets, determination of capital structure and sources of financing, management of research and development activities and management of investments.

In some types of entities, in depth analysis is required to identify relevant activities. For example, in case of structured entities, such as securitisation vehicle, in depth analysis might be required to identify relevant activities.

Relevant activities directed through voting rights

In case of those entities where decisions regarding relevant activities are made by the investee's board of directors, for example, if the investee is a limited liability company, voting rights are important, as directors are appointed or removed by shareholders.

More than 50% of voting rights of the investee

When an investor holds more than 50% of the voting rights of the investee, it enjoys the power to control the relevant activities of the investee, unless there are restrictions on exercising the voting right. For example, if Y Ltd. holds more than 50% of the voting rights of Z Ltd., it is straightforward to conclude that Y Ltd. controls Z Ltd. However, Y Ltd. should consider its substantive potential voting rights and the same of others.

Potential voting right

An example of potential voting right is call option on the shares of the investee. Call option gives the right to the holder to buy shares at a specified price on or before a specified date. Therefore, call option gives the holder potential voting right. If the holder has the current ability to exercise the option, the potential voting right is substantive. If the holder of the potential voting right does not have the current ability to exercise the right, the potential voting right is not substantive.

While evaluating its percentage of voting rights in the investee, the investor should consider its and other investors' substantive potential voting rights.

Example 21.1 (Potential voting rights)

The number of outstanding voting shares of Z Ltd. is 1,000. Y Ltd. holds 520 of the shares and K Ltd. holds 480 shares. K Ltd. also holds call option on the 200 shares of Z Ltd. and it has the current ability to exercise the option. Y Ltd. should consider percentage of its voting right, assuming that K Ltd. will exercise the call option. If, K Ltd. exercises the call option, its voting right will be (680/1,200) or 56.67%. Therefore, Y has no control over Z, although it currently holds 52% voting rights of Z Ltd. K Ltd. has power to control the relevant activities of Z Ltd.

Rights from other contractual arrangements

An investor should assess its contractual arrangement with other investors in assessing whether it has power to direct the relevant activities of the investee.

Example 21.2 (Contractual arrangement)

K Ltd. holds 60% voting rights in M Ltd. P Ltd. holds 20% voting rights in M Ltd. K Ltd. is primarily a financier and has no understanding of the business of M Ltd. K Ltd. and P Ltd. enters into an agreement under which K Ltd. agrees to vote in accordance with the wishes of P Ltd.

P Ltd., and not K Ltd., has the power to control the relevant activities of M Ltd.

Defacto power

An investor, that has less than 50% shareholding in the investee may have power to direct relevant activities of the investee even without agreements with other investors. When the investor holds significantly more voting rights than any other vote holder or organised group of vote holders, the investor is likely to have power to direct the relevant activities of the investee. Facts need to be considered in assessing whether the investor has defacto control over the investee.

Example 21.3 (Defacto power)

Y Ltd. holds 35% equity shares with voting rights of Z Ltd. The rest of the shares are held by thousands of dispersed shareholders. In this case, Y Ltd. (dominant shareholder) has power to direct the relevant activities of Z Ltd.

Example 21.4 (Defacto power)

Y Ltd. holds 35% equity shares with voting rights of Z Ltd. Institutional investors together hold 25% of the equity shares of Z Ltd. The rest of the shares are held by thousands of dispersed shareholders, none of whom individually holds more than 1% of equity shares. Past record shows that in recent meetings institutional investors reached an agreement and voted together either for or against a resolution. Only 3% of retail investors voted on resolutions. In this case, Y Ltd. (dominant shareholder) has power to direct the relevant activities of Z Ltd, as directors are appointed by simple majority (ordinary resolution).

Example 21.5 (Defacto power)

Y Ltd. holds 35% equity shares with voting rights of Z Ltd. Institutional investors together hold 25% of the equity shares of Z Ltd. The rest of the shares are held by thousands of dispersed shareholders, none of whom individually holds more than 1% of equity shares. Past record shows that in the recent meetings institutional investors reached an agreement and voted together either for or against a resolution. The 80% of retail investors voted on resolutions. In this case, Y Ltd. (dominant shareholder) does not have power to direct the relevant activities of Z Ltd.

Relevant activities not directed through voting rights

When voting rights are not relevant, the investor considers the following factors to assess whether it has control over the investee:

(i) Evidence of the practical ability to direct the relevant activities;
(ii) Indications of special relationship with the investee; and
(iii) Whether the investor has large exposure to variability of returns.

Examples of the practical ability to direct the relevant activities are: (i) the investor can appoint or approve the appointment of key management personnel of the investee; and (ii) the investor can direct the investee to enter into significant transactions for the benefit of the investor.

Examples of special relationship with the investee are: (i) key managerial personnel of the investee are ex-employees of the investor; (ii) the investor provides fund, critical technology, etc. and therefore, investee's operations are dependent on the investor; and (iii) a significant portion of the investee's activities are conducted on behalf of the investor.

Variability of Return

In order to have control for the purpose of business combination or preparation of consolidated financial statements, it is essential that the investor is exposed to variable returns from the involvement with the investee.

The GAAP (Ind AS) stipulates, "An investor is exposed, or has rights, to variable returns from its involvement with the investee when the investor's returns from its involvement have the potential to vary as a result of the investee's performance." The definition is very broad and is not limited to returns that might vary in their calculations.

Examples of variable returns are:

(i) Dividend from investment in equity issued by the investee, interest from investment in debt instruments issued by the investee and changes in the value of the investor's investment in the equity or debt securities of the investee;
(ii) Remuneration or fees receivable from investee from services provided to it;

NOTES

(iii) Tax benefits;

(iv) Residual interest in the investee's net assets in the situation of liquidation;

(v) Benefits that are available due to synergies between the operations of the investor and the investee.

The investor's returns can be only positive, only negative or both positive and negative.

In many situations an in-depth analysis is required to understand investor's exposure to variability of return from the relationship with the investee.

Linkage

An investor controls an investee if the investor not only has power over the investee and exposure or rights to variable returns from its involvement with the investee, but also has the ability to use its power to affect the investor's returns from its involvement with the investee.

If the investor is an agent, the linkage is missing.

In some cases, an in-depth analysis is required. For example, an in-depth analysis is required to assess whether the Fund Manager is acting as an agent or as a principal.

Key Terms
Control, Defacto power, Potential voting rights, Relevant activities, Substantive right, Variability of return

SUMMARY

An investor controls an investee when it is exposed, or has rights, to variable returns from its involvement with the investee and has the ability to affect those returns through its power over the investee. Control requires power, exposure to variability of returns and a linkage between the two. The investor has power if it has the current ability to direct relevant activities of the investee. An investor does not consider its protective rights in assessing whether it has power to direct the relevant activities. Protective rights are related to fundamental changes in the activities of an investee, or rights that apply only in exceptional circumstances.

Relevant activities are those activities, which significantly affect the investee's return. A range of operating and financing activities significantly affect the investee's return. In case of those entities where decisions regarding relevant activities are made by the investee's board of directors, for example, if the investee is a limited liability company, voting rights are important, as directors are appointed or removed by shareholders. While evaluating its percentage of voting rights in the investee, the investor should consider its and other investors' substantive potential voting rights. An investor should assess its contractual arrangement with other investors in assessing whether it has power to direct the relevant activities of the investee. An investor, which has less than 50% shareholding in the investee may have power to direct relevant activities of the investee even without agreements with other investors.

In order to have control for the purpose of business combination or preparation of consolidated financial statements, it is essential that the investor is exposed to variable returns from the involvement with the investee.

If the investor is an agent, the linkage between the power and right to variability of return is missing.

Self-Test Questions

Self-test question 21.2

State whether the following statements are true (T) or false (F):

(i) If the investor has no right or is not exposed to variable return from the investee, the question of control does not arise.

(ii) If decisions on relevant activities of the investee is taken using votes, the investor has control over the investee only if it holds more than 50% of the voting rights of the investee.

(iii) A potential voting right is substantive if that can be translated into present voting right (say, by exercising a call option) immediately when the decision is taken.
(iv) An investor should consider its own substantive potential voting rights only in determining whether it controls the investee.
(v) An investor might not have control over the investee if the investor holds less than 50% of the voting rights of the investee, even if all other shareholders are dispersed and cannot consult each other in exercising voting rights.
(vi) An investor should take into account past voting pattern of dispersed investors in assessing whether it has control over the investee.
(vii) An investor can enter into agreement with other investors to have control over the investee.
(viii) In an entity where decisions on relevant activities are not taken through voting, the investor control the investee if the investor can appoint or approve the appointment of key management personnel of the investee.
(ix) Usually, in order to have control over the investee, the investor should have practical ability to direct operating and financing activities of the investee, which significantly affect the return.
(x) Often fund managers act as an agent of the investor and therefore, do not control the investee.
(xi) An entity which has extended loan to another entity is exposed to variable return from that other entity.

BUSINESS COMBINATION

Business combination arises only when the transaction involves acquisition of business. Although the rules are applicable to all types of entities, we shall use the term company for easy understanding.

Business—The Concept

Acquisition of assets and group of assets

The acquisition of an asset or a group of assets may not constitute a business, as business is an integrated set of inputs (assets) and processes. If, the transaction does not involve acquisition of business, but acquisition of a group assets by paying a lump sum amount (often called *slump sale*), the acquirer (buyer) identifies and recognises the individual identifiable assets acquired, and liabilities assumed. It allocates the cost of the group to the individual identifiable assets and liabilities on the basis of their relative *fair values* at the date of purchase. Such a transaction or event does not give rise to goodwill.

Business

Ind As 103, Business Combination, defines business.

A business has two important components—inputs and processes. It is an integrated set of activities and assets (inputs), which is capable of producing output (e.g., goods and services).

Inputs

An input is any economic resource that creates, or has the ability to create, outputs when one or more processes are applied to it. Examples include non-current assets (including intangible assets or rights to use non-current assets), intellectual property, the ability to obtain access to necessary materials or rights and employees.

Process

Process is any system, standard, protocol, convention or rule that when applied to an input or inputs, creates or has the ability to create outputs. Examples include strategic management processes, operational processes and resource management processes. These processes typically are documented, but an organised workforce having the necessary skills and experience following rules and conventions may provide the necessary processes that are capable of being applied to inputs to create outputs. (Accounting, billing, payroll and other administrative systems typically are not processes used to create outputs.)

Output

Output is the result of inputs and processes applied to those inputs that provide or have the ability to provide a return in the form of dividends, lower costs or other economic benefits directly to investors or other owners, members or participants.

Essential components of a business are inputs and processes. However, a business need not include all of the inputs or processes that the seller used in operating that business if, market participants are capable of acquiring the business and continuing to produce outputs, for example, by integrating the business with their own inputs and processes.

CASE STUDY 21.1 Business Acquisition

K Electricals Limited (KEL) manufactures small transformers and power transformers in two different manufacturing facilities. The procurement and HR functions are centralised in the corporate office. N Ltd. (NL) decides to purchase the small transformer division with all the assets and processes and to retain senior executives. NL will integrate the operation of the small transformer business with its own centralised procurement and HR function.

Question

The CFO of NL seeks your advice on whether the transaction involves business acquisition.

Solution

The transaction involves business acquisition, NL has acquired the inputs (assets) and processes (by retaining senior executives) and it will integrate the inputs and processes acquired with its procurement and HR functions to produce output.

The nature of the elements of a business varies by industry and by the structure of an entity's operations (activities), including the entity's stage of development. Established businesses often have many different types of inputs, processes and outputs, whereas new businesses often have few inputs and processes and sometimes only a single output (product). Most of businesses also have liabilities, but a business need not have liabilities.

In the absence of evidence to the contrary, a particular set of assets and activities in which goodwill is present should be presumed to be a business. However, a business need not have goodwill. For example, if the purchase consideration is ₹1,00,000 and the fair value of net assets (assets less liabilities) acquired is ₹80,000, goodwill of (₹1,00,000 – 80,000) or ₹20,000 is present in the transaction. In this case no further evaluation is required to assess whether the transaction involves acquisition of business, provided the acquirer acquires the assets and the process (e.g., in the form of documents describing production process, Standards of operations, trade mark, etc.).

It is often not difficult to assess whether the transaction involves acquisition of business or acquisition of assets. But, in certain situations in-depth analysis is required to decide whether the transaction involves business acquisition.

NOTES

CASE STUDY 21.2 Assets Acquisition

J Ltd. (JL) was in the business of manufacturing biscuits. The facility manufacturing biscuits is closed for a long time as the company exited from biscuit production, as it was unable to compete with national and international brands. P Ltd (PL)., which produces a popular brand of biscuits, decides to acquire the biscuit manufacturing facility of JL at the purchase consideration of ₹1,00,000.

Question

The CFO of PL seeks your advice on whether the transaction involves business acquisition.

Solution

The transaction does not involve business acquisition, as PL has acquired only the assets (inputs) and not processes. The purchase consideration should be allocated to the assets acquired in proportion to the fair value of assets.

Acquisition Method

Ind AS 103 requires that a company should account for each business combination by applying the acquisition method. However, in a business combination involving group companies, the acquisition method is not applicable.

Acquisition method is also called the 'purchase method', because accounting is similar to accounting for purchases.

Applying the acquisition method requires:

(i) Identifying the acquirer;

(ii) Determining the *acquisition date;*

(iii) Recognising and measuring the identifiable assets acquired, the liabilities assumed and any non-controlling interest in the acquiree; and

(iv) Recognising and measuring goodwill or a gain from a bargain purchase.

Identifying Acquirer

Acquirer is the combining company which acquires the control of the other combining company or companies. In most business combinations identifying the acquirer is straightforward.

Combination effected primarily by transferring cash/other assets or by incurring liabilities

The acquirer is the company that transfer the cash or other assets or by incurring liabilities.

For example, if D Ltd. (DL) acquires control of Q Ltd. (QL), by transferring cash to its owners, then DL is the acquirer.

Combination effected primarily by issuing equity shares

The acquirer is the company that issues new equity shares. However, there are two exceptions. First, in case of reverse acquisitions, the issuing company is the acquiree. Second, when a new company is created to issue equity shares to effect business combination. We shall discuss both the exceptions separately.

Other factors

Sometimes various other factors, such as, relative voting rights, composition of the governing body, composition of senior management, relative sizes, etc. are considered to identify the acquirer.

NOTES

New entity formed to effect business combination

A new entity formed to effect a business combination is not necessarily the acquirer. If a new entity is formed to issue equity interests to effect a business combination, one of the combining entities that existed before the business combination shall be identified as the acquirer. In contrast, a new entity that transfers cash or other assets or incurs liabilities as consideration may be the acquirer.

For example, if three companies P, Q and S are combining to create Z and Z issues the equity shares, then Z is not the acquirer. One of the three combining companies will be identified as acquirer. This is important for two reasons. First, Z was not in existence when the deal was finalised and therefore, Z cannot be the acquirer. Second, as we shall see later, in acquisition accounting, the carrying amount of the assets and liabilities of the acquirer is not restated at fair value, while that of the acquiree is restated at fair value.

The acquirer is identified considering various factors, which have not been discussed in detail in this text. For example, if there is large minority voting interest and no other owner or organised group of owners have significant voting interest, then acquirer is usually the combining entity whose single owner or organised group of owners hold the largest minority voting interest in the combining entity. For example, if P owns 40% of the voting interest in the newly formed company and other six combining companies, each of which will hold 10% of equity interest in the newly formed company, P is the acquirer.

Reverse acquisition

A reverse acquisition occurs when the company that issues shares (the legal acquirer) is identified as the acquiree for accounting purposes. The company whose equity interests are acquired (the legal acquiree) must be the acquirer for accounting purposes for the transaction to be considered a reverse acquisition. For example, reverse acquisitions sometimes occur when a private limited company wants to become a listed company but does not want to register its equity shares. To accomplish that, the private company will arrange for a listed company to acquire its equity shares in exchange for the equity shares of the listed company. In this example, the listed company is the legal acquirer because it issued its equity shares, and the private limited company is the legal acquiree because its equity shares were acquired. However, application of the guidance in Ind AS 103 results in identifying:

(a) The listed company as the acquiree for accounting purposes (the accounting acquiree); and

(b) The private limited company as the acquirer for accounting purposes (the accounting acquirer).

The accounting acquiree must meet the definition of a business for the transaction to be accounted for as a reverse acquisition, and all of the recognition and measurement principles in Ind AS 103, including the requirement to recognise goodwill, apply.

Identifying Acquisition Date

Determining the acquisition date is important because it is the date on which the fair value of the consideration transferred by the acquirer and the assets acquired and liabilities assumed by it is estimated. This is the date on which Non-Controlling Interest (NCI, earlier called, minority interest) and goodwill are measured and recognised.

Acquisition date is the date on which the acquirer obtains control of the acquiree. In other words, acquisition date is the date on which the investor exposes itself to variable returns from its association with the investee and it acquires the ability to affect those returns through power over the relevant activities of the investee.

Determining the acquisition date is usually straightforward. However, sometimes, in-depth analysis is required because the acquirer (investor) and acquiree (investee) enter into an agreement much before the date the transaction is occurred, and, in many occasions, regulatory and other hurdles are to be passed before the companies can give effect to the transaction.

NOTES

Business combination achieved in stages (step acquisition)

Sometimes the acquirer acquires control over the acquires through successive purchases of shares. In that situation, the date of acquisition is the date the acquirer obtains control of the acquiree.

Consideration Transferred

Purchase consideration transferred should not include payment made for other elements of the transaction, that is payments that are not made to acquire control. For example, payment for settling pre-existing relationship, remunerating employees or former owners of the acquiree for future services or reimbursing the acquiree or its former owners for paying the acquirer's acquisition related costs are not part of the purchase consideration.

Acquisition related costs

Acquisition-related costs are the costs, which the acquirer incurs to effect a business combination. Those costs include finder's fees; advisory, legal, accounting, valuation and other professional or consulting fees; general administrative costs, including the costs of maintaining an internal acquisitions department; and costs of registering and issuing debt and equity securities. Those costs are not included in the purchase consideration. The acquirer should recognise them as expenses in the periods in which they are incurred, and the services are received, except that the costs to issue debt or equity securities should be recognised in accordance with accounting principles for the accounting for financial instruments.

Pre-existing relationship

Pre-existing relationships are effectively settled in business combination, because the acquirer consolidates the acquiree. Ind AS 103 provides various examples on the gain or loss on settlement of pre-existing relation due to business combination is calculated.

As a general principle, the acquirer assesses whether the settlement is favourable or unfavourable to it taking into account market perspective, measures gain or loss and adjust the purchase consideration by fair value or off-market consideration. We are providing few examples to explain the concept.

Example 21.6 (Pre-existing legal case)

Y Ltd. acquires Z Ltd. There is a court case going on between Y Ltd. and Z Ltd. Y is the defendant and Z is the plaintiff. Y has provided for the obligation at ₹10,000. The fair value of the obligation is ₹8,000. Therefore, the settlement, on consolidation, results in a gain of ₹2,000 which is recognised by Y. The purchase consideration should be reduced by the fair value of the obligation. If, the amount paid by Y to the earlier owners of Z is ₹1,00,000, the purchase consideration for calculating goodwill/capital reserve is (₹1,00,000 – 8,000) or ₹92,000.

Example 21.7 (Long-term contract)

Y Ltd. acquires Z Ltd. Y has a long-term, fixed-price supply contract with Z. On the acquisition date, the supply contract will run of another three years. The penalty to exit the contract is ₹1,00,000. On acquisition of Z by Y, the contract is settled. In such settlement the purchase consideration is reduced by the lower of the penalty and the compared market (off-market consideration) perspective. Assume that Y values the off-market consideration at ₹70,000. Therefore, Y will reduce the consideration by ₹70,000 and will recognise a loss of ₹70,000. Suppose that the penalty for exiting the contract is ₹50,000. Then, Y will reduce the consideration by ₹50,000 and will recognise a loss of ₹50,000.

NOTES

Valuation of purchase consideration

The purchase consideration transferred is measured at fair value. However, any portion of acquirer's share-based payment awards issued to replace awards held by the acquiree's employees are measured in accordance with Ind AS 102, Share-based payment.

Deferred consideration

Deferred payments are obligations to pay specified amounts at future dates. The fair value of the deferred consideration at the acquisition date is included in the purchase consideration. The unwinding of any interest element in the deferred consideration is recognised in profit or loss.

Contingent consideration

Contingent consideration is an obligation of the acquirer to transfer additional assets or equity interests to the former owners of an acquiree as part of the exchange for control of the acquiree if, specified future events occur or conditions are met. For example, the acquirer may be obliged to transfer additional cash or equity instrument if the post-combination earnings or share price exceeds the target.

Contingent consideration also may give the acquirer the right to the return of previously transferred consideration if, specified conditions are not met. For example, as per the agreement, the previous owners of the acquiree have the obligation to repay a part of the purchase consideration paid if, the post-combination performance target is not met.

The fair value of the contingent consideration at the acquisition date is included in the purchase consideration.

Asset transferred, or liabilities assumed by the acquirer

Assets transferred, or liabilities assumed by the acquirer as a part of the purchase consideration transferred in a business combination are measured at their acquisition date fair value. The gain or loss is recognised in profit or loss.

Business combination with no consideration transferred

A business combination can occur without the acquirer transferring consideration.

Example 21.8 (Business combination without transfer of consideration)

Y Ltd. had held 45% shares of Z Ltd. Z Ltd. bought back 20% of its shares in which Y Ltd. did not participate. Therefore, the shareholding of Y Ltd. in Z Ltd. has gone up from 45% to 56.25%. In the process Y Ltd. acquired control of Z Ltd. without transferring any consideration.

In a business combination achieved without the transfer of consideration, the acquirer must substitute the acquisition-date fair value of its interest in the acquiree for the acquisition-date fair value of the consideration transferred to measure goodwill or a capital reserve. In Example 21.8, Y Ltd. should consider the acquisition-date fair value of its 45% holding to measure goodwill or capital reserve.

Identifiable Assets Acquired, and Liabilities Assumed

Recognition of identifiable assets acquired, and liabilities assumed

On the acquisition date, the acquirer should recognise, the identifiable assets acquired, and the liabilities assumed. It recognises only those assets and liabilities, which meet the definition of asset and liability. For example, acquirer's plan to exit an activity of the acquiree or to terminate the employment of some employees under voluntary retirement scheme after acquisition does not result in an obligation at the acquisition date, and therefore, the acquirer does not recognise those costs as part of applying the acquisition method.

The acquirer also recognises separately goodwill, which is the excess of purchase consideration over the amount of net assets (identifiable assets recognised less identifiable liabilities recognised) and any non-controlling interest (NCI) in the acquiree. Earlier NCI used to be referred as 'minority interest'.

Measurement principle

The acquirer should measure the identifiable assets acquired and the liabilities assumed at their acquisition-date fair values. There are few exceptions. Discussion on all the exceptions is outside the scope of this book.

Contingent liability: Contingent liability in the books of the acquirer is recognised as a liability if it is a present obligation, in the sense 'more likely than not', and its fair value can be measured. The probability of payment is considered in estimating the fair value. For example, there is claim by the pollution control department, which is contested by the acquiree. This is a present obligation and the acquirer should recognise it as a liability at fair value. An example of a contingent liability that is not a present obligation is a performance guarantee issued by the acquirer.

Deferred taxes: The acquirer should recognise and measure a deferred tax asset or liability arising from the assets acquired and liabilities assumed in a business combination in accordance with Ind AS 12, *Income Taxes.*

Measurement of NCI

Non-controlling interest (NCI) is the equity in a subsidiary not attributable, directly or indirectly, to a parent. For example, Z Ltd. is a subsidiary of Y Ltd. Y holds 60% shares (equity) of Z. Therefore, 40% equity is held by entities other than Y. NCI is 40% equity of Z not attributable to parent (Y).

Classification of NCI

NCI has two components —'ordinary NCI' and 'other NCI'.

Ordinary NCI represents ownership interests that entitles the holder to proportionate share of the subsidiary company's net assets in liquidation.

NCI other than 'ordinary NCI' is classified as 'other NCI'. An example of other NCI is equity components of convertible bonds. When a convertible bond is issued, the proceeds is divided into liability and equity. Equity is presented as a component of 'other equity' in the balance sheet. However, if the company goes into liquidation before the conversion, total proceeds is repaid to the bond holder and shareholders do not have any claim on the equity component.

Many components of 'other equity' presented in the balance sheet are parts of 'ordinary NCI'.

Presence of 'ordinary NCI' and 'other NCI' makes the measurement little complicated. In our discussion in the following paragraphs, we shall assume that there is no 'other NCI'.

Measurement of ordinary NCI

NCI arises in the consolidated financial statements, only when the acquirer acquires less than 100% of the acquiree. A parent (acquirer) may hold 100% of the subsidiary (acquiree), if the subsidiary continues as a separate entity and maintains its own identity. NCI does not appear in the consolidated financial statements of a parent and its 100% subsidiary.

There are two options available for measuring NCI.

Option 1: NCI is valued at the fair value at the date of acquisition. It implies that goodwill or capital reserve (gain on a bargain purchase) includes a portion attributable to ordinary NCI.

NOTES

Example 21.9 (NCI is valued at fair value)

Y Ltd. acquires 60% of Z Ltd. for ₹1,100 for cash. The fair value of identifiable net assets of Z is ₹1,500. Fair value (assuming that the shares of Z is traded in the capital market, the market value) of the 40% share of NCI in Z is ₹650. Y decides to measure the NCI at fair value.

Y in its consolidated balance sheet will present the items as follows:

Assets:	
Identifiable net assets of Z:	₹1,500
Goodwill:	250
Cash	(1,100)
Liabilities and equity:	
NCI:	650

Cash is shown negative, as total cash is reduced by ₹1,100, as the acquisition is through cash.

Acquirer's (Y) share of goodwill is the excess of the purchase consideration (₹1,100) over Y's share of the fair value of net identifiable net assets (60% of ₹1,500 or ₹900), that is ₹200. NCI's share of goodwill is the difference between the fair value of NCI (₹650) and NCI's share in the fair value of identifiable net assets (40% of ₹1,500 or ₹600), that is ₹50.

Option 2: NCI is measured at the holders' proportionate amount of the recognised amount of the identifiable net assets of the acquirer. This implies that goodwill or capital reserve (gain on a bargain purchase) relates only to controlling interest acquired.

Example 21.10 (NCI is valued at holder's proportionate interest)

Considering the facts presented in Example 21.9, Y in its consolidated balance sheet will present the items as follows:

Assets:	
Identifiable net assets of Z:	₹1,500
Goodwill:	200
Cash	(1,100)
Liabilities and equity:	
NCI:	600

Cash is shown negative, as total cash is reduced by ₹1,000, as the acquisition is through cash. NCI is 40% of the fair value of the net identifiable assets (₹1,500). Goodwill is the excess of the purchase consideration (₹1,100) over Y's share of the fair value of net identifiable assets (60% of ₹1,500 or ₹900), that is ₹200. Therefore, goodwill has no share of NCI.

Measurement of other NCI

Other NCIs are measured at fair value in accordance with the relevant accounting standards (Ind AS).

Business Combination Achieved in Stages

When the acquirer acquires the acquiree through successive share purchases, it is referred as business combination achieved in stages. Obviously, at the acquisition date the acquirer holds some shares of the acquiree. For example, Y Ltd. holds 40% shares of Z Ltd. On June 30, 2019, Y purchases another 20% shares of Z. Thus, Y acquired Z in stages. First it acquired 40% shares of Z and then it purchased another 20% shares of Z to acquire control over Z. The acquisition date is June 30, 2019, which is the date on which Y acquires control of Z.

Accounting

The underlying assumption is that the non-controlling shares, which the acquirer holds at the acquisition date, is sold and repurchased along with the additional shares acquired at the acquisition date. Consequently, the difference between the fair value of the non-controlling shares at the acquisition date and the book value is recognised as gain or loss in the statement of profit and loss. The purchase consideration is the total of the fair value of the non-controlling shares held at the acquisition date and cost of new shares acquired at the acquisition date. For example, if Y holds 40% shares of Z at the acquisition date and acquires another 20% shares of Z to acquire control, it will use the following two steps:

(i) Estimate the fair value of 40% of shares held prior to acquisition and the difference between the book value and fair valė recognise as gain or loss in the statement or profit and loss;

(ii) Consider the total of the fair value of the 40% shares held prior to acquisition and the cost (fair value) of 20% shares purchased at the acquisition date as purchase consideration for estimating goodwill or capital reserve (gain on bargain purchase).

Measurement of Goodwill and Capital Reserve (Gain on Bargain Purchase)

Goodwill is the excess of the total of amounts against items listed in (A) below over the total of amounts against items listed in (B) below:

(A) **List of items**

(i) Purchase consideration transferred, which is usually measured at fair value;

(ii) Non-controlling interest (NCI); and

(iii) In a business combination achieved in stages, the acquisition date fair value of the acquirer's previously held equity interest in the investee.

(B) **List of items**

The fair value of the net identifiable assets (identifiable assets acquired less identifiable liabilities assumed) acquired. AS per Ind AS 103, some identifiable assets are not measured at fair value. In most situations those are not material. For our discussion, we have ignored those items.

A bargain purchase arises if the total amount of items listed in (B) exceeds the tòtal amount of items listed in (A).

Example 21.11 (Measurement of goodwill)

The fair value of consideration transferred by Y to acquire 60% of Z: ₹1,200

Fair value of identifiable net assets of Z over which Y acquired control: ₹1,000

NCI, measured at 40% of the fair value of identifiable net assets: ₹400

Goodwill = (₹1,200 + 400 – 1,000) or ₹600

The value of goodwill could be arrived as follows:

The fair value of consideration transferred by Y to acquire 60% of Z (₹1,200) less the 60% share of Y in the identifiable net assets of Z (0.60 × 1,000 or ₹600), that is, ₹600.

It is interesting to note that the goodwill of ₹600 relates only to controlling interest acquired.

Example 21.12 (Measurement of goodwill)

The fair value of consideration transferred by Y to shareholders of Z to acquire 60% of Z from the market: ₹1,200

Fair value of identifiable net assets of Z over which Y acquired control: ₹1,000

NCI, measured at fair value: ₹480

Goodwill = (₹1,200 + 480 – 1,000) or ₹680

It is interesting to note that the goodwill of ₹680 includes a portion attributable to ordinary NCI.

NOTES

Key Terms
Acquiree, Acquirer, Acquisition date, Bargain purchase, Business, Business combination, Contingent consideration, Goodwill, Measurement period, Non-controlling interest (NCI), Purchase consideration, reverse acquisition

Measurement Period

At the acquisition date, the acquirer may not be able to collect adequate information that is required to identify or measure:

(i) Consideration transferred;
(ii) The identifiable assets acquired, and liabilities assumed;
(iii) Any NCI;
(iv) Goodwill or capital reserve (the gain on a bargain purchase); and
(v) Any pre-existing equity interest of the acquirer in the acquiree.

Often estimating the fair value of assets and liabilities requires significant time. Valuation reports may not be available at the time of preparing and presenting the first financial statements after the business combination. If, adequate information is not available by the end of the reporting period in which the business combination occurs, the acquirer reports provisional figures in the financial statements. Subsequently, it collects more information after the reporting date and based on the new information, about facts and circumstances that existed as of the acquisition date, it changes the measurement of items listed in (i) to (v) above or recognises new items of assets and liabilities retrospectively. The period of collecting new information is called 'measurement period'. Measurement period ends when the management decides that no more new information would be available. However, the measurement period cannot exceed one year from the acquisition date.

SUMMARY

Business combination arises only when the transaction involves acquisition of business. Business is an integrated set of inputs (assets) and processes, which is capable of producing output. Process is any system, standard, protocol, convention or rule that when applied to an input or inputs, creates or has the ability to create outputs. Processes may be in writing (e.g., operation manual) or reside with employees as knowledge. In the absence of evidence to the contrary, a particular set of assets and activities in which goodwill is present should be presumed to be a business. However, a business need not necessarily have goodwill.

Acquirer is the combining company which acquires the control of the other combining company or companies. Acquirer is identified using various factors. If a new entity is formed to issue equity interests to effect a business combination, one of the combining entities that existed before the business combination shall be identified as the acquirer. In contrast, a new entity that transfers cash or other assets or incurs liabilities as consideration, may be the acquirer.

A reverse acquisition occurs when the company that issues shares (the legal acquirer) is identified as the acquiree for accounting purposes.

Acquisition date is the date on which the acquirer obtains control of the acquiree. In other words, acquisition date is the date on which the investor exposes itself to variable returns from its association with the investee and it acquires the ability to affect those returns through power over the relevant activities of the investee.

Acquisition-related costs are the costs, which the acquirer incurs to effect a business combination. Those costs are not included in the purchase consideration. The purchase consideration transferred is measured at fair value. However, any portion of acquirer's share-based payment awards issued to replace awards held by the acquiree's employees are measured in accordance with Ind AS 102, Share-based payment. The fair value of the deferred consideration at the acquisition date is included in the purchase consideration. The unwinding of any interest element in the deferred consideration is recognised in profit or loss. The fair value of the contingent consideration at the acquisition date is included in the purchase consideration. Assets transferred, or liabilities assumed by the acquirer as a part of the purchase consideration transferred in a business combination are measured at their acquisition date fair value. The gain or loss is recognised in profit or loss.

A business combination can occur without the acquirer transferring consideration.

NCI has two components—'ordinary NCI' and 'other NCI'. Ordinary NCI represents ownership interests that entitles the holder to proportionate share of the subsidiary company's net assets in liquidation. In 'other NCI' two options for measuring NCI are available. Option 1 is that NCI is valued at the fair value at the date of acquisition. Option 2 is to measure NCI at the holders' proportionate amount of the recognised amount of the identifiable net assets of the acquirer. Other NCIs are measured at fair value in accordance with the relevant accounting standard (Ind AS).

When the acquirer acquires the acquiree through successive share purchases, it is referred as business combination achieved in stages. The purchase consideration is the total of the fair value of the non-controlling shares held at the acquisition date and cost of new shares acquired at the acquisition date. The underlying assumption is that the non-controlling shares, which the acquirer holds at the acquisition date, is sold and repurchased along with the additional shares acquired at the acquisition date.

Goodwill is the excess of the total of amounts against items listed in (A) below over the total of amounts against items listed in (B) below:

(A) List of items: (i) Purchase consideration transferred, which is usually measured at fair value; (ii) Non-controlling interest (NCI); and (iii) In a business combination achieved in stages, the acquisition date fair value of the acquirer's previously held equity interest in the investee.

(B) List of items: The fair value of the net identifiable assets (identifiable assets acquired less identifiable liabilities assumed) acquired.

A bargain purchase arises if the total amount of items listed in (B) exceeds the total amount of items listed in (A).

Often it is difficult to estimate the fair value of purchase consideration and net assets. Therefore, first balance sheet is prepared with provisional figures. Companies determine the final figure within the measurement period, which cannot exceed one year from the acquisition date. The resulting adjustments are effected retrospectively.

Self-Test Questions

Self-test question 21.3

State whether the following statements are true (T) or false (F):

(i) In order to be classified as a business combination, the acquirer should necessarily acquire inputs (e.g., assets), processes and outputs.

(ii) Process is any system, standard, protocol, convention or rule that when applied to an input or inputs, creates or has the ability to create outputs, which are properly documented in writing.

(iii) When a new company is formed to run the combined business of two existing companies, the new company is identified as acquirer.

(iv) When in order to get listed in a stock exchange, a large private limited company arranges a small listed company to acquire its equity shares in exchange for the equity shares of the listed company, a reverse acquisition occurs.

(v) Acquisition date is the date on which the acquirer obtains control of the acquiree.

(vi) Acquisition related costs are included in the purchase consideration.

(vii) Pre-existing relationships are effectively settled in business combination and the fair value (market perspective) of the settlement amount is adjusted to the purchase consideration.

(viii) The fair value of the deferred consideration at the acquisition date is included in the purchase consideration.

(ix) The contingent consideration is not included in the purchase consideration.

(x) A business combination can occur without the acquirer transferring consideration.

(xi) Goodwill is measured at fair value.

(xii) Liabilities of the acquiree assumed by the acquirer are measured at fair value.

(xiii) A claim by the pollution control department, which is contested by the acquiree and presented as a contingent liability in its balance sheet, is recognised by the acquirer as a liability and is measured at fair value.

(xiv) Non-controlling interest (NCI) is the equity in a subsidiary not attributable, directly or indirectly, to a parent.

(xv) If the parent holds 60% of the acquiree, 40% of that portion of the convertible bond that is classified as equity and is included in 'other equity' in the acquiree's balance sheet is a part of 'ordinary NCI'.

(xvi) NCI appears in the consolidated financial statements even if the parent holds 100% of the subsidiary.

(xvii) In case of acquisition in stages, the purchase consideration is the total of the fair value of the non-controlling shares held at the acquisition date and cost of new shares acquired at the acquisition date.

CONSOLIDATED FINANCIAL STATEMENTS OF PARENT AND ITS SUBSIDIARIES

Consolidated financial statements present the performance and financial position of the group, which consists of the parent and its subsidiaries, *as if it is a single economic entity*. All the results and the assets and liabilities that are under the control of the parent are combined together to show single totals for each line item in the consolidated financial statements. Revenue and expenses, and assets and liabilities of the parent and subsidiaries are added together, line-by-line.

While consolidating the balance sheet, 'investment in subsidiary' in the balance sheet of the parent, which is usually measured at cost, is eliminated and the net asset (including goodwill) of the subsidiary is incorporated through line-by-line consolidation.

If the parent does not hold 100% of the net assets of the subsidiary, the portion that belongs to 'non-controlling shareholders' is presented in the consolidated balance sheet as a part of equity under the heading 'non-controlling interest' (NCI).

Similarly, in the consolidated statement of profit and loss, the share of the non-controlling interest in the net profit of the subsidiary is presented separately.

The principles of valuing identifiable net assets acquired, and liabilities assumed, measurement of goodwill or capital reserve and measurement of NCI, which are discussed in Section 21.3, are applicable in preparing the consolidated financial statements.

Consolidation of Balance Sheets

Example 21.13 (Consolidation of balance sheets)

On April 1, 2018, Y Ltd. purchased all the shares of Z Ltd. for ₹25,000, which was the fair value of the net assets of Z on the date of acquisition. The book value of net assets of Z was the same as their fair value. The net assets of Z were financed by equity (share capital ₹10,000 and retained earnings ₹15,000). The balance sheet of individual entities at March 31, 2019 were as follows:

	Y (₹)	Z (₹)
EQUITY		
Share capital	50,000	10,000
Retained earnings (Reserves and surplus)	60,000	20,000
Total	1,10,000	30,000
ASSETS		
Non-current Assets		
Property, plant and equipment	65,000	24,000
Investment in Z	25,000	Nil
	90,000	24,000
Net current assets	20,000	6,000
Total	1,10,000	30,000

Consolidated Balance Sheet of Y Ltd. and its subsidiary as at March 31, 2019

	₹	Comments
EQUITY		
Share capital	50,000	Y only
Retained earnings (Reserves and surplus)	65,000	Y + post-acquisition reserve of Z (₹5,000[1])
Total	1,15,000	
ASSETS		
Non-current Assets		
Property, plant and equipment	89,000	Y + Z
Investment	Nil	Eliminated
	89,000	
Net current assets	26,000	Y + Z
Total	1,15,000	

Notes:

1. Retained earnings of Z on acquisition date was ₹15,000. The same as at March 31, 2019 was ₹20,000. Thus, the post-acquisition reserve of Z was (₹20,000 – 15,000) or ₹5,000.
2. We assumed that the purchase consideration paid by Y to acquire Z equals the fair value of net assets of Z in order to avoid computation of goodwill.
3. We assumed that the fair value of net assets of Z was the same as book value in order to simplify the consolidation process. If, acquisition date fair value was different from the book value as on that, consolidation should be based on fair value and that cause complexity.

The elimination of intra-group balances and treatment of unrealised profits on assets bought from group companies

Ind AS 110 requires:

Eliminate in full intragroup assets and liabilities, equity, income, expenses and cash flows relating to transactions between entities of the group (profits or losses resulting from intragroup transactions that are recognised in assets, such as inventory and fixed assets, are eliminated in full). Intragroup losses may indicate an impairment that requires recognition in the consolidated financial statements.

Intra-group balances are likely to arise where the parent and the subsidiary trade with each other or if the parent has more than one subsidiary, the subsidiaries trade with each other. The consolidated financial statements present the result and the financial position of the group in a manner as if the group is a single entity. Therefore, the amount that the parent owes to subsidiaries or a subsidiary owes to the parent or another subsidiary appearing as payables/receivables in their respective balance sheets must be eliminated to avoid overstatement of receivables and payables.

NOTES

Intra-group unrealised profit is also eliminated, as it is incorrect to artificially boost the profits of the group by including profit made on transfers of inventories or other assets between the constituent entities. From the group perspective, only that part of the profit is realised, which relates to that part of the inventory or other asset, which is sold outside the group.

The amount of 'Non-controlling interest' (NCI) is reduced by NCI's share in the unrealised profit, if the profit was earned by the subsidiary. If, the parent earned the profit, NCI is not adjusted.

Example 21.14 (Consolidated balance sheet)

The following are the balance sheets of Y Ltd. and Z Ltd. as at March 31, 2019:

	P (₹)		S (₹)	
EQUITY AND LIABILITIES				
Equity				
Equity shares (₹1)		1,00,000		40,000
Retained earnings		90,000		32,000
		1,90,000		72,000
Non-current Liabilities				
Preference shares	50,000		10,000	
5% Borrowings	20,000	70,000	10,000	20,000
Current Liabilities				
Trade payables	39,000		18,000	
Intra-group payables	1,000	40,000	Nil	18,000
		3,00,000		1,10,000
ASSETS				
Non-Current Assets				
Property, plant and equipment		1,45,000		50,000
Investment in Z		53,000		Nil
		1,98,000		50,000
Current Assets				
Inventories	40,000		30,000	
Trade receivables	45,000		17,600	
Intra-group receivables	—		2,500	
Cash at bank	17,000	1,02,000	9,900	60,000
		3,00,000		1,10,000

Additional information:

1. The investment of Y in Z was acquired as follows:

30,000 equity shares of ₹1	₹44,000
4,000 preference shares	₹4,000
5,000 5% borrowings	₹5,000

   The equity shares were acquired when the retained earnings of Z were ₹12,000. Since acquisition, there is no impairment of goodwill. In effect Y acquired (30,000/40,000) or 75% shares of Z.
2. A remittance of ₹1,500, sent by Y to Z on 30 March 2019, was not recorded in the books of Z until 04 April 2019.
3. Goods had been sold at normal selling price by Z to Y during the year. The total sales of such goods during the year were for ₹80,000. The inventory of Y as at 31 March 2019 contained goods purchased from Z at a selling price of ₹16,000. Z earns 20% profit margin on sales to Y.
4. At the end of the year there was no liability outstanding in respect of loan interest or preference share dividend payable.

Consolidated balance sheet of P Group as at March 31, 2019

	₹	₹	Comments
EQUITY AND LIABILITIES			
Equity			
Equity share capital	1,00,000		P only
Retained earnings	1,02,600		Working 2
	2,02,600		
Non-controlling interest	17,200	2,19,800	Working 3
Non-current Liabilities			
Preference shares	56,000		Working 4
5% Borrowings	25,000	81,000	Working 4
Current Liabilities			
Trade payables		57,000	Y + Z
		3,57,800	
ASSETS			
Non-current Assets			
Goodwill	5,000		Working 1
Property, plant and equipment	1,95,000	2,00,000	Y + Z
Current Assets			
Inventories	66,800		Y + Z, adjusted for unrealised profit (₹3,200)
Trade receivables	62,600		Y + Z
Cash-in-transit	1,500		
Cash at bank	26,900	1,57,800	Y + Z
		3,57,800	

Working Notes:

1. *Goodwill*

Cost of investment in equity shares:	₹44,000
NCI (25% of 52,000, FV of net assets on acquisition date)	13,000
	57,000
Less, FV of net assets at the acquisition date	52,000
	₹5,000

In absence of information, it is assumed that the FV of net assets of Z at the acquisition date was the same as book value of net assets, which was calculated as follows: (Equity share capital ₹40,000 + retained earnings ₹12,000, as per additional information 1)

2. *Consolidated retained earnings*

Y	₹90,000
Z 75% of post-acquisition profit (32,000 – 12,000)	15,000
75% of unrealised profit earned by Z [0.75 × 20% of ₹16,000]	(2,400)
	₹1,02,600

3. *Non-controlling interest (NCI)*

NCI at acquisition date	₹13,000
Share of post-acquisition profit [25% of (32,000 – 12,000) or ₹20,000)]	5,000
25% of unrealised profit earned by Z [0.25 × 20% of ₹16,000)]	(800)
	₹17,200

NCI is adjusted for its share in the unrealised profit as Z earned the profit. Had Y earned the unrealised profit, the total unrealised profit would have been adjusted against consolidated retained earnings.

4. *Non-current liabilities*

	Preference shares	*Borrowings*
Y	₹50,000	₹20,000
Z (10,000 – 4,000*) & (10,000 – 5,000*)	6,000	5,000
	₹56,000	₹25,000

* Preference shares and borrowings held by Y as per additional information 1.

5. Investment in Z in the balance sheet of Y is eliminated.

NOTES

Consolidation of Statements of Profit and Loss

Consolidated statement of profit and loss presents the results of the group as if it is a single economic entity.

Majority of the figures are aggregation of the line items of the parent and its subsidiary.

From the consolidated revenue and other income, and expenses, inter-company transactions are eliminated. For example, a holding company may sell goods or services to its subsidiary, receives consultancy fees, commission, royalty, etc. These items are included in sales and other income of the holding company and in the expense items of the subsidiary. Alternatively, the subsidiary may also sell goods or services to the holding company. These inter-company transactions are to be eliminated in full.

The share of the non-controlling interest (NCI) in the group profit is presented separately in the consolidated statement of profit and loss.

Unrealised profit from intra-group revenue is eliminated from the value of the consolidated inventory to arrive at the consolidated profit. Where the unrealised profit is made by a subsidiary where there is NCI, the share of NCI in the unrealised profit is adjusted against share of profit or loss of NCI. Otherwise, the total of the unrealised profit is adjusted against the parent's share in the consolidated profit or loss.

Divided received/ receivable from a subsidiary is eliminated and the retained earnings in the balance sheet are adjusted. If, the dividend is received/receivable from pre-acquisition profit, the cost of investment is reduced by the amount of dividend.

Example 21.15 (Consolidated statement of profit and loss)

The following are the statements of profit and loss of Y Ltd. and Z Ltd. for the year ended March 31, 2019:

Particulars	Y (Amount in ₹)	Z(Amount in ₹)
Income		
Revenue	6,00,000	3,00,000
Other income (investment income)	4,000	—
Total income	6,04,000	3,00,000
Expenses		
Cost of sales	4,20,000	2,30,000
Operating expenses	1,00,000	47,000
Finance cost	8,000	3,000
Income tax expense	30,000	8,000
Total expense	5,58,000	2,88,000
Net profit	**46,000**	**12,000**

Summarised statements of changes in equity for the year ended March 31, 2019

Particulars	Y (Amount in ₹)	Z(Amount in ₹)
Balance at the start of the year	78,000	48,000
Profit for the year	46,000	12,000
Dividends on equity shares	(20,000)	(5,000)
Balance at the end of the year	1,04,000	55,000

Additional information

(i) Y purchased 16,000 shares of the 20,000 outstanding shares (par value ₹1) of Z on April 1, 2016 for ₹33,000.

(ii) The balance on Z's equity on the acquisition date was ₹35,000 (Share capital ₹20,000 plus retained earnings ₹15,000).

(iii) There has been no impairment of goodwill since acquisition.

Required: Prepare a consolidated statement of profit and loss and a statement of changes in equity for the Y group for the year ended March 31, 2019.

Solution: Z is a (16,000/20,000) × 100 or 80% subsidiary of Y.

Consolidated statement of profit and loss for the year ended March 31, 2019

Particulars	Amount in ₹	Comments
Income		
Revenue	9,00,000	Y + Z
Other income (investment income)	—	Eliminated, because it represents dividend received by Y from Z[1]
Total income	9,00,000	
Expenses		
Cost of sales	6,50,000	Y + Z
Operating expenses	1,47,000	Y + Z
Finance cost	11,000	Y + Z
Income tax expense	38,000	Y + Z
Total expenses	8,46,000	
Net profit	**54,000**	
Attributable to:		
Equity holders of Y (parent)	51,600	
Non-controlling interest	2,400	20% of profit of Z (₹12,000)

Note: Non-controlling shareholders of Z received dividend of ₹1,000 and their share of the carry forward equity is 20% of ₹55,000 or ₹11,000.

1. See statement of changes in equity for the year ended March 31, 2019

Example 21.16 (Consolidated statement of profit and loss)

The following are the statements of profit and loss of Y Ltd. and Z Ltd. for the year ended March 31, 2019:

Particulars	Y (Amount in ₹)	Z(Amount in ₹)
Income		
Revenue	6,20,000	3,07,000
Other income (Investment income: dividend and interest from Z)	6,000	—
Total income	6,26,000	3,07,000
Expenses		
Cost of sales	4,20,000	2,30,000
Operating expenses	1,00,000	47,000
Finance cost (including preference dividend)	11,000	7,000
Income tax expense	38,000	10,000
Total expense	5,69,000	2,94,000
Net profit	**57,000**	**13,000**

Summarised statements of changes in equity for the year ended March 31, 2019

Particulars	Y (Amount in ₹)	Z(Amount in ₹)
Balance at the start of the year	1,52,000	65,000
Profit for the year	57,000	13,000
Dividends on equity shares	(10,000)	(5,000)
Balance at the end of the year	1,99,000	73,000

Note: Redeemable preference shares are considered as liability. Therefore, it is not a part of equity. It is assumed that preference shares of Z Limited are redeemable preference shares. Therefore, statement of changes in equity does not include changes in preference shares.

Additional information:

(i) Y made investments in Z on April 1, 2016 when the balance sheet of Z showed the following:

Ordinary share capital (par value ₹1)	₹25,000
10% Preference share capital (par value ₹1)	₹20,000
Reserves	₹12,000
	₹57,000

(ii) The cost of investing in the shares of Z was: (i) ₹27,700 for 15,000 equity shares; and (ii) ₹5,200 for 5,000 10% preference shares.

(iii) On April 1, 2016 Y provided 50% of Z's loan.

(iv) The finance cost of ₹7,000 of Z is the total of loan interest (₹5,000) and preference dividend (₹2,000).

Required: Prepare a consolidated statement of profit and loss and a statement of changes in equity for the Y group for the year ended March 31, 2019.

Solution:

Notes:

(i) Z is a (15,000/25,000) × 100 or 60% subsidiary of Y.

(ii) Investment income of Y is income received from Z as per the following details: (a) Interest on loan (50% of ₹5,000) or ₹2,500; (b) Preference dividend (25% of ₹2,000) or ₹500; and dividend on equity shares (60% of ₹5,000) or ₹3,000.

Consolidated statement of profit and loss for the year ended March 31, 2019

Particulars	Amount in ₹	Comments
Income		
Revenue	9,29,000	Y + Z
Other income (investment income)	—	Eliminated, because it represents amount received by Y from Z[1]
Total income	9,29,000	
Expenses		
Cost of sales	6,50,000	Y + Z
Operating expenses	1,47,000	Y + Z
Finance cost	15,000	Y + Z, less intra-group finance cost of 3,000
Income tax expense	48,000	Y + Z
Total expenses	8,62,000	
Net profit	**67,000**	
Attributable to:		
Equity holders of Y (parent)	61,800	
Non-controlling interest	5,200	40% of profit of Z (₹13,000)

Summarised consolidated statements of changes in equity for the year ended March 31, 2019

Particulars	Y (Amount in ₹)	Non-controlling interest (Amount in ₹)	Total equity (Amount in ₹)
Balance at the start of the year	1,68,800[1]	18,000[2]	1,86,800
Profit for the year	61,800	5,200	67,000
Dividends on equity shares	(10,000)	(2,000)	(12,000)
Balance at the end of the year	2,11,000	73,000	2,40,800

1. Balance of equity at the start of the period attributable to equity shareholders of Y (parent): Y: ₹1,52,000 + share of post-acquisition profit of Z [0.60 × (₹65,000 – (57,000 – 20,000*)] = ₹1,68,800
2. Share attributable to equity: 40% × (65,000 – 20,000*) = ₹18,000

* Amount of preference shares at the acquisition date.

Example 21.17 (Consolidated statement of profit and loss)

The following are the statements of profit and loss of Y Ltd. and its subsidiary Z Ltd. for the year ended March 31, 2019:

Particulars	Y (Amount in ₹)	Z (Amount in ₹)
Income		
Revenue	1,25,000	50,000
Other income (Investment income)	3,180	
Total income	1,28,180	50,000
Expenses		
Cost of sales	50,000	20,000
Operating expenses	18,000	7,200
Finance cost	24,500	7,750
Tax expenses	14,000	7,000
Total expenses	1,06,500	41,950
Net profit	**21,680**	**8,050**

Summarised statement of changes in equity of Y and Z

Particulars	Y (Amount in ₹)	Z (Amount in ₹)
Balance on April 1, 2018	76,700	50,300
Net profit for the period	21,680	8,050
Equity dividend	(8,000)	(2,100)
	90,380	56,250

Additional information:

(i) Z supplies components to Y with a profit margin of 25% on cost. During the year 2018–19, revenue of Z includes sales of 5,000 to Y.

(ii) Inventories of Y includes components supplied by Z as per details below: (a) as at March 31, 2019: ₹800; and (b) March 31, 2018: ₹600.

(iii) Y bought 20,000 equity shares (par value ₹1) of Z's outstanding shares of 25,000 (par value ₹1) on the acquisition date at the purchase consideration of ₹27,000. On the acquisition date the balance sheet of Z showed (a) Equity ₹25,000; and (b) reserve of ₹22,500.

(iv) On the acquisition date Y also acquired 25% of the outstanding debentures of Z.

(v) Z's finance cost for the year 2018–19 comprises of the following: (a) interest on debentures: ₹6,000; and (b) interest payable on short-term borrowings: ₹1,750.

Required: Prepare consolidated statement of profit and loss of Y Group.

Solution:

Notes:

(i) Z is a (20,000/25,000) × 100 or 80% subsidiary of Y.

(ii) Investment income of Y consists of: (a) Interest on Z's debentures (25% of ₹6,000) or ₹1,500; and (b) dividend for Z (80% of ₹2,100) or 1,680. Thus, the total investment income Y is income from investments in Z.

(iii) Intra-group revenue (sale of Z to Y) of ₹5,000 should be reduced from both revenue and cost of sales.

(iv) (a) Unrealised profit in inventory as at March 31, 2018: [600 × (25/125)] or ₹120; (b) Unrealised profit in inventory as at March 31, 2019: [800 × (25/125)] or ₹160. This unrealised profit has increased by ₹40. Cost of sales should be increased by ₹40 and the carrying amount of inventories to be reduced by ₹40. Usually, a valuation allowance (provision for unrealised profit) is deducted from inventories.

Consolidated statement of profit and loss of Y Group for the year ended on March 31, 2019

Particulars	Amount (₹)	Comments
Incomes		
Revenue	1,70,000	Y + Z – ₹5,000
Investment income	—	Intra-group income eliminated
Total income	1,70,000	
Expenses		
Cost of sales	65,040	Y + Z – 5,000 + 40
Operating expenses	25,200	Y + Z
Finance cost	30,750	Y + Z – ₹1,500
Tax expenses	21,000	
Total expenses	1,41,990	
Net profit	28,010	
Attributable to:		
Equity holders of parent	26,408	
Non-controlling interest	1,602*	
	28,010	

*Z's net profit for the year:	₹8,050
Less increase in provision for unrealised profit	40
	₹8,010

20% of ₹8,010 or ₹1,602

Consolidated statement of changes in equity of the Y Group for the year ended March 31, 2019

	Attributable to equity shareholders of parent (Y) (₹)	Non-controlling shareholders' interest (₹)	Total
Balance at the start of the period	78,844	10,036	88,880
Profit for the period	26,408	1,602	28,010
Dividend	(8,000)	(420)	(8,420)
Balance at the end of the period	97,252	11,218	1,08,470

Self-Test Questions

Self-test question 21.4

Fill-in the blanks:

(i) Y Ltd. acquires 80% of Z Ltd. The fair value of the purchase consideration is ₹1,00,000 and the acquisition date fair value of the net assets of Z Ltd. is 1,00,000. Assuming that Y measures the NCI at the holders' proportionate amount of the recognised amount of the identifiable net assets of the acquirer, the goodwill should be recognised at ₹.....................

(ii) (i) Y Ltd. acquires 80% of Z Ltd. The fair value of the purchase consideration is ₹1,00,000 and the acquisition date fair value of the net assets of Z Ltd. is 1,00,000. Assuming that Y measures the NCI at the fair value (market value), which is ₹15,000, the goodwill should be recognised at ₹.....................

(iii) Z Ltd. is 80% subsidiary of Y Ltd. On the acquisition date the share capital and Reserves and Surplus of Y and Z were as follows:

Y: Share capital: ₹5,00,000; and Reserves and Surplus: ₹10,00,000

Z: Share capital: ₹2,00,000; and Reserves and Surplus: ₹3,50,000

On March 31, 2019 the share capital and Reserves and Surplus of Y and Z were as follows:

Y: Share capital: ₹5,00,000; and Reserves and Surplus: ₹20,00,000

Z: Share capital: ₹2,00,000; and Reserves and Surplus: ₹7,50,000

In the consolidated balance sheet of Y Group, the share capital should be presented at ₹................. and Reserves and Surplus to be presented at ₹....................

(iv) Z Ltd. is 70% subsidiary of Y Ltd. Z sold goods Y for ₹10,000, which has remained unsold and is included in the inventories of Y. Z sold the goods at the normal price and earned profit margin of 25% on cost. The inventories in the consolidated balance sheet of Y group should be the total of figures for inventories of in the balance sheets of Y and Z, reduced by ₹................., NCI should be adjusted by ₹................. and retained earnings should be adjusted by ₹.................

(v) Z Ltd. is 70% subsidiary of Y Ltd. Y sold goods Y for ₹10,000, 50% of which has remained unsold and is included in the inventories of Z. Y sold the goods at the normal price and earned profit margin of 20% on selling price. The inventories in the consolidated balance sheet of Y group should be the total of figures for inventories in the balance sheets of Y and Z, reduced by ₹................., NCI should be adjusted by ₹................. and retained earnings should be adjusted by ₹.................

(vi) Z Ltd. is a 70% subsidiary of Y Ltd. There is no borrowings in the balance sheet of Y. Z's balance sheet shows borrowings at ₹1,00,000, which represents the amount borrowed from Y. The consolidated balance sheet of Y Group should show borrowings of ₹...................

(vii) Z Ltd. is a 70% subsidiary of Y Ltd. Revenue of Y for the reporting period is ₹5,00,000. The same for Z is ₹3,00,000. During the year Y sold goods to Z for ₹1,00,000 on which it earned a profit of ₹20,000. The inventories of Z Ltd. at the end of the year do not include any item purchased from Y. The revenue in the consolidated statement of profit and loss should be ₹..................The cost of goods sold in the Y Group's statement of profit and loss should be total of cost of goods sold in the statements of profit and loss of Y and Z, reduced by ₹.................

EQUITY METHOD OF ACCOUNTING FOR INVESTMENT IN 'ASSOCIATES' AND 'JOINT VENTURES'

The applicable accounting standard is Ind AS 28, Investments in Associates and Joint Ventures.

Associate

An associate is an entity over which the investor has significant influence, but no control.

Significant influence is the power to participate in the financial and operating policy decisions of the investee but is not control or joint control of those policies. Significant influence is evidenced in one or more of the following ways:

(i) Representation on the board of directors;
(ii) Participation in policy-making process;
(iii) Material transaction between the investor and the investee;
(iv) Interchange of managerial personnel; and
(v) Provision for essential technical information.

If an entity holds, directly or indirectly (e.g., through subsidiaries), 20% or more of the voting power of the investee, it is presumed that the entity has significant influence over the investee, unless it can be clearly demonstrated that this is not the case. Conversely, if the entity holds, directly or indirectly (e.g., through subsidiaries), less than 20% of the voting power of the investee, it is presumed that the entity does not have significant influence, unless such influence can be clearly demonstrated. A substantial or majority ownership by another investor does not necessarily preclude an entity from having significant influence.

An entity may own share warrants, share call options, debt or equity instruments that are convertible into ordinary shares, or other similar instruments that have the potential, if exercised or converted, to give the entity additional voting power or to reduce another party's voting power over the financial and operating policies of another entity (i.e., potential voting rights). The existence and effect of potential voting rights that are currently exercisable or convertible, including potential voting rights held by other entities, are considered when assessing whether an entity has significant influence. Potential voting rights are not currently exercisable or convertible when, for example, they cannot be exercised or converted until a future date or until the occurrence of a future event.

Joint venture

A joint venture is a joint arrangement whereby the parties that have joint control of the arrangement have rights to the net assets of the arrangement.

A joint arrangement is an arrangement of which two or more parties have joint control.

Joint control is the contractually agreed sharing of control of an arrangement, which exists only when decisions about the relevant activities require the unanimous consent.

Equity method

When potential voting rights or other derivatives containing potential voting rights exist, an entity's interest in an associate or a joint venture is determined solely on the basis of existing ownership interests and does not reflect the possible exercise or conversion of potential voting rights and other derivative instruments.

Equity method procedures

Under the equity method, on initial recognition, the investment in an associate or a joint venture is recognised at cost, and the carrying amount is increased or decreased to recognise the investor's share of the profit or loss of the investee after the date of acquisition.

The investor's share of the investee's profit or loss is recognised in the investor's profit or loss.

Distributions (e.g., dividend) received from an investee reduce the carrying amount of the investment. Adjustments to the carrying amount may also be necessary for changes in the investor's proportionate interest in the investee arising from changes in the investee's other comprehensive income. Such changes include those arising from the revaluation of property, plant and equipment and from foreign exchange translation differences. The investor's share of those changes is recognised in the investor's other comprehensive income.

Transactions between the investor and associate/joint venture

Gains and losses resulting from 'upstream' and 'downstream' transactions between an entity (including its consolidated subsidiaries) and its associate or joint venture are recognised in the entity's financial statements only to the extent of unrelated investors' interests in the associate or joint venture.

'Upstream' transactions are, for example, sales of assets from an associate or a joint venture to the investor. 'Downstream' transactions are, for example, sales or contributions of assets from the investor to its associate or its joint venture.

The investor's share in the associate's or joint venture's gains or losses resulting from these transactions is eliminated.

Example 21.18 (Downstream sale of goods)

K Ltd. is 20% associate of Y Ltd. During the year 2017–18, Y sold goods to K for ₹210. Its cost of sales was 1/3rd of selling price. The goods remained unsold and was included in the year-end inventories of K. K sales the goods during 2018–19.

Required: Explain how Y should treat the transaction in financial statements for the years 2017–18 and 2018–19.

Solution:

2017–18

The share of unrealised profit of Y is to be eliminated. The total profit is (210 – 210 × 1/3) or 140. Thus, 20% of ₹140, which is the share of the unrealised profit of Y is to be eliminated.

In order to give effect to the above, Y will pass the following entries:

Revenue	Dr. 42 (20% of ₹210)	
To Cost of sales		Cr. 14 (20% of ₹70)
To Investment in associates		Cr. 28 (20% of ₹140)

Note that inventory is not credited, because inventory is in the balance sheet of Associate and the same is included in the balance sheet of Y in the line item 'investments in associates'.

2018–19

The goods are sold, and the profit is realised. Therefore, the entries that were passed in 217–18 should be reversed. The following entries should be passed:

Investment in associates	Dr. 28	
Cost of sales	Dr. 14 (20% of ₹70)	
To Revenue		Cr. 42

Example 21.19 (Upstream sale of goods)

K Ltd. is 20% associate of Y Ltd. During the year 2017–18, K sold goods to Y for ₹210. Its cost of sales was 1/3rd of selling price. The goods remained unsold and was included in the year-end inventories of Y. Y sales the goods during 2018–19.

Required: Explain how Y should treat the transaction in financial statements for the years 2017–18 and 2018–19.

Solution:

2017–18

Y's share of unrealised profit, which is 20% of (₹210 – 1/3 of 210) or ₹28 should be eliminated. The following entry should be passes:

Share of profit or loss of associate	Dr. ₹28	
To Investment in associate (or inventory)		Cr. ₹28

2018–19

On sale of the goods, the entry recorded in 2017–18 should be reversed by passing the following entry:

Investment in associates (or inventory)	Dr. 28	
To Share of profit or loss of associate		Cr. ₹28

Goodwill and capital reserve

On acquisition of the investment, any difference between the cost of the investment and the entity's share of the net fair value of the investee's identifiable assets and liabilities is accounted for as follows:

(a) Goodwill relating to an associate or a joint venture is included in the carrying amount of the investment. Amortisation of that goodwill is not permitted.

(b) Any excess of the entity's share of the net fair value of the investee's identifiable assets and liabilities over the cost of the investment is recognised directly in equity as capital reserve in the period in which the investment is acquired.

Fair value and impairment adjustments

Appropriate adjustments to the entity's share of the associate's or joint venture's profit or loss after acquisition are made in order to account, for example, for depreciation of the depreciable assets based on their fair values at the acquisition date. Similarly, appropriate adjustments to the entity's share of the associate's or joint venture's profit or loss after acquisition is made for impairment losses such as for goodwill or property, plant and equipment.

SUMMARY

If the investor has significant influence over the investee, the investee is called the associate of the investor. If the investor holds 20% of more (but not more than 50%) voting rights of the investee, it is assumed that the investee is the associate of the investor unless it is demonstrated otherwise. Similarly, if the investor holds less than 20% of the voting rights of the investee, it is assumed that the investee is not an associate of the investor unless it is demonstrated otherwise. In a joint venture financial and operating and financial decisions are taken by joint venturers jointly by arriving at a consensus. This is achieved through an arrangement between joint venturers. Relative shareholding of joint venturers is irrelevant.

The investor consolidates the financial statement of associates and joint ventures using the equity method, which is often referred as one-line consolidation.

Key Terms
Associate, Downstream transactions, Equity method, Joint venture, Significant influence, Upstream transactions

Self-Test Questions

Self-test question 21.5

State whether the following statements are true (T) or false (F):

(i) If an investor holds less than 20% of voting rights in the investee, the investee cannot be considered as an associate of the investor.

(ii) Under the equity method goodwill is included the line item 'investment in associates' in the consolidated balance sheet.

(iii) Under the equity method capital reserve is included the line item 'investment in associates' in the consolidated balance sheet.

(iv) Under the equity method the full unrealised gain from transactions between the associate and the investor (and/or its subsidiaries) are eliminated.

(v) Adjustments are required for the difference between the depreciation based on the book value of items of PP&E in the books of the associate and depreciation based on the acquisition date fair value of those items.

ANSWERS TO SELF-TEST QUESTIONS

21.1 (i) F; (ii) T; (iii) F; (iv) T; (v) T

21.2 (i) T; (ii) F; (iii) T; (iv) F; (v) T; (vi) T; (vii) T; (viii) T; (ix) T; (x) T; (xi) T

21.3 (i) F; (ii) F; (iii) F; (iv) T; (v) T; (vi) F; (vii) T; (viii) T; (ix) F; (x) T; (xi) F; (xii) T; (xiii) T; (xiv) T; (xv) F; (xvi) F; (xvii) T

21.4 (i) ₹20,000; (ii) ₹15,000; (iii) ₹5,00,000, ₹24,00,000; (iv) ₹600, ₹1,400; (v) Nil, ₹1,000; (vi) Nil; (vii) ₹1,00,000, ₹1,00,000

21.5 (i) F; (ii) T; (iii) F; (iv) F; (v) T

ASSIGNMENTS

Quiz

1. State whether the following statements are true (T) or false (F):
   (i) In a business combination one or more of the combining entities are necessarily dissolved.
   (ii) The terms 'business combination' and 'slump sale' are used interchangeably.
   (iii) In a demerger, the shareholders of the company, which hived off the business, become the shareholders of the new company, which is formed for demerger.
   (iv) The question of control arises when the investor is exposed, or has rights, to variable returns from its involvement with the investee.

(v) A lender (investor in the debt capital of the company) is not exposed to variable returns from its involvement with the investee, because it is entitled to a fixed return from investment and return of its investment.

(vi) Rights that can be exercised when the entity decides changing the constitution or selling an undertaking or commencing bankruptcy proceedings are protective rights.

(vii) Generally speaking the investor has power if it has the current ability to direct financial and operating activities of the investee.

(viii) If the investee's relevant activities are directed through voting rights, the investor can control the investee only by holding more than 50% voting rights.

(ix) In order to account for a transaction as business combination by the acquirer, it is essential that the acquirer retains the top-level employees of the acquiree, as business has two essential components—inputs and process.

(x) In a business combination in which a new company is created to carry on the combined business, the assets and liabilities of all the combining companies are restated at fair value.

(xi) Acquisition related costs are included in the purchase consideration for acquiring a business.

(xii) Contingent consideration is not included in the purchase consideration for acquiring a business.

(xiii) Business combination cannot occur without transfer of consideration.

(xiv) In case of business combination achieved in stages, the purchase consideration is the total of the book value of acquisition date non-controlling investment and additional investment to acquire control of the investee.

(xv) Measurement period cannot be longer than one year from the acquisition date.

(xvi) The portion of the net assets of the subsidiary that belongs to 'non-controlling shareholders' is presented in the consolidated balance sheet as a part of equity under the heading 'non-controlling interest' (NCI).

(xvii) While consolidating financial statements of the parent and subsidiaries only the parent's share of unrealised profit arising from intra-group transactions is eliminated.

(xviii) Only if the investor holds 20% or more, but not more than 50% of the equity shares (voting rights) of the investee, the investee is considered an 'associate' of the investor.

(xix) Equity method for consolidating financial statements of associates and joint ventures is also called 'one-line consolidation'.

(xx) Under the equity method for consolidating financial statements of the investor and its associate distributions (e.g., dividend) received from an investee reduce the carrying amount of the investment.

2. Fill-in the blanks

(i) Y Ltd. acquires 80% of Z Ltd. The fair value of the purchase consideration is ₹2,00,000 and the acquisition date fair value of the net assets of Z Ltd. is ₹1,50,000. Assuming that Y measures the NCI at the holders' proportionate amount of the recognised amount of the identifiable net assets of the acquirer, the goodwill should be recognised at ₹......................

(ii) (i) Y Ltd. acquires 80% of Z Ltd. The fair value of the purchase consideration is ₹2,00,000 and the acquisition date fair value of the net assets of Z Ltd. Is ₹1,50,000. Assuming that Y measures the NCI at the fair value (market value), which is ₹38,000, the goodwill should be recognised at ₹.....................

(iii) Z Ltd. is 80% subsidiary of Y Ltd. On the acquisition date the share capital and Reserves and Surplus of Y and Z were as follows:

Y: Share capital: ₹8,00,000; and Reserves and Surplus: ₹10,00,000

Z: Share capital: ₹2,00,000; and Reserves and Surplus: ₹5,00,000

On March 31, 2019 the share capital and Reserves and Surplus of Y and Z were as follows:

Y: Share capital: ₹8,00,000; and Reserves and Surplus: ₹20,00,000

Z: Share capital: ₹2,00,000; and Reserves and Surplus: ₹7,50,000

In the consolidated balance sheet of Y Group, the share capital should be presented at ₹................. and Reserves and Surplus to be presented at ₹....................

(iv) Z Ltd. is 70% subsidiary of Y Ltd. Z sold goods Y for ₹50,000, which has remained unsold and is included in the inventories of Y. Z sold the goods at the normal price and earned profit margin of 20% on sales. The inventories in the consolidated balance sheet of Y group should be the total of figures for inventories of in the balance sheets of Y and Z, reduced by ₹................., NCI should be adjusted by ₹.................. and retained earnings should be adjusted by ₹.................

(v) Z Ltd. is 70% subsidiary of Y Ltd. Y sold goods Y for ₹50,000, 50% of which has remained unsold and is included in the inventories of Z. Y sold the goods at the normal price and earned profit margin of 20% on selling price. The inventories in the consolidated balance sheet of Y group should be the total of figures for inventories in the balance sheets of Y and Z, reduced by ₹................., NCI should be adjusted by ₹................. and retained earnings should be adjusted by ₹.................

(vi) Z Ltd. is a 70% subsidiary of Y Ltd. There is no borrowings in the balance sheet of Y. Z's balance sheet shows borrowings at ₹5,00,000, which represents the amount borrowed from Y. The consolidated balance sheet of Y Group should show borrowings of ₹.................

(vii) Z Ltd. is a 70% subsidiary of Y Ltd. Revenue of Y for the reporting period is ₹8,00,000. The same for Z is ₹4,00,000. During the year Y sold goods to Z for ₹2,00,000 on which it earned a profit of ₹20,000. The inventories of Z Ltd. at the end of the year do not include any item purchased from Y. The revenue in the consolidated statement of profit and loss should be ₹................. . The cost of goods sold in the Y Group's statement of profit and loss should be total of cost of goods sold in the statements of profit and loss of Y and Z, reduced by ₹.................

(viii) K Ltd. is a 20% associate of Y Ltd. During the year 2017–18, Y sold good to K for ₹300. Its cost of sales was 1/3rd of selling price. The goods remained unsold and was included in the year-end inventories of K. In preparing the consolidated statement of profit and loss for the year 2017–18, revenue should be debited by ₹.........., cost of sales should be .... by ₹........... and investment in associates should be .... by ₹................

(ix) K Ltd. is a 20% associate of Y Ltd. During the year 2017–18, K sold good to Y for ₹300. Its cost of sales was 1/3rd of selling price. The goods remained unsold and was included in the year-end inventories of Y. The .... should be .... by ₹............... and .... should be .... by ₹.......................

Problems

3. The balance sheets as at March 31, 2019 of Y Ltd. and its subsidiary Z Ltd. are summarised below:

	Y (₹)		Z (₹)	
ASSETS				
Non-current Assets				
Property, plant and equipment	19,000		6,000	
Investment in Z	10,000	29,000	Nil	6,000
Current Assets				
Inventories	10,000		17,000	
Trade receivables	20,000		20,800	
Current account with Z	4,000		Nil	
Bank balance	17,000	51,000		37,800
Total assets		80,000		43,800
EQUITY AND LIABILITIES				
Equity				
Share capital (Par value ₹1 each)	40,000		8,000	
Reserves and surplus	30,000	70,000	12,000	20,000
Liabilities				
Non-current liabilities		Nil		
Current liabilities				
Trade payables	10,000		16,000	
Current account with Y	Nil		2,000	
Bank overdraft	Nil	10,000	5,800	23,800
Total equity and liabilities		80,000		43,800

Additional information:

(i) Many years ago, Y acquired 80% of Z. On the acquisition date, Z's reserves and surplus was ₹1,000. In an earlier year, on consolidation, goodwill had been written off after impairment review.

(ii) On March 31, 2019, there was cash in transit from Z to Y of ₹2,000.

Required: Prepare consolidated balance sheet of Y Group as at March 31, 2019.

4. The balance sheets of Y Ltd. and its subsidiary Z Ltd. as at March 31, 2019 are summarised below:

	Y (₹)		Z (₹)	
ASSETS				
Non-current Assets				
Property, plant and equipment	28,000		18,000	
Investment in Z	21,000	49,000	Nil	18,000
Current Assets				
Inventories	26,000		22,000	
Trade receivables	20,000		21,000	
Current account with Z	8,000		Nil	
Interest receivable from Z	250			
Bank balance	16,750	71,000		43,000
Total assets		**1,20,000**		**61,000**
EQUITY AND LIABILITIES				
Equity				
Share capital (Par value ₹1 each)	40,000		8,000	
Reserves and surplus	30,000	70,000	12,500	20,500
Liabilities				
Non-current liabilities				
Interest bearing borrowings		30,000		20,000
Current liabilities				
Trade payables	20,000		10,000	
Interest payable	Nil		500	
Current account with Y	Nil		6,000	
Bank overdraft	Nil	20,000	4,000	20,500
Total equity and liabilities		**1,20,000**		**61,000**

Additional information:

(i) Y acquired 75% of Z on April 1, 2016. The purchase consideration was ₹11,000. Reserves and surplus on the acquisition date in the balance sheet of Z was ₹4,000. Goodwill on consolidation is retained at cost in the group balance sheet, as there is no evidence of impairment since acquisition.

(ii) Investment of Y in Z includes interest-bearing long-term loan of ₹10,000.

(iii) On March 31, 2019 there was cash-in-transit from Z to Y of ₹2,000.

(iv) On March 31, 2019, the inventories of Z includes good purchased from Y at ₹5,000. Y invoiced it at the normal price, which is cost plus a margin of 25%.

Required: Prepare consolidated balance sheet of Y Group as at March 31, 2019.

CHAPTER

22

Topical Issues

LEARNING OBJECTIVES

This chapter aims to provide brief overview of basic accounting principles for accounting for changes in foreign exchange rates, accounting for leases, accounting for borrowing costs and accounting for share-based payments to employees. A detailed discussion is outside the scope of this book. After reading this chapter, you will learn the concepts of:

- Foreign exchange rate, functional currency, foreign currency and presentation currency
- Foreign currency transaction and exchange difference
- Reporting foreign currency transactions in functional currency
- Net investment in foreign operation
- Definition of lease, right to use asset, operating lease and finance lease
- Difference between the lease contract and service contract
- Accounting for lease by lessee and lessor
- Difference between operating lease and finance lease
- Accounting for sale and lease back transactions
- Accounting for borrowing costs, and
- Accounting for share-based payments to employees

Applicable Accounting Standard: *Ind AS 21, The Effects of Changes in Foreign Exchange Rate.*

NOTES

ACCOUNTING FOR CHANGES IN FOREIGN EXCHANGE RATES

Introduction

Foreign exchange rate is the ratio of exchange for two currencies. Exchange rate changes almost daily. Exchange rates are determined in the foreign exchange market. The spot exchange rate is the current exchange rate. Forward exchange rate is the rate quoted today for delivery and payment at a specified future date. Money dealers quote buying and selling rates. The 'buy rate' is the rate at which the dealer will buy the currency and 'sell rate' is the rate at which it will sell the currency. On December 30, 2018, Thomas Cook quotes USD/INR buy rate at 69.25 and sell rate at 70.95. These are spot rates. If a customer sells 1 USD to Thomas Cook, he/she will get ₹69.25. A customer can buy 1 USD by paying ₹70.95.

The Foreign Benchmarks India Private Limited (FBIL) issues reference rate for different currencies daily, except on Saturdays, Sundays and bank holidays in Mumbai. Reference rate is the official exchange rate. FBIL is jointly owned by the Fixed Income Money Market and Derivatives Association of India (FIMMDA), Foreign Exchange Dealers Association of India (FEDAI) and Indian Banks' Association (IBA). It was formed in December 2014 as a private limited company under the Companies Act 2013. Reference rate for USD/INR as at December 28, 2018 was 69.9786. No reference rate was published on December 30, 2018, as it was Sunday.

Functional Currency

The first step in accounting for changes in the foreign exchange rates is to determine the functional currency of the reporting entity. There is no concept of Group functional currency. The functional currency of a foreign branch or a subsidiary of the reporting entity might differ from the functional currency of the reporting entity. An entity maintains its accounting records in its functional currency.

Functional currency is the currency of the *primary economic environment* in which the company operates. A company's functional currency reflects the underlying transactions, events and conditions that are relevant to it. Accordingly, once determined, the functional currency is not changed unless there is a change in those underlying transactions, events and conditions. INR is the functional currency of most Indian companies. However, it is not necessary that the local currency of the country where the entity is domiciled should be its functional currency.

A truly global company having activities across different countries and transactions denominated in different currencies might find it difficult to determine the functional currency. When the functional currency is not obvious, management uses its *judgement* to determine the functional currency that most faithfully represents the economic effects of the underlying transactions, events and conditions.

Primary economic environment

The primary economic environment in which a company operates is normally the one in which it primarily generates and expends cash.

Ind AS 21 lists the following factors which a company should consider in determining its functional currency:

(i) The currency in which the sales prices for its goods and services are denominated and settled.

(ii) The currency of the country whose competitive forces and regulations mainly determine the sales prices of its goods and services.

(iii) The currency in which the costs of inputs (e.g., material and labour) are denominated and settled.

The following factors may also provide (secondary) evidence of a company's functional currency:

NOTES

(i) The currency in which funds from financing activities (i.e., issuing debt and equity instruments) are generated.

(ii) The currency in which receipts from operating activities are usually retained.

CASE STUDY 22.1 Functional Currency

Anugha Limited (AL) is domiciled in India. Its shareholders are located in India and it has obtained debt finance in INR from Indian financial institutions. It is classified as the healthcare industry, primarily focuses on herbal products. Its production facilities are located in India. The company imports a significant part of rare herbs from different countries and exports a major part of its products to USA and the European countries. Its sale prices are denominated in INR, US$ and Euro. The company maintains bank accounts in India and purchases foreign currency in INR to pay for inputs and converts sales proceeds denominated in foreign currency to INR.

Question

Determine the functional currency of AL.

Solution

The management of AL should form a judgement on its functional currency based on the factors stipulated in Ind AS 21. Its sale prices are denominated in INR, US$ and Euro. Consequently, there is no single currency which can be identified as the primary currency in which sale prices are denominated. Since its production takes place in India, the input costs, other than raw materials imported from different countries, are denominated in INR. It may be concluded that the primary currency in which input costs are denominated is INR. The AL is regulated by Indian laws because it is domiciled in India, its production facilities and shareholders are in India. Therefore, INR should be the functional currency of AL.

CASE STUDY 22.2 Functional Currency

Angarika Shipping Lines Limited (ASLL) is domiciled in India. It operates an international shipping line. Its sale prices are denominated in US$. The company pays wages to employees in INR. However, during the voyage of a ship, employees on board are paid various allowances in US$. Employees located in foreign offices are paid in the currency of the country in which the office is located. ASLL maintains bank accounts in all the locations where offices are situated. Its main bank account is at Standard Chartered Bank, New York (USA) branch. The company's shareholders are located in India. The company borrowed in US$ from financial institutions located in the USA.

Question

Explain what should be the functional currency of ASLL.

Solution

ASLL is domiciled in India and is governed by Indian laws and regulations. Investors of the company are located in India. Therefore, INR is a candidate for the designation of functional currency. The other candidate is US$, because the company's sale prices are denominated in US$, a part of the employee costs are paid in US$, and borrowings by the company are in US$. The company maintains bank account at Standard Chartered Bank, New York. This strengthens the claim of US$ for the designation of foreign currency.

In this case, the functional currency is not obvious. The management has to form judgement taking into account all the factors. From the facts presented in the illustration, it appears that US$ most faithfully represents the economic effects of the underlying transactions, events and conditions. Therefore, US$ should be designated as the functional currency.

NOTES

Foreign Currency

Foreign currency is a currency other than the functional currency of the company. For example, for a company, which has designated INR as its functional currency, currencies other than INR are foreign currencies.

Presentation Currency

Presentation currency is the currency in which the financial statements are presented.

Some countries allow companies to choose the currency for presentation of financial statements. A company often chooses the currency based on the location of its major stakeholder groups (e.g., customers and investors). Indian companies have no choice but to present their financial statements in INR.

Foreign Currency Transactions

Foreign currency transactions are transactions whose terms are denominated in a foreign currency or require settlement in a foreign currency. Examples of foreign currency transactions are:

(i) Purchases and sales of goods and services whose price is denominated in a foreign currency.

(ii) Borrowing and lending of funds when the accounts payable or receivable are denominated in a foreign currency.

(iii) Acquisition and disposal of assets, or assumption or settlement of liabilities, denominated in a foreign currency.

A change in foreign exchange rates directly affects cash flows to or from the entity that has entered into a foreign currency transaction.

For example, Y exports an item, priced at USD 100, to a customer in U.S.A. The USD/INR exchange rate at the date of despatch is ₹70. If, Y receives the payment immediately against Letter of credit, it receives ₹7,000. If, it receives payment after three months when USD/INR exchange rate is ₹68, it receives ₹6,800. Thus, the change in the exchange rate directly affects the cash inflow to the exporter. This is so in any foreign currency transaction.

The accounting principles for accounting for foreign currency transactions recognise that changes in exchange rates directly affect the operating result and cash flows to and from the entity. Ind AS 21 provides accounting principles and methods for recording foreign currency transactions and accounting for exchange difference.

Exchange difference

Exchange difference is the difference resulting from translating a given number of units of one currency into another currency at different exchange rates.

Foreign currency transactions are initially recorded in functional currency by translating the amount in foreign currency into functional currency using the spot exchange rate at the date on which the transaction is recorded in the books. For example, Y has exported goods for USD 100. Assume that the customer will pay after three months. Further assume that the USD/INR exchange rate was 70 on the date when the transaction was recorded and 68 when the payment was received. Y recorded the sales and receivables at (₹70 × 100) = ₹7,000. After three months Y received (₹68 × 100) = ₹6,800. Thus, (₹7,000 – 6,800) was the exchange difference. Y should recognise the exchange difference as a loss as the change in the exchange rate was unfavourable to Y, which is the exporter. If, instead of exporting, Y imported merchandise for USD 100 and the amount was payable to the vendor after three months. In that case, Y recorded purchase and payables at ₹7,000. After, three months, it paid the vendor ₹6,800. The change in the exchange rate was favourable to Y, which is the importer. Therefore, Y, which is the importer, should recognise the exchange difference as gain.

NOTES

In the above examples, INR strengthened against USD over a period of three months, as the price of 1 USD was reduced from INR 70 to INR 68. When the functional currency strengthens, importers gain and exporters lose. On the other hand, when the functional currency weakens, importers lose and exporters gain.

Reporting Foreign Currency Transactions in Functional Currency

Initial recognition

The foreign currency transactions should be recorded in the functional currency using the spot exchange rate between the functional currency and the foreign currency at the date of the transaction. For practical reasons, an entity may use a rate that approximates the actual rate at the date of the transaction. For example, in the absence of significant fluctuations in exchange rates, the average rate for a month or for a week might be used for all transactions during the period.

The initial measurement of asset or liability is adjusted if its acquisition or incurrence has been hedged with reference to foreign exchange risk. In case of 'fair value hedge' of firm commitment, the asset or liability resulting from meeting the firm commitment is adjusted to include the cumulative change in the fair value of the firm commitment attributable to the hedge risk that was recognised in the balance sheet. In case of 'cash flow hedge' of a forecast transaction, if the forecast transaction results in recognition of a non-financial item, the entire related amount accumulated in the 'cash flow hedge reserve' is removed and included in the initial cost or other carrying amount of the asset or liability.

Reporting at subsequent balance sheet dates

Accounting principle

The following are the general principles for translating foreign currency items into the reporting currency:

(i) Monetary items should be reported using the closing rate, that is, the closing spot rate at the balance sheet date.

(ii) Non-monetary items, which are carried at historical cost, should be reported using the exchange rate at the date of the transaction.

(iii) Non-monetary items (e.g., shares held for trading), which are carried at fair value, should be reported using exchange rates that existed when the values were determined.

Monetary and Non-monetary items

The essential feature of a monetary item is a right to receive (or an obligation to deliver) a fixed or determinable number of units of currency. Examples include: pensions and other employee benefits to be paid in cash; provisions that are to be settled in cash; and cash dividends that are recognised as a liability. Conversely, the essential feature of a non-monetary item is the absence of a right to receive (or an obligation to deliver) a fixed or determinable number of units of currency. Examples include: amounts prepaid for goods and services (e.g., prepaid rent); goodwill; intangible assets; inventories; property, plant and equipment; and provisions that are to be settled by the delivery of a non-monetary asset.

The appropriate treatment of deferred tax is not clear in Ind AS. Usually, it is being treated as monetary item, based on the view that deferred tax represents future amount of cash that will be paid to or received from tax authorities.

Exchange difference

Exchange difference arises from the following:

(i) Settlement of a foreign currency monetary item at an exchange rate different from that used in recording the item initially.

NOTES

(ii) Translating a foreign currency monetary item for reporting in financial statements using exchange rate different from that used in recording the item initially.

(iii) Settlement of a foreign currency monetary item at an exchange rate different from that used to translate it for reporting in previous financial statements.

(iv) Translating a foreign currency monetary item for reporting in financial statements at an exchange rate different from that used to translate it for reporting in previous financial statements.

Recognition of exchange difference (foreign exchange gains and losses)

Exchange differences arising from the settlement of monetary items or on translating monetary items at rates different from those at which they were translated on initial recognition during the period or in previous financial statements should be recognised as profit or loss in the period in which they arise, except exchange differences arising out of a monetary item that forms part of a reporting entity's net investment in a foreign operation.

When a gain or loss on a non-monetary item is recognised in other comprehensive income, any exchange component of that gain or loss should be recognised in other comprehensive income. Conversely, when a gain or loss on a non-monetary item is recognised in profit or loss, any exchange component of that gain or loss should be recognised in profit or loss.

Net Investment in Foreign Operation

A foreign operation is a company that is a subsidiary, associate, joint venture or branch of a reporting company, the activities of which are based or conducted in a country or currency other than those of the reporting company.

Functional currency of a foreign operation

The following additional factors are considered in determining the functional currency of a foreign operation, and whether its functional currency is the same as that of the reporting company (the reporting company, in this context, being the company that has the foreign operation as its subsidiary, branch, associate or joint venture):

(i) Whether the activities of the foreign operation are carried out as an extension of the reporting company, rather than being carried out with a significant degree of autonomy.

(ii) Whether transactions with the reporting company are a high or a low proportion of the foreign operation's activities.

(iii) Whether cash flows from the activities of the foreign operation directly affect the cash flows of the reporting company and are readily available for remittance to it.

(iv) Whether cash flows from the activities of the foreign operation are sufficient to service existing and normally expected debt obligations without funds being made available by the reporting entity.

For example, when the foreign operation only sells goods imported from the reporting entity and remits the proceeds to it, the functional currency of the foreign operation is the same as that of the reporting entity. When the operation accumulates cash and other monetary items, incurs expenses, generates income, and arranges borrowings, all substantially in its local currency, the functional currency of the foreign operation is the local currency, which is likely to be not the same as that of the reporting entity.

As an example, the functional currency of Hindustan Unilever Limited (HUL), a subsidiary of Unilever (UK/Netherlands) operating in India, which is INR, is different from that of Unilever. HUL operates with significant degree of autonomy from its parent, Unilever. The functional currency of most foreign branches of Indian banks is INR because often they operate as an extension of the Indian operations.

Net investment

Net investment in a foreign operation is the amount of the reporting company's interest in the net assets of that operation. Investment in the equity issued by a foreign operation (e.g., a foreign subsidiary) is a part of net investment in the subsidiary.

A company may have a monetary item that is receivable from or payable to a foreign operation. An item for which settlement is neither planned nor is likely to occur in the foreseeable future is, in substance, a part of the company's net investment in that foreign operation. Such monetary items may include long-term receivables or loans. They do not include trade receivables or trade payables. The company that has a monetary item receivable from or payable to a foreign operation may be any subsidiary of the group. For example, Solomon Limited (SL), domiciled in India, has a foreign operation in Italy. SL transferred INR 10,000,000 to the foreign operation in the form of interest-free loan, initially for five years. It has no intention to withdraw the money in the foreseeable future and intends to roll over the loan. The loan to the foreign operation is a part of SL's net investment in the foreign operation.

Exchange differences arising on a monetary item that forms a part of the reporting entity's net investment in a foreign operation should be recognised in profit or loss in the separate financial statements of the foreign entity or the individual financial statements of the foreign operation, as appropriate. In the financial statements that include the foreign operation and the reporting entity (e.g., consolidated financial statements when the foreign operation is a subsidiary), such exchange differences should be recognised in other comprehensive income and accumulated in equity. On disposal of the net investment, exchange differences accumulated in equity should be reclassified to profit or loss.

Translation of foreign currency financial statements

When a group contains an individual entity with a functional currency different from the presentation currency of the group, the balance sheet, profit and loss account, and cash flow statement are expressed in the presentation currency so that the consolidated financial statements can be presented in the presentation currency. For example, if an Indian company with INR as presentation currency has a subsidiary (located in USA), with US$ as functional currency, the balance sheet, the profit and loss account, and the cash flow statement prepared by the subsidiary from accounting records maintained in US$ (functional currency) are expressed in INR so that consolidated financial statements can be prepared.

Procedure

If the functional currency of a foreign operation is different from the presentation currency of the reporting firm, the reporting firm translates the results and financial position of that foreign operation into the presentation currency using the following procedure:

(i) The assets and liabilities, both monetary and non-monetary, should be translated using the closing rate.

(ii) Income and expense items should be translated using exchange rates at the dates of the transactions.

(iii) The resulting exchange differences should be recognised in other comprehensive income and is presented as a separate component of equity (e.g., in foreign currency translation reserve).

For practical reasons, a rate that approximates the actual exchange rates, for example, an average rate for the period, is often used to translate income and expense items of a foreign operation.

Exchange difference

The exchange differences result from translating (i) both the income and expenses at the exchange rates at the date of the transactions and assets and liabilities at the closing date, and (ii) the opening net assets at a closing rate that differs from the previous closing rate.

The reporting entity does not recognise these exchange differences in the statement of profit and loss, because the changes in exchange rates have little or no direct effect on the present and future cash flows from operations. The accumulated exchange difference is recognised in the statement of profit and loss on disposal of the foreign operation.

NOTES

SUMMARY

Foreign exchange rate is the ratio of exchange for two currencies. The Foreign Benchmarks India Private Limited (FBIL) issues reference rate for different currencies daily, except on Saturdays, Sundays and bank holidays in Mumbai. Reference rate is the official exchange rate. Functional currency is the currency of the *primary economic environment* in which the company operates. A company's functional currency reflects the underlying transactions, events and conditions that are relevant to it. Foreign currency is a currency other than the functional currency of the company. Presentation currency is the currency in which the financial statements are presented. Foreign currency transactions are those that are denominated in or require settlement in a foreign currency. The accounting principles for accounting for foreign currency transactions recognise that changes in exchange rates directly affect the operating result and cash flows to and from the entity. Exchange difference is the difference resulting from translating a given number of units of one currency into another currency at different exchange rates. Foreign currency transactions are initially recorded in functional currency by translating the amount in foreign currency into functional currency using the spot exchange rate at the date on which the transaction is recorded in the books. The initial measurement of asset or liability is adjusted if its acquisition or incurrence has been hedged with reference to foreign exchange risk. The following are the general principles for translating foreign currency items into the reporting currency: (i) Monetary items should be reported using the closing rate, that is, the closing spot rate at the balance sheet date; (ii) Non-monetary items, which are carried at historical cost, should be reported using the exchange rate at the date of the transaction; and (iii) Non-monetary items (e.g., shares held for trading), which are carried at fair value, should be reported using exchange rates that existed when the values were determined. Exchange differences arising from the settlement of monetary items or on translating monetary items at rates different from those at which they were translated on initial recognition during the period or in previous financial statements should be recognised as profit or loss in the period in which they arise, except exchange differences arising out of a monetary item that forms part of a reporting entity's net investment in a foreign operation.

A foreign operation is a company that is a subsidiary, associate, joint venture or branch of a reporting company, the activities of which are based or conducted in a country or currency other than those of the reporting company. Net investment in a foreign operation is the amount of the reporting company's interest in the net assets of that operation. Investment in the equity issued by a foreign operation (e.g., a foreign subsidiary) is a part of net investment in the subsidiary. In the financial statements that include the foreign operation and the reporting entity (e.g., consolidated financial statements when the foreign operation is a subsidiary), exchange differences arising from translating net investment should be recognised in other comprehensive income and accumulated in equity. On disposal of the net investment, exchange differences accumulated in equity should be reclassified to profit or loss.

If the functional currency of a foreign operation is different from the presentation currency of the reporting firm, the reporting firm translates the results and financial position of that foreign operation into the presentation currency using the following procedure: (i) The assets and liabilities, both monetary and non-monetary, should be translated using the closing rate; (ii) Income and expense items should be translated using exchange rates at the dates of the transactions; and (iii) The resulting exchange differences should be recognised in other comprehensive income and is presented as a separate component of equity (e.g., in foreign currency translation reserve).

Key Terms
Exchange difference, Foreign currency, Foreign currency transaction, Foreign exchange rate, Foreign operation, Functional currency, Net investment in a foreign operation, Presentation currency, Reference rate,

NOTES

Self-Test Questions

Self-test question 22.1

Indicate whether the following statements are true (T) or false (F):

(i) The local currency of the country in which a company is domiciled is necessarily its functional currency.

(ii) The functional currency of the parent and its subsidiaries should be the same.

(iii) The presentation currency of Indian companies is INR.

(iv) No exchange difference arises if, the date of recording the foreign exchange transaction and the date of receipt/payment coincides.

(v) Outstanding amount of advance to a vendor denominated in foreign currency should be translated at the closing spot rate for presentation in the balance sheet.

(vi) Trade receivables from a subsidiary is included in the net investment of the parent in the subsidiary.

(vii) Exchange difference arising from settling a liability, which relates to the acquisition of an item of PP&E, at an exchange rate different from the exchange rate at the date of recording the transaction, should be included in the cost of the asset.

(viii) Exchange difference arising from translating financial statements of a foreign operation having a functional currency other than that of the reporting entity, should be accumulated in equity through other comprehensive income.

(ix) The assets and liabilities, both monetary and non-monetary, of a foreign branch, whose functional currency is the same as that of the reporting entity, should be translated using the closing rate for presentation in the balance sheet.

(x) Borrowings denominated in a foreign currency should be translated using the closing rate for presentation in the balance sheet.

ACCOUNTING FOR LEASES

Applicable Accounting Standard

Leasing arrangements are quite common in business. For examples, firms take in lease office building, cars and other types of vehicles, computer servers, rail cars, space in shopping malls (e.g., by retailers), space in the airport (e.g., by airlines and merchandisers), aircrafts (e.g., by airlines) and medical equipment (e.g., hospitals and pathology labs). The lessee (who acquires the right to use the asset) and the lessor (who owns the asset) should account for the lease to provide relevant information in a manner that faithfully represents those transactions. This information gives a basis for users of financial statements to assess the effect that leases have on the financial position, financial performance and cash flows of an entity. Ind AS 116 stipulates the principles and methods for lease accounting, application of which requires judgement. In this section we shall discuss the fundamental principles of lease accounting without getting into details and application issues.

Ind AS 116, Leases, is applicable from the financial year commencing from or after April 1, 2019. Ind AS 17, Leases, is applicable for earlier periods. As per Ind AS 17, both the lessor and lessee classify leases into financial lease and operating lease. The principle of classification is the same that is discussed under 'accounting by lessor' in a subsequent section. The accounting by lessor under Ind AS 116 is similar to the accounting for financial lease by the lessor under Ind AS 17. The accounting for an operating lease by the lessee under Ind AS 17 is similar to the (optional) accounting for short-term leases and leases for low-cost items by the lessor under Ind AS 116 discussed later.

Scope exemption of Ind AS 116

Accounting principles and methods stipulated in Ind AS 116 are not applicable to:

(i) Leases to explore for or use minerals, oil, natural gas and similar non-regenerative resources;

NOTES

(ii) Leases of biological assets within the scope of Ind AS 41, *Agriculture,* held by a lessee;

(iii) Service concession arrangements within the scope of Appendix D, *Service Concession Arrangements,* of Ind AS 115, *Revenue from Contracts with Customer;*

(iv) Licences of intellectual property granted by a lessor within the scope of Ind AS 115, *Revenue from Contracts with Customers;* and

(v) Rights held by a lessee under licensing agreements within the scope of Ind AS 38, *Intangible Assets,* for such items as motion picture films, video recordings, plays, manuscripts, patents and copyrights.

Definition of Lease

Lease is defined as "a contract, or part of a contract, that conveys the right to use an asset (the underlying asset) for a period of time in exchange for consideration."

At inception of a contract, an entity shall assess whether the contract is, or contains, a lease. A contract is, or contains, a lease if the contract conveys the right to control the use of an identified asset for a period of time in exchange for consideration.

Inception of a contract

The inception date is earlier of the date of a lease agreement and the date of commitment by the parties to the principal terms and conditions of the lease. It may be different from the commencement date, which is the date on which a lessor makes an underlying asset available for use by a lessee.

Period of time

Period of time may be defined in terms of months (or years, days, hours, etc.) or in terms of production units.

Identified asset

Usually, the asset is specifically specified in the contract. An asset specified in the contract may not pass the test of identified asset. The asset specified in the contract is not an identified asset if the supplier has the substantive right to substitute the asset throughout the period of use.

A supplier's right to substitute an asset is substantive only if both of the following conditions exist:

(i) the supplier has the practical ability to substitute alternative assets throughout the period of use; and

(ii) the supplier would benefit economically from the exercise of its right to substitute the asset.

For example, Y leases BMW cars from Z and if the contract specifies the specification of the cars and their registration numbers, then the cars are identified assets and Z has no right to substitute those cars. On the other hand, if the contract does not specify the registration numbers of cars and cars are parked in Z's premises, when not in use, the cars are not identified assets, as Y can substitute the cars and the cost of substitution is minimal. In the first case the contract is a lease contract, assuming that all other conditions are fulfilled, and in the second case the contract is a service contract.

Let us take another example. J leases an aircraft from T. The contract requires that the interior of the aircraft should be decorated as per the specifications provided by J. The aircraft is an identified asset, as the cost of substitution is likely to exceed the benefits to T. The contract is a lease contract, if other conditions are fulfilled.

Usually, if the leased asset is located in the premised of the lessee, the asset is an identified asset, as the cost of substitution of the asset is likely to be higher than the benefits to the lessor.

NOTES

A capacity portion of an asset

A capacity portion of an asset can be an identified asset if it is physically distinct. For example, a floor of a building can be an identified asset. A capacity portion that is not physically distinct is an identified asset if it represents substantially all of the capacity of the entire asset. For example, the capacity portion of a fibre-optic cable is an identified asset only if it represents substantially all of the capacity of the entire asset.

Right to control the use of the asset

The lessee has the right to control the use of the asset if enjoys the right to:

(i) Obtain substantially all the economic benefits from using the asset throughout the period of use; and

(ii) Direct the use of the asset throughout the period.

Economic benefits

A lessee can obtain economic benefits from use of an asset directly or indirectly in many ways, such as by using, holding or sub-leasing the asset. The economic benefits from use of an asset include its primary output and by-products (including potential cash flows derived from these items), and other economic benefits from using the asset that could be realised from a commercial transaction with a third party.

When assessing the right to obtain substantially all of the economic benefits from the use of the asset, the customer should consider the economic benefits that result from use of the asset within the defined scope of its right to use the asset. For example, if the contract allows the customer to use the vehicle (identified asset within the contract) within Delhi, the customer should consider the economic benefits that result from use of the vehicle within Delhi.

Right to direct the use of the asset

A customer has the right to direct the use of an identified asset throughout the period of use only if the customer has the right to direct how and for what purpose the asset is used throughout the period of use.

The customer has the right to direct how and for what purpose the asset is used if it has the right to decide what output to be produced, in what quantity, where and when, within the defined scope of the customer's right of use. For example, a construction company takes on lease a bulldozer and as per the contract it can use the bulldozer in the National Capital Region (NCR). There is no other restriction and the construction company can decide when and in which site it will use the asset and for how many hours. It can also decide for what purpose (e.g., construction of buildings or construction of roads) it will use the asset. It may be concluded that the construction company has the right to direct to use the asset. Right to operating and maintaining the asset can be with the supplier or the customer and is considered in judging whether the customer has the right to direct the use of the asset.

How and for what purpose the asset is used are predetermined

When how and for what purpose the asset is used are predetermined, the customer has the right to direct the use of an identified asset throughout the period of use, if:

(i) the customer has the right to operate the asset (or to direct others to operate the asset in a manner that it determines) throughout the period of use, without the supplier having the right to change those operating instructions; or

(ii) the customer designed the asset (or specific aspects of the asset) in a way that predetermines how and for what purpose the asset will be used throughout the period of use.

NOTES

CASE STUDY 22.3 Retail Space

Y Ltd. (YL) is in the business of selling kid's products, such as readymade garments, educational toys and materials and school bags. It has entered into a contract with Z Ltd. (ZL), which is the owner of a large shopping mall in Vasant Kunj (Delhi) to take on rent a shopping space in the shopping mall. The contract:

(i) Specifies the size and exact location of the space;

(ii) Gives the right to ZL to relocate YL to another space;

(iii) Restricts YL from selling goods before and after the opening hours of the mall; and

(iv) Rent, which has two components—fixed monthly payment and a percentage of revenue.

At the inception of the lease, YL assesses that though ZL has the right to relocate YL, it is unlikely to happen, as ZL would derive economic benefits from that decision only if a new customer agrees to pay higher rent for the space occupied by YL than what it would pay for a vacant space.

Question

The CFO of YL seeks your advice on whether the contract with ZL is a lease contract.

Solution

The space is explicitly specified in the contract and the substitution right of ZL is not substantive, as it is unlikely to benefit economically from substitution. Therefore, the asset is an identified asset. The restriction on selling goods before or after the opening hours of the mall limits the scope, but does not preclude YL from deciding what goods and in what quantity to be sold at what price and when. Therefore, YL has the right to control the use of the asset. YL will enjoy substantially all the economic benefits from the use of the asset, although it has to pay a percentage of revenue to ZL as a part of rent.

In view of the above, the contract is a lease contract.

Accounting by Lessee

Lease term

An entity determines the lease term as the non-cancellable period of a lease, plus periods covered by an option to extend the lease if the lessee is reasonably certain to exercise that option; and periods covered by an option to terminate the lease if the lessee is reasonably certain not to exercise that option. In assessing the 'reasonable certainty' of exercising the option to extend the lease or not exercising the option to terminate the lease, an entity should consider all relevant facts and circumstances that create an economic incentive for such decisions. For example, it is more likely that a lessee will exercise an extension option if it has made significant investments to improve the leased asset or to tailor it for its special needs or by extending the lease it will avoid the cost of signing a replacement lease (e.g., negotiation costs, relocation costs, costs of integrating a new asset and costs of returning the original asset in a contractually specified condition or to a contractually specified location).

The lease term is reassessed only in limited circumstances.

Initial recognition and measurement

A lessee is required to recognise a *'right-of-use asset'* and a corresponding lease liability for almost all lease contracts at the commencement date.

Exemption

Lessees have option not to apply this accounting principle in case of short-term leases (lease term of 12 months or less) and leases for which the underlying asset is of low value (e.g., office furniture and IT equipment). A lessee, which decides to exercise the option recognises lease payments as expenses on a straight-line basis or another systematic basis that is more representative of the pattern of the lessee's benefit. For certain low value assets (such as assets that are dependent on, or highly interrelated with, other underlying assets), the exemption is not applicable.

Initial measurement of the lease liability

The lease liability is initially measured at an amount equal to the present value (PV) of the lease payments during the lease term that are not yet paid. The PV is calculated using the 'interest rate implicit in the lease' as the discount rate. If that rate cannot be readily determined, the lessee should use the lessee's 'incremental borrowing rate'.

Interest rate implicit in the lease

Interest rate implicit in the lease is the rate of interest that causes the PV of (i) the lease payments and (ii) the 'unguaranteed residual value' to equal the sum of (a) the fair value of the underlying asset and (b) any initial direct costs of the lessor. 'Unguaranteed residual value' is that portion of the residual value of the underlying asset, the realisation of which by a lessor is not assured or is guaranteed solely by a party related to the lessor.

Lease payments

Lease payments consist of the following components:

- Fixed payments (including in-substance fixed payments), less any lease incentives receivable;
- Variable lease payments that depend on an index or a rate;
- Amounts expected to be payable by the lessee under residual value guaranteed to the lessor or by a third party unrelated to the lessor;
- The exercise price of a purchase option (if the lessee is reasonably certain to exercise that option); and
- Payments of penalties for terminating the lease (if the lease term reflects the lessee exercising the option to terminate the lease).

Key Terms
Asset ceiling, Defined benefit plan, Defined contribution plan, Projected unit credit method

Contingent lease payments

Contingent lease payments are classified in the following three categories:

(i) Variable lease payments based on an index or a rate—Variable lease payments based on an index or a rate (for example, linked to a consumer price index, a benchmark interest rate or a market rental rate) are part of the lease liability. The lessee should initially measure variable lease payments based on an index or a rate using the index or the rate at the commencement date. Changes in rates/indices are taken into account at the point in time in which lease payments change. For example, if the contract stipulates that lease payments will be adjusted to reflect changes in the Consumer Price Index for the preceding 24 months, at the beginning of the third year, the lease liability has to be adjusted when the contractual cash flows will change. The revised measurement of the lease liability will be the present value of the revised payments, based on the Consumer Price Index at the date of change for the remainder of the term using the unchanged discount rate.

(ii) Variable lease payments based on any other variable—Variable lease payments not based on an index or a rate are not part of the lease liability. Examples of such payments are payments of a specified percentage of sales made from a retail store, payments based on the output of a solar or a wind farm, and payments if the

NOTES

lessee exceeds a specified mileage. Such payments are recognised in profit or loss in the period in which the event or condition that triggers those payments occurs.

(iii) In-substance fixed payments—Lease payments that, in form, contain variability but, in substance, are fixed are included in the lease liability. A lease payment is in-substance fixed if there is no genuine variability. For example, where payments must be made if the asset is proven to be capable of operating, or where payments must be made only if an event occurs that has no genuine possibility of not occurring.

Initial measurement of the right-to-use asset

The right-of-use asset is initially measured at cost, consisting of the amount of the initial measurement of the lease liability, plus (i) any lease payments made to the lessor at or before the commencement date less any lease incentives received, and (ii) the PV of the initial estimate of restoration costs and any initial direct costs incurred by the lessee. The provision for the restoration costs is recognised as a separate liability.

Initial direct costs

Initial direct costs are incremental costs that would not have been incurred if a lease had not been obtained. Examples are commissions or some payments made to existing tenants to obtain the lease. All initial direct costs are included in the initial measurement of the right-of-use asset.

Subsequent measurement of lease liability and right-to-use asset

The lessee measures the lease liability using the effective interest rate method. It depreciates the right-of-use asset as per its depreciation policy for assets that are similar to the asset covered under the lease. It also tests the same for impairment in accordance with the accounting standard that deals impairment. If, the lessee uses the straight line depreciation method, the combination of a straight-line depreciation of the right-of-use asset and the effective interest rate method applied to the lease liability results in a decreasing 'total lease expense' throughout the lease term. This effect is sometimes referred to as 'front loading'.

Alternative measurement model

A right-of-use asset *can* be subsequently measured at the revalued amount in accordance with Ind AS 16 if it relates to a class of property, plant and equipment and the lessee applies the revaluation model to all assets in that class.

Presentation and disclosures

On the balance sheet, the lessee has the option either to present the right-of-use asset separately or in the same line item in which the underlying asset would be presented. Similarly, the lessee has the option to present the lease liability either as a separate line item or together with other financial liabilities. If the right-of-use asset and the lease liability are not presented as separate line items, the lessee is required to disclose in the notes the carrying amount of those items and the line item in which they are included.

In the statement of profit or loss and other comprehensive income, the depreciation charge of the right-of-use asset should be presented in the same line item/items in which similar expenses (such as depreciation of property, plant and equipment) are shown. The interest expense on the lease liability should be presented as part of finance costs. The lessee is required to disclose the amount of interest expense on lease liabilities in the notes.

In the statement of cash flows, lease payments are classified consistently with payments on other financial liabilities:

- The part of the lease payment that represents cash payments for the principal portion of the lease liability is presented as a cash flow resulting from financing activities.
- The part of the lease payment that represents interest portion of the lease liability is presented as a cash flow resulting from financing activities.

NOTES

- Payments on short-term leases, for leases of low-value assets and variable lease payments not included in the measurement of the lease liability are presented as an operating cash flow.

To provide users with information that allows them to assess the amount, timing and uncertainty of lease payments, Ind AS 116 includes enhanced disclosure requirements.

Accounting by Lessor

The lessor classifies leases as either finance or operating lease. The lessor classifies the lease at the inception date. It reassesses the same only if there is a lease modification.

Lease classification

A lease is classified as a finance lease if it transfers substantially all the risks and rewards incidental to ownership of an underlying asset. A lease is classified as an operating lease if it does not transfer substantially all the risks and rewards incidental to ownership of an underlying asset. Whether a lease is a finance lease, or an operating lease depends on the substance of the transaction rather than the form of the contract. The following are the examples of situations that individually or in combination would normally lead to a lease being classified as a finance lease are:

(i) the lease transfers ownership of the underlying asset to the lessee by the end of the lease term;

(ii) the lessee has the option to purchase the underlying asset at a price that is expected to be sufficiently lower than the fair value at the date the option becomes exercisable for it to be reasonably certain, at the inception date, that the option will be exercised;

(iii) the lease term is for the major part of the economic life of the underlying asset even if title is not transferred;

(iv) at the inception date, the present value of the lease payments amounts to at least substantially all of the fair value of the underlying asset; and

(v) the underlying asset is of such a specialised nature that only the lessee can use it without major modifications.

Indicators of situations that individually or in combination could also lead to a lease being classified as a finance lease are:

(i) if the lessee can cancel the lease, the lessor's losses associated with the cancellation are borne by the lessee;

(ii) gains or losses from the fluctuation in the fair value of the residual accrue to the lessee (for example, in the form of a rent rebate equaling most of the sales proceeds at the end of the lease); and

(iii) the lessee has the ability to continue the lease for a secondary period at a rent that is substantially lower than market rent.

Recognition and measurement

Finance lease

For a finance lease, at the lease commencement, the lessor recognises a receivable at an amount equal to the net investment in the lease. The underlying asset does not appear in the balance sheet of the lessor. Net investment is the present value of the aggregate of lease payments receivable by the lessor and any unguaranteed residual value. The lessor uses the interest rate implicit in the lease to measure the net investment in the lease. The components of lease payments are discussed under 'accounting by lessee' above.

Subsequently, the lessor recognises finance income over the lease term, based on a pattern reflecting a constant periodic rate of return on the lessor's net investment in the lease. It applies the lease payments received from the lessee during the period against the 'gross investment in lease' to reduce the principal (receivable) and unearned interest. Gross investment in lease is the sum of: (i) the lease payments receivable by a lessor under a finance lease; and (ii) any unguaranteed residual value accruing to the lessor.

NOTES

Operating lease

If the contract is classified as an operating lease, the lessor continues to present the underlying asset. It recognises lease payments from operating leases as income on either a straight-line basis or another systematic basis. It applies another systematic basis if that basis is more representative of the pattern in which benefit from the use of the underlying asset is diminished. It recognises costs, including depreciation, incurred in earning the lease income as an expense.

Manufacturer/dealer vendor

Manufacturers or dealers often offer to customers the choice of either buying or leasing an asset. A finance lease of an asset by a manufacturer or dealer lessor gives rise to profit or loss equivalent to the profit or loss resulting from an outright sale of the underlying asset, at normal selling prices, reflecting any applicable volume or trade discounts.

At the commencement date, a manufacturer or dealer lessor recognises the following for each of its finance leases:

(i) Revenue—Revenue is the fair value (FV) of the underlying asset, or, if the present value of the lease payments accruing to the lessor, discounted using a market rate of interest, is lower, then the revenue is the PV of the lease payments;

(ii) Cost of sale—Cost of sale is the cost, or carrying amount if different, of the underlying asset less the present value of the unguaranteed residual value; and

(iii) Selling profit or loss—Profit or loss is the difference between revenue and the cost of sale recognised in accordance with an entity's policy for outright sales.

Sale and Leaseback Transaction

Transfer of the asset is a sale

Accounting by seller-lessee

If the buyer-lessor has obtained control of the underlying asset and the transfer is classified as a sale in accordance with Ind AS 115, the seller-lessee measures a right-of-use asset arising from the leaseback as the proportion of the previous carrying amount of the asset that relates to the right of use retained. The seller-lessee recognises the gain (or loss) that is limited to the proportion of the total gain (or loss) that relates to the rights transferred to the buyer-lessor.

If the consideration for the sale is not equal to the fair value of the asset, any resulting difference represents either a prepayment of lease payments (if the purchase price is below market terms) or an additional financing (if the purchase price is above market terms). The same logic applies if the lease payments are not at market rates.

The proportion of right to use retained is the ratio of the present value (PV) of lease payments to the fair value (FV) of the underlying asset. The ratio is calculated after adjusting the PV of the lease payments for the difference in the purchase price and FV of the underlying asset.

Accounting by buyer-lessor

The buyer-lessor accounts for the purchase in accordance with applicable standards (such as Ind AS 16 if the underlying asset is property, plant or equipment), and for the leaseback in accordance with Ind AS 116.

NOTES

ILLUSTRATION 22.1 Sale and Leaseback

K Ltd. (KL), the seller-lessee, sells a building to M Ltd. (ML), the buyer-lessor for cash of ₹20,00,000. The fair value of the building at the time of sale is ₹18,00,000. The carrying amount of the asset in the books of KL is ₹10,00,000. At the same time KL enters into a lease contract with ML to leaseback the building for 18 years with annual lease rent of ₹1,20,000, payable at the end of each year. KL's incremental borrowing rate is 4.5% per annum.

Question

Explain how the transaction (sale and leaseback) should be recorded by KL.

Solution

(i) The fair value of the building is ₹18,00,000, while the consideration for selling the asset to ML (ML's purchase price) is ₹20,00,000. Therefore, there is additional financing of (₹20,00,000 – 18,00,000) or ₹2,00,000 by ML to KL.

(ii) The present value of the annual lease payment of ₹1,20,000 discounted at the incremental borrowing rate of 4.5% per annum is ₹14,59,200.

(iii) A portion of the lease payments is towards the repayment of the additional financing. The PV of lease payments includes PV of payments towards repayment of additional financing of ₹2,00,000. Therefore, the PV of lease payments that relate to lease is (₹14,59,200 – 2,00,000) or ₹12,59,200.

(iv) The proportion of the asset retained is (₹12,59,200/18,00,000). KL should recognise the right-of-use asset at the retained proportion of the carrying amount, which is [(₹12,59,200/18,00,000) × ₹10,00,000] or ₹6,99,556.

(v) The cash received by KL on the sale of the asset, excluding additional financing of ₹2,00,000 is ₹18,00,000, which is the fair value of the asset. Thus, the total gain on the sale of the asset is (₹18,00,000 – 10,00,000) or ₹8,00,000. Out of the total gain, the gain that relates to the proportion of the right on the asset transferred to ML is [(₹18,00,000 – 12,59,200)/18,00,000] × ₹8,00,000 or ₹2,40,356. Therefore, KL should recognise the gain on sale of the asset at ₹2,40,356.

Journal entries at the commencement in the books of KL:

Cash	Dr. 20,00,000	
Right-to-use asset	Dr. 6,99,556	
To Building		Cr. 10,00,000
To Financing liability		Cr. 14,59,200
To Gain od sale-and-leaseback		Cr. 2,40,356

Transfer of the asset is not a sale

If the transfer is not a sale (i.e., the buyer-lessor does not obtain control of the asset in accordance with Ind AS 115), the seller-lessee does not derecognise the transferred asset and accounts for the cash received as a financial liability. The buyer-lessor does not recognise the transferred asset and, instead, accounts for the cash paid as a financial asset (receivable).

SUMMARY

A contract is, or contains, a lease if the contract conveys the right to control the use of an identified asset for a period of time in exchange for consideration. Usually, the asset is specifically specified in the contract. An asset specified in the contract may not pass the test of identified asset. The asset specified in the contract is not an identified asset if the supplier has the substantive right to substitute the asset throughout the period of use. A supplier's right to substitute an asset is substantive only if both of the following conditions exist: (i) the supplier has the practical ability to substitute alternative assets throughout the period of use; and (ii) the supplier would benefit economically from the exercise of its right to substitute the asset. A customer has the right to direct the use of an identified asset throughout the period of use only if the customer has the right to direct how and for what purpose the asset is used throughout the period of use.

An entity determines the lease term as the non-cancellable period of a lease, plus periods covered by an option to extend the lease if the lessee is reasonably certain to exercise that option; and periods covered by an option to terminate the lease if the lessee is reasonably certain not to exercise that option.

A lessee is required to recognise a *'right-of-use asset'* and a corresponding lease liability for almost all lease contracts at the commencement date. However, lessees have option not to apply this accounting principle in case of short-term leases and leases for which the underlying asset is of low value and recognise lease payments as expenses on a straight-line basis or another systematic basis that is more representative of the pattern of the lessee's benefit. For certain low value assets the exemption is not applicable.

Initially, lessees measure the lease liability at an amount equal to the present value (PV) of the lease payments during the lease term that are not yet paid. The PV is calculated using the 'interest rate implicit in the lease' as the discount rate. If that rate cannot be readily determined, a lessee should use the lessee's 'incremental borrowing rate'. Initially, the lessee measures the right-of-use asset at cost, consisting of the amount of the initial measurement of the lease liability, plus (i) any lease payments made to the lessor at or before the commencement date less any lease incentives received, and (ii) the PV of the initial estimate of restoration costs and any initial direct costs incurred by the lessee. The provision for the restoration costs is recognised as a separate liability. Subsequently, the lessee measures the lease liability using the effective interest rate method, and depreciates the right-of-use asset and also tests the same for impairment. The lessee can measure a right-of-use asset at the revalued amount in if it relates to a class of property, plant and equipment and the lessee applies the revaluation model to all assets in that class.

The lessor classifies leases as either finance or operating lease. A lease is classified as a finance lease if it transfers substantially all the risks and rewards incidental to ownership of an underlying asset. A lease is classified as an operating lease if it does not transfer substantially all the risks and rewards incidental to ownership of an underlying asset. For a finance lease, at the lease commencement, the lessor recognises a receivable at an amount equal to the net investment in the lease. Subsequently, the lessor recognises finance income over the lease term, based on a pattern reflecting a constant periodic rate of return on the lessor's net investment in the lease. It applies the lease payments received from the lessee during the period against the 'gross investment in lease' to reduce the principal (receivable) and unearned interest. Gross investment in lease is the sum of: (a) the lease payments receivable by a lessor under a finance lease; and (b) any unguaranteed residual value accruing to the lessor. If the contract is classified as an operating lease, the lessor continues to present the underlying asset. It recognises lease payments from operating leases as income on either a straight-line basis or another systematic basis. It recognises costs, including depreciation, incurred in earning the lease income as an expense.

A finance lease of an asset by a manufacturer or dealer lessor gives rise to profit or loss equivalent to the profit or loss resulting from an outright sale of the underlying asset, at normal selling prices, reflecting any applicable volume or trade discounts.

In a sale and leaseback transaction, if the buyer-lessor has obtained control of the underlying asset and the transfer is classified as a sale, the seller-lessee measures a right-of-use asset arising from the leaseback as the proportion of the previous carrying amount of the asset that relates to the right of use retained. The seller-lessee recognises the gain (or loss) that is limited to the proportion of the total gain (or loss) that relates to the rights transferred to the buyer-lessor. If the consideration for the sale is not equal to the fair value of the asset, any resulting difference represents either a prepayment of lease payments (if the purchase price is below market terms) or an additional financing (if the purchase price is above market terms). The same logic applies if the lease payments are not at market rates. The proportion of right to use retained is the ratio of the present value (PV) of lease payments to the fair value (FV) of the underlying asset. The ratio is calculated after adjusting the PV of the lease payments for the difference in the purchase price and FV of the underlying asset. The buyer-lessor accounts for the purchase in accordance with applicable standards (such as Ind AS 16 if the underlying asset is property, plant or equipment), and for the leaseback in accordance with Ind AS 116. If the transfer is not a sale, the seller-lessee does not derecognise the transferred asset and accounts for the cash received as a financial liability. The buyer-lessor does not recognise the transferred asset and, instead, accounts for the cash paid as a financial asset (receivable).

NOTES

Key Terms
Commencement of lease, Identified asset, Inception of lease, Lease, Lessee, Lessor, Right-of-use asset

Self-Test Questions

Self-test question 22.2

Indicate whether the following statements are true (T) or false (F):

(i) Usually, if the leased asset is located in the premises of the lessee, the asset is an identified asset.

(ii) In a lease contract, the period of time should be defined only in terms of months (or years, days, hours etc.).

(iii) If the customer has no right to decide how and for what purpose the asset is to be used, then the contract is a service contract.

(iv) Right to operate the asset by the customer is not construed as the right to direct the use of the asset unless the use of the asset is predetermined.

(v) At the inception of the lease, both the lessee and lessor classifies the lease either as an operating lease or a finance lease.

(vi) The terms inception of lease and commencement of lease are used interchangeably.

(vii) Right-of-use asset is an intangible asset.

(viii) Right-of-use asset is not depreciated/amortised and is tested for impairment periodically.

(ix) At the initial recognition, the lessee records the 'right-of-use asset' and the lease liability at the same amount.

(x) 'Right-of-use asset' is not tested for impairment.

(xi) If as per the lease agreement, the lessee (a retailer) has to pay a percentage of revenue to the lessor, the lesser should include the estimated PV of the same in the lease liability.

(xii) Payments on short-term leases, for leases of low-value assets and variable lease payments not included in the measurement of the lease liability are presented as an operating cash flow.

(xiii) The lessor is required to classify leases into operating lease and finance lease.

(xiv) A lease is a finance lease if the lessor transfers substantially the risks and returns incidental to the ownership of the asset to the lessee.

(xv) In case of finance lease, the underlying asset does not find place in the lessor's balance sheet.

(xvi) In case of finance lease, the lessor continues to charge depreciation on the leased asset.

(xvii) In case of operating lease, the lessor recognises the lease rent as income in the statement of profit and loss for the year in which the lease rent is accrued.

(xviii) When the seller/dealer leases an asset to a customer, it recognises the revenue at the fair value (FV) of the underlying asset, or, if the present value of the lease payments accruing to the lessor, discounted using a market rate of interest, is lower, then it recognises the revenue at the PV of the lease payments.

(xix) In a sale and lease back transaction, the seller-lessee recognises the gain (or loss) that is limited to the proportion of the total gain (or loss) that relates to the rights transferred to the buyer-lessor.

(xx) The proportion of right to use retained by the seller-lessee in a 'sale and lease back' transaction is the ratio of the present value (PV) of lease payments to the fair value (FV) of the underlying asset.

ACCOUNTING FOR BORROWING COSTS

Applicable accounting standard: Ind AS 23, Borrowing Costs.

General Principles

Borrowing cost is the total of interest and other costs that an entity incurs in connection with the borrowing of funds. Borrowing cost directly attributable to the acquisition of a qualifying asset, incurred during the construction or production period, is included in the cost of the asset. Other borrowing costs are recognised as an expense of the period in which they are incurred. The borrowing costs that are eligible for capitalisation are costs incurred by the entity. *They should not include notional costs*. The weighted average rate is used for capitalisation of borrowing costs unless a new borrowing is identified with a specific asset. The rate is applied on the average carrying amount of the asset during a period, including borrowing costs previously capitalised.

NOTES

Directly attributable

New borrowings made specifically for the purpose of acquisition, construction or production of a qualified asset is directly attributable to that asset. For example, if A Ltd. borrows ₹50 million to construct its administrative building, the borrowing is directly attributable to the construction of the administrative building. In order to be eligible for capitalisation of borrowing costs, it is not necessary to establish a direct relationship between the borrowing and the asset. A borrowing is directly attributable to a particular asset if that *would have been avoided* if the expenditure on the qualifying asset had not been made.

The amount of borrowing cost to be capitalised should be the amount that *theoretically* could have been avoided during the acquisition period if expenditures for the asset had not been made. The amount of borrowing cost that could be avoided is a measure of the *opportunity cost* of investment. Therefore, in assessing whether the borrowing could have been avoided, the entity should ascertain whether:

(i) Additional borrowing could be avoided if the expenditure on the qualifying asset had not been made, and

(ii) By using the fund expended for the qualifying asset, the company could repay a part of the borrowings outstanding at the end of the period.

It is true that investment of funds in the qualifying asset also entails rejection of a wide range of other possible uses of funds. Therefore, *borrowing cost that would have been avoided* constitutes only several measures of opportunity cost. But it is the measure that can be recognised in the present accounting framework.

The notion of *avoidable borrowing cost* is theoretical. The *practicality* of repaying individual borrowings is not considered in estimating the avoidable borrowing cost.

Qualifying asset

As a general principle, to qualify for capitalisation of borrowing costs, an asset must require a substantial period of time to get ready for its intended use or sale. Ordinarily, *a period of twelve months* is considered as substantial period of time unless a shorter or longer period can be justified on the basis of facts and circumstances of the case. The following assets usually take one year or more to get ready for intended use or sale unless the contrary can be proved by the entity:

(i) Assets that are constructed or otherwise produced for an enterprise's own use.

(ii) Assets intended for sale or lease that are constructed or otherwise produced as discrete projects such as ships or real estate developments.

(iii) Inventories where time is the major factor in bringing about a change in the condition of inventories such as production of wine.

Capitalisation Period

The capitalisation of borrowing costs commences when all the following conditions are satisfied:

(i) Expenditure for the acquisition, construction, or production of the asset is being incurred;

(ii) Borrowing costs are being incurred; and

(iii) Activities that are necessary to prepare the asset for its intended use or sale are in progress.

NOTES

Key Terms
Borrowing cost,
Capitalisation period,
Qualifying asset

Condition (iii) above should be interpreted broadly. Activities encompass more than the physical construction of the asset. They include technical and administrative work prior to the commencement of physical construction. Capitalisation continues as long as activities are in progress and ceases when the asset is substantially ready for use or sale. Capitalisation of borrowing costs is suspended during extended periods in which active development is interrupted. It is also suspended when acquisition or construction activities are suspended intentionally. However, when suspension or delay is inherent in the acquisition or construction process or it is imposed by external forces, capitalisation of borrowing costs is not suspended because interruptions on those situations are unavoidable. Brief, normal interruptions do not result in suspension of capitalisation of borrowing costs on the ground of immateriality. Acquisition or construction activities are construed broadly. Therefore, capitalisation of borrowing costs is not suspended during a period when substantial technical and administrative work is being carried out.

SUMMARY

Borrowing cost directly attributable to the acquisition of a qualifying asset, incurred during the construction or production period, is included in the cost of the asset. Other borrowing costs are recognised as an expense of the period in which they are incurred. They should not include notional costs. As a general principle, to qualify for capitalisation of borrowing costs, an asset must require a substantial period of time to get ready for its intended use or sale. The capitalisation of borrowing costs commences when all the following conditions are satisfied:

(i) Expenditure for the acquisition, construction, or production of the asset is being incurred;
(ii) Borrowing costs are being incurred; and
(iii) Activities that are necessary to prepare the asset for its intended use or sale are in progress. Capitalisation continues as long as activities are in progress and ceases when the asset is substantially ready for use or sale.

Self-Test Questions

Self-test question 22.3

Indicate whether the following statements are true (T) or false (F):

(i) Only the borrowing costs pertaining to the amount borrowed specifically for the production or construction of the asset should be added to the cost of the asset.
(ii) Only items of PP&E qualify for the capitalisation of borrowing costs.
(iii) Capitalisation of borrowing costs ceases when the asset is substantially ready for use.
(iv) When the construction or production of the asset is suspended for whatever reasons, the capitalisation of borrowing costs is also suspended.
(v) Capitalisation of borrowing costs is not suspended during a period when substantial technical and administrative work is being carried out.

ACCOUNTING FOR SHARE BASED PAYMENTS TO EMPLOYEES

Applicable accounting standard: Ind AS 102, Share Based Payments.

This section discusses the basic accounting principle very briefly and it does not discuss all the principles and methods stipulated in Ind AS 102.

General Principles

In a share-based payment transaction, an entity receives goods or services in exchange for consideration in the form of equity instruments, or cash or other assets for amounts that are based on the price (or value) of equity instruments.

NOTES

In many companies, share-based payment under the Employee Stock Ownership Plan (ESOP) is one of the components of the total compensation to an employee. Companies usually grant stock options to employees. An option gives the right to buy from the company its shares at a specified price at a specified date. For example, on 1 April 2019 (grant date), a company may grant option to its employees to buy from the company shares at ₹80 per share after 31 March 2024 (vesting date) but before 31 March 2027 (exercise date) if he continues his service with the company till 31 March 2024. An employee will exercise the option only if the share price moves beyond ₹80. For example, if the share price moves to ₹200 on a date after 31 March 2024 but before 31 March 2027, the payoff to the employee will be ₹120 (200 – 80) if she exercises the option on that date. Companies grant stock option to motivate employees to perform at the highest level of productivity so that the share price moves upward, which will benefit both the employees and the shareholders.

Accounting Principles

Goods or services received in a share-based payment transaction are measured at fair value of the goods or services received. Goods are recognised when they are obtained, and services are recognised over the period over which they are received. It recognises a corresponding increase in equity. When the goods or services received or acquired in a share-based payment transaction do not qualify for recognition as assets, they are recognised as expenses.

For equity-settled share-based payment transactions, the enterprise directly measures the goods or services received, and the corresponding increase in equity at the fair value of the goods or services received unless that fair value cannot be estimated reliably. If the entity cannot estimate reliably the fair value of the goods or services received, the company measures their value, and the corresponding increase in equity, indirectly, by reference to the fair value of the equity instruments granted.

Invariably, an enterprise cannot determine directly the fair value of services rendered by employees. Accordingly, it records the transaction at *the fair value of shares or options to acquire shares granted to employees.* The fair value of an option has two components—**intrinsic value** and the **time value**. Fair value of an option is usually estimated by using an economic model such as the Black-Scholes model. The intrinsic value is the difference between the exercise price and the price of the underlying stock on the date of valuation. For example, if the exercise price is ₹80 and the value of the underlying stock is ₹120, the intrinsic value is ₹40 (120–80). The time value of an option cannot be estimated directly. It is the difference between the fair value and the intrinsic value. For example, if the fair value is ₹100 and the intrinsic value is ₹40, the time value is ₹60 (100–40).

The fair value of the share or option is determined at the measurement date, which is the grant date in the case of employee stock option, based on the market price, if available, taking into consideration those terms and conditions upon which those equity instruments were granted.

Grant date

For transactions with employees, the measurement date is the grant date which is the date at which the company and the employee agree to a share-based payment arrangement. It is the date when the company and the employee have a shared understanding of the terms and conditions of the arrangement. On the grant date the company confers on the employee the right to equity instruments or other assets provided the specified vesting conditions and non-vesting conditions, if any, are met.

Vesting date, vesting period, vesting condition and non-vesting conditions

'Vest' means to become an entitlement. On the vesting date the equity instrument or the option to acquire equity instrument vests on an employee upon satisfaction of any specified vesting conditions. The period within which all the vesting conditions are to be satisfied is called the *vesting period.*

Vesting conditions are conditions that are to be satisfied to become entitled to the share-based payment. Vesting conditions include service conditions which require the employee to complete a specified period of service and performance conditions, which require specified performance targets to be met. Performance condition is a vesting condition that requires the employee to complete a specified period of service and specified performance target(s) to be met while services are rendered. Performance condition may be a market condition (e.g., achieving a certain share price target) or non-market performance (e.g., achieving a certain profit target).

Non-vesting conditions are unrelated to the requirement to deliver services to the entity. Even when all vesting conditions have been satisfied and the share-based payment vests, the employee does not receive the benefit of the share-based payment if a non-vesting condition is not met. Non-compete restriction, such as, the employee cannot join a competing enterprise within two years from the vesting date, is an example of non-vesting condition.

An employee has to fulfil both vesting and non-vesting conditions to be entitled for share-based payment and both types of conditions are considered in valuing the stock option.

Accounting method

If the share-based payment vests immediately, it is assumed that the payment is made for services already rendered. If the shared-based payment vests on satisfaction of vesting conditions during the vesting period, it is assumed that the payment is made for services to be rendered during the vesting period. In that case, the total fair value at the grant date of the number of stock options estimated to be vested to the employees at the end of the vesting period is amortised over the vesting period.

Each year employee benefits expense is recognised in the statement of profit and loss by credit to Stock Options Outstanding Account. The credit balance in that account is presented as a separate component of equity. If, at the end of the exercise period the option is not exercised, the accumulated balance in the Stock Options Outstanding Account is transferred to the general reserve. If the option is exercised, the total of the accumulated balance in the Stock Options Outstanding Account and the amount (exercise price) received from the employee is allocated to the share capital and share premium account.

ILLUSTRATION 22.2

On 1 January 2018 (Grant date) Rishika Ltd. (RL) grants 300 equity options to each of its 100 employees. The face value of each equity share is ₹10. RL estimates the fair value of options at the grant date, based on an option pricing model, at ₹20 per option. The contractual life (comprising the vesting period and the exercise period) of option granted is 6 years. The other relevant terms of the grant are:

Vesting period	3 years
Exercise period	3 years
Expected life	5 years
Exercise price ₹50	
Market price ₹50	

On 31 December 2018, RL estimates that only 95 employees will satisfy the vesting conditions at the vesting date. On 31 December 2019, RL estimates that only 98 employees will satisfy the vesting conditions at the vesting date. On 31 December 2020, only 90 employees met vesting conditions at the vesting date. In 2021, 40 employees exercised the option and, in 2022, 40 employees exercised the option; 10 employees allowed the option to expire.

Required

Explain the how RL should account for the stock options granted to employees.

Solution

Accounting in 2018. At 31 December 2018, RL estimates that only 95 employees will satisfy the vesting conditions at the vesting date. Therefore, expense for services to be received over the

NOTES

vesting period of three years is ₹5,70,000 (20 × 300 × 95). RL should allocate ₹5,70,000 over the vesting period of three years. Therefore, in the statement of profit and loss for 2018, it recognises the expense at ₹1,90,000 (5,70,000/3) with a corresponding credit to Stock Options Outstanding Account. The balance in the Stock Options Outstanding Account is presented in the balance sheet as at 31 December 2018 as a component of equity.

Accounting in 2019. On 31 December 2019, RL estimates that only 98 employees will satisfy the vesting conditions at the vesting date. Therefore, expense for services to be received over the vesting period of three years is ₹5,88,000 (20 × 300 × 98). RL should allocate ₹5,88,000 over the vesting period of three years. Therefore, cumulative expense to be recognised in the first two years is ₹3,92,000 (5,88,000/3) × 2. Thus, in 2019, RL should recognise the expense at ₹2,02,000 (3,92,000 – 1,90,000) with a corresponding credit to Stock Options Outstanding Account. The balance (₹3,92,000) in the Stock Options Outstanding Account is presented in the balance sheet as at 31 December 2019 as a component of equity.

Accounting in 2020. On 31 December 2020, only 90 employees met the vesting conditions. Therefore, the expense for services to be received over the vesting period of three years is ₹5,40,000 (20 × 300 × 90). Thus, cumulative expense to be recognized at the end of the third year is ₹5,40,000. Consequently, in 2020, RL should recognise the expense at ₹1,48,000 (5,40,000 – 3,92,000) with a corresponding credit to Stock Options Outstanding Account. The balance (₹5,40,000) in the Stock Options Outstanding Account is presented in the balance sheet as at 31 December 2020 as a component of equity.

Accounting in 2021. In the year, 40 employees exercised the option. Therefore, ₹2,40,000 (₹20 × 300 × 40) should be transferred from Stock Options Outstanding Account to share capital/share premium account. RL receives ₹6,00,000 (50 × 300 × 40) against issue of 12,000 shares. Thus, (₹6,00,000 + 2,40,000) or ₹8,40,000 is credited to: Share Capital Account: ₹1,20,000 (10 × 12,000 shares); and Share Premium Account: ₹7,20,000 [(50 + 20 – 10) × 12,000].

Accounting in 2022. In the year, 40 employees exercised the option. Therefore, ₹2,40,000 (20 × 300 × 40) should be transferred from Stock Options Outstanding Account to share capital/share premium account. RL receives ₹6,00,000 (50 × 300 × 40) against issue of 12,000 shares. Thus, ₹8,40,000 (6,00,000 + 2,40,000) is credited to: Share Capital Account: ₹1,20,000 (10 × 12,000 shares); and Share Premium Account: ₹7,20,000 [(50 + 20 – 10) × 12,000].

Accounting in 2023. In the year, 10 employees allowed their options to expire. Therefore, RL transfers the balance of ₹60,000 (5,40,000 – 2,40,000 – 2,40,000) from Stock Options Outstanding Account to General Reserve.

SUMMARY

Goods or services received in a share-based payment transaction are measured at fair value. Goods are recognised when they are obtained, and services are recognised over the period during which they are received. It recognises a corresponding increase in equity. When the goods or services received or acquired in a share-based payment transaction do not qualify for recognition as assets, they are recognised as expenses. An enterprise cannot determine directly the fair value of services rendered by employees. Accordingly, it records the transaction at *the fair value of shares or options to acquire shares granted to employees.* The fair value of the share or option is determined at the measurement date, which is the grant date in the case of employee stock option, based on the market price, if available, taking into consideration those terms and conditions upon which those equity instruments were granted. Vesting conditions include service conditions which require the employee to complete a specified period of service and performance conditions, which require specified performance targets to be met. Non-vesting conditions are unrelated to the requirement to deliver services to the entity. An employee has to fulfil both vesting and non-vesting conditions to be entitled for share-based payment and both types of conditions are considered in valuing the stock option. Each year employee benefits expense is recognised in the statement of profit and loss by credit to Stock Options Outstanding Account.

Key Terms

Exercise date, Grant date, Intrinsic value, Share-based payment, Vesting date, Vesting period

NOTES

Self-Test Questions

Self-test question 22.4

Indicate whether the following statements are true (T) or false (F):

(i) Goods or services received in a share-based payment transaction are measured at fair value of the goods or services received.

(ii) In case of ESOP, the services received from employees are measured at the fair value of share options granted at the grant date.

(iii) Non-vesting conditions are not considered in calculating the number of accounting periods over which the fair value of options granted is to be allocated.

(iv) The total fair value of options recognised over the vesting period is the fair value of the number of options granted irrespective of the number of options vested on employees.

(v) The accumulated balance in the Stock Options Outstanding Account is a component of 'other equity'

ANSWERS TO SELF-TEST QUESTIONS

22.1 (i) F; (ii) F; (iii) T; (iv) T; (v) F; (vi) F; (vii) F; (viii) T; (ix) F; (x) T

22.2 (i) T; (ii) F; (iii) T; (iv) T; (v) F; (vi) F; (vii) F; (viii) F; (ix) F; (x) F; (xi) F; (xii) T; (xiii) T; (xiv) T; (xv) T; (xvi) F; (xvii) T; (xviii) T; (xix) T; (xx) T

22.3 (i) F; (ii) F; (iii) T; (iv) F; (v) T

22.4 (i) T; (ii) T; (iii) T; (iv) F; (v) T

ASSIGNMENTS

Quiz

1. Write brief answers to the following questions:

   (i) Why is it not necessary that the functional currency should necessarily be the currency of the country in which the company is domiciled?

   (ii) What is the rationale behind translating the foreign currency monetary items into the functional currency using the closing rate at the balance sheet date for presentation in the balance sheet?

   (iii) Why borrowing cost for the period when the qualifying asset is ready for use and when it started commercial production should not be capitalised?

   (iv) Why is borrowing cost usually considered a non-inventoriable cost?

   (v) What are the important differences between a lease contract and a service contract?

   (vi) In what circumstances, a contract to provide space in an airport terminal, on rent, for retailing merchandise should not be considered as a lease contract?

   (vii) In what condition the contract that gives right to the customer for operating the equipment is considered a lease contract?

   (viii) Under what circumstances the amount at which the 'right-of-use asset' is recognised initially equals the amount of the lease liability recognised at the lease commencement?

   (ix) Why is the 'stock option outstanding account' presented as a part of other equity?

   (x) Why fair value of ESOP is being used to measure the value of services rendered by employees?

2. M Ltd. (ML), the seller-lessee, sells a building to P Ltd. (PL), the buyer-lessor for cash of ₹50,00,000. The fair value of the building at the time of sale is ₹40,00,000. The carrying amount of the asset in the books of KL is ₹10,00,000. At the same time KL enters into a lease contract with ML to leaseback the building for 20 years with annual lease rent of ₹2,00,000, payable at the end of each year. ML's incremental borrowing rate is 10% per annum.

   Required: Explain how the transaction (sale and leaseback) should be recorded by KL.

3. Explain how to establish that a part of the general borrowings is directly attributable to the acquisition of a qualified asset.

Index